AN INTRODUCTION TO SOCIAL SCIENCE IN LAW

by

JOHN MONAHAN
Henry and Grace Doherty Professor of Law and
Class of 1941 Research Professor
University of Virginia

LAURENS WALKER
T. Munford Boyd Professor of Law and
Caddell and Chapman Research Professor
University of Virginia

FOUNDATION PRESS
NEW YORK, NEW YORK
2006

THOMSON
™
WEST

© 2006 By FOUNDATION PRESS
     395 Hudson Street
     New York, NY 10014
     Phone Toll Free 1–877–888–1330
     Fax (212) 367–6799
     foundation-press.com
Printed in the United States of America

ISBN–13: 978–1–58778–987–8
ISBN–10: 1–58778–987–6

 *TEXT IS PRINTED ON 10% POST CONSUMER RECYCLED PAPER*

PREFACE TO THE COLLEGE EDITION

The substance of this book identifies four major uses of social science in law. In chapter one, Social Science Used to Determine Facts, we consider the first of these legal applications, the use of social science to determine factual issues specific to a particular case. In chapter two, Social Science Used to Make Law, we go on to consider the use of social research by courts to establish legal rules that will not only determine the outcome of a particular case, but will also govern a broad category of future cases. In the next chapter, Social Science Used to Provide Context, we consider a use of social science by courts that falls somewhere between the uses identified in chapters one and two: the use of general social science research to provide a context or background for the determination of a factual issue important only in a particular case. In the last chapter, Social Science Used to Plan the Litigation of a Case, we consider the efforts of attorneys to employ social science to prepare for trial. An Appendix contains the Supreme Court's landmark 1993 case on scientific evidence, Daubert v Merrill-Dow Pharmaceuticals, as well as those Federal Rules of Evidence most relevant to the involvement of social science in law.

While we have tried to write this book with only as much legal technicality as necessary, we assume a general familiarity with the American legal system (e.g., the distinction between a state and a federal court, or between a crime and a tort). Students lacking this familiarity, or those who wish to refresh their understanding, might want to read a general overview of the American legal system such as W. Burnham, Introduction to the Law and Legal System of the United States (1999); J. Calvi and S. Coleman, American Law and Legal Systems (2004); E. Farnsworth, An Introduction to the Legal System of the United States (1996); or J. Resnik, Processes of the Law: Understanding Courts and Their Alternatives (2004). In addition, students desiring an introduction to social science methodology and statistics may benefit from reading the primer on those topics contained in J. Monahan and L. Walker, Social Science in Law: Cases and Materials (6th ed. 2006), which also contains a detailed discussion of the jurisprudential origins of social science in law.

A word is necessary on several editorial conventions we have adopted. Many citations and footnotes that we considered non-essential in the reprinted material have been omitted without indication. Where footnotes are retained, they bear their original numbering. Omissions in the text of the cases and materials, except at the beginning of an excerpt, are indicated by bracketing the first letter of the succeeding word, rather than by a series of dots or asterisks. All extended quotations begin as a new paragraph. Finally, we would like to thank those authors and publishers who gave us permission to reprint in this edition from their works. They are as follows:

Excerpts from ABA Standards for Criminal Justice, Second Edition, copyright © 1980 by American Bar Association; reprinted by permission of the American Bar Association.

Excerpts from The Practice of Social Research, Seventh Edition by Earl Babbie, copyright © 1995 by Wadsworth Publishing Co.; reprinted by permission of the publisher.

Baldus, Woodworth, and Pulaski, Law and Statistics in Conflict: Reflections on McCleskey v. Kemp, in Handbook of Psychology and Law, 265-69 (Kagehiro and Laufer eds. 1992), reprinted with kind permission of Springer Science and Business Media.

Bazelon, Morality of the Criminal Law, 49 Southern California Law Review 1269 (1976); reprinted with the permission of the Southern California Law Review.

Belli, Melvin M., Modern Trials (2d ed. 1982); reprinted with the permission of the author.

Excerpt adapted from Readings in Social Psychology by Theodore M. Newcomb and Eugene L. Hartley, copyright © 1947 by Holt, Rinehart and Winston, Inc. and renewed 1975 by Theodore Newcomb and Eugene Hartley, reprinted by permission of the publisher.

Cook, Stuart W., Social Science and School Desegregation: Did We Mislead the Supreme Court?, 5 Personality and Social Psychology Bulletin 420 (1979), copyright © 1979 by Society for Personality and Social Psychology, Inc. Reprinted by permission of Sage Publications, Inc. and the author.

Davis, Kenneth Culp, Judicial, Legislative and Administrative Lawmaking: A Proposed Research Service for the Supreme Court, 71 Minnesota Law Review 1 (1986); reprinted with permission of the Minnesota Law Review and the author.

Davis, Kenneth Culp, Facts in Lawmaking, 80 Columbia Law Review 931, 931–42 (1980), copyright © 1980 by the Directors of the Columbia Law Review Association, Inc. All rights reserved. This article originally appeared at 80 Columbia Law Review 931 (1980). Reprinted by permission.

Davis, Kenneth Culp, An Approach to Problems of Evidence in the Administrative Process, 55 Harvard Law Review 364 (1942); reprinted by permission of the Harvard Law Review Association and the author. Copyright © 1942 by the Harvard Law Review Association.

Deciding on Death: Revising Jury Instructions to Improve Juror Comprehension of the Law, 7 Researching Law: An ABF Update 1 (1996), reprinted with permission of the American Bar Foundation.

Dentler, R. and M. Scott, Schools on Trial: An Inside Account of the Boston Desegregation Case (1981); reprinted with the permission of Abt. Books, Inc.

Deutscher, Max and Isador Chein, The Psychological Effects of Enforced Segregation: A Survey of Social Science Opinion. Journal of Psychology, volume 26, issue 2, pages 259-268 (1948). Reprinted with permission of the Helen Dwight Reid Educational Foundation. Published by Heldref Publications, 1319 Eighteenth St., NW, Washington, DC 20036-1802. www.heldref.org. Copyright © (1948).

Faigman, David L., David H. Kaye, Michael J. Saks and Joseph Sanders, Modern Scientific Evidence: The Law and Science of Expert Testimony (2nd Ed. 2002), reprinted with the permission of West Publishing Co.

Frederick, Jeffrey T., The Psychology of the American Jury (1987); reprinted with the permission of the Michie Company.

Gerard, Harold B., School Desegregation: The Social Science Role, 38 American Psychologist 869 (1983). Copyright © 1983 by the American Psychological Association. Reprinted by permission.

Gross, Samuel R., Overruled: Jury Neutrality in Capital Cases; reprinted from Stanford Lawyer, Vol. 21, No. 1 (Fall 1986). Copyright © 1986 by the Board of Trustees of the Leland Stanford Junior University. Reprinted with permission of the Stanford Lawyer and the author.

Haney, Banks, and Zimbardo, International Dynamics in a Simulated Prison, 1 International Journal of Criminology and Penology 69 (1973). Copyright © 1973 by Academic Press, Inc. (London) Limited; reprinted with the permission of the authors.

Haward, Forensic Psychology (1981); reprinted with the permission of Batsford (B.T.) Ltd.

Hill and Hill, Videotaping Children's Testimony: An Empirical View, 85 Michigan Law Review 809 (1987). Reprinted with permission of the Michigan Law Review and the authors.

Specified Excerpt from Simple Justice by Richard Kluger. Copyright © 1975 by Richard Kluger. Reprinted by permission of Alfred A. Knopf, Inc.

Lawrence, Robert, The Allure of Increased Conviction Rates: The Admissibility of Expert Testimony on Rape Trauma Syndrome in Criminal Proceedings, 70 Virginia Law Review 1657 (1984); reprinted with the permission of the Virginia Law Review and Fred B. Rothman & Co.

Linz, Daniel, S.D. Penrod, and E. Donnerstein, The Attorney General's Commission on Pornography: The Gaps Between Findings and "Facts", 1987 American Bar Foundation Research Journal 713. This material was first published in the American Bar Foundation Research Journal, Number 4, Fall 1987.

Loftus, Elizabeth F., Eyewitness Testimony, excerpts, reprinted by permission of the publisher from EYEWITNESS TESTIMONY, by Elizabeth F.

Schauer, Frederick, The Law of Obscenity, by Frederick F. Schauer, copyright © 1976 by the Bureau of National Affairs, Inc., Washington, D.C. 20037.

Schuller, Regina and Patricia Hastings, Battered Child Syndrome and Other Psychological Effects of Sexual and Physical Abuse of Children, in Modern Scientific Evidence: The Law and Science and Expert Testimony (2d ed. 2002), copyright © 2002 by West Group Publishing, reprinted with permission.

Stacy, The Search for the Truth in Constitutional Criminal Procedure, 91 Columbia Law Review 1369 (1991). This article originally appeared at 91 Colum. L. Rev. 1369 (1991). Reprinted by permission of the Columbia Law Review and Tom Stacy.

Tanford, The Law and Psychology of Jury Instructions, 69 Nebraska Law Review 71 (1990). Reprinted with permission of the Nebraska Law Review.

Underwood, Barbara, Law and the Crystal Ball: Predicting Behavior with Statistical Inference and Individualized Judgment (1979). Reprinted by permission of the Yale Law Journal Company and William S. Hein Company from The Yale Law Journal, Vol. 88, pages 1408-1448.

Walker and Monahan, Social Facts: Scientific Methodology and Legal Precedent, 76 California Law Review No. 4, July 1988, 877, 877–896. Copyright © 1988 by California Law Review, Inc. Reprinted with permission.

Walker and Monahan, Social Frameworks: A New Use of Social Science in Law, 73 Virginia Law Review 559 (1987); reprinted with the permission of the Virginia Law Review Association and Fred B. Rothman & Co.

J.M.
L.W.

Charlottesville, Virginia
September, 2005

*

SUMMARY OF CONTENTS

TABLE OF CONTENTS

CHAPTER THREE. Social Science Used to Provide Context 289

AN INTRODUCTION TO SOCIAL SCIENCE IN LAW

*

CHAPTER ONE

SOCIAL SCIENCE USED TO DETERMINE FACTS

In this chapter, we begin our examination of the uses of social science in law. We take as our point of departure the most straightforward and least controversial legal application of social science: its use to determine what Professor Kenneth Culp Davis called "adjudicative facts." Davis defined adjudicative facts as follows:

> When an agency [or court] finds facts concerning immediate parties—what the parties did, what the circumstances were, what the background conditions were—the agency [or court] is performing an adjudicative function, and the facts may conveniently be called adjudicative facts.

Davis, An Approach to Problems of Evidence in the Administrative Process, 55 Harvard Law Review 364, 402 (1942).

Adjudicative facts, in other words, are facts that apply only to the particular parties before the court. They are used to determine (or "adjudicate") what happened in a specific case, and not for some larger purpose, such as to argue that a law should be changed. What Davis called an adjudicative fact has been referred to by other commentators, e.g., T. Marvell, Appellate Courts and Lawyers (1978), as a "case fact," and by one court as "a plain, garden-variety fact." Bowling v. Department of Ins., 394 So.2d 165, 174 (Fla.Dist.Ct.App.1981).

The three areas we have chosen to explore the use of social science to determine adjudicative or case-specific facts involve trademarks, obscenity and damages.

SECTION I. TRADEMARKS

Trademarks identify products and producers. More precisely, the Trademark Act of 1946, known as the Lanham Act, as amended by the Trademark Law Revision Act of 1988, 15 U.S.C.A. § 1127, defines a trademark as follows:

> The term "trademark" includes any word, name, symbol, or device, or any combination thereof—
>
> > (1) used by a person, or

(2) which a person has a bona fide intention to use in commerce and applies to register on the principal register established by this Act,

to identify and distinguish his or her goods, including a unique product, from those manufactured or sold by others and to indicate the source of the goods, even if that source is unknown.

Thus, both "COKE" and the distinctive shape of the Coca-Cola bottle are trademarks of the Coca-Cola Company.

Trademarks can serve several valuable functions. First, they can serve an identifying function, indicating the source of the goods. This would facilitate determining the manufacturer if the product turned out to be defective. Second, trademarks can have a quality assurance function. Consumers who are impressed with the quality of a particular manufacturer's products may come to expect that repeat purchases from this manufacturer will be of similar quality. Finally, trademarks can have an advertising function. Repetition of the trademark through advertising may attract customers and create demand for the product. Thus, trademarks are an unusual form of property right in which the validity of the property interest depends on the reaction of third parties (i.e., consumers) rather than on the traditional indices of ownership such as possession. See E. Kitch and H. Perlman, Legal Regulation of the Competitive Process (4th ed. 1991).

Trademarks are often confused with two other forms of "intellectual property" rights, patents and copyrights, which together form much of the law prohibiting "unfair competition" in commerce. Patents, however, apply only to new inventions and copyrights apply only to original writings (or other forms of tangible expression, such as plays or films). In the case of a word processor, for example, the interior hardware may be protected by a patent, the instruction manual and software programs may be protected by a copyright, and the name of the word processor may be protected by a trademark. See S. Kane, Trademark Law: A Practitioner's Guide 7 (1987). Unlike patents and copyrights, which confer a monopoly only for time-limited periods (20 years in the case of patents, and the life of the author plus 70 years, in the case of copyrights), trademarks can confer a perpetual monopoly.

We focus here on only one issue in trademark law: "consumer confusion." The federal Patent and Trademark Office will refuse to register a new trademark if it so resembles a trademark already registered to another person "as to be likely, when used on or in connection with the goods of the applicant, to cause confusion or to cause mistake, or to deceive." 15 U.S.C.A. § 1052(d). A person who sells a product that is likely to cause confusion with an already trademarked product is liable for trademark infringement. If the plaintiff—the party with the existing trademark—can prove by a preponderance of the evidence that the defendant has caused consumers to be confused, an injunction can be issued by the court ordering the defendant to cease using the product designation in question, and civil damages can be awarded. See, in general, B. Pattishall and D. Hilliard, Trademarks (1987).

Before examining the ways that social science research has been used as evidence of consumer confusion, we first consider the rule of evidence that for many years barred the introduction of social science research in trademark cases: the "hearsay" rule.

A. SOCIAL SCIENCE EVIDENCE AND THE HEARSAY RULE

Rule 801(c) of the Federal Rules of Evidence defines "hearsay" as "a statement, other than one made by the declarant while testifying at the trial or hearing, offered in evidence to prove the truth of the matter asserted." Rule 802—the "hearsay rule"—states that "[h]earsay is not admissible" in court. Rule 803 states several exceptions to the hearsay rule. See Appendix A for the text of these rules.

When empirical data in the form of surveys first began to be introduced as evidence of consumer confusion in trademark cases, courts often rejected it as violating the hearsay rule: the subjects (or "respondents") in the surveys were seen as offering "statements" in evidence, despite the fact that they were not present at trial to testify and be cross-examined on the truth of those statements.

ELGIN NATIONAL WATCH CO. v. ELGIN CLOCK CO.

United States District Court, District of Delaware, 1928.
26 F.2d 376.

■ MORRIS, DISTRICT JUDGE:

In this suit, instituted by the Elgin National Watch Company against the Elgin Clock Company to obtain a decree enjoining and restraining the defendant, which manufactures or assembles clocks for automobiles, from using [a]ny corporate name or business style of which the word "Elgin" forms a part, the plaintiff [h]as presented its petition praying for an order granting it leave to file an affidavit of Arthur L. Lynn and the exhibits thereto annexed. The affidavit, submitted with the petition, purports to be that of an expert witness with respect to the meaning of the word "Elgin," as understood by the public when used in connection with timepieces, their manufacture or sale. [T]he affidavit reads thus:

"Arthur L. Lynn, being duly sworn, upon oath states as follows:

"I am a member of the advertising firm of Lennen & Mitchell, Inc. [I]n order to ascertain whether or not the word 'Elgin,' as applied to timepieces, means to retail jewelers the products of any particular concern, our company, under my supervision, mailed to representative retail jewelers throughout the United States a questionnaire which embraced the following questions:

"[1]. In connection with clocks and watches, does the name 'Elgin' mean to you and your customers the products of any particular concern or not? If so, whose?

"[2]. If you saw the name Elgin Clock Company on an automobile clock or watch, who would you think made it?

"[3]. Who would your customers think made such a clock or watch?

"[F]rom a careful examination of these questionnaires, I am of the opinion that the name 'Elgin,' used in connection with timepieces, means the Elgin National Watch Company, and that the name 'Elgin,' used in connection with the manufacture and sale of timepieces, would be taken by the public to mean the products of the Elgin National Watch Company."

[A]bout 2,000 returned questionnaires were submitted as exhibits with the affidavit.

The plaintiff concedes that its petition presents a case of first impression. It has found no judicial construction [t]o reveal or define the character of testimony which [m]ight be properly considered expert testimony in trademark cases.

[J. Cutler, On Passing Off (1904)] asserts that the plaintiff has to prove that to a considerable portion of the trade or of the public the trade-name means the plaintiff's goods and nothing else, and that such evidence can and ought to be given by traders and by members of the purchasing public. The author then says: "Of course, to call one such witness would be insufficient, as no court would place much, if any, reliance upon the evidence of one such witness. But then how many such witnesses ought the plaintiff to call? It may be stated that he ought to be prepared with from 20 to 30 such witnesses. * * * In selecting his 20 or 30 witnesses, the plaintiff must not take them all from one locality, but from different parts of the country, and in particular he ought to have some from the locality where the defendant's trade is carried on."

The plaintiff [proposes] to eliminate the necessity of calling, in cases of this character, numerous witnesses from all the different parts of the United States, and that apparently only by the procedure adopted by the plaintiff can such result be accomplished. While recognizing the practical difficulties presented in establishing, by satisfactory proof, what a trade-name nationally known denotes to the trade and to the public, I am not convinced [t]o make the innovation with respect to such proof that is here suggested by the plaintiff.

Were plaintiff's position sound, [there would be] a nullification of the long-established proposition that the rule against hearsay evidence finds no exception in the case of expert witnesses.

[T]he affidavit submitted for filing is one based, not upon personal knowledge of the affiant nor upon facts admitted in evidence, but, on the contrary, is predicated solely upon the unverified statements or opinions of persons not called as witnesses.

[I] am constrained to conclude that the prayer of plaintiff's petition must be denied, for the reason that a proper basis is wanting for the judgment or opinion of the affiant.

———

LIFE SAVERS CORP. v. CURTISS CANDY CO.

United States District Court, Northern District of Illinois, 1949.
87 F.Supp. 16.

■ SHAW, DISTRICT JUDGE:

The complaint in this case charges that the defendant [Curtiss Candy Co.] has infringed plaintiff's Trade-mark [b]y adopting a label for its candy mints. It is alleged to be a colorable imitation of the registered trade-mark and package used by Life Savers, resulting in actual confusion of goods between the products of the plaintiff and defendant in addition to the usual allegation of likelihood of confusion.

[T]here was a plethora of evidence from some 75 or 80 witnesses in numerous cities throughout the United States who testified that they had by confusion of goods accidentally picked up a package of Curtiss mints when they had wanted a package of Life Savers. [T]his evidence became cumulative in open court to such an extent that the court decided to hear no more of it, but afterwards discovered that there were depositions from about 60 people in different cities to the same effect. It is enough to say that it is evident that there has been some confusion of goods.

———

TRIANGLE PUBLICATIONS v. ROHRLICH

United States Court of Appeals, Second Circuit, 1948.
167 F.2d 969.

■ FRANK, CIRCUIT JUDGE, Dissenting.

[The plaintiff, Triangle Publications, published a magazine titled "Seventeen." The defendants, Joseph Rohrlich and others, began to produce girdles labeled "Miss Seventeen." A majority of the Court of Appeals affirmed the District Court's finding of trademark infringement based on likelihood of confusion.]

The [trial] judge's finding as to what was "likely" [to confuse] is nothing but a surmise, a conjecture, a guess. We are not bound by such a finding. We can guess as well as the trial judge.

I think that we should not pioneer in amplifying the trade-name doctrine on the basis of the shaky kind of guess in which the trial judge indulged. Like the trial judge's, our surmise must here rest on "judicial notice." As neither the trial judge nor any member of this court is (or resembles) a teen-age girl or the mother or sister of such a girl, our judicial notice apparatus will not work well unless we feed it with information directly obtained from "teen-agers" or from their female relatives accustomed to shop for them. Competently to inform ourselves, we should have a staff of investigators like those supplied to administrative agencies. As we have no such staff, I have questioned some adolescent girls and their mothers and sisters, persons I have chosen at random. I have been told uniformly by my questionees that no one could reasonably believe that any relation existed between plaintiff's magazine and defendants' girdles.

I admit that my method of obtaining such data is not satisfactory. But it does serve better than anything in this record to illuminate the pivotal fact. It convinces me that the plaintiff should bear a very heavy burden of proving that confusion is likely, a burden plaintiff did not discharge. For instance, plaintiff or the trial judge might have utilized, but did not, "laboratory" tests, of a sort now familiar, to ascertain whether numerous girls and women, seeing both plaintiff's magazine and defendants' advertisements, would believe them to be in some way associated.

NOTE

1. Judicial Notice. In his dissent in Triangle Publications v. Rohrlich, Judge Frank relied on an early form of the doctrine of "judicial notice" in conducting his "survey" of adolescent girls and their mothers and sisters. See Federal Rule of Evidence 201, "Judicial Notice of Adjudicative Facts," in Appendix A. This Rule—which was adopted in its current form in 1975, almost thirty years after the *Triangle* case—would seem to clearly bar independent judicial investigations of the type conducted by Judge Frank, since the degree to which consumers are confused between two products is not "generally known within the territorial jurisdiction of the trial court" and is not "capable of accurate and ready determination by resort to sources whose accuracy cannot reasonably be questioned."

ONEIDA v. NATIONAL SILVER

Supreme Court of New York, Madison County, 1940.
25 N.Y.S.2d 271.

■ DAVIS, JUSTICE.

The cause of action alleged by the plaintiff is one [f]or unfair competition. Its claim is that it being in the business of manufacturing silver plate and having originated a pattern or design called "Coronation," which had met with an extraordinary sale, the defendant, seeking to take advantage of the extensive advertising, sale and popularity of this particular pattern, copied or simulated the pattern, and sold in the market in competition with plaintiff, a pattern of its own called, "Princess Royal," thereby injuring unlawfully the plaintiff in its good will, its sales and profits. An injunction restraining these alleged unlawful acts, and an accounting are sought.

[F]ive [y]oung ladies [w]ere employed [t]o make what was called a "survey." They were given a book of fifty sheets upon each of which there were three questions. On the cover was one of the articles of the Princess Royal pattern with the backstamp concealed. These witnesses separately visited homes of what may be called the middle class of people, sought an interview with the housewife, explained that they had nothing to sell but were simply making a survey, showed the pattern and asked the housewife to identify it and to write and sign the answers. Two of the questions were in the following form: (1) Who do you think puts out this silverware? (2) If you wanted to buy a set of this silverware how would you ask for it? [T]hey interviewed 1,000 women and received a variety of answers, a considerable portion of which identified the article as that of plaintiff; and in only one instance was identification made as Princess Royal. More than one-third did not know the manufacturer or pattern.

When this evidence was offered I had doubts as to its competency, but took it subject to motion to strike out, or eventually to disregard it. I think that the evidence was competent. These persons, though not customers of a store, were members of the public and may be regarded as potential purchasers.

[T]he plaintiff did not rest alone upon this survey. From the housewives who had in the questionnaire identified the pattern as one of plaintiff or its manufacture, twenty-four women were called as witnesses who gave their reasons for being confused or deceived in identifying the Princess Royal pattern shown them. They were familiar with advertisements of silverware patterns. Such evidence has greater weight than that obtained in the "survey."

[I] reach the conclusion that the defendant, by [t]he fact that persons were readily confused and deceived, was engaged in acts of recognized unfair competition.

ZIPPO MANUFACTURING CO. v. ROGERS IMPORTS, INC.

United States District Court, Southern District of New York, 1963.
216 F.Supp. 670.

■ FEINBERG, DISTRICT JUDGE.

This case involves the attempt of a manufacturer of a popular cigarette lighter to keep others from imitating the lighters shape and appearance. Plaintiff Zippo Manufacturing Company ("Zippo"), a Pennsylvania corporation, alleges [t]rademark infringement [o]n the part of Rogers, Inc. ("Rogers"), a New York corporation, by reason of Rogers' sale of pocket lighters closely resembling Zippo's.

[P]laintiff has relied heavily on a consumer study to prove the elements of its case. [T]he purpose of the study was to determine [w]hether the similar physical attributes of the Rogers' lighters cause public confusion.

[T]he "universe" to be studied consisted of all smokers aged eighteen years and older residing in the continental United States, which the research project indicated was approximately 115,000,000 ("the smoking population"). All percentage results in the surveys represent projected percentages of the smoking population.

The three separate surveys were conducted across a national probability sample of smokers, with a sample size of approximately 500 for each survey. The samples were chosen on the basis of data obtained from the Bureau of Census.

[D]efendant objects to the admission of the surveys into evidence. It first contends that the surveys are hearsay. The weight of case authority, the consensus of legal writers, and reasoned policy considerations all indicate that the hearsay rule should not bar the admission of properly conducted public surveys. Although courts were at first reluctant to accept survey evidence or to give it weight, the more recent trend is clearly contrary. Surveys are now admitted over the hearsay objection on two technically distinct bases. Some cases hold that surveys are not hearsay at all; other cases hold that surveys are hearsay but are admissible because they are within the recognized exception to the hearsay rule for statements of present state of mind, attitude, or belief. Still other cases admit surveys without stating the ground on which they are admitted.

The cases holding that surveys are not hearsay do so on the basis that the surveys are not offered to prove the truth of what respondents said and, therefore, do not fall within the classic definition of hearsay.

[R]egardless of whether the surveys in this case could be admitted under the non-hearsay approach, they are admissible because the answers of respondents are expressions of presently existing state of mind, attitude, or belief. There is a recognized exception to the hearsay rule for such statements, and under it the statements are admissible to prove the truth of the matter contained therein.

––––––

NOTE

1. Non-Hearsay and Exceptions to the Hearsay Rule. Judge Feinberg gave two alternate grounds for admitting surveys as evidence. One was that surveys are not hearsay because they are not "offered in evidence to prove the truth of the matter asserted." Federal Rule of Evidence 801(c). That is, the fact that respondents confused Rogers lighters with Zippo lighters was not being offered to prove that Rogers, Inc., actually manufactured Zippos. The other ground for admitting surveys was that, even if they are hearsay, one of the exceptions to the hearsay rule is the "present sense impression," which allows the introduction of a statement "describing or explaining an event or condition made while the declarant was perceiving the event or condition, or immediately thereafter." Federal Rule of Evidence 803(1). See Appendix A.

B.   SOCIAL SCIENCE EVIDENCE OF CONSUMER CONFUSION

Zippo effectively marked the end of the hearsay objection to the introduction of survey evidence in trademark cases. *Zippo* also marked the beginning of the modern trend in trademark litigation in which the introduction of survey evidence has become the normal method of proving consumer confusion. In the following cases, we examine the range of methodologies that have been used by social scientists and accepted by courts to demonstrate that consumers are confused between two products or two producers.

ZIPPO MANUFACTURING CO. v. ROGERS IMPORTS, INC.

United States District Court, Southern District of New York, 1963.
216 F.Supp. 670.

■ FEINBERG, DISTRICT JUDGE.

[The allegations of the parties and descriptions of the survey sample are contained in the previous excerpt from this case.]

Defendant's [o]bjection to the surveys is that they should not have been conducted in respondents' homes but in stores, the actual places of purchase. While it may be that in general the store is the best place to measure the state of mind at the time of purchase, it would be virtually impossible to obtain a representative national sample if stores were used. An interview at a respondent's home is probative of his state of mind at the time of purchase, although the deviation from the actual purchase situation should be considered in weighing the force of this evidence. Therefore, the surveys are not inadmissible merely because they were conducted in homes.

[T]he [key] element of plaintiff's case is that the Rogers lighter is likely to cause prospective purchasers to regard it as a Zippo lighter. Plaintiff claims that this likelihood of confusion is established for the standard model principally by Survey C. [I]n Survey C, respondents were handed a standard Rogers lighter with all of its identifying marks, including the name on the bottom, and asked to identify its brand. 34.7 percent of respondents thought it was a Zippo lighter, and only 14.3 percent identified it as a Rogers. This would indicate that a substantial number of persons might confuse the Zippo and Rogers standard lighters because of their physical attributes, despite the appearance of the brand name on the lighters. Defendant's objections to the weight of this evidence must, of course, be seriously regarded, particularly its argument that no such confusion would exist in the store at the time of purchase because Rogers lighters are sold from display cards bearing the name "Rogers." This contention is buttressed by the fact that almost all of those who did correctly identify the Rogers lighter did so because they saw the brand name on the bottom, and the brand name would be more conspicuous on the display card. However, it is difficult to get away from the fact that the number of confused respondents was almost two and one-half times greater than those who recognized a Rogers as a Rogers, and a good portion of the confusion was due to the shape and style of the Rogers lighter.

[O]n all the evidence then, I find that plaintiff has established the likelihood of confusion—indeed actual confusion—between the Zippo and Rogers standard lighters.

AMSTAR CORPORATION v. DOMINO'S PIZZA

United States Court of Appeals, Fifth Circuit, 1980.
615 F.2d 252.

■ AINSWORTH, CIRCUIT JUDGE.

Amstar Corporation brought this suit asserting trademark infringement and unfair competition against Domino's Pizza, Inc. and several of its franchisees to enjoin their use of Amstar's federal registration of the "Domino" trademark. The complaint is based on allegations that defendants' use of the mark "Domino's Pizza" in connection with the sale of fast-food delivered hot pizza pies constitutes trademark infringement and a false designation of origin or representation in violation of the Trademark Act of 1946, 15 U.S.C.A. § 1051 et seq. [T]he district court ruled in favor of plaintiff, dismissed defendants' counterclaim, and permanently enjoined defendants use of the names "Domino" or "Domino's Pizza." Defendants then filed this appeal.

Standard of Review

[I]nitially, we must determine the appropriate standard of review applicable to the district court's finding of likelihood of confusion. [T]his circuit has held that likelihood of confusion is a question of fact which can only be set aside if clearly erroneous. The record in the present case indicates that the district court's finding of likelihood of confusion is clearly erroneous.

Likelihood of Confusion

[I]nfringement of a registered mark is governed by the provisions of 15 U.S.C.A. § 1114(1), which imposes liability against "use ... likely to cause confusion, or to cause mistake, or to deceive." [P]laintiff's claims against defendants, [t]herefore, turn on the determination of whether defendants' use of the mark "Domino's Pizza" is likely to cause confusion, mistake, or deception.

[D]issimilarities between the retail outlets for and the predominant consumers of plaintiff's and defendants' goods lessen the possibility of confusion, mistake, or deception. The dissimilarities here are substantial.

Plaintiff's "Domino" sugar products are distributed to the public primarily through grocery stores; defendants' pizzas and soft drinks are distributed exclusively through fast-food outlets specializing in home delivery or customer pickup, but offering no facilities for sit-down service.

[T]here are substantial dissimilarities between the predominant purchasers of plaintiff's and defendants' products. According to surveys presented at trial, "Domino's Pizza" patrons are primarily young (85.6% under 35 years of age), single (61%) males (63.3%). This coincides with the fact that 75% of the "Domino's Pizza" stores throughout the country are situated in college campus towns or around military bases where the advertising for "Domino's Pizza" is directed to the 18- to 34-year-old single male. In contrast, "Domino" sugar purchasers are predominantly middle-aged housewives.

[A]t trial, both parties introduced survey evidence on the issue of likelihood of confusion. The trial court characterized the defendants' survey as "about as contrived a survey as I have ever run across," but found plaintiff's survey "properly conducted and fair." Our own examination of the survey evidence convinces us that both surveys are substantially defective.

Plaintiff's survey was made by Dr. Russ Haley, Professor of Marketing at the University of New Hampshire. It was conducted in ten cities among female heads of household primarily responsible for making food purchases. Each participant was shown, in her own home, a "Domino's Pizza" box and was asked if she believed the company that made the pizza made any other product. If she answered yes, she was asked, "What products other than pizza do you think are made by the company that makes Domino's Pizza?" Seventy-one percent of those asked the second question answered "sugar."

While the possible confusion level shown by the Haley study is high, there are several defects in the survey which significantly reduce its probative value. First, one of the most important factors in assessing the validity of an opinion poll is the adequacy of the "survey universe," that is, the persons interviewed must adequately represent the opinions which are relevant to the litigation. The appropriate universe should include a fair sampling of those purchasers most likely to partake of the alleged infringer's goods or services. Of the ten cities in which the Haley survey was conducted, eight had no "Domino's Pizza" outlets, and the outlets in the remaining two had been open for less than three months. Additionally, the persons interviewed consisted entirely of women found at home during six daylight hours who identified themselves as the member of the household primarily responsible for grocery buying. As plaintiff's sugar is sold primarily in grocery stores, participants in the Haley survey would have been repeatedly exposed to plaintiff's mark, but would have had little, if any, exposure to defendants' mark. Furthermore, the survey neglected completely defendants' primary customers—young, single, male college students. Thus, we do not believe that the proper universe was examined, and the result of the survey must therefore be discounted.

[T]he trial court discounted defendants' survey for largely the same reasons just discussed—it was conducted on the premises of "Domino's Pizza" outlets and therefore did not examine a proper survey universe, and the questioning procedures used were improper. Thus, defendants' survey is likewise not probative of the presence or absence of confusion.

Accordingly, we conclude that the trial court was clearly in error when it held defendants' use of the trademark "Domino's Pizza" was likely to cause confusion, mistake, or deception.

[S]ince defendants' use of the mark "Domino's Pizza" is not likely to confuse, mislead, or deceive the public, the district court's order and injunction to the contrary are set aside, and the judgment is REVERSED.

————

THE SQUIRT COMPANY v. THE SEVEN-UP COMPANY

United States District Court, Eastern District of Missouri, 1979.
207 U.S. Patent Quarterly 12.

■ HARPER, DISTRICT JUDGE.

[The Squirt Company, producers of a grapefruit-flavored soft drink named "Squirt," charged the Seven-Up Company with trademark infringement in naming their lemonade-flavored soft drink "Quirst." A survey performed by the Maritz Company was introduced as evidence of consumer confusion.]

We turn now to the methodology followed in the execution of the Maritz Survey. At three Low Cost Grocery Stores located in and around Phoenix, Arizona a store intercept study was conducted on July 20, 21 and 22, 1978. During the three-day period in which the study or survey was conducted all three of the Low Cost Stores had the soft drinks, SQUIRT and QUIRST, available for sale at the reduced price of ninety-nine cents for a six-pack of 12-ounce cans. Upon entering the grocery store all customers were given a coupon worth fifty cents off the regular price of one six-pack of 12-ounce cans of any flavor of non-alcoholic beverage, with the exception of cola flavor. The primary purpose of the fifty-cent coupon was to stimulate the purchase of non-cola soft drinks and thus increase the efficiency of the three-day survey by having a large sample.

After a customer had completed his shopping, gone through the checkout line, had his groceries bagged and was preparing to leave the store, he was intercepted by an interviewer and asked the following questions which were contained in a questionnaire: Question #1. "Did you get a coupon like this on your way into the grocery store?" (At the time of asking the question the interviewer displayed the fifty-cent off coupon described above.)

If the answer to Question #1 was "Yes," the interview continued and the respondent was then asked: Question #2: "Did you use your coupon?"

If the answer to Question #2 was "Yes," the interview continued and the following question was directed to the respondent: Question #3: "What brands of six-pack 12-ounce cans of non-alcoholic beverage other than cola flavor did you buy?"

The answers to Question #3 were recorded verbatim by the interviewer on the questionnaire. Following the recording of the responses to Question #3 the respondent was issued the following request: Question #4: "May I see the six-pack(s) of (each brand in the order mentioned in Question #3) you bought? I know it is an inconvenience to unpack your groceries so I will give you a $3.00 gift certificate good on any purchase of $3.00 or more at this store through July 30th if you will show me the six-pack(s) you bought."

The interviewers were instructed to record verbatim the exact brands of 12-ounce canned, non-alcoholic beverages which were shown to them by the respondent.

[F]ollowing the completion of the entire survey a tabulation was made of the number of respondents who correctly identified the brand purchased and of respondents who did not correctly identify the brands they had just previously purchased.

A compilation of the Maritz Survey results disclosed that a total of 1,016 persons were in fact interviewed. Of this total, some 884 persons answered "Yes" to Question #2 and thus used their fifty-cent coupon. Of the 884 persons who used their coupon, 839 responded to Question #3 by identifying the brands they purchased and then responded to Question #4 by displaying their beverage purchases to the interviewer. Of the total of 839, there were 70 persons who stated in answer to Question 3 the soft drink SQUIRT. Of the 70 persons who said they had SQUIRT, 65 in fact were able to display SQUIRT in response to Question #4. Three persons who said they had purchased SQUIRT, in fact had purchased QUIRST, while two persons of the total of 70 who said they purchased SQUIRT, in fact purchased the soft drink SPRITE. Thus, approximately 4.3% of the respondents, three out of the 70 who said they had purchased SQUIRT, when asked to display their purchases in fact had purchased QUIRST.

[A]s a starting point in this Court's evaluation of the Maritz Survey, we would point out that we know of no cases containing an actual market survey of the Maritz variety wherein an actual purchaser is asked to list the brands he has just purchased, and then asked to display the brands he has named, in order to determine the accuracy of his listed purchases. The cases which contain survey evidence that have been cited by the parties in their briefs are not of the Maritz type wherein consumer action or behavior is evaluated. Rather, the cases cited to this Court entail "opinion" type surveys, where typically a specific number of interviews are conducted either in a "purchasing" environment, such as a store or shopping center, or in a "non-purchasing" environment, such as the home or laboratory, and the respondent will be asked to express his or her opinion with respect to specific marks and whether they originate from the same source, or whether there is any relationship at all between two marks, etc.

[T]his Court does believe that the results of the Maritz survey are strong evidence of a likelihood of confusion between SQUIRT and QUIRST. First of all, the fact that the survey was conducted in a live market environment and measured actual consumer purchasing behavior as opposed to being conducted in the home and measuring consumer opinion, lends greater reliability to the survey results. As Judge Wyzanski pointed out in American Luggage Works v. United States Trunk Co., Inc., 158 F.Supp. 50, 116 USPQ 188 (Mass.1957); aff'd 259 F.2d 69, 118 USPQ 424 (1st Cir.1958), at page 53, 116 USPQ at page 190–191:

> "If the interviewee is not in a buying mood but is just in a friendly mood answering a pollster, his degree of attention is quite different from what it would be had he his wallet in his hand. Many men do not take the same trouble to avoid confusion when they are responding to sociological investigators as when they spend their cash."

[T]his Court cannot say that the 4.3% (three out of seventy) level of error between SQUIRT and QUIRST is de minimus or statistically insignificant, when it is considered in the context of the entire soft drink industry. [T]hese considerations lead us to the conclusion that the defendants are infringing the plaintiff's SQUIRT trademarks because the name QUIRST is likely to cause confusion, mistake or deception.

THE KROGER CO. v. JOHNSON & JOHNSON

United States District Court, Southern District of Ohio, 1983.
570 F.Supp. 1055.

■ CARL B. RUBIN, CHIEF JUDGE.

[Johnson & Johnson claimed that the Kroger Company and others had infringed its trademark in the analgesic "Tylenol," by naming their analgesics "Actenol," "Supernol," and "Hydenol," and packaging them in a manner likely to cause consumer confusion.]

A survey performed by Bruno and Ridgeway Research Associates, Inc., a marketing and advertising research firm, demonstrated the potential for consumer confusion between Tylenol and the three accused products. The survey indicated not only the likelihood of confusion among these brands, but also a belief by substantial numbers of those interviewed that the accused products were manufactured by Tylenol.[6] Although defendants attacked the methodology of the Bruno survey at trial, we are satisfied that

---

6. In the survey, consumers were asked to view a shelf of products containing plaintiffs' products as well as other national brand pain relievers for approximately five seconds. Afterwards, they were asked to identify those products which they had seen. Between 17 and 24% of the respondents claimed that they had seen Tylenol, when in fact it was not present on the shelf. The interviewees were then shown the plaintiffs' respective products and asked who they believed made or manufactured that product. Twenty-three percent (23%) of the persons interviewed thought Actenol was manufactured by Tylenol. Forty percent (40%) of those persons interviewed with respect to Supernol and Hydenol likewise believed those products were manufactured by Tylenol.

it was conducted in a professional manner and may be considered as probative evidence on the issue of potential confusion.

[W]hile [Kroger] offered affidavits of 152 purchasers of Tylenol to the effect that they were not confused as to the nature of the product purchased or its origin, the Court does not find these affidavits controlling on the issue of potential confusion.[7]

[T]he preponderance of the evidence in this case establishes a likelihood of confusion between the plaintiffs' products and that of the defendant, as well as confusion as to the source of plaintiffs' products.

———

LA VICTORIA FOODS v. CURTICE-BURNS

United States District Court, Western District of Washington, 1986.
No. C85–1557MTB (Unpublished).

■ ROBERT J. BRYAN.

FINDINGS OF FACT

[1] The plaintiff has continuously produced and marketed a unique Mexican-style salsa product under the SALSA SUPREMA trademark since 1968. The unique salsa which the plaintiff markets under the SALSA SUPREMA trademark is the leading seller in the plaintiff's product line.

[2] The SALSA SUPREMA trademark is duly registered on the Principal Register of the United States Patent and Trademark Office under the Lanham Act of 1946, as amended, 15 U.S.C.A. § 1051 *et seq.,* to La Victoria Foods, Inc. on April 26, 1977 for "Hot Sauce". The plaintiff is the owner of that registration and of the mark so registered. [P]laintiff is entitled to all of the benefits of its incontestable registration.

[3] The plaintiff has continuously sold, advertised and promoted its SALSA SUPREMA-marked product since 1968. The sales of this product have steadily increased. In 1980 the sales were in excess of $2,000,000. In 1984 they were in excess of $5,000,000 and the rate of sales in early 1986 indicated expected sales in excess of $7,000,000 per year. Since July 1984, the plaintiff has sold hundreds of thousands of jars of the SALSA-SUPREMA-marked product in the States of Washington, Oregon, Idaho, Montana and Alaska. From June 1979 through May 1986, the plaintiff spent in excess of $12,000,000 advertising and promoting its products, a substantial part of which has emphasized the SALSA SUPREMA product.

---

7. Professor Dornoff noted the high probability of bias in the signing of these affidavits. The purchasers in question all mailed in and received a full rebate on the price paid for the product. They also received a double rebate if they consented to a personal interview. The affidavits were prepared by plaintiffs' counsel and the initial telephone interviews were conducted by counsel or members of his staff. Officials of SuperX obtained the affidavits during the personal interview. In view of the great probability of bias resulting from such techniques, as well as the unrepresentative nature of the sample, the Court attaches little weight to such evidence.

[4]   Defendant began marketing both a Mexican-style salsa product and a tortilla chip product under the LA SUPREMA trademark in July 1984. The LA SUPREMA-marked products have been sold and marketed continuously in the States of Washington, Oregon, Idaho, Montana and Alaska since July 1984. Defendant has sold in excess of 1,700,000 jars of LA SUPREMA-marked salsa products with gross sales in excess of $1,700,000.

[5]   The salsa products of plaintiff and defendant are sold in the same stores in the same geographic areas. The plaintiff's SALSA SUPREMA-marked salsa product is sold primarily as a general-purpose salsa in the Mexican food section of grocery stores and supermarkets. The SALSA SUPREMA product is also advertised and promoted as a dip. The defendant's LA SUPREMA-marked product is usually positioned in the chip and snack section of grocery stores and supermarkets and is primarily advertised and promoted as a dip.

[6]   Plaintiff presented evidence of a survey designed by Dr. Elizabeth Loftus and conducted through Mr. John Burshek of Herbert Research, Inc. The survey was designed to determine the incidence of actual confusion between LA SUPREMA salsa and SALSA SUPREMA where the prospective purchaser hears information about one or the other of the products and then attempts to purchase that product in a store. Shoppers were intercepted on a random basis as they entered three different supermarkets in the Seattle-Tacoma area. Prospective purchasers of the products involved were screened from non-prospective purchasers by being asked the question "How many times have you eaten Mexican food in the past year?" If the interviewee responded in the affirmative, that person was then offered an incentive of $2 to purchase a salsa product which the interviewer named verbally. The interviewer asked the respondent to purchase one of "SALSA SUPREMA" or "LA SUPREMA Salsa." Those who accepted the offer were given a card reflecting the offer. The card also bore a code known only to the interviewer that reflected which product the respondent had been asked to purchase. The respondent then proceeded into the store. The respondent was required to join the auditory stimuli given by the interviewer with a visual observation of the products in order to complete the test. When the respondent returned to the interviewer with a purchased product, the interviewer paid the promised $2 and recorded the name of the product purchased. The interviewer also recorded which product the interviewee had been asked to purchase. Three hundred and three people responded. One hundred and fifty three people were asked to purchase "SALSA SUPREMA" and one hundred and fifty were asked to purchase "LA SUPREMA salsa." The results were tabulated and a report was prepared.

[7]   The results of the plaintiff's auditory test indicated that there was an overall rate of actual confusion between the products in question of 11.9%. Both direct and reverse confusion were shown. Of those who were asked to purchase SALSA SUPREMA, 10.6% returned with LA SUPREMA Salsa, and 13.2% of those who were asked to purchase LA SUPREMA Salsa returned with SALSA SUPREMA. Dr. Loftus testified as to the design and

results of the survey and Mr. Burshek testified as to the conducting of the survey. Both witnesses were credible, particularly as compared to the defendant's survey expert.

[8] Dr. Loftus also approached ten grocery clerks at random in markets in the Seattle-Tacoma area and asked them where the "LA SUPREMA Salsa" was located. Seven of the ten directed her to the Mexican food section of the store when, in fact, the LA SUPREMA Salsa was located in the Chip and Snack section of the store. This is some evidence that those store personnel who are responsible for assisting the consuming public are themselves actually confused between these products and tends to confirm the results of the Loftus survey of prospective purchasers.

[9] The defendant also conducted a survey. Consumers selected by a random procedure were telephoned and asked whether they had purchased "Mexican-style sauces or dips" within the last six months, along with several other preliminary questions. Those who qualified were offered an incentive to come to the offices of the entity that conducted the survey. Those who accepted the invitations were taken into a room with the interviewer and seated at a table where a box was positioned between the interviewer and the respondent. After the respondent was seated, the box was removed to reveal a jar of the defendant's LA SUPREMA Salsa standing on the table at a distance of less than an arm's length from the respondent. The box was left off the product for the remainder of the interview. The respondent was asked the question "What is the name of this product?" and was allowed to look at the jar of the defendant's product for as long as was required to answer the question. After that question was answered, the respondent was asked, "Do you know who makes this product?" If the respondent answered in the affirmative, the question "Who is it that makes this product?" was then asked. The answers were recorded and the results were tabulated. Of the 201 people who were interviewed, 38.8% responded that the product was LA SUPREMA and another 20.5% responded with an answer which included LA SUPREMA or a close variant. Only 27 people said they knew who made the product. Of the 27 people, 21 said LA SUPREMA and one person said "Victoria."

[10] The defendant's survey did not measure likelihood of confusion with the plaintiff's product. It was, if anything, merely a measure of the respondent's ability to read the defendant's label. There was no fair opportunity for the respondent to reveal any confusion which might have existed. The fact that one person, even while looking directly at the defendant's label from a distance of less than arm's length, said "Victoria" is of some slight probative value that confusion is likely.

[11] The person who designed and conducted the defendant's survey testified with regard to that survey. His testimony was not credible. He appeared to be a partisan advocate. He was highly critical of the Loftus survey, but refused to acknowledge the very obvious substantial shortcomings in the design of his own survey and in the way in which it was conducted.

CONCLUSIONS OF LAW

[1] There exists a likelihood of confusion to some appreciable degree between the plaintiff's trademark "SALSA SUPREMA" and defendant's trademark "LA SUPREMA" when defendant's trademark is used in connection with the word "salsa."

[2] Defendant has infringed on plaintiff's "SALSA SUPREMA" trademark in violation of 15 U.S.C.A. § 1114 and 15 U.S.C.A. § 1125 in connection with the word "suprema." The appropriate remedy for such infringement is an injunction preventing the defendant from using the word "SUPREMA" or "SALSA SUPREMA" as a part of the brand name or trademark of any salsa product including their currently marketed product Bean Dip with salsa.

INDIANAPOLIS COLTS v. METROPOLITAN BALTIMORE FOOTBALL

United States Court of Appeals, Seventh Circuit, 1994.
34 F.3d 410.

■ POSNER, CHIEF JUDGE.

The Indianapolis Colts and the National Football League, to which the Colts belong, brought suit for trademark infringement (15 U.S.C.A. § 1051 et seq.) against the Canadian Football League's new team in Baltimore, which wants to call itself the "Baltimore CFL Colts." [T]he plaintiffs obtained a preliminary injunction against the new team's using the name "Colts," or "Baltimore Colts," or "Baltimore CFL Colts," in connection with the playing of professional football, the broadcast of football games, or the sale of merchandise to football fans and other buyers. The ground for the injunction was that consumers of "Baltimore CFL Colts" merchandise are likely to think, mistakenly, that the new Baltimore team is an NFL team related in some fashion to the Indianapolis Colts, formerly the Baltimore Colts. From the order granting the injunction the new team and its owners appeal to us under 28 U.S.C.A. § 1292(a)(1).

[A] bit of history is necessary to frame the dispute. [I]n 1984, the [Baltimore Colt's] team's owner, with the permission of the NFL, moved the team to Indianapolis, and it was renamed the "Indianapolis Colts." The move, sudden and secretive, outraged the citizens of Baltimore. [N]ine years later, the Canadian Football League granted a franchise for a Baltimore team. Baltimoreans clamored for naming the new team the "Baltimore Colts." And so it was named—until the NFL got wind of the name and threatened legal action.

[T]he Baltimore team wanted to call itself the "Baltimore Colts." To improve its litigating posture (we assume), it has consented to insert "CFL" between "Baltimore" and "Colts." A glance at the merchandise in the record explains why this concession to an outraged NFL has been made so readily. On several of the items "CFL" appears in small or blurred letters. And since the Canadian Football League is not well known in the United States—and "CFL" has none of the instant recognition value of "NFL"—the inclusion of the acronym in the team's name might have little impact on potential buyers even if prominently displayed. Those who know football well know that the new "Baltimore Colts" are a new CFL team wholly unrelated to the old Baltimore Colts; know also that the rules of Canadian football are different from those of American football and that teams don't move from the NFL to the CFL as they might from one conference within the NFL to the other. But those who do not know these things—and we shall come shortly to the question whether there are many of these football illiterates—will not be warned off by the letters "CFL." The acronym is a red herring, and the real issue is whether the new Baltimore team can appropriate the name "Baltimore Colts." The entire thrust of the defendants' argument is that it can.

[I]f everyone knows there is no contractual or institutional continuity, no pedigree or line of descent, linking the Baltimore-Indianapolis Colts and the new CFL team that wants to call itself the "Baltimore Colts" (or, grudgingly, the "Baltimore CFL Colts"), then there is no harm, at least no harm for which the Lanham Act provides a remedy, in the new Baltimore team's appropriating the name "Baltimore Colts" to play under and sell merchandise under. If not everyone knows, there is harm. Some people who might otherwise watch the Indianapolis Colts (or some other NFL team, for remember that the NFL, representing all the teams, is a coplaintiff) on television may watch the Baltimore CFL Colts instead, thinking they are the "real" Baltimore Colts, and the NFL will lose revenue. A few (doubtless very few) people who might otherwise buy tickets to an NFL game may buy tickets to a Baltimore CFL Colts game instead. Some people who might otherwise buy merchandise stamped with the name "Indianapolis Colts" or the name of some other NFL team may buy merchandise stamped "Baltimore CFL Colts," thinking it a kin of the NFL's Baltimore Colts in the glory days of Johnny Unitas rather than a newly formed team that plays Canadian football in a Canadian football league. It would be naive to suppose that no consideration of such possibilities occurred to the owners of the new Baltimore team when they were choosing a name, though there is no evidence that it was the dominant or even a major consideration.

Confusion thus is possible, and may even have been desired; but is it likely? There is great variance in consumer competence, and it would be undesirable to impoverish the lexicon of trade names merely to protect the most gullible fringe of the consuming public. The Lanham Act does not cast the net of protection so wide. The legal standard under the Act has been formulated variously, but the various formulations come down to whether it is likely that the challenged mark if permitted to be used by the defendant would cause the plaintiff to lose a substantial number of consumers. Pertinent to this determination is the similarity of the marks and of the parties' products, the knowledge of the average consumer of the product, the overlap in the parties' geographical markets, and the other factors that the cases consider. The aim is to strike a balance between, on the one hand, the interest of the seller of the new product, and of the consuming public, in an arresting, attractive, and informative name that will enable the new product to compete effectively against existing ones, and, on the other hand, the interest of existing sellers, and again of the consuming public, in consumers' being able to know exactly what they are buying without having to incur substantial costs of investigation or inquiry.

To help judges strike the balance, the parties to trademark disputes frequently as here hire professionals in marketing or applied statistics to conduct surveys of consumers. The battle of experts that ensues is frequently unedifying. Many experts are willing for a generous (and sometimes for a modest) fee to bend their science in the direction from which their fee is coming. The constraints that the market in consultant services for lawyers places on this sort of behavior are weak, as shown by the fact that both experts in this case were hired and, we have no doubt, generously remunerated even though both have been criticized in previous judicial opinions. The judicial constraints on tendentious expert testimony are inherently weak because judges (and even more so juries, though that is not an issue in a trademark case) lack training or experience in the relevant fields of expert knowledge. But that is the system we have. It might be improved by asking each party's hired expert to designate a third, a neutral expert who would be appointed by the court to conduct the necessary studies. The necessary authority exists, see Fed.R.Evid. 706, but was not exercised here.

Both parties presented studies. The defendants' was prepared by Michael Rappeport and is summarized in a perfunctory affidavit by Dr. Rappeport to which the district judge gave little weight. That was a kindness. The heart of Rappeport's study was a survey that consisted of three loaded questions asked in one Baltimore mall. Rappeport has been criticized before for his methodology, Jaret Int'l, Inc. v. Promotion in Motion, Inc., 826 F.Supp. 69, 73–74 (E.D.N.Y.1993), and we hope that he will take these criticisms to heart in his next courtroom appearance.

The plaintiffs' study, conducted by Jacob Jacoby, was far more substantial and the district judge found it on the whole credible. The 28-page report with its numerous appendices has all the trappings of social scientific rigor. Interviewers showed several hundred consumers in 24 malls scattered around the country, shirts and hats licensed by the defendants for sale to consumers. The shirts and hats have "Baltimore CFL Colts" stamped on them. The consumers were asked whether they were football fans, whether they watched football games on television, and whether they ever bought merchandise with a team name on it. Then they were asked, with reference to the "Baltimore CFL Colts" merchandise that they were shown, such questions as whether they knew what sport the team played, what teams it played against, what league the team was in, and whether the team or league needed someone's permission to use this name, and if so whose. If, for example, the respondent answered that the team had to get permission from the Canadian Football League, the interviewer was directed to ask the respondent whether the Canadian Football League had in turn to get permission from someone. There were other questions, none however obviously loaded, and a whole other survey, the purpose of which was to control for "noise," in which another group of mallgoers was asked the identical questions about a hypothetical team unappetizingly named the "Baltimore Horses." The idea was by comparing the answers of the two groups to see whether the source of confusion was the name "Baltimore Colts" or just the name "Baltimore," in which event the injunction would do no good since no one suggests that the new Baltimore team should be forbidden to use "Baltimore" in its name, provided the name does not also include "Colts."

Rappeport threw darts at Jacoby's study. Some landed wide. We are especially perplexed by the argument that survey research belongs to sociology rather than psychology (we leave the reader to guess the respective disciplines to which our rival experts belong); the courtroom is a peculiar site for academic turf wars. [B]ut Rappeport was right to complain that the choice of "Horses" for the comparison team loaded the dice and that some of Jacoby's questions were a bit slanted. That is only to say, however, that Jacoby's survey was not perfect, and this is not news. Trials would be very short if only perfect evidence were admissible.

Jacoby's survey of consumers' reactions to the "Baltimore CFL Colts" merchandise found rather astonishing levels of confusion not plausibly attributable to the presence of the name "Baltimore" alone, since "Baltimore Horses" engendered much less. (We don't like the name "Baltimore Horses," as we have said; but we doubt that a more attractive "Baltimore" name, the "Baltimore Leopards," for example, would have generated the level of confusion that "Baltimore CFL Colts" did.) Among self-identified football fans, 64 percent thought that the "Baltimore CFL Colts" was either the old (NFL) Baltimore Colts or the Indianapolis Colts. But perhaps this result is not so astonishing. Although most American football fans have heard of Canadian football, many probably are unfamiliar with the acronym "CFL," and as we remarked earlier it is not a very conspicuous part of the team logo stamped on the merchandise. Among fans who watch football on television, 59 percent displayed the same confusion; and even among those who watch football on cable television, which attracts a more educated audience on average and actually carries CFL games, 58 percent were confused when shown the merchandise. Among the minority not confused about who the "Baltimore CFL Colts" are, a substantial minority, ranging from 21 to 34 percent depending on the precise subsample, thought the team somehow sponsored or authorized by the Indianapolis Colts or the National Football League. It is unfortunate and perhaps a bit tricky that the subsample of consumers likely to buy merchandise with a team name on it was not limited to consumers likely to buy merchandise with a football team's name on it; the choice of the name "Baltimore Horses" for the comparison team was unfortunate; and no doubt there are other tricks of the survey researcher's black arts that we have missed. There is the more fundamental problem, one common to almost all consumer survey research, that people are more careful when they are laying out their money than when they are answering questions.

But with all this granted, we cannot say that the district judge committed a clear error (the standard, Scandia Down Corp. v. Euroquilt, Inc., supra, 772 F.2d at 1427–28) in crediting the major findings of the Jacoby study and inferring from it and the other evidence in the record that the defendants' use of the name "Baltimore CFL Colts" whether for the team or on merchandise was likely to confuse a substantial number of consumers. This means [t]hat the judge's finding concerning likelihood of confusion required that the injunction issue.

[A]FFIRMED.

———

KIS v. FOTO FANTASY

United States District Court, N.D. Texas, 2001.
204 F.Supp.2d 968.

■ LYNN, DISTRICT JUDGE.

Before the Court is Defendants' Motion to Strike the Expert Report of Dr. Daniel J. Howard and to Exclude His Testimony from Trial.

[I]. Background

Plaintiffs have filed suit against Defendants alleging, *inter alia,* that Defendants have violated the Lanham Act. Plaintiffs' Lanham Act claim stems from Defendants' use of drawings of Tom Cruise and Marilyn Monroe on the outside of their photo booths. Defendants and Plaintiffs both own photo booths that are placed inside malls around the country. The booths operate by allowing the user to either have a picture taken inside of the booth, or to insert a photo brought into the booth by the user, so that the machine can transform the picture into a sketch. On the outside of Defendants' booths (a.k.a. "Portrait Studios") are sketches of Tom Cruise and Marilyn Monroe. On one corner of these celebrities' sketch images reads the phrase, "SCAN IN YOUR FAVORITE CELEBRITIES." Plaintiffs claim that the placement of these sketches on Defendants' photo booths violates the Lanham Act because it creates confusion as to the "affiliation, connection, or association" of Tom Cruise and Marilyn Monroe with Defendants' booths. [P]laintiffs argue that this confusion leads users to utilize Defendants' booths more than Plaintiffs' booths. To support this claim, Plaintiffs hired Dr. Howard to perform a survey to determine the amount of actual confusion engendered by the pictures of these celebrities on the outside of Defendants' machines.

[D]r. Howard [c]onducted his mall study, or "field experiment." He went to NorthPark Mall and selected 224 consumers for questioning. Dr. Howard picked these individuals "to match the demographics of the users of the Portrait Studio published by Foto[ ]Fantasy on its web site, as well as the demographics of users and potential users [he] observed at the Portrait Studio" in Grapevine Mills Mall. He divided the group in half, randomly assigning each participant to either the "experimental" or the "control" group.

After dividing the participants into the experimental and control groups, Dr. Howard gave every group member an envelope that contained the survey materials. In order to "avoid any possible contamination of the process," he then stood out of sight while the respondents looked through the materials and answered the questions. The only difference between the materials given to the control group and to the experimental group was the inclusion of the Tom Cruise sketch in the experimental group's packet. "Since that would be the only factor that differentiated the two groups, any reliable differences in the answers that the two groups gave to the same questions could only be attributable to their exposure to the Tom Cruise sketch."

Based on the survey results, Dr. Howard concluded that

the Tom Cruise sketch on the outside of the Portrait Studios results in the Portrait Studios being significantly more likely to capture consumers' attention[, and] significantly more likely to arouse the interest of consumers in the Portrait Studio, and [therefore consumers are] significantly more likely to purchase portraits from the Portrait Studio. I am also of the opinion that the sketch of Tom Cruise on the Portrait Studio results in approximately half of the consuming public believing that Tom Cruise endorses or approves of the Portrait Studio. I arrive at this conclusion by deducting the 7.1% of those in the control group who said they believed it likely or very likely that Tom Cruise endorsed or approved of the Portrait Studio from the 56.3% of those in the experimental group who responded the same way. By deducting the 7.1% from the 56.3%, I conclude that the "net" or "incremental" confusion rate is 49.2%.

Defendants complain that Dr. Howard's conclusions are unreliable and should be disregarded by the Court for three reasons. First, [D]r. Howard did not utilize a proper survey universe; *i.e.,* his [s]urvey participants did not mirror the actual consumers of Defendants' product. Second, the survey included leading questions that suggested the answer to the participants and resulted in a "demand effect" that skewed the survey data. Last, Dr. Howard's methodology did not reflect actual market conditions, as he only showed the survey participants pictures of the photo booth instead of an actual photo booth.

[II]. Proper Survey Universe

Defendants argue that the survey universe [w]as improper:

Dr. Howard did not ... conduct the survey at a location that contains a photo booth, not to mention one owned or operated by any of the Defendants. Dr. Howard chose for his test location an upscale shopping mall in north Dallas that can hardly be said to reflect the consumer population to which his study should have been geared; that is, a population which is likely to encounter and utilize a Portrait Studio owned by Defendants. . . .

On the importance of a proper survey universe, Defendants rely primarily upon *Amstar Corp. v. Domino's Pizza, Inc.,* 615 F.2d 252 (5th Cir.1980), and *Jaret International, Inc. v. Promotion in Motion, Inc.,* 826 F.Supp. 69, 73–74 (E.D.N.Y.1993). These cases do not assist in proving Defendants' point, however.

Defendants quote *Amstar* for the proposition that "one of the most important factors in assessing the validity of an opinion poll is the adequacy of the 'survey universe,' that is, the persons interviewed must adequately represent the opinions which are relevant to the litigation." *Amstar,* 615 F.2d at 264. Indeed, the *Amstar* court did reject a survey proffered by the plaintiff in that case, who manufactured and sold Domino's Sugar. The plaintiff had introduced the survey to prove that consumers believed Domino's Sugar and Domino's Pizza were made by the same company or were related in some other way. The court rested its decision on the fact that the plaintiff's survey only polled "women found at home during six daylight hours who identified themselves as the member of the household primarily responsible for grocery buying." *Id.* The court found that, "[a]s plaintiff's sugar is sold primarily in grocery stores, participants in the . . . survey would have been repeatedly exposed to plaintiff's mark, but would have had little, if any, exposure to defendants' mark. Furthermore, the survey neglected completely defendants' primary customers[:] young, single, male college students." *Id.* In contrast, Dr. Howard attempted to replicate Defendants' consumer base. The claimed defects in Dr. Howard's survey universe are nothing like the flagrant methodological errors that inhered in the *Amstar* poll.

Thus, the cases cited by Defendants do not support the argument that the Court should disregard Dr. Howard's findings based on his survey universe. Although Dr. Howard could have improved the survey by conducting it at more than one mall, this is not a cause to throw out his findings. In fact, a similar report by Dr. Howard was held to survive a *Daubert* challenge for lack of geographic diversity. *See Harolds Stores, Inc. v. Dillard Dep't Stores, Inc.,* 82 F.3d 1533 (10th Cir.1996). In that case, Harold's Stores retained Dr. Howard to conduct a survey to " 'determine whether, and to what degree, Dillard's sale of Harold's copyrighted fabric designs inflicted damages to future sales of women's and men's clothing by Harold's.' " *Id.* at 1545. Dr. Howard's entire survey universe consisted of 1,231 female undergraduates at SMU. Dillard's objected to the universe of customers surveyed, arguing that it was too narrow. The court held, however, that Dr. Howard's testimony and report were admissible, finding that survey evidence should only be excluded "when the sample is clearly not representative of the universe it is intended to reflect." *See id.* at 1544 (internal quotation marks omitted). In contrast, "[t]echnical and methodological deficiencies in the survey, including the sufficiency of the universe sampled, bear on the weight of the evidence, not on the survey's admissibility." *Id.* The situation in *Harolds Stores* is much like the one at hand: In both, Dr. Howard attempted to assemble a survey participant group that conformed to the demographics supplied by Foto Fantasy. [A]lthough Dr. Howard could have conducted the survey with a larger respondent base, these defects go towards the weight, and not the admissibility, of the evidence.

III. *The Demand Effect*

Defendants argue that Dr. Howard's survey questions were leading and therefore tainted the participants' responses. The Court finds that the survey questions were not leading, however, as they did not suggest an answer to the respondents.[4] Defendants urge that even if the questions are not leading *per se,* they still suggest a possible association between Tom Cruise and the Portrait Studios that impermissibly influenced the participants' responses. In this argument, Defendants overlook the fact that Dr. Howard utilized a control group, one of the purposes of which was to monitor any possible demand effect the questions had on the respondents. As one district court found, "[t]he control cell is supposed to 'control' extraneous factors (known as 'noise')." *Novartis Consumer Health, Inc. v. Johnson & Johnson-Merck Consumer Pharm. Co.,* 129 F.Supp.2d 351, 365 n. 10 (D.N.J.2000). It further explained that " 'the control cell functions as a baseline and provides a measure of the degree to which respondents are likely to give an answer . . . because of other factors, such as the survey's questions, the survey's procedures, . . . or some other potential influence on a respondent's answer such as pre-existing beliefs.' " *Id.* (quoting the declaration of the expert who had conducted the survey). On this basis, Plaintiffs argue that, "[t]o the extent that something about the procedure or the questions in Dr. Howard's survey led consumers to see an endorsement where otherwise they might not have, that factor can be eliminated by subtracting the control group result from the test group result," which Dr. Howard purportedly did in determining the "net" confusion rate of 49.2%.

The Court finds that the use of the control group could have negated any real effect the form of the questions had on the participants. The fact that about 7% of the control group found it likely or very likely that Tom Cruise endorsed Defendants' Portrait Studios does suggest that something about the questions, the form of the survey, or something in the participants' background beliefs influenced them to find a relationship between the two even though they were not shown a picture of the Tom Cruise sketch that hangs outside Defendants' photo booths. Dr. Howard's subtracting of the 7.1% attributable to "noise" in arriving at his net estimation of confusion addresses this problem so that it does not present a reason for the Court to strike Dr. Howard's report and disregard his testimony.

---

4. Dr. Howard asked, among other things, "How likely or unlikely is it that Tom Cruise has endorsed, or approves of, the Portrait Studio?" The participants could choose from the following answers: very likely, likely, unsure, unlikely, and very unlikely.

IV.   Market Conditions

Defendants last argue that Dr. Howard's report fails to accurately reflect market conditions because [t]he survey participants were presented with an allegedly misleading picture of the Portrait Studio instead of with the actual Portrait Studio itself. [A]lthough it is clear from Dr. Howard's description of his experiment that it did not mirror actual market conditions in every possible way, Dr. Howard attempted, in his materials, to explain to the participants the mindset they should have in evaluating Defendants' photo booths. For example, the instructions to the questions told participants, "[w]hen answering these questions, assume that you were walking by a Portrait Studio." Dr. Howard also attempted to explain to the participants how the pictures of Tom Cruise and Marilyn Monroe fit into the overall design of the photo booths, stating that "[t]his 8 1/2 x 11 sketch is displayed on the outside of the Studio as an example of the Studio's work."

[I]n conclusion, the Court finds that Defendants' criticism of Dr. Howard's survey methodology, although it may be persuasive, goes only to the weight, and not the admissibility, of the evidence. Therefore, Defendants' Motion to Strike Dr. Howard's expert report and trial testimony is DENIED.

———

PHARMACIA CORP. v. ALCON LABORATORIES, INC.

United States District Court, D. New Jersey, 2002.
201 F.Supp.2d 335.

■ BASSLER, DISTRICT JUDGE.

Pharmacia initiated this civil action on March 30, 2001 under the Lanham (Trademark) Act of 1946 and New Jersey statutory and common law.

On April 16, 2001, Pharmacia moved for a preliminary injunction to enjoin defendant Alcon from infringing [P]harmacia's federally registered Xalatan trademark in connection with Alcon's use of the name Travatan for the sale of a prostaglandin-based product used for the treatment of the eye disease glaucoma.

[T]he Diamond Survey

Alcon produced evidence in the form of a survey of the relevant population, that the marketplace is not confused. A well-designed survey of ophthalmologists and optometrists conducted by Prof. Shari Seidman Diamond shows a net confusion rate of 1.5%. (there is "no evidence that the name of Alcon's product Travatan is likely to cause confusion with the name of Pharmacia's product Xalatan in the relevant population," *i.e.,* ophthalmologists and optometrists). Dr. Diamond also testified at the evidentiary hearing. The Court found her to be a very credible witness.

Professor Diamond is a professor of law and psychology at Northwestern University School of Law and a senior research fellow at the American Bar Foundation. She is the author of the *Reference Guide to Survey Research* contained in the Federal Judicial Center's *Reference Guide on Scientific Evidence* (1994, 2000), as well as a similar chapter in West Publishing's four volume treatise, *Modern Scientific Evidence* (1997, 2000), and several other well-respected articles in the field.

Professor Diamond chose to survey a nationwide population of ophthalmologists and optometrists because they are the market gatekeepers with respect to the prescription glaucoma medications at issue in this case. Ophthalmologists and optometrists thus make the ultimate determination as to which medications pharmacists will dispense and end-users—patients—will receive.

[I]n order to ensure that the population surveyed was representative of glaucoma prescribers, Professor Diamond considered several lists of doctors from which to draw interviewees, including the membership list for the American Ophthalmology Association. Professor Diamond ultimately used a list assembled by the National Data Center because it is widely used for research purposes within the pharmaceutical industry and because it provided enough information about potential respondents' practice size and years of experience to allow for a stratified random sample.

Because doctors are a particularly busy population of potential respondents, Professor Diamond arranged for each one to receive an advance letter, as well as follow-up phone calls, to schedule interviews at a convenient time.

The Diamond Survey tested for product source confusion. [T]here were two cells in the survey: (1) a test cell of 200 prescribers that used a Travatan advertisement as the stimulus; and (2) a control cell, also of 200 prescribers, that used an identical Lumigan ® advertisement as the stimulus. The stimulus was designed to focus the respondent's attention primarily on the name of the product.

The questions that Professor Diamond selected for the survey ("What company do you believe puts out the product whose advertisement you just saw?;" "Please tell me whether or not you believe the company whose advertisement you just saw puts out any other medications for the eye;" and "Please tell me whether or not you believe that the company whose advertisement you just saw needs authorization, permission or approval from some other company in order to put out the product advertised."), are a standard type and format of questions used to gauge confusion in trademark cases. Pharmacia's survey expert, Walter McCullough, used virtually identical questions in a trademark confusion survey he designed in a prior infringement case.

Five percent of the test cell respondents confused the source of Xalatan ® and Travatan and 3.5% of control cell respondents confused the source of Xalatan ® and Lumigan ®, yielding net confusion of 1.5%.

Professor Diamond selected the survey firm D.S. Howard & Associates ("D.S. Howard") to conduct the survey because it specializes in medical surveys and medical marketing research, fields surveys for pharmaceutical companies for approximately 60% of its work and is staffed by surveyors with an academic background and a reputation for attention to detail.

Interviewers were instructed to record absolute and accurate verbatim responses and capture every word and sound uttered by respondents, including the "humms" and "ahhs," even if doing so meant simultaneously transcribing the responses in less than perfect penmanship.

[A] review of all the questionnaires, as well as monitoring reports and tapes of the interviews, confirms that the responses were recorded accurately and completely. [T]he raw data collected for this survey, in the form of the verbatim responses of doctors, was preserved and was made available to Pharmacia and the Court for review.

[T]he Court is aware that Pharmacia is not legally required to conduct a confusion survey. But under the circumstances of this case, Pharmacia's failure to conduct any confusion survey weighs against its request for a preliminary injunction. Such a failure, particularly when the trademark owner is financially able, justifies an inference "that the plaintiff believes the results of the survey will be unfavorable." *Charles Jacquin et Cie, Inc. v. Destileria Serralles, Inc.*, 921 F.2d 467, 475 (3d Cir.1990).

Pharmacia's attempt to explain away its decision not to conduct a confusion survey (economics) further supports the appropriateness of such an inference, in light of the fact that from July 2000 forward, Pharmacia conducted numerous surveys concerning the Travatan mark, but never attempted to assess whether Travatan was likely to cause confusion with Xalatan. Moreover, the results of that research show that over 95% of ophthalmologists were aware of Travatan and Xalatan as distinct products. The enormous sums Pharmacia invested in market research to prepare for the Travatan launch stand in stark contrast to its failure to conduct a confusion survey here, and fully warrant a negative inference regarding likelihood of confusion.

[P]rofessor Diamond's well-designed survey of ophthalmologists and optometrists, showing a net confusion rate of 1.5%, provides further evidence to support the Court's conclusion that no confusion is likely. *Henri's Food Prods. Co. v. Kraft, Inc.*, 717 F.2d 352, 358–59 (7th Cir.1983) (holding that 7.6% confusion finding is "a factor weighing against infringement"); *Pfizer Inc. v. Astra Pharm. Prods., Inc.*, 858 F.Supp. 1305, 1326 (S.D.N.Y. 1994) (adjusted confusion rate of 7.27% in a survey is "low" and insufficient evidence of likelihood of confusion); *see also* 5 McCarthy § 32:188, at 32–311 (4th ed.2001) (generally, "figures below 20 percent become problematic because they can only be viewed against the background of other evidence . . . ").

[P]harmacia's Opinions Regarding Likelihood of Confusion

Because Pharmacia has no marketplace evidence of likely or actual confusion, it emphasizes evidence in the form of expert opinion testimony.

This evidence is insufficient to overcome the marketplace evidence that confusion is unlikely. Apart from consumer surveys, "[L]ay or even expert opinion about the likelihood of confusion is inadmissible or entitled to little weight." Richard L. Kirkpatrick, *Likelihood of Confusion in Trademark Law*, § 1.8.c, at 1–45 (PLI 1995); *Barnes Group*, 793 F.Supp. at 1293, 1301–02 (expert opinion that confusion was likely, offered without any supporting empirical data or marketplace observations, could not be relied on).

The opinions of Dr. Eisenberg and Mr. Di Domizio with regard to the likelihood of confusion between Travatan and Xalatan are based primarily on a subjective evaluation of the marks in light of their experience in the pharmaceutical industry (Di Domizio) or as an ophthalmologist (Eisenberg). There are no reported trademark cases in which a court has based its findings of a likelihood of confusion or dilution on the types of "opinions" on which Pharmacia relies. The bases for these opinions stand in stark contrast to the survey conducted by Professor Shari S. Diamond, J.D., Ph. D., which demonstrates persuasively a confusion rate of 1.5%.

[C]ONCLUSION

For the reasons discussed, the plaintiff's motion for a preliminary injunction is denied.

———

MANUAL FOR COMPLEX LITIGATION (4th Ed. 2004)
Federal Judicial Center.

Parties who propose to offer sampling or survey evidence may want to consider whether to disclose details of the proposed sampling or survey methods to the opposing parties before the work is done (including the specific questions that will be asked, the introductory statements or instructions that will be given, and other controls to be used in the interrogation process). Objections can then be raised promptly and corrective measures taken before the survey is completed. A meeting of the parties' experts can expedite the resolution of problems affecting admissibility.

———

REFERENCE GUIDE ON SURVEY RESEARCH
Shari Seidman Diamond.
In Reference Manual on Scientific Evidence (2d. 2000)

Purpose and Design of the Survey

A. Was the Survey Designed to Address Relevant Questions?

B. Was Participation in the Design, Administration, and Interpretation of the Survey Appropriately Controlled to Ensure the Objectivity of the Survey?

C.   Are the Experts Who Designed, Conducted, or Analyzed the Survey Appropriately Skilled and Experienced?

D.   Are the Experts Who Will Testify About Surveys Conducted by Others Appropriately Skilled and Experienced?

Population Definition and Sampling

A.   Was an Appropriate Universe or Population Identified?

B.   Did the Sampling Frame Approximate the Population?

C.   How Was the Sample Selected to Approximate the Relevant Characteristics of the Population?

D.   Was the Level of Nonresponse Sufficient to Raise Questions About the Representativeness of the Sample? If So, What Is the Evidence That Nonresponse Did Not Bias the Results of the Survey?

E.   What Procedures Were Used to Reduce the Likelihood of a Biased Sample?

F.   What Precautions Were Taken to Ensure That Only Qualified Respondents Were Included in the Survey?

Survey Questions and Structure

A.   Were Questions on the Survey Framed to Be Clear, Precise, and Unbiased?

B.   Were Filter Questions Provided to Reduce Guessing?

C.   Did the Survey Use Open-Ended or Closed-Ended Questions? How Was the Choice in Each Instance Justified?

D.   If Probes Were Used to Clarify Ambiguous or Incomplete Answers, What Steps Were Taken to Ensure That the Probes Were Not Leading and Were Administered in a Consistent Fashion?

E.   What Approach Was Used to Avoid or Measure Potential Order or Context Effects?

F.   If the Survey Was Designed to Test a Causal Proposition, Did the Survey Include an Appropriate Control Group or Question?

G.   What Limitations Are Associated with the Mode of Data Collection Used in the Survey?

> 1.   In-person interviews
>
> 2.   Telephone surveys
>
> 3.   Mail surveys
>
> 4.   Internet surveys

Surveys Involving Interviewers

A.   Were the Interviewers Appropriately Selected and Trained?

B.   What Did the Interviewers Know About the Survey and Its Sponsorship?

C. What Procedures Were Used to Ensure and Determine That the Survey Was Administered to Minimize Error and Bias?

Data Entry and Grouping of Responses

A. What Was Done to Ensure That the Data Were Recorded Accurately?

B. What Was Done to Ensure That the Grouped Data Were Classified Consistently and Accurately?

Disclosure and Reporting

A. When Was Information About the Survey Methodology and Results Disclosed?

B. Does the Survey Report Include Complete and Detailed Information on All Relevant Characteristics?

C. In Surveys of Individuals, What Measures Were Taken to Protect the Identities of Individual Respondents?

———

McCARTHY ON TRADEMARKS AND UNFAIR COMPETITION (4th Ed. 1996)

J. Thomas McCarthy.

It is notoriously easy for one survey expert to appear to tear apart the methodology of a survey taken by another. [O]ne must keep in mind that there is no such thing as a "perfect" survey. The nature of the beast is that it is a sample, albeit a scientifically constructed one. One must remain cognizant of the fact that, as Judge Anderson said of the survey evidence in the famous "Thermos" case, "any conclusion in this area cannot be reduced to a figure of unimpeachable accuracy but must, at best, be an approximation."[8] Like any scientific method related to statistics in the social sciences, every survey, no matter how carefully constructed and conducted, has some potential flaws somewhere. The proper approach is to view such evidence with some understanding of the difficulty of devising and running a survey and to use any technical defects only to lessen evidentiary weight, not to reject the results out-of-hand.

[P]robably, a part of a lingering judicial skepticism about survey evidence can be laid at the feet of parties and their attorneys who, in a desperate search for *some kind* of evidence, offer, with a straight face, a haphazard, self-serving "survey." It may not be surprising that many judges view such purported "scientific evidence" with distaste. They know that the techniques of testing and sampling buyer reactions have been developed to a fairly high degree of accuracy. Thus, there is no real excuse for a biased survey which attempts to measure buyer reaction by means of

8. American Thermos Products Co. v. Aladdin Industries, Inc. [207 F.Supp. 9, 21, 134 U.S.P.Q. (BNA) 98 (D.Conn.1962).]

leading or irrelevant questions asked in an environment far removed from the marketplace. The reason, of course, that accurate and scientifically precise surveys are not always offered is that they are costly. Perhaps the best that can be said is that no survey at all is better than a survey obtained "on the cheap." As weak arguments detract from even a strong case, a weak survey may detract from even the strongest case of trademark infringement.

SOCIAL FACTS: SCIENTIFIC METHODOLOGY AS LEGAL PRECEDENT

Laurens Walker and John Monahan.
76 California Law Review 877 (1988).

Under the Federal Rules of Evidence, the analysis of the admissibility of social science research to prove a case-specific fact begins—and usually ends—with the question of "relevance." According to Rule 401:

"Relevant evidence" means evidence having any tendency to make the existence of any fact that is of consequence to the determination of the action more probable or less probable than it would be without the evidence.

There are two components to this definition: To be relevant, evidence must bear on a fact that is "of consequence" to the case, and must make that fact "more probable or less probable" than it would otherwise be.

[A.] Materiality

While it was once mired in the strictures of pleading, the question of whether evidence is "of consequence" or "material" to a fact in issue is now generally treated as a component of relevance. Materiality concerns the relation between the proposition that the evidence is offered to demonstrate and the factual issues in the case. If the evidence is offered to prove a proposition that is not at issue, the evidence is immaterial and therefore irrelevant.

Whether proffered evidence is material depends upon the legal issue before the court: "[w]hat is 'in issue,' that is, within the range of the litigated controversy, is ... controlled by the substantive law."[32] In the context of social fact evidence, this means that even research flawlessly executed is inadmissible if the substantive law governing the case does not put in issue the fact that the research seeks to establish.

Questions of materiality are questions of substantive law, not questions of social science. Even without inquiring into the empirical merits of the evidence, it is proper for a court to exclude social science research that does not purport to demonstrate a fact with which the substantive law is concerned. Since judicial decisions based on the materiality prong of Rule

32. See C. McCormick, McCormick on Evidence — 185, at 541 (3d ed. 1984).

401 interpret the substantive law governing a case, they have the same precedential value as any other decisions of substantive law. Indeed, decisions on the materiality of social science evidence have uniformly been treated as precedent by subsequent courts.

[B.] Probative Value

To be relevant, evidence must make the existence of a fact "more probable or less probable" than it was before the evidence was offered. This component of relevance is usually referred to as "probative value" or "logical relevance." Evidence is logically relevant "only when the probability of finding that evidence given the truth of some hypothesis at issue in the case differs from the probability of finding the evidence given the falsity of the hypothesis at issue."[39] In the context of social science evidence, this means that even if the research directly addresses a fact of central concern to the substantive law, it will not be admitted unless the research data provides insight into the likelihood that the fact exists.

———

NOTES

1. Standard of Appellate Review. Both of the appellate cases included above—*Indianapolis Colts* and *Amstar*—applied the "clear error" standard for reviewing the trial court determination of consumer confusion. "Clear error" is the standard appellate courts normally use whenever they review a trial court determination of "adjudicative" fact. The reasons for this deference to trial courts have to do both with efficiency—so that appellate courts do not have to spend their time adjudicating factual issues already decided—and with accuracy—since the trial court actually observed the witnesses' testimony and the appellate court has only the "cold record" on which to rely, the trial court is generally in a better position to judge the facts. An appellate court makes its own findings of fact only to the extent that it determines what the facts are *not*—that the trial court was "clearly erroneous" in determining the facts based on the evidence in the record. In Amstar Corporation v. Domino's Pizza, for example, the appellate court held that the trial court was clearly in error when it held that the survey done by Amstar demonstrated consumer confusion between Domino's pizza and Domino's sugar.

2. Materiality and Probative Value. The "materiality" of social science evidence in trademark litigation is usually plain: the surveys address consumer confusion, which, given the language of the Lanham Act, is "of consequence" to the determination of trademark infringement. The dispute typically is whether the survey has probative value, that is, whether the survey makes it "more probable or less probable" that consumers are in fact confused. In La Victoria Foods v. Curtice-Burns, however, the court ruled that the defendant's survey—in which subjects were seated at a table

39. Lempert, Modeling Relevance, 75 Mich.L.Rev. 1021, 1026 (1977).

on which there was a bottle of LA SUPREMA salsa and asked "What is the name of this product?"—was immaterial: "The defendant's survey did not measure likelihood of confusion with plaintiff's product. It was, if anything, a measure of the respondent's ability to read the defendant's label."

3. Admissibility versus Weight of the Evidence. The court in *Zippo* distinguished the "admissibility" of the survey evidence from the "weight" to be accorded it in determining consumer confusion. The court in *KIS* and the commentary by McCarthy also raise this distinction. According to Federal Rule of Evidence 401, evidence is relevant if it has "any tendency" to make a material fact "more probable or less probable than it would be without the evidence." According to Rule 402, "[a]ll relevant evidence is admissible" (unless its admission violates some other laws or rules; see Appendix A). Therefore, it is not necessary for social science evidence to be determinative of a fact at issue in the case, or even to make the existence of a fact such as consumer confusion "more likely than not," for the evidence to be admitted. As long as it has "any" tendency to demonstrate the existence of consumer confusion, the evidence is relevant and therefore presumptively admissible. While a particular survey may be admissible because it has at least some tendency to demonstrate a fact like consumer confusion, the methodology of the survey, or the way that the methodology was carried out, may be sufficiently flawed that the survey evidence should not be given much "weight" in determining whether consumers are likely to be confused.

4. Other Uses of Social Science Evidence in Trademark Law. The use of social science evidence in trademark law is by no means limited to the determination of consumer confusion. The Lanham Act also prohibits the granting of a trademark to a "generic" term, and allows for the cancellation of a valid trademark to a term that becomes generic. A generic term is the common name for a type of product made by many companies, "the name of a particular genus or class of which an individual article or service is but a member." Vision Center v. Opticks, Inc., 596 F.2d 111, 115 (5th Cir. 1979). Examples of terms that have been held to be generic are aspirin, cellophane, escalator, and thermos. Examples of terms that have been challenged as generic but have been held by courts to be valid trademarks are COKE, LEVI'S, POLAROID, and TEFLON. Social science evidence is often used to determine whether a term is the common designation for a type of product made by many companies, or whether it is associated by the public with a particular product or producer. For an account of this and other uses of social science evidence in trademark litigation—including the "secondary meaning" that can be acquired by "descriptive" terms—see J. McCarthy, McCarthy on Trademarks and Unfair Competition (4th ed. 1996).

5. Consumer Perceptions and Deceptive Advertising. Issues analogous to consumer confusion in Lanham Act trademark cases also arise in Lanham Act deceptive advertising cases under 15 U.S.C.A. § 1125(a). Inconsistencies found between the literal message of an advertisement and the listeners' or viewers' perceptions of the message have been found relevant to the issues of "miscomprehension," "deception," and "misleadingness." The role played by social science research in determining facts in deceptive advertising litigation is discussed in Diamond and Dimitropoulos, Deception and Puffery in Advertising: Behavioral Science Implications for Regulation, in Advertising, Law and the Social Sciences (J. Lipton and B. Sales, eds., 1993), and Diamond, Using Psychology to Control Law: From Deceptive Advertising to Criminal Sentencing, 13 Law and Human Behavior 239 (1989).

EMPIRICAL QUESTIONS WITHOUT EMPIRICAL ANSWERS

John Monahan and Laurens Walker.
1991 Wisconsin Law Review 569 (1991).

[W]hat should a court do in trademark or similar cases when the parties contest a "social fact" but do not bring forth [s]ocial science evidence in support of their assertions? Since social facts are explicitly within the purview of the Federal Rules of Evidence and similar state codes, the answer, it would seem, is to be found by identifying the party with the burden of proof and then asking whether that burden has been met.

The substantive law, of course, identifies the party with the burden of proof and also specifies the type of evidence that will be sufficient to meet that burden. In trademark infringement cases, to continue our example, the plaintiff—the owner of a registered mark—bears the burden of proving by a preponderance of the evidence that the latecomer's product will cause "consumer confusion."

[W]hile social science studies are not the only form of evidence for proving consumer confusion,[27] they are clearly the preferred form of evidence for proving this "social fact." Failure of the plaintiff to introduce valid survey results may not be fatal to its claim of infringement, because other, less probative, forms of evidence bearing on consumer confusion may be available. But with courts beginning to draw adverse inferences from a lack of survey evidence, it will be a rare case where infringement is found in the absence of social science research.

More generally, failure to carry the burden of proof regarding an issue based on social fact will ordinarily result in victory for the opposing party, at least with respect to that issue in the case.

27. In Polaroid Corp. v. Polarad Elecs. Corp., 287 F.2d 492, 495 (2d Cir.1961), cert. denied, 368 U.S. 820 (1961), the Second Circuit specified a large number of factors of potential relevance in proving likely confusion, including the strength of the plaintiff's mark (for which advertising and sales figures are relevant evidence), defendant's bad faith adoption of the mark (for which instructions to a designer to imitate plaintiff's package are relevant evidence), and actual confusion (for which evidence of misdirected mail or phone calls is relevant). See S. Kane, Trademark Law: A Practitioner's Guide 117–37, 239–42 (1987).

SELECTED BIBLIOGRAPHY

Becker, Public Opinion Polls and Surveys as Evidence: Suggestions for Resolving Confusing and Conflicting Standards Governing Weight and Admissibility, 70 Oregon Law Review 463 (1991).

G. Dinwoodie and M. Janis, Trademarks and Unfair Competition: Law and Policy (2004).

P. Goldstein and E. Kitch, Unfair Competition, Trademark, Copyright, and Patent (2003).

E. Kitch and H. Perlman, Legal Regulation of the Competitive Process (4th ed. 1991).

J. McCarthy, Trademarks and Unfair Competition (4th ed. 1996).

M. Saks and R. Van Duizend, The Use of Scientific Evidence in Litigation (1983).

Section II.   Obscenity

In Interstate Circuit, Inc. v. Dallas, 390 U.S. 676, 88 S.Ct. 1298, 20 L.Ed.2d 225 (1968), Justice Harlan, dissenting, stated that "the subject of obscenity has produced a variety of views among members of the Court unmatched in any other course of constitutional adjudication. [In] 13 obscenity cases [i]n which signed opinions were written, [t]here has been a total of 55 separate opinions among the Justices." 390 U.S. at 704–705, 88 S.Ct. at 1314.

In Chapter Two, we deal with the controversial question of whether obscene materials are protected by the First Amendment. Here, we anticipate the Supreme Court's holding that "obscenity is not within the area of constitutionally protected speech or press," Roth v. United States, 354 U.S. 476, 485, 77 S.Ct. 1304, 1309, 1 L.Ed.2d 1498 (1957), and focus on the equally controversial question of how social science evidence can be used to determine whether a particular publication or film is obscene.

Before examining the ways that social science research has been used as evidence in obscenity litigation, we first consider whether social science evidence is admissible at all in such cases.

A.   The Admissibility of Social Science Evidence of Obscenity

Until the 1970's, two issues regarding the use of social science evidence in obscenity litigation were extensively debated by the United States Supreme Court and by lower courts. The first was whether the constitution *required* the prosecution to offer expert evidence of obscenity as part of proving its case beyond a reasonable doubt. The second was whether under the constitution the defense must be *permitted* to offer expert evidence to rebut the prosecution's case.

PEOPLE v. MULLER

Court of Appeals of New York, 1884.
96 N.Y. 408.

■ ANDREWS, J.

The defendant on the trial called as witnesses an artist who had practiced painting for many years, and also a person who had been engaged in the study of art. They were asked by defendant's counsel whether there was a distinguishing line, as understood by artists, between pure art and obscene and indecent art. The question was objected to by the prosecutor and excluded by the court.

[I]ndeed there is but little scope for proof bearing upon the issue of decency or obscenity, beyond the evidence furnished by the picture itself. The question which was excluded, if intended to bring out the fact that pictures might be either decent or indecent, and that the canons of pure art would accept those of one class and reject those of the other, was properly overruled as an attempt to prove a self-evident proposition. If the question was intended to be followed by proof that, according to the standard of judgment adopted and recognized by artists, the photographs in question were not obscene or indecent, it was properly rejected for the reason that the issue was not whether in the opinion of witnesses, or of a class of people, the photographs were indecent or obscene, but whether they were so in fact, and upon this issue witnesses could neither be permitted to give their own opinions, or to state the aggregate opinion of a particular class or part of the community. To permit such evidence would put the witness in the place of the jury, and the latter would have no function to discharge. The testimony of experts is not admissible upon matters of judgment within the knowledge and experience of ordinary jurymen. The question whether a picture or writing is obscene is one of the plainest that can be presented to a jury, and under the guidance of a discreet judge there is little danger of their reaching a wrong conclusion. The opinions of witnesses would not aid the jury in reaching a conclusion, and their admission would contravene the general rule that facts and not opinions are to be given in evidence.

JACOBELLIS v. OHIO

Supreme Court of the United States, 1964.
378 U.S. 184, 84 S.Ct. 1676, 12 L.Ed.2d 793.

*Oral Argument, April 1, 1964**

JUSTICE BLACK: How would you prove community standards?

* From Obscenity: The Complete Oral Arguments Before the Supreme Court in the   Major Obscenity Cases (L. Friedman, ed. 1970).

MR. CORRIGAN [Representing the State of Ohio]: You prove community standards, Your Honor, by putting in evidence people who are [experts].

You are able to have these people testify as to whether or not this material is below or above the community standards and subject them to cross-examination as to the basis for their opinion.

[J]USTICE WHITE: What is wrong with the jury just deciding? Why is not the jury itself a representative of community standards without having any evidence or testimony as to what they are? [I]f it is a local standard, is not the jury, in theory at least, and perhaps in fact, the better judges than the experts brought in from outside?

MR. CORRIGAN: Your Honor, you have to make a record upon which to appeal. You have to have something.

[J]USTICE WHITE: Well, you do have the obscene publication.

MR. CORRIGAN: Yes, sir.

JUSTICE WHITE: Now, do you think you have to have expert testimony in addition to that?

[M]R. CORRIGAN: I think it is helpful in making a determination as to what the community standard is.

JUSTICE HARLAN: I suppose what you are really doing is saying that perhaps every juryman who sits on these cases has not read quite as widely as some others have, and I suppose what you are doing with this evidence is to expose a juryman to at least the views of other individuals in the community in the name of "community standard," to tell him, "consider this before you say this book is obscene," or "you are to consider that before you say it is not obscene."

Is not that what it really comes down to?

MR. CORRIGAN: That is exactly right, Your Honor.

———

JACOBELLIS v. OHIO

Supreme Court of the United States, 1964.
378 U.S. 184, 84 S.Ct. 1676, 12 L.Ed.2d 793.

■ MR. JUSTICE STEWART, concurring.

I have reached the conclusion [t]hat under the First and Fourteenth Amendments criminal laws in this area are constitutionally limited to hard-core pornography. I shall not today attempt further to define the kinds of material I understand to be embraced within that shorthand description; and perhaps I could never succeed in intelligibly doing so. But I know it when I see it, and the motion picture involved in this case is not that.

———

SMITH v. CALIFORNIA

Supreme Court of the United States, 1959.
361 U.S. 147, 80 S.Ct. 215, 4 L.Ed.2d 205.

■ MR. JUSTICE FRANKFURTER, concurring.

[There is a] right of one charged with obscenity—a right implicit in the very nature of the legal concept of obscenity—to enlighten the judgment of the tribunal, be it the jury or as in this case the judge, regarding the prevailing literary and moral community standards and to do so through qualified experts. It is immaterial whether the basis of the exclusion of such testimony is irrelevance, or the incompetence of experts to testify to such matters. The two reasons coalesce, for community standards or the psychological or physiological consequences of questioned literature can as a matter of fact hardly be established except through experts. Therefore, to exclude such expert testimony is in effect to exclude as irrelevant evidence that goes to the very essence of the defense and therefore to the constitutional safeguards of due process. The determination of obscenity no doubt rests with judge or jury. Of course the testimony of experts would not displace judge or jury in determining the ultimate question whether the particular book is obscene, any more than the testimony of experts relating to the state of the art in patent suits determines the patentability of a controverted device.

There is no external measuring rod for obscenity. Neither, on the other hand, is its ascertainment a merely subjective reflection of the taste or moral outlook of individual jurors or individual judges. Since the law through its functionaries is "applying contemporary community standards" in determining what constitutes obscenity, Roth v. United States, 354 U.S. 476, 489, 77 S.Ct. 1304, 1311, 1 L.Ed.2d 1498, it surely must be deemed rational, and therefore relevant to the issue of obscenity, to allow light to be shed on what those "contemporary community standards" are. Their interpretation ought not to depend solely on the necessarily limited, hit-or-miss, subjective view of what they are believed to be by the individual juror or judge. It bears repetition that the determination of obscenity is for juror or judge not on the basis of his personal upbringing or restricted reflection or particular experience of life, but on the basis of "contemporary community standards." Can it be doubted that there is a great difference in what is to be deemed obscene in 1959 compared with what was deemed obscene in 1859? The difference derives from a shift in community feeling regarding what is to be deemed prurient or not prurient by reason of the effects attributable to this or that particular writing. Changes in the intellectual and moral climate of society, in part doubtless due to the views and findings of specialists, afford shifting foundations for the attribution. What may well have been consonant "with mid-Victorian morals, does not seem to me to answer to the understanding and morality of the present time." United States v. Kennerley, 209 F. 119, 120. This was the view of Judge Learned Hand decades ago reflecting an atmosphere of propriety much closer to mid-Victorian days than is ours. Unless we disbelieve that the literary, psychological or moral standards of a community can be made fruitful and illuminating subjects of inquiry by those who give their life to such inquiries, it was violative of "due process" to exclude the constitutionally relevant evidence proffered in this case. [F]or the reasons I have indicated, I would make the right to introduce such evidence a requirement of due process in obscenity prosecutions.

MILLER v. CALIFORNIA

Supreme Court of the United States, 1973.
413 U.S. 15, 93 S.Ct. 2607, 37 L.Ed.2d 419.

■ MR. CHIEF JUSTICE BURGER delivered the opinion of the Court.

This is one of a group of "obscenity-pornography" cases being reviewed by the Court in a re-examination of standards enunciated in earlier cases involving what Mr. Justice Harlan called "the intractable obscenity problem." Interstate Circuit, Inc. v. Dallas, 390 U.S. 676, 704, 88 S.Ct. 1298, 1313, 20 L.Ed.2d 225 (1968) (concurring and dissenting).

Appellant conducted a mass mailing campaign to advertise the sale of illustrated books, euphemistically called "adult" material. After a jury trial, he was convicted of violating California Penal Code — 311.2(a), a misdemeanor, by knowingly distributing obscene matter.

[T]he basic guidelines for the trier of fact must be: (a) whether "the average person, applying contemporary community standards" would find that the work, taken as a whole, appeals to the prurient interest, (b) whether the work depicts or describes, in a patently offensive way, sexual conduct specifically defined by the applicable state law; and (c) whether the work, taken as a whole, lacks serious literary, artistic, political, or scientific value.

[D]uring the trial, both the prosecution and the defense assumed that the relevant "community standards" in making the factual determination of obscenity were those of the State of California, not some hypothetical standard of the entire United States of America. Defense counsel at trial never objected to the testimony of the State's expert on community standards[12] or to the instructions of the trial judge on "statewide" standards.

[N]othing in the First Amendment requires that a jury must consider hypothetical and unascertainable "national standards" when attempting to determine whether certain materials are obscene as a matter of fact.

---

12. The record simply does not support appellant's contention, belatedly raised on appeal, that the State's expert was unqualified to give evidence on California "community standards." The expert, a police officer with many years of specialization in obsceni- ty offenses, had conducted an extensive statewide survey and had given expert evidence on 26 occasions in the year prior to this trial. Allowing such expert testimony was certainly not constitutional error.

[I]t is neither realistic nor constitutionally sound to read the First Amendment as requiring that the people of Maine or Mississippi accept public depiction of conduct found tolerable in Las Vegas, or New York City.

PARIS ADULT THEATRE I v. SLATON

Supreme Court of the United States, 1973.
413 U.S. 49, 93 S.Ct. 2628, 37 L.Ed.2d 446.

■ MR. CHIEF JUSTICE BURGER delivered the opinion of the Court.

It should be clear from the outset that we do not undertake to tell the States what they must do, but rather to define the area in which they may chart their own course in dealing with obscene material.

[But it was not] error [for the trial court] to fail to require "expert" affirmative evidence that the materials were obscene when the materials themselves were actually placed in evidence. The films, obviously, are the best evidence of what they represent.[6]

KAPLAN v. CALIFORNIA

Supreme Court of the United States, 1973.
413 U.S. 115, 93 S.Ct. 2680, 37 L.Ed.2d 492.

■ MR. CHIEF JUSTICE BURGER delivered the opinion of the Court.

In Miller v. California, 413 U.S. 15, 93 S.Ct. 2607, 37 L.Ed.2d 419, the Court today holds that the " 'contemporary community standards of the State of California,' "as opposed to "national standards," are constitutionally adequate to establish whether a work is obscene. We also reject in Paris Adult Theatre I v. Slaton [413 U.S. 49, 93 S.Ct. 2628, 37 L.Ed.2d 446 (1973)] any constitutional need for "expert" testimony on behalf of the prosecution, or for any other ancillary evidence of obscenity, once the allegedly obscene material itself is placed in evidence. Paris Adult Theatre I, supra, 413 U.S., at 56, 93 S.Ct., at 2634–2635. The defense should be free to introduce appropriate expert testimony, see Smith v. California, 361 U.S. 147, 164–165, 80 S.Ct. 215, 224–225, 4 L.Ed.2d 205 (1959) (Frankfurter, J.,

---

6. This is not a subject that lends itself to the traditional use of expert testimony. Such testimony is usually admitted for the purpose of explaining to lay jurors what they otherwise could not understand. Cf. 2 J. Wigmore, Evidence __ 556, 559 (3d ed. 1940). No such assistance is needed by jurors in obscenity cases; indeed the "expert witness" practices employed in these cases have often made a mockery out of the otherwise sound concept of expert testimony. See *United States v. Groner*, 479 F.2d 577, 585–586 (C.A.5 1973); *id.*, at 587–588 (Ainsworth, J., concurring). "Simply stated, hard core pornography ... can and does speak for itself." *United States v. Wild*, 422 F.2d 34, 36 (C.A.2 1969), cert. denied, 402 U.S. 986, 91 S.Ct. 1644, 29 L.Ed.2d 152 (1971). We reserve judgment, however, on the extreme case, not presented here, where contested materials are directed at such a bizarre deviant group that the experience of the trier of fact would be plainly inadequate to judge whether the material appeals to the prurient interest.

concurring), but in "the cases in which this Court has decided obscenity questions since *Roth*, it has regarded the materials as sufficient in themselves for the determination of the question." *Ginzburg v. United States*, 383 U.S. 463, 465, 86 S.Ct. 942, 944, 16 L.Ed.2d 31 (1966).

HAMLING v. UNITED STATES

Supreme Court of the United States, 1974.
418 U.S. 87, 94 S.Ct. 2887, 41 L.Ed.2d 590.

■ Mr. Justice Rehnquist delivered the opinion of the Court.

Our holding in *Miller* that California could constitutionally proscribe obscenity in terms of a "statewide" standard did not mean that any such precise geographic area is required as a matter of constitutional law. [S]ince this case was tried in the Southern District of California, and presumably jurors from throughout that judicial district were available to serve on the panel which tried petitioners, it would be the standards of that "community" upon which the jurors would draw.

B.   Social Science Evidence of "Community Standards"

When *Miller, Paris Adult Theatre I,* and *Kaplan* were decided by the United States Supreme Court on the same day in 1973, the law regarding the admissibility of social science evidence in obscenity litigation was settled: the Constitution did not require the prosecution to offer expert evidence as part of proving its case, and the Constitution did require that the defense be permitted to offer expert evidence to rebut the prosecution's case.

In Pope v. Illinois, 481 U.S. 497, 107 S.Ct. 1918, 95 L.Ed.2d 439 (1987), the Supreme Court reaffirmed that "the first and second prongs of the *Miller* test—appeal to prurient interest and patent offensiveness—are issues of fact for the jury to determine applying contemporary community standards." 481 U.S. at 500, 107 S.Ct. at 1920. In the following cases, we examine the use of social science evidence to help determine these "community standards."

PEOPLE v. NELSON

Appellate Court of Illinois, Second District, 1980.
88 Ill.App.3d 196, 43 Ill.Dec. 476, 410 N.E.2d 476.

■ Seidenfeld, Presiding Justice.

Timothy D. Nelson was convicted after a jury trial of the offense of criminal obscenity. He was sentenced to a term of 45 days in jail and fined $1,000. Defendant appeals, contending that the trial court prejudicially erred in refusing to admit a public opinion poll on the issue of community standards and the proffered testimony of an expert witness analyzing the results of the poll.

[T]he witness is a Ph.D. and a social scientist who specializes in survey research methodology and the conducting of public opinion polls. His expertise as a social scientist and professional pollster were stipulated. [T]he target for the poll was the adult population of the State of Illinois. The sample was 770 persons. The State was divided into 77 areas of approximately equal population, and then using a random selection technique, representatives were sent out to conduct 770 interviews.

[T]he summary of the questions and results is included as an Appendix to this opinion. Dr. Bell described the concept of "consensus", stating that approximately 75% of the population would have to agree on a proposition before one could say there was a consensus. In analyzing the results of the 1978 Illinois community standard survey, he found that there was no consensus about whether it was acceptable or not acceptable to have depictions of sexually explicit materials provided under certain circumstances described in the questions. As the result of his expert analysis he concluded that there was no community standard regarding such depictions.

The prosecution objected to the expert analysis on the ground that there was no community standard shown by the survey and therefore that the testimony based on the inconclusive survey would invade the jury's province. The trial court ruled that both the survey evidence and the analysis invaded the province of the jury and that they were thus inadmissible.

[C]learly, a state-wide "community standard" based upon public acceptance of material claimed to be obscene is an essential element of proof of the charge.

Section 11–20(c)(4) of the Illinois Criminal Code provides, as relevant:

"In any prosecution for an offense under this Section evidence shall be admissible to show: * * * (4) The degree, if any, of public acceptance of the material in this State; * * * ". Ill.Rev.Stat.1977, ch. 38, par. 11–20(c)(4).

In view of the fact that no objections were made to the methodology or partiality of the survey the statutory provision makes the evidence admissible in our view since the results show "the degree if any, of the public acceptance of the [material]." It is apparent from the survey that the questions were framed with reference to Section 11–20(c)(4), since the members of the public are asked to state whether they feel it would be acceptable for the average adult in Illinois to see or buy sexually explicit materials. The questions and answers were relevant in that they showed that a majority of Illinois residents find depictions of "nudity and actual or pretended sexual activities" acceptable. This is relevant to the question of whether such depictions are "patently offensive" (for by definition acceptable materials are not offensive), and to the question whether such material appeals to "prurient interest."

[T]he survey results are strong evidence that the community standards would accept or at least would not reject the portrayal of sexually explicit material in movies when the access to the movies is limited to adult viewers. In fact, survey evidence may be the only way to prove degrees of acceptability of a product or material, as distinct from its availability. The State does not have the burden of introducing any evidence as to what the state-wide community standard is. But that cannot justify a court in denying the defendant the right to introduce the best evidence he can gather on this issue. Essentially the result of refusing the proffered evidence left the jurors with no way of knowing what the State standard might be. Particularly in this case, in which the jury *voir dire* showed that most of the jurors had lived all of their lives in the community of Rockford, did not read a paper from any other community within the State of Illinois and read few national magazines, it appears that the jurors would have little practical experience on which to base their opinion of what the state-wide community standard might be. This raises the great danger that the jurors may have applied a personal standard rather than a state-wide community standard. We conclude that the exclusion of the survey testimony was harmful and prejudicial error and requires that the case be remanded for a new trial.

The trial court, however, properly ruled that the commentary of the expert, exclusive of his foundation testimony, was inadmissible. The testimony of the expert that the survey results showed that there was no "consensus" in public opinion and therefore that there is no community standard by which to judge the obscenity of the material, is confusing for the jury. This comment is based on a social science concept which may be foreign to the jury. Further it focuses their attention on the nature and existence of the crime, perhaps thereby distracting them from a determination of guilt or innocence in the case at bar. Moreover, the survey results are clear and self-explanatory so that the jurors should have no difficulty in interpreting the results without expert aid.

[T]he judgment is therefore reversed and the cause remanded for a new trial in accordance with this opinion.

APPENDIX
SUMMARY—ILLINOIS COMMUNITY STANDARDS SURVEY

QUESTION: Is it your opinion that in recent years the standards in Illinois have changed so that depictions of nudity and sexual activities in movies and publications available only to adults are now more acceptable or less acceptable?

More acceptable 60.5%; less acceptable 25.7%; neither 7.8%; don't know 4.4%; no answer 1.3%; other .2%.

QUESTION: Do you think it is acceptable or not acceptable in Illinois for the average adult to see any depiction of actual or pretended sexual activities shown in movies and publications that he or she wants to?

Acceptable 58.1%; not acceptable 33.2%; neither 5.2%; no answer 3.5%.

GENERAL QUESTION

In your opinion, is it now all right or not all right in the State of Illinois for:

QUESTION: Adults who want to view them, to purchase magazines that depict nudity and actual or pretended sexual activities?

All right 63.1%; not all right 31.0%; neither 2.2%; no answer 3.6%.

QUESTION: Movie theaters, restricting attendance to adults only, to show films that depict nudity and actual or pretended sexual activities for adults who want to attend?

All right 59.2%; not all right 32.1%; neither 4.3%; no answer 4.4%.

QUESTION: Bookstores that restrict admittance to adults only to sell publications and movies depicting nudity and actual or pretended sexual activities for adults who want to go inside and purchase them?

All right 54.8%; not all right 37.3%; neither 4.0%; no answer 3.9%.

QUESTION: Arcades that restrict admittance to adults only to show films that depict nudity and actual or pretended sexual activities?

All right 48.7%; not all right 42.1%; neither 3.5%; no answer 5.7%.

QUESTION: Adults who want to, in the privacy of their homes, to see movies and publications that depict nudity and actual or pretended sexual activities?

All right 67.4%; not all right 25.7%; neither 2.9%; no answer 4.0%.

QUESTION: We have used the phrases "nudity" and "sexual activities" in the interview. What we mean by these terms is total male and/or female nudity, and sexual intercourse including all kinds of sexual variations. Is that what you understood we meant, or did you think we meant something else?

Understood 93.4%; something else 3.0%; neither 1.8%; no answer 1.8%.

———

CARLOCK v. STATE

Court of Criminal Appeals of Texas, 1980.
609 S.W.2d 787.

■ ROBERTS, JUDGE.

A jury found the appellant guilty [of commercial obscenity] and assessed his punishment at 120 days confinement and a fine of $1000.00

[T]he appellant contends that the trial court erred in excluding from evidence a public opinion survey dealing with community standards regarding obscenity. The appellant called only one witness during the guilt-innocence stage of the trial, Dr. Roderick Bell. At a hearing out of the presence of the jury, Dr. Bell testified that in May and June of 1977, he conducted a poll of Dallas County regarding that community's standards as to explicit sexual materials.

[T]he State advances several arguments in support of its contention that the trial court properly excluded the appellant's expert evidence. It first asserts that the assistance of an expert witness is not needed for a juror to determine community standards and, therefore, exclusion of such evidence is within the trial court's discretion. The State's argument is premised upon Paris Adult Theatre I v. Slaton, 413 U.S. 49, 93 S.Ct. 2628, 37 L.Ed.2d 446 (1973), in which the United States Supreme Court held that expert testimony on behalf of the prosecution is not constitutionally required because the allegedly obscene material itself is sufficient evidence for the determination of the question of obscenity. But that holding cannot justify denying a defendant the right to introduce the best evidence he can produce upon a material element of the statutory definition of obscenity. Indeed, in another opinion delivered the same day as *Paris Adult Theater I*, the Supreme Court expressed the view that while expert affirmative evidence upon relevant community standards is not required, a defendant should be free to introduce appropriate expert testimony. Kaplan v. California, 413 U.S. 115, 93 S.Ct. 2680, 37 L.Ed.2d 492 (1973); see also Smith v. California, 361 U.S. 147, 80 S.Ct. 215, 4 L.Ed.2d 205 (1959).

[A]lthough such expert evidence is not required from either the State or the defendant, it is certainly relevant to the determination of a material fact issue. We therefore reject the State's first contention that the trial court could properly exclude the appellant's expert evidence as to contemporary community standards in the exercise of judicial discretion.

The State next contends that the exclusion of the public opinion survey from evidence was proper because the poll was taken in May and June of 1977, and, therefore, did not reflect the community standards of August 11, 1976, the date of the alleged offense. The State did not present any evidence in support of its contention, and it is doubtful that the standards at issue did in fact change significantly in this relatively short period of time. But regardless of whether the State's claim is or is not correct, any such alleged defect in the manner in which a poll was conducted should affect only the weight to be accorded the survey results rather than the admissibility of the survey itself. Since the jury is the exclusive judge of the weight to be given to the testimony, the trial court should have permitted the jury to hear and consider the appellant's opinion survey.

The State also contends that the public opinion survey was inadmissible because it dealt with only general opinions regarding obscenity rather than the community's opinion of the particular magazine in question. Although we do not decide the question, it is arguable that the survey would have been more probative if it had asked whether the particular magazine in question appealed to the prurient interest of the average person. Even so, this would not authorize the trial court to exclude from evidence the public opinion survey offered in this case. The expert evidence would not be rendered inadmissible simply because more probative questions could have been incorporated into the poll. Rather the weakness perceived by the State in appellant's evidence goes only to its weight.

————

SALIBA v. STATE

Court of Appeals of Indiana, Second District, 1985.
475 N.E.2d 1181.

■ SHIELDS, JUDGE.

Saliba was charged with exhibiting an obscene film in his adult book store in Indianapolis on November 12, 1981. The film which formed the basis for Saliba's conviction depicted three males involved in various homosexual activities. Prior to trial, Saliba employed Dr. Roderick Bell of California to conduct a public opinion poll to determine community standards in Marion County regarding the depiction of sexual activities in movies and publications. At trial and out of the jury's presence, Saliba offered into evidence the results of the poll designed by Dr. Bell. In support of the offer, Dr. Bell testified to his qualifications and explained the general nature of public opinion polls. Dr. Bell then extensively discussed the scientific methodology generally employed in conducting polls and detailed the specific techniques employed in conducting the poll at issue. Based on the design, execution, tabulation and verification of the instant poll, Dr. Bell opined that the poll was a valid measure of the degree of public acceptance of sexually explicit materials in Marion County.

The State objected to the poll's validity and [t]he trial judge ruled the poll inadmissible.

[S]urvey Evidence in Obscenity Prosecutions

As the State contends, the obscene character of materials may be determined by the jury based on a viewing of the allegedly offensive material. The State need not present an expert witness or other evidence of community standards.

However, expert evidence on this issue may be highly relevant. The jurors are not instructed to evaluate obscenity based on their personal opinions but are charged with applying contemporary community standards. In the absence of expert testimony, the jury's determination of contemporary community standards runs the risk of incorporating the individual juror's "necessarily limited, hit-or-miss subjective view" "on the basis of his personal upbringing or restricted reflection or particular experience of life." Smith v. California, 361 U.S. 147, 165, 80 S.Ct. 215, 225, 4 L.Ed.2d 205 (1959) (Frankfurter, J., concurring). Consequently, the defendant in an obscenity prosecution is entitled to introduce relevant and appropriate expert testimony on the issue of contemporary community standards. Kaplan v. California, 413 U.S. 115, 93 S.Ct. 2680, 37 L.Ed.2d 492.

Expert testimony based on a public opinion poll is uniquely suited to a determination of community standards. Perhaps no other form of evidence is more helpful or concise. [T]he alternative modes of introducing such evidence are less desirable Zippo Manufacturing Co. v. Rogers Imports, Inc., 216 F.Supp. 670 (S.D.N.Y.1963) (leading case on survey evidence). For example, the presentation of in-court testimony from the entire target population or even a representative sample is patently impractical. And the use of an expert witness to testify regarding his or her opinion on community standards is not as direct or accurate as a public poll, even assuming an expert could qualify on the subject. The nature of public opinion polls renders them better suited to demonstrate contemporary community standards.

Admissibility of Survey Evidence

In the instant case, the State objected to the admission of the public opinion poll both on the grounds of relevancy and trustworthiness. Specifically, the State argued the poll's focus on overall community standards did not determine whether the film in question was obscene. Alternatively, the State argued the poll was improperly conducted and therefore unreliable. We will address each contention in turn.

A.   Relevancy

[O]ur probe into relevance is two-pronged. Were the questions in the poll relevant to a determination of 1) community standards in general and 2) the community's acceptance of viewing the particular film in question.

1.   General Community Standards

We first determine whether the questions in the poll were relevant to a determination of community standards. For example, question seven asked: "Do you personally think it is acceptable or not acceptable for the average adult to see any depiction of actual or pretended sexual activities shown in movies and publications that he or she wants to?" The balance of the questions in the poll merely changed the type and location of access to such materials to movies, books, or magazines and theaters, bookstores, or arcades. The poll therefore questioned the interviewees regarding their view of community acceptance of sexually explicit materials rather than their personal acceptance of such materials.

We must emphasize the majority of the community need not desire to view sexually explicit materials in order to establish community acceptance or tolerance of such materials. Rather, the issue concerns the population's perception of what is generally acceptable in the community considering the intended and probable recipients of the materials. The questions in the poll parallel the statutorily mandated standard; matter is "obscene" if "the average person, applying contemporary community standards" finds the material as a whole appeals to the prurient interest in sex. The poll's results were relevant evidence of the community standards which the jury was obligated to apply.

2. Acceptance of Particular Film

We must also determine if the community acceptance of viewing "nudity and actual or pretended sexual activity", as phrased throughout the poll, is relevant to a determination of the acceptance of viewing the film in question. We also answer this inquiry in the affirmative. The poll defines "nudity and pretended or actual sexual activity" as "total male and/or female nudity, and sexual intercourse including all kinds of sexual variation." The sexual activity portrayed in the instant film fell within the definition of "nudity and actual or pretended sexual activity."

Although the poll did not present the interviewees with the ultimate question to be decided by the jury (i.e., whether the particular film was obscene), the poll was relevant to an application of community standards. [T]he failure to poll the population on the ultimate issue does not negate relevancy. The population's general opinion is probative, although not determinative, of community standards and, consequently, of the population's specific opinion of the film in question.

B. Trustworthiness

Although the poll was relevant, we must also determine whether it was admissible. Relevant public opinion polls and other survey evidence are widely accepted as generally admissible if properly conducted. See generally Zippo, 216 F.Supp. at 682. Objections to admissibility usually arise because the contents of public opinion polls are generally not within the firsthand knowledge of the submitting witness; they may also constitute hearsay.

Several theories, however, have been advanced to justify the admission of public opinion polls. Some authorities classify polls as falling under the state of mind exception to the hearsay rule. Others characterize polls as hearsay but conclude the need for the evidence at trial and the circumstantial guarantees of trustworthiness justify admission. Still other authorities classify survey evidence as non-hearsay, and therefore directly rely on the rules governing admission of expert testimony generally. Id. In any event, it is now generally accepted neither the hearsay rule nor the requirement of firsthand knowledge bars the admission of properly conducted public opinion polls or surveys. As explained in the Advisory Committee's Note to Fed.R.Evid. 703: "Attention is directed to the validity of the techniques employed rather than the relatively fruitless inquiries whether hearsay is involved." 51 F.R.D. 404 (1971).

The admissibility of a public opinion poll depends primarily upon the presence of circumstantial guarantees of trustworthiness. 1 J. Moore, Moore's Federal Practice 2.712 (1982). Public opinion polls are surveys designed to elicit the state of mind of a targeted population ("universe") through an examination of a representative portion ("sample") of the universe. Through accepted statistical analysis, the sample data is used to project the opinion of the entire targeted population. In short, the circumstantial guarantees of trustworthiness are premised on 1) the use of generally accepted surveying techniques in conducting the poll and 2) adherence to statistically correct methods in conducting the poll and evaluating the results.

This twofold inquiry has led to the judicial development of [seven] foundational criteria which are generally accepted as scientifically necessary to insure a poll's reliability and, consequently, its admissibility. The proponent of a poll has the burden of establishing: 1) the poll was conducted by an expert in the field of surveying; 2) the relevant universe was examined; 3) a representative sample was drawn from the relevant universe; 4) the mode of questioning was "correct" (mail, telephone, personal interview, etc.); 5) the sample, questionnaire, and the interviews were designed in accordance with generally accepted standards; 6) the data gathered was accurately reported; and 7) the data was analyzed in a statistically correct manner. J. Moore, supra at 138. The adherence to this generally accepted methodology renders the poll's results admissible in the form of expert opinion.

Once these foundational requirements are established, subject to cross-examination, the poll is admissible. [G]iven an adequate foundation, questions regarding the technical adequacy of a poll affect the poll's weight only.

[D]r. Bell's foundation testimony explained the typical methodology used in conducting opinion polls and described the methodology employed in conducting the instant poll. Dr. Bell identified the "universe" as the adult population of Marion County. This "universe" was sampled by telephone using a random digit dialing technique, the currently preferred method of telephone interviewing. This technique used a list of telephone numbers randomly generated by computer in proportion to the number of lines for existing telephone prefixes. During the first two weeks of February, 1982, five hundred (500) adults from Marion County were questioned by interviewers from Herron Associates of Indianapolis, a field service. The interviewers were instructed and supervised by Dr. Bell. Dr. Bell prepared the questionnaire through the use of extensive "pretesting" techniques designed to insure the questions were understood by the interviewees. The interviewers were instructed to read the questionnaire to the interviewees and record the responses as designated by the accompanying "code sheet" or answer key. Once the interviews were complete, a subset of the sample was recontacted by the field supervisor to verify the interview took place and the responses were accurately coded. Dr. Bell then drew a subset of the subset to reverify. Dr. Bell testified this form of spot checking is the only accepted verification technique. The raw data was keyed into a computer for tabulation; Dr. Bell also supervised this data input. The results of the poll were 98% repeatable within a margin of error of 3% to 4%. Dr. Bell testified that the definitions, standards and methodologies described were used by "practically all" national polling organizations including Lou Harris. Dr. Bell's testimony alone provided a complete foundation for admission of the poll.

[T]he State's objections merely affected the poll's weight, not its admissibility. The survey was erroneously excluded.

Judgment reversed and cause remanded for a new trial.

———

COMMONWEALTH v. TRAINOR

Supreme Judicial Court of Massachusetts, Suffolk, 1978.
374 Mass. 796, 374 N.E.2d 1216.

■ WILKINS, JUSTICE.

The individual defendant and the corporate defendant were found guilty in February, 1976, after a jury waived trial, on all counts of indictments charging them with having possession of obscene matter in June, 1975, with intent to disseminate it.

[W]e come [t]o an issue with which this court has not dealt previously. The appellants argue that the judge improperly excluded a public opinion survey from evidence. Although, as will be seen, public opinion surveys are admissible in certain circumstances, we agree with the judge's decision to exclude the appellants' public opinion survey.

A properly conducted public opinion survey, offered through an expert in conducting such surveys, is admissible in an obscenity case if it tends to show relevant standards in the Commonwealth. We see no meaningful distinction between a properly conducted public opinion survey offered to show community norms and the testimony of an expert who states his views on the opinion of the public concerning the portrayal of certain allegedly obscene conduct. We have already recognized the admissibility of expert testimony of the latter type. We have said, citing Paris Adult Theatre I v. Slaton, 413 U.S. 49, 56, 93 S.Ct. 2628, 37 L.Ed.2d 446 (1973), that triers of fact "may consider expert testimony on the subject of Statewide standards, if any is offered in evidence, but also may disregard such evidence because the matter at issue may be per se sufficient evidence for a finding of prurience in most cases." Commonwealth v. 707 Main Corp., 357 N.E.2d 753, 761 (1976). Although expert testimony may be excluded, in the judge's discretion, if a subject is within the common knowledge of the average juror, the line between matters of common knowledge and matters beyond common knowledge often is not precise. If such expert testimony may give the jury appreciable assistance in resolving a fact question, it is admissible in the judge's discretion. Where the question is whether portrayals of sexual conduct are "obscene" under the statutory definition, it would be a rare case in which testimony from a qualified expert should be excluded on the ground that it would not be helpful to the trier of fact. Similarly, a properly conducted public opinion survey should be admitted. The question then is what is a properly conducted public opinion survey.

If the universe surveyed is relevant, if the sample questioned is representative of the relevant universe, if the questions are in a form appropriate to obtain unbiased answers within a reasonable margin of error, and if the pollster is qualified, the weight of authority supports the admission of a public opinion survey tending to prove a fact relevant to a material issue. See the leading, oft-cited case, Zippo Mfg. Co. v. Rogers Imports, Inc., 216 F.Supp. 670, 682 et seq. (S.D.N.Y.1963). However, where the methodology of the survey is deficient, the trial judge should exclude it.

We are not inclined to pause long to resolve whether a survey of people's opinions is hearsay and, if it is, whether it is admissible under the state of mind exception to the hearsay rule. Numerous authorities have admitted particular surveys under that hearsay exception. The focus should be on the techniques employed rather than on whether hearsay is involved. See Fed.R.Evid. 703 and Note of the Advisory Committee, 56 F.R.D. 183, 283 (1972). A properly conducted public opinion survey itself adequately ensures a good measure of trustworthiness, and its admission may be necessary in the sense that no other evidence would be as good as the survey evidence or perhaps even obtainable as a practical matter. Of course, the judge will have to determine in his discretion whether the methodology of the survey was adequate to justify its admission. In certain instances, any weaknesses in the manner in which a poll was conducted might affect only the weight to be accorded the survey results rather than the admissibility of the survey in evidence.

In light of these principles, we consider the public opinion survey prepared for the defendants in this case. The defendants made an offer of proof of the testimony and exhibits relating to their survey. Two hundred adults, all residents of Boston, divided evenly by sex, were obtained from all sections of Boston by telephone solicitations conducted evenings, and each was interviewed. Each was offered $10 to come to an office in downtown Boston for an interview on an undisclosed subject relating to a pending court case. Trained personnel conducted the interviews shortly before trial. The defendants intended to introduce the results of the survey through an expert experienced in conducting public opinion surveys, who would have testified that the margin of error in the survey ranged from 6% to 10%.

The questions largely sought the personal views of each person interviewed: whether, in particular circumstances, he or she would be willing to have motion picture films shown or magazines sold depicting human sexual conduct. One question asked, for example, whether the individual would "personally be willing to have motion picture films or magazines showing human sexual intercourse between members of the opposite sex (*sic*) shown or sold" in (a) residential neighborhoods of Boston, (b) general commercial or business areas in Boston, (c) Boston adult entertainment districts, (d) under conditions where minors were excluded, or (e) in places clearly marked so that anyone not wanting to see them could avoid them. The interviewer suggested three answers: would be willing, would not be willing, or "[d]on't care one way or the other." If other answers such as no opinion or a qualified approval, were given, those answers also were tabulated. Similar questions were asked concerning each subject's willingness to allow the sale or showing of films or magazines depicting human masturbation, oral sex, or homosexual acts. Two other questions inquired into each subject's willingness to allow the sale of particular magazines which were shown to him or her. One of those magazines was the subject of one count in an indictment in this case.

As would be expected, the willingness of the subjects interviewed to have such films shown, or magazines sold, increased as the suggested place of the showing or sale moved from residential to adult entertainment areas, when minors were excluded from involvement, and when the nature of the material to be shown or sold was plainly indicated. In general, males were more willing to allow the showing or sale of such materials than females.

It is important to note certain facts not set forth in the offer of proof. There was no indication that the method of selection of the subjects to be interviewed assured a representative sample of the citizens of Boston. One might suspect that certain persons would decline to participate because of the method by which they were approached or because of their unwillingness or inability to take the time to participate in such interviews. The selection process was not shown to be free from producing a bias in the survey results.

The interrogation of residents of only Boston raises the question whether the survey results are competent to prove the standards of the Commonwealth as a whole. However, because the obscenity statute assumes the existence of a uniform, Statewide standard, we should not reject a representative and otherwise valid survey limited to a population as large as that of Boston.

Finally, and most significantly, we note the absence of any indication that the willingness, the lack of willingness, or the indifference of a group to the sale of sexually explicit magazines or the showing of sexually explicit films has any relevance to any issue material to this case. The survey results apparently were offered as bearing on the question whether the films and magazines involved in this case displayed sexual conduct in a patently offensive way. The offer of proof made no attempt to connect an acceptance of, or an indifference to, the showing or sale of that material with whether the particular sexual conduct involved in this case was depicted or described in a patently offensive way. Perhaps many people would not object to others' seeing such material, although they themselves regard that material as patently offensive. The offer of proof did not explain the relationship of the offered evidence to this fundamental factual question of patent offensiveness.

Because the offer of proof failed to demonstrate the representativeness of the persons interviewed and failed to show that the survey results were relevant to any material issue in the case, the judge was warranted in excluding the survey and expert testimony concerning it.

———

UNITED STATES v. PRYBA

United States District Court, Eastern District of Virginia, 1988.
678 F.Supp. 1225.

■ ELLIS, DISTRICT JUDGE.

Defendants sought to introduce the testimony of Dr. Joseph Scott, a sociologist with a background in statistical methodology. Dr. Scott conducted an "ethnographical" study which allegedly showed that the materials here in question are accepted by the adult community in the Alexandria division. According to Dr. Scott, an ethnographic study "looks at what is going on in the community." To get a look at "what is going on" in the Alexandria Division of the Eastern District of Virginia, Dr. Scott did the following:

(1) He viewed the subject materials.

(2) He "probably went" to eighty or ninety bookstores, approximately sixty-nine of which sold what Dr. Scott described as "male sophisticate" magazines. He also visited about seventy-five video stores, of which forty-three sold adult videotapes.

(3) He talked to the operators and customers of the stores he visited about sexually explicit (male sophisticate) materials.

(4) He called newspaper editors and discussed with them the number and content of "letters to the editors" to ascertain the number and type of complaints relating to sexually explicit material.

As a result of this "ethnography," Dr. Scott was prepared to offer the jury his opinion that the "overwhelming majority" of adults in the community have at one time or another viewed sexually explicit material and that such materials, including the materials here in question, are readily acceptable by the average adult in the community. He prepared no report; he had only his notes. To reach his sweeping conclusion, Dr. Scott, who has never lived in Virginia, required only eight days.

The issue is whether such testimony is competent expert evidence of the prevailing community standards.[12] It is not.

[R]ule 104(a): Witness Must be Qualified

The Court holds that the bases of Dr. Scott's opinion are insufficient to qualify him as an expert either on contemporary community standards of obscenity in the Alexandria Division, or on the question whether the materials in issue are accepted by the community. Dr. Scott admits that ethnography is a "new approach" in the study of sexual mores. He described ethnography as a qualitative analysis of a community, a method

---

12. Dr. Scott conceded that ethnography is a new approach to the study of community acceptance of sexually explicit material, but claimed that it is generally accepted in the social science field. Yet general acceptance of ethnography in the social sciences, even if true, does not mean that Dr. Scott's ethnography in this case qualifies him as an expert in the contemporary community standards of the Alexandria Division. Cf. Frye v. United States, 293 F. 1013 (D.C.Cir.1923). The problem here is that Dr. Scott's ethnography is not scientific in the sense understood in *Frye*. There is a difference between scientific studies and methodologies in the natural sciences and studies found acceptable in the social sciences. The former must typically meet more rigorous standards and be subject to reliable replication. Put more directly, Dr. Scott's interviews of adult video store clerks, store managers, and customers over an eight-day period is simply not science.

used to "assess" community standards. "Ethnography is the work of describing a culture." J. Spradley, The Ethnographic Interview 3 (1979). The issue is whether Scott's ethnographic evidence properly reflects contemporary community standards. It does not. Stripped of its scientific disguise, Dr. Scott's so-called "ethnography" is shown to be nothing more than a series of interviews with dealers of sexually explicit materials and their customers. This is neither science, nor work requiring expertise. Moreover, Scott did not visit churches, community centers, garden clubs, Rotary Clubs or the like to develop a basis for his opinion. Also, Dr. Scott did not show the films or magazines here in issue to those whom he interviewed, but instead discussed only those sexually explicit materials sold in the stores that he visited. In sum, defendants have failed to establish how Scott's ethnography is related to the general community's acceptance of the specific materials in issue.

[A]lso, Scott's testimony must be excluded because it is predicated solely upon qualitative rather than quantitative analysis. Scott's analysis, i.e., talking to customers and vendors of sexually explicit material and reviewing letters to the editors of various publications, in no way demonstrates community acceptance of the materials here in issue. Scott's testimony, although perhaps reflecting availability of the materials surveyed, fails to evidence community acceptance. It is well-settled that mere availability does not equate with community acceptance. Scott offers no *quantitative* analysis for much of his male sophisticate material, such as sale or distribution figures, which might have been probative of community acceptance. Dr. Scott's ethnography, in essence, constitutes nothing more than a one-man, eight-day, unscientific poll of purveyors and purchasers of smut. To permit this so-called "study" to masquerade as expert testimony on Northern Virginia's contemporary community standards of obscenity is ludicrous. This "study" did not and could not make Dr. Scott a competent, reliable expert on the contemporary community standards on sexually explicit material in Northern Virginia. Accordingly, the Court excluded Dr. Scott's testimony as falling far short of even minimal standards under Rules 702 and 104 of the Federal Rules of Evidence.

THE LAW OF OBSCENITY (1976)

Fredrick Schauer.

One interpretation [of the term "patently offensive" in the *Miller* test of obscenity] asks whether the materials themselves would actually offend the average member of the community, or the majority of the community, or the community as a whole. [B]ut there is another possible interpretation, that asks not whether the materials offend the community or the average person, but whether the community or the average person is offended by the materials being available to those who wish to see them. In other words, are the community standards tolerant, even though most members of the community might themselves be offended by the materials. If so, it can be argued that the materials are not offensive to the community because they are restricted only to those who choose to see them. [T]hus, the survey may ask the respondents whether *they* are offended by the material, or whether they are offended by its availability in the community to those who want it.

ESTIMATING COMMUNITY STANDARDS: THE USE OF SOCIAL SCIENCE EVIDENCE IN AN OBSCENITY PROSECUTION

Daniel Linz, Edward Donnerstein, Kenneth C. Land, Patricia L. McCall, Joseph Scott, Bradley J. Shafer, Lee J. Klein, and Larry Lance.
55 Public Opinion Quarterly 80 (1991).*

The study reported here was proffered as evidence in the State of North Carolina v. Cinema Blue of Charlotte, Inc., 392 S.E.2d 136 (N.C.App. 1990). In this study, an attempt was made to gather social science data to inform the jury as to whether the average adult in Mecklenburg County, NC, applying contemporary community standards, would find that five movies and one magazine alleged to be obscene by the state, either appealed to a prurient interest in sex or were patently offensive.

[A] sample of Mecklenburg County residents were contacted by telephone. The sample was compiled through random digit dialing using a list of digits, not weighted by prefix, obtained from Survey Sampling Inc., Fairfield, Connecticut. Potential respondents who could not be reached were called back three times with next-day calling staggered by time. Once contacted, the respondents were administered an interview that involved four components: (1) selection of an adult respondent in the household 18 years old or over; (2) assessment of demographic characteristics including: age, education, race, and sex (the interviewers were instructed to recruit within quotas corresponding to the proportions within each of these demographic categories in the population); (3) subject recruitment "to possibly view a movie . . . and fill out a questionnaire about it?" and (4) subject recruitment to possibly view "adult, X-rated sexually explicit films." Once respondents agreed to participate in the study, they were informed that they would receive $50.00 upon completion of the project, which, they were told, would last approximately two-and-a-half hours. Participants were then given the address of the study site.

[A] total of 614 adults completed the initial telephone interview. Of these, 380 respondents indicated that they would be willing to participate in a film-viewing project; 8 indicated they were "not sure," and 226 declined participation. From this group, a total of 284 respondents agreed to participate in the study once they were informed that they might be asked to watch an X-rated video. Of these respondents, 244 were scheduled for a film-viewing session. One hundred thirty-two subjects reported for a film-viewing session. One subject left once the video began, and two were dismissed with payment because all video viewing set-ups were being used simultaneously. A total of 129 subjects participated in the film [e]valuation study.

[S]ubjects reported to the viewing sessions not knowing if they would be asked to watch an X-rated film or a nonexplicit film. Subjects were randomly assigned to view either one of five sexually explicit films [o]r a nonexplicit control film.

Prefilm Questionnaire Administration

Subjects were [g]iven a questionnaire and instructed to take it to one of ten separate video viewing rooms and complete it. They were asked to indicate length of residence in Mecklenburg County, newspaper subscription, video movie consumption, cable subscription, political affiliation, political attitudes, religiosity, religious service attendance, attitudes about current events, education level, age, and religious affiliation. Most important, the following set of instructions were given and questions asked.

> The next few questions deal with X-rated videos and adult movies and magazines. The nudity and sex shown in these types of adult material include: nude bodies and close-up graphic depictions of a variety of sexual activities, such as sexual intercourse, ejaculation, bondage, oral sex, anal sex, group sex, and variations of these acts by adult performers.

> Do you think it *is* or *is not* tolerated in your community for the average adult to see adult movies, video cassettes, and magazines showing nudity and sex if they should want to?

>   Tolerated   1 2 3 4 5 6 7 8   Not Tolerated

> Do you believe you *should* be able to see any such showing of actual sex acts in adult movies, video cassettes, or magazines if you should want to?

>   Definitely No   1 2 3 4 5 6 7 8   Definitely Yes

> Some adult movies, video cassettes, and magazines show actual sex acts in great detail and with close-ups of sexual organs. Would viewing this type of material appeal to an unhealthy, shameful, or morbid interest in sex?

>   Definitely Yes   1 2 3 4 5 6 7 8   Definitely No

Film Viewing

Upon completing the prefilm questionnaire, subjects were instructed to return it to one of the staff members. The subject was then taken to the viewing room and shown how to turn off the video cassette recorder (VCR). Subjects were instructed at that time to turn off the VCR once they had viewed the videocassette and report to the staff person. The staff person then started the VCR and left the room. All subjects viewed the film alone, and their viewing was timed to ensure that they had viewed the film in its entirety.

Postfilm Questionnaire

When subjects returned from their movie viewing room, they were given a postfilm questionnaire and instructed to return to their room, alone, to complete it. This questionnaire assessed subject attitudes on a number of current issues, including gun control, censorship, and religious tolerance. Most important, they were given the following instructions and questions.

> In the first questionnaire you filled out, we asked you about X-rated videos, adult movies, and adult magazines. We said that the nudity and sex shown in these adult materials include: nude bodies and close-up graphic depictions of a variety of sexual activities. This includes: sexual intercourse, ejaculation, bondage, oral sex, anal sex, group sex, and variations of these acts by adult performers.
>
> Was the movie you saw today what you expected to see, given this definition of X-rated videos, adult movies, and magazines?
>
> Definitely No   1   2   3   4   5   6   7   8   Definitely Yes
>
> The next few questions deal *only* with the X-rated video that you saw today. The scenes you saw in this film may have included nude bodies and close-up graphic depictions of a variety of sexual activities, including: sexual intercourse, ejaculation, oral sex, anal sex, group sex, and variations of these acts by adult performers.

[T]his question was followed by questions on community tolerance and personal tolerance that were similar to those in the pretest. The appeal to prurient interest question was not preceded by the sentence concerning adult movies and videotapes in general, and reference was made, rather, to the particular film just viewed.

[C]ontrol Film Subjects

Control subjects [v]iewed a nonexplicit film (*Nothing in Common*). Their postfilm questionnaire did not include questions on whether the film they viewed met their definition of an "X-rated" film, and they were asked the prurient appeal question with the preface sentence in both the pre-and postfilm questionnaire. Otherwise, control subjects were treated in an identical manner to the sexually explicit film-viewing subjects.

Results

Subject Responses After Film Viewing and Comparisons Pre-and Postfilm Viewing

Table 4. Comparison of "[B]efore" and "After" Film Viewing (X-rated film viewing subjects only) on Beliefs About Community Tolerance, Viewing Materials, and Appeal to Shameful and Morbid Interest in Sex

	Before Film	After Film
	"Do you think it *is* or *is not* tolerated in your community for the average adult to obtain and see adult movies, video cassettes, and magazines showing nudity and sex if they want to?"	
Tolerated	59.1%	52.7%
N	65	58
Not tolerated	40.9%	47.3%
N	45	52
	"Do you believe you *should* be able to see any such showing of actual sex acts in adult movies, video cassettes, or magazines if you want to?"	
Definitely yes	74.5%	75.19%
N	82	86
Definitely no	25.5%	24.81%
N	28	24
	"Some adult movies, videocassettes, and magazines show actual sex acts in great detail and with close-ups of sexual organs. Would viewing this type of material appeal to an unhealthy, shameful, or morbid interest in sex?"	
Definitely yes	43.6%	16.4%
N	48	18
Definitely no	56.4%	83.6%
N	62	92

Column [2] of table 4 shows the responses of subjects to the three critical questions after viewing the films. (It is important to remember that subjects were instructed to answer these questions *only* with reference to the film they had viewed that day.) For these analyses, responses were summed across all of the X-rated film-viewing conditions. As can be seen from the table, a majority of subjects believe that it is tolerated in their community for the average adult to obtain and see the adult video cassettes charged in the case. Seventy-five percent believe they personally should be able to see any such showing of actual sex acts in adult movies, video cassettes, or magazines, and 16% believe viewing the type of material charged in the case appealed to an unhealthy, shameful, or morbid interest in sex.

Changes pre-and postfilm viewing (again, summed across the five sexually explicit film conditions) were also examined for each of the three outcome variables by comparing the mean differences from pre-to postviewing. Comparisons of pre-and postfilm subject responses on the belief that these materials are tolerated in the community showed no significant change from pre-to postfilm viewing ($p > .15$). Likewise, there was no statistically significant change in subjects' opinions about whether they should be allowed to see such materials ($p > .50$). There was, however, a statistically significant change in subjects' perception that the materials appealed to a shameful, unhealthy, or morbid interest in sex before and after viewing. Subjects were less likely to find the materials appealed to such interests after viewing ($p < .0001$). Forty-four percent of the subjects believed that such material appealed to morbid, shameful, or unhealthy interest in sex before seeing a film. After they viewed a film, the percentage dropped to 16%.

Further Substantiation of the Findings

[I]t is necessary to rule out the possibility that answering the questions about tolerance/patent offensiveness and prurient appeal twice, once in the prefilm questionnaire and again in the postfilm questionnaire, might have caused subjects to think more carefully about these issues than they normally would, and lead them to change their opinion as a result of this reflection (a testing-effect bias). Specifically, it may be the case that the significant change from pre-to postfilm viewing on the questionnaire item about unhealthy, shameful, or morbid interest in sex that we observed was the result of subjects giving this question further consideration from the time of completing the prefilm questionnaire to the time they completed the postfilm questionnaire, and not the result of changing their opinions because they had seen the film. To test this possibility, we compared the responses of the neutral-film control group subjects before and after the film viewing on this questionnaire item. The results of this statistical test revealed a nonsignificant change between pre-and postfilm evaluations for the control group on the prurient appeal question ($p > .26$).

[D]iscussion

[A]t least two types of "tolerance" can be measured through a community survey—the opinions of a representative sample of persons about what they *think* the *community* tolerates, and the collective opinions of these same individuals about what they *personally* should be allowed to view. In this study, we asked subjects about both. The findings reported here (see table 4) indicate that a much lower percentage of people think the hypothetical "community" tolerates the films they just viewed than is the case when people are asked to report on what they personally tolerate (what they should be allowed to view). If we define community tolerance as the sum of individual responses about what people personally would tolerate, we would conclude that the community of Mecklenburg County is *overwhelmingly* tolerant of these materials, by a margin of 3 to 1.

[I]t might be informative to jurors for a social scientist to present evidence about *both* perceptions of the community and individual levels of tolerance. It should be acknowledged, however, that most policy decision making based on public opinion research relies on the summation of individual opinions rather than "guesses" by respondents about others' opinions and behaviors. As social scientists, we place far more confidence in a procedure whereby we ask people if they should personally be free to engage in a specific behavior (such as watching a movie) and summing these individual responses in order to obtain "the average" response, than we would be in asking people to report on what they *perceive* the "average" person would do in the same situation.

ST. JOHN v. STATE OF NORTH CAROLINA PAROLE COMMISSION

United States District Court, Western District of North Carolina, 1991.
764 F.Supp. 403.

■ ROBERT D. POTTER, DISTRICT JUDGE.

[Petitioners were convicted in a state court of selling obscene video-tapes and sentenced to six years in prison. Having exhausted their appeals in state court, they filed a petition in federal court for a writ of habeas corpus. The Respondent—the Parole Commission that maintained custody of petitioners—moved for summary judgment dismissing the petition.]

[P]etitioners believe the following argument support[s] their contention that relief is available:

The trial court excluded Petitioners' expert evidence in violation of Petitioners' right of confrontation and compulsory process pursuant to the Sixth Amendment and their due process rights pursuant to the Fourteenth Amendment.

[F]ilm Evaluation Study.

Petitioners attempted to introduce at trial a study involving focus groups that reviewed the films named in the indictment. According to Petitioners, the admission of such a study has never been attempted at an obscenity trial. Because the materials presented in the study were the films actually at issue, Petitioners argue that the trial court had no basis in law to exclude these studies.

Admittedly, the procedures utilized in the film evaluation study were designed to lead to the introduction of more relevant evidence than the other studies. Nonetheless, the Court does not believe that this fact alone requires the admission of the study. The proffered expert testimony revealed that only 20 to 24 people viewed each of the videotapes at issue.[11] Given the fact that the study was conducted in conditions exclusively in the control of Petitioners, the Court does not believe that Judge Gray was in error in finding that this evidence would be of no assistance to the 12 members of the community comprising the jury. Simply put, the Court believes that the record in this matter raises serious questions regarding whether those selected to participate in the study were "average" members of the community. The Court can envision large numbers of the community refusing to participate in a study that would expose them to the filth contained in the films at issue here. Even if it could be demonstrated that the focus groups were comprised of "average" citizens, the Court doubts

---

11. Petitioners argue that the Court should not consider the small composition of the focus groups because the district attorney threatened to prosecute the experts for disseminating obscenity if the films were shown to the focus groups. [J]udge McMillan entered an order enjoining the district attorney from prosecuting the experts. However, the Fourth Circuit vacated that order as being unlawful. The Court does not believe that Petitioners can complain of the size of the focus groups in light of the Fourth Circuit's opinion.

whether the opinion of 20 to 24 persons would be of great assistance to the jury in deciding what in effect is a jury question—whether the films were obscene. Thus, the Court believes that the trial court did not deprive Petitioners of any constitutional right in excluding this study.

[R]espondents' motion for summary judgment is GRANTED.

NOTES

1. Focus Groups? The court referred to the conditions in the true experimental study later published by Linz et al as "focus groups." D. Stewart and P. Shamdasani, Focus Groups: Theory and Practice (1990), however, describe focus groups as follows: "The contemporary focus group interview generally involves 8 to 12 individuals who discuss a particular topic under the direction of a moderator who promotes interaction and assures that the discussion remains on the topic of interest." Id. at 10. Since the subjects in the Linz et al study watched a film in private and completed a written post-film questionnaire—never discussing their reactions to the film with another subject or with a "moderator"—"focus groups" would appear an inapt description of the methodology of the study the Petitioners had attempted to introduce at trial.

2. Obscenity Prosecutions. *Daubert v. Merrell Dow Pharmaceuticals* was decided in 1993. As of mid-2005, there are no reported opinions in which a court has subjected a survey of community standards of obscenity to a *Daubert* analysis. This becomes less surprising when one realizes that there have been few obscenity prosecutions in recent years. This state of affairs may be about to change, however. The first issue of *DOJ [Department of Justice] Obscenity Prosecution News* (Spring 2005) stated that "From calendar years 1993 through 2000, CEOS [DOJ's Child Exploitation and Obscenity Section] handled only 4 obscenity prosecutions. From calendar year 2001 through February 1, 2005, CEOS has obtained convictions in 11 obscenity prosecutions; [h]as pending indictments in 5 cases; and is currently handling 15 active investigations, with many more in preliminary stages. These numbers reflect a more than 675% increase in CEOS obscenity prosecutions over the prior eight years."

SELECTED BIBLIOGRAPHY

Bedard and Gertz, Differences in Community Standards for the Viewing of Heterosexual and Homosexual Pornography, 12 International Journal of Public Opinion Research 324 (2000).

Obscenity and Pornography Decisions of the United States Supreme Court (M. Harrison and S. Gilbert eds. 2000).

Imwinkelried, The "Bases" of Expert Testimony: The Syllogistic Structure of Scientific Testimony, 67 North Carolina Law Review 1 (1988).

Lindgren, Defining Pornography, 141 University of Pennsylvania Law Review 1153 (1993).

F. Schauer, The Law of Obscenity (1976).

SECTION III.   DAMAGES

The law of remedies is concerned with the kind of relief to be given to a plaintiff who has established that a defendant has violated a substantive right. An injunction, for example, can be issued by a court commanding a defendant to act or to avoid acting in a certain way (e.g., to cease using a given term as a trademark for a product), and disobeying the court's order can result in a fine or imprisonment for contempt. Another common remedy is damages. A person who suffers a legally recognized harm is often entitled to an award of damages. Damages are given to the plaintiff in the form of money, even if the plaintiff's injury was not pecuniary (e.g., pain and suffering). The primary purpose of damages is a compensatory one: to make up to the plaintiff for what he or she has lost. Separate from compensatory damages, a plaintiff may also be awarded punitive damages, whose common purpose is to punish the defendant in the case of particularly aggravated misconduct on the defendant's part. See D. Dobbs, Remedies (2nd ed. 1993).

Compensatory damages have traditionally been decided on an individual basis, with the jury or judge setting the amount of money to be awarded in rough proportion to the extent of the plaintiff's injury. See Robinson and Abraham, Collective Justice in Tort Law, 78 Virginia Law Review 1481, 1481–1490 (1992). In the case of "mass torts," however, in which large numbers of plaintiffs have been injured by a defendant or group of defendants, determining the amount of damages to be awarded to each individual plaintiff has threatened to overwhelm the legal system. Some courts have recently attempted to deal with this problem in a creative way: by employing sampling techniques derived from the social sciences.

HAROLDS STORES, INC. v. DILLARD DEPARTMENT STORES

United States Court of Appeals, Tenth Circuit, 1996.
82 F.3d 1533.

■ BALDOCK, CIRCUIT JUDGE.

This appeal arises from a jury verdict entered in a copyright infringement action. Plaintiffs Harold's Stores, Inc. ("Harold's") and CMT Enterprises, Inc. ("CMT") filed suit against Defendant Dillard Department Stores, Inc. ("Dillard") alleging that Dillard infringed Harold's copyrighted fabric designs contained on women's garments, predominately skirts. [A] jury returned a verdict for Harold's. [D]illard appeals, arguing that [t]he district court erroneously admitted consumer survey evidence, and that it was entitled to judgment as a matter of law after trial.

[D]illard is a retail department store, operating 218 stores in 17 states. Harold's is a retail clothing store with 22 stores in 7 states, including 6 in

Oklahoma and 7 in Texas. Women's clothing forms the majority of Harold's business. With the assistance of CMT, a garment manufacturer, Harold's designs and manufactures private label women's clothing, including skirts, that feature original print fabric designs. Harold's annually develops 70 to 80 print fabrics from original art that it purchases from art studios in Italy and New York. [H]arold's represents to its customers that the original print fabric garments are available solely from Harold's.

[O]n May 10, 1993, Rebecca Casey, C.E.O. of Harold's, received information that Dillard stores in Norman and Tulsa, Oklahoma were offering for sale skirts with print fabric patterns identical to print skirts that Harold's had sold during the previous 1991 to 1992 sales season. Ms. Casey dispatched two employees to a Dillard store to investigate. The employees returned with "sacks of garments" purchased at Dillard that upon first examination appeared identical to print skirts that Harold's had developed from original art and offered for sale at $78.00 to $80.00 apiece the year before. The Dillard skirts were priced at $28.00 to $30.00. Over the next few days, Harold's personnel discovered skirts substantially similar to Harold's own offered for sale in 26 different Dillard stores.

[P]rior to trial, Dillard stipulated that it had infringed 19 of Harold's copyrighted print fabrics. Dillard offered for sale a total of 22,000 garments manufactured using Harold's copyrighted print fabric designs, and placed advance orders for 15,000 more. Thus, Dillard offered for sale or had ordered a total of 37,000 garments which infringed Harold's copyrights.

The district court conducted a six-day jury trial on Harold's damages claims. To establish its damages, Harold's submitted opinion testimony from [D]r. Daniel Howard. [D]r. Howard, a marketing professor from Southern Methodist University ("SMU"), estimated Harold's damages. Based on the results of a survey of college-aged women who had visited a Harold's store or examined a Harold's catalog and visited a Dillard store during the relevant time, Dr. Howard calculated the damages Harold's suffered nationwide due to Dillard's infringement of Harold's copyrights. [O]ver Dillard's motion in limine and objections, the district court admitted Dr. Howard's survey, report, and testimony.

[D]illard contends the district erred in admitting Dr. Howard's survey. Dillard argues the district court abused its discretion in admitting the survey because: (1) Dr. Howard failed to survey a relevant universe of consumers, and (2) the survey was not material or probative to establish copyright damages.

We allow the admission of survey evidence "as an exception to the hearsay rule if the survey is material, more probative on the issue than other evidence and if it has guarantees of trustworthiness." Brunswick Corp. v. Spirit Reel Co., 832 F.2d 513, 522 (10th Cir.1987) (citing Fed. R.Evid. 803(24)); see also 5 Jack B. Weinstein & Margaret A. Berger, Weinstein's Evidence P 901(b)(9)[03] at 901–140 (1995) ("The admissibility of survey or sampling results depends upon two factors: necessity and trustworthiness."); Manual for Complex Litigation, Third, s 21.493 at 101 (1995) ("In some cases, sampling techniques may provide the only practicable means to collect and present relevant data.''). "A survey is trustworthy if it is shown to have been conducted according to generally accepted survey principles." (Brunswick Corp., 832 F.2d at 522)

The survey should sample an adequate or proper universe of respondents. Exxon Corp. v. Texas Motor Exchange of Houston, Inc., 628 F.2d 500, 507 (5th Cir.1980). "[T]hat is, the persons interviewed must adequately represent the opinions which are relevant to the litigation." Amstar Corp. v. Domino's Pizza, Inc., 615 F.2d 252, 264 (5th Cir.), cert. denied, 449 U.S. 899, 101 S.Ct. 268, 66 L.Ed.2d 129 (1980). The district court should exclude the survey "when the sample is clearly not representative of the universe it is intended to reflect." Bank of Utah v. Commercial Sec. Bank, 369 F.2d 19, 27 (10th Cir.1966), cert. denied, 386 U.S. 1018, 87 S.Ct. 1374, 18 L.Ed.2d 456 (1967). Technical and methodological deficiencies in the survey, including the sufficiency of the universe sampled, bear on the weight of the evidence, not the survey's admissibility. We review the district court's admission of a survey for an abuse of discretion.

At trial, Harold's claimed that Dillard's sale in 1993 of copyrighted skirts that Harold's sold in 1991 and 1992 injured Harold's reputation and goodwill, and damaged Harold's relations and future sales with present and prospective customers. Harold's retained Dr. Howard to offer opinion testimony in support of Harold's damages claims. As a basis for his testimony, Dr. Howard surveyed 1,231 female undergraduates at SMU in October 1993 using a single-page survey. The complete survey is set forth in the margin.[7] 578 of the 1,231 respondents reported that they had visited a Harold's store or looked at a Harold's catalog and visited a Dillard store during the relevant time periods. Dr. Howard used the universe of female undergraduates who were exposed to both Harold's and Dillard during the times at issue to "determine whether, and to what degree, Dillard's sale of Harold's copyrighted fabric designs inflicted damages to future sales of women's and men's clothing by Harold's." Aplee. Supp.App. at 2441, 2472.

7. Shopping Survey Instructions: Please respond to the following questions by placing a "x" in the space that most closely reflects your memories and your feelings about the issues addressed.

(1) Have you visited a Harold's store or looked at a Harold's catalog in the past two years (in 1991 or 1992)?

___yes ___no ___unsure

(2) Did you visit a Dillard's department store from May to August of this year(1993)?

___yes ___no ___unsure

CONTINUE THE SURVEY ONLY IF YOU ANSWERED "YES" TO #1 AND #2

(3) On any of your recent visits to Dillard's, have you seen any print skirts with patterns you thought of as being unique to Harold's?

___yes ___no ___unsure

(4) On any of your recent visits to Dillard's, have you seen any women's purses with designs you thought of as being unique to Harold's?

___yes ___no ___unsure

(5) How likely or unlikely is it that you will purchase clothes from Harold's within the next year?

very likely __:__:__:__:__ very unlikely

(6) Is this the first time you have answered these questions?

___yes ___no ___unsure

Dillard maintains the district court abused its discretion in admitting the survey because the group surveyed was too narrow. Dillard argues that because Dr. Howard surveyed only female undergraduates at SMU, and from their responses extrapolated damages for all consumers that potentially would shop at a Harold's store, the survey was fatally flawed. According to Dillard, the proper universe encompasses "Harold's overall customers." Aplt. Reply Br. at 21.

On this record, we cannot conclude the district court abused its discretion in admitting the survey. The district court conducted an extensive voir dire of Dr. Howard and satisfied itself that the survey was material, probative to the issue of copyright infringement damages, and conducted according to generally accepted survey principles. The record also reflects that Harold's laid an adequate foundation to admit the survey.

[W]e also conclude that Dr. Howard surveyed an adequate universe of respondents. Ms. Casey, CEO of Harold's, testified that college-aged women represent a critically important group to Harold's overall sales. Ms. Casey also testified that Harold's first store was located on a college campus and that Harold's intentionally locates its stores near college campuses to target the college market, primarily undergraduate women. Ms. Casey observed that in her view, the buying patterns of college-age women are "identical to our older customers." Aplt.App. at 1676. Testimony before the district court also established that purchasing patterns, consumer preferences, and the demand for Harold's products were similar for all Harold's stores, regardless of geographic location.

Because testimony before the district court established that college-age women comprise Harold's core customer base, this survey does not amount to an instance "when the sample is clearly not representative of the universe it is intended to reflect." Bank of Utah, 369 F.2d at 27. Instead, the record demonstrates that the universe of college-age women who had visited a Dillard store and either visited a Harold's store or looked at a Harold's catalog during the relevant time periods "represent the opinions which are relevant to the litigation." Amstar, 615 F.2d at 264. That is, the survey respondents' opinions are probative on the issue of whether and to what degree Dillard's infringement and sale of Harold's copyrighted fabric designs damaged Harold's future clothing sales. Thus, Dillard's contention that the survey was not probative or material to the issue of copyright infringement damages fails.

In sum, we hold the district court did not abuse its discretion in admitting the survey because Dr. Howard surveyed an adequate universe of respondents according to generally accepted survey principles. Consequently, any technical or methodological deficiencies in the manner in which Dr. Howard conducted the survey bear on the weight—not the admissibility—of the survey. We therefore reject Dillard's argument that the district court erred in admitting the survey because the survey respondents did not encompass "Harold's overall customers" and because the survey was, according to Dillard, not material or probative.

[D]illard [also] [m]aintains the district court erred in denying its Rule 50 (b) renewal motion for judgment as a matter of law because the evidence was insufficient to support the copyright damages award. Dillard contends that the survey evidence attested to by Dr. Howard did not provide reliable evidence of present or future reduced sales revenue as a result of reduced purchase intentions.

[H]arold's offered opinion testimony from Dr. Howard in support of its copyright infringement damages claims. Dr. Howard based his damages estimates on the survey. Of the universe of undergraduate women who had visited a Dillard store in 1993, (when Dillard offered the infringing skirts for sale), and visited a Harold's store or looked at a Harold's catalog in 1991 or 1992, Dr. Howard testified that the survey detected a reduced future purchase intention by respondents who saw print skirts at Dillard that they thought were unique to Harold's. Specifically, Dr. Howard testified that women who saw the infringing skirts at Dillard were somewhat unlikely to purchase clothes from Harold's within the next year. In contrast, women who visited both stores but did not see skirts they thought of as unique to Harold's were, on the whole, fairly likely to shop at Harold's in the future. Dr. Howard reported that the women who saw the garments at issue at Dillard were 33.1% less likely to purchase garments at Harold's than women who visited both stores at the relevant time but did not view the infringing skirts.

Dr. Howard analyzed the survey data and estimated the damages Harold's suffered nationwide from Dillard's copyright infringement. Dr. Howard testified that Harold's suffered damages to goodwill, reputation, and sales to future and prospective customers in the range of $226,367.00 to $517,809.00.

Based on this evidence, the jury awarded Harold's and CMT actual damages of $312,000.00 on the copyright infringement claim. Viewing the evidence in the light most favorable to Harold's and drawing all reasonable inferences therefrom, SCFC ILC, Inc., 36 F.3d at 962, we conclude there was substantial evidence tending to support the jury's damages award on Harold's copyright infringement claim.

[I]n sum, we hold the district court did not err by [a]dmitting Dr. Howard's survey and [d]enying Dillard's renewal motion for judgment as a matter of law after trial.

[A]FFIRMED.

CIMINO v. RAYMARK INDUSTRIES, INC.

United States District Court, Eastern District of Texas, 1990.
751 F.Supp. 649.

■ Robert M. Parker, Chief Judge.

The odyssey of asbestos litigation in the Eastern District of Texas has now entered its third decade. The trek started by Clarence Borel and

Claude Tomplait has been marked by aimless wandering through the legal wilderness. The journey has taken its predicted toll. Raymark, Forty-Eight Insulations, Unarco, Standard Asbestos, Johns-Manville, Eagle-Picher, and now Celotex are bankrupt. Other defendants are clearly in the twilight of their participation. Four hundred and forty-eight members of the class have died waiting for their cases to be heard. The departed companies and plaintiffs have all been victims of a system that has seen a substantial majority of the compensation dollar go to witnesses and lawyers in the form of transaction costs. Transaction costs consumed $.61 of each asbestos-litigation dollar with $.37 going to defendants litigation costs; the plaintiffs receive only $.39 from each litigation dollar.

[T]he Court has now witnessed an evolution in defense strategy. [Defendants] have adopted a "fortress mentality" and are attempting to avoid liability by obstructing the Court's ability to provide a forum in these cases. It is a strategy that is not unique to East Texas, but is one that is being utilized all across the country. They assert a right to individual trials in each case and assert the right to repeatedly contest in each case every contestable issue involving the same products, the same warnings, and the same conduct. The strategy is a sound one; the defendants know that if the procedure in *Cimino* is not affirmed, these cases will never be tried.

If the Court could somehow close thirty cases a month, it would take six and one-half years to try these cases and there would be pending over 5,000 untouched cases at the present rate of filing. Transaction costs would be astronomical.

The great challenge presented to the Court by this litigation is to provide a fair and cost effective means of trying large numbers of asbestos cases.

[D]uring the course of the *Cimino* trial while the question of whether asbestos products were unreasonably dangerous was being litigated once again in Beaumont, the federal courtroom in Tyler was being used by the State Court of Appeals Judges because men in spacesuits were removing asbestos from their chambers.

THE PLAN

[O]n February 19, 1990, this Court certified a class under Fed.R.Civ.P. 23(b)(3) consisting of 3,031 plaintiffs with existing cases in the Eastern District of Texas, all claiming an asbestos-related injury or disease result- ing from exposure to defendants' asbestos containing insulation products. Seven hundred thirty-three cases were removed as a result of being dismissed, severed or settled. The class consisting of 2,298 plaintiffs went to trial against Pittsburgh-Corning, Fibreboard, Celotex, Carey-Canada, and ACL.

PHASE I

[T]he issues were whether each asbestos containing insulation product manufactured by each defendant, settling and non-settling, was defective and unreasonably dangerous, the adequacy of warnings, the state of the art defense and the fiber type defense.

[P]HASE II

Phase II required a jury finding for each of nineteen worksites during certain time periods regarding which asbestos containing insulation products were used, which crafts were sufficiently exposed to asbestos fibers from those products for such exposure to be a producing cause of an asbestos-related injury or disease and an apportionment of causation among defendants, settling and non-settling.

In other words, the exposure questions to be submitted would be specific as to time, place, craft, and amounts of exposure.

PHASE III

Phase III is the damage issue. The 2,298 class members were divided into five disease categories based on the plaintiff's injury claims. The Court selected a random sample from each disease category as follows:

	SAMPLE SIZE	DISEASE CATEGORY POPULATION
Mesothelioma	15	32
Lung Cancer	25	186
Other Cancer	20	58
Asbestosis	50	1,050
Pleural Disease	50	972
TOTAL	160	2,298

The damage case of each trial sample class member randomly drawn was then submitted to a jury. Each plaintiff whose damage case was submitted to the jury is to be awarded his individual verdict and the average verdict for each disease category will constitute the damage award for each non-sample class member.

Plaintiffs have agreed to the procedure, thereby waiving their rights to individual damage determinations.

THE TRIAL

Phase I began with jury selection on February 6, 1990 and the verdict was returned March 29, 1990. The Court then granted the parties' request for additional preparation time between Phase I and Phases II and III. Two juries were selected on July 3, 1990. The juries sat together for the first five trial days which were devoted to general medical testimony. The juries were then divided and began hearing testimony on groups of plaintiffs and returning damage verdicts. The last verdict for the 160 individual damages cases was received October 5, 1990.

In all, the trial consumed 133 days of trial time and produced 25,348 pages of transcript prepared as daily copy. The docket sheet in the Clerk's office is 529 pages long. The Court has entered 373 signed Orders.

Prior to trial 1,885 sets of interrogatories were answered by the parties and 2,354 depositions were taken, with an additional 800 being taken during trial. Independent medical examinations were conducted of 1,400 plaintiffs.

During the course of the trial, 271 expert witnesses and 292 fact witnesses testified, 6,176 exhibits were received in evidence constituting 577,000 pages of documents. Fifty-eight individual lawyers participated in the in-court presentation of this case which was presided over in varying degrees by four district judges and three magistrates.

If all that is accomplished by this is the closing of 169 cases, then it was not worth the effort and will not be repeated.

PHASE II—STIPULATION

[P]rior to the Court drafting a verdict form for Phase II, the parties agreed to stipulate as to what the jury findings would have been had Phase II been tried to a jury. The parties stipulated that the jury would have apportioned causation among the defendants in the amounts of 10% causation for each of the non-settling defendants and 13% causation for the settling defendant Johns-Manville Corporation.

STATISTICS

Phase III of the plan utilizes the science of statistics, or more specifically, inferential statistics.

[A]cceptance of statistical evidence is now commonplace in the Courts. The following illustrations demonstrate the diverse legal contexts in which statistics, particularly random sampling, has been used. In trademark infringement suits, statistical sampling is useful in determining consumer product identification and confusion regarding trademarks. See Processed Plastic Co. v. Warner Communications, Inc., 675 F.2d 852, 854–58 (7th Cir.1982) (survey of children between the ages of 6 and 12 in order to determine if Plaintiff's toy car was confused with Defendant's "Dukes of Hazzard" toy car); Exxon Corp. v. Texas Motor Exchange, Inc., 628 F.2d 500 (5th Cir.1980) (survey of 515 licensed drivers indicated high possibility of confusion between "Texon" and "Exxon"); Zippo Manufacturing Co. v. Rogers Imports, Inc., 216 F.Supp. 670 (S.D.N.Y.1963).

[I]n the area of torts, statistics have been used to prove both liability and damages. The New Jersey Supreme Court has, in at least two cases, relied upon statistics showing the correlation between the theft of cars with keys left in the ignition and automobile accidents in the liability phase of a trial. See Hill v. Yaskin, 75 N.J. 139, 380 A.2d 1107 (1977); Zinck v. Whelan, 120 N.J.Super. 432, 294 A.2d 727 (1972). Courts frequently permit evidence of life-expectancy or mortality tables when determining damages. See Ageloff v. Delta Airlines, Inc., 860 F.2d 379 (11th Cir.1988); Espana v. United States, 616 F.2d 41 (2d Cir.1980); Larsen v. International Business Machines Corp., 87 F.R.D. 602 (E.D.Pa.1980) (use of work-life tables). Statistical evidence has proven to be particularly useful in the determination of lost or future revenues, profits or earnings. See In re Knickerbocker,

827 F.2d 281, 288–89 (8th Cir.1987) (court allowed expert to testify as to future revenues, based upon historical analysis and price predictions).

[T]he reasons the courts have come to rely on statistics are the same reasons that society embraces the science. It has been proved to provide information with an acceptable degree of accuracy and economy.

[A]gainst this backdrop, defendants assert that statistical methodology is somehow inappropriate for mass tort cases. This contention fails when examined under the same microscope used in other cases. The method incorporated into Phase III produces a level of economy in terms of both judicial resources and transaction cost that needs no elaboration. Moreover, defendants cannot possibly suggest that no form of statistical evidence is appropriate in this case. They frequently used statistics during this trial. At the outset, Owens-Illinois submitted a statistical analysis of a telephone survey conducted by Jury Analyst, Inc. on a sample of 500 people from each division in this district in support of its Motion to Transfer Venue. Defendants Fibreboard and Pittsburgh-Corning subsequently adopted that motion. The voluminous medical literature offered by both sides contains innumerable examples of statistical surveys and analysis.

Defendant Pittsburgh-Corning relied upon the testimony of Dr. Thomas Robert Savings to estimate the percentage of Pittsburgh-Corning products in the Golden Triangle area. Dr. Savings made an extensive statistical analysis to compute the estimated market share for Pittsburgh-Corning which was then extrapolated to the chemical plants in the area. The Court is of the opinion that defendants' extensive reliance upon statistical analysis and extrapolation considerably weakens their argument against the use of the same by the Court.

[D]UE PROCESS

Defendants object to the Court's plan and assert that due process, even in the asbestos context, entitles defendants to a traditional one-on-one trial in each of the 2,298 cases. In defendants' eyes there are no common issues, irrespective of the fact that the products in each trial would be identical, the warnings would be identical, and the exposure evidence for each worksite during the time periods inquired about for each craft would be identical.

[I]t is this Court's opinion that due process in the asbestos context should not be analyzed in the narrow, traditional, one-sided view of defendants, but should also encompass the impact on plaintiffs and even the obvious societal interest involved.

[D]amages must be determined in the aggregate. Whether it is by the mechanism of the Court's plan or by some other procedure approved or suggested by the Court of Appeals, without the ability to determine damages in the aggregate, the Court cannot try these cases.

IN RE ESTATE OF FERDINAND E. MARCOS HUMAN RIGHTS LITIGATION

United States District Court, District of Hawai'i, 1995.
910 F.Supp. 1460.

■ Real, District Judge.

Victims of torture, summary execution and disappearance filed suits for damages, in the form of a class action as well as individual direct actions, against the Estate of the former President of the Philippines, Ferdinand E. Marcos (MARCOS), for human rights violations.

[I]n 1986 MARCOS fled the Philippines and arrived in the State of Hawaii. MARCOS was a resident of Hawaii at the time he was served with the complaints that are the subject of this litigation but he died during the pendency of these actions. The Estate of Ferdinand E. Marcos (the ES-TATE) has been substituted in MARCOS' place; his widow, Imelda Marcos, and his son, Ferdinand E. Marcos, Jr., have appeared before this Court as representatives of the ESTATE.

The action was tried in the three phases: (1) liability, (2) exemplary [i.e., punitive] damages, and (3) compensatory damages, over a nine year period—from 1986 to 1995. In the compensatory damages phase, Phase III, this Court allowed the jury to consider the damages to a random sample of plaintiffs as representative of the injuries suffered by those in the three subclasses; i.e. (1) plaintiffs who were tortured; (2) the families of those individuals who were the subjects of summary execution; and (3) the families of those who disappeared as the result of the actions of MARCOS.

[C]LASS ACTION

On September 22, 1992, in the liability phase of the trial, the jury found defendants liable to 10,059 plaintiffs, for the acts of torture, summary execution and disappearance. On February 23, 1994 the jury awarded plaintiffs $1.2 billion in exemplary damages.

In the compensatory damages phase, the class action plaintiffs present-ed their case to the jury by using damages sustained by a random sample of plaintiffs as representative of damages suffered by the entire class.

[A]t this time there are two issues before this Court. The primary question is whether the use by this Court of a random sample of plaintiffs, as representative of the injuries suffered by others in the class, violates defendant's due process rights. The second question is whether use of the random sample violates the defendant's Seventh Amendment right to a jury trial.

The ESTATE asserts random sampling is inappropriate for this case, and each claim should be individually tried. This Court holds otherwise. The use of aggregate procedures, with the help of an expert in the field of inferential statistics, for the purpose of determining class compensatory damages is proper.

James Dannemiller, an expert in the field of inferential statistics and survey sampling for twenty five years, assisted in this case. [M]r. Dannemiller testified that inferential statistics is a recognized science which uses mathematical equations to infer the probability of events occurring or not occurring. One branch of that science is the sampling theory, which deals with the selection of sample sizes sufficient to produce results that can be applied to a larger population from which the sample was selected with a specified probability of error. The formula Dannemiller used in this case is a well-known statistical tool that is found in Leslie Kish, Survey Sampling 53 (New York, John Wiley and Sons 1962) (KISH FORMULA).

Mr. Dannemiller testified under the KISH FORMULA, 137 randomly selected valid claims examined from a larger population of 9,541 validly submitted claims by class members would produce a 95% confidence level. The Court then considered the details of deposing 137 randomly selected claimants.

This Court appointed a Special Master, to facilitate the taking of depositions of 137 randomly selected plaintiffs. The Special Master's appointment had a three-fold purpose: first, he supervised the taking of the 137 depositions in the Philippines; second, he served as a court-appointed expert on damages, under Federal Rule of Evidence 706, to review the deposition transcripts along with the claim forms; finally, he made recommendations on compensatory damages for the 137 claimants as well as the remaining class members to the jury.

The depositions which the Special Master oversaw were noticed and taken in accordance with the Federal Rules of Civil Procedure. Although having notice of the depositions of the 137 class member sample and the names of the individual class members, the ESTATE chose not to participate and did not appear at any of the depositions, which were taken during October and November of 1994. Nor did the ESTATE choose to depose any of the 9,541 class members to test the procedure employed by the Court, or to acquire evidence to refute the fairness to the defendant of this random selection process using inferential statistical methodology.

The Special Master was directed by this Court to review the depositions for the following three elements: (1) whether the abuse claimed fell within one of the three definitions, with which the Court charged the jury at the liability phase of the trial; (2) whether the Philippine military or paramilitary was involved in such abuse; and (3) whether the abuse occurred during the period of September 1972 through February 1986.

[O]f the 137 randomly sampled claims, 67 were torture victims, 52 were execution victims and 18 were disappearance victims. Based upon the depositions of each of the 137 randomly selected class member's claims and review of all the claims of the remaining class members, the Special Master recommended damages under Philippine, International, and American law, for each of the three categories of claims. During the Special Master's testimony, the Court advised the jury that they, in determining damages, could accept, modify or reject the recommendations of the Special Master. The jury was also instructed that they could, independently, on the basis of the depositions of the 137 randomly chosen class members, make their own judgment as to the individual damages of the 137 claimants and the aggregate damages suffered by the class. [A]fter five days of deliberations, the jury returned a verdict of over $766 million, approximately $1 million less than the Special Master had recommended.

In his report and testimony, the Special Master made damage determinations for torture victims by ranking each claim from 1–5, with 5 representing the worst abuses and suffering. The torture claims were evaluated based upon Judge Real's decision in Trajano v. Imee Marcos-Manotoc, aff'd, In re: Estate of Ferdinand E. Marcos Litigation, 978 F.2d 493 (9th Cir. 1992), cert. denied, 508 U.S. 972, 113 S.Ct. 2960, 125 L.Ed.2d 661 (1993), as part of this matter, and the following considerations: (1) physical torture, including what methods were used and/or abuses were suffered; (2) mental abuse, including fright and anguish; (3) amount of time torture lasted; (4) length of detention, if any; (5) physical and/or mental injuries; (6) victim's age; and (7) actual losses, including medical bills. Although each claim of torture could have been but were not totally unique, as the Court Appointed Expert on damages, the Special Master, was able to determine that there were sufficient similarities within a rating category to recommend a standard damage amount to each victim within that grouping.

[F]or computing the total amount of damages for summary execution and disappearance victims, depending on the individual facts, there were different variables which went into the equation: (1) torture prior to death or disappearance; (2) the actual killing or disappearance; (3) the victim's family's mental anguish; and (4) lost earnings.

[T]he utilization of random sampling was fully examined in Cimino v. Raymark Industries, Inc., 751 F.Supp. 649 (E.D.Tex.1990), an asbestos class action.

[D]ue Process

In a case such as this one, where there are 9,541 class members, most of whom live in other areas of the world, a balancing of interests must occur to obtain justice to the parties. A due process analysis must weigh defendant's claim to the right to trial in each individual case against judicial economy and manageability by use of a valid statistical procedure. [T]his Court was moved by the same concerns as Chief Judge Parker in Cimino. Here, individual trials for each of the 9,541 plaintiffs would take decades. Most of that time would be wasted since the nature of the injuries would be similar, if not identical, the testimony would be largely duplicative. Utilizing the procedure employed by the Court the injuries could be accurately categorized, and the source of the injuries would be identical. [I]nferential statistics with random sampling produces an acceptable due process solution to the troublesome area of mass tort litigation.

The issue remains whether this Court's use of inferential statistics in using aggregate procedures, denied defendant's their constitutional due process right to a one-on-one trial. This Court believes, "the aggregate trial is, in some vital respects, superior to the individual trial"[15] and does not violate the substantive or procedural due process rights of either the plaintiffs or the defendant.

This Court finds persuasive the analysis of Professors Saks and Blanck in their discussion that aggregate trials do not violate due process.

[S]eventh Amendment

The issue here is whether the use of random samples, in an aggregate trial, violates the Seventh Amendment right to a jury trial. [T]he Seventh Amendment provides no formula for the procedures to be used in a trial by jury. Rather, it is the rules of evidence and procedure that impact jury trials. Pragmatic application of these rules, consistent with justice, is all that is necessary for the presentation of the facts necessary for a jury determination. To claim otherwise certainly raises form over substance to a new level in today's jurisprudential world.

Here, the jury did determine the facts of the case, as the substance of the action was presented to the jury. There would be no benefit to either side in having the entire class testify given the repetition in the claims. Rule 23 of the Federal Rule of Civil Procedure does not mandate the presence of each member of the class. Therefore, by choosing a random sample of 137 claimants in an aggregate trial, neither side was deprived of even the form of their right to a jury trial. [D]efendant was given its day in court with the jury, by procedures facilitating the presentation of evidence by use of random sampling in an aggregate damage trial.

[C]ONCLUSION

The use of an aggregate procedure for determining compensatory damages, under the procedures followed in this litigation, was neither a violation of the parties' due process rights nor their right to a jury trial under the Seventh Amendment. The aggregation of compensatory damage claims vindicates important federal and international policies, permits justice to be done without unduly clogging the court system, and was shown to be fair to the defendant.

Judgment shall be entered for plaintiffs.

———

HILAO v. ESTATE OF MARCOS

United States Court of Appeals, Ninth Circuit, 1996.
103 F.3d 789.

■ FLETCHER, CIRCUIT JUDGE:

The Estate of Ferdinand E. Marcos appeals from a final judgment entered against it in a class-action suit after a trifurcated jury trial on the

---

15. Michael J. Saks and Peter David Blanck, "Justice Improved: The Unrecognized Benefits of Aggregation and Sampling in Mass Torts", 44 STAN.L.REV. 815, 827 (1992).

damage claims brought by a class of Philippine nationals (hereinafter collectively referred to as "Hilao") who were victims of torture, "disappearance", or summary execution under the regime of Ferdinand E. Marcos. [T]he district court allowed the use of a statistical sample of the class claims in determining compensatory damages.

[T]he Estate's challenge to the procedure used by the district court is very narrow. It challenges specifically only "the method by which [the district court] allowed the validity of the class claims to be determined": the master's use of a representative sample to determine what percentage of the total claims were invalid.

The grounds on which the Estate challenges this method are unclear. It states that to its knowledge this method "has not previously been employed in a class action". This alone, of course, would not be grounds for reversal, and in any case the method has been used before in an asbestos class-action case, the opinion in which apparently helped persuade the district court to use this method. See Cimino v. Raymark Indus., Inc., 751 F.Supp. 649, 659–667 (E.D.Tex.1990).

The Estate also argues that the method was "inappropriate" because the class consists of various members with numerous subsets of claims based on whether the plaintiff or his or her decedent was subjected to torture, "disappearance", or summary execution. The district court's methodology, however, took account of those differences by grouping the class members' claims into three subclasses.

Finally, the Estate appears to assert that the method violated its rights to due process because "individual questions apply to each subset of claims, i.e., whether the action was justified, the degree of injury, proximate cause, etc." It does not, however, provide any argument or case citation to explain how the methodology violated its due-process rights. Indeed, the "individual questions" it identifies—justification, degree of injury, proximate cause—are irrelevant to the challenge it makes: the method of determining the validity of the class members' claims. The jury had already determined that Philippine military or paramilitary forces on Marcos' orders—or with his conspiracy or assistance or with his knowledge and failure to act—had tortured, summarily executed, or "disappeared" untold numbers of victims and that the Estate was liable to them or their survivors. The only questions involved in determining the validity of the class members' claims were whether or not the human-rights abuses they claim to have suffered were proven by sufficient evidence.

Although poorly presented, the Estate's due-process claim does raise serious questions. Indeed, at least one circuit court has expressed "profound disquiet" in somewhat similar circumstances. In re Fibreboard Corp., 893 F.2d 706, 710 (5th Cir.1990). [O]n the other hand, the time and judicial resources required to try the nearly 10,000 claims in this case would alone make resolution of Hilao's claims impossible. See Cimino, 751 F.Supp. at 652–53 ("If the Court could somehow close thirty cases a month, it would take six and one-half years to try these [2,298] cases ... "). The similarity in the injuries suffered by many of the class members would make such an effort, even if it could be undertaken, especially wasteful, as would the fact that the district court found early on that the damages suffered by the class members likely exceed the total known assets of the Estate.

While the district court's methodology in determining valid claims is unorthodox, it can be justified by the extraordinarily unusual nature of this case. " 'Due process,' unlike some legal rules, is not a technical conception with a fixed content unrelated to time, place and circumstances". Cafeteria and Restaurant Workers Union, Local 473 v. McElroy, 367 U.S. 886, 895, 81 S.Ct. 1743, 1748, 6 L.Ed.2d 1230 (1961). In Connecticut v. Doehr, 501 U.S. 1, 10, 111 S.Ct. 2105, 2112, 115 L.Ed.2d 1 (1991), a case involving prejudgment attachment, the Supreme Court set forth a test, based on the test of Mathews v. Eldridge, 424 U.S. 319, 96 S.Ct. 893, 47 L.Ed.2d 18 (1976), for determining whether a procedure by which a private party invokes state power to deprive another person of property satisfies due process: [F]irst, consideration of the private interest that will be affected by the [procedure]; second, an examination of the risk of erroneous deprivation through the procedures under attack and the probable value of additional or alternative safeguards; and third, ... principal attention to the interest of the party seeking the [procedure], with, nonetheless, due regard for any ancillary interest the government may have in providing the procedure or forgoing the added burden of providing greater protections. 501 U.S. at 11, 111 S.Ct. at 2112. The interest of the Estate that is affected is at best an interest in not paying damages for any invalid claims. If the Estate had a legitimate concern in the identities of those receiving damage awards, the district court's procedure could affect this interest. In fact, however, the Estate's interest is only in the total amount of damages for which it will be liable: if damages were awarded for invalid claims, the Estate would have to pay more. The statistical method used by the district court obviously presents a somewhat greater risk of error in comparison to an adversarial adjudication of each claim, since the former method requires a probabilistic prediction (albeit an extremely accurate one) of how many of the total claims are invalid. The risk in this case was reduced, though, by the fact that the proof-of-claim form that the district court required each class member to submit in order to opt into the class required the claimant to certify under penalty of perjury that the information provided was true and correct. Hilao's interest in the use of the statistical method, on the other hand, is enormous, since adversarial resolution of each class member's claim would pose insurmountable practical hurdles. The "ancillary" interest of the judiciary in the procedure is obviously also substantial, since 9,541 individual adversarial determinations of claim validity would clog the docket of the district court for years. Under the balancing test set forth in Mathews and Doehr, the procedure used by the district court did not violate due process. [T]he judgment of the district court is therefore

AFFIRMED.

■ RYMER, CIRCUIT JUDGE, concurring in part and dissenting in part:

Because I believe that determining causation as well as damages by inferential statistics instead of individualized proof raises more than "serious questions" of due process, I must dissent from [that Part] of the majority opinion.

[T]here is little question that Marcos caused tremendous harm to many people, but the question is which people, and how much. That, I think, is a question on which the defendant has a right to due process. If due process in the form of a real prove-up of causation and damages cannot be accomplished because the class is too big or to do so would take too long, then (as the Estate contends) the class is unmanageable and should not have been certified in the first place. As Judge Becker recently wrote for the Third Circuit in declining to certify a 250,000-member class in an asbestos action: "Every decade presents a few great cases that force the judicial system to choose between forging a solution to a major social problem on the one hand, and preserving its institutional values on the other. This is such a case." Georgine v. Amchem Prod., Inc., 83 F.3d 610, 617 (3d Cir.1996).

So is this. I think that due process dictates the choice: a real trial. I therefore dissent.

IN RE CHEVRON U.S.A.

United States Court of Appeals, Fifth Circuit, 1997.
109 F.3d 1016.

■ Robert M. Parker, Circuit Judge:

This controversy arose out of the alleged injuries suffered by over 3,000 plaintiffs and intervenors ("Plaintiffs"), who claim damages for personal injuries, wrongful death, and property contamination allegedly caused by Chevron's acts and omissions. The Plaintiffs and their allegedly contaminated property are located in the Kennedy Heights section of Houston, Texas. The Plaintiffs contend that their subdivision was constructed on land used in the 1920's by Chevron for a crude oil storage waste pit. According to the Plaintiffs, when Chevron ceased using the property as a tank farm, it failed to take appropriate measures to secure the site, thereby allowing other waste to be deposited on the land. Later, Chevron sold the property for residential development knowing that the land was contaminated. Various developers filled these waste pits without remediating the land. Plaintiffs assert that the hazardous substances which were stored in the waste pits have migrated into the environment, including the drinking water supply for the Kennedy Heights section. As a result, Plaintiffs claim personal injuries and property damage.

[O]n December 19, 1996, the district court approved a trial plan. The trial plan provided for a unitary trial on the issues of "general liability or causation" on behalf of the remaining plaintiffs, as well as the individual causation and damage issues of the selected plaintiffs, and ordered the selection of a bellwether group of thirty (30) claimants, fifteen (15) to be chosen by the plaintiffs and fifteen (15) to be chosen by Chevron. Chevron contends that the goal of the "unitary trial" was to determine its liability, or lack thereof, in a single trial and to establish bellwether verdicts to which the remaining claims could be matched for settlement purposes. It is this selection process which Chevron argues will not result in a representative group of bellwether plaintiffs.

Chevron filed with the district court the affidavit of Ronald G. Frankiewicz, Ph.D. which evaluated the district court's trial plan for selecting the thirty plaintiffs, concluding that such a plan was "not representative." Instead, Frankiewicz detailed the "stratified selection process" which should be used by the district court in selecting the bellwether group which would result in a representative group of plaintiffs. The district court however struck Frankiewicz's affidavit as untimely filed and redundant in substance. On January 7, 1997, the district court denied Chevron's request to certify an interlocutory appeal. This Petition for Writ of Mandamus[1] ensued.

DISCUSSION

[1]. The Plan

The district court, after designating the case as complex, then articulated the goals of its trial plan as seeking to achieve the greatest efficiency and expedition in the resolution of all issues involved in the case. Pursuant to those goals, it structured the trial as follows:

1. Composed of thirty (30) plaintiffs, fifteen (15) chosen by the plaintiffs and fifteen (15) chosen by the defendants. The thirty (30) plaintiffs chosen shall come from the lists submitted by the parties to the state court in April of 1996. However, each side is permitted to substitute or replace not more than five (5) plaintiffs, within its discretion, on or before January 1, 1997.

2. All chosen plaintiffs shall be adults, to the exclusion of minor children, unless the children are part of a household represented by at least one adult.

3. Each individual shall be counted as a single plaintiff, as opposed to a household as a single plaintiff.

4. The trial shall focus on the individual claims of each of the selected plaintiffs and on the issue of the existence or nonexistence of liability on the part of Chevron for the pollutants that, allegedly, give rise to all of the plaintiffs' claims. Thus, a unitary trial on the issues of general liability or causation as well as the individual causation and damage issues of the selected plaintiff shall occur.

5. The Court reserves the right to: (a) place a time limit on the length of the trial, limit the testimony of certain witnesses, limit the number of witnesses to be called on a particular issue, amend this Order, and issue additional orders.

---

1. [Ed. Note: An order requiring the trial court judge to take certain action.]

Initially, we note the obvious. The trial plan, while clearly designed to resolve the issue of liability on the part of Chevron to all the plaintiffs by referring to a unitary trial on the issues of general liability or causation, does not identify any common issues or explain how the verdicts in the thirty (30) selected cases are supposed to resolve liability for the remaining 2970 plaintiffs. It is impossible to discern from the district court's order what variables may exist that will impact on both the property and personal injury claims in this litigation. Similar litigation typically contains property issue variables that are related to time, proximity, and contamination levels of exposure to any pollutants that may be present, and personal injury claims that contain a mix of alleged exposure related maladies that also may be affected by time, proximity, and exposure levels. We, however, may not speculate on the homogeneity of the mix of claims, the uniformity of any exposure that may have existed and what diseases, if any, may be related to that exposure. Instead our review is restricted to the record and to an examination of the district court's order.

[2].   A Bellwether Trial

The term bellwether is derived from the ancient practice of belling a wether (a male sheep) selected to lead his flock. The ultimate success of the wether selected to wear the bell was determined by whether the flock had confidence that the wether would not lead them astray, and so it is in the mass tort context.

The notion that the trial of some members of a large group of claimants may provide a basis for enhancing prospects of settlement or for resolving common issues or claims is a sound one that has achieved general acceptance by both bench and bar. References to bellwether trials have long been included in the Manual for Complex Litigation. See MANUAL FOR COMPLEX LITIGATION — 33.27–.28 (3d ed.1995). The reasons for acceptance by bench and bar are apparent. If a representative group of claimants are tried to verdict, the results of such trials can be beneficial for litigants who desire to settle such claims by providing information on the value of the cases as reflected by the jury verdicts. Common issues or even general liability may also be resolved in a bellwether context in appropriate cases.

Whatever may be said about the trial contemplated by the district court's December 19, 1996 order, one thing is clear. It is not a bellwether trial. It is simply a trial of fifteen (15) of the "best" and fifteen (15) of the "worst" cases contained in the universe of claims involved in this litigation. There is no pretense that the thirty (30) cases selected are representative of the 3,000 member group of plaintiffs.

A bellwether trial designed to achieve its value ascertainment function for settlement purposes or to answer troubling causation or liability issues common to the universe of claimants has as a core element representativeness—that is, the sample must be a randomly selected one of sufficient size so as to achieve statistical significance to the desired level of confidence in the result obtained. Such samples are selected by the application of the science of inferential statistics. The essence of the science of inferential statistics is that one may confidently draw inferences about the whole from a representative sample of the whole. The applicability of inferential statistics have long been recognized by the courts.

The selected thirty (30) cases included in the district court's "unitary trial" are not cases calculated to represent the group of 3,000 claimants. Thus, the results that would be obtained from a trial of these thirty (30) cases lack the requisite level of representativeness so that the results could permit a court to draw sufficiently reliable inferences about the whole that could, in turn, form the basis for a judgment affecting cases other than the selected thirty. While this particular sample of thirty cases is lacking in representativeness, statistical sampling with an appropriate level of representativeness has been utilized and approved. As recognized by the Ninth Circuit, "[i]nferential statistics with random sampling produces an acceptable due process solution to the troublesome area of mass tort litigation." In re Estate of Marcos Human Rights Litigation, 910 F.Supp. 1460, 1467 (D.Haw.1995), aff'd. sub. nom. Hilao v. Estate of Marcos, 103 F.3d 767 (9th Cir.1996) (holding that the random sampling procedures used by the district court do not violate due process).

We, therefore, hold that before a trial court may utilize results from a bellwether trial for a purpose that extends beyond the individual cases tried, it must, prior to any extrapolation, find that the cases tried are representative of the larger group of cases or claims from which they are selected. Typically, such a finding must be based on competent, scientific, statistical evidence that identifies the variables involved and that provides a sample of sufficient size so as to permit a finding that there is a sufficient level of confidence that the results obtained reflect results that would be obtained from trials of the whole. See Hilao, 103 F.3d at 786; Michael J. Saks & Peter David Blanck, Justice Improved: The Unrecognized Benefits of Aggregation and Sampling in Mass Torts, 44 STAN. L.REV. 815 (1992). It is such findings that provide the foundation for any inferences that may be drawn from the trial of sample cases. Without a sufficient level of confidence in the sample results, no inferences may be drawn from such results that would form the basis for applying such results to cases or claims that have not been actually tried.

[C]ONCLUSION

The petition, therefore, for mandamus as it relates to the trial of the thirty (30) selected cases is DENIED. Whether the district court wishes to proceed with that trial, to secure thirty (30) individual judgments, is a matter within the discretion of the trial court. Likewise, whether the trial judge wishes to [c]onduct a bellwether trial based on a properly selected sample are matters also within the discretion of the district court. [T]he petition for mandamus is GRANTED insofar as it relates to utilization of the results obtained from the trial of the thirty (30) selected cases for any purpose affecting issues or claims of, or defenses to, the remaining untried cases.

■ EDITH H. JONES, CIRCUIT JUDGE, specially concurring:

I [h]ave serious doubts about the major premise of Judge Parker's opinion, i.e., his confidence that a bellwether trial of representative cases is permissible to extrapolate findings relevant to and somehow preclusive upon a larger group of cases. [I] have serious doubts about the procedure even where, as here, Chevron agreed to use of a statistically sound bellwether trial process.

[T]he only case cited in the Manual for Complex Litigation concerning a bellwether strategy was tried by Judge Parker when he sat on the district court. Cimino v. Raymark, 751 F.Supp. 649, 653, 664–65 (E.D.Tex.1990), cited in Manual for Complex Litigation — 33.27–.28 (3d Ed.1995). One other recent case, affirmed in a split verdict of the Ninth Circuit, also used a bellwether technique. Hilao v. Estate of Marcos, 103 F.3d 767 (9th Cir.1996). These are not necessarily the only examples of bellwether trials, but they appear to be most unusual.

The use of statistical sampling as a means to identify and resolve common issues in tort litigation has, however, been severely criticized. See Hilao, supra at 787–88 (Rymer, Judge, concurring in part and dissenting in part). Among other things, the technique may deprive nonparties of their Seventh Amendment jury trial right. [A]dditionally, as Judge Higginbotham cautioned in In re Fibreboard Corp. [893 F.2d 706 (5th Cir.1990)], there is a fine line between deriving results from trials based on statistical sampling and pure legislation. Judges must be sensitive to stay within our proper bounds of adjudicating individual disputes. We are not authorized by the Constitution or statutes to legislate solutions to cases in pursuit of efficiency and expeditiousness. Essential to due process for litigants, including both the plaintiffs and Chevron in this non-class action context, is their right to the opportunity for an individual assessment of liability and damages in each case. Nowhere did the district court explain how it was authorized to make the results of this bellwether trial unitary for any purposes concerning the 2,970 other plaintiffs' cases pending before him. In sum, I simply do not share Judge Parker's confidence that bellwether trials can be used to resolve mass tort controversies.

———

CIMINO v. RAYMARK INDUSTRIES, INC.

Unites States Court of Appeals, Fifth Circuit, 1998.
151 F.3d 297

■ GARWOOD, CIRCUIT JUDGE:

We begin by stating some very basic propositions. These personal injury tort actions for monetary damages are "a prototypical example of an action at law, to which the Seventh Amendment applies." Wooddell v. Intern. Broth. of Elec. Workers, 112 S.Ct. 494, 498 (1991). The Seventh Amendment applies notwithstanding that these are diversity cases. But because these are diversity cases, the Rules of Decision Act, 28 U.S.C. § 1652, and Erie R. Co. v. Tompkins, 58 S.Ct. 817, 822–23 (1938), with its seeming constitutional underpinning, mandate that the substantive law applied be that of the relevant state, here Texas. Substantive law includes not only the factual elements which must be found to impose liability and fix damages, but also the burdens of going forward with evidence and of persuasion thereon.

[T]hus, the question becomes: did the implemented trial plan include a litigated determination, consistent with the Seventh Amendment, of the Texas-law mandated issues of whether, as to each individual plaintiff, Pittsburgh Corning's product was a cause of his complained-of condition and, if so, the damages that plaintiff suffered as a result.

[W]ith one exception, noted below, we are aware of no appellate decision approving such a group, rather than individual, determination of cause in a damage suit for personal injuries to individuals at widely different times and places.

[W]e [do not] consider that In Re Chevron U.S.A., Inc., 109 F.3d 1016 (5th Cir.1997), justifies the instant trial plan. [W]hile the majority opinion (one judge specially concurred) contains language generally looking with favor on the use of bellwether verdicts when shown to be statistically representative, this language is plainly dicta, certainly insofar as it might suggest that representative bellwether verdicts could properly be used to determine individual causation and damages for other plaintiffs. To begin with, no such question was before this Court, as the trial plan contemplated that individual causation and damages issues would not be controlled by the thirty individual bellwether verdicts, which would be used to encourage settlement. Moreover, what we did—our *holding*—was to prevent any preclusive use of the unitary trial results (whether for general causation or individual causation or otherwise) in cases other than those of the thirty selected plaintiffs. [C]learly, In Re Chevron U.S.A. does not control the result here, and this panel is not bound by its dicta.

In Hilao v. Estate of Marcos, 103 F.3d 767 (9th Cir.1996), a divided panel of the Ninth Circuit in a rule 23(b)(3) class action permitted recoverable tort damages to be determined in a lump sum for the entire class. [H]ilao is distinguishable here; it did not operate under the constraints of the Rules of Decision Act or Erie; the present case, by contrast, does operate under those constraints. If Hilao is not thus distinguishable it is simply contrary to Fibreboard [893 F.2d 706 (5th Cir.1990)], which binds us and which in our opinion is in any event correct. Further, Hilao did not address—and there was apparently not presented to it any contention concerning—the Seventh Amendment. Finally, we find ourselves in agreement with the thrust of the dissenting opinion there. Id. at 788 ("Even in the context of a class action, individual causation and individual damages must still be proved individually").

In sum, as Fireboard held, under Texas law causation must be determined as to "individuals, not groups." And, the Seventh Amendment gives the right to a jury trial to make that determination.

[W]e do not act in ignorance or disregard of the asbestos crises. In Amchem Products, Inc. v. Windsor, 117 S.Ct. 2231, 2237–38 (1997), the Supreme Court called attention to the report of the Judicial Conference's Ad Hoc Committee on Asbestos Litigation, stating that "Real reform, the report concluded, required federal legislation creating a national asbestos-dispute resolution scheme." Id. at 2238. The Court also observed, "The argument is sensibly made that a nationwide administrative claims processing regime would provide the most secure, fair, and efficient means of compensating victims of asbestos exposure. Congress, however, has not adopted such a solution." Id. at 2252 (footnote omitted). Nevertheless, the Court refused to stretch the law to fill the gap resulting from congressional inaction. As we said in Fibreboard, federal courts must remain faithful to Erie and must maintain "the separation of powers between the judicial and legislative branches." Id. at 711.(52) "The Judicial Branch can offer the trial of lawsuits. It has no power or competence to do more." Id. at 712.

We accordingly reverse the judgments before us.

IN RE SIMON II LITIGATION

United States District Court, Eastern District of New York, 2002
211 F.R.D. 86

MEMORANDUM AND ORDER

■ WEINSTEIN, SENIOR DISTRICT JUDGE

[S]mokers have alleged and demonstrated in many suits that, had they not been misled by the industry, they would not have started smoking or would have quit earlier, thus eliminating or reducing cigarette-caused damage to their health. In the main, the industry has won these litigations, which present substantial factual and legal barriers to recovery, but a trend in favor of plaintiffs seems to be developing.

One of the problems for claimants has been the enormous expense of trying the cases, making them unattractive to plaintiffs' attorneys suing for individual clients on a contingency fee basis. Class or consolidated actions for compensatory damages have been difficult to justify because of the varied individual circumstances of the smokers. Yet statistical analysis based upon the law of large numbers, together with extensive demographic and epidemiological data and sampling techniques, arguably provide a basis for computing an appropriate approximation of total compensatory damages that could be awarded were all those injured to sue as a single class.

[The] use of statistical evidence and methods in the American justice system to establish liability and damages is appropriate, particularly in mass injury cases such as this one. *See, e.g., In re Chevron U.S.A., Inc.,* 109 F.3d 1016, 1019–20 (5th Cir.1997) (use of statistics to draw inferences about the claims of 3,000 plaintiffs and intervenors who claimed wrongful death, personal injury, and property contamination from defendant's storage of hazardous substances which had leaked from crude oil waste pits and migrated into the plaintiffs' drinking water supply). *But see Hilao v. Estate of Marcos,* 103 F.3d 767, 788 (9th Cir.1996) (Rymer, J., dissenting) ("I cannot believe that a summary review of transcripts of a selected sample of victims who were able to be deposed for the purpose of inferring the type of abuse, by whom it was inflicted, and the amount of damages proximately caused thereby, comports with fundamental notions of due process."); *In re Fibreboard Corp.,* 893 F.2d 706, 710 (5th Cir.1990) ("[T]he *assumption* of plaintiffs' argument is that its proof of omnibus damages is in fact achievable; that statistical measures of representativeness and commonality will be sufficient for the jury to make informed judgments concerning damages.")

Greater reliance on statistical methods is required by the profound evolution in our economic communication and data compilation and retrieval systems in recent decades. Manufacturers now mass produce goods for consumption by millions using new chemical compounds and processes, creating the potential for mass injury. Modern adjudicatory tools must be adapted to allow the fair, efficient, effective and responsive resolution of the claims of these injured masses.

[A]gainst this backdrop, the use of statistical evidence in the instant case violates neither the Constitutional guarantee of due process nor the Constitutional right to a jury trial. *See In re Chevron U.S.A., Inc.,* 109 F.3d at 1020 ("[t]he applicability of inferential statistics have long been recognized by the courts"; collecting cases); Laurens Walker & John Monahan, *Sampling Damages,* 83 Iowa L.Rev. 545, 546 (1998) ("[A] complete solution of the numbers problem in mass torts can only be achieved by ... randomly sampling damages without apology.")

[D]ue Process

[W]hether a procedural device utilized where a private party invokes state authority to deprive another person or entity of property comports with due process is determined by a balancing of interests:

> [F]irst, consideration of the private interest that will be affected by the [procedure]; second, an examination of the risk of erroneous deprivation through the procedures under attack and the probable value of additional or alternative safeguards; and third, ... principal attention to the interest of the party seeking the [procedure], with, nonetheless, due regard for any ancillary interest the government may have in providing the procedure or forgoing the added burden of providing greater protections.

Connecticut v. Doehr, 501 U.S. 1, 11, 111 S.Ct. 2105, 115 L.Ed.2d 1 (1991); *see also Hilao,* 103 F.3d at 786.

Consideration of the private interests at issue counsels in favor of utilizing statistical methods. Tobacco companies admittedly have an interest in not paying for damages in excess of what alleged misconduct may have caused; that interest would be furthered by their confronting (before a jury) each of the hundreds of thousands of plaintiffs who suffered smoking-related illnesses with respect to their reliance on tobacco company misstatements and omissions, and about their discovery of their injuries (so as to precisely determine in each instance when the statute of limitations started to run).

Practical considerations temper the weight of tobacco companies' interest, however. If such an individualized process were undertaken, it would have to continue beyond all lives in being. Assuming tobacco companies were willing to expend the resources and monies necessary both in discovery and at trial to mount such an undertaking, the litigation costs in doing so would far exceed any monies saved by avoiding erroneous payments especially given appropriate statutes of limitations.

[T]he interest of plaintiffs in avoiding the additional litigation costs that would arise if defendants were permitted to confront each possible plaintiff at trial is enormous. The necessary additional litigation costs plaintiffs would have to bear would consume much of any recovery from defendants, making continued pursuit of the litigation fruitless. *See, e.g., Hilao,* 103 F.3d at 786 ("[Plaintiffs'] interest in the use of the statistical method ... is enormous[ ] since adversarial resolution of each class member's claim would pose insurmountable practical hurdles.").

The interests of the injured plaintiffs must be considered. Requiring individual proof as to each claim would unnecessarily intrude on the lives of hundreds of thousands of people. Examining each grain of sand is too burdensome in a survey of a beach.

The second element of the due process balancing test—examination of the risk of erroneous deprivation through the procedures under attack and the probable value of additional or alternative safeguards—also supports allowance of the proffered statistical proof, subject to appropriate *Daubert* challenges. *See Daubert v. Merrell Dow Pharmaceuticals,* 509 U.S. 579, 113 S.Ct. 2786, 125 L.Ed.2d 469 (1993); *see also Falise v. American Tobacco Co.,* 107 F.Supp.2d 200 (E.D.N.Y.2000); *cf. International Bhd. of Teamsters, Local 734 v. Philip Morris Inc.,* 196 F.3d 818, 823 (7th Cir.1999) ("Statistical methods could provide a decent answer—likely a more accurate answer than is possible when addressing the equivalent causation question in a single person's suit.").

[T]he third due process consideration—regard for any interest the government may have in procedures—heavily weighs in support of allowing plaintiffs to rely on statistical evidence. A consolidated trial with full presentation of the individual facts of each of plaintiffs' claims relating to smoking-related illnesses before a single jury would be unmanageable. *See Manual for Complex Litigation* § 22.3, at 136 ("Although the presentation of the evidence at trial is normally controlled by the strategies and tactics of counsel, in complex litigation other considerations also require attention, primarily jury comprehension and the length of the trial. These are not unrelated concepts, since a shorter trial promotes jury comprehension, and effective presentation saves time."); Joe S. Cecil, Valerie P. Hans & Elizabeth C. Wiggins, *Citizen Comprehension of Difficult Issues: Lessons from Civil Jury Trials,* 40 Am. U.L.Rev. 727, 764 (1991) ("[T]he overall picture of the jury [in complex cases] that emerges from the available data indicates that juries are capable of deciding even very complex cases, especially if procedures to enhance jury competence are used."). Hundreds-of-thousands of separate trials brought by individuals who suffered a smoking-related illness would prove unnecessarily burdensome; it would "clog the docket of the district court for years." *Hilao,* 103 F.3d at 786–87; *see also* Laurens Walker & John Monahan, *Sampling Liability,* 85 Va. L.Rev. 329, 343 (1999) ("Individualized information should be used where it is practical—i.e., cost effective—to obtain. If individual information is not practical to obtain, however, sampling should be used so that a judgment can be reached efficiently and expeditiously.").

Under the balancing test set forth in *Doehr,* the use of statistical evidence (subject to satisfaction of the *Daubert* criteria) by plaintiffs does not violate due process strictures. *See* Michael J. Saks & Peter David Blanck, *Justice Improved: The Unrecognized Benefits of Aggregation and Sampling in the Trial of Mass Torts,* 44 Stan. L.Rev. 815, 826–832 (1992) (statistical sampling comports with due process in mass aggregation cases).

Jury Right

The use of aggregated proof in plaintiffs' claims does not violate the Seventh Amendment. A contrary view would require concluding that the Constitution establishes fixed limitations on the methods of proof a particular party may offer. Requiring such a horse and buggy interpretation for trials in a computer-guided-rocket age seems somewhat far-fetched. Courts cannot ignore and deny themselves what the rest of the world relies upon in fact-finding.

———

NOTE

1. **On Appeal**. Judge Weinstein's trial plan for Simon II provided, as the excerpt above suggests, for the certification of a class action. Defendants appealed his certification decision and the circuit court held, 407 F.3d 125 (2d Cir. 2005) that Judge Weinstein had employed a type of class action which was not permitted, under the circumstances, by the rules of civil procedure. Although on appeal defendants had objected to the sampling plan, the appeals court did not rule on this aspect of the case. The circuit court described an alternative procedure which might be used for certification and remanded to the district court for further proceedings.

———

SAMPLING DAMAGES*

Laurens Walker and John Monahan.
83 Iowa Law Review 545 (1998).

The astonishing number of claimants in mass tort litigation overwhelms traditional commitment to individual, case by case, adjudication of

———

* Laurens Walker and John Monahan, Sampling Damages, 83 Iowa L. Rev. 545 (1998) (reprinted with permission).

compensatory damage claims. Some cases have involved millions of claimants and many cases have involved thousands of injured persons seeking compensation. Numbers such as these rule out any serious consideration of individual trials and have prompted controversial experimentation by courts with various forms of aggregation. Among these experiments are three district courts which have endorsed a form of aggregation that centered on statistical sampling as a solution to what might be called the numbers problem. In Cimino v. Raymark Industries, Inc., the compensatory damage claims of 2298 persons were adjudicated by trying a random sample of 160 cases and applying the results to all of the remaining cases. A panel of the Fifth Circuit rejected the implemented plan. In re Estate of Marcos Human Rights Litigation involved the compensatory damage claims of 10,059 persons which were adjudicated by deposing a random sample of 137 claimants, aggregating the results, and presenting the depositions and the aggregated information to a jury at one trial. A panel of the Ninth Circuit upheld this implemented plan. In re Chevron, U.S.A. Inc. addressed three-thousand compensatory damage claims which were the subject of a plan to try a sample of thirty cases to provide a basis for disposing of the rest. The court of appeals rejected the plan because the proposed sample was not randomly drawn, but approved the use of random sampling.

Cimino, *Marcos* and *Chevron* involved important steps toward solution of the numbers problem in mass tort litigation, but they incorporate cautious, tentative measures that fail to realize the full potential of statistical sampling to solve many of the problems posed by throngs of claimants. The difficulty in all three cases is that the pretense of individual adjudication is maintained. In all three, time and money were wasted in an effort to provide a few claimants "individual" adjudication, while using a survey to resolve other claims. Our thesis is that a complete solution of the numbers problem in mass torts can only be achieved by abandoning any pretense of individual adjudication and randomly sampling damages without apology.

[T]he first step would be certification of a class of plaintiffs co-extensive with the population to be surveyed. This step would provide plaintiffs a class representative who could, with expert assistance, produce a survey and present it at a class trial. [A]fter certification, the class representative, charged with the burden of proof on damages, would employ an expert to conduct the damage survey. This choice would not need to be approved by the court or by the opposing party because the class representative would only be engaging in the traditional collection of evidence for use at trial.

[I]n our proposal, the trial judge would not take a role in planning or carrying out the survey. Instead, the class representative would ask the court to approve the admission at trial of the survey results. At that time, opposing parties would be invited to examine the survey and make any objections. Both the court and opposing parties would be presented a comprehensive report of the survey. The trial judge would apply the

Daubert standards using the *Survey Research Guide* [see Diamond, above, p. 119] criteria, and either permit or refuse expert testimony describing the survey and results to the jury.

[T]he defendant would also have access to survey methodology to collect evidence regarding damages. In cases involving large stakes, the defendant might well choose to employ an expert and survey the opposing class members about their damages.

[F]inally, and in stark contrast to the *Cimino* and *Chevron* or *Marcos* models, under our proposal the results of the survey or surveys, if permitted by the court under *Daubert*, would be presented by expert testimony to the jury with the data aggregated to suggest a total amount of compensation to be divided among the class or among subclasses. No individual data would be presented to the jury and no individual damage verdicts would be required or permitted.

NOTE

1. Sampling Liability. Walker and Monahan, Sampling Liability, 85 Virginia Law Review 329 (1999), have suggested that sampling techniques used to determine damages might also be used to determine issues of liability:

> We propose as a model for determining liability in complex cases that the method of proof be determined by the cost of collecting information. Individualized information should be used where it is practical—i.e., cost effective—to obtain. If individual information is not practical to obtain, however, sampling should be used so that a judgment can be reached efficiently and expeditiously. The fundamental justification for this model is found in its capacity to avoid outcomes determined by the cost of gathering information. In a situation where critical information about liability is costly to obtain, one side can prevail simply because the relevant information costs too much for the other side to gather and not because of the merits as established by law.

Id. at 343.

SELECTED BIBLIOGRAPHY

Bone, Statistical Adjudication Rights, Justice, and Utility in a World of Process Scarcity, 46 Vanderbilt Law Review 561 (1993).

Mullenix, Beyond Consolidation: Postaggregative Procedure in Asbestos Mass Tort Litigation, 32 William and Mary Law Review 475 (1991).

Robbennolt, Punitive Damage Decision Making: The Decisions of Citizens and Trial Court Judges, 26 Law and Human Behavior 315 (2002).

Robinson and Abraham, Collective Justice in Tort Law, 78 Virginia Law Review 1481 (1992).

Saks and Blanck, Justice Improved: The Unrecognized Benefits of Aggregation and Sampling in the Trial of Mass Torts, 44 Stanford Law Review 815 (1992).

Saks, Hollinger, Wissler, Evans, and Hart, Reducing Variability in Civil Jury Awards, 21 Law and Human Behavior 243 (1997).

Willging, Beyond Maturity: Mass Tort Case Management in the Manual for Complex Litigation, 148 University of Pennsylvania Law Review 2225 (2000).

Wissler, Hart, and Saks, Decisionmaking About General Damages: A Comparison of Jurors, Judges, and Lawyers, 98 Michigan Law Review 751 (1999).

Wissler, Rector, and Saks, The Impact of Jury Instructions on the Fusion of Liability and Compensatory Damages, 25 Law and Human Behavior 125 (2001).

CHAPTER TWO

SOCIAL SCIENCE USED TO MAKE LAW

In this chapter, we turn our attention to a second and much more controversial legal application of social science: its use to determine what Professor Kenneth Culp Davis called "legislative facts." Davis defined legislative facts as follows:

> When an agency [or court] wrestles with a question of law or policy, it is acting legislatively, [a]nd the facts which inform its legislative judgment may conveniently be denominated legislative facts.

Davis, An Approach to Problems of Evidence in the Administrative Process, 55 Harvard Law Review 364, 402 (1942).

Legislative facts, in other words, are facts that courts use when they make law (or "legislate"), rather than simply apply settled doctrine to resolve a dispute between particular parties to a case. While the determination of adjudicative facts affects only the litigants before the court, the determination of legislative facts influences the content of legal doctrine itself, and therefore affects many parties in addition to those who brought the case.

We begin our examination of the use of social science to make law by considering in more detail Professor Davis' concept of legislative fact. We then explore the law-making use of social science in both constitutional and common law. Finally, we present our own effort to reconceptualize legislative fact as "social authority."

SECTION I. LEGISLATIVE FACTS

In the sixty years since it was first articulated, the notion of legislative fact "has been widely accepted in the federal appellate courts." Broz v. Schweiker, 677 F.2d 1351, 1357 (11th Cir.1982). The United States Supreme Court as well has invoked the term on numerous occasions, e.g., Concerned Citizens v. Pine Creek Conservancy Dist., 429 U.S. 651, 97 S.Ct. 828, 51 L.Ed.2d 116 (1977); Lockhart v. McCree, 476 U.S. 162, 106 S.Ct. 1758, 90 L.Ed.2d 137 (1986).

AN APPROACH TO PROBLEMS OF EVIDENCE IN THE ADMINISTRATIVE PROCESS

Kenneth Culp Davis.
55 Harvard Law Review 364 (1942).

The rules of evidence for finding facts which form the basis for creation of law and determination of policy should differ from the rules for finding facts which concern only the parties to a particular case.

[W]hen an agency finds facts concerning immediate parties—what the parties did, what the circumstances were, what the background conditions were—the agency is performing an adjudicative function, and the facts may conveniently be called adjudicative facts. When an agency wrestles with a question of law or policy, it is acting legislatively, just as judges have created the common law through judicial legislation, and the facts which inform its legislative judgment may conveniently be denominated legislative facts. The distinction is important; the traditional rules of evidence are designed for adjudicative facts, and unnecessary confusion results from attempting to apply the traditional rules to legislative facts.

The courts have generally treated legislative facts differently from adjudicative facts, even though the distinction has not been clearly articulated and explanations have been beclouded by an erroneous use of the concept of judicial notice. The distinction between legislative and adjudicative facts apparently has been clearly recognized only in constitutional cases, in which a category of "constitutional facts" has emerged. Often referred to as "social and economic data," constitutional facts are those which assist a court in forming a judgment on a question of constitutional law. [I]n *Muller v. Oregon,* for example, the Court considered factual information contained in a brief filed by Mr. Louis D. Brandeis, including "extracts from over ninety reports of committees, bureaus of statistics, commissioners of hygiene, inspectors of factories, both in this country and in Europe...." [208 U.S. 412, 420, 28 S.Ct. 324, 326, 52 L.Ed. 551 (1908)] After Brandeis became a justice he continued his extensive factual studies and wrote many opinions saturated with facts brought to light through his own researches.

[T]he Court's reliance on extra-record constitutional facts has become fairly familiar. But what has not been so generally recognized is that constitutional facts are only one manifestation of a larger category of facts which are utilized for informing a court's legislative judgment on questions of law and policy. In non-constitutional cases courts often use a similar type of legislative facts not developed through the evidence.

[N]ot only have Supreme Court justices frequently relied upon extra-record facts, but the facts relied upon in many instances do not come within the scope of judicial notice. Many of the facts used, for instance, clearly are not covered by the language of the American Law Institute's proposed *Code of Evidence:* "The judge may of his own motion take judicial notice of ... (b) specific facts so notorious as not to be the subject of reasonable dispute, and (c) specific facts and propositions of generalized knowledge which are capable of immediate and accurate demonstration by resort to easily accessible sources of indisputable accuracy...." [T]he boundaries of judicial notice prescribed by the proposed *Code* may, of course, be perfectly appropriate for adjudicative facts; they seem to me wholly inappropriate for legislative facts.

[T]he agency must be free to go outside the record and beyond the limits of judicial notice in informing itself of facts which enter into its judgment in molding law and formulating policy.

It is neither possible nor desirable to immunize adjudicators from acquiring new factual knowledge; they should have more of it, not less.

It is, after all, the facts which concern the parties to a particular proceeding, rather than generalized information, which best lend themselves to the usual processes of cross-examination and rebuttal. Briefs and oral arguments are often (though not always) better vehicles for presentation of legislative facts than testimony and documents. And when a court or administrative tribunal makes its own investigation, the safeguard usually lies in the petition for reargument (new briefs and oral arguments) rather than in the petition for a rehearing (new evidence).

———

NOTE

1.   Judicial Notice. The Code of Evidence proposed by the American Law Institute was a precursor of the Federal Rules of Evidence enacted by Congress in 1975. Rule 201, "Judicial Notice of Adjudicative Facts", explicitly incorporates the distinction between legislative and adjudicative facts proposed by Davis in his 1942 article. The Advisory Committee appointed by the Supreme Court notes that Rule 201 "is the only evidence rule on the subject of judicial notice. It deals only with judicial notice of 'adjudicative' facts. No rule deals with judicial notice of 'legislative' facts." See Appendix A. Professors Saltzburg, Martin and Capra have stated that "[t]he most serious problem with Rule 201 may be its total failure to address legislative facts." S. Saltzburg, M. Martin, and D. Capra, Federal Rules of Evidence Manual 201–7 (8th ed. 2001).

———

FACTS IN LAWMAKING

Kenneth Culp Davis.
80 Columbia Law Review 931 (1980).

The ingredients of all lawmaking have to be policy ideas and facts, but the policy ideas are necessarily dependent, immediately or remotely, on facts. Two interrelated questions [a]re: (1) Should law require lawmakers to develop the facts that are relevant to their lawmaking? (2) Should law require lawmakers, before using facts in lawmaking, to allow interested parties to challenge the assumed facts?

[T]he judgment is an easy one that at least *sometimes* the law should require the relevant facts to be developed and should require them to be available to opposing persons for a pre-decision response. But when?

[W]hen facts used in lawmaking are (1) narrow and specific, (2) central or critical, (3) controversial, (4) unmixed with judgment or policy, (5) provable, and (6) in some degree about the parties or known mainly by them, the parties clearly should have a pre-decision chance to challenge them, and the requirement may even be imposed in the name of due process. But when the facts are (1) broad and general, (2) background or peripheral, (3) noncontroversial, (4) mixed with judgment or policy, (5) not easily provable, and (6) wholly unrelated to the parties, a court or agency may use them without even adverting to any possible problem of procedural fairness. When the six items are mixed—some at one end of the scale, some at the other, some toward the middle—the two questions of how much support the facts should have and of what procedural protection to give the parties may be difficult. Law cannot feasibly provide for all combinations and permutations, and in each instance a judgment must be made.

––––––

JUDICIAL, LEGISLATIVE, AND ADMINISTRATIVE LAWMAKING: A PROPOSED RESEARCH SERVICE FOR THE SUPREME COURT

Kenneth Culp Davis.
71 Minnesota Law Review 1 (1986).

The Supreme Court is often at its best on complex thinking problems, on philosophical or ethical or moral issues, on analysis or reasoning, and on issues of interpretation. The Court may often be at its worst on policy issues that are dependent upon understanding or instincts about legislative facts. Indeed, my impression is that, typically, the Court is basically baffled in trying to deal with legislative facts. The Court's treatment of legislative facts may be an especially weak area in its whole performance, and it seems to be fully aware of that weakness.

[W]hen the Supreme Court in deliberating about a case realizes that it needs legislative facts it does not have, what should it do? [A]nd what does it do?

What it does not do is easier to state. It *never* assigns the problem to a qualified staff for a study or investigation; it *never* gets the parties' response to such a study or investigation; and it *never* uses notice and comment procedure.

What the Supreme Court affirmatively does is quite various. It has no system. It tries one method after another, almost always with unsatisfactory results.

[W]hat sort of system might be established to supply the Court with needed studies of legislative facts? Brandeis briefs should be encouraged; the Court now welcomes them, but not many are filed. Perhaps law offices should more often engage appropriate scientific or professional specialists to contribute to the preparation of briefs. That would help but at best would be only a partial solution. The Supreme Court might employ specialists in sciences and social sciences to assist the Justices in somewhat the way law clerks do. But the Court is not geared to employing and managing such a staff, and a small staff would lack the needed diversification. Although having such a staff might be preferable to not having it, a much better idea is creation of a research organization outside the Court to make studies at the Court's request.

[I] propose that the Supreme Court after due deliberation should formally ask Congress to explore the potential for creating a research service to assist the Court. The sole purpose should be to increase the Court's freedom to obtain whatever research assistance it decides it needs. The Court should have the privilege of asking for research either on a problem about a pending case or about a narrow or broad area of law.

[T]he Court's use of the research service would rarely delay decisions. The service might be used in only about a half dozen decisions in each term, although it might be quite important in some of those cases.

SELECTED BIBLIOGRAPHY

D. Faigman, The Use and Misuse of Science in the Law (1999).

D. Faigman, Laboratory of Justice: The Supreme Court's 200-Year Struggle to Integrate Science and the Law (2005).

Faigman and Monahan, Psychological Evidence at the Dawn of the Law's Scientific Age, 56 Annual Review of Psychology 631 (2005).

Handbook of Psychology in Legal Contexts 2d (R. Bull and D. Carson eds. 2003).

Psychology and Law: An Empirical Perspective (N. Brewer and K. Williams eds. 2005).

A. Smith, Law, Social Science, and the Criminal Courts (2004).

SECTION II. CONSTITUTIONAL LAW

A large portion of the lawmaking uses of social science have occurred in the context of constitutional law. In particular, decisions involving the First, Sixth, Eighth, and Fourteenth Amendments have often invoked social science to support a finding of "legislative fact." For historical reasons, we begin our analysis with the Fourteenth Amendment.

A. THE FOURTEENTH AMENDMENT: SCHOOL SEGREGATION

Section 1 of the Fourteenth Amendment to the Constitution, ratified in 1868, reads, in part:

No State shall make or enforce any law which shall abridge the privileges or immunities of citizens of the United States; nor shall any State deprive any person of life, liberty, or property, without due process of law; nor deny to any person within its jurisdiction the equal protection of the laws.

While many constitutional lawmaking uses of social science implicate the Fourteenth Amendment, none do so more directly than cases finding that the segregation of public schools by race or gender violates the Amendment's "equal protection" clause.

1.   SEGREGATION BY RACE

The lawmaking uses of social science in litigation on the racial segregation of public schools fall into two categories. The first and earlier type of case dealt with the issue of whether the statutory segregation of schools by race violated the Fourteenth Amendment. The second and more recent type of case concerns the question of whether remedies for schools that have violated the Fourteenth Amendment can take into account affected parties' likely reactions to those remedies.

(a) "Separate but Equal"

Surely the best known use of social science in any area of law occurred when the United States Supreme Court in Brown v. Board of Education, 347 U.S. 483, 74 S.Ct. 686, 98 L.Ed. 873 (1954), cited several social science studies in overturning Plessy v. Ferguson, 163 U.S. 537, 16 S.Ct. 1138, 41 L.Ed. 256 (1896) to find that the racial segregation of public schools violates the equal protection clause of the Fourteenth Amendment. The court cited the studies in what has been called "the most controversial footnote in American constitutional law." Rosen, History and State of the Art of Applied Social Research in the Courts, in The Use/Nonuse/Misuse of Applied Social Research in the Courts 9 (M. Saks and C. Barron, eds. 1980). *Brown* is generally regarded as the beginning of the modern era in the use of social science in law.

PLESSY v. FERGUSON

Supreme Court of the United States, 1896.
163 U.S. 537, 16 S.Ct. 1138, 41 L.Ed. 256.

■ MR. JUSTICE BROWN delivered the opinion of the court.

This case turns upon the constitutionality of an act of the General Assembly of the State of Louisiana, passed in 1890, providing for separate railway carriages for the white and colored races.

The first section of the statute enacts "that all railway companies carrying passengers in their coaches in this State, shall provide equal but separate accommodations for the white, and colored races, by providing two or more passenger coaches for each passenger train, or by dividing the passenger coaches by a partition so as to secure separate accommodations: Provided, That this section shall not be construed to apply to street railroads. No person or persons, shall be admitted to occupy seats in coaches, other than, the ones, assigned, to them on account of the race they belong to."

[T]he information filed in the criminal District Court charged in substance that Plessy, being a passenger between two stations within the State of Louisiana, was assigned by officers of the company to the coach used for the race to which he belonged, but he insisted upon going into a coach used by the race to which he did not belong. [Plessy] was ordered by the conductor to vacate said coach and take a seat in another assigned to persons of the colored race, and having refused to comply with such demand he was forcibly ejected with the aid of a police officer, and imprisoned in the parish jail to answer a charge of having violated the above act.

The constitutionality of this act is attacked upon the ground that it conflicts [w]ith the [F]ourteenth Amendment, which prohibits certain restrictive legislation on the part of the States.

[B]y the Fourteenth Amendment, all persons born or naturalized in the United States, and subject to the jurisdiction thereof, are made citizens of the United States and of the State wherein they reside; and the States are forbidden from making or enforcing any law which shall abridge the privileges or immunities of citizens of the United States, or shall deprive any person of life, liberty or property without due process of law, or deny to any person within their jurisdiction the equal protection of the laws.

[T]he object of the amendment was undoubtedly to enforce the absolute equality of the two races before the law, but in the nature of things it could not have been intended to abolish distinctions based upon color, or to enforce social, as distinguished from political equality, or a commingling of the two races upon terms unsatisfactory to either. Laws permitting, and even requiring, their separation in places where they are liable to be brought into contact do not necessarily imply the inferiority of either race to the other, and have been generally, if not universally, recognized as within the competency of the state legislatures in the exercise of their police power. The most common instance of this is connected with the establishment of separate schools for white and colored children, which has been held to be a valid exercise of the legislative power even by courts of States where the political rights of the colored race have been longest and most earnestly enforced.

[W]e consider the underlying fallacy of the plaintiff's argument to consist in the assumption that the enforced separation of the two races stamps the colored race with a badge of inferiority. If this be so, it is not by reason of anything found in the act, but solely because the colored race chooses to put that construction upon it.

[L]egislation is powerless to eradicate racial instincts or to abolish distinctions based upon physical differences, and the attempt to do so can only result in accentuating the difficulties of the present situation. If the civil and political rights of both races be equal one cannot be inferior to the other civilly or politically. If one race be inferior to the other socially, the Constitution of the United States cannot put them upon the same plane.

THE PSYCHOLOGICAL EFFECTS OF ENFORCED SEGREGATION: A SURVEY OF SOCIAL SCIENCE OPINION

Max Deutscher and Isidor Chein.
26 The Journal of Psychology 259 (1948).

Final decision on the legality of enforced segregation, regardless of equal facilities, has not yet been rendered by the Supreme Court. Here too, social science evidence may be a significant if not crucial factor. For social scientists interested in "social engineering," this represents a concrete opportunity to apply the relevant findings of social science data.

The Problem

The present report is an attempt to gather the current opinions of social scientists about one aspect of the problem: namely, the psychological effects of enforced segregation, both on the group which enforces the segregation and on the group which is segregated. Since the purpose of the study was to gather material which would be relevant to a court decision, the focus was on aspects pertinent to the legal questions involved.

[S]ince anthropologists, psychologists, and sociologists have been most concerned with the development of individuals and their socialization, these were the social scientists whose views were sought.

[A] questionnaire and a covering letter were prepared for distribution to these 849 social scientists. Every effort was made to present the issue and to formulate the questions in as unbiased and unleading manner as possible.

[T]he questionnaire asked for opinions about the psychological effect of enforced segregation on both the segregated and segregating groups. About the effect on the segregated groups, respondents were asked to check one of the three following statements:

I believe that enforced segregation has detrimental psychological effects on members of racial and religious groups which are segregated, even if equal facilities are provided.

I believe that enforced segregation does not have detrimental psychological effects on members of racial and religious groups which are segregated, if equal facilities are provided.

I have not as yet formed an opinion on this issue.

In regard to the effect on the segregating groups, respondents were asked to check one of the three following statements:

I believe that enforced segregation has a detrimental psychological effect on the group which enforces the segregation, even if that group provides equal facilities for the members of the racial and religious groups which are segregated.

I believe that enforced segregation does not have a detrimental psychological effect on the group which enforces the segregation, if that group provides equal facilities for the members of the racial and religious groups which are segregated.

I have not as yet formed an opinion on this issue.

Results

[T]he results pertinent to Question 1 on the questionnaire are[:]

Ninety per cent of the total sample express the opinion that enforced segregation has detrimental psychological effects *on the segregated groups.* Two per cent believe that it has no harmful effects on the segregated group. Four per cent indicate that they have no opinion on this issue, while another 4 per cent did not answer this item even though they returned the questionnaire.

Opinions about the effects on the segregating groups (Question 2) show a similar distribution. Eighty-three per cent of the respondents believe that enforced segregation has detrimental psychological effects *on the group which enforces the segregation.* Four per cent express the opinion that it does not have harmful effects on the segregating group. Nine per cent say that they have not formed an opinion on this issue, and 5 per cent did not answer this item.

[I]t seems safe, therefore, to conclude from the above reported results that substantial majorities of social scientists who may be said to have some competence with regard to the matters under inquiry agree that enforced segregation is psychologically detrimental to both the segregated and enforcing groups even when equal facilities are provided.

———

RACIAL IDENTIFICATION AND PREFERENCE IN NEGRO CHILDREN*

Kenneth B. Clark and Mamie P. Clark.
In Readings in Social Psychology (1947).
(T. Newcomb and E. Hartley, eds.)

The specific problem of this study is an analysis of the genesis and development of racial identification as a function of ego development and self-awareness in Negro children.

* Excerpts adapted from READINGS IN SOCIAL PSYCHOLOGY, by Theodore M. Newcomb and Eugene L. Hartley, copyright 1947 by Holt, Rinehart and Winston, and

[D]olls Test. The subjects were presented with four dolls, identical in every respect save skin color. Two of these dolls were brown with black hair and two were white with yellow hair. In the experimental situation these dolls were unclothed except for white diapers. The position of the head, hands, and legs on all the dolls was the same. For half of the subjects the dolls were presented in the order: white, colored, white, colored. For the other half the order of presentation was reversed. In the experimental situation the subjects were asked to respond to the following requests by choosing *one* of the dolls and giving it to the experimenter:

1. Give me the doll that you like to play with—(*a*) like best.

2. Give me the doll that is a nice doll.

3. Give me the doll that looks bad.

4. Give me the doll that is a nice color.

[S]ubjects

Two hundred fifty-three Negro children formed the subjects of this experiment. One hundred thirty-four of these subjects (southern group) were tested in segregated nursery schools and public schools in Hot Springs, Pine Bluff, and Little Rock, Arkansas. These children had had no experience in racially mixed school situations. One hundred nineteen subjects (northern group) were tested in the racially mixed nursery and public schools of Springfield, Massachusetts.

[N]orth-South Differences. From Table 8 it is clear that the southern children in segregated schools are less pronounced in their preference for the white doll, compared to the northern children's definite preference for this doll. Although still in a minority, a higher percentage of southern children, compared to northern, prefer to play with the colored doll or think that it is a "nice" doll.

TABLE 8

CHOICES OF SUBJECTS IN NORTHERN (MIXED SCHOOLS) AND SOUTHERN (SEGREGATED SCHOOLS) GROUPS (REQUESTS 1 THROUGH 4)*

Choice	North, percent	South, Percent
Request 1 (play with)		
colored doll	28	37
white doll..	72	62

renewed 1975 by Theodore M. Newcomb and Eugene L. Hartley, reprinted by permission of the publisher.

[Ed. Note: This is the original report of the data later included in K.B. Clark, Effect of Prejudice and Discrimination on Personality Development (Midcentury White House Conference on Children and Youth, 1950).]

* Individuals failing to make either choice not included, hence some percentages add to less than 100.

Choice	North, percent	South, Percent
Request 2 (nice doll)		
colored doll	30	46
white doll	68	52
Request 3 (looks bad)		
colored doll	71	49
white doll	17	16
Request 4 (nice color)		
colored doll	37	40
white doll	63	57

A significantly higher percentage (71) of the northern children, compared to southern children (49) think that the brown doll looks bad. Also a slightly higher percent of the southern children think that the brown doll has a "nice color," while more northern children think that the white doll has a "nice color."

In general, it may be stated that northern and southern children in these age groups tend to be similar in the degree of their preference for the white doll—with the northern children tending to be somewhat more favorable to the white doll than are the southern children. The southern children, however, in spite of their equal favorableness toward the white doll, are significantly less likely to reject the brown doll (evaluate it negatively), as compared to the strong tendency for the majority of the northern children to do so.

———

NOTE

1. Interpretations of the Doll Data. The results of the Clark and Clark 1947 "doll study", to which Professor Kenneth Clark testified in one of the cases joined with *Brown,* were otherwise interpreted in van den Haag, Social Science Testimony in the Desegregation Cases—A Reply to Professor Kenneth Clark, 6 Villanova Law Review 69, 77 (1960):

> Whether it be granted that his tests show psychological damage to Negro children, the comparison between the responses of Negro children in segregated and in nonsegregated schools shows that "they do not differ" except that *Negro children in segregated schools "are less pronounced in their preference for the white doll" and more often think of the colored dolls as "nice" or identify with them.* In short, if Professor Clark's tests do demonstrate damage to Negro children, then they demonstrate that the damage is *less* with segregation and *greater* with congregation. Yet, Professor Clark told the Court that he was proving that "segregation inflicts injuries upon the Negro" by the very tests which, if they prove anything—which is doubtful—prove the opposite!

R. Kluger, Simple Justice (2004) at 356, described the interpretation Professor Clark placed on these data:

The finding that Southern segregated black children showed much less inclination to reject the brown doll seemed a spot of special vulnerability, which Clark of course chose to avoid in his courtroom testimony. "Thurgood Marshall was very worried about that point," Clark comments. "But I believe, and I so argued at the time, that what the findings show is that the black children of the South were more adjusted to the feeling that they were not as good as whites and, because they felt defeated at an early age, did not bother using the device of denial. But that's not health. Adjusting to pathology is not health. The way the Northern kids were fighting it can be seen as a better sign. The little Southern children would point to the black doll and say, 'oh, yeah, that's me there—that's a nigger—I'm a nigger,' and they said it almost cheerfully. In the Northern cities, the question clearly threw the kids into a much more emotional state and often they'd point to the white doll."

Marshall had weighed the risks of Clark's findings and decided that on balance they demonstrated injury to segregated Negro youngsters. "I wanted this kind of evidence on the record," he had said.

SIMPLE JUSTICE (REVISED AND EXPANDED ED. 2004)

Richard Kluger.

[A]fter sketching out his background and projective test methods with dolls [as an expert witness in Briggs v. Elliott, 98 F.Supp. 529 (E.D.S.C. 1951), later joined with Brown v. Board of Education, 347 U.S. 483, 74 S.Ct. 686, 98 L.Ed. 873 (1954)], Clark gave the essence of his findings as presented in his White House conference paper of the previous year: "I have reached the conclusion from the examination of my own results and from an examination of the literature in the entire field that discrimination, prejudice and segregation"—good to his word, he refused to single out school segregation—"have definitely detrimental effects on the personality development of the Negro child." He went on:

> The essence of this detrimental effect is a confusion in the child's concept of his own self-esteem—basic feelings of inferiority, conflict, confusion in his self-image, resentment, hostility towards himself, hostility towards whites, intensification of ... a desire to resolve his basic conflict by sometimes escaping or withdrawing.

[C]lark then applied his general statements to the specific test results he obtained in Clarendon County: eleven of the sixteen black children thought the brown doll looked "bad"; ten of them considered the white doll the "nice" one [a]nd seven of the sixteen picked the white doll as the one like themselves.

> The conclusion which I was forced to reach was that these children in Clarendon County, like other human beings who are subjected to an

obviously inferior status in the society in which they live, have been definitely harmed in the development of their personalities; that the signs of instability in their personalities are clear, and I think that every psychologist would accept and interpret these signs as such.

It was a careful, low-key recitation, all the more stark for Clark's modulated manner. The psychologist hurriedly caught his breath and then braced himself for a relentless cross-examination. "I wasn't prepared for Mr. Figg's Southern gentility," he recalls.

Figg had sized up Clark's testimony and decided it would not adversely affect his case. He snipped away, trying to trivialize it rather than bludgeon it into inconsequence. No, Clark said, nobody else was present in the room while he tested each youngster. Yes, Clark said, he and his wife primarily had developed these particular tests, which had been given to about 400 children all together over the years. There was only a single sharp exchange between them as Figg tried to invoke the racist ideology of William Graham Sumner and other early sociologists that had prevailed half a century earlier but had been almost totally discredited by the academic world in the past two decades.

Q. Do you recognize the psychology that people, based upon the "universal consciousness of kind," social heritage and the degree of visibility of differences between the races and so forth—enters into the problem of dealing with the existence of two different races in great numbers in a particular area?

A. I do not recognize that at all, sir.

Q. You don't recognize that?

A. I do not recognize it as a principle which should govern democratic relations.

Q. Do you recognize that there is an emotional facet in the problem of two different races living in large numbers together in the same area?

A. I have just given you results which indicate the consequences of that kind of emotional tension.

Confronted with a determined and obviously quick-witted witness with expertise in an area that Figg knew relatively little about, the defense attorney did not force the issue. "You don't cross-examine in a probing way if you're not sure what the answers are going to be," notes Figg, who by then had had a dozen years' experience as a state prosecutor and knew the territory. "I was concerned about findings of fact, and once we determined that his testimony was based on very few children, that there were no witnesses to the tests, and that this was his own test method and not a well-established one, I didn't press the matter. His numbers were small and unimposing, so why should I have pushed it? In the courtroom, his manner was quiet and matter-of-fact. Nobody took it seriously."

The essence of Kenneth Clark's testimony, though, would be taken very seriously indeed before *Briggs* was finally resolved.

———

NOTE

1. Doll Studies Reconsidered. Gray-Little and Hafdahl, Factors Influencing Racial Comparisons of Self-Esteem: A Quantitative Review, 126 Psychological Bulletin 26 (2000) reviewed research on racial differences in self-esteem since the Clark and Clark studies. Their conclusions were as follows:

> Early research in this area, exemplified by the doll studies of racial preference, was viewed as demonstrating that Blacks have less self-regard than Whites. However, a meta-analytic synthesis of 261 comparisons, based largely on self-esteem scales and involving more than half a million respondents, revealed *higher* scores for Black than for White children, adolescents, and young results. Id. at 26 (emphasis added).

————

THE EFFECTS OF SEGREGATION AND THE CONSEQUENCES OF DESEGREGATION: A SOCIAL SCIENCE STATEMENT*

Appendix to Appellants' Briefs

BROWN v. BOARD OF EDUCATION OF TOPEKA

Supreme Court of the United States, 1954.
347 U.S. 483, 74 S.Ct. 686, 98 L.Ed. 873.

The problem of the segregation of racial and ethnic groups constitutes one of the major problems facing the American people today. It seems desirable, therefore, to summarize the contributions which contemporary social science can make toward its resolutions. There are, of course, moral and legal issues involved with respect to which the signers of the present statement cannot speak with any special authority and which must be taken into account in the solution of the problem. There are, however, also factual issues involved with respect to which certain conclusions seem to be justified on the basis of the available scientific evidence. It is with these issues only that this paper is concerned. Some of the issues have to do with the consequences of segregation, some with the problems of changing from segregated to unsegregated practices.

[I]

At the recent Mid-century White House Conference on Children and Youth, a fact-finding report on the effects of prejudice, discrimination and segregation on the personality development of children was prepared as a

---

* This statement was drafted and signed by the following sociologists, anthropologists, psychologists and psychiatrists, who have worked in the area of American race relations: [32 names are given].

basis for some of the deliberations.[2] This report brought together the available social science and psychological studies which were related to the problem of how racial and religious prejudices influenced the development of a healthy personality. It highlighted the fact that segregation, prejudices and discriminations, and their social concomitants potentially damage the personality of all children—the children of the majority group in a somewhat different way than the more obviously damaged children of the minority group.

The report indicates that as minority group children learn the inferior status to which they are assigned—as they observe the fact that they are almost always segregated and kept apart from others who are treated with more respect by the society as a whole—they often react with feelings of inferiority and a sense of personal humiliation.

[T]he report indicates that minority group children of all social and economic classes often react with a generally defeatist attitude and a lowering of personal ambitions. This, for example, is reflected in a lowering of pupil morale and a depression of the educational aspiration level among minority group children in segregated schools. In producing such effects, segregated schools impair the ability of the child to profit from the educational opportunities provided him.

[T]he preceding view is consistent with the opinion stated by a large majority (90%) of social scientists who replied to a questionnaire concerning the probable effects of enforced segregation under conditions of equal facilities. This opinion was that, regardless of the facilities which are provided, enforced segregation is psychologically detrimental to the members of the segregated group.[12]

[II]

Segregation is at present a social reality. Questions may be raised, therefore, as to what are the likely consequences of desegregation.

One such question asks whether the inclusion of an intellectually inferior group may jeopardize the education of the more intelligent group by lowering educational standards or damage the less intelligent group by placing it in a situation where it is at a marked competitive disadvantage. Behind this question is the assumption, which is examined below, that the presently segregated groups actually are inferior intellectually.

The available scientific evidence indicates that much, perhaps all, of the observable differences among various racial and national groups may be adequately explained in terms of environmental differences. It has been found, for instance, that the differences between the average intelligence

2. Clark, K.B., Effect of Prejudice and Discrimination on Personality Development, Fact Finding Report Mid-century White House Conference on Children and Youth, Children's Bureau, Federal Security Agency, 1950 (mimeographed).

12. Deutscher, M. and Chein, I., The Psychological Effects of Enforced Segregation: A Survey of Social Science Opinion, J. Psychol., 1948, 26, 259–287.

test scores of Negro and white children decrease, and the overlap of the distribution increases, proportionately to the number of years that the Negro children have lived in the North. Related studies have shown that this change cannot be explained by the hypothesis of selective migration. It seems clear, therefore, that fears based on the assumption of innate racial differences in intelligence are not well founded.

[A] second problem that comes up in an evaluation of the possible consequences of desegregation involves the question of whether segregation prevents or stimulates interracial tension and conflict and the corollary question of whether desegregation has one or the other effect.

The most direct evidence available on this problem comes from observations and systematic study of instances in which desegregation has occurred. Comprehensive reviews of such instances clearly establish the fact that desegregation has been carried out successfully in a variety of situations although outbreaks of violence had been commonly predicted. Extensive desegregation has taken place without major incidents in the armed services in both Northern and Southern installations and involving officers and enlisted men from all parts of the country, including the South.

[U]nder certain circumstances desegregation not only proceeds without major difficulties, but has been observed to lead the emergence of more favorable attitudes and friendlier relations between races. Relevant studies may be cited with respect to housing, employment, the armed services and merchant marine, recreation agency, and general community life.

Much depends, however, on the circumstances under which members of previously segregated groups first come in contact with others in unsegregated situations. Available evidence suggests, first, that there is less likelihood of unfriendly relations when the change is simultaneously introduced into all units of a social institution to which it is applicable—e.g., all of the schools in a school system or all of the shops in a given factory. When factories introduced Negroes in only some shops but not in others the prejudiced workers tended to classify the desegregated shops as inferior, "Negro work." Such objections were not raised when complete integration was introduced.

The available evidence also suggests the importance of consistent and firm enforcement of the new policy by those in authority. It indicates also the importance of such factors as: the absence of competition for a limited number of facilities or benefits; the possibility of contacts which permit individuals to learn about one another as individuals; and the possibility of equivalence of positions and functions among all of the participants within the unsegregated situation. These conditions can generally be satisfied in a number of situations, as in the armed services, public housing developments, and public schools.

[III]

The problem with which we have here attempted to deal is admittedly on the frontiers of scientific knowledge. Inevitably, there must be some differences of opinion among us concerning the conclusiveness of certain items of evidence, and concerning the particular choice of words and placement of emphasis in the preceding statement. We are nonetheless in agreement that this statement is substantially correct and justified by the evidence, and the differences among us, if any, are of a relatively minor order and would not materially influence the preceding conclusions.

BROWN v. BOARD OF EDUCATION OF TOPEKA

Supreme Court of the United States, 1954.
347 U.S. 483, 74 S.Ct. 686, 98 L.Ed. 873.

■ Mr. Chief Justice Warren delivered the opinion of the Court.

We come [t]o the question presented: Does segregation of children in public schools solely on the basis of race, even though the physical facilities and other "tangible" factors may be equal, deprive the children of the minority group of equal educational opportunities? We believe that it does.

[T]o separate them from others of similar age and qualifications solely because of their race generates a feeling of inferiority as to their status in the community that may affect their hearts and minds in a way unlikely ever to be undone. The effect of this separation on their educational opportunities was well stated by a finding in the Kansas case by a court which nevertheless felt compelled to rule against the Negro plaintiffs:

> "Segregation of white and colored children in public schools has a detrimental effect upon the colored children. The impact is greater when it has the sanction of the law; for the policy of separating the races is usually interpreted as denoting the inferiority of the negro group. A sense of inferiority affects the motivation of a child to learn. Segregation with the sanction of law, therefore, has a tendency to [retard] the educational and mental development of negro children and to deprive them of some of the benefits they would receive in a racial[ly] integrated school system."

Whatever may have been the extent of psychological knowledge at the time of Plessy v. Ferguson, this finding is amply supported by modern authority.[11] Any language in Plessy v. Ferguson contrary to this finding is rejected.

We conclude that in the field of public education the doctrine of "separate but equal" has no place. Separate educational facilities are

---

11. K.B. Clark, Effect of Prejudice and Discrimination on Personality Development (Midcentury White House Conference on Children and Youth, 1950); Witmer and Kotinsky, Personality in the Making (1952), c. VI; Deutscher and Chein, The Psychological Effects of Enforced Segregation: A Survey of Social Science Opinion, 26 J. Psychol. 259 (1948); Chein, What are the Psychological Effects of Segregation Under Conditions of Equal Facilities?, 3 Int. J. Opinion and Attitude Res. 229 (1949); Brameld, Educational Costs, in Discrimination and National Welfare (MacIver, ed., 1949), 44–48; Frazier, The Negro in the United States (1949), 674–681. And see generally Myrdal, An American Dilemma (1944).

inherently unequal. Therefore, we hold that the plaintiffs and others similarly situated for whom the actions have been brought are, by reason of the segregation complained of, deprived of the equal protection of the laws guaranteed by the Fourteenth Amendment.

JURISPRUDENCE*

Edmond Cahn.
30 New York University Law Review 150 (1955).

In the months since the utterance of the *Brown* [opinion], the impression has grown that the outcome, either entirely or in major part, was caused by the testimony and opinions of the scientists, and a genuine danger has arisen that even lawyers and judges may begin to entertain this belief. The word "danger" is used advisedly, because I would not have the constitutional rights of Negroes—or of other Americans—rest on any such flimsy foundation as some of the scientific demonstrations in these records.

[O]bviously, the *Brown* [opinion is] susceptible of more than one interpretation. My views do not agree with those of some very able commentators, who consider that the opinions show important marks of the psychologists' influence. Granting this variety of interpretations, does it really matter whether the Supreme Court relies or does not rely on the psychologists' findings? Does it make any practical difference?

I submit it does. In the first place, since the behavioral sciences are so very young, imprecise, and changeful, their findings have an uncertain expectancy of life. Today's sanguine asseveration may be cancelled by tomorrow's new revelation—or new technical fad. It is one thing to use the current scientific findings, however ephemeral they may be, in order to ascertain whether the legislature has acted reasonably in adopting some scheme of social or economic regulation; deference here is shown not so much to the findings as to the legislature. It would be quite another thing to have our fundamental rights rise, fall, or change along with the latest fashions of psychological literature. Today the social psychologists—at least the leaders of the discipline—are liberal and egalitarian in basic approach. Suppose, a generation hence, some of their successors were to revert to the ethnic mysticism of the very recent past; suppose they were to present us with a collection of racist notions and label them "science." What then would be the state of our constitutional rights? Recognizing as we do how sagacious Mr. Justice Holmes was to insist that the Constitution be not tied to the wheels of any economic system whatsoever, we ought to keep it similarly uncommitted in relation to the other social sciences.

---

* Cahn, Jurisprudence, 30 New York University Law Review 150, 157–58, 167 (1955); reprinted with permission of the New York University Law Review.

STELL v. SAVANNAH-CHATHAM COUNTY BOARD OF EDUCATION

United States District Court, Southern District of Georgia, 1963.
220 F.Supp. 667.

■ SCARLETT, DISTRICT JUDGE:

This is a class action in the right of the minor Negro plaintiffs as students in public schools of Savannah-Chatham County to enjoin defendant Board of Education from operating a bi-racial school system.

[T]he defendants [c]onceded the existence of a dual school system for white and Negro students in the City and County.

[A] motion to intervene on behalf of themselves and their class was made by minor white school children alleging that the separation of Negro and white children in the public schools was not determined solely by race or color but rather upon racial traits of educational significance as to which racial identity was only a convenient index.

Among these significant factors for consideration in devising a rational program best suited to the peculiar educational needs of Negro and white school children in separate schools were:

(a) differences in specific capabilities, learning progress rates, mental maturity, and capacity for education in general;

(b) differences in physical, psychical and behavioral traits.

The differences were alleged to be of such magnitude as to make it impossible for Negro and white children of the same chronological age to be effectively educated in the same classrooms.

It was alleged that to congregate children of such diverse traits in schools in the proportion and under the conditions existing in Savannah would seriously impair the educational opportunities of both white and Negro and cause them grave psychological harm.

[I]ntervenors [p]roduced Dr. Ernest van den Haag, a Professor of Social Philosophy at New York University and lecturer on sociology and social philosophy at the New School for Social Research. As with the other witnesses presented by the intervenors, plaintiffs conceded that Dr. van den Haag was an authority in his field. This witness reviewed for the Court a number of educational studies which investigated sources of group conflicts in the classroom and the patterns of association among students which affect their educational achievement. These studies, in whose conclusions Professor van den Haag concurred, show that inter-racial associational distinctions arise spontaneously in pre-school children without regard to whether they live in an area of segregated or integrated schooling. This is one aspect of group identification which every individual makes.

[A]ccording to this witness, any group having self-identification or associational preference closes its ranks in the presence of other groups. Prejudices, whether ethnic, religious or racial, increase rather than decrease in proportion to the degree of non-voluntary contact between separately identifiable groups. This is a psychological phenomenon which was noted in the time of Periclean Greece. Studies made of actual intermixing of groups in classrooms confirm the predicted result that an increase in cross-group contacts increases pre-existing racial hostility rather than ameliorates it. This group tension effect is greatest where obvious group identity criteria exist, such as physical appearance or variations in learning rate. Such groupings prevent a class having a natural homogeneity, multiply disciplinary problems in the classroom, and decrease attention to study.

Dr. van den Haag stated that acceptable group identifications are essential to the well-being of the individual. Any attempt to de-identify one's self with a natural grouping would be harmful.

[T]he proofs closed, plaintiffs renewed their objection of irrelevancy and moved to strike the evidence submitted by intervenors.

[I]n stating the basis for the objection to this evidence, counsel for plaintiffs said:

> " * * * the law is settled by the Supreme Court in the Brown case that segregation itself injures negro children in the school system. That is what the Supreme Court's decision is all about, so we do not have to prove that."

A ruling on plaintiffs' objection therefore made it essential to consider the legal parameters of the Supreme Court's Brown decision.

[I]t is [a]pparent that the governance of the present issues by Brown is the question of whether the applicable portion of the determination in that case—the injury occurring through segregation as plaintiffs put it—is a finding of fact or a conclusion of law. For this let us look to the words and record in Brown.

[I]n Brown the Supreme Court stated for itself the nature of its inquiry:

> "We come then to the question presented: Does segregation of children in public schools solely on the basis of race, even though the physical facilities and other 'tangible' factors may be equal, deprive the children of the minority group of equal educational opportunities?" (347 U.S. p. 493, 74 S.Ct. p. 691)

Although it would appear sufficiently clear on its face that this calls for a conclusion of fact rather than law, we are confirmed when we find that Court looking to the testimonial and other evidence in the records before it and to a submission of scientific opinion rather than seeking the answer to this question in the law books.

From the Kansas record, the Court read:

> " * * * the policy of separating the races is usually interpreted as denoting the inferiority of the negro group. A sense of inferiority affects the motivation of a child to learn. Segregation with the sanction of law, therefore, has a tendency to [retard] the educational and mental development of Negro children and to deprive them of some of the benefits they would receive in a racial[ly] integrated school system."

These are facts, not law. To make these findings the Kansas District Judge considered evidence—not cases. Whether Negroes in Kansas believed that separate schooling denoted inferiority, whether a sense of inferiority affected their motivation to learn and whether motivation to learn was increased or diminished by segregation was a question requiring evidence for decision. That was as much a subject for scientific inquiry as the braking distance required to stop a two-ton truck moving at ten miles an hour on dry concrete.

[T]he Supreme Court put at rest any residual question on the nature of its inquiry when it indicated its reliance on scientific information:

"Whatever may have been the extent of psychological knowledge at the time of Plessy v. Ferguson, [163 U.S. 537, 16 S.Ct. 1138, 41 L.Ed. 256,] this finding is amply supported by modern authority." 347 U.S. p. 494, 74 S.Ct. p. 692.

The teachings of psychology in 1896, in 1954, or in 1963 are inquiries requiring evidence in the same sense as repeated determinations of "seaworthiness." Actually, the non-legal authority to which the Court referred was neither testimonial nor documentary in character but came from a "Brandeis" type brief filed directly in the Supreme Court by the National Association for the Advancement of Colored People.

[T]he Supreme Court in Brown also had placed before it statements by scientists that separate schooling caused psychic injury to the Negro child. Here again the evidence in this case shows the contrary to be the fact. In this case, each witness testified that no such injury had been observed by him and in fact a dual school system is more favorable to the children involved in a psychological sense, avoids the injurious conflict arising from loss of racial identity, and results in a more successful educational program for the students of both races.

[T]he Court accordingly accepts the evidence given in the present case as having somewhat stronger indicia of truth than that on which the findings of potential injury were made in Brown.

[O]n the law these pupils of both races in Savannah-Chatham County are entitled to the best education available and on the unassailable facts that education is best given in separate schools adapted to their varying abilities. On the mandate of that law this Court gives judgment dismissing the complaint.

———

STELL v. SAVANNAH-CHATHAM COUNTY BOARD OF EDUCATION

United States Court of Appeals, Fifth Circuit, 1964.
333 F.2d 55.

■ GRIFFIN B. BELL, CIRCUIT JUDGE:

The District Court was bound by the decision of the Supreme Court in Brown. We reiterate that no inferior federal court may refrain from acting as required by that decision even if such a court should conclude that the Supreme Court erred either as to its facts or as to the law.

[W]e do not read the major premise of the decision of the Supreme Court in the first Brown case as being limited to the facts of the cases there presented. We read it as proscribing segregation in the public education process on the stated ground that separate but equal schools for the races were inherently unequal. This being our interpretation of the teaching of that decision, it follows that it would be entirely inappropriate for it to be rejected or obviated by this court.

[W]e hold that the District Court erred in failing to grant the preliminary injunction in the Savannah case.

———

NOTE

1. "Establishing" Social Science Findings: The Effect of Higher Courts on Lower Courts. In a study of seventeen school desegregation cases litigated during the 1970's, Sanders, Rankin-Widgeon, Kalmuss, and Chesler, The Relevance of "Irrelevant" Testimony: Why Lawyers Use Social Science Experts in School Desegregation Cases, 16 Law and Society Review 403 (1982), found that social scientists testifying for defendant school systems sometimes tried to reopen the legislative fact question addressed by the Supreme Court in footnote 11 of *Brown*. Perhaps because of the Fifth Circuit's decision in *Stell*, however, trial judges treated footnote 11 as dispositive. Sanders et al., id. at 414, quote one social scientist as follows:

> The legal doctrine is cast in concrete, and that's been one of my frustrations—it's as though the evidence is really immaterial. [I] remember in one case, I was talking with the judge from the witness box, and questioning some of the [social science] testimony in *Brown*. He asked me, "are you questioning the facts of *Brown*?" And I said, "yes," and he said, "well, that's not admissible for you to be doing that."

Professors Perry and Melton, Precedential Value of Judicial Notice of Social Facts: Parham as an Example, 22 Journal of Family Law 633, 666–67 (1984), in this regard, make the following observation:

> It is well settled that findings of fact are not included in the *stare decisis* doctrine and have no precedential value beyond the original case. [H]owever, [w]hen a legal conclusion seems to rest on empirical assumptions (e.g., the psychological harm of school segregation), then those assumptions may become de facto conclusions of law which are not disputable.

———

FORCED JUSTICE: SCHOOL DESEGREGATION AND THE LAW (1995)*

David J. Armor.

The research on black self-esteem is of particular historical interest, given the original emphasis on this issue by the 1952 social science statement and the Supreme Court's decision in *Brown*. At that time low self-esteem was seen as the major psychological mechanism contributing to lower academic performance of black children (or any group of children, for that matter), and that view is still popular among many educators and some social scientists today.

The early versions of self-esteem theory, as applied to racial segregation, emerged from studies that used indirect or projective measures of self-esteem (the doll-playing techniques of Kenneth and Mamie Clark being the most prominent). During this period black children's preferences for white dolls were interpreted as rejection of their race and hence rejection of themselves. As the research on self-esteem became more extensive and more sophisticated during the 1960s, studies came to rely more on direct (self-report) measures of self-esteem, and earlier interpretations gave way to what came to be seen as a much more complex process. [T]he vast majority of these studies find that black self-esteem is either higher than or equal to white self-esteem.

[P]ossibly the results of the early doll studies were misinterpreted, and segregated black students did not in fact have lower personal self-esteem than white students at the time of *Brown*. Unfortunately, the theory that black self-esteem differed before *Brown* cannot be tested because no known studies using direct assessment of personal self-esteem were conducted during that period. What is known, with considerable certainty, is that from at least mid-1960s forward there is little evidence that black students have lower self-esteem than white students.

If school segregation does not create low black self-esteem in the first place, then the question of whether desegregation raises black self-esteem may be somewhat academic. Nonetheless, numerous social science studies have compared the self-esteem of segregated and desegregated black students, and several reviews of these studies have been compiled. [O]f nearly fifty studies of desegregation and black self-esteem identified by these reviewers, only six had consistently positive effects. A much larger number—seventeen separate studies—found that school desegregation has adverse effects on black self-esteem.

[S]everal theories have been advanced to explain the adverse effects of desegregation on self-esteem. Most explanations rely on one of two possibilities: a social comparison phenomenon or racial prejudice. Desegregated black students may for the first time find themselves at a disadvantage academically or economically in comparison with white students, and these unfavorable comparisons lead to a lowered personal sense of worth. De-

* Reprinted by permission of Oxford University Press.

segregated black students may also experience racial prejudice or acts of discrimination for the first time, which may also have an impact on their personal self-esteem.

SOCIAL SCIENCE AND SCHOOL DESEGREGATION: DID WE MISLEAD THE SUPREME COURT?

Stuart W. Cook.
5 Personality and Social Psychology Bulletin 420 (1979).

During the deliberations prior to its school desegregation decision in 1954 the Supreme Court had before it a Social Science Statement on the effects of segregation and desegregation. This article reassesses the quality of that Statement 25 years later. Key points in the Statement are compared to the results of subsequent research. Some points, e.g., no negative effect on the school achievement of white students, have been supported. Others, e.g., improvement in black self-esteem, are difficult to evaluate due to inconsistent and uninterpretable research findings. Still others, e.g., more favorable racial attitudes, cannot be compared to the research findings because desegregation was not carried out in accord with conditions that were specified as conducive to the outcomes predicted in the Statement.

[In sum,] there seems little reason to doubt the soundness of the information provided to the Supreme Court in the Social Science Statement of 1954. Regrettably, social scientists in the 1960's and 1970's misdirected their efforts, devoting countless hours to an unrewarding study of the confusing outcomes of desegregation carried out under conditions already known to minimize its effectiveness.

SCHOOL DESEGREGATION: THE SOCIAL SCIENCE ROLE

Harold B. Gerard.
38 American Psychologist 869 (1983).

In his recent article [quoted above] Cook answers the question, Did we mislead the Court? His answer is No—principally, he goes on to say, because the conditions for real integration, which were outlined in the statement, are rarely met in the typical mixed classroom, although the framers argued that these conditions "can generally be satisfied in the public schools." Thirty-two prominent social scientists signed the statement. If I had been asked to do so, I probably would have signed it, too.

In retrospect, however, it was extraordinarily quixotic to assume that the following conditions specified in the statement [as conducive to successful desegregation] would or could be met in the typical school system: (a) firm and consistent endorsement by those in authority; (b) the absence of competition among the representatives of the different racial groups; © the equivalence of positions and functions among all participants in the desegregated setting; and (d) interracial contacts of the type that permit learning about one another as individuals. What could the framers have been thinking about while believing that the conjunction of these four conditions could be met in the typical American school? [F]or the four conditions to be met in the typical school, the teacher would have to be a social engineering whiz. How many of us with our supposed sophistication in group dynamics would undertake the task? The truly embarrassing question is, what do we actually know about intergroup contact that could really make a difference in the way a desegregation program is implemented?

[The authors of the statement] also argued that since President Eisenhower, as one of his first executive orders on entering the White House in 1953, desegregated the armed services, desegregation of the schools could also be successfully accomplished by government decree. This ignored marked differences between the military situation where men and women, black and white, were facing a common enemy in Korea and the complex nexus of circumstances represented by school desegregation, especially in the North. It also ignored the fact that in school desegregation the participants are children, and this engenders a good deal of emotion in their parents.

In his article, Cook attempted to evade the bad predictions [in the Social Science Statement] by blaming the system, but it was that self-same system about which the predictions were made, a system with which the framers were intimately acquainted. Excuse not accepted.

(b) "White Flight"

The constitutionality of "separate but equal" public schools having been resolved in the negative, much contemporary litigation concerns the remedies courts can order when they find a school system to be segregated. One issue that courts have had to confront repeatedly is whether, in fashioning a remedy, the Fourteenth Amendment permits them to take into account social science research on the likely behavioral reactions of the parties affected by the remedy. More plainly put, the question has been whether busing will result in "white flight," and, if so, whether this empirical conclusion should play any role in the decision to order busing.

———

MORGAN v. KERRIGAN

United States District Court, District of Massachusetts, 1975.
401 F.Supp. 216.

■ GARRITY, DISTRICT JUDGE.

[The district court had previously issued an opinion holding that Boston's public schools were unconstitutionally segregated according to race. The court then began extended consideration of a proposal to end this segregation. Among its requirements, this plan called for mandatory busing of approximately 21,000 students. During consideration of the proposed remedy, the Boston Home and School Association, an organization of parents, pointed out alleged defects in the plan, including its failure to allow for what the association claimed to be the predictable resegregative effects of white flight. The district court refused to consider the possibility of white flight.]

Inevitably, the court's primary concern in a desegregation case conflicts with other legitimate concerns. The remedy must accommodate these other interests. But the accommodation must reflect the primacy of the need to achieve equal opportunity in education. In its respect for a variety of interests, a desegregation plan resembles other equitable remedies. The Supreme Court has stated concisely a rough guideline for reconciling these interests.

> Having once found a violation, the district judge or school authorities should make every effort to achieve the greatest possible degree of actual desegregation, taking into account the practicalities of the situation. Davis v. Board of School Commissioners of Mobile County, 1971, 402 U.S. 33, 37, 91 S.Ct. 1289, 1292, 28 L.Ed.2d 577.

[S]ome of the parties have urged that the court limit the extent of actual desegregation lest children from middle class white families leave the public school system and to prevent racial turmoil and violence in Boston's schools and communities. The plaintiffs have argued, just as vigorously, that the court may not consider either "white flight" or the prospect of resistance to desegregation, in formulating the remedy. These prophecies of "white flight" and racial turmoil, like opposition itself, are not "practicalities" that can be weighed against the rights of the plaintiffs.[7] Opposition to a lawful desegregation remedy reflects no legitimate interest. Expression of that opposition constitutes a problem, of course, which the desegregation plan must confront in its implementation. But it does not constitute one of the "practicalities" to which the plan itself properly can make an accommodation. The court may not limit desegregation in deference to such opposition. To hold otherwise would be to trade away the constitutional rights of children to receive a desegregated education in order to appease parents and voters who prefer segregation to desegregation which involves forced busing, i.e., assignments to schools beyond walking distance. The impropriety of such an accommodation has long since been decided. The rule of law must prevail.

---

7. Another ground for refusing to limit a remedy for fear of "white flight" is that a court would be presumptuous to try to predict the effect upon long-term trends in population movement of its adoption of a particular element, otherwise constitutionally required, in a desegregation plan. The masters received expert testimony on the subject of "white flight" from Boston's public schools during the current school year and concluded that the contention was a "misleading fiction."

MORGAN v. KERRIGAN

United States Court of Appeals, First Circuit, 1976.
530 F.2d 401.

■ COFFIN, CHIEF JUDGE.

[Judge Garrity's treatment of the white flight issue was one subject of appeal concerning the desegregation plan.]

These appeals present varied challenges to orders of the district court implementing a plan of desegregation for the public schools of Boston. The consolidated cases concern the remedy phase of litigation initiated by plaintiffs-appellees, representing a class of all black public school students and their parents, against, principally, the Boston School Committee and the Superintendent of Boston Public Schools. The liability phase came to an end in 1974 with a district court finding of substantial segregation in the entire school system intentionally brought about and maintained by official action over the years. Morgan v. Hennigan, 379 F.Supp. 410 (D.Mass.1974). We affirmed, Morgan v. Kerrigan, 509 F.2d 580 (1st Cir. 1974), and the Supreme Court denied certiorari, 421 U.S. 963, 95 S.Ct. 1950, 44 L.Ed.2d 449 (1975).

[T]he "White Flight" Controversy.

The district court ruled that "white flight," defined as the departure of white children from the Boston city schools to parochial, private, or suburban school systems, is not a practicality for which the plan must make an accommodation. Morgan v. Kerrigan, 401 F.Supp. at 233–34. The Mayor and the Association challenge this ruling as an abuse of discretion, claiming that "white flight" alters the effectiveness of a desegregation plan and leads to "resegregation" of the schools.

White flight is an expression of opposition by individuals in the community to desegregation of the school system. From the inception of school desegregation litigation, accommodation of opposition to desegregation by failing to implement a constitutionally necessary plan has been impermissible.

Appellants contend, however, that white flight differs from other forms of opposition, because its effects, the withdrawal of white pupils from the school system, alter the effectiveness of the desegregation plan. The school system, they claim is "resegregated": the city school system largely black and other minority; the private and suburban systems, largely white.[29] To

---

29. Subsequent to the district court decision, we allowed to be filed, subject to a determination of relevance, voluminous affidavits and other materials by social scientists on the subject of white flight.

The admissibility of these submissions have been attacked as being outside the record, F.R.A.P. 10(a), and as hearsay. The materials have been defended as sociological data in the nature of "legislative facts" relevant to a determination of the law governing the district court in this matter.

For reasons we discuss in the text, we reject all these materials as irrelevant to the issues before us on this appeal. We include a brief synopsis of these materials to illustrate the difficulty in evaluating white flight if it were relevant.

prevent this result, appellants claim that the district court should consider white flight a "practicality", and limit the amount of desegregation to that level which would enjoy acceptance in the white community.[30]

The data submitted initially by the Association consists of an affidavit and report prepared by James S. Coleman, Professor of Sociology at the University of Chicago. Dr. Coleman states that his recent study shows that while there is decreasing segregation within school districts, segregation between school districts in the same metropolitan area is increasing; that rapid increase in loss of white children from central city schools follows immediately after school desegregation; and that as a consequence, desegregation has not significantly raised the levels of academic achievement of blacks.

Plaintiffs counter with the transcript of testimony given by Jane R. Mercer, Associate Professor of Sociology, University of California at Riverside, in a case involving Indianapolis. Her testimony shows that she studied desegregation in school districts throughout the state of California; that white exit to private schools is a short term phenomenon; and that declines in white population in the cities are part of a long term demographic trend independent of desegregation. The plaintiffs also submit a paper written by Meyer Weinberg, Editor of *Integrated Education* magazine, which summarizes other studies showing white flight to be an avoidable phenomenon, not an inevitable consequence of mandatory desegregation. Weinberg's paper and another paper written by Professors Green of Michigan State University and Pettigrew of Harvard University, criticize Dr. Coleman's methodology, claiming that the source of his raw data is unknown; that failure to evaluate large cities which have been subject to massive desegregation orders separately from large cities which have not been subject to court orders undermines the study's relevancy; and that failure to control for other variables, which may be correlated with white flight, jeopardizes the validity of his conclusions.

Dr. Coleman replies in an affidavit filed with a copy of a working paper, "Trends in School Segregation, 1968–73". In his affidavit, Dr. Coleman states that the report previously filed with the court was prepared for oral delivery and was based on the attached working paper. He defends his methodology, states that his conclusions are consistent with the findings of the studies cited by Weinberg, and the studies conducted by Dr. Mercer. Dr. Coleman states that his study shows that massive white flight will occur when there is a significant decrease in segregation in a city where there is a high proportion of blacks in the central city and suburbs of a significantly different racial composition.

Plaintiffs, in rebuttal, file another study prepared by Christine H. Rossell, of Boston University. The Rossell study, prepared from data on 86 northern school districts subject to court ordered or legislatively enacted school desegregation, suggests that white flight is minimal and a temporary reaction to school desegregation. Plaintiffs claim that Dr. Rossell's study differs from Dr. Coleman's in that Dr. Rossell deals only with northern school districts subject to desegregation plans while Dr. Coleman does not distinguish between forms of desegregation.

In the final submission, Dr. Coleman defends his study against the Rossell findings, suggesting that her analysis is inadequate to examine the effects of desegregation on a core city school system. He further claims that his model has proved accurately predictive of the Boston experience.

Throughout this series of submissions this court has been burdened with reports written for sociologists by sociologists utilizing sophisticated statistical and mathematical techniques. We lack the expertise to evaluate these studies on their merits. We do come to one conclusion, however. The relationship between white flight and court ordered desegregation is a matter of heated debate among experts in sociology, and a firm professional consensus has not yet emerged.

Appellants have also filed with this court copies of the Boston School Department's current census of students according to race and minority group. The figures facially suggest loss of a significant number of white enrollees. We note, however, that the district court is currently studying the accuracy of past enrollment data. We decline to make any conclusions concerning the existence or nonexistence of white flight on the sparse figures available to us.

30. Appellants suggested approach would necessarily involve the district court in

There are two endemic flaws in this argument. First, in the trial on liability, evidence was presented that feeder patterns, district lines, and open transfer policies were established for the purpose of satisfying purported white community desires. This evidence resulted in a finding that the Boston schools were administered in violation of the Fourteenth Amendment. Appellants now ask that the district court, in devising a remedy for these violations, respond in the same way as the Boston School Committee did to the same perceived community attitudes: draw district lines, assign pupils to schools, and limit racial mixture to reduce "white flight". In other words, while appellants dwell upon the unpleasant prospect of an inner city black school system surrounded by suburban white school systems, the prospect contemplated by their approach is that of an inner city segregated system, created unlawfully, but permitted to endure because the apprehension of massive white flight has made legal what had once been in violation of the constitution.

Second, appellants' claim that white flight destroys the effectiveness of the school desegregation plan, because of "resegregation" of the school system, founders on the constitutional definition of unlawful segregation. The Supreme Court has recently reemphasized that the constitutional right is to attend school in a unitary, non-discriminatory, public school system. It is not to attend school in a system which is comprised of students of a racial balance which exists in the general geographical area.

What the layman calls "resegregation" is not constitutionally recognized segregation. It is racial isolation imposed by historic school district boundaries or by individual choices to attend private institutions. This racial isolation becomes constitutionally significant only when the district boundaries are drawn with segregative intent, or when the state participates in the private institutions.

The constitution cannot solve all problems. On the contrary, to the extent that it demands that rights which have previously been overridden

something like the following analysis: (1) take evidence concerning the prospects of white flight under the various plans proposed; (2) exclude the causes of such flight attributable to any historic trend, or such factors as overcrowding, transportation difficulties, deteriorated housing, taxes, crime, pollution, industrial migration, etc.; (3) make a judgment as to the effect which different levels of desegregation would have on white flight; and (4) select or devise that plan which will incorporate enough desegregation to bring about the maximum amount of inter-racial contact in the schools after taking account of the white flight such desegregation would be expected to induce.

The experts have difficulty in attempting to justify conclusions as to the effect of past desegregation plans on white flight, see note 29 supra; the task of making estimates of expected exodus of whites attributable to varying future desegregation plans would seem to be more difficult. Conceivably, public attitude sampling could be undertaken, using various hypotheses. This might involve questioning parents in a particular section or school district whether they would be likely to place their child elsewhere, or move, if the child were to attend a school which was x, y, or z percent black. The possibility is a real one that surveys would indicate that the prospect of any substantial amount of desegregation or busing would provoke sufficient expressions of intent to flee as to negate any desegregation plan. Alternatively, if expressed intentions were to be heavily discounted, their utility would accordingly diminish.

be enforced, it creates social problems. It inconveniences, sometimes substantially, law enforcement officers, prison wardens, university administrators, and government bureaucrats. And, when it allows tasteless books to be sold or movies shown, many are offended. But expectable individual, official or group reaction does not outweigh constitutional rights. We therefore must agree with another court which said, "concern over 'white flight' . . . cannot become the higher value at the expense of rendering equal protection of the laws the lower value." Mapp v. Board of Education of Chattanooga, [525 F.2d 169], quoting 366 F.Supp. 1257, 1260 (E.D.Tenn. 1973).

The bright note in this otherwise somber picture is the care and imagination that the district court has displayed in structuring a diversified educational system offering superior opportunities for children, both white and black. The plan is not a mechanical device to ensure that the races share equally, but serves its constitutional goals within a framework offering educational hope for the children of the city. Nevertheless, federal courts have a limited jurisdiction and competence. To the extent that reorienting the Boston school system involves social expenses, it must be paid for in coin less dear than the constitutional rights of the city's citizens. Here as elsewhere, the Boston community must look to other institutions, city, state, federal and private, to contribute to an effort to vindicate the constitutional rights of its citizens at a minimum of social cost.

[W]e therefore affirm.

———

NOTES

1. Subsequent Research on White Flight in Boston. In R. Dentler and M. Scott, Schools on Trial: An Inside Account of the Boston Desegregation Case 224–226 (1981), the authors, who were appointed by Judge Garrity as experts to assist in designing the final desegregation plan in 1975, reflected upon the "white flight" issue in light of subsequent experience:

> White flight [in Boston] began in 1973 and reached a high velocity in 1975. Enrollments went from about 55 percent white in 1973 to 36 percent in 1980. Our efforts to account for this change lead us to think that roughly half of it was associated, however directly or indirectly, with desegregation.

> [T]here is no question as to whether white flight is occurring, although early in 1975 we were not able to foresee its scale and were tempted to downplay its importance in our public statements. [W]e did not anticipate the relocation of thousands of households to places far removed from the Greater Boston metropolitan area.

> Heavy white flight took place and it damaged not only school desegregation but also the income mix of students and the tax base of Boston.

During the 2005–06 academic year, 14 percent of the students enrolled in Boston public schools were white.

2. More Recent Research. D. Armor, Forced Justice: School Desegregation and the Law (1995),* summarized more recent research on white flight and white attitudes toward school desegregation as follows:

> The consensus at this point is that school desegregation contributes to white flight and that the flight can be quite large for some school systems, especially those systems that are larger, have higher minority concentrations, and have suburban or private school systems that can serve as alternatives for those who flee a desegregation plan or for new residents who want to avoid one. There is less consensus about whether some types of desegregation plans create more white flight than others and about the long-term consequences of white flight on effectiveness [of desegregation plans].

> The studies also show strong white parental support for various voluntary desegregation techniques such as magnet schools [a]nd no significant opposition to increasing the minority enrollment in their children's current schools. A significant fraction of white parents would object to sending their children to predominantly minority schools, however, and a large majority remain strongly opposed to the technique of mandatory busing—or to any method that would reassign their child to a distant school in a black neighborhood. Id. at 180, 203–204.

————

ANDERSON EX REL. DOWD v. CITY OF BOSTON

United States Court of Appeals, First Circuit, 2004.
375 F.3d 71.

■ Lipez, Circuit Judge.

At the outset of its penultimate ruling in this protracted litigation, the district court observed: "This case may possibly be the concluding chapter in thirty years of litigation over the effort to desegregate the Boston Public Schools." *Boston's Children First v. Boston School Comm., 260 F.Supp.2d 318, 319 (D.Mass.2003).* That cautious prediction may be accurate.

[I]n quick review, thirty years ago the Massachusetts federal district court held that the City of Boston promoted and maintained a racially segregated dual public school system in violation of constitutionally guaranteed rights. After twelve years of supervision by the district court, the court returned control over student assignments to BPS [Boston Public Schools], declaring that BPS's student assignment system had achieved unitariness, *Morgan v. Nucci, 831 F.2d 313, 318 (1st Cir.1987),* "i.e. a fully integrated,

---

non-segregated system." *Id. at 316.* At that point, BPS adopted an assign-ment system known as the Controlled Choice Student Assignment Plan, (the "Old Plan"), which went into effect for the 1989–90 academic year.

The Old Plan

[B]oston is divided into three Attendance Zones—the North, East, and West Zones—for purposes of the elementary and middle school assignments at issue in this case. These zones were drawn by the district court as part of its desegregation orders, and the lines largely hew to major transporta-tion routes to keep traditional neighborhoods intact as much as possible. Students are eligible to attend any of the schools located in the Attendance Zone in which the students reside.

[U]nder the Old Plan, BPS assigned students to schools using the following criteria: the student's rank preference for the school; whether a sibling already attended the school; whether the student lived within the school's walk zone; whether the student had already matriculated at the school on a temporary basis; and, as a tie-breaker, the student's random number, with a lower random number winning out over higher numbers. Assignments under the Old Plan operated with one additional constraint— the "ideal racial percentage" for each grade's population, as calculated by the racial and ethnic composition of the student population in that grade within each of the three Attendance Zones. If admitting a student would cause a deviation of more than 15% from the "ideal racial percentage," that student would not be admitted. The Old Plan operated largely without change for ten years, from 1989 through 1999.

[T]he New Plan

Based in no small part on [BPS] Superintendent Payzant's frank assessment to the School Committee that, in light of *Wessmann [v. Gittens, 160 F.3d 790 (1st Cir.1998)]* and other reverse discrimination lawsuits, plaintiffs in this case would almost certainly prevail in their challenge to the Old Plan, the School Committee voted on July 14, 1999, to discontinue the use of the racial classifications in the Old Plan. At the time of this vote, the School Committee also charged the Superintendent with developing a new student assignment plan that did not consider "race as a factor in making student assignments."

[C]ourse of Litigation Below

[F]ollowing a bench trial on the merits, the district court issued a ruling in [Boston's Children First v. Boston School Committee, *260 F.Supp.2d 318, "BCF IV"*] on April 23, 2003. The court found that (1) the New Plan [w]as facially race-neutral, (2) there was no evidence that the policy was applied in a discriminatory manner, and (3) plaintiffs did not show that the policy was adopted with a discriminatory intention and applied in a way that had a discriminatory effect. [I]n consequence, the court entered judgment for defendants.

The Constitutionality of the New Plan

[S]ince race-based classifications are not in play and plaintiffs failed to show that the New Plan was adopted with a discriminatory purpose, the New Plan must only survive rational basis review: as long as the plan is rationally related to a legitimate governmental interest, it must be upheld. [D]efendants adopted the New Plan to foster "excellence, equity and diversity through access and educational opportunity throughout the Boston Public Schools." All of those goals are legitimate state interests, and the assignment process of the New Plan is rationally related to achieving them. [A]ccordingly, we reject plaintiffs' claims that the New Plan violates their rights under the Equal Protection Clause of the Fourteenth Amendment, Title VI, or § § 1981 and 1983.

[I]t is not surprising that this case and those that preceded it have inspired deep passions among the parties and their supporters. Indeed, in histories already written about the aftermath of *Brown* in our large cities, Boston has often been cited as a city that resisted fiercely the mandate of *Brown* and the measures required to dismantle a public school system segregated by government action.

Hopefully, future histories will also tell the rest of the story. Attitudes in Boston have evolved, policies have changed, institutions have reorganized. In many ways, the social fabric has been re-knit. But this healing has not lowered the stakes in public education. People of good faith, harboring only the best of intentions, can—and do—disagree about the ultimate resolution of the difficult legal and social issues that surround public education generally and school assignment systems specifically. These continuing disagreements do not diminish all that has been accomplished.

[F]or all of the foregoing reasons, the judgments of the district court are AFFIRMED in all respects.

2. SEGREGATION BY GENDER

Almost thirty years after *Brown* held that the segregation of public schools by race violated the Equal Protection clause of the Fourteenth Amendment, the Supreme Court addressed the question of whether the segregation of public schools by gender was also unconstitutional. The question arose in the context of a state-supported nursing school.

———

MISSISSIPPI UNIVERSITY FOR WOMEN v. HOGAN

Supreme Court of the United States, 1982.
458 U.S. 718, 102 S.Ct. 3331, 73 L.Ed.2d 1090.

■ JUSTICE O'CONNOR delivered the opinion of the Court.

[Respondent Joe Hogan applied for admission to the Mississippi University for Women School of Nursing. Since by statute the University limited its enrollment to women applicants, Hogan was denied admission.

The district court denied Hogan preliminary injunctive relief and the court of appeals reversed.]

This case presents the narrow issue of whether a state statute that excludes males from enrolling in a state-supported professional nursing school violates the Equal Protection Clause of the Fourteenth Amendment.

[T]he State's primary justification for maintaining the single-sex admissions policy of MUW's School of Nursing is that it compensates for discrimination against women and, therefore, constitutes educational affirmative action. As applied to the School of Nursing, we find the State's argument unpersuasive.

[M]ississippi has made no showing that women lacked opportunities to obtain training in the field of nursing or to attain positions of leadership in that field when the MUW School of Nursing opened its door or that women currently are deprived of such opportunities. In fact, in 1970, the year before the School of Nursing's first class enrolled, women earned 94 percent of the nursing baccalaureate degrees conferred in Mississippi and 98.6 percent of the degrees earned nationwide. United States Department of Health, Education, and Welfare, Earned Degrees Conferred: 1969–1970, 388 (1972). That year was not an aberration; one decade earlier, women had earned all the nursing degrees conferred in Mississippi and 98.9 percent of the degrees conferred nationwide. United States Department of Health, Education, and Welfare, Earned Degrees Conferred 1959–1960: Bachelor's and Higher Degrees 135 (1960). As one would expect, the labor force reflects the same predominance of women in nursing. When MUW's School of Nursing began operation, nearly 98 percent of all employed registered nurses were female. United States Bureau of the Census, 1981 Statistical Abstract of the United States 402 (1981).

Rather than compensate for discriminatory barriers faced by women, MUW's policy of excluding males from admission to the School of Nursing tends to perpetuate the stereotyped view of nursing as an exclusively woman's job.[15] By assuring that Mississippi allots more openings in its state-supported nursing schools to women than it does to men, MUW's admissions policy lends credibility to the old view that women, not men, should become nurses, and makes the assumption that nursing is a field for women a self-fulfilling prophecy. Thus, we conclude that, although the State recited a "benign, compensatory purpose," it failed to establish that the alleged objective is the actual purpose underlying the discriminatory classification.

The policy is invalid also because it fails the second part of the equal protection test, for the State has made no showing that the gender-based classification is substantially and directly related to its proposed compensa-

---

15. Officials of the American Nurses Association have suggested that excluding men from the field has depressed nurses' wages. Hearings Before the United States Equal Employment Opportunity Commission on Job Segregation and Wage Discrimination 510–511, 517–518, 523 (April 1980). To the extent the exclusion of men has that effect, MUW's admissions policy actually penalizes the very class the State purports to benefit.

tory objective. To the contrary, MUW's policy of permitting men to attend classes as auditors fatally undermines its claim that women, at least those in the School of Nursing, are adversely affected by the presence of men.

MUW permits men who audit to participate fully in classes. Additionally, both men and women take part in continuing education courses offered by the School of Nursing, in which regular nursing students also can enroll. Deposition of Dr. James Strobel 56–60 and Deposition of Dean Annette K. Barrar 24–26. The uncontroverted record reveals that admitting men to nursing classes does not affect teaching style, Deposition of Nancy L. Herban 4, that the presence of men in the classroom would not affect the performance of the female nursing students, Tr. 61 and Deposition of Dean Annette K. Barrar 7–8, and that men in coeducational nursing schools do not dominate the classroom. Deposition of Nancy Herban 6. In sum, the record in this case is flatly inconsistent with the claim that excluding men from the School of Nursing is necessary to reach any of MUW's educational goals.

Thus, considering both the asserted interest and the relationship between the interest and the methods used by the State, we conclude that the State has fallen far short of establishing the "exceedingly persuasive justification" needed to sustain the gender-based classification. Accordingly, we hold that MUW's policy of denying males the right to enroll for credit in its School of Nursing violates the Equal Protection Clause of the Fourteenth Amendment.

■ CHIEF JUSTICE BURGER, dissenting.

I agree generally with Justice Powell's dissenting opinion. I write separately, however, to emphasize that the Court's holding today is limited to the context of a professional nursing school. Since the Court's opinion relies heavily on its finding that women have traditionally dominated the nursing profession, it suggests that a State might well be justified in maintaining, for example, the option of an all-women's business school or liberal arts program.

■ JUSTICE BLACKMUN, dissenting.

While the Court purports to write narrowly, declaring that it does not decide the same issue with respect to "separate but equal" undergraduate institutions for females and males or with respect to units of MUW other than its School of Nursing, there is inevitable spillover from the Court's ruling today. That ruling, it seems to me, places in constitutional jeopardy any state-supported educational institution that confines its student body in any area to members of one sex, even though the State elsewhere provides an equivalent program to the complaining applicant. The Court's reasoning does not stop with the School of Nursing of the Mississippi University for Women.

■ JUSTICE POWELL, with whom JUSTICE REHNQUIST joins, dissenting.

[C]oeducation, historically, is a novel educational theory. From grade school through high school, college, and graduate and professional training, much of the nation's population during much of our history has been educated in sexually segregated classrooms.

[T]he sexual segregation of students has been a reflection of, rather than an imposition upon, the preference of those subject to the policy. It cannot be disputed, for example, that the highly qualified women attending the leading women's colleges could have earned admission to virtually any college of their choice. Women attending such colleges have chosen to be there, usually expressing a preference for the special benefits of single-sex institutions. Similar decisions were made by the colleges that elected to remain open to women only.[4]

The arguable benefits of single-sex colleges also continue to be recognized by students of higher education. The Carnegie Commission on Higher Education has reported that it "favor[s] the continuation of colleges for women. They provide an element of diversity . . . and [an environment in which women] generally . . . speak up more in their classes, . . . hold more positions of leadership on campus, . . . and have more role models and mentors among women teachers and administrators." Carnegie Report, quoted in K. Davidson, R. Ginsburg, & H. Kay, Sex-Based Discrimination 814 (1975 ed.). A 10-year empirical study by the Cooperative Institutional Research Program of the American Counsel of Education and the University of California, Los Angeles also has affirmed the distinctive benefits of single-sex colleges and universities. As summarized in A. Astin, Four Critical Years 232 (1977), the data established that

"[b]oth [male and female] single-sex colleges facilitate student involvement in several areas: academic, interaction with faculty, and verbal aggressiveness. . . . Men's and women's colleges also have a positive effect on intellectual self-esteem. Students at single-sex colleges are more satisfied than students at coeducational colleges with virtually all aspects of college life. . . . The only area where students are less satisfied is social life."[5]

---

4. In announcing Wellesley's decision in 1973 to remain a women's college, President Barbara Newell said that "[t]he research we have clearly demonstrates that women's colleges produce a disproportionate number of women leaders and women in responsible positions in society; it does demonstrate that the higher proportion of women on the faculty the higher the motivation for women students." Carnegie Report, supra, in Babcock et al., Sex Discrimination and the Law, at 1014. Similarly rejecting coeducation in 1971, the Mount Holyoke Trustees Committee on Coeducation reported that "the conditions that historically justified the founding of women's colleges" continued to justify their remaining in that tradition. Ibid.

5. In this Court the benefits of single-sex education have been asserted by the stu-

dents and alumnae of MUW. One would expect the Court to regard their views as directly relevant to this case: "[I]n the aspect of life known as courtship or mate-pairing, the American female remains in the role of the pursued sex, expected to adorn and groom herself to attract the male. Without comment on the equities of this social arrangement, it remains a sociological fact.

"An institution of collegiate higher learning maintained exclusively for women is uniquely able to provide the education atmosphere in which some, but not all, women can best attain maximum learning potential. It can serve to overcome the historic repression of the past and can orient a woman to function and achieve in the still male dominated economy. It can free its students of the burden of playing the mating game while attend-

[A] distinctive feature of America's tradition has been respect for diversity. [A]t stake in this case as I see it is the preservation of a small aspect of this diversity. But that aspect is by no means insignificant, given our heritage of available choice between single-sex and coeducational institutions of higher learning. The Court answers that there is discrimination. [B]ut, having found "discrimination," the Court finds it difficult to identify the victims. It hardly can claim that women are discriminated against. A constitutional case is held to exist solely because one man found it inconvenient to travel to any of the other institutions made available to him by the State of Mississippi. In essence he insists that he has a right to attend a college in his home community. This simply is not a sex discrimination case. The Equal Protection Clause was never intended to be applied to this kind of case.

———

ASSOCIATION AND ASSIMILATION

Deborah L. Rhode.
81 Northwestern University Law Review 106 (1986).

Contemporary justifications for sex-segregated schools generally take two forms. One rationale is remedial: gender segregation, like gender preference in affirmative action programs, serves the short-term objective of overcoming women's historic disadvantages in educational and vocational pursuits. A second and broader rationale involves pluralism: single-sex education promotes values of cultural diversity and personal association analogous to those that traditionally have enjoyed first amendment protection.

The majority in *Hogan* chose to address only the first of these rationales. [P]articularly since this was the Court's first full opinion on single-sex schools, its analysis left much to be desired. As Justice Powell's dissent and Mississippi University for Women's brief noted, a substantial body of empirical research suggests that certain all-female learning environments serve remedial objectives. Compared with coeducational institutions, women's colleges reportedly have fostered greater verbal assertiveness, higher career aspirations, more intellectual self-esteem, expanded leadership opportunities, enhanced faculty-student contact, greater access to female role models, and more opportunities for women faculty or administrators. Presumably the state might have an interest in promoting some of these characteristics even for those in female-dominated professions. Why the Court declined even to mention this research, and instead relied on two witnesses' more speculative opinions, is not self-evident. It may be, as one amicus brief implied, that the university failed to make an adequate factual showing at trial. Alternatively, nursing schools have characteristics that

ing classes, thus giving academic rather than sexual emphasis. Consequently, many such institutions flourish and their graduates make significant contributions to the arts, professions and business." Brief for Mississippi University for Women Alumnae Assn. as Amicus Curiae 2–3.

cast doubt on the relevance of certain data regarding undergraduate programs; for example, their students are older, the percentage of male enrollees is unusually small, and opportunities for female faculty and access to female role models already are present. In either case, the majority's analysis begs for qualifications.

Equally problematic was the dissenting opinions' unqualified embrace of the university's remedial claim. Extolling the virtues of single-sex education, Justice Powell, joined by Chief Justice Burger and Justice Rehnquist, set forth a selective and superficial account of the available research. Moreover, as the Coalition of Women's Colleges has noted, much of the empirical data on which the dissent or its authorities relied is "outdated and generally insufficient to support a coherent argument." For example, it is unclear how attributes like greater verbal assertiveness and intellectual self-esteem in single-sex environments affect women's capacity to function in mixed environments.

[T]he pluralist defense of single-sex schools raises similar difficulties. It is true, as Justice Powell noted in *Hogan,* that generations of distinguished Americans have found "distinct advantages" in sexually segregated education. Yet comparable claims were made about racially segregated schools and clubs—claims that often rested on comparable stereotypes. Moreover, nothing in the standard pluralist argument serves to distinguish all-female from all-male schools as an antidote for "needless conformity."

[T]hus, the enhancement of some students' choices can come only at the cost of restricting others', and history leaves little doubt about which sex has paid the greater price for segregation. Even assuming that the pluralist defense somehow could be limited to women's schools, one cannot further suppose, as did the dissenters in *Hogan,* that perpetuating these institutions unequivocally "expands women's choices." To affirm the "honored traditions" of Mississippi University for Women, which focused on typing, teaching, nursing, and needlework, is to reinforce expectations that have constrained, not expanded, women's options. Lumping all women's schools into the same abstract category ignores the diversity in experience that such institutions have fostered.

[I]n the face of such competing concerns and conflicting data, the courts have steered a muddled course, and the prospects for improvement are not encouraging. Separate-but-equal as educational policy remains a perplexing misnomer. In some respects separate is better. In other respects it is worse. But never is it likely to be equal.

NOTES

1.   Standard of Review. Mississippi University for Women v. Hogan has been cited hundreds of times by lower courts, but not for its specific holding regarding the segregation by gender of nursing schools. Rather, the case has been cited as the definitive affirmation by the Supreme Court of an "intermediate" standard for reviewing the constitutionality of any state action involving gender. State action involving economic transactions—such as the maximum hour legislation at issue in Muller v. Oregon—is to be reviewed under a "rational basis" test: the legislation is to be upheld unless the means provided for achieving a legislative purpose bear no rational relationship to that purpose. Virtually all legislation passes this test. State action involving "fundamental" rights, such as freedom of speech, or "suspect" classifications, such as race, are subject to "strict scrutiny" by the courts: the legislation will be upheld only if there is a "compelling interest" at stake. Virtually all legislation fails this test. See Wilkinson, The Supreme Court, The Equal Protection Clause, and the Three Faces of Constitutionality, 61 Virginia Law Review 945 (1975). After *Hogan,* state action involving gender is reviewed according to a standard more demanding than rationality, but less demanding than strict scrutiny: the legislation will be upheld only if the State can show an "exceedingly persuasive justification" for a gender-based classification, which the State in *Hogan* failed to do.

2. The Conclusions of Sociologists. In The Trial of a Mississippi Lawyer, The New York Times, May 15, 1983, § 6 (Magazine), at 62, 69, Wilbur Colom, Hogan's attorney at the oral argument before the Supreme Court, described one of the "ironic moments" of the case in which Colom, an African-American lawyer, invoked Edmond Cahn's criticism, above, of the *Brown* decision:

> Thurgood Marshall, in 1954, arguing in *Brown,* had convinced the court to outlaw racial segregation in schools and base its decision on studies by social scientists that demonstrated segregated education adversely affected minorities. In the Hogan case, various studies were being used by those arguing for single-sex education to demonstrate that women learn better in an environment free from the disturbing influence of men. Turning to Justice Marshall, I contended that I did not want "my or anyone else's" constitutional rights to depend on the conclusions of sociologists.

3. Women's Colleges and Women Leaders. In footnote 4 of his dissent in Mississippi University for Women v. Hogan, Justice Powell cites approvingly the statement of Wellesley President Barbara Newell that "[t]he research we have clearly demonstrates that women's colleges produce a disproportionate number of women leaders and women in responsible positions in society." This research, however, is susceptible to other, less clear, interpretations. Tidball, Perspective on Academic Women and Affirmative Action, 54 Educational Record 130 (1973) is one of the most frequently cited studies asserting a causal relationship between attending a women's college and later achievement. She reported that all-female colleges produced a higher percentage of those listed in *Who's Who of American Women* between 1910 and 1950 than did coeducational institutions. As Rhode, Association and Assimilation, 81 Northwestern University Law Review 106, 139 (1986), notes:

As a threshold matter, to view *Who's Who* listings as an adequate measure of achievement is to accept what many feminists have criticized as an impoverished understanding of individual worth, an understanding that historically has devalued women's contributions. But even assuming *arguendo* that an entry in *Who's Who* is an appropriate indication of success, one cannot infer a causal relationship from a correlation without controlling for a host of variables that Tidball's research failed to acknowledge. From her data, it is impossible to separate the effects of single-sex schools from the higher socioeconomic status and career orientation of their students. For example, had Ivy League institutions been open to women during the period of Tidball's study, the percentage of achievers from coeducational schools might have been substantially different.

4.   The Constitutionality of Gender-Segregated, State-Supported, Elementary Schools. In Garrett v. Board of Education of the School District of the City of Detroit, 775 F.Supp. 1004 (E.D.Mich.1991), the district court, relying on Mississippi University for Women v. Hogan, ruled that Detroit could not open three public elementary schools that would offer an Afrocentric curriculum and would admit only males. "This Court views the purpose for which the Academies came into being as an important one. It acknowledges the status of urban males as an 'endangered species.' The purpose, however, is insufficient to override the rights of females to equal opportunities." Id. at 1014.

UNITED STATES v. COMMONWEALTH OF VIRGINIA

United States District Court, Western District of Virginia, 1991.
766 F.Supp. 1407.

■ KISER, DISTRICT JUDGE.

It was in May of 1864 that the United States and the Virginia Military Institute (VMI) first confronted each other. That was a life-and-death engagement that occurred on the battlefield at New Market, Virginia. The combatants have again confronted each other, but this time the venue is in this court. Nonetheless, VMI claims the struggle is nothing short of a life-and-death confrontation—albeit figurative.

The conflict between the parties arises out of the United States' challenge to VMI's all-male admissions policy. The United States asserts that as a state-supported college, VMI's refusal to admit females to the Institute, regardless of their qualifications, violates the Equal Protection Clause of the Fourteenth Amendment. VMI counters by saying that although it discriminates against women, the discrimination is not invidious but rather to promote a legitimate state interest—diversity in education.

[Mississippi University for Women v.]Hogan involved admission of a single student into the nursing school, and the Court did not purport to extend its ruling to cover other programs at the school. 458 U.S. at 733, 102 S.Ct. at 3340 (Chief Justice Burger dissenting). These determinations

require a fact-intensive examination of the practical considerations underlying the challenged policy. Many of the facts underlying the Supreme
Court's rejection of the justification proffered in Hogan are not present
here. In Hogan, Justice O'Connor's majority opinion emphasized that the

> uncontroverted record reveals that admitting men to nursing classes
> does not affect teaching style, ... that the presence of men in the
> classroom would not affect the performance of the female nursing
> students, ... and that men in coeducational nursing schools do not
> dominate the classroom.... In sum, the record in this case is flatly
> inconsistent with the claim that excluding men from the School of
> Nursing is necessary to reach any of MUW's educational goals.

Hogan, 458 U.S. at 731, 102 S.Ct. at 3339. The record in this case is
directly to the contrary. The record is replete with testimony that single
gender education at the undergraduate level is beneficial to both males and
females. Moreover, the evidence establishes that key elements of the
adversative VMI educational system, with its focus on barracks life, would
be fundamentally altered, and the distinctive ends of the system would be
thwarted, if VMI were forced to admit females and to make changes
necessary to accommodate their needs and interests.

One of the most striking differences in the two cases is the reasons
proffered to justify the discrimination. In Hogan, Mississippi maintained
that a female-only admission policy at MUW was affirmative action which
was justified to compensate women for past discrimination whereas, here,
Virginia urges that a male-only admission policy at VMI promotes diversity
within its statewide system of higher education. The Court found that
Mississippi's proffered explanation failed both prongs of the intermediate
scrutiny test, i.e., that it was not an important governmental objective and
that the means of advancing the objective were not substantially related to
the achievement of that objective. In contrast, diversity in education has
been recognized both judicially and by education experts as being a legitimate objective. The sole way to attain single-gender diversity is to maintain
a policy of admitting only one gender to an institution.

[O]ne empirical study in evidence, not questioned by any expert,
demonstrates that single-sex colleges provide better educational experiences than coeducational institutions. Students of both sexes become more
academically involved, interact with faculty frequently, show larger increases in intellectual self-esteem and are more satisfied with practically all
aspects of college experience (the sole exception is social life) compared with
their counterparts in coeducational institutions. Attendance at an all-male
college substantially increases the likelihood that a student will carry out
career plans in law, business and college teaching, and also has a substantial positive effect on starting salaries in business. Women's colleges increase the chances that those who attend will obtain positions of leadership, complete the baccalaureate degree, and aspire to higher degrees.
Alexander Astin, Four Critical Years, (1977). This research was cited
favorably by Justice Powell in his dissenting opinion in Hogan, 458 U.S. at
738–39, 102 S.Ct. at 3343–44. Viewed in the light of this very substantial
authority favoring single-sex education, the VMI Board's decision to main-

tain an all-male institution is fully justified even without taking into consideration the other unique features of VMI's method of teaching and training. [W]hen one considers VMI's methods of education and the effect that admission of women into the institution will have, the Board's decision to remain an all-male institution is further reinforced. Expert testimony established that, even though some women are capable of all of the individual activities required of VMI cadets, a college where women are present would be significantly different from one where only men are present.

[P]hysical education requirements would have to be altered, at least for the women. The current program, where every student must pass precisely the same physical test before graduation, would prevent a disproportionate number of women from graduating, thus forcing VMI either to establish different requirements for women, or to eliminate or substantially reduce the requirements so that they could be applied to both sexes, which would remove one important part of the VMI system of education. The introduction of women into VMI would add a new set of stresses on the cadets, of a very different kind than the cadets now face. The belief that this would affect the educational program is well-founded in empirical evidence, and not based on an archaic stereotype.

[C]onclusion

Through its Board of Visitors at VMI, Virginia has set an objective of providing single-gender education for males. The evidence in the case, which is virtually uncontradicted, supports Virginia's view that substantial educational benefits flow from a single-gender environment, be it male or female, that cannot be replicated in a coeducational setting. This adds a measure of diversity to Virginia's overall system of education that would be missing if VMI were coeducational. The diversity is further enhanced by VMI's unique method of instruction which was applauded by all of the educational experts who testified. Thus, Virginia has sustained the requirement that gender discrimination serves an important state educational objective. Virginia also met the second prong of the Hogan test by proving that the objective of diversity of education is met by providing single-gender education. Obviously, the only means of attaining this goal is to exclude women from the all-male institution—VMI. But Virginia did not stop there. It enlarged on the single-gender diversity by maintaining an institution whose method of instruction is unique in all the world.

VMI is a different type of institution. It has set its eye on the goal of citizen-solider and never veered from the path it has chosen to meet that goal. VMI truly marches to the beat of a different drummer, and I will permit it to continue to do so.

APPENDIX: FINDINGS OF FACT
[D]ifferences Between Men and Women

A. Gender-Based Physiological Differences

[1]. High maximal lifting capacity refers to the ability to lift 50 kilograms to a height of 132 centimeters of distance, which corresponds to the tail board

of a military truck. Approximately 7% of median college-age females possess high maximal lifting capacity, as compared with approximately 80% of males. Approximately 50% of median college-age females can engage in activities requiring a medium maximal lifting capacity, while 100% of median college-age males can engage in such activities.

[2]. On the average, college-age females perform a two-mile run approximately three minutes slower than the median for college-age males.

[3]. The median college-age female is not capable of performing push-ups equivalent to that of the median college-age male. Of the females tested, none was able to come close to meeting the push-up requirement of the VMI physical fitness test. The maximum number of push-ups by a female was 18, compared with a minimum requirement of 45 push-ups on the VMI fitness test.

[4]. Comparison of the United States Military Academy classes of 1989 and 1981 male and female cadets on the Army physical fitness tests, USMA indoor obstacle course test, and the USMA physical ability test, shows the following:

(a) Seven of eight physical tests show half (50th percentile) of the women performed below the bottom five percent of the men. The single exception is the Army physical fitness sit-up test, which was almost identical for the two groups.

(b) Three-quarters (75th percentile) of the women performed below the bottom five percent of the men in the indoor obstacle course and physical ability test push-up, standing long jump, modified basketball throw, and 300-yard shuttle run test.

(c) The 75th percentile of women for the class of 1989 Army physical fitness test push-up performance was equal to the 8th percentile performance for the men; and the 75th percentile women for the class of 1981 performance was equal to the 13th percentile performance for the men.

B.   Gender-Based Developmental Differences

1.   According to Dr. Richardson [an expert witness for VMI], the "nature of an experience that is growth-producing for a majority of women, according to the literature, is one that is supportive, is one that emphasizes positive motivation. I'm not saying that some women don't do well under adversative model, undoubtedly there are some who do, but you [do not] design educational experiences around the exception. You have to design them around the rule, and I think you would find that the doubting model ... the adversative model ... would have to be gradually adapt[ed] so that it incorporated more of the positive motivation, positive reenforcement."

2.   A substantial body of contemporary scholarship and research supports the proposition that, although males and females have significant areas of developmental overlap, they also have differing developmental needs that are deep-seated.

[3]. Given these developmental differences females and males characteristically learn differently. Males tend to need an atmosphere of adversativeness or ritual combat in which the teacher is a disciplinarian and a worthy competitor. Females tend to thrive in a cooperative atmosphere in which the teacher is emotionally connected with the students.

[4]. Commenting on the scholarly literature and empirical evidence that single-sex education is desirable in light of gender-based developmental differences, the government's expert, Dr. Conrad [an expert witness for the United States], described the gender differences identified by researchers as "tendencies." He emphasized that the attributes of males and females in individual cases may diverge from these average tendencies. In other words, there are exceptions to the general rule.

UNITED STATES v. COMMONWEALTH OF VIRGINIA

United States Court of Appeals, Fourth Circuit, 1992.
976 F.2d 890.

■ NIEMEYER, CIRCUIT JUDGE:

The United States contends on appeal that enhancing diversity by offering a distinctive single-sex education to men only is not a legitimate state objective and that the Commonwealth and VMI have not established a sufficient justification for VMI's male-only admissions policy.

[T]he mission of VMI is to produce "citizen-soldiers, educated and honorable men who are suited for leadership in civilian life and who can provide military leadership when necessary." Focusing primarily on character development and leadership training through a unique and intense process, characterized as an "adversative" educational model drawn from earlier military training and English public schools, VMI's educational method emphasizes physical rigor, mental stress, absolute equality of treatment, absence of privacy, minute regulation of behavior, and indoctrination of values. The process is designed to foster in VMI cadets doubts about previous beliefs and experiences and to instill in cadets new values which VMI seeks to impart.

[T]he district court began its opinion by noting that in May 1864, during the Civil War, VMI cadets bravely fought Union troops at New Market, Virginia. The court continued, "the combatants have again confronted each other, but this time the venue is in this court." What was not said is that the outcome of each confrontation finds resolution in the Equal Protection Clause.

[T]o conduct the appropriate Fourteenth Amendment analysis in this case, we must determine whether the state policy of excluding women from admission to VMI is substantially related to an important policy or objective of Virginia. [W]e must first decide whether VMI's male-only admissions policy, maintained pursuant to state-delegated authority, is a classification justified by a fair and substantial relationship with the institution's mission of developing citizen soldiers, and this in turn leads to an examination of whether VMI's mission would be materially altered by the admission of women.

Much of the debate between the parties relates to the physiological differences between men and women and the question of a woman's ability to perform and endure the physical training included in VMI's program. While it is agreed by the parties that *some* women can meet the physical standards now imposed on men, it is also agreed that a smaller percentage of women can do so. Based on evidence about the experience of the service academies and the Marine Corps, the district court was justified in finding that if women were to be admitted, VMI would have to convert to a dual-track physical training program in order to subject women to a program equal in effect to that of men, and that, as found by a study conducted at West Point, cadets of both sexes would nevertheless perceive the treatment of them as unequal, leading to jealousy and resentment.

All the parties also agree that men and women would and should be entitled to some degree of privacy, at least to the extent that men and women not, in all respects, be exposed to each other. While again there was much debate among the parties as to the changes that might be required to accommodate this at VMI with the admission of women, all agreed that some accommodation would be necessary.

Finally, the parties have debated extensively the effect of cross-sexual confrontations that the adversative program would produce. Testimony was received that the deliberate harassment that upperclassmen give to "rats" [i.e., new cadets] would play out differently when the upperclassman is of one sex and the "rat" another. While the government attributed the predicted effect of this as stereotyping, the evidence supported the district court's finding that cross-sexual confrontation and interaction introduces additional elements of stress and distraction which are not accommodated by VMI's methodology. The court relied on testimony by experts and similar such observations made in the West Point study.

The sum of the changes that could be expected prompted the district court to conclude that if VMI became coeducational, it would offer "neither males nor females the VMI education that now exists." The court observed that "equal treatment would necessarily give way to fair treatment, thus undermining egalitarianism," which is a critical characteristic that now pervades several aspects of VMI's methodology. And the record supports the district court's findings that at least these three aspects of VMI's program—physical training, the absence of privacy, and the adversative approach—would be materially affected by coeducation, leading to a substantial change in the egalitarian ethos that is a critical aspect of VMI's training.

The district court's conclusions that VMI's mission can be accomplished only in a single-gender environment and that changes necessary to accommodate coeducation would tear at the fabric of VMI's unique methodology are adequately supported. And the district court was not clearly erroneous in concluding that if a court were to require the admission of women to VMI to give them access to this unique methodology, the decision would deny those women the very opportunity they sought because the unique characteristics of VMI's program would be destroyed by coeducation. The Catch-22 is that women are denied the opportunity when excluded from VMI and cannot be given the opportunity by admitting them, because the change caused by their admission would destroy the opportunity.

It is not the maleness, as distinguished from femaleness, that provides justification for the program. It is the homogeneity of gender in the process, regardless of which sex is considered, that has been shown to be related to the essence of the education and training at VMI.

The argument by the government that VMI's existing program is maintained as the result of impermissible stereotyping and overly broad generalizations, without a more detailed analysis, might lead, if accepted, to a finding that would impose a conformity that common experience rejects. Men and women are different, and our knowledge about the differences, physiological and psychological, is becoming increasingly more sophisticated. Indeed the evidence in this case amply demonstrated that single-genderedness in education can be pedagogically justifiable.

For instance, in a ten-year empirical study reported by Alexander W. Astin in *Four Critical Years: Effects of College on Beliefs, Attitudes, and Knowledge* (San Francisco: Jossey-Bass 1977), it was found that single-sex colleges have advantages over coeducational colleges in numerous areas. A summary of the report provided by the parties in this case states:

> Single-sex colleges show a pattern of effects on both sexes that is almost uniformly positive. Students of both sexes become more academically involved, interact with faculty frequently, show large increases in intellectual self-esteem, and are more satisfied with practically all aspects of college experience (the sole exception is social life) compared with their counterparts in coeducational institutions.

J.A.1830. In addition to providing substantial benefits to college students, single-sex education also has been found to have salutary consequences for sexual equality in the job market. In a study conducted by Marvin Bressler and Peter Wendell, *The Sex Composition of Selective Colleges and Gender Differences in Career Aspirations,* 51 J. Higher Educ. 650, 662 (1980), the authors observed that in single-sex colleges, the students were more likely to set aside initial, stereotypical job aspirations in favor of more sex-neutral aspirations. They concluded from their data,

> The available evidence thus fails to support the hypothesis that coeducation is a useful instrument for altering the imbalance in career aspirations of academically superior men and women undergraduates.

* * *

> [I]f all selective residential colleges reverted to single sex status, a notable fraction of all men and an even larger proportion of all women would probably renounce initial career commitments, a development

which would have salutary consequences for sexual equality in the job market.

The experts for both sides in this case appear to agree with the conclusions reached in these studies.

Thus, while the data support a pedagogical justification for a single-sex education, they do not materially favor either sex. Both men *and* women appear to have benefited from single-sex education in a materially similar manner. The evidence about the VMI system suggests no differently. The problems that could be anticipated by coeducation at VMI, which are suggested by VMI generally to arise from physiological differences between men and women, needs for privacy, and cross-sexual confrontations, would not be anticipated in an all-female program with the same mission and methodology as that of VMI.

In summary, the record supports the conclusion that single-sex education is pedagogically justifiable, and VMI's system, which the district court found to include a holistic formula of training, even more so. It is not remarkable therefore that the government in its brief conceded, "[I]t is not our position that the Fourteenth Amendment embodies a per se bar to public single-sex education."

While this conclusion answers the question of whether VMI's male-only policy is justified by its institutional mission, the argument does not answer the larger question of whether the unique benefit offered by VMI's type of education can be denied to women by the state under a policy of diversity, which has been advanced as the justification and which was relied on by the district court.

The parties agree that VMI offers a unique combination of education and training that makes a positive contribution offered by no other institution. And the district court found, apparently without exception from any party, that "VMI's military program is absolutely unique. No other school in Virginia or in the United States, public or private, offers the same kind of rigorous military training as is available at VMI." The decisive question in this case therefore transforms to one of why the Commonwealth of Virginia offers the opportunity only to men. While VMI's institutional mission justifies a single-sex program, the Commonwealth of Virginia has not revealed a policy that explains why it offers the unique benefit of VMI's type of education and training to men and not to women. Although it is readily apparent from the evidence that the rigor of the physical training at VMI is tailored to males, in the context of a single-sex female institution, it could be adjusted without detrimental effect. No other aspect of the program has been shown to depend upon maleness rather than single-genderedness.

[I]f VMI's male-only admissions policy is in furtherance of a state policy of "diversity," the explanation of how the policy is furthered by affording a unique educational benefit only to males is lacking. A policy of diversity which aims to provide an array of educational opportunities, including single-gender institutions, must do more than favor one gender.

[I]n short, VMI has adequately defended a single-gender education and training program to produce "citizen soldiers," but it has not adequately explained how the maintenance of one single-gender institution gives effect to, or establishes the existence of, the governmental objective advanced to support VMI's admissions policy, a desire for educational diversity.

We are thus left with three conclusions: (1) single-gender education, and VMI's program in particular, is justified by a legitimate and relevant institutional mission which favors neither sex; (2) the introduction of women at VMI will materially alter the very program in which women seek to partake; and (3) the Commonwealth of Virginia, despite its announced policy of diversity, has failed to articulate an important policy that substantially supports offering the unique benefits of a VMI-type of education to men and not to women.

[I]n light of our conclusions and the generally recognized benefit that VMI provides, we do not order that women be admitted to VMI if alternatives are available. But VMI's continued status as a state institution is conditioned on the Commonwealth's satisfactorily addressing the findings we affirm and bringing the circumstances into conformity with the Equal Protection Clause of the Fourteenth Amendment. By commenting on the potential benefits of single-gender education while discussing the alleged governmental interest in support of VMI's admissions policies, we do not mean to suggest the specific remedial course that the Commonwealth should or must follow hereafter. Rather, we remand the case to the district court to give to the Commonwealth the responsibility to select a course it chooses, so long as the guarantees of the Fourteenth Amendment are satisfied. Consistent therewith, the Commonwealth might properly decide to admit women to VMI and adjust the program to implement that choice, or it might establish parallel institutions or parallel programs, or it might abandon state support of VMI, leaving VMI the option to pursue its own policies as a private institution. While it is not ours to determine, there might be other more creative options or combinations.

VACATED AND REMANDED FOR FURTHER PROCEEDINGS.

UNITED STATES v. VIRGINIA

Supreme Court of the United States, 1996.
518 U.S. 515, 116 S.Ct. 2264, 135 L.Ed.2d 735.

■ Justice Ginsburg delivered the opinion of the Court.

In response to the Fourth Circuit's ruling, Virginia proposed a parallel program for women: Virginia Women's Institute for Leadership (VWIL). The 4-year, state-sponsored undergraduate program would be located at Mary Baldwin College, a private liberal arts school for women, and would be open, initially, to about 25 to 30 students. Although VWIL would share VMI's mission—to produce "citizen-soldiers"—the VWIL program would differ, as does Mary Baldwin College, from VMI in academic offerings, methods of education, and financial resources.

[V]irginia returned to the District Court seeking approval of its proposed remedial plan, and the court decided the plan met the requirements of the Equal Protection Clause. The District Court again acknowledged evidentiary support for these determinations: "[T]he VMI methodology could be used to educate women and, in fact, some women . . . may prefer the VMI methodology to the VWIL methodology." [852 F. Supp.], at 481. But the "controlling legal principles," the District Court decided, "do not require the Commonwealth to provide a mirror image VMI for women." Ibid. The court anticipated that the two schools would "achieve substantially similar outcomes." Ibid.

A divided Court of Appeals affirmed the District Court's judgment. 44 F.3d 1229 (C.A.4 1995). This time, the appellate court determined to give "greater scrutiny to the selection of means than to the [State's] proffered objective." Id., at 1236. The official objective or purpose, the court said, should be reviewed deferentially.

"[P]roviding the option of a single-gender college education may be considered a legitimate and important aspect of a public system of higher education," the appeals court observed, id., at 1238; that objective, the court added, is "not pernicious," id., at 1239.

[H]aving determined, deferentially, the legitimacy of Virginia's purpose, the court considered the question of means. Exclusion of "men at Mary Baldwin College and women at VMI," the court said, was essential to Virginia's purpose, for without such exclusion, the State could not "accomplish [its] objective of providing single-gender education." Ibid.

[T]he cross-petitions in this case present two ultimate issues. First, does Virginia's exclusion of women from the educational opportunities provided by VMI—extraordinary opportunities for military training and civilian leadership development—deny to women "capable of all of the individual activities required of VMI cadets," 766 F.Supp., at 1412, the equal protection of the laws guaranteed by the Fourteenth Amendment? Second, if VMI's "unique" situation, id., at 1413—as Virginia's sole single-sex public institution of higher education—offends the Constitution's equal protection principle, what is the remedial requirement?

[T]o summarize the Court's current directions for cases of official classification based on gender: Focusing on the differential treatment or denial of opportunity for which relief is sought, the reviewing court must determine whether the proffered justification is "exceedingly persuasive." The burden of justification is demanding and it rests entirely on the State. See Mississippi Univ. for Women, 458 U.S., at 724, 102 S.Ct., at 3336. The State must show "at least that the [challenged] classification serves 'important governmental objectives and that the discriminatory means employed' are 'substantially related to the achievement of those objectives.'" Ibid. (quoting Wengler v. Druggists Mutual Ins. Co., 446 U.S. 142, 150, 100 S.Ct. 1540, 1545, 64 L.Ed.2d 107 (1980)). The justification must be genuine, not hypothesized or invented post hoc in response to litigation. And it must not rely on overbroad generalizations about the different talents, capacities, or preferences of males and females.

[I]n support of its initial judgment for Virginia, a judgment rejecting all equal protection objections presented by the United States, the District Court made "findings" on "gender-based developmental differences." 766 F.Supp., at 1434–1435. These "findings" restate the opinions of Virginia's expert witnesses, opinions about typically male or typically female "tendencies." Id., at 1434. For example, "[m]ales tend to need an atmosphere of adversativeness," while "[f]emales tend to thrive in a cooperative atmosphere." Ibid. "I'm not saying that some women don't do well under [the] adversative model," VMI's expert on educational institutions testified, "undoubtedly there are some [women] who do"; but educational experiences must be designed "around the rule," this expert maintained, and not "around the exception." Ibid.

The United States does not challenge any expert witness estimation on average capacities or preferences of men and women. Instead, the United States emphasizes that time and again since this Court's turning point decision in Reed v. Reed, 404 U.S. 71, 92 S.Ct. 251, 30 L.Ed.2d 225 (1971), we have cautioned reviewing courts to take a "hard look" at generalizations or "tendencies" of the kind pressed by Virginia, and relied upon by the District Court. See O'Connor, Portia's Progress, 66 N.Y.U.L.Rev. 1546, 1551 (1991). State actors controlling gates to opportunity, we have instructed, may not exclude qualified individuals based on "fixed notions concerning the roles and abilities of males and females." Mississippi Univ. for Women, 458 U.S., at 725, 102 S.Ct., at 3336.

[V]irginia and VMI trained their argument on "means" rather than "end," and thus misperceived our precedent. Single-sex education at VMI serves an "important governmental objective," they maintained, and exclusion of women is not only "substantially related," it is essential to that objective. By this notably circular argument, the "straightforward" test Mississippi Univ. for Women described, see 458 U.S., at 724–725, 102 S.Ct., at 3336–3337, was bent and bowed.

The State's misunderstanding and, in turn, the District Court's, is apparent from VMI's mission: to produce "citizen-soldiers," individuals

> " 'imbued with love of learning, confident in the functions and attitudes of leadership, possessing a high sense of public service, advocates of the American democracy and free enterprise system, and ready ... to defend their country in time of national peril.' " 766 F.Supp., at 1425 (quoting Mission Study Committee of the VMI Board of Visitors, Report, May 16, 1986).

Surely that goal is great enough to accommodate women, who today count as citizens in our American democracy equal in stature to men. Just as surely, the State's great goal is not substantially advanced by women's categorical exclusion, in total disregard of their individual merit, from the State's premier "citizen-soldier" corps. Virginia, in sum, "has fallen far short of establishing the 'exceedingly persuasive justification,' "Mississippi Univ. for Women, 458 U.S., at 731, 102 S.Ct., at 3340, that must be the solid base for any gender-defined classification.

[I]n the second phase of the litigation, Virginia presented its remedial plan—maintain VMI as a male-only college and create VWIL as a separate program for women. [A] remedial decree, this Court has said, must closely fit the constitutional violation; it must be shaped to place persons unconstitutionally denied an opportunity or advantage in "the position they would have occupied in the absence of [discrimination]." See Milliken v. Bradley, 433 U.S. 267, 280, 97 S.Ct. 2749, 2757, 53 L.Ed.2d 745 (1977) (internal quotation marks omitted). The constitutional violation in this case is the categorical exclusion of women from an extraordinary educational opportunity afforded men. A proper remedy for an unconstitutional exclusion, we have explained, aims to "eliminate [so far as possible] the discriminatory effects of the past" and to "bar like discrimination in the future." Louisiana v. United States, 380 U.S. 145, 154, 85 S.Ct. 817, 822, 13 L.Ed.2d 709 (1965).

Virginia chose not to eliminate, but to leave untouched, VMI's exclusionary policy. For women only, however, Virginia proposed a separate program, different in kind from VMI and unequal in tangible and intangible facilities.

[V]WIL affords women no opportunity to experience the rigorous military training for which VMI is famed. [V]WIL students participate in ROTC and a "largely ceremonial" Virginia Corps of Cadets, see 44 F.3d, at 1234, but Virginia deliberately did not make VWIL a military institute. The VWIL House is not a military-style residence and VWIL students need not live together throughout the 4-year program, eat meals together, or wear uniforms during the school day. [V]WIL students receive their "leadership training" in seminars, externships, and speaker series, see 852 F.Supp., at 477, episodes and encounters lacking the "[p]hysical rigor, mental stress, . . . minute regulation of behavior, and indoctrination in desirable values" made hallmarks of VMI's citizen-soldier training.

[V]irginia maintains that these methodological differences are "justified pedagogically," based on "important differences between men and women in learning and developmental needs," "psychological and sociological differences" Virginia describes as "real" and "not stereotypes." Brief for Respondents 28 (internal quotation marks omitted).

[I]n contrast to the generalizations about women on which Virginia rests, we note again these dispositive realities: VMI's "implementing methodology" is not "inherently unsuitable to women," 976 F.2d, at 899; "some women . . . do well under [the] adversative model," 766 F.Supp., at 1434 (internal quotation marks omitted); "some women, at least, would want to attend [VMI] if they had the opportunity," id., at 1414; "some women are capable of all of the individual activities required of VMI cadets," id., at 1412, and "can meet the physical standards [VMI] now impose[s] on men," 976 F.2d, at 896. It is on behalf of these women that the United States has instituted this suit, and it is for them that a remedy must be crafted,[19] a remedy that will end their exclusion from a state-supplied educational opportunity for which they are fit, a decree that will "bar like discrimination in the future." Louisiana, 380 U.S., at 154, 85 S.Ct., at 822.

[V]irginia, in sum, while maintaining VMI for men only, has failed to provide any "comparable single-gender women's institution." Id., at 1241. Instead, the Commonwealth has created a VWIL program fairly appraised as a "pale shadow" of VMI in terms of the range of curricular choices and faculty stature, funding, prestige, alumni support and influence. [V]irginia's remedy does not match the constitutional violation; the State has shown no "exceedingly persuasive justification" for withholding from women qualified for the experience premier training of the kind VMI affords.

[F]or the reasons stated, the initial judgment of the Court of Appeals, 976 F.2d 890 (C.A.4 1992), is affirmed, the final judgment of the Court of Appeals, 44 F.3d 1229 (C.A.4 1995), is reversed, and the case is remanded for further proceedings consistent with this opinion.

It is so ordered.

■ JUSTICE SCALIA, dissenting.

The question to be answered [i]s whether the exclusion of women from VMI is "substantially related to an important governmental objective."

It is beyond question that Virginia has an important state interest in providing effective college education for its citizens. That single-sex instruction is an approach substantially related to that interest should be evident enough from the long and continuing history in this country of men's and women's colleges. But beyond that, as the Court of Appeals here stated: "That single-gender education at the college level is beneficial to both sexes is a *fact established in this case*." 44 F.3d 1229, 1238 (C.A.4 1995) (emphasis added).

The evidence establishing that fact was overwhelming—indeed, "virtually uncontradicted" in the words of the court that received the evidence, 766 F.Supp. 1407, 1415 (W.D.Va.1991). As an initial matter, Virginia demonstrated at trial that "[a] substantial body of contemporary scholarship and research supports the proposition that, although males and females have significant areas of developmental overlap, they also have differing developmental needs that are deep-seated." Id., at 1434. While no one questioned that for many students a coeducational environment was nonetheless not inappropriate, that could not obscure the demonstrated benefits of single-sex colleges. For example, the District Court stated as

---

19. Admitting women to VMI would undoubtedly require alterations necessary to afford members of each sex privacy from the other sex in living arrangements, and to adjust aspects of the physical training programs. See Brief for Petitioner 27–29; cf. note following 10 U.S.C.A. § 4342 (academic and other standards for women admitted to the Military, Naval, and Air Force Academies "shall be the same as those required for male individuals, except for those minimum essential adjustments in such standards required because of physiological differences between male and female individuals"). Experience shows such adjustments are manageable.

follows: "One empirical study in evidence, not questioned by any expert, demonstrates that single-sex colleges provide better educational experiences than coeducational institutions. Students of both sexes become more academically involved, interact with faculty frequently, show larger increases in intellectual self-esteem and are more satisfied with practically all aspects of college experience (the sole exception is social life) compared with their counterparts in coeducational institutions. Attendance at an all-male college substantially increases the likelihood that a student will carry out career plans in law, business and college teaching, and also has a substantial positive effect on starting salaries in business. Women's colleges increase the chances that those who attend will obtain positions of leadership, complete the baccalaureate degree, and aspire to higher degrees." Id., at 1412. See also id., at 1434–1435 (factual findings). "[I]n the light of this very substantial authority favoring single-sex education," the District Court concluded that "the VMI Board's decision to maintain an all-male institution is fully justified even without taking into consideration the other unique features of VMI's teaching and training." Id., at 1412. This finding alone, which even this Court cannot dispute, should be sufficient to demonstrate the constitutionality of VMI's all-male composition.

[T]he Court [d]ismisses the District Court's " 'findings' on 'gender-based developmental differences' "on the ground that "[t]hese 'findings' restate the opinions of Virginia's expert witnesses, opinions about typically male or typically female 'tendencies.' "(quoting 766 F.Supp., at 1434–1435). How remarkable to criticize the District Court on the ground that its findings rest on the evidence (i.e., the testimony of Virginia's witnesses)! That is what findings are supposed to do.

NO CHILD LEFT BEHIND ACT: GUIDE TO FREQUENTLY ASKED QUESTIONS (2005)

Committee on Education and the Workforce, United States House of Representatives.

On March 3, 2004, the Department of Education proposed to clarify its regulations regarding when single-sex classes and schools are permitted at the elementary and secondary school levels. [T]he proposal addresses two specific areas—single sex classes and single sex schools. With regard to classes, current regulations prohibit school districts (and private schools that receive federal assistance) from offering single-sex classes except in areas involving physical education, sex education, or chorus. The proposed changes would allow these schools and districts to offer single-sex classes when the single-sex nature of the class is substantially related (a) to providing a diversity of educational options or (b) to meeting the particular, identified needs of students. Schools and districts must treat male and female students evenhandedly in providing single-sex classes. Student participation in single-sex classes would be on a *voluntary* basis. A substantially equal coeducational class in the same subject would always be required. Schools and districts would be required to evaluate single-sex classes periodically to ensure consistency with these nondiscrimination requirements. While currently a school district may provide a single-sex public school when it offers comparable benefits and opportunities to students of the other sex in another school, the Department has interpreted this provision to require two comparable single-sex schools, one for boys and one for girls. The proposed change would clarify that a district that provides a single-sex public school may offer the required substantially equal benefits and opportunities to students of the other sex in either a single-sex school or coeducational school.

B.   THE FIRST AMENDMENT: OBSCENITY

In Chapter One, we considered the use of social science evidence to determine the factual question of whether a given film or publication violated "community standards", and hence fulfilled one of the Supreme Court's criteria for obscenity. Here, we examine the logically prior lawmaking question: can the State, consistent with the First Amendment, proscribe obscene material at all? The First Amendment to the Constitution states that "Congress shall make no law ... abridging the freedom of speech, or of the press."

UNITED STATES v. ROTH

United States Court of Appeals, Second Circuit, 1956.
237 F.2d 796.

■ CLARK, CHIEF JUDGE.

[Samuel Roth was convicted by a district court jury of four counts of mailing materials alleged to be "obscene, lewd, lascivious, filthy and of an indecent character." He was sentenced to five years imprisonment. On appeal, he attacked the statute as violating the First Amendment.]

We can understand all the difficulties of censorship of great literature, and indeed the various foolish excesses involved in the banning of notable books, without feeling justified in casting doubt upon all criminal prosecutions, both state and federal, of commercialized obscenity. A serious problem does arise when real literature is censored; but in this case no such issues should arise, since the record shows only salable pornography. But even if we had more freedom to follow an impulse to strike down such legislation in the premises, we should need to pause because of our own lack of knowledge of the social bearing of this problem, or consequences of such an act;[4] and we are hardly justified in rejecting out of hand the

4. See Fuld, J., in Brown v. Kingsley Books, Inc., 1 N.Y.2d 177, 151 N.Y.S.2d 639, 641, note 3, 134 N.E.2d 461, 463: "It is noteworthy that studies are for the first time being made, through such scientific skills as exist, concerning the impact of the obscene, in writings and other mass media, on the mind and behavior of men, women and children. (See, e.g., Jahoda and Staff of Research Center for Human Relations, New York University [1954]. The Impact of Literature: A Psychological Discussion of Some Assumptions in the Censorship Debate.)"

strongly held views of those with competence in the premises as to the very direct connection of this traffic with the development of juvenile delinquency. We conclude, therefore, that the attack on constitutionality of this statute must here fail.

■ FRANK, CIRCUIT JUDGE (concurring).

[Appendix to concurring opinion.]

As a judge of an inferior court, I am constrained by opinions of the Supreme Court concerning the obscenity statute to hold that legislation valid. Since, however, I think [t]hat none of those opinions has carefully canvassed the problem in the light of the Supreme Court's interpretation of the First Amendment, especially as expressed by the Court in recent years, I deem it not improper to set forth, in the following, factors which I think deserve consideration in passing on the constitutionality of that statute.

[N]o adequate knowledge is available concerning the effects on the conduct of normal adults of reading or seeing the "obscene"

Suppose we assume, *arguendo,* that sexual thoughts or feelings, stirred by the "obscene," probably will often issue into overt conduct. Still it does not at all follow that that conduct will be anti-social. For no sane person can believe it socially harmful if sexual desires lead to normal, and not anti-social, sexual behavior since, without such behavior, the human race would soon disappear.

Doubtless, Congress could validly provide punishment for mailing any publications if there were some moderately substantial reliable data showing that reading or seeing those publications probably conduces to seriously harmful sexual conduct on the part of normal adult human beings. But we have no such data.

Suppose it argued that whatever excites sexual longings might *possibly* produce sexual misconduct. That cannot suffice: Notoriously, perfumes sometimes act as aphrodisiacs, yet no one will suggest that therefore Congress may constitutionally legislate punishment for mailing perfumes.

[E]ffect of "obscenity" on adult conduct

To date there exist, I think, no thorough-going studies by competent persons which justify the conclusion that normal adults' reading or seeing of the "obscene" probably induces anti-social conduct. Such competent studies as have been made do conclude that so complex and numerous are the causes of sexual vice that it is impossible to assert with any assurance that "obscenity" represents a ponderable causal factor in sexually deviant adult behavior. [W]hat little competent research has been done, points definitely in a direction precisely opposite to that assumption.

[T]he following is a recent summary of studies of [the relationship of obscenity to juvenile delinquency][33] "(1) Scientific studies of juvenile delin-

---

33. Lockhart & McClure, Literature.   38 Minn.L.Rev. (1954), 295, 385–386.
The Law of Obscenity and the Constitution,

quency demonstrate that those who get into trouble, and are the greatest concern of the advocates of censorship, are far less inclined to read than those who do not become delinquent. [(2)] Sheldon and Eleanor Glueck, who are among the country's leading authorities on the treatment and causes of juvenile delinquency, have recently published the results of a ten-year study of its causes. They exhaustively studied approximately 90 factors and influences that might lead to or explain juvenile delinquency; but the Gluecks gave no consideration to the type of reading material, if any were read by the delinquents. This is, of course, consistent with their finding that delinquents read very little. When those who know so much about the problem of delinquency among youth—the very group about whom the advocates of censorship are most concerned—conclude that what delinquents read has so little effect upon their conduct that it is not worth investigating in an exhaustive study of causes, there is good reason for serious doubts concerning the basic hypothesis on which obscenity censorship is dependent. (3) The many other influences in society that stimulate sexual desire are so much more frequent in their influence and so much more potent in their effect that the influence of reading is likely, at most, to be relatively insignificant in the composite of forces that lead an individual into conduct deviating from the community sex standards.... And the studies demonstrating that sex knowledge seldom results from reading indicates the relative unimportance of literature in sexual thoughts and behavior as compared with other factors in society."

Judge Clark, however, speaks of "the strongly held views of those with competence in the premises as to the very direct connection" of obscenity "with the development of juvenile delinquency." He cites and quotes from a recent opinion of the New York Court of Appeals and an article by Judge Vanderbilt, which in turn, cite the writings of persons thus described by Judge Clark as "those with competence in the premises." One of the cited writings is a report, by Dr. Jahoda and associates, entitled The Impact of Literature: A Psychological Discussion of Some Assumptions in the Censorship Debate (1954). I have read this report (which is a careful survey of all available studies and psychological theories). I think it expresses an attitude quite contrary to that indicated by Judge Clark. In order to avoid any possible bias in my interpretation of that report, I thought it well to ask Dr. Jahoda to write her own summary of it, which, with her permission, I shall quote. (In doing so, I am following the example of Mr. Justice Jackson who, in Federal Trade Commission v. Ruberoid Co., 343 U.S. 470, 485, 72 S.Ct. 800, 809, 96 L.Ed. 1081, acknowledged that he relied on "an unpublished treatise", i.e., one not available to the parties. If that practice is proper, I think it similarly proper to quote an author's unpublished interpretation of a published treatise.) Dr. Jahoda's summary reads as follows:

"Persons who argue for increased censorship of printed matter often operate on the assumption that reading about sexual matters or about violence and brutality leads to anti-social actions, particularly to juvenile delinquency. An examination of the pertinent psychological literature has led to the following conclusions:

"1.   There exists no research evidence either to prove or to disprove this assumption definitively.

"2.   In the absence of scientific proof two lines of psychological approach to the examination of the assumption are possible: (a) a review of what is known on the causes of juvenile delinquency; and (b) review of what is known about the effect of literature on the mind of the reader.

"3.   In the vast research literature on the causes of juvenile delinquency there is no evidence to justify the assumption that reading about sexual matters or about violence leads to delinquent acts. Experts on juvenile delinquency agree that it has no single cause. Most of them regard early childhood events, which precede the reading age, as a necessary condition for later delinquency. At a later age, the nature of personal relations is assumed to have much greater power in determining a delinquent career than the vicarious experiences provided by reading matter. Juvenile delinquents as a group read less, and less easily, than non-delinquents. Individual instances are reported in which so-called 'good' books allegedly influenced a delinquent in the manner in which 'bad' books are assumed to influence him.

"Where childhood experiences and subsequent events have combined to make delinquency psychologically likely, reading could have one of two effects: it could serve a trigger function releasing the criminal act or it could provide for a substitute outlet of aggression in fantasy, dispensing with the need for criminal action. There is no empirical evidence in either direction.

"4.   With regard to the impact of literature on the mind of the reader, it must be pointed out that there is a vast overlap in content between all media of mass communication. The daily press, television, radio, movies, books and comics all present their share of so-called 'bad' material, some with great realism as reports of actual events, some in clearly fictionalized form. It is virtually impossible to isolate the impact of one of these media on a population exposed to all of them. Some evidence suggests that the particular communications which arrest the attention of an individual are in good part a matter of choice. As a rule, people do not expose themselves to everything that is offered, but only to what agrees with their inclinations."

[M]aybe some day we will have enough reliable data to show that obscene books and pictures do tend to influence children's sexual conduct adversely. Then a federal statute could be enacted which would avoid constitutional defects by authorizing punishment for using the mails or interstate shipments in the sale of such books and pictures to children.

———

NOTES

1.   Judicial Notice. In his concurring opinion in United States v. Roth, Judge Frank "thought it well to ask Dr. Jahoda to write her own summary" of the research on the relationship between obscenity and crime. See Federal Rule of Evidence 201 and the Advisory Committee Note in Appendix A and the American Bar Association's Code of Judicial Conduct (1999), which provides in Canon 3:

> A judge shall not initiate, permit, or consider ex parte communications, or consider other communications made to the judge outside the presence of the parties concerning a pending or impending proceeding.

In Commentary, the Code states "An appropriate and often desirable procedure for a court to obtain the advice of a disinterested expert on legal issues is to invite the expert to file a brief amicus curiae."

In this regard, T. Marvell, in a major study of appellate courts, *Appellate Courts and Lawyers* (1978), reported numerous instances of judges seeking informal expert assistance. For example, one judge said that he talked to his doctor during an annual physical examination about the practical effect a proposed ruling would have on surgeons' dealings with their patients. Marvell noted, id. at 98, 99:

> Some judges send their clerks to professors rather than go themselves, and clerks are not likely to get advice without being directed to do so. [T]his advice is ordinarily obtained over the telephone or in informal meetings; written communication about the cases outside regular channels is uncommon.

> [M]uch, if not most of the information sought [i]s information about [legislative] facts, such as the practical consequences of a proposed ruling. [T]heoretically, outsiders are not supposed to know anything about the court's deliberations. But by asking for advice a judge would imply that he is writing on the case, and he may disclose how he is leaning. For this reason questions are generally posed in the abstract without giving the name or specific facts of the case.

2.   Burden of Proof. The Supreme Court ultimately upheld the Second Circuit's Roth decision, 354 U.S. 476, 77 S.Ct. 1304, 1 L.Ed.2d 1498 (1957), with Justice Brennan writing for the court and concluding that "obscenity is not within the area of constitutionally protected speech or press." Justice Douglas (joined by Justice Black) dissented, however, citing at 510–511, 77 S.Ct. at 1322–1323 the same data as Judge Frank in his concurrence:

> If we were certain that impurity of sexual thoughts impelled to action, we would be on less dangerous ground in punishing the distributors of this sex literature. But it is by no means clear that obscene literature, as so defined, is a significant factor in influencing substantial deviations from the community standards. [T]he absence of dependable information on the effect of obscene literature on human conduct should make us wary. It should put us on the side of protecting society's interest in literature, except and unless it can be said that the particular publication has an impact on action that the government can control.

––––––––

REPORT OF THE COMMISSION ON OBSCENITY AND PORNOGRAPHY (1970)

A number of empirical studies conducted recently by psychiatrists, psychologists, and sociologists attempted to assess the effects of exposure to explicit sexual materials. [T]he findings of available research are summarized below.

[C]riminal and Delinquent Behavior

Delinquent and nondelinquent youth report generally similar experiences with explicit sexual materials. Exposure to sexual materials is widespread among both groups. The age of first exposure, the kinds of materials to which they are exposed, the amount of their exposure, the circumstances of exposure, and their reactions to erotic stimuli are essentially the same, particularly when family and neighborhood backgrounds are held constant. There is some evidence that peer group pressure accounts for both sexual experience and exposure to erotic materials among youth. A study of a heterogeneous group of young people found that exposure to erotica had no impact upon moral character over and above that of a generally deviant background.

Statistical studies of the relationship between availability of erotic materials and the rates of sex crimes in Denmark indicate that the increased availability of explicit sexual materials has been accompanied by a decrease in the incidence of sexual crime. Analysis of police records of the same types of sex crimes in Copenhagen during the past 12 years revealed that a dramatic decrease in reported sex crimes occurred during this period and that the decrease coincided with changes in Danish law which permitted wider availability of explicit sexual materials. Other research showed that the decrease in reported sexual offenses cannot be attributed to concurrent changes in the social and legal definitions of sex crimes or in public attitudes toward reporting such crimes to the police, or in police reporting procedures.

Statistical studies of the relationship between the availability of erotic material and the rates of sex crimes in the United States presents a more complex picture. During the period in which there has been a marked increase in the availability of erotic materials, some specific rates of arrest for sex crimes have increased (e.g., forcible rape) and others have declined (e.g., overall juvenile rates). For juveniles, the overall rate of arrests for sex crimes decreased even though arrests for nonsexual crimes increased by more than 100%. For adults, arrests for sex offenses increased slightly more than did arrests for nonsex offenses. The conclusion is that, for America, the relationship between the availability of erotica and changes in sex crime rates neither proves nor disproves the possibility that availability of erotica leads to crime, but the massive overall increases in sex crimes that have been alleged do not seem to have occurred.

Available research indicates that sex offenders have had less adolescent experience with erotica than other adults. They do not differ significantly from other adults in relation to adult experience with erotica, in relation to reported arousal or in relation to the likelihood of engaging in sexual behavior during or following exposure. Available evidence suggests that sex offenders' early inexperience with erotic material is a reflection of their more generally deprived sexual environment. The relative absence of experience appears to constitute another indicator of atypical and inadequate sexual socialization.

In sum, empirical research designed to clarify the question has found no evidence to date that exposure to explicit sexual materials plays a significant role in the causation of delinquent or criminal behavior among youth or adults. The Commission cannot conclude that exposure to erotic materials is a factor in the causation of sex crime or sex delinquency.

Dissent by Commissioners Morton A. Hill, S.J., and Winfrey C. Link, Concurred in by Charles H. Keating, Jr.

We feel impelled to issue this report in vigorous dissent.

The conclusions and recommendations in the majority report will be found deeply offensive to Congress and to tens of millions of Americans. And what the American people do not know is that the scanty and manipulated evidence contained within this report is wholly inadequate to support the conclusions and sustain the recommendations. Thus, both conclusions and recommendations are, in our view, fraudulent.

What the American people have here for the two million dollars voted by Congress, and paid by the taxpayer, is a shoddy piece of scholarship that will be quoted ad nauseam by cultural polluters and their attorneys within society.

The fundamental "finding" on which the entire report is based is: that "empirical research" has come up with "no reliable evidence to indicate that exposure to explicitly sexual materials plays a significant role in the causation of delinquent or criminal behavior among youth or adults."

The inference from this statement, i.e., pornography is harmless, is not only insupportable on the slanted evidence presented; it is preposterous. How isolate one factor and say it causes or does not cause criminal behavior? How determine that one book or one film caused one man to commit rape or murder? A man's entire life goes into one criminal act. No one factor can be said to have caused that act.

The Commission has deliberately and carefully avoided coming to grips with the basic underlying issue. The government interest in regulating pornography has always related primarily to the prevention of moral corruption and *not* to prevention of overt criminal acts and conduct, or the protection of persons from being shocked and/or offended.

The basic question is whether and to what extent society may establish and maintain certain moral standards. If it is conceded that society has a legitimate concern in maintaining moral standards, it follows logically that government has a legitimate interest in at least attempting to protect such standards against any source which threatens them.

[W]e believe it is impossible, and totally unnecessary, to attempt to prove or disprove a cause-effect relationship between pornography and criminal behavior.

———

PARIS ADULT THEATRE I v. SLATON

Supreme Court of the United States, 1973.
413 U.S. 49, 93 S.Ct. 2628, 37 L.Ed.2d 446.

■ MR. CHIEF JUSTICE BURGER delivered the opinion of the Court.

[In two cases decided on the same day, Miller v. California, 413 U.S. 15, 93 S.Ct. 2607, 37 L.Ed.2d 419 (1973), and Paris Adult Theatre I v. Slaton, the Supreme Court established the obscenity "test" currently in use. Chief Justice Burger, writing in *Miller* for five members of the court, stated, "The basic guidelines for the trier of fact must be: (a) whether 'the average person, applying contemporary community standards' would find that the work, taken as a whole, appeals to the prurient interest, (b) whether the work depicts or describes, in a patently offensive way, sexual conduct specifically defined by the applicable state law; and (c) whether the work, taken as a whole, lacks serious literary, artistic, political, or scientific value." 413 U.S. at 24, 93 S.Ct. at 2614. The Supreme Court considered the empirical issues raised by obscenity statutes in *Paris,* which concerned a Georgia civil proceeding to enjoin the showing of allegedly obscene films at two "adult" theaters in Atlanta. The trial judge had dismissed the complaint, and the Georgia Supreme Court had reversed the dismissal.]

We hold that there are legitimate state interests at stake in stemming the tide of commercialized obscenity, even assuming it is feasible to enforce effective safeguards against exposure to juveniles and to passersby. Rights and interests "other than those of the advocates are involved." Breard v. Alexandria, 341 U.S. 622, 642 (1951). These include the interest of the public in the quality of life and the total community environment, the tone of commerce in the great city centers, and, possibly, the public safety itself. The Hill-Link Minority Report of the Commission on Obscenity and Pornography indicates that there is at least an arguable correlation between obscene material and crime.[8]

8. The Report of the Commission on Obscenity and Pornography 390–412 (1970). For a discussion of earlier studies indicating "a division of thought [among behavioral scientists] on the correlation between obscenity and socially deleterious behavior," Memoirs v. Massachusetts, [383 U.S. 413, 86 S.Ct. 975, 16 L.Ed.2d 1 (1966)] at 451, and references to expert opinions that obscene material may induce crime and antisocial conduct, see id., at 451–453 (Clark, J., dissenting). Mr. Justice Clark emphasized:

"While erotic stimulation caused by pornography may be legally insignificant in itself, there are medical experts who believe that such stimulation frequently manifests itself in criminal sexual behavior or other antisocial conduct. For example, Dr. George W. Henry of Cornell University has expressed the opinion that obscenity, with its exaggerated and morbid emphasis on sex, particularly abnormal and perverted practices, and its unrealistic presentation of sexual behavior and attitudes, may induce antisocial conduct

[B]ut, it is argued, there are no scientific data which conclusively demonstrate that exposure to obscene material adversely affects men and women or their society. It is urged on behalf of the petitioners that, absent such a demonstration, any kind of state regulation is "impermissible." We reject this argument. It is not for us to resolve empirical uncertainties underlying state legislation, save in the exceptional case where that legislation plainly impinges upon rights protected by the Constitution itself. Mr. Justice Brennan, speaking for the Court in Ginsberg v. New York, 390 U.S. 629, 642–643, 88 S.Ct. 1274, 1282, 20 L.Ed.2d 195 (1968), said: "We do not demand of legislatures 'scientifically certain criteria of legislation.' Noble State Bank v. Haskell, 219 U.S. 104, 110 (31 S.Ct. 186, 187) 55 L.Ed. 112." Although there is no conclusive proof of a connection between antisocial behavior and obscene material, the legislature of Georgia could quite reasonably determine that such a connection does or might exist. In deciding *Roth,* this Court implicitly accepted that a legislature could legitimately act on such a conclusion to protect *"the social interest in order and morality."* Roth v. United States, 354 U.S., at 485, 77 S.Ct. at 1309, quoting Chaplinsky v. New Hampshire, 315 U.S. 568, 572, 62 S.Ct. 766, 769, 86 L.Ed. 1031 (1942) (emphasis added in *Roth*).

From the beginning of civilized societies, legislators and judges have acted on various unprovable assumptions. Such assumptions underlie much lawful state regulation of commercial and business affairs. [O]n the basis of these assumptions both Congress and state legislatures have, for example, drastically restricted associational rights by adopting antitrust laws, and have strictly regulated public expression by issuers of and dealers in securities. [U]nderstandably those who entertain an absolutist view of the First Amendment find it uncomfortable to explain why rights of association, speech, and press should be severely restrained in the marketplace of goods and money, but not in the marketplace of pornography.

Likewise, when legislatures and administrators act to protect the physical environment from pollution and to preserve our resources of forests, streams, and parks, they must act on such imponderables as the impact of a new highway near or through an existing park or wilderness area. [T]he fact that a congressional directive reflects unprovable assumptions about what is good for the people, including imponderable aesthetic assumptions, is not a sufficient reason to find that statute unconstitutional.

If we accept the unprovable assumption that a complete education requires the reading of certain books, and the well nigh universal belief that good books, plays, and art lift the spirit, improve the mind, enrich the human personality, and develop character, can we then say that a state

by the average person. A number of sociologists think that this material may have adverse effects upon individual mental health, with potentially disruptive consequences for the community.

"Congress and the legislatures of every State have enacted measures to restrict the distribution of erotic and pornographic material, justifying these controls by reference to evidence that antisocial behavior may result in part from reading obscenity." Id., at 452–453, 86 S.Ct., at 994–995 (footnotes omitted).

legislature may not act on the corollary assumption that commerce in obscene books, or public exhibitions focused on obscene conduct, have a tendency to exert a corrupting and debasing impact leading to antisocial behavior?

[T]he sum of experience, including that of the past two decades, affords an ample basis for legislatures to conclude that a sensitive, key relationship of human existence, central to family life, community welfare, and the development of human personality, can be debased and distorted by crass commercial exploitation of sex. Nothing in the Constitution prohibits a State from reaching such a conclusion and acting on it legislatively simply because there is no conclusive evidence or empirical data.

FACTS IN LAWMAKING

Kenneth Culp Davis.
80 Columbia Law Review 931 (1980).

The Court in *Paris* relied on a 1970 minority report of two of the nineteen members of the Commission on Obscenity and Pornography, and said that the question of legislative fact was "arguable" on one side, without saying whether it was "arguable" on the other side.

[T]he Court's inaccurate factfinding in the *Paris* case is obviously deplorable, but the deficiencies run much deeper: (1) The Court should recognize its affirmative responsibility to assure that reasonably available legislative facts that may affect its lawmaking are adequately developed. (2) When facts presented by the parties are inadequate, it should, unless it does its own research, either request factual briefs on designated questions or remand for factual development on those questions. (3) When extra record facts are crucial in its lawmaking, it should address the question whether procedural fairness requires that parties be given a pre-decision chance to challenge the facts it uses.

NEW YORK v. FERBER

Supreme Court of the United States, 1982.
458 U.S. 747, 102 S.Ct. 3348, 73 L.Ed.2d 1113.

■ JUSTICE WHITE delivered the opinion of the Court.

[Paul Ferber, the proprietor of a Manhattan bookstore, sold an undercover police officer two films of young boys masturbating. He was convicted under a state statute prohibiting promotion of a sexual performance by a child under sixteen years old. The New York Court of Appeals reversed, holding that the statute—which did not require proof that the performance be obscene—violated the First Amendment. The Supreme Court granted certiorari "presenting the single question: 'To prevent the abuse of children who are made to engage in sexual conduct for commercial purposes, could the New York State Legislature, consistent with the First Amendment, prohibit the dissemination of material which shows children engaged in sexual conduct, regardless of whether such material is obscene?' ''']

Like obscenity statutes, laws directed at the dissemination of child pornography run the risk of suppressing protected expression by allowing the hand of the censor to become unduly heavy. For the following reasons, however, we are persuaded that the States are entitled to greater leeway in the regulation of pornographic depictions of children.

First. It is evident beyond the need for elaboration that a state's interest in "safeguarding the physical and psychological well being of a minor" is "compelling." [T]he prevention of sexual exploitation and abuse of children constitutes a government objective of surpassing importance. [S]uffice it to say that virtually all of the States and the United States have passed legislation proscribing the production of or otherwise combatting "child pornography." The legislative judgment, as well as the judgment found in the relevant literature, is that the use of children as subjects of pornographic materials is harmful to the physiological, emotional, and mental health of the child.[9] That judgment, we think, easily passes muster under the First Amendment.

Second. The distribution of photographs and films depicting sexual activity by juveniles is intrinsically related to the sexual abuse of children in at least two ways. First, the materials produced are a permanent record of the children's participation and the harm to the child is exacerbated by their circulation.[10] Second, the distribution network for child pornography

---

9. "[T]he use of children as ... subjects of pornographic materials is very harmful to both the children and the society as a whole." S.Rep. No. 95–438, p. 5 (1978). It has been found that sexually exploited children are unable to develop healthy affectionate relationships in later life, have sexual dysfunctions, and have a tendency to become sexual abusers as adults. Schoettle, Child Exploitation: A Study of Child Pornography, 19 J.Am.Acad. Child Psych. 289, 296 (1980) (hereafter cited as Child Exploitation); Schoettle, Treatment of the Child Pornography Patient, 137 Am.J.Psych. 1109, 1110 (1980); Densen-Gerner, Child Prostitution and Child Pornography: Medical, Legal and Societal Aspects of the Commercial Exploitation of Children, reprinted in U.S. Dept. of Health and Human Services, Sexual Abuse of Children: Selected Readings 77, 80 (1980) (hereafter cited as Commercial Exploitation) (sexually exploited children predisposed to self-destructive behavior such as drug and alcohol abuse or prostitution). See generally A. Burgess & L. Holmstrom, Accessory-to-Sex: Pressure, Sex and Secrecy, in A. Burgess, A. Groth, L. Holmstrom, and S. Sgroi, Sexual Assault of Children and Adolescents 85, 94 (1978); V. DeFrancis, Protecting the Child Victim of Sex Crimes Committed by Adults, 169 (1969); Ellerstein & Canavan, Sexual Abuse of Boys, 134 Am.J.Diseases of Children 255, 256–257 (1980); Finch, Adult Seduction of the Child: Effects on the Child, Med. Aspects of Human Sexuality 170, 185 (Mar.1973); Groth, Sexual Trauma in the Life Histories of Rapists and Child Molesters, 4 Victimology 10 (1979). Sexual molestation by adults is often involved in the production of child sexual performances. Sexual Exploitation of Children, A Report to Illinois General Assembly by the Illinois Legislative Investigatory Comm'n at 30–31 (1980) (hereafter cited as Ill.Comm'n). When such performances are recorded and distributed, the child's privacy interests are also invaded.

10. As one authority has explained:

"[P]ornography poses an even greater threat to the child victim than does sexual abuse or prostitution. Because the child's actions are reduced to a recording, the pornog-

must be closed if the production of material which requires the sexual exploitation of children is to be effectively controlled. Indeed, there is no serious contention that the legislature was unjustified in believing that it is difficult, if not impossible, to halt the exploitation of children by pursuing only those who produce the photographs and movies.

[T]hird. The advertising and selling of child pornography provides an economic motive for and is thus an integral part of the production of such materials, an activity illegal throughout the Nation. "It rarely has been suggested that the constitutional freedom for speech and press extends its immunity to speech or writing used as an integral part of conduct in violation of a valid criminal statute." Giboney v. Empire Storage & Ice Co., 336 U.S. 490, 498, 69 S.Ct. 684, 688, 93 L.Ed. 834 (1949).

[F]ourth. The value of permitting live performances and photographic reproductions of children engaged in lewd sexual conduct is exceedingly modest, if not *de minimis*. We consider it unlikely that visual depictions of children performing sexual acts or lewdly exhibiting their genitals would often constitute an important and necessary part of a literary performance or scientific or educational work.

[F]ifth. Recognizing and classifying child pornography as a category of material outside the protection of the First Amendment is not incompatible with our earlier decisions. "The question whether speech is, or is not, protected by the First Amendment often depends on the content of the speech." Young v. American Mini Theatres, 427 U.S. 50, 66, 96 S.Ct. 2440, 2450, 49 L.Ed.2d 310 (Opinion of JUSTICE STEVENS, joined by THE CHIEF JUSTICE, JUSTICE WHITE, and JUSTICE REHNQUIST). [T]hus it is not rare that a content-based classification of speech has been accepted because it may be appropriately generalized that within the confines of the given classification, the evil to be restricted so overwhelmingly outweighs the expressive interests, if any, at stake, that no process of case-by-case adjudication is required. When a definable class of material such as that covered by § 263.15, bears so heavily and pervasively on the welfare of children engaged in its production we think the balance of competing interests is clearly struck and that it is permissible to consider these materials as without the protection of the First Amendment.

---

raphy may haunt him in future years, long after the original misdeed took place. A child who has posed for the camera must go through life knowing that the recording is circulating within the mass distribution system for child pornography." Shouvlin, Preventing the Sexual Exploitation of Children: A Model Act, 17 Wake Forest L.Rev. 535, 545 (1981).

See also Schoettle, Child Exploitation, at 292 ("[I]t is the fear of exposure and the tension of keeping the act secret that seem to have the most profound emotional repercussions"); Note, Protection of Children from Use in Pornography: Toward Constitutional and Enforceable Legislation, 12 U.Mich.J. Law Reform 295, 301 (1979) (hereafter cited as Use in Pornography) (interview with child psychiatrist) ("The victims knowledge of publication of the visual material increases the emotional and psychic harm suffered by the child.").

NOTE

1. Case Studies and Retrospective Surveys. Among the authorities Justice White cited in support of his statement that "it has been found that sexually exploited children are unable to develop healthy affectionate relationships in later life, have sexual dysfunctions, and have a tendency to become sexual abusers as adults," is Schoettle, Treatment of the Child Pornography Patient, 137 American Journal of Psychiatry 1109 (1980). That article is a brief case study of "Kathy," a 12-year old girl who, along with her siblings, engaged in photographed sexual acts with adults and with each other. The principal findings of this report are as follows, id. at 1109–1110:

> After police investigation of the child pornography ring, Kathy and her family were referred to our sex abuse clinic for psychiatric evaluation and weekly therapy. At the first session Kathy's complaints related to feeling guilty about being accused of involving her younger siblings in the sexual exploration schemes. [K]athy's history and presentation were consistent with a diagnosis of sexual deviation with associate depression.

Another study Justice White cited is Groth, Sexual Trauma in the Life Histories of Rapists and Child Molesters, 4 Victimology 10, 11 (1979), where the author stated:

> The subjects for this study consisted of 348 men convicted of sexual assault and referred to a security treatment center for diagnostic observation. Most of these offenders were recidivists. [D]ata pertaining to sexual trauma in the life histories of these men were retrieved through interviews with these subjects and/or a study of their clinical records. Sexual trauma was operationally defined as any sexual activity witnessed or experienced which was emotionally upsetting or disturbing to the subject. As a comparison group, sixty-two male law enforcement officers were administered an anonymous questionnaire in regard to sexual trauma experienced during their development. This police sample was roughly comparable to the offender sample in regard to age and socio-economic background.

> [E]vidence of some form of sexual trauma during their developmental years (ages one-fifteen) was found in the life histories of 106 (31 percent) of the subjects. No evidence of any sexual trauma was found for 203 (58 percent) of the subjects, and no data were available for thirty-nine (11 percent) of the subjects in this study. In comparison, only two (3 percent) of the sample of law enforcement officers reported any history of sexual trauma during their formative years.

REPORT OF THE ATTORNEY GENERAL'S COMMISSION ON PORNOGRAPHY (1986)

Summary for Violent and Nonviolent Sexually Explicit Materials.

In evaluating the results for sexually violent material, it appears that exposure to such materials (1) leads to a greater acceptance of rape myths and violence against women; (2) have more pronounced effects when the victim is shown enjoying the use of force or violence; (3) is arousing for rapists and for some males in the general population; and (4) has resulted in sexual aggression against women in the laboratory.

[R]esearch has further demonstrated that such attitudes as rape myth acceptance and acceptance of violence against women are correlated with arousal to such materials and with "real-world" sexual aggression and that subjects who have demonstrated sexual aggression in the laboratory are also more likely to report using coercion and force in their actual sexual interactions. The validation of the measures used in his studies, the use of physiological measures of arousal, and the attempt to systematically examine patterns among different populations with a variety of measures, arousal, attitudinal and behavioral, all tend to provide the type of convergent validation we feel is required of social science evidence.

We are less confident about the findings for nonviolent sexually explicit materials and we hasten to add that this is not necessarily because this class of materials has no effects but because the wide variety of effects obtained needs to be more systematically examined and explained.

[I]t is clear that the conclusion of "no negative effects" advanced by the 1970 Commission is no longer tenable. It is also clear that catharsis, as an explanatory model for the impact of pornography, is simply unwarranted by evidence in this area, nor has catharsis fared well in the general area of mass media effects and anti-social behavior.

This is not to say, however, that the evidence as a whole is comprehensive enough or definitive enough. While we have learned much more since 1970, even more areas remain to be explored.

What do we know at this point?

—It is clear that many sexually explicit materials, particularly of the commercial variety, that are obviously designed to be arousing, *are,* in fact, arousing, both to offenders and nonoffenders.

—Rapists appear to be aroused by both forced as well as consenting sex depictions while nonoffenders (our college males) are less aroused by depictions of sexual aggression. On the other hand, when these portrayals show the victim as "enjoying" the rape, these portrayals similarly elicit high arousal levels.

—Arousal to rape depictions appears to correlate with attitudes of acceptance of rape myths and sexual violence and both these measures likewise correlate with laboratory-observed aggressive behaviors.

—Depictions of sexual violence also increase the likelihood that rape myths are accepted and sexual violence toward women condoned. Such attitudes have further been found to be correlated with laboratory aggression toward women. Finally, there is also some evidence that laboratory aggression toward women correlates with self-reported sexually aggressive behaviors.

What we know about the effects of nonviolent sexually explicit material is less clear. There are tentative indications that negative effects in the areas of attitudes might also occur, particularly from massive exposure. The mechanics of such effects need to be elaborated more fully, however, particularly in light of more recent findings that suggest that degrading themes might have effects that differ from non violent, non-degrading sexually explicit materials. This is clearly an area that deserves further investigation.

—There are suggestions that pornography availability may be one of a nexus of socio-cultural factors that has some bearing on rape rates in this country. Other cross-cultural data, however, offer mixed results as well so these findings have to be viewed as tentative at best.

—We still know very little about the causes of deviancy and it is important to examine the developmental patterns of offenders, particularly patterns of early exposure. We do have some convergence on the data from some rapists and males in the general population in the areas of arousal and attitudes but again, this remains to be examined more closely.

Clearly, the need for more research remains as compelling as ever.

STATEMENT OF DR. JUDITH BECKER AND ELLEN LEVINE

The Commission sought to break down pornography into the various types of sexually explicit material available in our society. Unfortunately, social science research to date has not uniformly followed any such categorization (although we certainly suggest that future researchers consider this option), and the attempt to force the available social science data to fit the Commission's categories is fruitless. That is why in this statement the conclusions and interpretations of what the social science data *says* and *does not say* follow the research, not the Commission, categories.

First, it is essential to state that the social science research has not been designed to evaluate the relationship between exposure to pornography and the commission of sexual crimes; therefore efforts to tease the current data into proof of a causal link between these acts simply cannot be accepted. Furthermore, social science does not speak to harm, on which this Commission report focuses. Social science research speaks of a relationship among variables or effects that can be positive or negative.

Research has evaluated adults rather than children, and it is the latter who are most likely to be influenced by pornography. Studies have relied almost exclusively on male college student volunteers, which means that the "generalizability" of this data is extremely limited. The only other category studied in depth is sex offenders. Information from the sex-offender population must be interpreted with care because it may be self-serving. The research conducted to date has been correlational and experimental. Despite these limitations, the research data can be interpreted to indicate the following:

A. In a laboratory setting, exposure to sexually violent stimuli has a negative effect on research subjects as measured by acceptance of rape myth and aggression and callousness toward women. We do not know, however, how long this attitudinal change is sustained without further stimulation; more importantly, we do not know whether and why such an attitudinal change might transfer into a behavioral change. There is reason for concern about these findings because we do know that experience with sex offenders indicates they harbor belief systems and attitudes consistent with deviant sexual practices (e.g. "women enjoy being raped" or "sexual acts with a child are a way of showing love and affection to that child"). We know further that such attitudes appear to be a precursor and maintainer of actual deviant behavior in an offender population. Although we believe the potential exists for attitudinal changes to translate into behavioral changes in some circumstances, this possibility needs considerable additional investigation.

B. Very little social-science research has been conducted evaluating the impact of non-violent degrading material on the average adult. Furthermore, there is a problem of definition about what constitutes "degrading material." We strongly encourage further research to define and evaluate the impact of such material.

C. Although research findings are far from conclusive, the preponderance of existing data indicates that non-violent and non-degrading sexually explicit materials do not have a negative effect on adults.

D. In documents attached to the main report mention has been made of a possible relationship between circulation rates of pornographic magazines and sex crime rates. One of the authors of the study on which the Commission has based its conclusion, Murray Straus, has written to explain his own research, which he suggested was being misinterpreted. "I do not believe that this research demonstrates that pornography causes rape.... In general the scientific evidence clearly indicates that if one is concerned with the effects of media on rape, the problem lies in the prevalence of violence in the media, not on sex in the media."

E. To date there is no single comprehensive theory that is agreed upon to explain the development of paraphilic behavior. Human behavior is complex and multi-causal. To say that exposure to pornography in and of itself causes an individual to commit a sexual crime is simplistic, not supported by the social science data, and overlooks many of the other variables that may be contributing causes. Research must be conducted on the development of sexual interest patterns if we are to understand and control paraphilic behavior.

F.   Unfortunately, little is known about the impact of sexually explicit material on children. Ethically and morally one could not and would not conduct experiments to examine such a relationship. We do know that adolescents and young adults are large consumers of these materials, and little is yet known about its impact on this population. We underscore the statement made in the main body of the Commission's report regarding social science research: "In many respects, research is still at a fairly rudimentary stage, and with few attempts to standardize categories of analysis, self-reporting questionnaires, types of stimulus materials, description of stimulus materials, measurement of effects and related problems. We recommend that moneys be made available to fund further research on this topic."

THE ATTORNEY GENERAL'S COMMISSION ON PORNOGRAPHY: THE GAPS BETWEEN "FINDINGS" AND FACTS

Daniel Linz, Steven D. Penrod, and Edward Donnerstein.
1987 American Bar Foundation Research Journal 713 (1987).

The Commission maintains that there is a "causal relationship" between exposure to sexually violent pornography and negative changes in certain attitudes toward and perceptions of women, as well as increased aggression toward women. This statement is accurate as long as it refers to the results of laboratory studies examining sexually violent images. In the typical study, men are first exposed to depictions that show the female victim "enjoying" or reacting in a positive fashion to her mistreatment, and they are then asked to report on their attitudes and beliefs about rape victims and/or administer electric shocks or other forms of "punishment" to a female victim. The results of these studies have generally indicated that male subjects exposed to sexual violence of this sort show (1) changes in the perception of a rape victim (e.g., seeing her as less injured and more responsible for her assault); (2) changes in the perception of a rapist (e.g., seeing him as less responsible for his actions and as deserving less punishment); (3) greater acceptance of certain "rape myths"; and (4) more aggressive behavior toward a female target than control subjects. Depictions involving victims who abhor their experience *produce similar outcomes* depending on the population exposed to these materials.

However, there are at least two important considerations that should be kept in mind when applying the results of these social psychological experiments to legal decision making about pornography and obscenity. The first consideration is whether the changes in attitudes and behaviors following exposure to sexually violent material are due primarily to the sexually explicit context in which the violence is depicted, or to the violence itself, regardless of sexual explicitness. The second consideration is a methodological qualification that involves a familiar criticism of laboratory investigations of aggressive behavior.

Is Sexual Explicitness Necessary for Harmful Effects to Occur?

Depictions of women "enjoying" the application of force and of women as the deserving victims of sexual and nonsexual violence are pervasive in the mass media.

In a [r]ecent pair of studies, two of the authors of this essay systematically examined the relative contributions of the aggressive and sexual components of violent pornography. In the first study, male college students were angered by either a male or a female confederate and were then shown one of four different films. The first film [contained] aggressive pornography. The second was X-rated but contained no aggression or sexual coercion. Subjects rated the second film just as sexually and physiologically arousing as the first film. The third film contained scenes of aggression against women but without any sexual content. Subjects rated it as less sexually and physiologically arousing than the previous two films. The final film was of neutral content.

After viewing the films, the men were given the opportunity to aggress against male or female confederates of the experiment. The results showed that the men who viewed the film that was both aggressive and pornographic displayed the highest level of aggression against the woman, but the aggression-only film produced more aggression against the woman than did the sexually explicit film that contained no violence or coercion. In fact, there were no differences in aggression against the female target for subjects in the sex-only film condition and in the neutral film condition. In the second study, subjects who viewed the combination of sex and violence displayed higher levels of aggressive behavior than subjects in the sex-only group, and subjects exposed to the violence-only depiction also exhibited higher levels of aggression than the sex-only group.

[G]eneralizations From Laboratory Experiments

In addition to the fact that many of the experimental studies upon which the Commission bases its findings did not employ obscene or pornographic stimuli, the Commission also fails to exercise proper caution about generalizing the results of these studies to violent behavior outside the laboratory. Despite the higher level of causal certainty accorded the laboratory experiment relative to other forms of investigation, laboratory assessments of the effects of violent mass media on behavior are susceptible to many criticisms concerning external validity—for example, the extent to which findings obtained under laboratory conditions can be applied to persons, situations, and times outside the laboratory.

[T]he Commission should have acknowledged at least a few of the most important of those criticisms. Among them would be: (1) laboratory subjects may not perceive themselves as inflicting harm when experimenters ask them to perform very artificial forms of aggression in their interactions with a confederate; (2) outside the laboratory violence is not sanctioned, but inside the laboratory aggression is condoned, even encouraged, after the subject has viewed violent material; (3) all the studies examine subjects from a very narrow segment of the general population; (4) laboratory experiments may be generally susceptible to what has been termed an "experimenter demand effect," wherein subjects attempt to guess and then confirm the experimenter's hypothesis; (5) usually only studies that obtain positive results are published; and (6) no one yet has been able to come up with either an acceptable operational definition of aggressive behavior on the part of the subject who is supposedly reacting to the film or other media event, or an acceptable definition of what actually constitutes violence in the media depiction itself.

––––––

NOTES

1. External Validity of Research on Violent Pornography. One of the dependent measures in the research on violent pornography has been a question asking subjects the likelihood they would commit a rape "if they could not get caught." One study found that 51 percent of undergraduate males responded that their likelihood of committing a rape under these conditions was greater than zero. "It would seem highly inappropriate to argue that those subjects who indicated a possibility of engaging in rape, particularly under the hypothetical circumstances of being assured of not being caught, are actually likely to rape. This self-report, however, may be an indication of a tendency that in combination with other factors and in an exaggerated form may indeed be predictive of such assaults." Malamuth, Haber, and Feshbach, Testing Hypotheses Regarding Rape: Exposure to Sexual Violence, Sex Differences, and the "Normality" of Rapists, 14 Journal of Research in Personality 121, 134 (1980).

2. Ethics of Research on Violent Pornography. Clearly, the researchers conducting the studies described above could not terminate the research at the point that the subjects reported an increase in the likelihood of committing a rape, even under the hypothetical condition of not being caught. Rather, at the conclusion of the research, the "experimenter then brought the subject a debriefing sheet, which, for subjects who were exposed to rape depictions, stressed the violent nature of rape and presented several points designed to dispel rape myths. [A]ssessments of the effectiveness of such debriefings [c]onducted as long as 4 months following research participation [c]onsistently show that the overall impact of research participation that includes exposure to rape portrayals followed by debriefings is a reduction in subjects' acceptance of rape myths." Malamuth and Check, Sexual Arousal to Rape Depictions: Individual Differences, 92 Journal of Abnormal Psychology 55, 59 (1983).

3. Moral Decay and Social Harm. Linz, Donnerstein, Shafer, Land, McCall, and Graesser, Discrepancies between the Legal Code and Community Standards for Sex and Violence: An Empirical Challenge to Traditional Assumptions in Obscenity Law, 29 Law and Society Review 127 (1995), report a study in which residents of western Tennessee were randomly assigned to view sexually explicit films at issue in an obscenity case, violent films, or control films (neither sexually explicit nor violent). The researchers report finding tolerance for depictions of consensual sexual behavior, but substantial disapproval of violent sexual behavior such as rape or bondage. "Obscenity law with its emphasis on 'moral decay' appears to lie outside the community's scope of concern. Instead, the possible harms of exposure to violence appear most troubling." Id at 160–161. Linz et al conclude that these and other research results now "suggest that prosecutions most closely aligned with both community standards and harmful effects as identified by empirical research would involve materials that feature rape or other forms of sexual violence rather than consenting sexual depictions." Id at 162.

UNITED STATES v. EXTREME ASSOCIATES, INC.

United States District Court, Western District of Pennsylvania, 2005.
325 F.Supp.2d 578.

■ GARY L. LANCASTER, DISTRICT JUDGE.

This is a criminal prosecution charging nine counts of violating the federal obscenity statutes and one count of conspiracy based on that conduct. The United States has charged defendants Extreme Associates, Inc., Robert Zicari, and Janet Romano with distribution of obscene material via the mails and the Internet. Defendants are in the business of producing and selling sexually explicit films. Defendants have filed a motion to dismiss the indictment arguing that the federal obscenity laws infringe on the rights of liberty and privacy guaranteed by the due process clause of the United States Constitution.

[D]efendants do not dispute, for purposes of this motion, that the films involved in this case are obscene [a]s that term is defined in *Miller v. California,* 413 U.S. 15 (1973).

[T]he government contends that because the federal obscenity statutes have withstood constitutional attack for more than thirty-five years, this court lacks the authority to find that they are unconstitutional. On the merits, the government argues that there is no fundamental right involved in this case and that this court should not create a "new" fundamental right to commercially distribute obscene material. Because we find that the federal obscenity statutes place a burden on the exercise of the fundamental rights of liberty, privacy and speech recognized by the Supreme Court in *Stanley v. Georgia [394 U.S. 557, 568 (1969)],* we have applied the strict scrutiny test.

Recently, in a much publicized and analyzed case, the Supreme Court relied on a substantive due process analysis to strike down Texas' homosexual sodomy law. *Lawrence v. Texas,* 539 U.S. 558 (2003). The decision opens with the Court's declaration that "[l]iberty protects the person from unwarranted government intrusions into a dwelling or other private places." *Id.* at 562. [T]he Supreme Court found that a person's decisions about what personal relationships, including homosexual relationships, he will have in his own home are not to be controlled or criminalized by the government because the government finds such relationships to be immoral. *Id.* at 564–66, 578–79. Instead, the Court deemed such decisions to lie within a "realm of personal liberty which the government may not enter." *Id.* at 578 (citing *Casey,* 505 U.S. at 847). Because the case involved two consenting adults engaged in sexual activity in the privacy of their own home and not minors, persons who might be coerced or injured, public conduct, or prostitution, the Court found that no state interest—including promoting a moral code—could justify the law's intrusion into the personal and private life of the individuals involved. *Id.* at 578.

[T]he *Lawrence* decision [is] important to this case. It can be reasonably interpreted as holding that public morality is not a legitimate state interest sufficient to justify infringing on adult, private, consensual, sexual conduct even if that conduct is deemed offensive to the general public's sense of morality.

[T]he government has identified two state interests in this case: 1) the protection of unwitting adults from exposure to obscene materials; and 2) the protection of children from exposure to obscene materials.

a.   *Protection of Unwitting Adults*

It cannot be seriously disputed that, historically, the government's purpose in completely banning the distribution of sexually explicit obscene material, including to consenting adults, was to uphold the community sense of morality.[1] That is, to prevent, to the extent possible, individuals from entertaining lewd or lustful thoughts stimulated by viewing material that appeals to one's[2] prurient interests. Harboring such thoughts, the government deems, is immoral conduct even when done by consenting adults in private. Indeed, one of, if not the, principle underpinning of *Roth v. California,* in which the Supreme Court held that obscenity is not within the area of constitutionally protected speech, was the Court's unquestioned assumption that such material offends the community sense of morality. *Roth,* 354 U.S. at 485 (" . . . any benefit that may be derived from [lewd and obscene material] is clearly outweighed by the social interest in order and morality").

After *Lawrence,* however, upholding the public sense of morality is not even a legitimate state interest that can justify infringing one's liberty interest to engage in consensual sexual conduct in private. *Lawrence,* 539 U.S. at 578–79. Therefore, this historically asserted state interest certainly

---

1. The government admitted as much when it advanced as its compelling interest at oral argument "prohibiting the proliferation of obscenity in the community."

2. The court's use of the word "one's" is an understatement of great proportion. The pornography industry in the United States is estimated annually to be between $10 billion and $14 billion; generating more revenue than professional football, basketball and baseball put together, more than Hollywood's domestic box office receipts and larger than all the revenues generated by rock and country music recordings. Allison [Sanctioning Sodomy: The Supreme Court Liberates Gay Sex and Limits State Power to Vindicate the Moral Sentiments of the People, 39 Tulsa L. Rev 95 (2003)] at 148.

cannot rise to the level of a compelling interest, as is required under the strict scrutiny test.

Even if the government's asserted interest in keeping unwitting adults from inadvertently viewing this material could rise to the level of being a compelling state interest, the obscenity laws, as applied to these defendants, are not narrowly tailored to advance that interest. As such, they would nevertheless fail the strict scrutiny test.

Access to the video clips for which defendants are being prosecuted is limited to those people who: 1) access defendants' website; 2) join the members-only section of defendants' website, which requires a name and address; 3) pay a membership fee [of $89.95 for 90 days, renewable automatically], which requires a credit card; 4) are issued a password; 5) use the password to gain access to the obscene material; and, finally, 6) either view or download the material that they wish to view on a computer.

Therefore, due to the Internet access technology used by these defendants to distribute the video tapes and video clips charged in this case, the interest of protecting unwitting adults from inadvertent exposure to their material is not advanced at all, let alone by the least restrictive means possible. That is, defendants' mechanism of distributing the materials charged in this case dictate that only those individuals who want to see defendants' films, indeed, want to see them badly enough that they are willing to pay to see them, are able to do so.

[b]. Protection of Minors

Finally, the government asserts that protecting minors from exposure to obscene material is a governmental interest justifying a total ban on its distribution. We find that even if this interest qualifies as a compelling one, as applied to this case, the federal obscenity statutes are not narrowly drawn to serve that interest. [T]here are numerous ways to protect minors from exposure to obscene materials that are less restrictive than a complete ban on the distribution of such material to consenting adults. [C]omputer software is available that parents, or other supervising adults, can install on their computers that would effectively filter sexually explicit material when minors are surfing the Internet. This software allows the adult user to disable the filtering device when the computer is being used by an adult, if desired. Such software was recognized as an effective means of shielding minors from exposure to inappropriate material by the Supreme Court in *United States v. American Library Ass'n, Inc.*, 539 U.S. 194 (2003). [A]s was required by these defendants, prepayment with credit cards is another effective way to restrict access to inappropriate materials by minors. Significantly, the Federal Communications Commission has already determined that requiring prepayment by credit card effectively restricts minors' access to live 'dial-a-porn' messages. The Commission reasoned that because credit cards are not routinely issued to minors,[3] services which require credit card payment are usually limited to adults.

---

3. A review of the websites of the major credit card issuers such as Master Card, Visa, American Express and Discover, shows that all require that applicants be at least 18

[C]ONCLUSION

We find that the federal obscenity statutes burden an individual's fundamental right to possess, read, observe, and think about what he chooses in the privacy of his own home by completely banning the distribution of obscene materials. As such, we have applied the strict scrutiny test to those statutes. The federal obscenity statutes fail the strict scrutiny test because they are not narrowly drawn to advance the asserted governmental interests of protecting minors and unwitting adults from exposure to obscene materials, as applied to these defendants and the facts of this case. Because the federal obscenity statutes are unconstitutional as applied, defendants' indictment must be dismissed.

———

NOTE

1. **Government Appeal**. The Justice Department has appealed the District Court's decision in *Extreme Associates* to the Third Circuit. The Brief for the United States, dated April 11, 2005, states:

> The Court's recent decision in Lawrence v. Texas, 539 U.S. 558 (2003), does nothing to alter the Court's prior precedents. The holding of the Lawrence decision was based upon, and limited to, intimate sexual conduct between consenting adults in the privacy of their bedroom. [C]onsequently, the federal prohibition on the distribution of obscene material is subject to rational basis review, rather than the strict scrutiny which the district court incorrectly applied. And, the federal statutes prohibiting the distribution of obscenity easily pass rational basis review. [A]s the government argued below, in addition to its interest in protecting children and unwilling adults from exposure to obscenity, the government also has an interest in prohibiting the proliferation of obscenity in the community, upholding community standards, and protecting public morality. [T]he government's concern with the proliferation of obscenity and with preserving a decent and moral society remains not only a legitimate governmental interest, but also of utmost concern.[4]

years of age before being issued a credit card. *See* mastercard.com, usa.visa.com, discovercard.com, and americanexpress.com.

4. For example, recent testimony presented to the U.S. Senate Judiciary Subcommittee on the Constitution on February 16, 2005, reflects this concern, citing "compelling evidence" of the "horrible devastation," including "unhealthy, harmful sexual addiction, suicide, rape, and other crimes of violence," that "commercial pandering of obscene materials has on families and the moral fabric of our nation. That such material is linked to criminal, dangerous and unhealthy conduct is now well-established. We know the material restricted by federal obscenity statutes is horrifically harmful and devastatingly dangerous, especially to children." (Hearing Before the Senate Judiciary Subcommittee on the Constitution (statement of Professor William Wagner) (citing H.R. Rep. No. 105–775 at 11 (1998); Hearings, 105th Cong. 55–57, 84 (1998) (statement of Dr. Mary Anne Layden); and S. Rep. No. 106–141, at 1 (1999))).

C. THE SIXTH AMENDMENT: JURIES AND WITNESSES

The Sixth Amendment to the Constitution reads in part as follows:

In all criminal prosecutions, the accused shall enjoy the right to a speedy and public trial, by an impartial jury of the State and district wherein the crime shall have been committed, [and] to be confronted with the witnesses against him.

Social science research has been heavily implicated in three Sixth Amendment issues in recent years. The first concerns the minimum size of the group that constitutes a "jury." The second concerns whether juries that decide capital cases are "impartial." The third concerns whether a defendant is "confronted" with witnesses when those witnesses testify via videotape.

1. JURY SIZE

The number of decision-makers varies dramatically in different procedural systems. In some cultures, it is traditional to assemble an entire community to render a verdict; in other cultures, a single judge hears cases. The number of persons necessary to constitute a jury for purposes of the Sixth Amendment has been the focus of a number of Supreme Court cases since 1970.

WILLIAMS v. FLORIDA

Supreme Court of the United States, 1970.
399 U.S. 78, 90 S.Ct. 1893, 26 L.Ed.2d 446.

■ MR. JUSTICE WHITE delivered the opinion of the Court.

[After trial to a six-member jury, petitioner was convicted in a Florida court of robbery, and sentenced to life imprisonment. Petitioner challenged the Florida law which required that a six-member jury try all non-capital criminal cases as contrary to the Sixth and Fourteenth Amendments of the U.S. Constitution.]

In Duncan v. Louisiana, 391 U.S. 145, 88 S.Ct. 1444, 20 L.Ed.2d 491 (1968), we held that the Fourteenth Amendment guarantees a right to trial by jury in all criminal cases that—were they to be tried in a federal court—would come within the Sixth Amendment's guarantee. Petitioner's trial for robbery on July 3, 1968, clearly falls within the scope of that holding. The question in this case then is whether the constitutional guarantee of a trial by "jury" necessarily requires trial by exactly 12 persons, rather than some lesser number—in this case six. We hold that the 12-man panel is not a necessary ingredient of "trial by jury," and that respondent's refusal to impanel more than the six members provided for by Florida law did not violate petitioner's Sixth Amendment rights as applied to the States through the Fourteenth.

We had occasion in Duncan v. Louisiana, supra, to review briefly the oft-told history of the development of trial by jury in criminal cases. That history revealed a long tradition attaching great importance to the concept of relying on a body of one's peers to determine guilt or innocence as a safeguard against arbitrary law enforcement. That same history, however, affords little insight into the considerations that gradually led the size of that body to be generally fixed at 12. Some have suggested that the number 12 was fixed upon simply because that was the number of the presentment jury from the hundred, from which the petit jury developed. Other, less circular but more fanciful reasons for the number 12 have been given, "but they were all brought forward after the number was fixed," and rest on little more than mystical or superstitious insights into the significance of "12." Lord Coke's explanation that the "*number of twelve* is much respected *in holy writ,* as 12 *apostles,* 12 *stones,* 12 *tribes, etc.,*" is typical. In short, while sometime in the 14th century the size of the jury at common law came to be fixed generally at 12, that particular feature of the jury system appears to have been a historical accident, unrelated to the great purposes which gave rise to the jury in the first place. The question before us is whether this accidental feature of the jury has been immutably codified into our Constitution.

[T]here is absolutely no indication in "the intent of the framers" [of the Constitution] of an explicit decision to equate the constitutional and common-law characteristics of the jury.

Nothing in this history suggests, then, that we do violence to the letter of the Constitution by turning to other than purely historical considerations to determine which features of the jury system, as it existed at common law, were preserved in the Constitution. The relevant inquiry, as we see it, must be the function that the particular feature performs and its relation to the purposes of the jury trial. Measured by this standard, the 12-man requirement cannot be regarded as an indispensable component of the Sixth Amendment.

The purpose of the jury trial, as we noted in *Duncan,* is to prevent oppression by the Government. "Providing an accused with the right to be tried by a jury of his peers gave him an inestimable safeguard against the corrupt or overzealous prosecutor and against the complaint, biased, or eccentric judge." Duncan v. Louisiana, supra, at 156. Given this purpose, the essential feature of a jury obviously lies in the interposition between the accused and his accuser of the commonsense judgment of a group of laymen, and in the community participation and shared responsibility that results from that group's determination of guilt or innocence. The performance of this role is not a function of the particular number of the body that makes up the jury. To be sure, the number should probably be large enough to promote group deliberation, free from outside attempts at intimidation, and to provide a fair possibility for obtaining a representative cross-section of the community. But we find little reason to think that these goals are in any meaningful sense less likely to be achieved when the jury numbers six, than when it numbers 12—particularly if the requirement of unanimity is retained. And, certainly the reliability of the jury as a factfinder hardly seems likely to be a function of its size.

It might be suggested that the 12-man jury gives a defendant a greater advantage since he has more "chances" of finding a juror who will insist on acquittal and thus prevent conviction. But the advantage might just as easily belong to the State, which also needs only one juror out of twelve insisting on guilt to prevent acquittal. What few experiments have occurred—usually in the civil area—indicate that there is no discernible difference between the results reached by the two different-sized juries.[48] In short, neither currently available evidence nor theory[49] suggests that the 12-man jury is necessarily more advantageous to the defendant than a jury composed of fewer members.

[W]e conclude, in short, as we began: the fact that the jury at common law was composed of precisely 12 is a historical accident, unnecessary to effect the purposes of the jury system and wholly without significance "except to mystics." Duncan v. Louisiana, supra, 391 U.S., at 182, 88 S.Ct. at 1466 (Harlan, J., dissenting). To read the Sixth Amendment as forever codifying a feature so incidental to the real purpose of the Amendment is to ascribe a blind formalism to the Framers which would require considerably more evidence than we have been able to discover in the history and language of the Constitution or in the reasoning of our past decisions. [C]onsistent with this holding, we conclude that petitioner's Sixth Amendment rights, as applied to the States through the Fourteenth Amendment, were not violated by Florida's decision to provide a six-man rather than a 12-man jury.

---

48. See Wiehl, [The Six Man Jury, 4 Gonzaga Law Review 35, 40–41 (1968)]; Tamm, [The Five-Man Civil Jury, 51 Geo.L.J. 120, 134–136 (1962)]; Cronin, Six-Member Juries Tried in Massachusetts District Court, 42 J.Am.Jud.Soc., 136 (1958). See also New Jersey Experiments with Six-Man Jury, 9 Bull. of the Section of Jud.Admin. of the ABA (May 1966); Phillips, A Jury of Six in All Cases, 30 Conn.B.J. 354 (1956).

49. Studies of the operative factors contributing to small group deliberation and decisionmaking suggest that jurors in the minority on the first ballot are likely to be influenced by the proportional size of the majority aligned against them. See H. Kalven & H. Zeisel, The American Jury 462–463, 488–489 (1966); C. Hawkins, Interaction and Coalition Realignments in Consensus-Seeking Groups: A Study of Experimental Jury Deliberations 13, 146, 156, Aug. 17, 1960 (unpublished thesis on file at Library of Congress); cf. Asch, Effects of Group Pressure Upon the Modification and Distortion of Judgments in Readings in Social Psychology 2 (G. Swanson, T. Newcomb & E. Hartley et al., eds., 1952). See generally Note, On Instructing Deadlocked Juries, 78 Yale L.J. 100, 108 and n. 30 (and authorities cited), 110–111 (1968). Thus if a defendant needs initially to persuade four jurors that the State has not met its burden of proof in order to escape ultimate conviction by a 12-man jury, he arguably escapes by initially persuading half that number in a six-man jury: random reduction, within limits, of the absolute number of the jury would not affect the outcome. See also C. Joiner, Civil Justice and the Jury 31, 83 (1962) (concluding that the deliberative process should be the same in either the six-or 12-man jury).

COLGROVE v. BATTIN

Supreme Court of the United States, 1973.
413 U.S. 149, 93 S.Ct. 2448, 37 L.Ed.2d 522.

■ MR. JUSTICE BRENNAN delivered the opinion of the Court.

In Williams v. Florida, 399 U.S. 78, 90 S.Ct. 1893, 26 L.Ed.2d 446 (1970), the Court sustained the constitutionality of a Florida statute providing for six-member juries in certain criminal cases. The constitutional challenge rejected in that case relied on the guarantees of jury trial secured the accused by Art. III, § 2, cl. 3, of the Constitution and by the Sixth Amendment. We expressly reserved, however, the question whether "additional references to the 'common law' that occur in the Seventh Amendment might support a different interpretation" with respect to jury trial in civil cases. Id., at 92 n. 30, 90 S.Ct., at 1901. We conclude that they do not.

The pertinent words of the Seventh Amendment are: "In Suits at common law ... the right of trial by jury shall be preserved...." On its face, this language is not directed to jury characteristics, such as size, but rather defines the kind of cases for which jury trial is preserved, namely, "suits at common law."

[C]onsistently with the historical objective of the Seventh Amendment, our decisions have defined the jury right preserved in cases covered by the Amendment, as "the substance of the common-law right of trial by jury, as distinguished from mere matters of form or procedure...." Baltimore & Carolina Line, Inc. v. Redman, 295 U.S. 654, 657, 55 S.Ct. 890, 891, 79 L.Ed. 1636 (1935). The Amendment, therefore, does not "bind the federal courts to the exact procedural incidents or details of jury trial according to the common law in 1791," Galloway v. United States, 319 U.S. 372, 390, 63 S.Ct. 1077, 1087, 87 L.Ed. 1458 (1943).

[O]ur inquiry turns, then, to whether a jury of 12 is of the substance of the common-law right of trial by jury. Keeping in mind the purpose of the jury trial in criminal cases to prevent government oppression, *Williams,* 399 U.S., at 100, 90 S.Ct., at 1905, and, in criminal and civil cases, to assure a fair and equitable resolution of factual issues, Gasoline Products Co. v. Champlin Co., 283 U.S. 494, 498, 51 S.Ct. 513, 514, 75 L.Ed. 1188 (1931), the question comes down to whether jury performance is a function of jury size. In *Williams,* we rejected the notion that "the reliability of the jury as a factfinder ... [is] a function of its size," 399 U.S., at 100–101, 90 S.Ct., at 1906, and nothing has been suggested to lead us to alter that conclusion. Accordingly, we think it cannot be said that 12 members is a substantive aspect of the right of trial by jury.

[T]here remains, however, the question whether a jury of six satisfies the Seventh Amendment guarantee of "trial by jury." We had no difficulty reaching the conclusion in *Williams* that a jury of six would guarantee an accused the trial by jury secured by Art. III and the Sixth Amendment. Significantly, our determination that there was "no discernible difference between the results reached by the two different-sized juries," 399 U.S., at 101, 90 S.Ct., at 1906, drew largely upon the results of studies of the operations of juries of six in civil cases. Since then, much has been written about the six-member jury, but nothing that persuades us to depart from the conclusion reached in *Williams*.[15] Thus, while we express no view as to whether any number less than six would suffice,[16] we conclude that a jury of six satisfies the Seventh Amendment's guarantee of trial by jury in civil cases.

---

15. Arguments, pro and con, on the effectiveness of a jury of six compared to a jury of 12 will be found in Devitt, [The Six Man Jury in the Federal Court, 53 F.R.D. 273 (1971)]; Augelli, [Six-Member Juries in Civil Actions in the Federal Judicial System, 3 Seton Hall L.Rev. 281 (1972)]; Croake, [Memorandum on the Advisability and Constitutionality of Six Man Juries and ⅚ Verdicts in Civil Cases, 44 N.Y.State B.J. 385 (1972)]; Fisher, [The Seventh Amendment and the Common Law: No Magic in Numbers, 56 F.R.D. 507 (1973)]; Bogue & Fritz, The Six-Man Jury, 17 S.D.L.Rev. 285 (1972); Moss, The Twelve Member Jury in Massachusetts—Can it be Reduced?, 56 Mass.L.Q. 65 (1971); Zeisel, . . . And Then There Were None: The Diminution of the Federal Jury, 38 U.Chi. L.Rev. 710 (1971); Zeisel, The Waning of the American Jury, 58 A.B.A.J. 367 (1972); Gibbons, The New Minijuries: Panacea or Pandora's Box?, 58 A.B.A.J. 594 (1972); Kaufman, The Harbingers of Jury Reform, 58 A.B.A.J. 695 (1972); Whalen, Remarks on Resolution of 7th Amendment Jury Trial Requirement, 54 F.R.D. 148 (1972); Note, Right to Twelve-Man Jury, 84 Harv.L.Rev. 165 (1970); Note, Reducing the Size of Juries, 5 U.Mich.J.L.Reform 87 (1971); Note, The Effect of Jury Size on the Probability of Conviction: An Evaluation of Williams v. Florida, 22 Case W.Res.L.Rev. 529 (1971); Comment, Defendant's Right to a Jury Trial—Is Six Enough?, 59 Ky.L.J. 997 (1971).

Professor Zeisel has suggested that the six-member jury is more limited than the 12-member jury in representing the full spectrum of the community, and this in turn may result in differences between the verdicts reached by the two panels. Zeisel, supra, 38 U.Chi.L.Rev., at 716–719.

On the other hand, one study suggests that the decrease in the size of the jury from 12 to six is conducive to a more open discussion among the jurors, thereby improving the quality of the deliberative process. Note, supra, 5 U.Mich.J.L.Reform, at 99–106. See also

C. Joiner, Civil Justice and the Jury 31, 83 (1962) (concluding prior to *Williams* that the deliberative process should be the same in either six-or 12-member juries).

In addition, four very recent studies have provided convincing empirical evidence of the correctness of the *Williams* conclusion that "there is no discernible difference between the results reached by the two different-sized juries." Note, Six-Member and Twelve-Member Juries: An Empirical Study of Trial Results, 6 U.Mich.J.L.Reform 671 (1973); Institute of Judicial Administration, A Comparison of Six- and Twelve-Member Civil Juries in New Jersey Superior and County Courts (1972); Note, An Empirical Study of Six- and Twelve-Member Jury Decision-Making Processes, 6 U.Mich.J.L.Reform 712 (1973); Bermant & Coppock, Outcomes of Six- and Twelve-Member Jury Trials: An Analysis of 128 Civil Cases in the State of Washington, 48 Wash.L.Rev. 593 (1973).

16. What is required for a "jury" is a number large enough to facilitate group deliberation combined with a likelihood of obtaining a representative cross section of the community. Williams v. Florida, 399 U.S., at 100, 90 S.Ct., at 1905. It is undoubtedly true that at some point the number becomes too small to accomplish these goals, but, on the basis of presently available data, that cannot be concluded as to the number six. See Tamm, A Proposal for Five-Member Civil Juries in the Federal Courts, 50 A.B.A.J. 162 (1964); Tamm, The Five-Man Civil Jury: A Proposed Constitutional Amendment, 51 Geo.L.J. 120 (1962).

IGNORANCE OF SCIENCE IS NO EXCUSE*

Michael Saks.
10 Trial 18 (1974).

The briefs presented by opposing counsel [in Williams v. Florida and Colgrove v. Battin] were oblivious to well established social science findings and/or methodological principles which would have supported the appellant. In short, the law's confrontation with some relatively simple empirical questions was simply an embarrassment. Let us look with some care at the treatment of the jury size issue.

Defendant Williams was convicted of a crime which, under Florida law, was tried to a jury of six rather than 12. Williams appealed on grounds that included the fact that his conviction was by what he argued was an unconstitutionally small jury. When the case reached the US Supreme Court, the Court asserted that an answer to the question lay not in law nor in history, but in a functional analysis of the jury purpose. That is, do the characteristics or behavior of a six-person jury differ in such a way or to such a degree from that of a 12-person jury that the former will not fulfill the jury's purpose as well as the latter. Although the opinion stated that the case entirely turned on this set of empirical questions, it dealt with them in only three paragraphs. The Court concluded that there were no differences—that either size would do as well in providing a representative cross-section of the community, in being reliable and accurate, in providing for the jury minority's ability to resist majority pressure, that there would be equal amounts of deliberation, and that the likelihood of conviction would remain the same.

How did the Court know the answers to these questions? It knew because "experiments" on the effects of reduced jury size in the civil area all showed "no discernible difference." Footnote 48 of the Court's opinion cites six such "experiments." One reference consisted of an unsupported assertion that there would be no differences; three were reports of haphazard observations by officials in courts using six-member juries, who said they saw no differences; another was a report that a jurisdiction was trying out six-member juries; and the sixth was an article on the economic advantages to be expected from reduced jury size. As Professor Hans Zeisel commented in a critique of this use by the Court of non-studies, "this is scant evidence by any standards."[8] Not one of the references even began to address competently the empirical questions the Court posed for itself.

Footnote 49 is perhaps more incredible. A number of genuine empirical studies were cited to support the contention that " ... jurors in the minority ... are likely to be influenced by the proportional size of the majority aligned against them." That is to say, a jury split 10–2 is equivalent to one split 5–1 in terms of the minority's ability to defend its view, because both represent 83%–17% splits. Each of the studies cited,

---

* Reprinted with the permission of TRIAL (November–December 1974). Copyright: The Association of Trial Lawyers of America.

8. Zeisel, ... And Then There Were None: Diminution of the Federal Jury, 38 Chicago L.Rev. 710 (1974).

however, found exactly the opposite to be true.[9] They found that it is the absolute rather than the relative size of the opposition that determined factional influence, and that having an ally (10–2) as compared to having no ally (5–1) makes an enormous difference. This is a classic and widely known finding in social psychology research on conformity. The presence of an ally is one of the most powerful known facilitators of minority resistance to conformity pressure.

In asserting that there would be a negligible difference in the ability of 12-member and six-member juries to provide a representative cross-section of the community, the court ignored what is obvious to every social scientist: that when sampling from heterogeneous populations, sample size (12 versus 6) determines how well minority groups in the population will be represented. In sampling from a population stratified 90%/10%, for example, we can predict from our knowledge of sampling theory that 72% of 12-member juries will include one or more members of the minority, but that only 47% of the 6-member samples will. Still, this is only a statistical prediction, and a sincere empiricist would want to see empirical evidence. In my own experiments on 12-member versus six-member juries I compared the number of large and the number of small juries that had one or more blacks present. Blacks composed 10% of the population from which these jurors were drawn. Instead of the 72% to 47% contrast predicted, I found an 82% to 32% difference.[10] Not many people would term this difference "negligible."

After the decision in Williams v. Florida, the first empirical studies aimed directly at the effects of group size on jury behavior were conducted. By the time Colgrove v. Battin was heard, four such studies had been published and were considered by the Court. This might be viewed as progress. The Court did look at empirical studies and did understand the stated findings.

What the Court did not realize was that not all empirical studies are equal. As Zeisel and Shari Diamond make clear in a recent paper[12], the validity of empirical studies differs, and the intelligent use of empirical evidence requires a critical evaluation of the research. An empirical finding is only as good as the methods used to find it. Thus, the methods used in an empirical study must be scrutinized. The importance of method cannot be overstressed. Method is the overlooked, but more important term, in the phrase "scientific method." Studies using poor methods tell one nothing; but they can seriously mislead because their findings still may properly be called "empirical."

The four empirical studies cited in Colgrove v. Battin, because of their faulty methods, said much less than the Court thought they were saying.

---

9. [These studies are discussed in detail in M. Saks, Jury Verdicts, 16–18 (1977).]

10. [Reported in M. Saks, Jury Verdicts (1977).]

12. Zeisel & Diamond, "Convincing Empirical Evidence" on the Six-member Jury, 41 Chicago L.Rev. 281 (1974).

Two of the studies[13] compared the behavior of six-member and 12-member civil juries in two jurisdictions where litigants were able to choose which jury size the case would be tried to. The studies found no difference in outcomes that exceeded chance levels.

One of the studies examined more than just the verdicts reached. It found that the 12-member jury, compared to the six-member, deliberated longer, awarded three times as much damages, and, most curiously, required about twice as much trial time. The researchers correctly discounted these differences by noting that attorneys did not choose their jury size carelessly. Attorneys tended to select 12-member juries for cases involving large amounts of damages sought and/or more complex issues. That accounts for the difference in trial times and awards. And the notion is fully supported by the additional findings that in cases scheduled for trial before 12-member juries, there were significantly more settlements, and those settlements were for triple the amount of settlements in six-member juries.

What is operating here is known in social science jargon as a "confound." A confound exists when several potential causes vary simultaneously. Under such conditions it is difficult and usually impossible to know which potential cause is responsible for changes in performance. Thus, in comparing large juries hearing more complex and more costly cases to small juries hearing less complex and less costly cases, one cannot know whether it is jury size, complexity, or damages sought which is responsible for the various observed differences.

The researchers are probably correct in suggesting that it is complexity and not jury size that created all of those undesirable differences. What they ignore, however, is that while the confound (differential complexity and damages sought) can create differences that are not due to the variable of major interest (jury size), it can mask a difference that is in fact caused by the major variable. When the researchers saw a difference they didn't like, they explained it away by pointing to the confound. When they saw a non-difference they did like, they made believe the confound wasn't there. Given the procedures by which the data were collected and analyzed, one is simply unable to know what effect, if any, jury size did have.

A third study compared a sample of 12-member jury decisions made prior to a statutory reduction in jury size to a sample of six-person jury decisions made after the change.[14] Here, attorney choice of jury size could not be a factor since attorneys had no choice. But there were other potential confounds. The most serious was that not only did the jury size change, but a mediation board was created to try to settle auto negligence cases. The vital data are not provided by the study, but a plausible possibility is that lawyers, in keeping with their behavior in the study

13. Bermant, G. & Coppock, R. Outcomes of Six-and Twelve-member Jury Trials: An Analysis of 128 Civil Cases in the State of Washington, 48 Washington Law Review 593 (1973); Institute of Judicial Administration, A Comparison of Six-and Twelve-member Juries in New Jersey Superior and County Courts (1972).

14. Mills, Six-member and Twelve-member Juries: An Empirical Study of Trial Results, 6 University of Michigan Journal of Law Reform 671 (1973).

discussed above, tended to use the mediation board to settle the expensive and/or complex cases, rather than trust them to a jury. Thus, after the statutory changes, expensive or complex cases would be siphoned off, and the cases tried to six-member juries would therefore tend to be less complex. And we are back where we were in the previous two studies. The study's findings that no difference occurred in the direction of verdicts is still unreliable. We cannot *know* that there was a difference due to jury size, but, given the available data, we cannot be assured that a change in the kinds of cases that went to trial did not mask an actual difference due to jury size.

A fundamental strategy for avoiding the problem of confounds is to do a "true experiment." This was what the fourth study did.[15] In a true experiment the research procedures assure that only the variables of interest are permitted to vary systematically. In the study under discussion, the same case was presented to all juries by videotape and jurors were randomly assigned to sit as a six-member jury or a twelve-member jury. This assured that the only difference between the six-member and 12-member juries was their size.

But the achieving of such non-ambiguity is often at a cost. An obvious cost in this experiment is the fact that the study is now of mock juries and not real juries making decisions about real defendants. That is less of a problem than it seems at first blush; such "laboratory" studies are virtually never contradicted by "real-world" studies of the same phenomena. But there are other costs that a controlled experiment can—but need not—fall victim to.

The study in question did not avoid these heavy losses. College undergraduates were used rather than adult jurors. The number of juries used was only 16—8 large and 8 small. All competent social scientists know that the ability of a study to detect effects is determined in part by the sample size. A good way to guarantee that a study will find "no differences" is to use a very small sample size. If there is in reality a 1% difference between large and small juries in the number of verdicts favoring the defendant, it would require about 10,000 juries to insure statistically reliable detection of that difference. A sample size of 16 can be sure of detecting differences between proportions of verdicts only if the difference is 25% or greater. Also, the videotaped trial that was used happened to be so heavily weighted to the defendant that not a single verdict favored the plaintiff. If there is no variability in a dependent variable (verdicts), there is no possible way to see how jury size affects the variability. These are only the major flaws in this experiment, but it should be clear that they alone are adequate to insure that the only finding that could have come from this study was "no difference between the different-sized juries."

Interestingly enough, these empirical studies note that in Williams v. Florida the Court made its conclusions on the question of jury size effects

---

15. Kessler, An Empirical Study of Six-member and Twelve-member Jury Decision-making Processes, 6 University of Michigan Journal of Law Reform 712 (1973).

without the benefit of empirical evidence. That's why the studies were conducted—to provide such empirical evidence. But because of glaring shortcomings, these studies contribute nothing to establishing the answer. The final irony is that in Colgrove v. Battin the Court referred to these studies as "convincing empirical evidence." As Zeisel and Diamond point out in their analysis of that "convincing empirical evidence," the expertise required to spot the major flaws in that empirical research is modest. And the expertise required to know when one is dealing with empirical evidence and when one is dealing with bald assertions is even easier to come by. Yet the Court and the respective advocates have consistently failed to exercise the modest expertise that could have prevented this remarkable incompetence. The Court currently believes the matter of equality of performance for different-size juries is now well established, when in truth there is still no evidence to support such a conclusion.

———

BALLEW v. GEORGIA

Supreme Court of the United States, 1978.
435 U.S. 223, 98 S.Ct. 1029, 55 L.Ed.2d 234.

■ MR. JUSTICE BLACKMUN announced the judgment of the Court and delivered an opinion in which MR. JUSTICE STEVENS joined.

[Ballew was the manager of the Paris Adult Theatre in Atlanta, Georgia. He was charged in a two-count misdemeanor accusation with "distributing obscene materials in violation of Georgia Code Section 26–2101 in that the said accused did, knowing the obscene nature thereof, exhibit a motion picture film entitled 'Behind the Green Door' that contained obscene and indecent scenes." Ballew was brought to trial in the Criminal Court of Fulton County; the practice of this court was to try misdemeanor cases before juries of five persons, pursuant to Georgia law. Ballew's motion that the court impanel a twelve-person jury was denied, and the trial proceeded with the smaller jury panel, which returned guilty verdicts on both counts. Ballew's state appeals, on several grounds, including a Sixth Amendment challenge of the five-person jury, were unsuccessful. The United States Supreme Court granted certiorari.]

This case presents the issue whether a state criminal trial to a jury of only five persons deprives the accused of the right to trial by jury guaranteed to him by the Sixth and Fourteenth Amendments. Our resolution of the issue requires an application of principles enunciated in Williams v. Florida, 399 U.S. 78, 90 S.Ct. 1893, 26 L.Ed.2d 446 (1970), where the use of a six-person jury in a state criminal trial was upheld against constitutional attack.

[W]hen the Court in *Williams* permitted the reduction in jury size—or, to put it another way, when it held that a jury of six was not unconstitutional—it expressly reserved ruling on the issue whether a number smaller than six passed constitutional scrutiny. Id., at 91 n. 28, 90 S.Ct., at 1901.

The Court refused to speculate when this so-called "slippery slope" would become too steep. We face now, however, the two-fold question whether a further reduction in the size of the state criminal trial jury does make the grade too dangerous, that is, whether it inhibits the functioning of the jury as an institution to a significant degree, and, if so, whether any state interest counterbalances and justifies the disruption so as to preserve its constitutionality.

Williams v. Florida and Colgrove v. Battin, 413 U.S. 149, 93 S.Ct. 2448, 37 L.Ed.2d 522 (1973) (where the Court held that a jury of six members did not violate the Seventh Amendment right to a jury trial in a civil case), generated a quantity of scholarly work on jury size.[10] These writings do not draw or identify a bright line below which the number of jurors would not be able to function as required by the standards enunciated in *Williams*. On the other hand, they raise significant questions about the wisdom and constitutionality of a reduction below six. We examine these concerns:

10. E.g., M. Saks, Jury Verdicts (1977) (hereinafter cited as Saks); Bogue & Fritz, The Six-Man Jury, 17 S.D.L.Rev. 285 (1972); Davis, Kerr, Atkin, Holt, & Mech, The Decision Processes of 6- and 12-Person Mock Juries Assigned Unanimous and Two-Thirds Majority Rules, 32 J. of Personality & Soc. Psych. 1 (1975); Diamond, A Jury Experiment Reanalyzed, 7 U.Mich.J.L. Reform 520 (1974); Friedman, Trial by Jury: Criteria for Convictions, Jury Size and Type I and Type II Errors, 26–2 Am.Stat. 21 (Apr.1972) (hereinafter cited as Friedman); Institute of Judicial Administration, A Comparison of Six- and Twelve-Member Civil Juries in New Jersey Superior and County Courts (1972). Lempert, Uncovering "Nondiscernible" Differences: Empirical Research and the Jury-Size Cases, 73 Mich.L.Rev. 643 (1975) (hereinafter cited as Lempert); Nagel & Neef, Deductive Modeling to Determine an Optimum Jury Size and Fraction Required to Convict, 1975 Wash.U.L.Q. 933 (hereinafter cited as Nagel & Neef); New Jersey Criminal Law Revision Commission, Six-Member Juries (1971); Pabst, Statistical Studies of the Costs of Six-Man versus Twelve-Man Juries, 14 Wm. & Mary L.Rev. 326 (1972) (hereinafter cited as Pabst); Saks, Ignorance of Science Is No Excuse, 10 Trial 18 (Nov.–Dec.1974); Thompson, Six Will Do!, 10 Trial 12 (Nov.–Dec. 1974); Zeisel, Twelve is Just, 10 Trial 13 (Nov.–Dec.1974); Zeisel, . . . And Then There Were None: The Diminution of the Federal Jury, 38 U.Chi.L.Rev. 710 (1971) (hereinafter cited as Zeisel); Zeisel, The Waning of the American Jury, 58 A.B.A.J. 367 (1972); Zeisel

& Diamond, "Convincing Empirical Evidence" on the Six Member Jury, 41 U.Chi. L.Rev. 281 (1974) (hereinafter cited as Zeisel & Diamond); Note, The Effect of Jury Size on the Probability of Conviction: An Evaluation of Williams v. Florida, 22 Case W.Res.L.Rev. 529 (1971) (hereinafter cited as Note, Case W.Res.); Note, Six-Member and Twelve-Member Juries: An Empirical Study of Trial Results, 6 U.Mich.J.L. Reform 671 (1973); Note, An Empirical Study of Six- and Twelve-Member Jury Decision-Making Processes, 6 U.Mich.J.L. Reform 712 (1973).

Some of these studies have been pressed upon us by the parties. Brief for Petitioner 7–9; Tr. of Oral Arg. 26–27.

We have considered them carefully because they provide the only basis, besides judicial hunch, for a decision about whether smaller and smaller juries will be able to fulfill the purpose and functions of the Sixth Amendment. Without an examination about how juries and small groups actually work, we would not understand the basis for the conclusion of Mr. Justice Powell that "a line has to be drawn somewhere." We also note that The Chief Justice did not shrink from the use of empirical data in Williams v. Florida, 399 U.S. 78, 100–102, 105, 90 S.Ct. 1893, 1905–1907, 1908, 26 L.Ed.2d 446 (1970), when the data were used to support the constitutionality of the six-person criminal jury, or in Colgrove v. Battin, 413 U.S. 149, 158–160, 93 S.Ct. 2448, 2453–2454, 37 L.Ed.2d 522 (1973), a decision also joined by Mr. Justice Rehnquist.

First, recent empirical data suggest that progressively smaller juries are less likely to foster effective group deliberation. At some point, this decline leads to inaccurate fact-finding and incorrect application of the common sense of the community to the facts. Generally, a positive correlation exists between group size and the quality of both group performance and group productivity.[11] A variety of explanations have been offered for this conclusion. Several are particularly applicable in the jury setting. The smaller the group, the less likely are members to make critical contributions necessary for the solution of a given problem.[12] Because most juries are not permitted to take notes, see Forston, Sense and Non-Sense: Jury Trial Communication, 1975 B.Y.U.L.Rev. 601, 631–633, memory is important for accurate jury deliberations. As juries decrease in size, then, they are less likely to have members who remember each of the important pieces of evidence or argument.[13] Furthermore, the smaller the group, the less likely it is to overcome the biases of its members to obtain an accurate result.[14] When individual and group decisionmaking were compared, it was seen that groups performed better because prejudices of individuals were frequently counterbalanced, and objectivity resulted. Groups also exhibited increased motivation and self-criticism. All these advantages, except, perhaps, self-motivation, tend to diminish as the size of the group diminishes.[15] Because juries frequently face complex problems laden with value choices, the benefits are important and should be retained. In particular, the counterbalancing of various biases is critical to the accurate application of the common sense of the community to the facts of any given case.

Second, the data now raise doubts about the accuracy of the results achieved by smaller and smaller panels. Statistical studies suggest that the risk of convicting an innocent person (Type I error) rises as the size of the jury diminishes.[16] Because the risk of not convicting a guilty person (Type II error) increases with the size of the panel,[17] an optimal jury size can be selected as a function of the interaction between the two risks. Nagel and Neef concluded that the optimal size, for the purpose of minimizing errors, should vary with the importance attached to the two types of mistakes. After weighting Type I error as 10 times more significant than Type II, perhaps not an unreasonable assumption, they concluded that the optimal jury size was between six and eight. As the size diminished to five and

---

11. Two researchers have summarized the findings of 31 studies in which the size of groups from 2 to 20 members was an important variable. They concluded that there were no conditions under which smaller groups were superior in the quality of group performance and group productivity. Thomas & Fink, Effects of Group Size, 60 Psych.Bull. 371, 373 (1963), cited in Lempert 685. See Saks 77 et seq., 107.

12. See Faust, Group versus Individual Problem-Solving, 59 J.Ab. & Soc.Psych. 68, 71 (1959), cited in Lempert 685 and 686.

13. Saks 77 et seq.; see Kelley & Thibaut, Group Problem Solving, 4 Handbook of Soc.Psych. 68–69 (2d ed., G. Lindzey & E. Anderson 1969) (hereinafter cited as Kelley & Thibaut).

14. Lempert 687–688, citing Barlund, A Comparative Study of Individual, Majority, and Group Judgment, 58 J.Ab. & Soc.Psych. 55, 59 (1959); see Kelley & Thibaut 67.

15. Lempert 687–688, citing Barlund, supra n. 14, pp. 58–59.

16. Friedman; Nagel & Neef.

17. Nagel & Neef 945.

below, the weighted sum of errors increased because of the enlarging risk of the conviction of innocent defendants.[18]

Another doubt about progressively smaller juries arises from the increasing inconsistency that results from the decreases. Saks argued that the "more a jury type fosters consistency, the greater will be the proportion of juries which select the correct (i.e., the same) verdict and the fewer 'errors' will be made." Saks 86–87. From his mock trials held before undergraduates and former jurors, he computed the percentage of "correct" decisions rendered by 12-person and 6-person panels. In the student experiment, 12-person groups reached correct verdicts 83% of the time; 6-person panels reached correct verdicts 69% of the time. The results for the former-juror study were 71% for the 12-person groups and 57% for the 6-person groups. Ibid. Working with statistics described in H. Kalven & H. Zeisel, The American Jury 460 (1966), Nagel and Neef tested the average conviction propensity of juries, that is, the likelihood that any given jury of a set would convict the defendant.[19] They found that half of all 12-person juries would have average conviction propensities that varied by no more than 20 points. Half of all six-person juries, on the other hand, had average conviction propensities varying by 30 points, a difference they found significant in both real and percentage terms.[20] Lempert reached similar results when he considered the likelihood of juries to compromise over the various views of their members, an important phenomenon for the fulfillment of the commonsense function. In civil trials averaging occurs with respect to damages amounts. In criminal trials it relates to numbers of counts and lesser included offenses.[21] And he predicted that compromises would be more consistent when larger juries were employed. For example, 12-person juries could be expected to reach extreme compromises in 4% of the cases, while 6-person panels would reach extreme results in 16%.[22] All three of these *post*-Williams studies, therefore, raise significant doubts about the consistency and reliability of the decisions of smaller juries.

Third, the data suggest that the verdicts of jury deliberation in criminal cases will vary as juries become smaller, and that the variance amounts to an imbalance to the detriment of one side, the defense. Both Lempert and Zeisel found that the number of hung juries would diminish

---

18.   Id., at 946–948, 956, 975. Friedman reached a similar conclusion. He varied the appearance of guilt in his statistical study. The more guilty the person appeared, the greater the chance that a 6-member panel would convict when a 12-member panel would not. As jury size was reduced, the risk of Type I error would increase, Friedman said, without a significant corresponding advantage in reducing Type II error. Friedman 23.

19.   Nagel & Neef 952, 971, concluded that the average juror had a propensity to convict more frequently than to acquit, a

tendency designated by the figure .677. In other words, if the average jury considered the average case 67.7% of the jurors would vote to convict.

20.   With the average juror having a conviction propensity of .677, the average 12-member jury propensities ranged from .579 to .775. The average six-member jury propensities ranged from .530 to .830. Id., at 971–972.

21.   Lempert 680.

22.   Accord, Zeisel 718; Note, Case W.Res. 547.

as the panels decreased in size. Zeisel said that the number would be cut in half—from 5% to 2.4% with a decrease from 12 to 6 members.[23] Both studies emphasized that juries in criminal cases generally hang with only one, or more likely two, jurors remaining unconvinced of guilt.[24] Also, group theory suggests that a person in the minority will adhere to his position more frequently when he has at least one other person supporting his argument.[25] In the jury setting the significance of this tendency is demonstrated by the following figures: If a minority viewpoint is shared by 10% of the community, 28.2% of 12-member juries may be expected to have no minority representation, but 53.1% of 6-member juries would have none. Thirty-four percent of 12-member panels could be expected to have two minority members, while only 11% of 6-member panels would have two.[26] As the numbers diminish below six, even fewer panels would have one member with the minority viewpoint and still fewer would have two. The chance for hung juries would decline accordingly.

Fourth, what has just been said about the presence of minority viewpoint as juries decrease in size foretells problems not only for jury decisionmaking, but also for the representation of minority groups in the community. The Court repeatedly has held that meaningful community participation cannot be attained with the exclusion of minorities or other identifiable groups from jury service.

[A]lthough the Court in *Williams* concluded that the six-person jury did not fail to represent adequately a cross-section of the community, the opportunity for meaningful and appropriate representation does decrease with the size of the panels. Thus, if a minority group constitutes 10% of the community, 53.1% of randomly selected six-member juries could be expected to have no minority representative among their members, and 89% not to have two.[27] Further reduction in size will erect additional barriers to representation.

Fifth, several authors have identified in jury research methodological problems tending to mask differences in the operation of smaller and larger juries.[28] For example, because the judicial system handles so many clear cases, decisionmakers will reach similar results through similar analyses most of the time. One study concluded that smaller and larger juries could disagree in their verdicts in no more than 14% of the cases.[29] Disparities, therefore, appear in only small percentages. Nationwide, however, these small percentages will represent a large number of cases. And it is with respect to those cases that the jury trial right has its greatest value. When the case is close, and the guilt or innocence of the defendant is not readily

23. Zeisel 720; accord Lempert 676. But see Saks 89–90.

24. Lempert 674–677; Zeisel 719.

25. Asch, Effects of Group Pressure upon the Modification and Distortion of Judgments in Group Dynamics Research and Theory, 189, 195–197 (2d ed., 1960), cited in Lempert 673.

26. Id., at 669, 677.

27. Ibid.; Saks 90.

28. Lempert 648–653; Nagel & Neef 934–937; Saks, Ignorance of Science Is No Excuse, supra n. 10, at 19; Zeisel & Diamond 283–291; Note, Case W.Res. 535.

29. Lempert 648–653.

apparent, a properly functioning jury system will insure evaluation by the sense of the community and will also tend to insure accurate factfinding.[30]

Studies that aggregate data also risk masking case-by-case differences in jury deliberations. The authors, H. Kalven and H. Zeisel, of The American Jury (1966), examined the judge-jury disagreement. They found that judges held for plaintiffs 57% of the time and that juries held for plaintiffs 59%, an insignificant difference. Yet case-by-case comparison revealed judge-jury disagreement in 22% of the cases. Id., at 63, cited in Lempert 656. This casts doubt on the conclusion of another study that compared the aggregate results of civil cases tried before 6-member juries with those of 12-member jury trials.[31] The investigator in that study had claimed support for his hypothesis that damages awards did not vary with the reduction in jury size. Although some might say that figures in the aggregate may have supported this conclusion, a closer view of the cases reveals greater variation in the results of the smaller panels, i.e., a standard deviation of $58,335 for the 6-member juries, and of $24,834 for the 12-member juries.[32] Again, the averages masked significant case-by-case differences that must be considered when evaluating jury function and performance.

While we adhere to, and reaffirm our holding in *Williams v. Florida,* these studies, most of which have been made since *Williams* was decided in 1970, lead us to conclude that the purpose and functioning of the jury in a criminal trial is seriously impaired, and to a constitutional degree, by a reduction in size to below six members. We readily admit that we do not pretend to discern a clear line between six members and five. But the assembled data raise substantial doubt about the reliability and appropriate representation of panels smaller than six. Because of the fundamental importance of the jury trial to the American system of criminal justice, any

---

30. Zeisel and Diamond have criticized one of the more important studies supporting smaller juries. See n. 34, infra. In Note, An Empirical Study of Six-and Twelve-Member Jury Decision-Making Processes, 6 U.Mich. J.L. Reform 712 (1973), the author tested the deliberations of larger and smaller panels by showing to sets of both sizes the video tape of a single mock civil trial. The case concerned an automobile accident and turned on whether the plaintiff had been speeding. If so, Michigan law precluded recovery because of contributory negligence. Of the 16 juries tested, not one found for the plaintiff. This led Zeisel and Diamond to conclude: "The evidence in the case overwhelmingly favored the defendant.... This overpowering bias makes the experiment irrelevant. On the facts of this case, any jury under any rules would probably have arrived at the same verdict. Hence, to conclude from this experiment that jury size generally has no effect on the verdict is impermissible." Zeisel & Diamond 287.

See also Diamond, A Jury Experiment Reanalyzed, 7 U.Mich.J.L. Reform 520 (1974). The criticized study was cited and relied upon by the Court in Colgrove v. Battin, 413 U.S. 149, 159, n. 15, 93 S.Ct. 2448, 2454, 37 L.Ed.2d 522 (1973).

31. See Note, Six-Member and Twelve-Member Juries: An Empirical Study of Trial Results, 6 U.Mich.J.L. Reform 671 (1973). This also was cited and relied upon in Colgrove v. Battin, 413 U.S., at 159 n. 15, 93 S.Ct. 2448, n. 15.

32. Zeisel & Diamond 289–290. These authors also criticized the Michigan study because it ignored two other important changes that had occurred when the size of civil juries was decreased from 12 to 6 members: A mediation board, which encouraged settlements, had been introduced, and rules that permitted discovery of insurance policy limits had taken effect. See Saks 43.

further reduction that promotes inaccurate and possibly biased decision-making, that causes untoward differences in verdicts, and that prevents juries from truly representing their communities, attains constitutional significance.

[T]he empirical data cited by Georgia do not relieve our doubts. The State relies on the Saks study for the proposition that a decline in the number of jurors will not affect the aggregate number of convictions or hung juries. Tr. of Oral Arg. 27. This conclusion, however, is only one of several in the Saks study; that study eventually concludes:

> "Larger juries (size twelve) are preferable to smaller juries (six). They produce longer deliberations, more communication, far better community representation, and, possibly, greater verdict reliability (consistency)." Saks 107.

Far from relieving our concerns, then, the Saks study supports the conclusion that further reduction in jury size threatens Sixth and Fourteen Amendment interests.

Methodological problems prevent reliance on the three studies that do purport to bolster Georgia's position. The reliability of the two Michigan studies cited by the State has been criticized elsewhere.[34] The critical problem with the Michigan laboratory experiment, which used a mock civil trial, was the apparent clarity of the case. Not one of the juries found for the plaintiff in the tort suit; this masked any potential difference in the decisionmaking of larger and smaller panels. The results also have been doubted because in the experiment only students composed the juries, only 16 juries were tested, and only a video tape of the mock trial was presented.[35] The statistical review of the results of actual jury trials in Michigan erroneously aggregated outcomes. It is also said that it failed to take account of important changes of court procedure initiated at the time of the reduction in size from 12 to 6 members.[36] The Davis study, which employed a mock criminal trial for rape, also presented an extreme set of facts so that none of the panels rendered a guilty verdict.[37] None of these three reports, therefore, convinces us that a reduction in the number of jurors below six will not affect to a constitutional degree the functioning of juries in criminal trials.

With the reduction in the number of jurors below six creating a substantial threat to Sixth and Fourteenth Amendment guarantees, we must consider whether any interest of the State justifies the reduction. We

---

34. Note, Six-Member and Twelve-Member Juries: An Empirical Study of Trial Results, 6 U.Mich.J.L. Reform 671 (1973) (a statistical study of actual jury results), and Note, An Empirical Study of Six-and Twelve-Member Jury Decision-Making Processes, 6 U.Mich.J.L. Reform 712 (1973) (a laboratory experiment using a mock trial), were both criticized in Saks 43–46, and in Zeisel & Diamond 286–290. The second study was criticized in Diamond, A Jury Experiment Reanalyzed, 7 U.Mich.J.L. Reform 520 (1974). The Michigan studies were advanced by the State at oral argument. Tr. of Oral Arg. 27.

35. Saks 45.

36. Id., at 43–44; Zeisel & Diamond 288–290.

37. Davis, et al., supra n. 10, at 7, criticized in Saks 49–51.

find no significant state advantage in reducing the number of jurors from six to five.

The States utilize juries of less than 12 primarily for administrative reasons. Savings in court time and in financial costs are claimed to justify the reductions.[38] The financial benefits of the reduction from 12 to 6 are substantial; this is mainly because fewer jurors draw daily allowances as they hear cases.[39] On the other hand, the asserted saving in judicial time is not so clear. Pabst in his study found little reduction in the time for voir dire with the six-person jury because many questions were directed at the veniremen as a group.[40] Total trial time did not diminish, and court delays and backlogs improved very little. The point that is to be made, of course, is that a reduction in size from six to five or four or even three would save the States little. They could reduce slightly the daily allowances, but with a reduction from six to five the saving would be minimal. If little time is gained by the reduction from 12 to 6, less will be gained with a reduction from 6 to 5. Perhaps this explains why only two States, Georgia and Virginia, have reduced the size of juries in certain nonpetty criminal cases to five. Other States appear content with six members or more. In short, the State has offered little or no justification for its reduction to five members.

Petitioner, therefore, has established that his trial on criminal charges before a five-member jury deprived him of the right to trial by jury guaranteed by the Sixth and Fourteenth Amendments.

■ Mr. Justice POWELL, with whom The Chief Justice and Mr. Justice Rehnquist join, concurring in the judgment.

I concur in the judgment, as I agree that use of a jury as small as five members, with authority to convict for serious offenses, involves grave questions of fairness. As the opinion of Mr. Justice Blackmun indicates, the line between five-and six-member juries is difficult to justify, but a line has to be drawn somewhere if the substance of jury trial is to be preserved. [I] have reservations as to the wisdom—as well as the necessity—of Mr. Justice Blackmun's heavy reliance on numerology derived from statistical studies. Moreover, neither the validity nor the methodology employed by the studies cited was subjected to the traditional testing mechanisms of the adversary process. The studies relied on merely represent unexamined findings of persons interested in the jury system.

---

38. See New Jersey Criminal Law Revision Commission, Six-Member Juries (1971); Bogue & Fritz, The Six-Man Jury, 17 S.D.L.Rev. 285 (1972).

39. It has been said that a reduction from 12 jurors to 6 throughout the federal system could save at least $4 million annually. Zeisel, Twelve is Just, 10 Trial 13 (Nov.–Dec. 1974). Another study calculated a saving in jury man-hours of 41.9% with the reduction to six members. Pabst, Statistical Stud-

ies of the Costs of Six-Man versus Twelve-Man Juries, 14 Wm. & Mary L.Rev. 326, 328 (1972).

40. Id., at 327; Zeisel, Twelve is Just, supra. But see Institute of Judicial Administration, A Comparison of Six-and Twelve-Member Civil Juries in New Jersey Superior and County Courts 27–28 (1972); New Jersey Criminal Law Revision Commission, Six-Member Juries 3–4 (1971); Thompson, Six Will Do, 10 Trial 12, 14 (Nov.–Dec. 1974).

For these reasons I concur only in the judgment.

PEOPLE v. DISTRICT COURT

Supreme Court of Colorado, 1981.
634 P.2d 44.

Larry J. Dirgo was charged by information in the District Court of Boulder County with the offense of criminal mischief. [T]he case was set for a jury trial on May 14, 1981. On the day before the trial the defendant Dirgo moved the court for a trial to a jury of one person. His motion was based upon section 18–1–406(4), C.R.S. 1973 (1978 Repl. Vol. 8), which provides:

> "(4) Except as to class 1 felonies, the defendant in any felony or misdemeanor case may, with the approval of the court, elect, at any time before verdict, to be tried by a number of jurors less than the number to which he would otherwise be entitled."

The statutorily prescribed jury to which one accused of a felony is entitled is a jury of twelve persons. Section 18–1–406(1), C.R.S.1973 (1978 Repl. Vol. 8). The district court, although expressing doubts about the wisdom of the procedure, concluded that the statute permitted a jury of one person and therefore the court granted Dirgo's motion. The district attorney sought relief from this order and we issued our rule to show cause.

It is fundamental that one accused of a felony is constitutionally entitled to a jury trial. It is also clear that the accused may waive his constitutional right to a jury.

The preliminary question for determination is whether under section 18–1–406(4) above set forth, one accused of a felony, other than a class 1 felony, may, with the approval of the court, elect to be tried by a number of jurors less than the number to which he would otherwise be entitled.

In Williams v. Florida, 399 U.S. 78, 90 S.Ct. 1893, 26 L.Ed.2d 446 (1970), the validity of a Florida statute was challenged, which provided for a jury of six in all criminal cases except capital cases where a jury of twelve was constitutionally mandated. The Supreme Court held as follows:

> " ... The question in this case then is whether the constitutional guarantee of a trial by 'jury' necessarily requires trial by exactly 12 persons, rather than some lesser number—in this case six. We hold that the 12-man panel is not a necessary ingredient of 'trial by jury,' and that respondent's refusal to impanel more than the six members provided for by Florida law did not violate petitioner's Sixth Amendment rights as applied to the States through the Fourteenth."

It is thus not constitutionally impermissible under the United States Constitution to impanel a jury of six rather than twelve to try a felony case other than a capital case.

We find no language in the Colorado Constitution which mandates that one accused of a felony may not elect to be tried by a jury numbering less than twelve persons. The enactment of the statute under consideration, section 18–1–406(4), is a recognition that public policy does not demand a jury of twelve in non-capital felony cases. Reinforced by the rationale of *Williams, supra,* we hold that one accused of a felony, other than a capital offense, may at his election, subject to the statutorily required approval of the court, be tried to a jury of less than twelve persons.

We next consider the validity of the trial court's determination that the defendant could be tried by a jury of one. We hold that the court's ruling was erroneous.

Initially, we observe that section 18–1–406(4) does not speak in terms of a single juror, but rather of a "number of *jurors* less than the number to which he would otherwise be entitled." (Emphasis added.) More importantly, the term "jury" connotes a deliberative body of persons. The word "jury" has been defined as:

"A body of men sworn to give a verdict upon some matter submitted to them; ... a body of men selected according to law, impaneled and sworn to inquire into and try any matter of fact, and to give their verdict according to the evidence legally produced." Webster's Third New International Dictionary, 1966.

In *Williams,* supra, the Supreme Court speaking to the size of a jury stated:

" ... the essential feature of a jury obviously lies in the interposition between the accused and his accuser of the commonsense judgment of a *group of laymen,* and in the community participation and shared responsibility that results from that group's determination of guilt or innocence. The performance of this role is not a function of the particular number of the body that makes up the jury. To be sure, the number should probably be large enough to promote group deliberation, free from outside attempts at intimidation, and to provide a fair possibility for obtaining a representative cross-section of the community...." (Emphasis added.)

It is thus obvious that a jury may not be composed of a single person. If the accused desires a one person determination of his guilt or innocence, he may waive the jury and be tried by the court.

We are thus left with the question of what minimum number of persons may compose a constitutional jury in a non-capital felony case if a defendant elects under the statute to be tried by a jury of less than the number to which he is entitled. We are guided in our determination by the decision in Ballew v. Georgia, 435 U.S. 223, 98 S.Ct. 1029, 55 L.Ed.2d 234 (1978). In that case the petitioner was accused of a misdemeanor which under the Georgia statute was triable by a jury of five persons. He contended he was entitled to a jury of twelve. The Supreme Court held that a jury of less than six persons substantially threatens Sixth and Fourteenth Amendment guarantees and held that the Georgia statute was unconstitutional.

The essence of the Court's reasoning, as previously expounded in *Williams v. Florida,* supra, was that since the purpose of a jury trial is to prevent oppression by the government and to safeguard against corrupt and overzealous prosecution, that purpose could be attained by participation of the community in the determination of guilt and by the application of the common sense of laymen who as jurors consider the case. This function could only be served by a jury of sufficient size to promote group deliberation, to insulate the members of the jury from outside intimidation, and to provide a representative cross section of the community. The Supreme Court held in *Williams* that a jury of six could adequately perform that function and satisfy the underlying purposes of a jury.

In *Ballew,* supra, the Court had before it numerous empirical studies concerning the minimum size below which the number of jurors would not be able to function as required by the standards enunciated in *Williams, supra.* The Court in *Ballew* concluded as follows:

> "While we adhere to, and reaffirm our holding in *Williams v. Florida,* these studies, most of which have been made since *Williams* was decided in 1970, lead us to conclude that the purpose and functioning of the jury in a criminal trial is seriously impaired, and to a constitutional degree, by a reduction in size to below six members. We readily admit that we do not pretend to discern a clear line between six members and five. But the assembled data raise substantial doubt about the reliability and appropriate representation of panels smaller than six. Because of the fundamental importance of the jury trial to the American system of criminal justice, any further reduction that promotes inaccurate and possibly biased decisionmaking, that causes untoward differences in verdicts, and that prevents juries from truly representing their communities, attains constitutional significance."

The defendant Dirgo in the present case is not asserting a denial of a constitutional jury. However, in our view, to allow Dirgo to elect to be tried by a jury of less than six persons would submit the issue of his guilt or innocence to a body of persons insufficient in number to function in accordance with the standards set forth in *Williams,* supra, and thus not qualify as a valid jury.

For the foregoing reasons we draw the line at six persons and hold that one accused of a non-capital felony who elects, pursuant to section 18–1–406(4), to be tried by a jury of less than twelve persons may not be tried by a jury of less than six persons. It follows that a jury of one as requested and ordered in this case is no jury at all.

———

OPINION OF THE JUSTICES

Supreme Court of New Hampshire, 1981.
121 N.H. 480, 431 A.2d 135.

The following request of the Senate for an opinion of the justices was adopted on May 27, 1981, and filed with the supreme court on June 3, 1981:

"Whereas, the Senate has under consideration HB 698 which reduces the number of persons serving on juries in civil cases from 12 to 6; and

"Whereas, some members of the Senate question the constitutionality of certain aspects of the proposed legislation;

"Now, therefore, be it

"Resolved by the Senate;

"That the Justices of the Supreme Court are respectfully requested to give their opinion and answer the following question:

"Do any provisions of HB 698 in the form as passed by the House of Representatives violate any provision of the United States Constitution or of the New Hampshire Constitution?"; and

"That the clerk of the Senate transmit copies of this resolution and HB 698 as passed by the House of Representatives, to the Justices of the Supreme Court."

The following answer was returned.

To the Honorable Senate:

The undersigned justices of the supreme court reply as follows to your request filed in this court on June 3, 1981.

We need not devote considerable discussion to your inquiry regarding the constitutionality of House bill 698 under the federal constitution. In passing, however, we note that the Justices of the Supreme Court of the United States have expressed divergent views in their individual opinions on the subject matter.

In Williams v. Florida, 399 U.S. 78, 90 S.Ct. 1893, 26 L.Ed.2d 446 (1970), the Supreme Court of the United States in considering a Sixth Amendment question sustained a Florida statute providing for the use of unanimous six-member juries in all but capital cases, holding that the twelve-member jury is not a necessary ingredient of a "trial by jury." In Colgrove v. Battin, 413 U.S. 149, 159–60, 93 S.Ct. 2448, 2454, 37 L.Ed.2d 522 (1973), the Supreme Court of the United States held that a *federal district court* procedural rule providing for six-member juries in civil cases did not violate the Seventh Amendment's guarantee of trial by jury in civil cases.

Since the *Williams,* supra and *Colgrove,* supra decisions, writings of legal scholars with empirical studies, leading to considerable debate regarding the impact of six-member juries, have been legion. For a listing of several of these articles, see Ballew v. Georgia, 435 U.S. 223, 231 n. 10, 98 S.Ct. 1029, 1034 n. 10, 55 L.Ed.2d 234 (1978). In *Ballew,* supra, the Supreme Court held that a jury of less than six in a criminal trial violated the Sixth and Fourteenth Amendments to the Constitution. When Justice Blackmun wrote the majority opinion in *Ballew,* he had the benefit of the post-*Williams* data, and he discussed several studies that suggested: "that progressively smaller juries are less likely to foster effective group deliberation," and that "[a]t some point, this decline leads to inaccurate fact-finding and incorrect application of the common sense of the community to the facts," 435 U.S. at 232, 98 S.Ct. at 1035; "that the risk of convicting an innocent person . . . rises as the size of the jury diminishes," id. at 234, 98 S.Ct. at 1036; that "[t]he chance for hung-juries would decline," id. at 236, 98 S.Ct. at 1037; and that "[f]urther reduction in size will erect additional barriers to [minority] representation," id. at 237, 98 S.Ct. at 1037. *See generally* Note, The Jury Size Question in Pennsylvania: Six of One and a Dozen of the Other, 53 Temple L.Q. 89, 90 n. 5–7 (1980) (discussing studies regarding these problems).

Although Justice Blackmun's majority opinion in *Ballew* expressed these concerns in the context of a decision regarding a further reduction of criminal trial juries from six to five, we note that these problems may also arise in the context of reducing the size of juries in civil cases from twelve to six.

Justice Marshall, in a footnote to his dissent in *Colgrove,* supra, noted that "the Seventh Amendment is one of the few remaining provisions in the Bill of Rights which has not been held to be applicable to the states" through the Fourteenth Amendment. 413 U.S. at 169 n. 4, 93 S.Ct. at 2459 n. 4. Accordingly, although House Bill 698 might pass muster under the federal constitution, the determination of its propriety falls squarely within this State's power to apply its own constitutional provisions regarding trial by jury. See First Nat'l Bank of Olathe v. Clark, 226 Kan. 619, 622, 602 P.2d 1299, 1302 (1979).

In 1859, the New Hampshire House of Representatives asked the justices of this court whether the legislature had the power to change the law to provide for petit juries numbering less than twelve. In responding to the House of Representatives this court stated:

> "We regard it as a well settled and unquestioned rule of construction that the language used by the legislature, in the statutes enacted by them, and that used by the people in the great paramount law which controls the legislature as well as the people, is to be always understood and explained *in that sense in which it was used at the time when the constitution and the laws were adopted.*"

Opinion of the Justices, 41 N.H. 550, 551 (1860). (Emphasis added.) The court examined the meaning of the terms "jury" and "trial by jury" at the time of the adoption of our constitution, concluding that:

> "[W]e are of opinion that no body of less than twelve men, though they should be by law denominated a jury, would be a jury within the meaning of the constitution; nor would a trial by such a body, though called a trial by jury, be such, within the meaning of that instrument. *We think, therefore, that the legislature have no power so to change the law in relation to juries, as to provide that petit juries may be composed of a less number than twelve,* nor to provide that a number of the petit jury, less than the whole number, can render a verdict. . . ."

Id. at 552 (emphasis added); see Copp v. Henniker, 55 N.H. 179, 193 (1875). We reaffirm this decision, believing that the vitality of its conclusion remains today, especially in light of the number of empirical studies that have questioned the impact of the six-member jury on our court system. We therefore answer your question as it pertains to the New Hampshire Constitution, N.H. Const., Pt. I, Art. 20, in the affirmative.

————

NOTE

1. **Recent Development.** In 2005, the American Bar Association approved a set of recommended Principles for Juries and Jury Trials. Principle 3, "Juries Should Have 12 members," reads:

A.   Juries in civil cases should be constituted of 12 members wherever feasible and under no circumstances fewer than six members.

B.   Juries in criminal cases should consist of:

1.   Twelve persons if a penalty of confinement for more than six months may be imposed upon conviction;

2.   At least six persons if the maximum period of confinement that may be imposed upon conviction is six months or less.

C.   At any time before verdict, the parties, with the approval of the court, may stipulate that the jury shall consist of fewer jurors than required for a full jury, but in no case fewer than six jurors. In criminal cases the court should not accept such a stipulation unless the defendant, after being advised by the court of his or her right to trial by a full jury, and the consequences of waiver, personally waives the right to a full jury either in writing or in open court on the record.

The Principles are available at http://www.abanet.org/juryprojectstandards/principles.pdf

2.   DEATH-QUALIFIED JURIES

In many states, in cases in which the death penalty is a statutory option, juries render two verdicts in a "bifurcated" or split trial. The first verdict, after the "guilt phase" of the trial, is whether the defendant is guilty or not guilty (or not guilty by reason of insanity) of the crime charged or of a lesser crime. If the defendant is found guilty of the capital offense charged, the second verdict, after the "sentencing phase" of the trial, is whether the defendant should receive the death penalty or a prison sentence. The same jury renders both verdicts.

In all criminal cases, potential jurors are screened by the prosecutor, defense counsel, and the judge during a proceeding known as "voir dire." Potential jurors can be eliminated "for cause" if the judge finds reason to believe that they may not be able to render a fair verdict, for example, if they are related to, or friends of, the defendant or the victim. (Each side also has a limited number of "peremptory" challenges by which it can strike a juror without giving any reason.)

In capital cases, an additional form of screening is employed in many states in which potential jurors are eliminated from both the guilt phase and the penalty phase—that is, from the entire trial—if they state during voir dire that they are so opposed to the death penalty that they will not consider voting for execution if the defendant is found guilty. This form of screening is known as "death-qualification."

WITHERSPOON v. ILLINOIS

Supreme Court of the United States, 1968.
391 U.S. 510, 88 S.Ct. 1770, 20 L.Ed.2d 776.

■ Mr. Justice Stewart delivered the opinion of the Court.

The petitioner was brought to trial in 1960 in Cook County, Illinois, upon a charge of murder. The jury found him guilty and fixed his penalty at death. At the time of his trial an Illinois statute provided:

> "In trials for murder it shall be a cause for challenge of any juror who shall, on being examined, state that he has conscientious scruples against capital punishment, or that he is opposed to the same."

[T]he issue before us is a narrow one. It does not involve the right of the prosecution to challenge for cause those prospective jurors who state that their reservations about capital punishment would prevent them from making an impartial decision as to the defendant's guilt. Nor does it involve the State's assertion of a right to exclude from the jury in a capital case those who say that they could never vote to impose the death penalty or that they would refuse even to consider its imposition in the case before them. For the State of Illinois did not stop there, but authorized the prosecution to exclude as well all who said that they were opposed to capital punishment and all who indicated that they had conscientious scruples against inflicting it.

[T]he petitioner contends that a State cannot confer upon a jury selected in this manner the power to determine guilt. He maintains that such a jury, unlike one chosen at random from a cross-section of the community, must necessarily be biased in favor of conviction, for the kind of juror who would be unperturbed by the prospect of sending a man to his death, he contends, is the kind of juror who would too readily ignore the presumption of the defendant's innocence, accept the prosecution's version of the facts, and return a verdict of guilt. To support this view, the petitioner refers to what he describes as "competent scientific evidence that death-qualified jurors are partial to the prosecution on the issue of guilt or innocence."[10]

---

10. In his brief, the petitioner cites two surveys, one involving 187 college students, W.C. Wilson, Belief in Capital Punishment and Jury Performance (Unpublished Manu- script, University of Texas, 1964), and the other involving 200 college students, F.J. Goldberg, Attitude Toward Capital Punishment and Behavior as a Juror in Simulated

The data adduced by the petitioner, however, are too tentative and fragmentary to establish that jurors not opposed to the death penalty tend to favor the prosecution in the determination of guilt.[11] We simply cannot conclude, either on the basis of the record now before us or as a matter of judicial notice, that the exclusion of jurors opposed to capital punishment results in an unrepresentative jury on the issue of guilt or substantially increases the risk of conviction. In light of the presently available information, we are not prepared to announce a *per se* constitutional rule requiring the reversal of every conviction returned by a jury selected as this one was.

It does not follow, however, that the petitioner is entitled to no relief. For in this case the jury was entrusted with two distinct responsibilities: first, to determine whether the petitioner was innocent or guilty; and second, if guilty, to determine whether his sentence should be imprisonment or death. It has not been shown that this jury was biased with respect to the petitioner's guilt. But it is self-evident that, in its role as arbiter of the punishment to be imposed, this jury fell woefully short of that impartiality to which the petitioner was entitled under the Sixth and Fourteenth Amendments.

If the State had excluded only those prospective jurors who stated in advance of trial that they would not even consider returning a verdict of death, it could argue that the resulting jury was simply "neutral" with respect to penalty. But when it swept from the jury all who expressed conscientious or religious scruples against capital punishment and all who opposed it in principle, the State crossed the line of neutrality. In its quest for a jury capable of imposing the death penalty, the State produced a jury uncommonly willing to condemn a man to die.

[S]pecifically, we hold that a sentence of death cannot be carried out if the jury that imposed or recommended it was chosen by excluding venire-

---

Capital Cases (Unpublished Manuscript, Morehouse College, undated). In his petition for certiorari, he cited a study based upon interviews with 1,248 jurors in New York and Chicago. A preliminary, unpublished summary of the results of that study stated that "a jury consisting only of jurors who have no scruples against the death penalty is likely to be more prosecution prone than a jury on which objectors to the death penalty sit," and that "the defendant's chances of acquittal are somewhat reduced if the objectors are excluded from the jury." H. Zeisel, Some Insights Into the Operation of Criminal Juries 42 (Confidential First Draft, University of Chicago, November 1957).

11. During the post-conviction proceedings here under review, the petitioner's counsel argued that the prosecution-prone character of "death-qualified" juries presented "purely a legal question," the resolution of

which required "no additional proof" beyond "the facts ... disclosed by the transcript of the voir dire examination...." Counsel sought an "opportunity to submit evidence" in support of several contentions unrelated to the issue involved here. On this issue, however, no similar request was made, and the studies relied upon by the petitioner in this Court were not mentioned. We can only speculate, therefore, as to the precise meaning of the terms used in those studies, the accuracy of the techniques employed, and the validity of the generalizations made. Under these circumstances, it is not surprising that the *amicus curiae* brief filed by the NAACP Legal Defense and Educational Fund finds it necessary to observe that, with respect to bias in favor of the prosecution on the issue of guilt, the record in this case is "almost totally lacking in the sort of factual information that would assist the Court."

men for cause simply because they voiced general objections to the death penalty or expressed conscientious or religious scruples against its infliction. No defendant can constitutionally be put to death at the hands of a tribunal so selected.

Whatever else might be said of capital punishment, it is at least clear that its imposition by a hanging jury cannot be squared with the Constitution. The State of Illinois has stacked the deck against the petitioner. To execute this death sentence would deprive him of his life without due process of law.

———

GRIGSBY v. MABRY

United States District Court, Eastern District of Arkansas, 1983.
569 F.Supp. 1273.

■ Eisele, Chief Judge:

Pending before the Court are the habeas corpus petitions of James T. Grigsby [a]nd Ardia McCree, who have been in the custody of the Arkansas Department of Correction since their convictions for capital murder. Each petitioner contends that his conviction must be set aside due to the exclusion for cause at the guilt determination phase of his trial of certain venirepersons who during *voir dire* professed adamant scruples against the death penalty.

[A]s a result of *Witherspoon* both those who are able to make an impartial decision on the defendant's guilt and those who are not are excluded from participating in that decision if they, on *voir dire,* express adamant opposition to the death penalty, i.e., if they would, at any later sentencing phase, "automatically" vote against the death penalty without regard to the evidence in the case. Jurors possessing such strong scruples against the death penalty are referred to as "*Witherspoon* Excludables" or "WEs." [T]he petitioner in *Witherspoon* attempted to persuade the Supreme Court on the basis of logic and intuition that those persons who expressed attitudes in favor of the death penalty would, as jurors, "favor the prosecution in the determination of guilt." [T]he petitioner in *Witherspoon* expressly declined the "opportunity to submit evidence" on the guilt-proneness issue. It is true that at the appellate level the petitioner asked the Supreme Court to judicially notice summaries of some early social scientific research. [T]he Supreme Court found this data "too tentative and fragmentary to establish that jurors not opposed to the death penalty tend to favor the prosecution in the determination of guilt." Indeed, those data were very "tentative and fragmentary."

[T]he Supreme Court noted in *Witherspoon* that the items which it was asked to judicially notice had not been introduced into evidence or subjected to the fact-finding process. Therefore, the Court was left to: " ... speculate ... as to the precise meaning of the terms used in the studies, the accuracy of the techniques employed and the validity of the generalizations made." Id. at 517 n. 11, 88 S.Ct. at 1774 n. 11. The Court ultimately refused to find, based upon the record or judicial notice, "that the exclusion of jurors opposed to capital punishment results in an unrepresentative jury on the issue of guilt. . . ." Id. at 517–18, 88 S.Ct. at 1774–75. By this determination the Supreme Court refused to adopt a *per se* guilt phase rule. Instead, it invited further study, leaving it open for future defendants to attempt to prove that juries death-qualified by *Witherspoon* standards were "less than neutral with respect to guilt." See id. at 518, 88 S.Ct. at 1775.

The petitioners in the case at bar have responded to the Supreme Court's invitation with a plethora of well-documented scientific research that does not suffer from the numerous deficiencies attributed to the research in *Witherspoon*.

[After Witherspoon, these] questions remained: (1) Are there among those in the group adamantly opposed to the death penalty (the WEs) persons who could fairly and impartially try the guilt/innocence issue if they did not have to participate in the sentencing phase, and (2), if so, does the exclusion of such persons deprive the defendant at the guilt phase of a representative jury, or result in a jury that is more prone to convict than would be a jury from which such persons were not excluded?

The term "nullifier" is used to describe a prospective juror who states that he would be unable to try the issue of the defendant's guilt/innocence upon the basis of the evidence and the law. In the death-penalty context this is the person who would say, "I cannot vote a defendant guilty regardless of the evidence if I know that, should he be convicted, someone else [the court or some other jury] might impose the death penalty." These nullifiers are described in *Witherspoon* as those persons who make it unmistakably clear that their attitude toward the death penalty "would prevent them from making an impartial decision as to the defendant's guilt." See 391 U.S. at 513, 88 S.Ct. at 1772. It is, of course, agreed by all that "nullifiers" are properly excluded from both the guilt/innocence phase and the sentencing phase of a capital case. But it is urged that no proper reason exists for the exclusion of the impartial WEs at the guilt/innocence phase. For this reason they are sometimes referred to as "Guilt-Phase Includables."

Using this terminology all "*Witherspoon* Excludables" (WEs) may be divided into "Nullifiers" and "Guilt Phase Includables."

This court must decide on the basis of the evidence presented if there are differences, material to jury performance, between those qualified to serve under *Witherspoon* standards and those who are excluded by such standards.

[Research on this topic has been] undertaken by Dr. Phoebe Ellsworth and her colleagues Dr. Joan C. Harrington, Dr. William Thompson, Dr. Claudia Cowan and Raymond M. Bukaty in 1979. The studies were designed to replicate the results of earlier studies using more sophisticated experimental and control techniques and to attempt to gain some insight into the reasons that death-qualified jurors might be more conviction prone than non-death qualified jurors who could fairly try the issue of guilt-innocence in capital trials.

The transcript of Dr. Ellsworth's testimony in the *Hovey* case [Hovey v. Superior Court, 28 Cal.3d 1, 168 Cal.Rptr. 128, 616 P.2d 1301 (1980)] was received in evidence here. Dr. Haney relied upon that transcript together with the studies themselves for the purpose of explaining the full thrust and effect of those studies. It will be recalled that the California Supreme Court found Dr. Ellsworth's work very persuasive.

The subjects of the five *Ellsworth* studies were all drawn from the same panel of 288 adult, jury-eligible citizens in Santa Clara and San Mateo counties in California. They were recruited by using a jury list from the local court and by advertising for volunteers. Forty-five percent had prior jury service. Each subject was read an introductory statement and was asked to assume that he or she was a prospective juror in a criminal case being questioned by a judge. The statement explained the bifurcated process by which capital trials are presently conducted in this country. Each was then asked the following question:

Which of the following expresses what you would do if you were a juror for the first (guilt/innocence) part of the trial?

a.   I would follow the judge's instructions and decide the question of guilt or innocence in a fair and impartial manner based on the evidence and the law or

b.   I would not be fair and impartial in deciding the question of guilt or innocence, knowing that if the person was convicted he or she might get the death penalty.

Those who chose (b) were then excluded from participation in any of the studies. This eliminated the "nullifiers," leaving only those who could sit as impartial jurors at the guilt-innocence phase of capital trials.

The subjects were also inquired of as follows:

The judge will ask you this question:

Is your attitude toward the death penalty such that as a juror you would never be willing to impose it in any case, no matter what the evidence was or would you consider voting to impose it in at least some cases?

a.   I would be unwilling to impose it in any case.

b.   I would consider voting to impose it in some cases.

The answers identified the *Witherspoon* Excludables, or, more precisely, the "Guilt Phase Includables" (since the nullifiers had already been removed) on the one hand and identified those who were death-qualified on the other hand. With this information Dr. Ellsworth and her colleagues were able to compare the voting behavior of the subjects in all five studies. The final sample was composed of 258 death-qualified subjects and 30 WEs.

The *Ellsworth* studies did not use random sampling techniques. In fact they often restricted the number of WEs so that, in the deliberation studies, simulated juries could be composed of differing percentages of WEs, i.e., so that such 12-person juries could have 0, 1, 2, 3 or 4, but not more than 4 WEs.

Since random techniques were not employed no claim is made that it is possible to generalize from the numbers of WEs and death-qualified in the subject pool to the population at large.

In the *Ellsworth Conviction Proneness Study 1979,* [t]he stimulus used was a 2-hour videotape re-enactment of an actual murder trial in Massachusetts. It was prepared by Dr. Hastie for use in his own work and was loaned to Dr. Ellsworth for her study. She revised it somewhat and substituted California jury instructions. The tape included opening statements, the direct and cross-examination of seven witnesses, closing arguments and one-half hour of jury instructions. It was filmed in a Massachusetts courtroom using a judge, a prosecutor and a defense attorney to portray those same roles in the film. Probably no simulation, even of an actual trial, will be completely satisfactory to an experienced judge or lawyer. But the Court finds this videotape to be a high quality and realistic stimulus. The tape is in evidence in its entirety.

After viewing the videotape each subject was asked to vote for one of four verdicts: (1) guilty of first degree murder, (2) guilty of second degree murder, (3) guilty of voluntary manslaughter, or (4) not guilty by reason of self-defense or excusable homicide. The results were as follows:

ELLSWORTH CONVICTION-PRONENESS STUDY

DISTRIBUTION OF INITIAL VERDICTS

(BY DEATH-QUALIFIED/EXCLUDABLE)

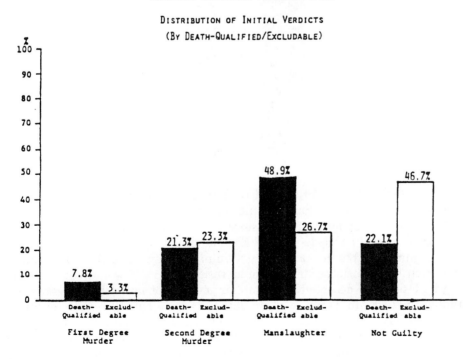

It will be seen that most voted for manslaughter or acquittal. Few voted for first or second degree murder. Among these there were no significant differences but when the manslaughter and not guilty votes are considered the typical pattern emerges. About half of the death-qualified jurors voted to convict of manslaughter while only approximately one-fourth of the *Witherspoon* excludables so voted. Put another way 46.7% of WEs voted to acquit as compared with 22.1% of the death-qualified.

Considering only guilty and not guilty votes this study shows a 25% greater guilty vote by death-qualified subjects compared to WEs (77.9% versus 53.3%). Note the following graph:

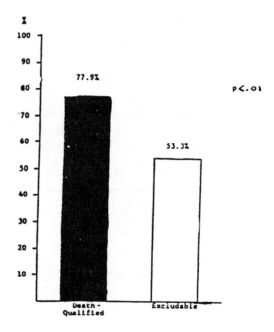

ELLSWORTH CONVICTION-PRONENESS STUDY
PERCENT VOTING GUILTY
(BY DEATH-QUALIFIED/EXCLUDABLE)

Dr. Ellsworth then proceeded to determine the effect that systematic exclusion of WEs would have on the number of not guilty votes in a case such as that portrayed. She assumed that 17.2% of the jury eligible population would be made up of WEs. The Court finds this to have been a valid assumption based upon the attitudinal surveys. She then determined that such systematic exclusion would result in 31% fewer initial votes to acquit. Using the accepted and familiar method of multiple regression (so frequently used in racial discrimination cases), Dr. Ellsworth excluded other possibly relevant factors that might arguably account for such differences, e.g., age, gender, area of residence, or prior jury experience. This study provides strong evidence for the opinion, so often expressed by petitioners' experts, that death penalty attitudes are a far better predictor of juror voting behavior than any other single characteristic.

The results of this study are significant and demonstrate that persons who are death-qualified by *Witherspoon* standards are substantially more likely to vote to acquit than are persons excluded by those standards.* This study marks the culmination of some fifteen years of research demonstrating the divergent juror voting propensities of death-qualified versus excludable jurors.

Can the behavior of *juries* be predicted from the results of studies revealing the attitudes and voting behavior of individual *jurors*? Dr. Hastie answers this in the affirmative, basing his opinion in part upon the findings of Hans Zeisel and Harry Kalven in *The American Jury* [(1966)]. One of those findings, based upon extensive empirical investigation, is that the first ballot preferences of a majority of jurors in a given case is the single most accurately predictive factor in determining the final verdict outcome by that jury. Since first ballots are frequently taken prior to any extensive jury deliberations, the attitudes which each juror brings to the jury room turn out to be very important in explaining the differences that surface upon the initial ballot. The evidence shows that there is a strong propensity for *initial majority* verdicts to be the same as the *final unanimous* verdict. Therefore, studies of individual juror attitudes provide reliable information about final jury verdicts.

Dr. Hastie's own studies also support his opinion. His research shows that "initial faction size" constitutes the best predictive factor in determining final verdict outcomes, i.e., the verdict initially selected by the largest faction will most likely become the jury's final verdict. So the extent of initial agreement, prior to jury deliberation, is most often decisive of the final outcome.

The Court finds that the systematic exclusion of WEs from capital juries will reduce the number of cases with an initial majority, or largest faction, in favor of acquittal or in favor of a lesser included offense and will thereby substantially lessen the likelihood of acquittal and the likelihood of a vote of guilty to a lesser-included offense when the final unanimous jury verdict comes in.

[T]he phrase "fireside induction" has been used to refer to "those common sense empirical generalizations about human behavior which derive from introspection, anecdotal evidence, and culturally transmitted beliefs."[14]

[H]ere the fireside inductions clearly support the contentions of petitioners. If asked, "Does the removal of all prospective jurors with adamant objections to the death penalty result in a jury more prone to convict?" Trial lawyers and judges will answer, "yes, of course." If asked, "Does the

---

* [Ed. Note: There appears to be a typographical error in this sentence. Either "death-qualified" should be "disqualified," or "acquit" should be "convict."]

14. Meehl, Law and Fireside Inductions: Some Reflections of a Clinical Psychologist, in Law Justice and the Individual in Society (J. Tapp & F. Levine Eds.1977).

usual process of death qualification itself, as observed time and again, prejudice the defendant?" The answer, "yes, clearly."

Yet it is always possible that our dearly held "fireside induction" may be proved to have been in error, to be nothing more than professional superstition. And the U.S. Supreme Court in *Witherspoon* itself counsels against embracing *per se* rules based upon judicial notice or intuition without the benefit of empirical studies.

The research has been done. The studies have been introduced into evidence and explained. What do they show? They prove that what we "knew" all along is in fact true. The trial lawyers and judges could have been wrong but in this case at least they were right.

[M]r. Grigsby is now deceased. The Court will therefore set aside the conviction of Mr. McCree only and direct the respondent, within 90 days, to retry him or to set him free.

——————

LOCKHART v. McCREE

Supreme Court of the United States, 1986.
476 U.S. 162, 106 S.Ct. 1758, 90 L.Ed.2d 137.

■ Justice Rehnquist delivered the opinion of the Court.

In this case we address the question left open by our decision nearly 18 years ago in Witherspoon v. Illinois, 391 U.S. 510, 88 S.Ct. 1770, 20 L.Ed.2d 776 (1968): Does the Constitution prohibit the removal for cause, prior to the guilt phase of a bifurcated capital trial, of prospective jurors whose opposition to the death penalty is so strong that it would prevent or substantially impair the performance of their duties as jurors at the sentencing phase of the trial? We hold that it does not.

[T]he District Court held a hearing on the "death qualification" issue in July 1981, receiving in evidence numerous social science studies concerning the attitudes and beliefs of "*Witherspoon*-excludables," along with the potential effects of excluding them from the jury prior to the guilt phase of a bifurcated capital trial. In August 1983, the court concluded, based on the social science evidence, that "death qualification" produced juries that "were more prone to convict" capital defendants than "non-death-qualified" juries. Grigsby v. Mabry, 569 F.Supp., at 1323. The court ruled that "death qualification" thus violated both the fair cross-section and impartiality requirements of the Sixth and Fourteenth Amendments, and granted McCree habeas relief.

The Eighth Circuit found "substantial evidentiary support" for the District Court's conclusion that the removal for cause of "*Witherspoon*-excludables" resulted in "conviction-prone" juries, and affirmed the grant of habeas relief on the ground that such removal for cause violated McCree's constitutional right to a jury selected from a fair cross-section of the community. Grigsby v. Mabry, 758 F.2d, at 229.

[B]efore turning to the legal issues in the case, we are constrained to point out what we believe to be several serious flaws in the evidence upon which the courts below reached the conclusion that "death qualification" produces "conviction-prone" juries.[3] McCree introduced into evidence some fifteen social science studies in support of his constitutional claims, but only six of the studies even purported to measure the potential effects on the guilt-innocence determination of the removal from the jury of "*Witherspoon*-excludables."[4] Eight of the remaining nine studies dealt solely with generalized attitudes and beliefs about the death penalty and other aspects of the criminal justice system, and were thus, at best, only marginally relevant to the constitutionality of McCree's conviction.[5] The fifteenth and final study dealt with the effects on prospective jurors of *voir dire* questioning about their attitudes toward the death penalty,[6] an issue McCree raised

3. McCree argues that the "factual" findings of the District Court and the Eighth Circuit on the effects of "death qualification" may be reviewed by this Court only under the "clearly erroneous" standard of Federal Rule of Civil Procedure 52(a). Because we do not ultimately base our decision today on the invalidity of the lower courts' "factual" findings, we need not decide the "standard of review" issue. We are far from persuaded, however, that the "clearly erroneous" standard of Rule 52(a) applies to the kind of "legislative" facts at issue here. See generally Dunagin v. City of Oxford, Mississippi, 718 F.2d 738, 748, n. 8 (C.A.5 1983) (en banc) (plurality opinion of Reavley, J.). The difficulty with applying such a standard to "legislative" facts is evidenced here by the fact that at least one other Court of Appeals, reviewing the same social science studies as introduced by McCree, has reached a conclusion contrary to that of the Eighth Circuit. See Keeten v. Garrison, 742 F.2d 129, 133, n. 7 (C.A.4 1984) (disagreeing that studies show relationship between generalized attitudes and behavior as jurors), cert. pending, No. 84—187.

4. The Court of Appeals described the following studies as "conviction-proneness surveys": H. Zeisel, Some Data on Juror Attitudes Toward Capital Punishment (University of Chicago Monograph 1968) (Zeisel); W. Wilson, Belief in Capital Punishment and Jury Performance (unpublished manuscript, University of Texas, 1964) (Wilson); Goldberg, Toward Expansion of *Witherspoon:* Capital Scruples, Jury Bias, and Use of Psychological Data to Raise Presumptions in the Law, 5 Harv.Civ.Rights–Civ.Lib.L.Rev. 53 (1970) (Goldberg); Jurow, New Data on the Effect of a "Death Qualified" Jury on the Guilt Determination Process, 84 Harv.L.Rev.

567 (1971) (Jurow); and Cowan, Thompson, & Ellsworth, The Effects of Death Qualification on Jurors' Predisposition to Convict and on the Quality of Deliberation, 8 Law & Hum.Behav. 53 (1984) (Cowan–Deliberation). In addition, McCree introduced evidence on this issue from a Harris Survey conducted in 1971. Louis Harris & Associates, Inc., Study No. 2016 (1971) (Harris–1971).

5. The Court of Appeals described the following studies as "attitudinal and demographic surveys": Bronson, On the Conviction Proneness and Representativeness of the Death-Qualified Jury: An Empirical Study of Colorado Veniremen, 42 U.Colo.L.Rev. 1 (1970); Bronson, Does the Exclusion of Scrupled Jurors in Capital Cases Make the Jury More Likely to Convict? Some Evidence from California, 3 Woodrow Wilson L.J. 11 (1980); Fitzgerald & Ellsworth, Due Process vs. Crime Control: Death Qualification and Jury Attitudes, 8 Law & Hum.Behav. 31 (1984); and Precision Research, Inc., Survey No. 1286 (1981). In addition, McCree introduced evidence on these issues from Thompson, Cowan, Ellsworth, & Harrington, Death Penalty Attitudes and Conviction Proneness, 8 Law & Hum.Behav. 95 (1984); Ellsworth, Bukaty, Cowan, & Thompson, The Death-Qualified Jury and the Defense of Insanity, 8 Law & Hum.Behav. 81 (1984); A. Young, Arkansas Archival Study (unpublished, 1981); and various Harris, Gallup, and National Opinion Research Center polls conducted between 1953 and 1981.

6. McCree introduced evidence on this issue from Haney, On the Selection of Capital Juries: The Biasing Effects of the Death-Qualification Process, 8 Law & Hum.Behav. 121 (1984).

in his brief to this Court but that counsel for McCree admitted at oral argument would not, standing alone, give rise to a constitutional violation.[7]

Of the six studies introduced by McCree that at least purported to deal with the central issue in this case, namely, the potential effects on the determination of guilt or innocence of excluding "*Witherspoon*-excludables" from the jury, three were also before this Court when it decided *Witherspoon, supra.*[8] There, this Court reviewed the studies and concluded:

> "The data adduced by the petitioner ... are too tentative and fragmentary to establish that jurors not opposed to the death penalty tend to favor the prosecution in the determination of guilt. We simply cannot conclude, either on the basis of the record now before us or as a matter of judicial notice, that the exclusion of jurors opposed to capital punishment results in an unrepresentative jury on the issue of guilt or substantially increases the risk of conviction. In light of the presently available information, we are not prepared to announce a *per se* constitutional rule requiring the reversal of every conviction returned by a jury selected as this one was." Id., at 517–518, 88 S.Ct., at 1774–75 (footnote omitted).

It goes almost without saying that if these studies were "too tentative and fragmentary" to make out a claim of constitutional error in 1968, the same studies, unchanged but for having aged some eighteen years, are still insufficient to make out such a claim in this case.

Nor do the three post-*Witherspoon* studies introduced by McCree on the "death qualification" issue provide substantial support for the "*per se* constitutional rule*" McCree asks this Court to adopt. All three of the "new" studies were based on the responses of individuals randomly selected from some segment of the population, but who were not actual jurors sworn under oath to apply the law to the facts of an actual case involving the fate of an actual capital defendant.[9] We have serious doubts about the value of these studies in predicting the behavior of actual jurors. In addition, two of the three "new" studies did not even attempt to simulate the process of jury deliberation,[10] and none of the "new" studies was able to predict to what extent, if any, the presence of one or more "*Witherspoon-*

---

7. We would in any event reject the argument that the very process of questioning prospective jurors at *voir dire* about their views of the death penalty violates the Constitution. McCree concedes that the State may challenge for cause prospective jurors whose opposition to the death penalty is so strong that it would prevent them from impartially determining a capital defendant's guilt or innocence. *Ipso facto,* the State must be given the opportunity to identify such prospective jurors by questioning them at *voir dire* about their views of the death penalty.

8. The petitioner in *Witherspoon* cited the Wilson and Goldberg studies, and a prepublication draft of the Zeisel study.

9. The Harris–1971 study polled 2,068 adults from throughout the United States, the Cowan-Deliberation study involved 288 jury-eligible residents of San Mateo and Santa Clara Counties in California, and the Jurow study was based on the responses of 211 employees of the Sperry Rand Corporation in New York.

10. The Harris–1971 and Jurow studies did not allow for group deliberation, but rather measured only individual responses.

excludables" on a guilt-phase jury would have altered the outcome of the guilt determination.[11]

Finally, and most importantly, only one of the six "death qualification" studies introduced by McCree even attempted to identify and account for the presence of so-called "nullifiers," or individuals who, because of their deep-seated opposition to the death penalty, would be unable to decide a capital defendant's guilt or innocence fairly and impartially.[12] McCree concedes, as he must, that "nullifiers" may properly be excluded from the guilt-phase jury, and studies that fail to take into account the presence of such "nullifiers" thus are fatally flawed.[13] Surely a *"per se* constitutional rule" as far-reaching as the one McCree proposes should not be based on the results of the lone study that avoids this fundamental flaw.

Having identified some of the more serious problems with McCree's studies, however, we will assume for purposes of this opinion that the studies are both methodologically valid and adequate to establish that "death qualification" in fact produces juries somewhat more "conviction-prone" than "non-death-qualified" juries. We hold, nonetheless, that the Constitution does not prohibit the States from "death qualifying" juries in capital cases.

The Eighth Circuit ruled that "death qualification" violated McCree's right under the Sixth Amendment, as applied to the States via incorporation through the Fourteenth Amendment, to a jury selected from a representative cross-section of the community. But we do not believe that the fair cross-section requirement can, or should, be applied as broadly as that court attempted to apply it. We have never invoked the fair cross-section principle to invalidate the use of either for-cause or peremptory challenges to prospective jurors, or to require petit juries, as opposed to jury panels or venires, to reflect the composition of the community at large.

---

11. Justice Marshall's dissent refers to an "essential unanimity" of support among social-science researchers and other academics for McCree's assertion that "death qualification" has a significant effect on the outcome of jury deliberations at the guilt phase of capital trials. See post, at 6. At least one of the articles relied upon by the dissent candidly acknowledges, however, that its conclusions ultimately must rest on "[a] certain amount of . . . conjecture" and a willingness "to transform behavioral suspicions into doctrine." Finch & Ferraro, The Empirical Challenge to Death Qualified Juries: On Further Examination, 65 Neb.L.Rev. 21, 67 (1986). As the authors of the article explain:

"[U]ncertainty inheres in every aspect of the capital jury's operation, whether one focuses on the method of identifying excludables or the deliberative process through which verdicts are reached. So it is that, some seventeen years after *Witherspoon,* no

definitive conclusions can be stated as to the frequency or the magnitude of the effects of death qualification.

* * *

"Nor is it likely that further empirical research can add significantly to the current understanding of death qualification. The true magnitude of the phenomenon of conviction proneness is probably unmeasurable, given the complexity of capital cases and capital adjudication." Id., at 66–67.

12. Only the Cowan-Deliberation study attempted to take into account the presence of "nullifiers."

13. The effect of this flaw on the outcome of a particular study is likely to be significant. The Cowan-Deliberation study revealed that approximately 37% of the *"Witherspoon*-excludables" identified in the study were also "nullifiers."

[B]ut even if we were willing to extend the fair cross-section requirement to petit juries, we would still reject the Eighth Circuit's conclusion that "death qualification" violates that requirement. The essence of a "fair cross-section" claim is the systematic exclusion of "a 'distinctive' group in the community." [Duren v. Missouri] 439 U.S., at 364, 99 S.Ct., at 668. In our view, groups defined solely in terms of shared attitudes that would prevent or substantially impair members of the group from performing one of their duties as jurors, such as the "*Witherspoon*-excludables" at issue here, are not "distinctive groups" for fair cross-section purposes.

[T]he group of "*Witherspoon*-excludables" involved in the case at bar differs significantly from the groups we have previously recognized as "distinctive." "Death qualification," unlike the wholesale exclusion of blacks, women, or Mexican-Americans from jury service, is carefully designed to serve the State's concededly legitimate interest in obtaining a single jury that can properly and impartially apply the law to the facts of the case at both the guilt and sentencing phases of a capital trial. There is very little danger, therefore, and McCree does not even argue, that "death qualification" was instituted as a means for the State to arbitrarily skew the composition of capital-case juries.

Furthermore, unlike blacks, women, and Mexican-Americans, "*Witherspoon*-excludables" are singled out for exclusion in capital cases on the basis of an attribute that is within the individual's control. It is important to remember that not all who oppose the death penalty are subject to removal for cause in capital cases; those who firmly believe that the death penalty is unjust may nevertheless serve as jurors in capital cases so long as they state clearly that they are willing to temporarily set aside their own beliefs in deference to the rule of law. Because the group of "*Witherspoon*-excludables" includes only those who cannot and will not conscientiously obey the law with respect to one of the issues in a capital case, "death qualification" hardly can be said to create an "appearance of unfairness."

Finally, the removal for cause of "*Witherspoon*-excludables" in capital cases does not prevent them from serving as jurors in other criminal cases, and thus leads to no substantial deprivation of their basic rights of citizenship. They are treated no differently than any juror who expresses the view that he would be unable to follow the law in a particular case.

In sum, "*Witherspoon*-excludables," or for that matter any other group defined solely in terms of shared attitudes that render members of the group unable to serve as jurors in a particular case, may be excluded from jury service without contravening any of the basic objectives of the fair cross-section requirement. It is for this reason that we conclude that "*Witherspoon*-excludables" do not constitute a "distinctive group" for fair cross-section purposes, and hold that "death qualification" does not violate the fair cross-section requirement.

McCree argues that, even if we reject the Eighth Circuit's fair cross-section holding, we should affirm the judgment below on the alternative ground, adopted by the District Court, that "death qualification" violated his constitutional right to an impartial jury. McCree concedes that the individual jurors who served at his trial were impartial, as that term was defined by this Court in cases such as Irvin v. Dowd, 366 U.S. 717, 723, 81 S.Ct. 1639, 1643, 6 L.Ed.2d 751 (1961) ("It is sufficient if the juror can lay aside his impression or opinion and render a verdict based on the evidence presented in court"), [I]nstead, McCree argues that his jury lacked impartiality because the absence of "*Witherspoon*-excludables" "slanted" the jury in favor of conviction.

We do not agree. McCree's "impartiality" argument apparently is based on the theory that, because all individual jurors are to some extent predisposed towards one result or another, a constitutionally impartial *jury* can be constructed only by "balancing" the various predispositions of the individual *jurors*. Thus, according to McCree, when the State "tips the scales" by excluding prospective jurors with a particular viewpoint, an impermissibly partial jury results. We have consistently rejected this view of jury impartiality, including as recently as last Term when we squarely held that an impartial *jury* consists of nothing more than "*jurors* who will conscientiously apply the law and find the facts." Wainwright v. Witt, 469 U.S. 412, 423, 105 S.Ct. 844, 852, 83 L.Ed.2d 841 (1985) (emphasis added).

The view of jury impartiality urged upon us by McCree is both illogical and hopelessly impractical. McCree characterizes the jury that convicted him as "slanted" by the process of "death qualification." But McCree admits that exactly the same twelve individuals could have ended up on his jury through the "luck of the draw," without in any way violating the constitutional guarantee of impartiality. Even accepting McCree's position that we should focus on the *jury* rather than the individual *jurors,* it is hard for us to understand the logic of the argument that a given jury is unconstitutionally partial when it results from a State-ordained process, yet impartial when exactly the same jury results from mere chance. On a more practical level, if it were true that the Constitution required a certain mix of individual viewpoints on the jury, then trial judges would be required to undertake the Sisyphean task of "balancing" juries, making sure that each contains the proper number of Democrats and Republicans, young persons and old persons, white-collar executives and blue-collar laborers, and so on. Adopting McCree's concept of jury impartiality would also likely require the elimination of peremptory challenges, which are commonly used by both the State and the defendant to attempt to produce a jury favorable to the challenger.

[I]n our view, it is simply not possible to define jury impartiality, for constitutional purposes, by reference to some hypothetical mix of individual viewpoints. Prospective jurors come from many different backgrounds, and have many different attitudes and predispositions. But the Constitution presupposes that a jury selected from a fair cross-section of the community is impartial, regardless of the mix of individual viewpoints actually represented on the jury, so long as the jurors can conscientiously and properly carry out their sworn duty to apply the law to the facts of the particular case. We hold that McCree's jury satisfied both aspects of this constitutional standard. The judgment of the Court of Appeals is therefore

Reversed.

■ JUSTICE MARSHALL, with whom JUSTICE BRENNAN and JUSTICE STEVENS join, dissenting.

With a glib nonchalance ill-suited to the gravity of the issue presented and the power of respondent's claims, the Court upholds a practice that allows the State a special advantage in those prosecutions where the charges are the most serious and the possible punishments, the most severe. The State's mere announcement that it intends to seek the death penalty if the defendant is found guilty of a capital offense will, under today's decision, give the prosecution license to empanel a jury especially likely to return that very verdict. Because I believe that such a blatant disregard for the rights of a capital defendant offends logic, fairness, and the Constitution, I dissent.

[I]n the wake of *Witherspoon,* a number of researchers set out to supplement the data that the Court had found inadequate in that case. The results of these studies were exhaustively analyzed by the District Court in this case, see Grigsby v. Mabry (*Grigsby II*), 569 F.Supp. 1273, 1291–1308 (E.D.Ark.1983), and can be only briefly summarized here.[2] The data strongly suggest that death qualification excludes a significantly large subset—at least 11% to 17%—of potential jurors who could be impartial during the guilt phase of trial.[3] Among the members of this excludable class are a disproportionate number of blacks and women.

The perspectives on the criminal justice system of jurors who survive death qualification are systematically different from those of the excluded jurors. Death-qualified jurors are, for example, more likely to believe that a defendant's failure to testify is indicative of his guilt, more hostile to the insanity defense, more mistrustful of defense attorneys, and less concerned

---

2. Most of the studies presented here were also comprehensively summarized in Hovey v. Superior Court [28 Cal.3d 1, 168 Cal.Rptr. 128, 616 P.2d 1301 (1980)]. Because the California Supreme Court found the studies had not accounted for jurors who could be excluded because they would automatically vote for the death penalty where possible, that court ultimately rejected a defendant's constitutional challenge to death qualification. But see Kadane, After *Hovey:* A Note on Taking Account of the Automatic Death Penalty Jurors, 8 Law & Hum.Behav. 115 (1984).

3. Bronson, On the Conviction Proneness and Representativeness of the Death-Qualified Jury: An Empirical Study of Colorado Veniremen, 12 U.Colo.L.Rev. 1 (1970) (using classification only approximating *Witherspoon* standard, and finding 11% of subjects *Witherspoon*-excludable); Bronson, Does the Exclusion of Scrupled Jurors in Capital Cases Make the Jury More Likely to Convict? Some Evidence from California, 3 Woodrow Wilson L.J. 11 (1980) (using more appropriate *Witherspoon* question and finding 93% overlap of "strongly opposed" group in prior Bronson study with *Witherspoon*-excludables); Jurow, New Data on the Effect of a "Death Qualified Jury" on the Guilt Determination Process, 84 Harv.L.Rev. 567 (1971) (finding only 10% of sample excludable, but likely to have underestimated size of class in general population because sample 99% white and 80% male); Fitzgerald & Ellsworth, Due Process vs. Crime Control: Death Qualification and Jury Attitudes, 8 Law & Hum.Behav. 31 (1984) (random sample with nullifiers screened out finding 17% still excludable under *Witherspoon*); A. Young, Arkansas Archival Study (unpublished, 1981) (14% of jurors questioned in *voir dire* transcripts excludable); Precision Research, Inc., Survey No. 1286 (1981) (11% excludable, not counting nullifiers).

about the danger of erroneous convictions. This pro-prosecution bias is reflected in the greater readiness of death-qualified jurors to convict or to convict on more serious charges. And, finally, the very process of death qualification—which focuses attention on the death penalty before the trial has even begun—has been found to predispose the jurors that survive it to believe that the defendant is guilty.

The evidence thus confirms, and is itself corroborated by, the more intuitive judgments of scholars and of so many of the participants in capital trials—judges, defense attorneys, and prosecutors.

[R]espondent's case would of course be even stronger were he able to produce data showing the prejudicial effects of death qualification upon actual trials. Yet until a State permits two separate juries to deliberate on the same capital case and return simultaneous verdicts, defendants claiming prejudice from death qualification should not be denied recourse to the only available means of proving their case, recreations of the *voir dire* and trial processes. See Grigsby v. Mabry, 758 F.2d, at 237 ("[I]t is the courts who have often stood in the way of surveys involving real jurors and we should not now reject a study because of this deficiency").

The chief strength of respondent's evidence lies in the essential unanimity of the results obtained by researchers using diverse subjects and varied methodologies. Even the Court's haphazard jabs cannot obscure the power of the array. Where studies have identified and corrected apparent flaws in prior investigations, the results of the subsequent work have only corroborated the conclusions drawn in the earlier efforts. Thus, for example, some studies might be faulted for failing to distinguish within the class of *Witherspoon*-excludables, between nullifiers (whom respondent concedes may be excluded from the guilt phase) and those who could assess guilt impartially. Yet their results are entirely consistent with those obtained after nullifiers had indeed been excluded. See, *e.g.*, Cowan, Thompson, & Ellsworth, The Effects of Death Qualification on Jurors Predisposition to Convict and on the Quality of Deliberation, 8 Law & Hum.Behav. 53 (1984). And despite the failure of certain studies to "allow for group deliberations," the value of their results is underscored by the discovery that initial verdict preferences, made prior to group deliberations, are a fair predictor of how a juror will vote when faced with opposition in the jury room. See Cowan, Thompson, & Ellsworth, supra, at 68–69; see also R. Hastie, S. Penrod, & N. Pennington, Inside the Jury 66 (1983); H. Kalven & H. Zeisel, The American Jury 488 (1966).

The evidence adduced by respondent is quite different from the "tentative and fragmentary" presentation that failed to move this Court in *Witherspoon*. 391 U.S., at 517, 88 S.Ct., at 1774. Moreover, in contrast to *Witherspoon*, the record in this case shows respondent's case to have been "subjected to the traditional testing mechanisms of the adversary process," Ballew v. Georgia, 435 U.S. 223, 246, 98 S.Ct. 1029, 1042, 55 L.Ed.2d 234 (1978) (Powell, J., concurring in judgment). At trial, respondent presented three expert witnesses and one lay witness in his case in chief, and two additional lay witnesses in his rebuttal. Testimony by these witnesses permitted the District Court, and allows this Court, better to understand the methodologies used here and their limitations. Further testing of respondent's empirical case came at the hands of the State's own expert witnesses. Yet even after considering the evidence adduced by the State, the Court of Appeals properly noted: "there are no studies which contradict the studies submitted [by respondent]; in other words, all of the documented studies support the district court's findings." 758 F.2d, at 238.

[F]aced with the near unanimity of authority supporting respondent's claim that death qualification gives the prosecution a particular advantage in the guilt phase of capital trials, the majority here makes but a weak effort to contest that proposition. Instead, it merely assumes for the purposes of this opinion "that 'death-qualification' in fact produces juries somewhat more 'conviction-prone' than 'non-death-qualified' juries," and then holds that this result does not offend the Constitution. This disregard for the clear import of the evidence tragically misconstrues the settled constitutional principles that guarantee a defendant the right to a fair trial and an impartial jury whose composition is not biased toward the prosecution.

OVERRULED: JURY NEUTRALITY IN CAPITAL CASES

Samuel R. Gross.
21 Stanford Lawyer 11 (1986).

At the outset, I should make my point of view clear. I argued the *Lockhart* case in the Supreme Court on behalf of the respondent, Mr. Ardia McCree, and I lost. Needless to say, I am not a detached observer.

[I]n the Supreme Court, the American Psychological Association filed a brief amicus curiae evaluating the social scientific evidence, and concluded that "without credible exception, the research studies show that death-qualified juries are prosecution prone [and] unrepresentative," and that "the research clearly satisfies the criteria for evaluating the methodological soundness, reliability and utility of empirical research." But the Supreme Court finds fault.

The Court begins its discussion of the empirical record by observing that "McCree introduced into evidence some fifteen social science studies. . . . "; five paragraphs later the Court concludes that it should not base its holding on the one "lone study" that it found worthy of consideration. I will mention only a few of the steps in the remarkable winnowing process that happens in between:

Several of the studies show that jurors who are excluded by death qualification differ greatly from those who remain, in their attitudes toward the criminal justice system—on questions such as whether a defendant who does not testify in his own defense is probably guilty. The Court immediately dismisses these studies as "at best, only marginally relevant" because they "dealt solely with generalized attitudes," and never considers them again.

Three of the remaining studies—which show directly that death-qualified jurors are more likely to vote to convict than those who are excluded—had been presented to the Supreme Court in *Witherspoon*. Therefore, the Court says, "[I]t goes almost without saying that if these studies were 'too tentative and fragmentary' . . . in 1968, the same studies, unchanged but having aged some eighteen years, are still insufficient." [B]ut [t]he fact that these studies were *insufficient* to prove a claim *by themselves* hardly means that they can be written off and ignored entirely when they are presented together with other evidence—which is exactly what the Supreme Court does.

One of McCree's studies shows that the *process* of questioning jurors about their death penalty attitudes predisposes them to believe that the defendant is guilty. The Court disposes of this study by pointing out that "counsel for McCree admitted at oral argument" that this problem "would not, standing alone, give rise to a constitutional violation." Needless to say, the effects of this type of questioning do not occur (and were not litigated) "standing alone"—they are an inseparable aspect of the process of identifying and excluding death penalty opponents—but the Supreme Court, having made this apparently irrelevant observation, acts as if it has one less study to think about.

The most striking thing about the Supreme Court's method of treating the social scientific studies on death qualification is what the Court does *not* do. The Court never even attempts to weigh all the evidence collectively, and reach a decision on the underlying facts. On this claim, that would have been easy: the evidence in support is uncommonly strong—and it is supported by anecdotal wisdom and common sense—while the evidence in opposition is non-existent. Instead, the Supreme Court shops around to find some objection to each study, and having found one, however tenuous, it rules that study out of bounds.

[M]cCree argued that because death qualification increases the likelihood of conviction, it undermines the impartiality of the jury. The Court finds this argument "both illogical and hopelessly impractical" because "McCree admits that exactly the same twelve individuals [who convicted him] could have ended up on his jury through the 'luck of the draw,' without in any way violating the constitutional guarantee of impartiality. . . .[I]t is hard for us to understand the logic of the argument that a given jury is unconstitutionally partial when it results in a State-ordained process, yet impartial when exactly the same jury results from mere chance." I have difficulty believing that the Court really means this. All-white juries can occur by chance; does that make them constitutional if they "result from a State-ordained process"? And what is the reach of this test? Residential segregation could occur by chance; so could an all-male work force. Does that make the arguments against them illogical and impractical when it is proven that chance had nothing to do with it?

[T]he Court could have held, as a matter of law, that the biasing effects of death qualification are immaterial, without taking on the task of contradicting a body of proof that no one seriously doubts. But that would have made their legal argument sound callous: "You may have proven that your jury was biased toward conviction, but it doesn't matter, not even if you are executed as a result." On the other hand, the Court could have held that the evidence is still insufficient without adding a tortuous legal holding— but that would have posed even greater difficulties. Such a decision would have rested on a single shaky leg: on an empirical question where the scientific community is uncommonly single minded, the Supreme Court has little credibility to assert the opposite. Worse, a holding based solely on the insufficiency of the evidence would have been an invitation for future litigation based on additional studies and even fuller records, and the last thing the Court wanted was to face this claim again.

NOTE

1. External Validity. The amicus brief filed by the American Psychological Association in the *Lockhart* case addressed the issue of the generalization of the research findings to actual juries:

[One] criticism concerns the fact that the studies compared death-qualified and excludable jurors, rather than death-qualified and typical criminal juries. Inevitably, juries composed of a mixture of death-qualified and GPI [Guilt Phase Includable] jurors will fall somewhere between a jury composed solely of GPIs or DQs [Death-Qualifieds]. Death-qualified jurors are more conviction prone than such mixed juries would be. Thus, the size of the difference between the pure WE [Witherspoon-Excludable] and pure DQ groups in the research studies cannot be taken as an accurate estimate of the size of the difference between jury verdicts, although the existence and direction of the effect is clear from the studies. The precise magnitude of difference in a given case will change as a result of many variables, e.g., quality of lawyering, first ballot verdict, number of WEs on mixed juries, strength of the evidence.

The research demonstrates that the composition of juries in terms of death penalty attitudes is an important variable and that over the long run eliminating GPIs will increase the number of guilty verdicts.

UNITED STATES v. GREEN

United States District Court, District of Massachusetts, 2004.
343 F.Supp.2d 23.

■ GERTNER, D.J.

Count Sixteen of the superceding indictment in the above entitled case alleges that Branden Morris ("Morris") and Darryl Green killed Terrell

Gethers for the purpose of maintaining and increasing position in the Enterprise, which was an Enterprise engaged in racketeering activity ... " whose goal was to engage in the sale of crack cocaine and marijuana, to seek to prevent others from interfering with their sales, and specifically, to carry on a violent dispute with a rival gang, the Franklin Hill Giants. That dispute allegedly led to a number of murders and attempted murders during a one year period in 2000 and 2001.

[T]he issue before me principally concerns the conduct of the trials of the two death penalty defendants, Morris and Darryl Green. [S]hould a penalty phase be necessary, there is no question that the government is entitled to death-qualify the *punishment* jury. *Witherspoon*, 391 U.S. at 520. Specifically, the government may ask whether the venireman's views about the death penalty "would prevent or substantially impair the performance of his duties as a juror in accordance with his instructions and his oath." *Wainwright v. Witt,* 469 U.S. 412, 424, 105 S.Ct. 844, 83 L.Ed.2d 841 (1985) (internal quotations omitted); *Witherspoon,* 391 U.S. at 520.

Since the usual practice is to have a guilt trial followed by a penalty trial before the same jury, the usual result is that the Court death-qualifies the guilt jury as well. Section 3593, for example, codifies this practice by providing that the capital hearing "shall be conducted—(1) before the jury that determined the defendant's guilt," or "before a jury impaneled for the purpose of the hearing if the jury that determined defendant's guilt was discharged for good cause." 18 U.S.C. § 3593(b).

But the usual practice of death-qualifying a single jury charged with hearing both liability and punishment is neither constitutionally nor statutorily required. It has simply evolved as a standard practice. Nothing prevents this Court from fashioning a different procedure more suited to the facts of this case, to the exigencies of the Court's calendar, and to the promotion of fairness to both sides.

Unitary Jury Versus Two Juries

In *Lockhart v. McCree,* 476 U.S. 162, 106 S.Ct. 1758, 90 L.Ed.2d 137 (1986), the Court finally addressed, albeit indirectly, the question of whether the Constitution permits or prohibits a unitary jury or dual juries. In *Lockhart* the court concluded that the practice of death-qualifying the unitary jury did not violate a defendant's rights. [D]eath-qualification of the unitary jury, in short, on the record then presented to the Court, did not raise constitutional issues.

But that conclusion did not suggest its opposite, which the government argues here—that a court *must* have a unitary jury, that the unitary jury *must be* death-qualified in all cases, and indeed, that the government has a right to a death-qualified unitary jury. The precise question in *Lockhart* was whether "the Constitution prohibit[s] the removal for cause, prior to the guilt phase of a bifurcated capital trial, of prospective jurors whose opposition to the death penalty is so strong that it would prevent or substantially impair the performance of their duties as jurors at the sentencing phase of the trial." *Id.* at 165. The Court held that the Constitution did not *prohibit* the removal of death penalty opponents for cause. Importantly, it did not hold that the Constitution *requires* the removal of death penalty opponents prior to the guilt phase.

[U]nique Complexity of Death-Qualifying a Massachusetts Jury

[S]tudies suggest that death-qualification leads to the exclusion of a disproportionate number of black and female jurors, especially in this Commonwealth. Defendant's preliminary data suggests that African-Americans are under-represented in the jury venire in the Eastern Division of Massachusetts, by as much as half their representation in the community—particularly that 7.8%—9.1% of residents in the Eastern Division of Massachusetts are in whole or in part African-American, that a significantly smaller percentage are included in the jury venire, that in the United States population 48% of black people (but only 22% of whites) oppose the death penalty, and that 45% of Massachusetts voters overall oppose the death penalty. *See Green,* 324 F.Supp.2d at 329. Death-qualifying a jury could significantly deplete the already paltry number of minority jurors in the Eastern District.

Initial data gathered by defendants indicates that economic status and racial compositions of cities are closely connected to the return rates of the local census, which determines which names are placed on the Master Jury Wheel. Potential jurors whose names are placed on the Master Wheel by the Federal Jury Commissioner are mailed a jury summons and a juror questionnaire. Further preliminary research by defendants indicates that only approximately half of the summonses mailed are returned with completed questionnaires, and that, of the questionnaires returned over the last three years, the percentage returned by African-Americans was around 3%.

These two factors—the large percentage of African-Americans who are opposed to the death penalty and the disproportionately small number of African-Americans in the Eastern District of Massachusetts jury venire—de facto exclude all or most African-Americans from a death-qualified jury.

This result was clear in *United States v. Gilbert* (98–cr–30044–MAP), where of the 600 people who completed questionnaires, the court conducted voir dire of 203 jurors to qualify sixty-four. Only eight black individuals were voir dired—six opposing the death penalty (75%) and two favoring the death penalty only in special circumstances (25%). *No black jurors were seated.* The result was the same in *United States v. Sampson,* (01–cr–10384–MLW)[16] where of the 498 jurors that completed questionnaires only twenty-three identified themselves as black (4.6%). Of the potential black

16. The defense team in *Sampson* also compiled data on gender and attitudes towards the death penalty. Forty-three percent of the women, as opposed to 31.4% of the men were opposed to the death penalty. These numbers indicate a more pronounced differential than nationwide statistics indicating that 30% of women and 22% of men oppose the death penalty.

jurors, ten (43.5%) were opposed to the death penalty, one (4.3%) was in favor of the death penalty, and ten were neutral (43.5%). *No black jurors were seated on that jury either.*[17]

Moreover, similar studies raise the serious concern that death-qualified juries are more conviction prone. In both of the cases where it considered the issue—*Witherspoon* and *Lockhart*—the Supreme Court has rejected this argument citing "tentative and fragmentary" data. *Lockhart* at 170 (citing *Witherspoon* at 517–18). Notably, the Court did not wholly foreclose any constitutional infirmities stemming from conviction-prone death-qualified juries. *See Witherspoon* at 517–518 ("We simply cannot conclude . . . *on the basis of the record now before us* . . . *In light of the presently available information* . . ." that excluding jurors opposed to capital punishment increases the risk of conviction to the level of constitutional infirmity) (emphasis added). In the years since *Witherspoon* and *Lockhart* were decided, significant social science research has been devoted to studying the effect of death-qualification on jurors.

Updated data presented by defendants in this case overwhelmingly shows that death-qualified jurors are significantly more conviction prone than jurors who are not death qualified. For example, nearly one half (49.2%) of all death-qualified capital jurors make their sentencing decision before the penalty phase of the trial even begins. Darryl Green and Branden Morris's Supplemental Memorandum On the Issue of Impaneling Separate Juries, filed September 10, 2004, at p. 6. Several qualitative studies found that jurors who were exposed to the potential punishment during jury selection have a propensity to believe that the subtext of the voir dire is that the trial is not about whether the defendant committed the underlying crime but about what punishment the defendant should receive. *Id.* at 9–10 (citing Craig Haney, *On the Selection of Capital Juries: The Biasing Effects of the Death-Qualification Process,* 8 Law & Human Behavior 121 (1984); *Examining Death Qualification: Further Analysis of the Process Effect,* 8 Law & Human Behavior 133 (1984); Haney, Hurado & Vega, *"Modern" Death Qualification: New Data on Its Biasing Effects,* 18 Law & Human Behavior 619 (1994)). These findings represent just a sliver of the recent data indicating that death-qualified jurors are skewed to be conviction-prone.

While this decision does not rest on the conviction-prone juror problem, and its constitutional implications, it surely affects my obligations as a trial judge. Death penalty qualification hinders my responsibility to facili-

---

17. These numbers present a stark comparison with the attitudes of potential white jurors who completed questionnaires. In *Gilbert,* 170 jurors identified themselves as white, Caucasian, or of European origin— fifty-eight (34.1%) were opposed to the death penalty, fifty-six (32.9%) were generally in favor of the death penalty, and twenty-three (13.5%) approved of the death penalty in certain circumstances. In *Sampson,* 451 (90.1%) identified themselves as white—181 (40.1%) were in favor of the death penalty, 100 (22.2%) were neutral, and 170 (37.7%) were opposed. While I recognize the limitations of these statistics—the small sampling size, the limited amount of data available on the reasons for dismissal, the opinion characterizations created by defense counsel—these numbers give me great pause.

tate, to the best of my ability, a fair trial on guilt. It provides an additional "good cause" justifying bifurcating the juries in the trials of the capital defendants before me.

CONCLUSION

For all the above reasons, I will impanel a jury to decide guilt/innocence and, if necessary, a separate jury to decide penalty. I will "death-qualify" only the latter jury.

UNITED STATES v. GREEN

United States Court of Appeals, First Circuit, 2005.
407 F.3d 434.

■ SELYA, CIRCUIT JUDGE.

The district court's primary justification for its dual jury order rests with its interpretation of the relevant section of the FDPA [Federal Death Penalty Act]. The court concluded that 18 U.S.C. § 3593(b) permits a court to decide, before trial commences, that good cause exists to discharge the original jury once it has adjudicated the defendant's guilt and then empanel a new jury for the penalty phase.

18 U.S.C. § 3593(b) provides that if a defendant is found guilty or pleads guilty to a capital offense, there "shall" be a separate sentencing hearing. Id. The statute further provides that "[t]he hearing shall be conducted before the jury that determined the defendent's guilt." Id. § 3593(b)(1). The statute proceeds to carve out a series of exceptions [including] "(C) the jury that determined the defendant's guilt was discharged for good cause."

[T]he question before us concerns the proper interpretation of section 3593(b)(2)(C). The government argues that this is a narrow jury-discharge provision that only comes into play if, *after a finding of guilt*, good cause to discharge the original jury arises. The defendants argue that this is a broader, more malleable provision, one that should be construed against the backdrop of a trial court's extensive case management powers. On this basis, the defendants exhort us to hold that section 3593(b)(2)(C) requires only that the discharge of the guilt phase jury must occur before a new penalty phase jury is empaneled. As a necessary corollary of this interpretation, the defendants reason that the district court may decide at any time—even in advance of trial—that it will discharge the guilt phase jury for what it deems to be good cause and empanel a new jury for the penalty phase.

[T]he bottom line is this: where Congress has provided a specific panoply of rules that must be followed, the district court's discretionary powers simply do not come into play. Because this is such an instance, there is no reason to distort the plain meaning of the statutory text in an effort to preserve those powers. We hold, therefore, that the language of the exception in section 3593(b)(2)(C), ("the jury that determined the defendant's guilt was discharged for good cause . . .'') refers exclusively to a jury that has returned a guilty verdict in a federal capital case.

[T]he government invites us to pass upon the validity of the district court's suggestion that it might defer death-qualification altogether until after it takes a verdict on the issue of guilt or innocence. We decline the invitation. [F]ederal courts [cannot] issue advisory opinions. The suggestion against which the government seeks protection is not embodied in an order and the defendants have thus far decried the concept. Consequently, there is no live controversy as to that suggestion.

[I]nasmuch as the central issue presented in this case is novel, of great importance, likely to recur, and otherwise apt to evade review, we grant the government's petition for a writ of mandamus, vacate the dual jury order, and remand the case for further proceedings consistent with this opinion.

3.   VIDEOTAPED WITNESSES

Recent concern about the incidence of sexual abuse of children has, in turn, prompted concern about the process for taking the testimony of children in court. Many have contended that face-to-face courtroom encounters with an alleged abuser will be harmful to children and will likely impede their testimony. Reacting to this concern, a number of states have sought to employ videotape as an innovation for taking the testimony of children in such cases. Yet, defendants have insisted on strict application of the ''confrontation clause'' of the Sixth Amendment.

STATE v. JARZBEK

Supreme Court of Connecticut, 1987.
204 Conn. 683, 529 A.2d 1245.

■ PETERS, CHIEF JUSTICE.

The sole issue in this appeal is whether, in a criminal prosecution involving alleged sexual abuse of children, a minor victim may testify through the use of a videotape made outside the physical presence of the defendant.

[B]efore we address the merits of the defendant's attack on the videotaped evidence taken outside his physical presence, we must first identify the process by which that videotape was sought, the videotaping procedure that the trial court authorized, and the role that the videotaped testimony played at the defendant's trial. A detailed understanding of the record is essential to put the defendant's claims into focus.

The trial court permitted videotaping of the testimony of the alleged victims, T, and her brother, I, in response to a pretrial motion by the state. In support of its motion, the state presented the testimony of two clinical psychologists who opined that the children would be psychologically and emotionally traumatized if they were to be required to testify in open court in the presence of the defendant. The defendant called no witnesses of his own, although he did cross-examine the state's witnesses.

In granting the state's motion, the trial court framed the issue as "whether or not the videotaping of the testimony of these four and five year old witnesses outside the presence of the defendant and the jury in a case alleging sexual molesting by their father violates the defendant's sixth amendment right of confrontation." The court noted the widespread prevalence of child sexual abuse and the "tremendous rise" in the number of such cases in recent years. Relying upon the testimony of the psychologists, and upon the state's assertion that sexually abused children suffer further trauma when forced to testify in the presence of their alleged abusers, the court concluded that the children's testimony could be videotaped outside the physical presence of the defendant without violating his constitutional right of confrontation.

The trial court's order set out specific procedures designed to balance the needs of the children to testify without trauma and the right of the defendant to confront the witnesses against him. The court designated those who would be permitted to be present when one of the children testified: the child's mother, the judge, the state's attorney and one defense counsel. The court required the videotaping to take place in a setting comparable to a child psychology laboratory, consisting of a witness room connected by a one-way mirror to a monitoring room. The defendant, in the monitoring room, would not be visible from the witness room, but would be able to observe the witness fully and directly and to hear the testimony as it was given. The court recognized that the defendant was entitled to access to his counsel for the purpose of cross-examining the witness, and ordered that the witness room and the monitoring room be electronically linked by a communications device, such as an ear attachment, that would permit the defendant to communicate instantly with his counsel. To further the defendant's meaningful participation in cross-examination, the court also provided that the defendant should have the assistance of co-counsel while he was observing the videotaping from the monitoring room.

After a competency hearing, only T, the defendant's daughter, was deemed competent to testify at trial.[3] T's testimony was videotaped for trial in accordance with the court's order. Although the court's order would have enabled the defendant to observe the taping in the monitoring room, he chose not to attend the hearing. Defense counsel had a full opportunity to cross-examine T at the hearing at which her testimony was taped.

[A]lthough we conclude that neither a hearsay argument nor a theory of waiver provides a persuasive analogy legitimating the videotaped procedure that was used in this case, we accept the proposition that other compelling state interests may justify dispensing with the constitutionally mandated requirement of physical confrontation. The state has proffered two possible interests as justification for an impairment of the defendant's constitutional confrontation rights. First, the state contends that its interest in combating sexual abuse of children and minimizing the trauma

---

3. The younger witness, I, appeared at the competency hearing but refused to testify, despite the efforts of the trial court and the state's attorney to elicit testimony from him.

experienced by child victims when they participate in the judicial process outweighs the interests served by constitutional confrontation requirements. Second, it maintains that videotaping the testimony of a minor victim outside the physical presence of the accused is necessary to encourage minor victims of sex crimes to come forward and provide accurate testimony. According to the state, these two interests justify the adoption of a per se rule, applicable to all prosecutions involving sexual abuse of children, which would allow the videotaping of the testimony of a minor victim outside the physical presence of the defendant.

[T]he state's first rationale rests on the interest of the state, acting as parens patriae, in safeguarding the welfare of children. The underlying assumption is that sexually abused children who testify in open court, in the presence of their alleged abusers, suffer severe trauma and are thereby victimized a second time by the judicial system itself. See J. Parker, "The Rights of Child Witnesses: Is the Court A Protector or Perpetrator?" 17 New Eng.L.Rev. 643, 647–56 (1982); G. Melton, "Psychological Issues in Child Victim's Interaction with the Legal System," 5 Victimology 274–75 (1980); D. Libai, "The Protection of the Child Victim of a Sexual Offense in the Criminal Justice System," 15 Wayne L.Rev. 977, 983–84 (1969). That rationale further assumes that children are uniquely vulnerable witnesses who must be treated more delicately than adult witnesses in order to protect their psychological and emotional well-being. See L. Berliner & M. Barbieri, "The Testimony of the Child Victim of Sexual Assault," 40 J.Soc.Issues 125, 128 (1984).

We acknowledge that protecting the physical and psychological well-being of children is a compelling state interest. As the defendant accurately points out, however, it is by no means clear that sexually abused children are harmed, psychologically or otherwise, by the experience of testifying in the presence of their alleged abusers. To date, there is no empirical data that unequivocally supports the state's sweeping generalization that minor victims are inevitably traumatized by that experience. To the contrary, experts in child psychology who have studied sexually abused children are divided on the issue of whether they suffer undue trauma and further harm in facing the accused at trial. G. Melton, supra, 274; G. Goodman, "The Child Witness: Conclusions and Future Directions for Research and Legal Practice," 40 J.Soc.Issues 157, 167–68 (1984); D. Whitcomb, E. Shapiro & L. Stellwagen, "When the Victim is a Child: Issues for Judges and Prosecutors," National Institute of Justice (1985) pp. 17–18; L. Berliner & M. Barbieri, supra. Moreover, recent studies indicate that some minor victims actually benefit from their participation in proceedings that give them a sense of power over those who have violated them and afford them a long awaited opportunity to achieve vindication. G. Melton, "Sexually Abused Children and the Legal System: Some Policy Recommendations," 13 Am.J.Family Therapy 61, 64–65 (1985); L. Berliner & M. Barbieri, supra, 135; C. Rogers, "Child Sexual Abuse and the Courts: Preliminary Findings," Social Work and Child Sexual Abuse (Conte & Shore Eds.1982) pp. 145, 150.

Just as the United States Supreme Court, in Globe Newspaper Co. v. Superior Court, [457 U.S. 596] at 609, 102 S.Ct. at 2621 [73 L.Ed.2d 248 (1982)] rejected the generalization that sexually abused children invariably suffer traumatic injury by testifying in the presence of the press and the general public, we reject the generalization that these children will be traumatized by testifying in the presence of the accused. Given the lack of consensus among recognized authorities as to the effect on a minor victim of a face-to-face confrontation with the accused, we conclude that the state's interest in protecting the well-being of children, in and of itself, does not justify a per se rule that infringes on a defendant's right of confrontation.

The second rationale proffered by the state focuses on the difficulty of persuading minor victims to testify in sexual abuse cases and on the credibility of their testimony. The state claims that allowing minor victims to testify outside the physical presence of the accused encourages victims to cooperate with law enforcement authorities and, more importantly, enhances the reliability of their testimony. The defendant responds that the state's claim regarding the enhanced reliability of testimony taken outside the physical presence of the accused is too speculative to justify depriving a criminal defendant of his constitutional right of confrontation on that basis.

We have decided to pursue a middle ground in order to accommodate the competing concerns of the state and the defendant. Taking as our point of departure the truth-enhancing goals of the confrontation clauses, we conclude that they should not be construed so strictly as to preclude the state, in particular circumstances, from establishing a compelling need to have a minor victim of tender years testify outside the physical presence of his or her alleged sexual assaulter. We cannot discount the possibility that such a witness might be intimidated, or for any number of reasons inhibited, by the presence of the accused. For example, a minor victim may refuse to testify or may distort his or her testimony because he or she has been threatened by the defendant or is overwhelmed by feelings of guilt. In such instances, affording the defendant the right of physical confrontation would undermine the purpose of confrontation, instead of advancing its truth-seeking goals.

We conclude that, in criminal prosecutions involving the alleged sexual abuse of children of tender years, the practice of videotaping the testimony of a minor victim outside the physical presence of the defendant is, in appropriate circumstances, constitutionally permissible. Our holding that appropriate circumstances may warrant a departure from strict compliance with confrontation requirements does not, however, signal a relaxation of the underlying evidentiary requirement that appropriate circumstances be proven to exist. We emphatically reject the proposal of the state that, in every case allegedly involving the sexual abuse of children, we should presume that the credibility of a minor victim's testimony will be improved by excluding the defendant from the witness room during that witness's testimony. There is no constitutional justification for automatically depriving all criminal defendants of the right of physical confrontation during the videotaping of a minor victim's testimony. We instead mandate a case-by-case analysis, whereby a trial court must balance the individual defendant's right of confrontation against the interest of the state in obtaining reliable testimony from the particular minor victim in question.

––––––

VIDEOTAPING CHILDREN'S TESTIMONY: AN EMPIRICAL VIEW

Paula E. Hill and Samuel M. Hill.
85 Michigan Law Review 809 (1987).

The authors of this Note conducted an empirical investigation to test the hypothesis that children's recall, or their willingness to report recall, differs with setting. The authors hypothesized that if children were questioned in a small setting by only one unfamiliar person, they could recount a greater amount of accurate information that they had witnessed on a videotape than if they were questioned in a typical courtroom setting. The children watched a simulated father-daughter confrontation on videotape. Their ability to recall was then tested in one of two settings. One-half of the children testified in a small room that contained two one-way mirrors and a microphone suspended from the ceiling. This setting accurately reflects how videotaped testimony might be taken in an actual child sexual abuse case. The authors tested the recall of the remaining children either at a county courthouse or in the University of Michigan Law School moot courtroom. The study tested free recall, with separate scores for central items, irrelevant details, and inaccuracies. After the free recall, children were asked specific questions concerning details of the videotape. Answers to these questions were scored as "correct," "incorrect," and "do not know."

The results of those analyses, which either indicated a trend toward, or actually attained statistical significance, indicated that, compared to children in a courtroom, children in a small room tend to (1) relate more central items in free recall; (2) answer specific questions correctly more often; and (3) say "I don't know" or give no answer when asked specific questions significantly less often. A possible explanation for the different responses in each setting is that children in the courtroom gave no answer to questions that children in the small room answered correctly. The responses of children in a small room were more complete than those of children in the courtroom.

The present findings lend support to the argument that current courtroom procedures militate against eliciting complete testimony from children. There were several aspects of the courtroom situation that, when compared with the small room, may have contributed to this effect: the courtroom was large; the child had to sit farther from her parent(s); several people were present; the child witness was questioned by three unfamiliar men; the robed judge sat very close to the child; and the child was facing, and in close proximity to, the unpleasant man from the videotaped portrayal. The combined effects of these variables evoked anxiety in the children, as demonstrated by their conversations with an experimenter after testifying. In addition, the "attorneys" informally noted many instances of nervousness in the children testifying in court (e.g., twisting hair, attempting to leave the witness stand or the courtroom before the end of the session, shaking, and in one instance crying).

When asked to point to the man from the videotape, only nine children positively identified the "defendant" in the courtroom, although three others glanced at him often throughout the session. Either these three children did not recognize the man, or they did not admit that they did.

The poor identification results of the study probably understate the effects of stress on the child's willingness or ability to testify; in actual abuse cases, the testifying child-victim usually knows the defendant. In the present study, the child witness was not a victim of the defendant; thus, the child did not suffer the trauma of confronting a recognized person who had assaulted her. The children participating in the study were not victims of, or witnesses to an actual crime. For children who are victims of sexual abuse, or who are in some way traumatized, it is likely that the problems indicated in this study would be much more pronounced and extend beyond reluctance to identify the assailant. In an actual trial, child sexual abuse victims must face the alleged abuser; this study could not allow so stressful a condition.

NOTE

1. Necessity. In Maryland v. Craig, 497 U.S. 836, 110 S.Ct. 3157, 111 L.Ed.2d 666 (1990) the U.S. Supreme Court considered whether child witnesses in a sexual abuse case were properly permitted to testify "outside the defendant's physical presence, by one-way closed circuit television." 497 U.S. at 840, 110 S.Ct. at 3160. Justice O'Connor wrote for a majority of five justices who held that the procedure was acceptable. The majority decided that the Sixth Amendment did not establish an absolute right to face-to-face confrontation, but, instead, created a preference for that procedure, a preference that could be abrogated by a demonstration that an alternative procedure was necessary to further important state interests. The majority concluded that, "a State's interest in the physical and psychological well-being of child abuse victims may be sufficiently important to outweigh, at least in some cases, defendant's right to face his or her accusers in court." 497 U.S. at 853, 110 S.Ct. at 3167. Justice O'Connor also observed that "where face-to-face confrontation causes significant emotional distress in a child witness, there is evidence that such confrontation would in fact *disserve* the Confrontation Clause's truth seeking goal." 497 U.S. at 857, 110 S.Ct. at 3169. Among other sources, Justice O'Connor cited the videotaping study by Hill and Hill. Justice Scalia, writing for four dissenting justices, concluded that the Court "has applied 'interest-balancing' analysis where the text of the Constitution simply does not permit it." 497 U.S. at 870, 110 S.Ct. at 3176.

D. THE EIGHTH AMENDMENT: THE DEATH PENALTY

The Eighth Amendment to the Constitution reads as follows:

Excessive bail shall not be required, nor excessive fines imposed, nor cruel and unusual punishments inflicted.

Social science research has been used in recent years to address the "cruel" and the "unusual" prongs of the Eighth Amendment. The "cruelty" issue arises in cases that consider whether the death penalty deters crime. The "unusual" issue is the focus of cases contending that the death penalty is applied in a discriminatory manner. In addition, most recently, courts have used social science to address the issue of whether the execution of certain kinds of offenders constitutes an "excessive" sanction.

1. DETERRENCE

The "cruelty" prong of the Eighth Amendment has been invoked in arguments that the death penalty results in the gratuitous infliction of suffering since execution lacks the penological justification of deterring crime. Social science research has been heavily emphasized by both sides in this debate.

FURMAN v. GEORGIA

Supreme Court of the United States, 1972.
408 U.S. 238, 92 S.Ct. 2726, 33 L.Ed.2d 346.

■ PER CURIAM.

Certiorari was granted limited to the following question: "Does the imposition and carrying out of the death penalty in [these cases] constitute cruel and unusual punishment in violation of the Eighth and Fourteenth Amendments?" 403 U.S. 952, 91 S.Ct. 2287, 29 L.Ed.2d 863 (1971). The Court holds that the imposition and carrying out of the death penalty in these cases constitute cruel and unusual punishment in violation of the Eighth and Fourteenth Amendments. The judgment in each case is therefore reversed insofar as it leaves undisturbed the death sentence imposed, and the cases are remanded for further proceedings.

■ JUSTICE MARSHALL, concurring.

The most hotly contested issue regarding capital punishment is whether it is better than life imprisonment as a deterrent to crime.

[T]horsten Sellin, one of the leading authorities on capital punishment, has urged that [t]he death penalty [does not deter murderers. Sellin's] evidence has its problems, however. One is that there are no accurate figures for capital murders; there are only figures on homicides and they, of course, include noncapital killings. A second problem is that certain murders undoubtedly are misinterpreted as accidental deaths or suicides, and there is no way of estimating the number of such undetected crimes. A third problem is that not all homicides are reported. Despite these difficulties, most authorities have assumed that the proportion of capital murders in a State's or nation's homicide statistics remains reasonably constant, and that the homicide statistics are therefore useful.

Sellin's statistics demonstrate that there is no correlation between the murder rate and the presence or absence of the capital sanction. He compares States that have similar characteristics and finds that irrespective of their position on capital punishment, they have similar murder rates. In the New England States, for example, there is no correlation between executions and homicide rates. The same is true for Midwestern States, and for all others studied. Both the United Nations and Great Britain have acknowledged the validity of Sellin's statistics.

Sellin also concludes that abolition and/or reintroduction of the death penalty had no effect on the homicide rates of the various States involved. This conclusion is borne out by others who have made similar inquiries and by the experience of other countries. Despite problems with the statistics, Sellin's evidence has been relied upon in international studies of capital punishment.

[D]espite the fact that abolitionists have not proved non-deterrence beyond a reasonable doubt, they have succeeded in showing by clear and convincing evidence that capital punishment is not necessary as a deterrent to crime in our society. This is all that they must do. We would shirk our judicial responsibilities if we failed to accept the presently existing statistics and demanded more proof. It may be that we now possess all the proof that anyone could ever hope to assemble on the subject. But, even if further proof were to be forthcoming, I believe there is more than enough evidence presently available for a decision in this case.

[I]n light of the massive amount of evidence before us, I see no alternative but to conclude that capital punishment cannot be justified on the basis of its deterrent effect.

■ MR. CHIEF JUSTICE BURGER, with whom MR. JUSTICE BLACKMUN, MR. JUSTICE POWELL and MR. JUSTICE REHNQUIST join, dissenting.

[A] controversial question is whether the death penalty acts as a superior deterrent. Those favoring abolition find no evidence that it does.[21] Those favoring retention start from the intuitive notion that capital punishment should act as the most effective deterrent and note that there is no convincing evidence that it does not. Escape from this empirical stalemate is sought by placing the burden of proof on the States and concluding that they have failed to demonstrate that capital punishment is a more effective deterrent than life imprisonment. Numerous justifications have been advanced for shifting the burden, and they are not without their rhetorical appeal. However, these arguments are not descended from established

21. See, e.g., Sellin, Homicides in Retentionist and Abolitionist States, in Capital Punishment 135 et seq. (T. Sellin ed. 1967); Schuessler, The Deterrent Influence of the Death Penalty, 284 Annals 54 (1952).

constitutional principles, but are born of the urge to bypass an unresolved factual question. Comparative deterrence is not a matter that lends itself to precise measurement; to shift the burden to the States is to provide an illusory solution to an enormously complex problem. If it were proper to put the States to the test of demonstrating the deterrent value of capital punishment, we could just as well ask them to prove the need for life imprisonment or any other punishment. Yet I know of no convincing evidence that life imprisonment is a more effective deterrent than 20 years' imprisonment, or even that a $10 parking ticket is a more effective deterrent than a $5 parking ticket. In fact, there are some who go so far as to challenge the notion that any punishments deter crime. If the States are unable to adduce convincing proof rebutting such assertions, does it then follow that all punishments are suspect as being "cruel and unusual" within the meaning of the Constitution? On the contrary, I submit that the questions raised by the necessity approach are beyond the pale of judicial inquiry under the Eighth Amendment.

[I]f today's opinions demonstrate nothing else, they starkly show that this is an area where legislatures can act far more effectively than courts.

[T]he preference for legislative action is justified by the inability of the courts to participate in the debate at the level where the controversy is focused. The case against capital punishment is not the product of legal dialectic, but rests primarily on factual claims, the truth of which cannot be tested by conventional judicial processes. The five opinions in support of the judgments differ in many respects, but they share a willingness to make sweeping factual assertions, unsupported by empirical data, concerning the manner of imposition and effectiveness of capital punishment in this country. Legislatures will have the opportunity to make a more penetrating study of these claims with the familiar and effective tools available to them as they are not to us.

The highest judicial duty is to recognize the limits on judicial power and to permit the democratic processes to deal with matters falling outside of those limits.

GREGG v. GEORGIA

Supreme Court of the United States, 1976.
428 U.S. 153, 96 S.Ct. 2909, 49 L.Ed.2d 859.

■ JUSTICE STEWART announced the judgment of the Court.

[This case presented the question of whether the imposition of the death sentence under a Georgia statute would be "cruel and unusual" punishment under the Eighth and Fourteenth Amendments of the Constitution. The case was, to some extent, a successor to Furman v. Georgia, 408 U.S. 238, 92 S.Ct. 2726, 33 L.Ed.2d 346 (1972), where the court held that a prior version of the statute was unconstitutional because of the broad discretion it accorded juries to impose or withhold the death penalty. In

Gregg, one consideration was whether the death sentence resulted in the gratuitous infliction of suffering because it lacked the penological justification of deterring crime. The presence of this issue led members of the court to consider the deterrent effect, if any, of the death sentence.]

Statistical attempts to evaluate the worth of the death penalty as a deterrent to crimes by potential offenders have occasioned a great deal of debate.[31] The results simply have been inconclusive. As one opponent of capital punishment has said:

> "[A]fter all possible inquiry, including the probing of all possible methods of inquiry, we do not know, and for systematic and easily visible reasons cannot know, what the truth about this 'deterrent' effect may be. . . .

> "The inescapable flaw is . . . that social conditions in any state are not constant through time, and that social conditions are not the same in any two states. If an effect were observed (and the observed effects, one way or another, are not large) then one could not at all tell whether any of this effect is attributable to the presence or absence of capital punishment. A 'scientific'—that is to say, a soundly based— conclusion is simply impossible, and no methodological path out of this tangle suggests itself." C. Black, Capital Punishment: The Inevitability of Caprice and Mistake 25–26 (1974).

Although some of the studies suggest that the death penalty may not function as a significantly greater deterrent than lesser penalties,[32] there is no convincing empirical evidence either supporting or refuting this view. We may nevertheless assume safely that there are murderers, such as those who act in passion, for whom the threat of death has little or no deterrent effect. But for many others, the death penalty undoubtedly is a significant deterrent. There are carefully contemplated murders, such as murder for hire, where the possible penalty of death may well enter into the cold calculus that preceded the decision to act. And there are some categories of murder, such as murder by a life prisoner, where other sanctions may not be adequate.[34]

---

31. See, e.g., Peck, The Deterrent Effect of Capital Punishment: Ehrlich and His Critics, 85 Yale L.J. 359 (1976); Baldus & Cole, A Comparison of the Work of Thorsten Sellin and Isaac Ehrlich on the Deterrent Effect of Capital Punishment, 85 Yale L.J. 170 (1975); Bowers & Pierce, The Illusion of Deterrence in Isaac Ehrlich's Research on Capital Punishment, 85 Yale L.J. 187 (1975); Ehrlich, The Deterrent Effect of Capital Punishment: A Question of Life and Death, 65 Am.Econ.Rev. 397 (June 1975); Hook, The Death Sentence, in The Death Penalty in America 146 (H. Bedau ed. 1967); T. Sellin, The Death Penalty, A Report for the Model Penal Code Project of the American Law Institute (1959).

32. See, e.g., The Death Penalty in America, supra, at 258–332; Report of the Royal Commission on Capital Punishment, 1949–1953, Cmd. 8932.

34. We have been shown no statistics breaking down the total number of murders into the categories described above. The overall trend in the number of murders committed in the nation, however, has been upward for some time. In 1964, reported murders totaled an estimated 9,250. During the ensuing decade, the number reported increased 123%, until it totaled approximately 20,600 in 1974. In 1972 the year *Furman* was announced, the total estimated was 18,520. Despite a fractional decrease in 1975 as com-

The value of capital punishment as a deterrent of crime is a complex factual issue the resolution of which properly rests with the legislatures, which can evaluate the results of statistical studies in terms of their own local conditions and with a flexibility of approach that is not available to the courts. Furman v. Georgia, [408 U.S.] at 403–405, 92 S.Ct., at 2810–2812 (Burger, C.J., Dissenting). Indeed, many of the post-*Furman* statutes reflect just such a responsible effort to define those crimes and those criminals for which capital punishment is most probably an effective deterrent.

■ JUSTICE MARSHALL, dissenting.

[I]n *Furman,* I canvassed the relevant data on the deterrent effect of capital punishment. 408 U.S. at 347–354, 92 S.Ct. at 2781–2785.[2] The state of knowledge at that point, after literally centuries of debate, was summarized as follows by a United Nations Committee:

> "It is generally agreed between the retentionists and abolitionists, whatever their opinions about the validity of comparative studies of deterrence, that the data which now exist show no correlation between the existence of capital punishment and lower rates of capital crime."[3]

The available evidence, I concluded in *Furman,* was convincing that "capital punishment is not necessary as a deterrent to crime in our society." Id. at 353.

The Solicitor General in his *amicus* brief in these cases relies heavily on a study by Isaac Ehrlich,[4] reported a year after *Furman,* to support the contention that the death penalty does deter murder. Since the Ehrlich study was not available at the time of *Furman* and since it is the first scientific study to suggest that the death penalty may have a deterrent effect, I will briefly consider its import.

The Ehrlich study focused on the relationship in the Nation as a whole between the homicide rate and "execution risk"—the fraction of persons convicted of murder who were actually executed. Comparing the differences in homicide rate and execution risk for the years 1933 to 1969, Ehrlich found that increases in execution risk were associated with increases in the homicide rate.[5] But when he employed the statistical technique of multiple regression analysis to control for the influence of other variables posited to

---

pared with 1974, the number of murders increased in the three years immediately following *Furman* to approximately 20,400, an increase of almost 10%. See FBI, Uniform Crime Reports, for 1964, 1972, 1974, and 1975, Preliminary Annual Release.

2. See e.g., T. Sellin, The Death Penalty, A Report for the Model Penal Code Project of the American Law Institute (1959).

3. United Nations, Department of Economic and Social Affairs, Capital Punishment, pt. II, & 159, p. 123 (1968).

4. I. Ehrlich, The Deterrent Effect of Capital Punishment: A Question of Life and Death (Working Paper No. 18, National Bureau of Economic Research, Nov. 1973); Ehrlich, The Deterrent Effect of Capital Punishment: A Question of Life and Death, 65 Am. Econ.Rev. 397 (June 1975).

5. Id. at 409.

have an impact on the homicide rate,[6] Ehrlich found a negative correlation between changes in the homicide rate and changes in execution risk. His tentative conclusion was that for the period from 1933 to 1967 each additional execution in the United States might have saved eight lives.[7]

The methods and conclusions of the Ehrlich study have been severely criticized on a number of grounds.[8] It has been suggested, for example, that the study is defective because it compares execution and homicide rates on a nationwide, rather than a state-by-state, basis. The aggregation of data from all States—including those that have abolished the death penalty—obscures the relationship between murder and execution rates. Under Ehrlich's methodology, a decrease in the execution risk in one State combined with an increase in the murder rate in another State would, all other things being equal, suggest a deterrent effect that quite obviously would not exist. Indeed, a deterrent effect would be suggested if, once again all other things being equal, one State abolished the death penalty and experienced no change in the murder rate, while another State experienced an increase in the murder rate.

The most compelling criticism of the Ehrlich study is that its conclusions are extremely sensitive to the choice of the time period included in the regression analysis. Analysis of Ehrlich's data reveals that all empirical support for the deterrent effect of capital punishment disappears when the five most recent years are removed from his time series—that is to say, whether a decrease in the execution risk corresponds to an increase or a decrease in the murder rate depends on the ending point of the sample period. This finding has cast severe doubts on the reliability of Ehrlich's tentative conclusions. Indeed, a recent [s]tudy, based on Ehrlich's theoretical model but using cross-section state data for the years 1950 and 1960, found no support for the conclusion that executions act as a deterrent.

The Ehrlich study, in short, is of little, if any, assistance in assessing the deterrent impact of the death penalty. The evidence I reviewed in *Furman* remains convincing, in my view, that "capital punishment is not

---

6. The variables other than execution risk included probability of arrest, probability of conviction given arrest, national aggregate measures of the percentage of the population between age 14 and 24, the unemployment rate, the labor force participation rate, and estimated per capita income.

7. Id. at 398, 414.

8. See Passell & Taylor, The Deterrent Effect of Capital Punishment: Another View (unpublished Columbia University Discussion Paper 74–7509, Mar.1975), reproduced in Brief for Petitioner App. E in Jurek v. Texas, O.T.1975, No. 75–5844; Passell, The Deterrent Effect of the Death Penalty: A Statistical Test, 28 Stan.L.Rev. 61 (1975); Baldus & Cole, A Comparison of the Work of Thorsten Sellin & Isaac Ehrlich on the Deterrent Ef-

fect of Capital Punishment, 85 Yale L.J. 170 (1975); Bowers & Pierce, The Illusion of Deterrence in Isaac Ehrlich's Research on Capital Punishment, 85 Yale L.J. 187 (1975); Peck, The Deterrent Effect of Capital Punishment: Ehrlich and His Critics, 85 Yale L.J. 359 (1976). See also Ehrlich, Deterrence: Evidence and Inference, 85 Yale L.J. 209 (1975); Ehrlich, Rejoinder, 85 Yale L.J. 368 (1976). In addition to the items discussed in text, criticism has been directed at the quality of Ehrlich's data, his choice of explanatory variables, his failure to account for the interdependence of those variables, and his assumptions as to the mathematical form of the relationship between the homicide rate and the explanatory variables.

necessary as a deterrent to crime in our society." 408 U.S., at 353, 92 S.Ct., at 2784. The justification for the death penalty must be found elsewhere.

————

DETERRENCE AND INCAPACITATION: ESTIMATING THE EFFECTS OF CRIMINAL SANCTIONS ON CRIME RATES

Panel on Research on Deterrent and Incapacitative Effects.
National Academy of Sciences (1978).

The question of whether capital punishment has any additional deterrent effect beyond that associated with imprisonment has been a subject of intense debate for generations. Periodically, this debate emerges as a matter of major public concern. This has happened most recently in the series of U.S. Supreme Court decisions[54] regarding the constitutionality of capital punishment. In the most recent of the Supreme Court decisions, complex technical evidence on the deterrent effect of capital punishment was brought into the debate by the Solicitor General, who introduced an analysis by Ehrlich in his *amicus curiae* brief.

The Ehrlich analysis showed a negative association over time between United States national homicide rates and the number of executions per homicide conviction, a proxy for the probability of execution. This association has been interpreted as demonstrating that capital punishment deters homicide and has been carried to the point of estimating the number of homicides averted per execution. Ehrlich's analysis contradicted earlier analyses that found no evidence that capital punishment deters homicide.

[W]hile all the earlier studies failed to find evidence of a deterrent effect, they suffer from a number of methodological weaknesses. The most serious flaw was the general failure to control adequately for the variety of demographic, cultural, and socioeconomic factors, other than the death penalty, that influence murder rates. Examining "similar" contiguous states or the same jurisdiction over short time periods represents some effort to hold these factors constant, but, when dealing with rare events like homicides and executions where the numbers are quite small, the crudeness of these controls could easily mask any effects that may exist. In addition, there were no controls for differences in noncapital sanctions, which could also influence homicide rates.

In some studies, different jurisdictions were compared on the basis of their statutes regarding capital punishment rather than by their practice, when the latter may be the more relevant factor affecting deterrence. Additionally, these analyses usually failed to separate the number of capital homicides (those homicides for which capital punishment was a legal sanction) from total homicides as the dependent variable, and variations in

54. Furman v. Georgia, 408 U.S. 238 (1972); Fowler v. North Carolina, 95 Sup.Ct. 223; Jurek v. Texas, 96 Sup.Ct. 2950; Wood-son v. North Carolina, 96 Sup.Ct. 2978; Proffitt v. Florida; 96 Sup.Ct. 2976; and Gregg v. Georgia, 96 Sup.Ct. 2909.

the larger number of noncapital homicides in the total could have masked a deterrent effect.

[E]hrlich, using time-series data for 1933–1969 in which homicides and executions were aggregated for the entire United States, reports a deterrent effect for executions. There have been a number of reanalyses of data equivalent to that used by Ehrlich. All of these reanalyses have shown that Ehrlich's findings are sensitive to minor technical variations in the analysis. These variations include changes in the mathematical form of the relationship of homicide rates to their determinants (e.g., a multiplicative form compared to a linear one) and the variables included as determinants of homicide (e.g., including the aggregate crime index as a determinant). These reanalyses either reversed the direction of the presumed effect or greatly reduced its magnitude.

The most striking sensitivity of Ehrlich's findings is to the time period over which the analysis is conducted. No negative association is found for 1933–1961, so that the results are determined by the effect in 1962–1969. But during those eight years, *all* crime rates rose dramatically, and the frequency of executions declined (and had ceased by 1968). Thus, to conclude that a deterrent effect exists, one must assume that the steady rise in homicides over this eight-year period was caused at least in part by the decline in executions and that the trends in executions and in homicides were not generated either independently or by some common third cause, which might also account for the rise in other crimes. If one makes these assumptions, statistical analyses contribute no further information to the test of the deterrence hypothesis. Moreover, the failure to discern any deterrent effect in the earlier 1933–1961 period, when there was more fluctuation in both homicide and execution rates, still remains unexplained.

In summary, the flaws in the null-effect results and the sensitivity of the Ehrlich results to minor variations in model specification and their serious temporal instability lead the Panel to conclude that the results of the analyses on capital punishment provide no useful evidence on the deterrent effect of capital punishment.

Our conclusion should not be interpreted as meaning that capital punishment does not have a deterrent effect, but rather that there is currently no evidence for determining whether it does have a deterrent effect. Furthermore, we are skeptical that the death penalty, so long as it is used relatively rarely, can ever be subjected to the kind of statistical analysis that would validly establish the presence or absence of a deterrent effect.

Our conclusion on the current evidence does not imply that capital punishment should or should not be imposed. The deterrent effect of capital punishment and its magnitude reflect only one aspect of the many considerations involved in the choice of the use of the death penalty. Those considerations include issues related to the value of human life, the moral justification of killing by government, and the appropriate form of public outrage at heinous crimes—all of which are likely to dominate policy decisions in comparison to inevitably crude estimates of the deterrent effects.

2. DISCRIMINATION

The "unusual" prong of the Eighth Amendment has been the focus of arguments that the death penalty is invoked with disproportionate frequency on defendants whose victims have been white. The issue here has revolved around one major social science study of the application of the death penalty.

McCLESKEY v. KEMP

Supreme Court of the United States, 1987.
481 U.S. 279, 107 S.Ct. 1756, 95 L.Ed.2d 262.

■ JUSTICE POWELL delivered the opinion of the Court.

McCleskey, a black man, was convicted of two counts of armed robbery and one count of murder in the Superior Court of Fulton County, Georgia, on October 12, 1978. McCleskey's convictions arose out of the robbery of a furniture store and the killing of a white police officer during the course of the robbery.

[T]he jury recommended that he be sentenced to death on the murder charge and to consecutive life sentences on the armed robbery charges. The court followed the jury's recommendation and sentenced McCleskey to death.

On appeal, the Supreme Court of Georgia affirmed the convictions and the sentences.

McCleskey [f]iled a petition for a writ of habeas corpus in the federal District Court for the Northern District of Georgia. His petition raised 18 claims, one of which was that the Georgia capital sentencing process is administered in a racially discriminatory manner in violation of the Eighth and Fourteenth Amendments to the United States Constitution. In support of his claim, McCleskey proffered a statistical study performed by Professors David C. Baldus, George Woodworth, and Charles Pulaski (the Baldus study) that purports to show a disparity in the imposition of the death sentence in Georgia based on the race of the murder victim and, to a lesser extent, the race of the defendant. The Baldus study is actually two sophisticated statistical studies that examine over 2,000 murder cases that occurred in Georgia during the 1970s. The raw numbers collected by Professor Baldus indicate that defendants charged with killing white persons received the death penalty in 11% of the cases, but defendants charged with killing blacks received the death penalty in only 1% of the cases. The raw numbers also indicate a reverse racial disparity according to the race of the defendant: 4% of the black defendants received the death penalty, as opposed to 7% of the white defendants.

Baldus also divided the cases according to the combination of the race of the defendant and the race of the victim. He found that the death penalty was assessed in 22% of the cases involving black defendants and white victims; 8% of the cases involving white defendants and white victims; 1% of the cases involving black defendants and black victims; and 3% of the cases involving white defendants and black victims. Similarly, Baldus found that prosecutors sought the death penalty in 70% of the cases involving black defendants and white victims; 32% of the cases involving white defendants and white victims; 15% of the cases involving black defendants and black victims; and 19% of the cases involving white defendants and black victims.

Baldus subjected his data to an extensive analysis, taking account of 230 variables that could have explained the disparities on nonracial grounds. One of his models concludes that, even after taking account of 39 nonracial variables, defendants charged with killing white victims were 4.3 times as likely to receive a death sentence as defendants charged with killing blacks. According to this model, black defendants were 1.1 times as likely to receive a death sentence as other defendants. Thus, the Baldus study indicates that black defendants, such as McCleskey, who kill white victims have the greatest likelihood of receiving the death penalty.

The District Court held an extensive evidentiary hearing on McCleskey's petition. Although it believed that McCleskey's Eighth Amendment claim was foreclosed by the Fifth Circuit's decision in Spinkellink v. Wainwright, 578 F.2d 582, 612–616 (1978), cert. denied, 440 U.S. 976, 99 S.Ct. 1548, 59 L.Ed.2d 796 (1979), it nevertheless considered the Baldus study with care. It concluded that McCleskey's "statistics do not demonstrate a prima facie case in support of the contention that the death penalty was imposed upon him because of his race, because of the race of the victim, or because of any Eighth Amendment concern." McCleskey v. Zant, 580 F.Supp. 338, 379 (N.D.Ga.1984). As to McCleskey's Fourteenth Amendment claim, the court found that the methodology of the Baldus study was flawed in several respects. Because of these defects, the Court held that the Baldus study "fail[ed] to contribute anything of value" to McCleskey's claim. Id., at 372 (emphasis omitted). Accordingly, the Court dismissed the petition. [T]he Court of Appeals affirmed the dismissal by the District Court of McCleskey's petition for a writ of habeas corpus, with three judges dissenting as to McCleskey's claims based on the Baldus study. We granted certiorari, and now affirm.

McCleskey's first claim is that the Georgia capital punishment statute violates the Equal Protection Clause of the Fourteenth Amendment.[7]

7. Although the District Court rejected the findings of the Baldus study as flawed, the Court of Appeals assumed that the study is valid and reached the constitutional issues. Accordingly, those issues are before us. As did the Court of Appeals, we assume the study is valid statistically without reviewing the factual findings of the District Court. Our assumption that the Baldus study is statistically valid does not include the assumption that the study shows that racial considerations actually enter into any sentencing decisions in Georgia. Even a sophisticated multiple regression analysis such as the Baldus study can only demonstrate a *risk* that the factor of race entered into some capital sentencing decisions and a necessarily lesser risk

[O]ur analysis begins with the basic principle that a defendant who alleges an equal protection violation has the burden of proving "the existence of purposeful discrimination." Whitus v. Georgia, 385 U.S. 545, 550, 87 S.Ct. 643, 646, 17 L.Ed.2d 599 (1967). A corollary to this principle is that a criminal defendant must prove that the purposeful discrimination "had a discriminatory effect" on him. Wayte v. United States, 470 U.S. 598, 608, 105 S.Ct. 1524, 1531, 84 L.Ed.2d 547 (1985). Thus, to prevail under the Equal Protection Clause, McCleskey must prove that the decision-makers in his case acted with discriminatory purpose. He offers no evidence specific to his own case that would support an inference that racial considerations played a part in his sentence. Instead, he relies solely on the Baldus study.[11] McCleskey argues that the Baldus study compels an inference that his sentence rests on purposeful discrimination. McCleskey's claim that these statistics are sufficient proof of discrimination, without regard to the facts of a particular case, would extend to all capital cases in Georgia, at least where the victim was white and the defendant is black.

The Court has accepted statistics as proof of intent to discriminate in certain limited contexts. First, this Court has accepted statistical disparities as proof of an equal protection violation in the selection of the jury venire in a particular district. [S]econd, this Court has accepted statistics in the form of multiple regression analysis to prove statutory violations under Title VII.

But the nature of the capital sentencing decision, and the relationship of the statistics to that decision, are fundamentally different from the corresponding elements in the venire-selection or Title VII cases. Most importantly, each particular decision to impose the death penalty is made by a petit jury selected from a properly constituted venire. Each jury is unique in its composition, and the Constitution requires that its decision rest on consideration of innumerable factors that vary according to the characteristics of the individual defendant and the facts of the particular capital offense. Thus, the application of an inference drawn from the general statistics to a specific decision in a trial and sentencing simply is not comparable to the application of an inference drawn from general statistics to a specific venire-selection or Title VII case. In those cases, the statistics relate to fewer entities, and fewer variables are relevant to the challenged decisions. [A]ccordingly, we reject McCleskey's equal protection claims.

McCleskey also argues that the Baldus study demonstrates that the Georgia capital sentencing system violates the Eighth Amendment.

that race entered into any particular sentencing decision.

11. McCleskey's expert testified:

"Models that are developed talk about the effect on the average. They do not depict the experience of a single individual. What they say, for example, [is] that on the average, the race of the victim, if it is white, increases on the average the probability ... (that) the death sentence would be given.

"Whether in a given case that is the answer, it cannot be determined from statistics." 580 F.Supp., at 372.

[I]n light of our precedents under the Eighth Amendment, McCleskey cannot argue successfully that his sentence is "disproportionate to the crime in the traditional sense." See Pulley v. Harris, 465 U.S. 37, 43, 104 S.Ct. 871, 875, 79 L.Ed.2d 29 (1984). He does not deny that he committed a murder in the course of a planned robbery, a crime for which this Court has determined that the death penalty constitutionally may be imposed. Gregg v. Georgia, 428 U.S., at 187, 96 S.Ct., at 2931. His disproportionality claim "is of a different sort." Pulley v. Harris, supra, 465 U.S., at 43, 104 S.Ct., at 875. McCleskey argues that the sentence in his case is disproportionate to the sentences in other murder cases.

[T]o evaluate McCleskey's challenge, we must examine exactly what the Baldus study may show. Even Professor Baldus does not contend that his statistics prove that race enters into any capital sentencing decisions or that race was a factor in McCleskey's particular case. Statistics at most may show only a likelihood that a particular factor entered into some decisions. There is, of course, some risk of racial prejudice influencing a jury's decision in a criminal case. There are similar risks that other kinds of prejudice will influence other criminal trials. The question "is at what point that risk becomes constitutionally unacceptable," Turner v. Murray, 476 U.S. 28, 36, n. 8, 106 S.Ct. 1683, 1688, n. 8, 90 L.Ed.2d 27 (1986). McCleskey asks us to accept the likelihood allegedly shown by the Baldus study as the constitutional measure of an unacceptable risk of racial prejudice influencing capital sentencing decisions. This we decline to do.

[A]t most, the Baldus study indicates a discrepancy that appears to correlate with race. Apparent disparities in sentencing are an inevitable part of our criminal justice system. The discrepancy indicated by the Baldus study is "a far cry from the major systemic defects identified in *Furman*," Pulley v. Harris, 465 U.S., at 54, 104 S.Ct., at 881. As this Court has recognized, any mode for determining guilt or punishment "has its weaknesses and the potential for misuse." Singer v. United States, 380 U.S. 24, 35, 85 S.Ct. 783, 790, 13 L.Ed.2d 630 (1965). Specifically, "there can be 'no perfect procedure for deciding in which cases governmental authority should be used to impose death.'" Zant v. Stephens, 462 U.S. 862, 884, 103 S.Ct. 2733, 2746, 77 L.Ed.2d 235 (1983) (quoting Lockett v. Ohio, 438 U.S., at 605, 98 S.Ct., at 2965 (plurality opinion of Burger, C.J.)). Despite these imperfections, our consistent rule has been that constitutional guarantees are met when "the mode [for determining guilt or punishment] itself has been surrounded with safeguards to make it as fair as possible." Singer v. United States, supra, 380 U.S., at 35, 85 S.Ct., at 790. Where the discretion that is fundamental to our criminal process is involved, we decline to assume that what is unexplained is invidious. In light of the safeguards designed to minimize racial bias in the process, the fundamental value of jury trial in our criminal justice system, and the benefits that discretion provides to criminal defendants, we hold that the Baldus study does not demonstrate a constitutionally significant risk of racial bias affecting the Georgia capital-sentencing process.

Two additional concerns inform our decision in this case. First, McCleskey's claim, taken to its logical conclusion, throws into serious question the principles that underlie our entire criminal justice system. The Eighth Amendment is not limited in application to capital punishment, but applies to all penalties. Thus, if we accepted McCleskey's claim that racial bias has impermissibly tainted the capital sentencing decision, we could soon be faced with similar claims as to other types of penalty.[38] Moreover, the claim that his sentence rests on the irrelevant factor of race easily could be extended to apply to claims based on unexplained discrepancies that correlate to membership in other minority groups, and even to gender.[40] Similarly, since McCleskey's claim relates to the race of his victim, other claims could apply with equally logical force to statistical disparities that correlate with the race or sex of other actors in the criminal justice system, such as defense attorneys[41], or judges. Also, there is no logical reason that such a claim need be limited to racial or sexual bias. If arbitrary and capricious punishment is the touchstone under the Eighth Amendment, such a claim could—at least in theory—be based upon any arbitrary variable, such as the defendant's facial characteristics,[43] or the physical attractiveness of the defendant or the victim,[44] that some statistical study indicates may be influential in jury decisionmaking. As these examples illustrate, there is no limiting principle to the type of challenge brought by McCleskey. The Constitution does not require that a State

38. Studies already exist that allegedly demonstrate a racial disparity in the length of prison sentences. See, e.g., Spohn, Gruhl, & Welch, The Effect of Race on Sentencing: A Reexamination of an Unsettled Question, 16 Law & Soc.Rev. 71 (1981–1982); Unnever, Frazier & Henretta, Race Differences in Criminal Sentencing, 21 Sociological Q. 197 (1980).

40. See Chamblin, The Effect of Sex on the Imposition of the Death Penalty (paper presented at a symposium of the Amer. Psych. Assn., entitled "Extra-legal Attributes Affecting Death Penalty Sentencing," New York City, Sept., 1979); Steffensmeier, Effects of Judge's and Defendant's Sex on the Sentencing of Offenders, 14 Psychology 3 (1977).

41. See Johnson, Black Innocence and the White Jury, 83 Mich.L.Rev. 1611, 1625–1640, and n. 115 (1985) (citing Cohen & Peterson, Bias in the Courtroom: Race and Sex Effects of Attorneys on Juror Verdicts, 9 Social Behavior & Personality 81 (1981)); Hodgson & Pryor, Sex Discrimination in the Courtroom: Attorney's Gender and Credibility, 55 Psychological Rep. 483 (1984).

43. See Kerr, Bull, MacCoun, & Rathborn, Effects of victim attractiveness, care and disfigurement on the judgments of Amer-

ican and British mock jurors, 24 Brit. J. Social Psych. 47 (1985); Johnson, supra, 1638, n. 128 (citing Shoemaker, South, & Lowe, Facial Stereotypes of Deviants and Judgments of Guilt or Innocence, 51 Social Forces 427 (1973)).

44. Some studies indicate that physically attractive defendants receive greater leniency in sentencing than unattractive defendants, and that offenders whose victims are physically attractive receive harsher sentences than defendants with less attractive victims. Smith & Hed, Effects of Offenders' Age and Attractiveness on Sentencing by Mock Juries, 44 Psychological R. 691 (1979); Kerr, Beautiful and Blameless: Effects of Victim Attractiveness and Responsibility on Mock Jurors' Verdicts, 4 Personality and Social Psych. Bull. 479 (1978). But see Baumeister & Darley, Reducing the Biasing Effect of Perpetrator Attractiveness in Jury Simulation, 8 Personality and Social Psych. Bull. 286 (1982); Schwibbe & Schwibbe, Judgment and Treatment of People of Varied Attractiveness, 48 Psychological R. 11 (1981); Weiten, The Attraction-Leniency Effect in Jury Research: An Examination of External Validity, 10 J. Applied Social Psych. 340 (1980).

eliminate any demonstrable disparity that correlates with a potentially irrelevant factor in order to operate a criminal justice system that includes capital punishment. As we have stated specifically in the context of capital punishment, the Constitution does not "plac[e] totally unrealistic conditions on its use." Gregg v. Georgia, 428 U.S., at 199, n. 50, 96 S.Ct., at 2937, n. 50.

Second, McCleskey's arguments are best presented to the legislative bodies. It is not the responsibility—or indeed even the right—of this Court to determine the appropriate punishment for particular crimes. It is the legislatures, the elected representatives of the people, that are "constituted to respond to the will and consequently the moral values of the people." Furman v. Georgia, 408 U.S., at 383, 92 S.Ct., at 2800 (Burger, C.J., dissenting). Legislatures also are better qualified to weigh and "evaluate the results of statistical studies in terms of their own local conditions and with a flexibility of approach that is not available to the courts," Gregg v. Georgia, supra, 428 U.S., at 186, 96 S.Ct., at 2931. Capital punishment is now the law in more than two thirds of our States. It is the ultimate duty of courts to determine on a case-by-case basis whether these laws are applied consistently with the Constitution. Despite McCleskey's wide ranging arguments that basically challenge the validity of capital punishment in our multi-racial society, the only question before us is whether in his case, the law of Georgia was properly applied. We agree with the District Court and the Court of Appeals for the Eleventh Circuit that this was carefully and correctly done in this case.

■ JUSTICE BRENNAN, dissenting.

It is important to emphasize at the outset that the Court's observation that McCleskey cannot prove the influence of race on any particular sentencing decision is irrelevant in evaluating his Eighth Amendment claim. Since Furman v. Georgia, 408 U.S. 238, 92 S.Ct. 2726, 33 L.Ed.2d 346 (1972), the Court has been concerned with the *risk* of the imposition of an arbitrary sentence, rather than the proven fact of one. *Furman* held that the death penalty "may not be imposed under sentencing procedures that create a substantial risk that the punishment will be inflicted in an arbitrary and capricious manner." Godfrey v. Georgia, 446 U.S., at 427, 100 S.Ct., at 1764.

[T]he Court assumes the statistical validity of the Baldus study, and acknowledges that McCleskey has demonstrated a risk that racial prejudice plays a role in capital sentencing in Georgia. Nonetheless, it finds the probability of prejudice insufficient to create constitutional concern. Close analysis of the Baldus study, however, in light of both statistical principles and human experience, reveals that the risk that race influenced McCleskey's sentence is intolerable by any imaginable standard.

The Baldus study indicates that, after taking into account some 230 nonracial factors that might legitimately influence a sentencer, the jury *more likely than not* would have spared McCleskey's life had his victim been black. The study distinguishes between those cases in which (1) the jury exercises virtually no discretion because the strength or weakness of aggravating factors usually suggests that only one outcome is appropriate; and (2) cases reflecting an "intermediate" level of aggravation, in which the jury has considerable discretion in choosing a sentence. McCleskey's case falls into the intermediate range. In such cases, death is imposed in 34% of white-victim crimes and 14% of black-victim crimes, a difference of 139% in the rate of imposition of the death penalty.

In other words, just under 59%—almost 6 in 10—[of the] defendants comparable to McCleskey would not have received the death penalty if their victims had been black.

Furthermore, even examination of the sentencing system as a whole, factoring in those cases in which the jury exercises little discretion, indicates the influence of race on capital sentencing. For the Georgia system as a whole, race accounts for a six percentage point difference in the rate at which capital punishment is imposed. Since death is imposed in 11% of all white-victim cases, the rate in comparably aggravated black-victim cases is 5%. The rate of capital sentencing in a white-victim case is thus 120% greater than the rate in a black-victim case. Put another way, over half— 55%—of defendants in white-victim crimes in Georgia would not have been sentenced to die if their victims had been black. Of the more than 200 variables potentially relevant to a sentencing decision, race of the victim is a powerful explanation for variation in death sentence rates—as powerful as nonracial aggravating factors such as a prior murder conviction or acting as the principal planner of the homicide.

These adjusted figures are only the most conservative indication of the risk that race will influence the death sentences of defendants in Georgia. Data unadjusted for the mitigating or aggravating effect of other factors show an even more pronounced disparity by race. The capital sentencing rate for all white-victim cases was almost *11 times* greater than the rate for black-victim cases. Furthermore, blacks who kill whites are sentenced to death at nearly *22 times* the rate of blacks who kill blacks, and more than *7 times* the rate of whites who kill blacks.

In addition, prosecutors seek the death penalty for 70% of black defendants with white victims, but for only 15% of black defendants with black victims, and only 19% of white defendants with black victims. Since our decision upholding the Georgia capital-sentencing system in *Gregg*, the State has executed 7 persons. All of the 7 were convicted of killing whites, and 6 of the 7 executed were black. Such execution figures are especially striking in light of the fact that, during the period encompassed by the Baldus study, only 9.2% of Georgia homicides involved black defendants and white victims, while 60.7% involved black victims.

McCleskey's statistics have particular force because most of them are the product of sophisticated multiple-regression analysis. Such analysis is designed precisely to identify patterns in the aggregate, even though we may not be able to reconstitute with certainty any individual decision that goes to make up that pattern. Multiple-regression analysis is particularly well-suited to identify the influence of impermissible considerations in sentencing, since it is able to control for permissible factors that may explain an apparent arbitrary pattern. While the decision-making process of a body such as a jury may be complex, the Baldus study provides a massive compilation of the details that are most relevant to that decision. As we held in the Title VII context last term in Bazemore v. Friday, 478 U.S. 385, 106 S.Ct. 3000, 92 L.Ed.2d 315 (1986), a multiple-regression analysis need not include every conceivable variable to establish a party's case, as long as it includes those variables that account for the major factors that are likely to influence decisions. In this case, Professor Baldus in fact conducted additional regression analyses in response to criticisms and suggestions by the District Court, all of which confirmed, and some of which even strengthened, the study's original conclusions.

The statistical evidence in this case thus relentlessly documents the risk that McCleskey's sentence was influenced by racial considerations. This evidence shows that there is a better than even chance in Georgia that race will influence the decision to impose the death penalty; a majority of defendants in white-victim crimes would not have been sentenced to die if their victims had been black. In determining whether this risk is acceptable, our judgment must be shaped by the awareness that "[t]he risk of racial prejudice infecting a capital sentencing proceeding is especially serious in light of the complete finality of the death sentence." Turner v. Murray, 476 U.S. 28, 35, 106 S.Ct. 1683, 1688, 90 L.Ed.2d 27 (1986), and that "[i]t is of vital importance to the defendant and to the community that any decision to impose the death sentence be, and appear to be, based on reason rather than caprice or emotion." Gardner v. Florida, 430 U.S. 349, 358, 97 S.Ct. 1197, 1204, 51 L.Ed.2d 393 (1977). In determining the guilt of a defendant, a state must prove its case beyond a reasonable doubt. That is, we refuse to convict if the chance of error is simply less likely than not. Surely, we should not be willing to take a person's life if the chance that his death sentence was irrationally imposed is *more* likely than not. In light of the gravity of the interest at stake, petitioner's statistics on their face are a powerful demonstration of the type of risk that our Eighth Amendment jurisprudence has consistently condemned.

LAW AND STATISTICS IN CONFLICT: REFLECTIONS ON McCLESKEY v. KEMP*

David C. Baldus, George Woodworth, and Charles A. Pulaski, Jr. In Handbook of Psychology and Law.
(D.K. Kagehiro and W.S. Laufer eds. 1992).

We believe that the Court's refusal in *McCleskey* to accept the normal rules of statistical inference reflects considerations going well beyond the methodological justifications by Justice Powell. One factor working against McCleskey's equal protection arguments may have been that the principle

* Baldus, Woodworth, and Pulaski, Law and Statistics in Conflict: Reflections on McCleskey v. Kemp, in Handbook of Psychol-ogy and Law, 265–69 (Kagehiro and Laufer eds. 1992), reprinted with kind permission of Springer Science and Business Media.

of racial equality underlying the equal protection clause of the Fourteenth Amendment was not as heavily implicated in his case as it is in more typical civil rights cases. As a convicted murderer, McCleskey did not enjoy the same status of an "oppressed minority" as claimants in housing, employment, and school discrimination cases.

In addition, the principal basis of *McCleskey's* discrimination claims was not evidence of discrimination against black defendants, but rather against defendants whose victims were white. This difference constitutes another deviation from the typical civil rights model in which the claimants suffered adverse treatment or denial of benefits on the basis of their gender or race, factors over which they had no control. It may appear inappropriate to allow a defendant who "chose" his victim to invoke that person's race as a basis for obtaining relief under the Constitution.

To be sure, to the extent that capital punishment produces benefits for either the white or black community, race-of-victim discrimination does adversely affect the black community as a whole. Specifically, discrimination on the basis of the race of the victim means that any beneficial effects produced by capital punishment are disproportionately allocated to the white community. Also, race-of-victim discrimination represents a distinct insult to the black community in that it conveys the message that black lives are worth less than white lives, regardless of the motivation for the differential in treatment. Nevertheless, as a class, black murder defendants are not adversely affected by race-of-victim discrimination. In fact, because most killers of black victims are blacks themselves, the suppressed rate of death sentencing in black-victim cases means that fewer black defendants receive the death sentence than would otherwise be the case.

We do not intend to suggest, however, that the Court cares little about race-of-victim discrimination. Indeed, Justice Powell's opinion in Booth v. Maryland [482 U.S. 496, 107 S.Ct. 2529, 96 L.Ed.2d 440 (1987)], decided two months after McCleskey, reflects the Court's continuing concerns. *Booth* held that Maryland's use of detailed Victim Information Statements (VIS) in penalty trials violated the Eighth Amendment.

> The VIS in this case provided the jury with two types of information. First, it described the personal characteristics of the victims and the emotional impact of the crimes on the family. Second, it set forth the family members' opinions and characterizations of the crimes and the defendant. For the reasons stated below, we find that this information is irrelevant to a capital-sentencing decision, and that its admission creates a constitutionally unacceptable risk that the jury may impose the death penalty in an arbitrary and capricious manner. [Id. at 503, 107 S.Ct. at 2533].

Moreover, Justice Powell explained his concern about the Victim Information Statements' description of the personal characteristics of the decedent in the following footnote:

> We are troubled by the implication that defendants whose victims were assets to their community are more deserving of punishment

than those whose victims are perceived to be less worthy. Of course, our system of justice does not tolerate such distinctions. [Id. at 506, n. 8, 107 S.Ct. at 2534, n. 8].

This language clearly demonstrates a continuing commitment to a principled nondiscriminatory death-sentencing system, especially as it applies to the characteristics of the victim. Certainly, if the Court condemned jury consideration of the victim's character, it clearly would condemn the consideration of the victim's race by either prosecutors or jurors.

Of course, the *Booth* decision does raise an obvious question: How can one reconcile the Court's decision in *Booth* which, on the basis of a completely undocumented risk, invalidated the use of Victim Impact Statements, with the Court's ruling two months earlier in *McCleskey* that empirical evidence was incapable of proving a "constitutionally significant risk of racial bias"? It may also be relevant that, in cases like *Booth,* the Court can comfortably assess the risk of arbitrariness and capriciousness in individual cases based solely on unproven hunches about the effects of certain rules and procedures without recourse to empirical evidence about those effects. This preference for hunches or intuition may very well reflect an insecurity about the Justices' own abilities to assess properly quantitative evidence of the type presented in *McCleskey.* The Court may fear that subsequent analysis will demonstrate that it incorrectly interpreted the empirical data on which its findings were based. Furthermore, one can understand why relatively untrained judges, confronted with massive quantities of data and conflicting expert opinions about the validity and probative force of statistically derived inferences, might have greater confidence in intuitively derived conclusions than the pronouncements of statisticians. If the Court felt more confident about its ability to distinguish good from bad empirical studies, it might be more willing to accept such studies as a basis for its decisions. Certainly, without such confidence, one can understand a reluctance to rely upon an empirical study, no matter how well-regarded by the experts.

Uncertainty about the validity of empirical research does not, however, appear to offer a plausible explanation for the Court's rejection of McCleskey's claim and its seemingly contrary ruling in *Booth*. The likely explanation, we think, is that cases like *Booth,* which vacate death sentences on ad hoc grounds, will at most affect only a few defendants and lack any potential for producing a large-scale disruptive effect on state death-sentencing systems generally. A ruling for McCleskey, in contrast, carried the potential for a serious disruption of current death-sentencing practices both in Georgia and in other death-sentencing jurisdictions.

[A] ruling in McCleskey's favor could have seriously disrupted the U.S. death-sentencing system. The United States Supreme Court has labored for 15 years to develop a body of doctrine which would allow the states to resume routine executions under standards which would satisfy the requirements of the Constitution. In the eyes of many proponents of the death penalty, however, the Court's efforts have been woefully ineffective and have merely frustrated the desires of the people to get on with the executions. At the time of the *McCleskey* decision, more than 3,000 death sentences had been imposed, but fewer than 100 had been actually carried out through the execution. A finding in favor of McCleskey, whether based upon the jury discrimination model or an employment discrimination model, which would have led to the scrutiny of each individual death sentence, would likely have led to the wholesale staying of executions until each jurisdiction's death-sentencing could be legitimated through an empirical study. A delay of 5 years in executions as a consequence would not have seemed unlikely. The outcry against the Court from such a policy would have been predictable.

[Justice Powell] suggested a final possible explanation for the Court's decision. In it, he indicated that because the Eighth Amendment applies to the entire criminal justice system, a holding that evidence of race or sex discrimination in a criminal justice system could expose it to a successful Eighth Amendment challenge would potentially jeopardize the entire criminal justice system. He envisioned a virtual invasion of statisticians and social scientists who could potentially bring the entire criminal justice system to its knees.

To be sure, as noted above, a ruling favorable to McCleskey would have disrupted the death-sentencing systems of some states, at least for the short term; but Justice Powell's apprehension of a parade of social scientists and statisticians disrupting the courts appears to be greatly exaggerated. In the first place, the only social science research relevant to judicial proceedings would be field research conducted in actual courts. Most of the social science studies cited by Justice Powell were not field studies but experiments that used students as mock jurors. In the second place, field research of the type Justice Powell fears is expensive, extremely time-consuming, and, because of its applied nature, generally not favored by funding sources. The relatively small amount of judicial field research done to date is suggestive of the few incentives that the system offers to produce it. Third, most of the field research conducted to date tends to undercut the farfetched claims Justice Powell thinks social scientists would be inclined to support. That research does not suggest that the criminal justice system is systematically biased or invidious, or that it characteristically functions arbitrarily or irrationally. To be sure, there is substantial evidence of sentencing disparities among similarly situated offenders, but most of the available evidence does not suggest that these disparities are correlated with sex, physical appearance, or any of the other factors hypothesized by the Court. In fact, with respect to the issue of discrimination against minority defendants, the literature suggests that further empirical inquiry may increase public confidence in the basic fairness of the system.

Finally, we find it distressing that a majority of the Supreme Court would choose to reject a claim based upon invidious racial discrimination because of the work load that a ruling in the claimant's favor might entail in later cases. Former Chief Justice Burger frequently urged Congress to conduct a "judicial impact study" before enacting new legislation. Justice

Powell's avowed concerns in *McCleskey* have the same flavor, but, given the constitutional character of the rights asserted, seem much less appropriate.

JUSTICE LEWIS F. POWELL, JR. (1994)*

John C. Jeffries, Jr.

Powell stated his position most succinctly in an early memorandum urging his colleagues not to hear McCleskey's case. First, it was hard to know what to make of statistics. "[S]entencing judges and juries are constitutionally *required* to consider a host of individual-specific circumstances in deciding whether to impose capital punishment. No study can take all of these individual circumstances into account, precisely because they are fact-specific as to each defendant." Of course, taking all factors into account was precisely what Baldus and his colleagues had tried to do, but Powell was uneasy with this kind of evidence. As he said elsewhere, "[m]y understanding of statistical analysis ... ranges from limited to zero."

He also did not know what constitutional weight to give to the statistical effect of the *victim's* race. "[O]ne would expect that if there were race-based sentencing, the Baldus study would show a bias based on the *defendant's* race," but the "study suggests *no* such effect...." Differential treatment of defendants based on the race of their victims was hard to understand as racial bias against defendants.

Finally, Powell thought the overall picture revealed by the figures was decidedly positive. The "study tends to show that the system operates rationally as a general matter: The death penalty was most likely in those cases with the most severe aggravating factors and the least mitigating factors, and least likely in the opposite cases. The pattern suggests precisely the kind of careful balancing of individual factors that the Court required in *Gregg*,"

[P]owell did not see the case as condoning racism but simply as recognizing the inevitable variations in any nonmandatory death penalty.

[I]n conversation with the author in the summer of 1991, Powell was asked whether he would change his vote in any case:

"Yes, *McCleskey v. Kemp*."

"Do you mean you would now accept the argument from statistics?"

"No, I would vote the other way in any capital case."

"In *any* capital case?"

"Yes."

* Reprinted with the permission of Scribner, a Division of Simon and Schuster, from LOUIS F. POWELL, JR.: A BIOGRAPHY by John C. Jeffries, Jr. Copyright © 1994 by John C. Jeffries, Jr., and with the permission of the author.

"Even in *Furman v. Georgia*?"

"Yes. I have come to think that capital punishment should be abolished."

————

NOTES

1. Court-Ordered Research. The defendant in People v. Jackson, 28 Cal.3d 264, 168 Cal.Rptr. 603, 618 P.2d 149 (1980), an African-American male, was convicted of murdering two white women and sentenced to death. The California Supreme Court affirmed the conviction but appointed a retired state appellate justice as a referee and ordered him "to take evidence and make findings of fact with respect to defendant's contentions that death sentences in California have been discriminatorily imposed on the basis of (1) the race of the victim, (2) the race of the defendant, and/or (3) the gender of the defendant." In re Jackson, Crim. 22165, Minutes of the California Supreme Court, May 3, 1984. After the referee had spent three years and one million dollars commissioning this research, a new majority of the California Supreme Court quashed the study. "Our order, dated May 3, 1984, expanding the reference to include claims of discriminatory application of the death penalty in California on the basis of race and sex, is vacated without prejudice to a renewed application for an expanded or separate reference which alleges a prima facie case not inconsistent with McCleskey v. Kemp (1987), 481 U.S. 279, 95 L.Ed.2d 262." In re Jackson, Crim. 22165, Minutes of the California Supreme Court, October 27, 1987.

2. Certificates of Non-Discrimination. The Omnibus Drug Initiative of 1988, Pub.L. 100–690, codified at 21 U.S.C.A. § 848(*o*)(1), "Death Penalty for Drug-Related Killings," states as follows:

> In any hearing held before a jury under this section, the court shall instruct the jury that in its consideration of whether the sentence of death is justified it shall not consider the race, color, religious beliefs, national origin, or sex of the defendant or the victim, and that the jury is not to recommend a sentence of death unless it has concluded that it would recommend a sentence of death for the crime in question no matter what the race, color, religious beliefs, national origin, or sex of the defendant, or the victim, may be. The jury shall return to the court a certificate signed by each juror that consideration of the race, color, religious beliefs, national origin, or sex of the defendant or the victim was not involved in reaching his or her individual decision, and that the individual juror would have made the same recommendation regarding a sentence for the crime in question no matter what the race, color, religious beliefs, national origin, or sex of the defendant, or the victim, may be.

3. EXCESSIVE SANCTION

In Atkins v. Virginia, 536 U.S. 304, 122 S.Ct. 2242, 153 L.Ed.2d 335 (2002), the Supreme Court held that executing people with mental retardation constituted an "excessive" sanction in violation of the Eighth and Fourteenth Amendments to the Unites States Constitution. Three years later, the court applied a similar analysis, informed by social science, to hold that the execution of offenders who were under the age of 18 when they committed their crimes was also unconstitutional.

ROPER v. SIMMONS

Supreme Court of the United States, 2005.
543 U.S. ___, 125 S.Ct. 1183, 161 L.Ed.2d 1.

■ Justice Kennedy delivered the opinion of the Court.

This case requires us to address...whether it is permissible under the Eighth and Fourteenth Amendments to the Constitution of the United States to execute a juvenile offender who was older than 15 but younger than 18 when he committed a capital crime. [A]t the age of 17, when he was still a junior in high school, Christopher Simmons, the respondent here, committed murder. About nine months later, after he had turned 18, he was tried and sentenced to death.

[B]ecause the death penalty is the most severe punishment, the Eighth Amendment applies to it with special force. *Thompson*, 487 U.S., at 856 (O'CONNOR, J., concurring in judgment). Capital punishment must be limited to those offenders who commit "a narrow category of the most serious crimes" and whose extreme culpability makes them "the most deserving of execution." *Atkins [536 U.S. 304 (2002)]* at 319.

[T]hree general differences between juveniles under 18 and adults demonstrate that juvenile offenders cannot with reliability be classified among the worst offenders. First, as any parent knows and as the scientific and sociological studies respondent and his *amici* cite tend to confirm, "[a] lack of maturity and an underdeveloped sense of responsibility are found in youth more often than in adults and are more understandable among the young. These qualities often result in impetuous and ill-considered actions and decisions." *Johnson [509 U.S. 350 (1993)]*, at 367; see also *Eddings*, *[455 U.S. 104 (1982)]*, at 115–116 ("Even the normal 16-year-old customarily lacks the maturity of an adult"). It has been noted that "adolescents are overrepresented statistically in virtually every category of reckless behavior." Arnett, Reckless Behavior in Adolescence: A Developmental Perspective, 12 Developmental Review 339 (1992). In recognition of the comparative immaturity and irresponsibility of juveniles, almost every State prohibits those under 18 years of age from voting, serving on juries, or marrying without parental consent.

The second area of difference is that juveniles are more vulnerable or susceptible to negative influences and outside pressures, including peer pressure. *Eddings*, *supra*, at 115 ("Youth is more than a chronological fact. It is a time and condition of life when a person may be most susceptible to influence and to psychological damage"). This is explained in part by the prevailing circumstance that juveniles have less control, or less experience with control, over their own environment. See Steinberg & Scott, Less Guilty by Reason of Adolescence: Developmental Immaturity, Diminished Responsibility, and the Juvenile Death Penalty, 58 Am. Psychologist 1009, 1014 (2003) (hereinafter Steinberg & Scott) ("As legal minors, [juveniles] lack the freedom that adults have to extricate themselves from a criminogenic setting").

The third broad difference is that the character of a juvenile is not as well formed as that of an adult. The personality traits of juveniles are more transitory, less fixed. See generally E. Erikson, Identity: Youth and Crisis (1968).

These differences render suspect any conclusion that a juvenile falls among the worst offenders. The susceptibility of juveniles to immature and irresponsible behavior means "their irresponsible conduct is not as morally reprehensible as that of an adult." *Thompson, supra,* at 835 (plurality opinion). Their own vulnerability and comparative lack of control over their immediate surroundings mean juveniles have a greater claim than adults to be forgiven for failing to escape negative influences in their whole environment. The reality that juveniles still struggle to define their identity means it is less supportable to conclude that even a heinous crime committed by a juvenile is evidence of irretrievably depraved character. From a moral standpoint it would be misguided to equate the failings of a minor with those of an adult, for a greater possibility exists that a minor's character deficiencies will be reformed. Indeed, "the relevance of youth as a mitigating factor derives from the fact that the signature qualities of youth are transient; as individuals mature, the impetuousness and recklessness that may dominate in younger years can subside." *Johnson, supra,* at 368; see also Steinberg & Scott 1014 ("For most teens, [risky or antisocial] behaviors are fleeting; they cease with maturity as individual identity becomes settled. Only a relatively small proportion of adolescents who experiment in risky or illegal activities develop entrenched patterns of problem behavior that persist into adulthood").

In *Thompson,* a plurality of the Court recognized the import of these characteristics with respect to juveniles under 16, and relied on them to hold that the Eighth Amendment prohibited the imposition of the death penalty on juveniles below that age. 487 U.S., at 833–838. We conclude the same reasoning applies to all juvenile offenders under 18.

Once the diminished culpability of juveniles is recognized, it is evident that the penological justifications for the death penalty apply to them with lesser force than to adults. We have held there are two distinct social purposes served by the death penalty: " 'retribution and deterrence of capital crimes by prospective offenders.' " *Atkins,* 536 U.S., at 319 (quoting *Gregg* v. *Georgia,* 428 U.S. 153, 183 (1976) (joint opinion of Stewart, Powell, and STEVENS, JJ.)). As for retribution, we remarked in *Atkins* that "if the culpability of the average murderer is insufficient to justify the most extreme sanction available to the State, the lesser culpability of the mentally retarded offender surely does not merit that form of retribution." 536 U.S., at 319. The same conclusions follow from the lesser culpability of the juvenile offender. Whether viewed as an attempt to express the community's moral outrage or as an attempt to right the balance for the wrong to the victim, the case for retribution is not as strong with a minor as with an adult. Retribution is not proportional if the law's most severe penalty is imposed on one whose culpability or blameworthiness is diminished, to a substantial degree, by reason of youth and immaturity.

As for deterrence, it is unclear whether the death penalty has a significant or even measurable deterrent effect on juveniles, as counsel for the petitioner acknowledged at oral argument. In general we leave to legislatures the assessment of the efficacy of various criminal penalty schemes. Here, however, the absence of evidence of deterrent effect is of special concern because the same characteristics that render juveniles less culpable than adults suggest as well that juveniles will be less susceptible to deterrence. In particular, as the plurality observed in *Thompson*, "the likelihood that the teenage offender has made the kind of cost-benefit analysis that attaches any weight to the possibility of execution is so remote as to be virtually nonexistent." 487 U.S., at 837. To the extent the juvenile death penalty might have residual deterrent effect, it is worth noting that the punishment of life imprisonment without the possibility of parole is itself a severe sanction, in particular for a young person.

In concluding that neither retribution nor deterrence provides adequate justification for imposing the death penalty on juvenile offenders, we cannot deny or overlook the brutal crimes too many juvenile offenders have committed. Certainly it can be argued, although we by no means concede the point, that a rare case might arise in which a juvenile offender has sufficient psychological maturity, and at the same time demonstrates sufficient depravity, to merit a sentence of death. Indeed, this possibility is the linchpin of one contention pressed by petitioner and his *amici*. They assert that even assuming the truth of the observations we have made about juveniles' diminished culpability in general, jurors nonetheless should be allowed to consider mitigating arguments related to youth on a case-by-case basis, and in some cases to impose the death penalty if justified.

[W]e disagree. The differences between juvenile and adult offenders are too marked and well understood to risk allowing a youthful person to receive the death penalty despite insufficient culpability. [I]t is difficult even for expert psychologists to differentiate between the juvenile offender whose crime reflects unfortunate yet transient immaturity, and the rare juvenile offender whose crime reflects irreparable corruption. See Steinberg & Scott 1014–1016. As we understand it, this difficulty underlies the rule forbidding psychiatrists from diagnosing any patient under 18 as having antisocial personality disorder, a disorder also referred to as psychopathy or sociopathy, and which is characterized by callousness, cynicism, and contempt for the feelings, rights, and suffering of others. American Psychiatric Association, Diagnostic and Statistical Manual of Mental Disorders 701–706 (4th ed. text rev. 2000); see also Steinberg & Scott 1015. If trained psychiatrists with the advantage of clinical testing and observation refrain, despite diagnostic expertise, from assessing any juvenile under 18 as having antisocial personality disorder, we conclude that States should refrain from asking jurors to issue a far graver condemnation—that a juvenile offender merits the death penalty. When a juvenile offender commits a heinous crime, the State can exact forfeiture of some of the most basic liberties, but the State cannot extinguish his life and his potential to attain a mature understanding of his own humanity.

[T]he Eighth and Fourteenth Amendments forbid imposition of the death penalty on offenders who were under the age of 18 when their crimes were committed. The judgment of the Missouri Supreme Court setting aside the sentence of death imposed upon Christopher Simmons is affirmed.

■ Justice Scalia, with whom The Chief Justice and Justice Thomas join, dissenting.

[T]oday's opinion provides a perfect example of why judges are ill equipped to make the type of legislative judgments the Court insists on making here. To support its opinion that States should be prohibited from imposing the death penalty on anyone who committed murder before age 18, the Court looks to scientific and sociological studies, picking and choosing those that support its position. It never explains why those particular studies are methodologically sound; none was ever entered into evidence or tested in an adversarial proceeding. As The Chief Justice has explained:

> "Methodological and other errors can affect the reliability and validity of estimates about the opinions and attitudes of a population derived from various sampling techniques. Everything from variations in the survey methodology, such as the choice of the target population, the sampling design used, the questions asked, and the statistical analyses used to interpret the data can skew the results." *Atkins, supra,* at 326–327 (dissenting opinion) (citing R. Groves, Survey Errors and Survey Costs (1989); 1 C. Turner & E. Martin, Surveying Subjective Phenomena (1984)).

In other words, all the Court has done today, to borrow from another context, is to look over the heads of the crowd and pick out its friends.

We need not look far to find studies contradicting the Court's conclusions. As petitioner points out, the American Psychological Association (APA), which claims in this case that scientific evidence shows persons under 18 lack the ability to take moral responsibility for their decisions, has previously taken precisely the opposite position before this very Court. In its brief in *Hodgson* v. *Minnesota,* 497 U.S. 417 (1990), the APA found a "rich body of research" showing that juveniles are mature enough to decide whether to obtain an abortion without parental involvement. Brief for APA as *Amicus Curiae,* O. T. 1989, No. 88–805 etc., p. 18. The APA brief, citing psychology treatises and studies too numerous to list here, asserted: "By middle adolescence (age 14–15) young people develop abilities similar to adults in reasoning about moral dilemmas, understanding social rules and laws, [and] reasoning about interpersonal relationships and interpersonal problems." *Id.,* at 19–20 (citations omitted). Given the nuances of scientific methodology and conflicting views, courts—which can only consider the limited evidence on the record before them—are ill equipped to determine which view of science is the right one. Legislatures "are better qualified to weigh and 'evaluate the results of statistical studies in terms of their own local conditions and with a flexibility of approach that is not available to the courts.' " *McCleskey* v. *Kemp,* 481 U.S. 279, 319 (1987) (quoting *Gregg, supra,* at 186).

Even putting aside questions of methodology, the studies cited by the Court offer scant support for a categorical prohibition of the death penalty for murderers under 18. At most, these studies conclude that, *on average,* or *in most cases,* persons under 18 are unable to take moral responsibility for their actions. Not one of the cited studies opines that all individuals under 18 are unable to appreciate the nature of their crimes.

Moreover, the cited studies describe only adolescents who engage in risky or antisocial behavior, as many young people do. Murder, however, is more than just risky or antisocial behavior. It is entirely consistent to believe that young people often act impetuously and lack judgment, but, at the same time, to believe that those who commit premeditated murder are—at least sometimes—just as culpable as adults. Christopher Simmons, who was only seven months shy of his 18th birthday when he murdered Shirley Crook, described to his friends *beforehand*—"in chilling, callous terms," as the Court puts it, *ante,* at 1—the murder he planned to commit. He then broke into the home of an innocent woman, bound her with duct tape and electrical wire, and threw her off a bridge alive and conscious.

[N]or does the Court suggest a stopping point for its reasoning. If juries cannot make appropriate determinations in cases involving murderers under 18, in what other kinds of cases will the Court find jurors deficient? We have already held that no jury may consider whether a mentally deficient defendant can receive the death penalty, irrespective of his crime. See *Atkins,* 536 U.S., at 321. Why not take other mitigating factors, such as considerations of childhood abuse or poverty, away from juries as well? Surely jurors "overpowered" by "the brutality or cold-blooded nature" of a crime, *ante,* at 19, could not adequately weigh these mitigating factors either.

SELECTED BIBLIOGRAPHY

A.   The Fourteenth Amendment: School Desegregation

Cowan, Distinguishing Private Women's Colleges from the *VMI* Decision, 30 Columbia Journal of Law and Social Problems 137 (1997).

W. Cross, Shades of Black: Diversity in African-American Identity (1991).

J. Jackson, Social Scientists for Social Justice: Making the Case Against Segregation (2001).

Jackson, The Scientific Attack on *Brown v. Board of Education*, 1954–1964, 59 American Psychologist 530 (2004).

Kalmuss, Chesler, and Sanders, Political Conflict in Applied Scholarship: Expert Witnesses in School Desegregation Litigation, 30 Social Problems 168 (1982).

W. Loh, Social Research in the Judicial Process: Cases, Readings, and Text (1984).

Lucas and Paret, Law, Race, and Education in the United States, 1 Annual Review of Law and Science 203 (2005).

Note, Inner-City Single-Sex Schools: Educational Reform or Invidious Discrimination? 105 Harvard Law Review 1741 (1992).

Race, Law, and Culture: Reflections on *Brown v. Board of Education* (A. Sarat, ed. 1997).

Ryan, Schools, Race, and Money, 109 Yale Law Journal 249 (1999).

Ryan, The Limited Influence of Social Science Evidence in Modern Desegregation Cases, 81 North Carolina Law Review 1161 (2003).

Sanders, *Brown v. Board of Education*: An Empirical Reexamination of Its Effects on Federal District Courts. 29 Law and Society Review 731 (1995).

Schofield and Hausmann, School Desegregation and Social Science Research, 59 American Psychologist 538 (2004).

Simson, Separate But Equal and Single-Sex Schools, 90 Cornell Law Review 443 (2005).

Stephan, The Effects of School Desegregation: An Evaluation 30 Years After *Brown*, in Advances in Applied Social Psychology, Vol. 3 (M. Saks and L. Saxe eds. 1986).

P. Strum, Women in the Barracks: The VMI Case and Equal Rights (2002).

Weber, Immersed in an Educational Crisis: Alternative Programs for African-American Males, 45 Stanford Law Review 1099 (1993).

B. The First Amendment: Obscenity

E. Donnerstein, D. Linz, and S. Penrod, The Question of Pornography (1987).

Koppelman, Does Obscenity Cause Moral Harm?, 105 Columbia Law Review 1635 (2005).

Linz, Blumenthal, Donnerstein, Kunkel, Shafer, and Lichtenstein, Testing Legal Assumptions Regarding the Effects of Dancer Nudity and Proximity to Patron on Erotic Expression, 24 Law and Human Behavior 507 (2000).

Linz, Land, Ezell, Paul, and Williams, An Examination of the Assumption that Adult Businesses Are Associated with Crime in Surrounding Areas: A Secondary Effects Study in Charlotte, North Carolina, 38 Law and Society Review 69 (2004).

Mullin and Linz, Desensitization and Resensitization to Violence Against Women: Effects of Exposure to Sexually Violent Films on Judgments of Domestic Violence Victims, 69 Journal of Personality and Social Psychology 449 (1995).

Obscenity and Pornography Decisions of the United States Supreme Court (M. Harrison and S. Gilbert eds. 2000).

Seto, Maric, and Barbaree, The Role of Pornography in the Etiology of Sexual Aggression, 6 Aggression and Violent Behavior 35 (2001).

C. The Sixth Amendment: Juries

Brewer, Race and Jurors' Receptivity to Mitigation in Capital Cases: The Effect of Jurors', Defendants', and Victims' Race in Combination, 28 Law and Human Behavior 529 (2004).

Butler and Moran, The Role of Death Qualification in Venirepersons' Evalutions of Aggravating and Mitigating Circumstances in Capital Trials, 26 Law and Human Behavior 175 (2002).

Diamond, Truth, Justice, and the Jury, 26 Harv. J. of Law & Public Policy 143 (2003).

Diamond and Rose, Real Juries, 1 Annual Review of Law and Social Science 255 (2005).

Diamond, Rose, and Murphy, Revisiting the Unanimity Requirement: The Behavior of the Non-Unanimous Civil Jury, ___ Northwestern Law Review (in press).

Diamond, Saks, and Landsman, Juror Judgments About Liability and Damages: Sources of Variability and Ways To Increase Consistency, 48 DePaul Law Review 301 (1998).

Diamond, Vidmar, Rose, Ellis, and Murphy, Jury Discussions During Civil Trials: Studying an Arizona Innovation. 45 University of Arizona Law Review 1 (2003).

N. Finkel, Commonsense Justice: Jurors' Notions of the Law (1998).

FosterLee and Horowitz, The Effects of Juror-Aid Innovations on Juror Performance in Complex Civil Trials, 86 Judicature 184 (2003).

Goodman, Tobey, Batterman-Faunce, Orcutt, Thomas, Shapiro, and Sachsenmaier, Face-to-Face Confrontation: Effects of Closed-Circuit Technology on Children's Eyewitness Testimony and Jurors' Decisions, 22 Law and Human Behavior 165 (1998).

V. Hans, Business on Trial: The Civil Jury and Corporate Responsibility (2000).

V. Hans and N. Vidmar, Judging the Jury (1986).

Heuer and Penrod, Juror Notetaking and Question Asking During Trials: A National Field Experiment, 18 Law and Human Behavior 121 (1994).

Kaye, And Then There Were Twelve: Statistical Reasoning, the Supreme Court, and the Size of the Jury, 68 California Law Review 1004 (1980).

Kaye and Koehler, Can Jurors Understand Probabilistic Evidence?, 154 Journal of the Royal Statistical Association 75 (1991).

London and Nunez, The Effect of Jury Deliberations on Jurors' Propensity to Disregard Inadmissible Evidence, 85 Journal of Applied Psychology 932 (2000).

Mott, Hans, and Simpson, What's Half a Lung Worth? Civil Jurors' Accounts of Their Award Decision Making, 24 Law and Human Behavior 401 (2000).

Reifman, Gusick, and Ellsworth, Real Jurors' Understanding of the Law in Real Cases, 16 Law and Human Behavior 539 (1992).

Saks, The Smaller the Jury, The Greater the Unpredictability. 79 Judicature 263 (1996).

Saks, What Jury Experiments Tell Us About How Juries (Should) Make Decisions, 6 Southern California Interdisciplinary Law Journal 1 (1998).

Saks and Marti, A Meta-Analysis of the Effects of Jury Size, 21 Law and Human Behavior 451 (1997)

Schuller, Expert Evidence and Hearsay: The Influence of "Secondhand" Information on Jurors' Decisions, 19 Law and Human Behavior 345 (1995)

Slobogin, Should Juries and the Death Penalty Mix?: A Prediction About the Supreme Court's Answer, 70 Indiana Law Journal 1249 (1995).

Slobogin, Is Justice Just Us?, 87 Journal of Criminal law and Criminology 101 (1996).

Sommers, On Racial Diversity and Group Decision-Making: Identifying Multiple Effects of Racial Composition on Jury Deliberations. Journal of Personality and Social Psychology (in press).

Sommers and Ellsworth, White Juror Bias: An Investigation of Prejudice Against Black Defendants in American Courtrooms, 7 Psychology, Public Policy, and Law 201 (2001).

Sommers and Ellsworth, How Much do we Really Know About Race and Juries? A Review of Social Science Theory and Research, 78 Chicago-Kent Law Review 997 (2003).

Sorenson, Wrinkle, Brewer, and Marquart, Capital Punishment and Deterrence: Examining the Effect of Executions on Murder in Texas, 45 Crime and Delinquency 481 (1999).

Vidmar, Expert Evidence, the Adversary System, and the Jury, 95 American Journal of Public Health S137 (2005).

Zeisel and Diamond, "Convincing Empirical Evidence" on the Six Member Jury, 41 University of Chicago Law Review 281 (1974).

D.   The Eighth Amendment: The Death Penalty

Allen, Mabry, and McKelton, Impact of Juror Attitudes About the Death Penalty on Juror Evaluations of Guilt and Punishment: A Meta-Analysis, 22 Law and Human Behavior 715 (1998).

Baldus, The Death Penalty Dialog Between Law and Social Science. 70 Indiana Law Journal 1033 (1995).

D. Baldus, G. Woodworth, and C. Pulaski, Equal Justice and the Death Penalty: A Legal and Empirical Analysis (1990).

Baldus, Woodworth, and Pulaski, Reflections on the "Inevitability" of Racial Discrimination in Capital Sentencing and the "Impossibility" of its Prevention, Detection, and Correction. 51 Washington and Lee Law Review 359 (1994).

Baldus, Woodworth, Zuckerman, Weiner, and Broffitt, Racial Discrimination and the Death Penalty in the Post-*Furman* Era: An Empirical and Legal Overview, With Recent Findings from Philadelphia, 83 Cornell Law Review 1638 (1998).

Beck and Shumsky, A Comparison of Retained and Appointed Counsel in Cases of Capital Murder, 21 Law and Human Behavior 525(1997).

Blume, Eisenberg, and Johnson, Post-*McCleskey* Racial Discrimination Claims in Capital Cases, 83 Cornell Law Review 1771 (1998).

Conley, Turnier, and Rose, The Racial Ecology of the Courtroom: An Experimental Study of Juror Response to the Race of Criminal Defendants, 2000 Wisconsin Law Review 1185 (2000).

Crosby, Britner, Jodl and Portwood, The Juvenile Death Penalty and the Eighth Amendment: An Empirical Investigation of Societal Consensus and Proportionality, 19 Law and Human Behavior 245 (1995)

Diamond and Casper, Empirical Evidence and the Death Penalty: Past and Future, 50 Journal of Social issues 177 (1994).

Ehrlich, The Deterrent Effect of Capital Punishment—A Question of Life and Death, 65 American Economic Review 397 (1975).

Ehrlich, On Positive Methodology, Ethics, and Polemics in Deterrence Research, 22 British Journal of Criminology 124 (1982).

Eisenberg, Death Sentence Rates and County Demographics: An Empirical Study, 90 Cornell Law Review 347 (2005).

Eisenberg, Garvey, and Wells, The Deadly Paradox of Capital Jurors, 74 Southern California Law Review 371 (2001).

Ellsworth, Unpleasant Facts: The Supreme Court's Response to Empirical Research on Capital Punishment, in Challenging Capital Punishment: Legal and Social Science Approaches (K. Haas and J. Inciardi eds. 1988).

Finkel, Prestidigitation, Statistical Magic, and Supreme Court Numerology in Juvenile Death Penalty Cases, 1 Psychology, Public Policy, and Law 612 (1995).

Gross and Ellsworth, Second Thoughts: Americans' Views on the Death Penalty at the Turn of the Century, in Capital Punishment and the American Future (S. Garvey, ed. 2001).

C. Haney, Death by Design: Capital Punishment as a Social Psychological System (2005).

Hans, Death by Jury, in Challenging Capital Punishment: Legal and Social Science Approaches (K. Haas and J. Inciardi eds. 1988).

Heilbrun, Foster, and Golden, The Death Sentence in Georgia, 1974–1987: Criminal Justice or Racial Injustice?, 16 Criminal Justice and Behavior 139 (1989).

Kennedy, McCleskey v. Kemp: Race, Capital Punishment, and the Supreme Court, 101 Harvard Law Review 1388 (1988).

McAdams, Racial Disparity and the Death Penalty, 61 Law and Contemporary Problems, 153 (1998).

Nadler, Flouting the Law, 83 Texas Law Review 1399 (2005).

Nebraska Death Penalty Study: An Interdisciplinary Symposium, 81 Nebraska Law Review 479 (2002).

Weisberg, The Death Penalty Meets Social Science: Deterrence and Jury Behavior Under New Scrutiny, 1 Annual Review of Law and Social Science 151 (2005).

SECTION III. COMMON LAW

While the bulk of the lawmaking uses of social science clearly have occurred in the area of constitutional law, common law has also seen the application of empirical research. We consider here two topics where social science studies have been relied upon to change the course of the common law. The first concerns rules of evidence. The second deals with tort liability.

A.   RULES OF EVIDENCE

1.   THE EXCLUSIONARY RULE

The Fourth Amendment to the Constitution reads as follows:

The right of the people to be secure in their persons, houses, papers, and effects, against unreasonable searches and seizures, shall not be violated, and no Warrants shall issue, but upon probable cause, supported by Oath or affirmation, and particularly describing the place to be searched, and the persons or things to be seized.

Weeks v. United States, 232 U.S. 383, 34 S.Ct. 341, 58 L.Ed. 652 (1914) held that evidence seized in violation of the Fourth Amendment could not be used against the defendant in federal criminal prosecutions. Since the time of *Weeks,* this has been known as the "exclusionary rule."

WOLF v. COLORADO

Supreme Court of the United States, 1949.
338 U.S. 25, 69 S.Ct. 1359, 93 L.Ed. 1782.

■ Mr. Justice Frankfurter delivered the opinion of the Court.

The precise question for consideration is this: Does a conviction by a State court for a State offense deny the "due process of law" required by the Fourteenth Amendment, solely because evidence that was admitted at the trial was obtained under circumstances which would have rendered it inadmissible in a prosecution for violation of a federal law in a court of the United States because there deemed to be an infraction of the Fourth Amendment as applied in Weeks v. United States, 232 U.S. 383, 34 S.Ct. 341, 58 L.Ed. 652?

[T]he security of one's privacy against arbitrary intrusion by the police—which is at the core of the Fourth Amendment—is basic to a free society. It is therefore implicit in "the concept of ordered liberty" and as such enforceable against the States through the Due Process Clause. The knock at the door, whether by day or by night, as a prelude to a search, without authority of law but solely on the authority of the police, did not need the commentary of recent history to be condemned as inconsistent with the conception of human rights enshrined in the history and the basic constitutional documents of English-speaking peoples.

Accordingly, we have no hesitation in saying that were a State affirmatively to sanction such police incursion into privacy it would run counter to the guaranty of the Fourteenth Amendment. But the ways of enforcing such a basic right raise questions of a different order. How such arbitrary conduct should be checked, what remedies against it should be afforded, the means by which the right should be made effective, are all questions that are not to be so dogmatically answered as to preclude the varying solutions which spring from an allowable range of judgment on issues not susceptible of quantitative solution.

In Weeks v. United States, supra, this Court held that in a federal prosecution the Fourth Amendment barred the use of evidence secured through an illegal search and seizure. [T]he immediate question is whether the basic right to protection against arbitrary intrusion by the police demands the exclusion of logically relevant evidence obtained by an unreasonable search and seizure because, in a federal prosecution for a federal crime, it would be excluded. As a matter of inherent reason, one would suppose this to be an issue as to which men with complete devotion to the protection of the right of privacy might give different answers. When we find that in fact most of the English-speaking world does not regard as vital to such protection the exclusion of evidence thus obtained, we must hesitate to treat this remedy as an essential ingredient of the right. The contrariety of views of the States is particularly impressive in view of the careful reconsideration which they have given the problem in the light of the *Weeks* decision. [T]he [state] jurisdictions which have rejected the *Weeks* doctrine have not left the right to privacy without other means of protection. Indeed, the exclusion of evidence is a remedy which directly serves only to protect those upon whose person or premises something incriminating has been found. We cannot, therefore, regard it as a departure from basic standards to remand such persons, together with those who emerge scatheless from a search, to the remedies of private action and such protection as the internal discipline of the police, under the eyes of an alert public opinion, may afford. Granting that in practice the exclusion of evidence may be an effective way of deterring unreasonable searches, it is not for this Court to condemn as falling below the minimal standards assured by the Due Process Clause a State's reliance upon other methods which, if consistently enforced, would be equally effective.

[W]e hold, therefore, that in a prosecution in a State court for a State crime the Fourteenth Amendment does not forbid the admission of evidence obtained by an unreasonable search and seizure.

■ Mr. Justice Murphy, dissenting.

The conclusion is inescapable that but one remedy exists to deter violations of the search and seizure clause. That is the rule which excludes illegally obtained evidence. Only by exclusion can we impress upon the zealous prosecutor that violation of the Constitution will do him no good. And only when that point is driven home can the prosecutor be expected to emphasize the importance of observing constitutional demands in his instructions to the police.

If proof of the efficacy of the federal rule were needed, there is testimony in abundance in the recruit training programs and in-service courses provided the police in states which follow the federal rules.[5] St. Louis, for example, demands extensive training in the rules of search and seizure, with emphasis upon the ease with which a case may collapse if it depends upon evidence obtained unlawfully. Current court decisions are digested and read at roll calls. The same general pattern prevails in Washington, D.C. In Dallas, officers are thoroughly briefed and instructed that "the courts will follow the rules very closely and will detect any frauds." In Milwaukee, a stout volume on the law of arrest and search and seizure is made the basis of extended instruction. Officer preparation in the applicable rules in Jackson, Mississippi, has included the lectures of an Associate Justice of the Mississippi Supreme Court. The instructions on evidence and search and seizure given to trainees in San Antonio carefully note the rule of exclusion in Texas, and close with this statement: "Every police officer should know the laws and the rules of evidence. Upon knowledge of these facts determines whether the ... defendant will be

---

5. The material which follows is gleaned from letters and other material from Commissioners of Police and Chiefs of Police in twenty-six cities. Thirty-eight large cities in the United States were selected at random, and inquiries directed concerning the instructions provided police on the rules of search and seizure. Twenty-six replies have been received to date. Those of any significance are mentioned in the text of this opinion. The sample is believed to be representative, but it cannot, of course, substitute for a thoroughgoing comparison of present-day police procedures by a completely objective observer. A study of this kind would be of inestimable value.

convicted or acquitted.... When you investigate a case ... remember throughout your investigation that only admissible evidence can be used."

But in New York City, we are informed simply that "copies of the State Penal Law and Code of Criminal Procedure" are given to officers, and that they are "kept advised" that illegally obtained evidence may be admitted in New York courts. In Baltimore, a "Digest of Laws" is distributed, and it is made clear that the statutory section excluding evidence "is limited in its application to the trial of misdemeanors.... It would appear ... that ... evidence illegally obtained may still be admissible in the trial of felonies." In Cleveland, recruits and other officers are told of the rules of search and seizure, but "instructed that it is admissible in the courts of Ohio. The Ohio Supreme Court has indicated very definitely and clearly that Ohio belongs to the 'admissionist' group of states when evidence obtained by an illegal search is presented to the court." A similar pattern emerges in Birmingham, Alabama.

The contrast between states with the federal rule and those without it is thus a positive demonstration of its efficacy. There are apparent exceptions to the contrast—Denver, for example, appears to provide as comprehensive a series of instructions as that in Chicago, although Colorado permits introduction of the evidence and Illinois does not. And, so far as we can determine from letters, a fairly uniform standard of officer instruction appears in other cities, irrespective of the local rule of evidence. But the examples cited above serve to ground an assumption that has motivated this Court since the *Weeks* case: that this is an area in which judicial action has positive effect upon the breach of law; and that, without judicial action, there are simply no effective sanctions presently available.

————

MAPP v. OHIO

Supreme Court of the United States, 1961.
367 U.S. 643, 81 S.Ct. 1684, 6 L.Ed.2d 1081.

■ Mr. Justice Clark delivered the opinion of the court.

[A]fter declaring that the "security of one's privacy against arbitrary intrusion by the police" is "implicit in 'the concept of ordered liberty' and as such enforceable against the States through the Due Process Clause," and announcing that it "stoutly adhere[d]" to the *Weeks* decision, the Court decided [in Wolf v. Colorado] that the *Weeks* exclusionary rule would not then be imposed upon the States as "an essential ingredient of the right." 338 U.S., at 27–29, 69 S.Ct., at 1362. The Court's reasons for not considering essential to the right to privacy, as a curb imposed upon the States by the Due Process Clause, that which decades before had been posited as part and parcel of the Fourth Amendment's limitation upon federal encroachment of individual privacy, were bottomed on factual considerations.

While they are not basically relevant to a decision that the exclusionary rule is an essential ingredient of the Fourth Amendment as the right it embodies is vouch-safed against the States by the Due Process Clause, we will consider the current validity of the factual grounds upon which *Wolf* was based.

The Court in *Wolf* first stated that "[t]he contrariety of views of the States" on the adoption of the exclusionary rule of *Weeks* was "particularly impressive" (338 U.S. at page 29, 69 S.Ct. at page 1362); and, in this connection, that it could not "brush aside the experience of States which deem the incidence of such conduct by the police too slight to call for a deterrent remedy ... by overriding the [States'] relevant rules of evidence." At pages 31–32 of U.S., at page 1363 of 69 S.Ct. While in 1949, prior to the *Wolf* case, almost two-thirds of the States were opposed to the use of the exclusionary rule, now, despite the *Wolf* case, more than half of those since passing upon it, by their own legislative or judicial decision, have wholly or partly adopted or adhered to the *Weeks* rule.

Significantly, among those now following the rule is California, which, according to its highest court, was "compelled to reach that conclusion because other remedies have completely failed to secure compliance with the constitutional provisions...." People v. Cahan, 44 Cal.2d 434, 445, 282 P.2d 905, 911 (1955). In connection with this California case, we note that the second basis elaborated in *Wolf* in support of its failure to enforce the exclusionary doctrine against the States was that "other means of protection" have been afforded "the right to privacy." 338 U.S., at page 30, 69 S.Ct., at page 1362. The experience of California that such other remedies have been worthless and futile is buttressed by the experience of other States.

[I]t, therefore, plainly appears that the factual considerations supporting the failure of the *Wolf* Court to include the *Weeks* exclusionary rule when it recognized the enforceability of the right to privacy against the States in 1949, while not basically relevant to the constitutional consideration, could not, in any analysis, now be deemed controlling.

[T]oday we once again examine *Wolf's* constitutional documentation of the right to privacy free from unreasonable state intrusion, and, after its dozen years on our books, are led by it to close the only courtroom door remaining open to evidence secured by official lawlessness in flagrant abuse of that basic right, reserved to all persons as a specific guarantee against that very same unlawful conduct. We hold that all evidence obtained by searches and seizures in violation of the Constitution is, by that same authority, inadmissible in a state court.

———

UNITED STATES v. LEON

Supreme Court of the United States, 1984.
468 U.S. 897, 104 S.Ct. 3405, 82 L.Ed.2d 677.

■ JUSTICE WHITE delivered the opinion of the Court.

[Acting on the basis of information from a confidential informant who claimed to have witnessed a drug sale take place at a given address approximately five months previously, officers of the Burbank, California, Police Department began a surveillance of the address. During this surveillance, a number of persons with previous drug convictions were observed entering a home and leaving with small packages. A police officer applied for a warrant to search the homes and automobiles of the individuals observed. The application, which had been reviewed by several Deputy District Attorneys, was granted by a state superior court judge. The ensuing searches produced large quantities of cocaine, and Antonio Leon and several others were indicted on drug-related charges. The defendants filed motions to suppress the evidence seized pursuant to the warrant. The District Court found that, while the police had acted reasonably and in good faith, the warrant upon which their search was based was insufficient to establish probable cause for a search, because it failed to establish the credibility of the confidential informant and because the information provided by the informant was "stale." The District Court, therefore, suppressed much of the evidence as having been obtained in violation of the Fourth Amendment. The government appealed to the Court of Appeals for the Ninth Circuit, which affirmed the District Court. The government's petition for certiorari to the Supreme Court presented the question "[w]hether the Fourth Amendment exclusionary rule should be modified so as not to bar the admission of evidence seized in reasonable, good faith reliance on a search warrant that is subsequently held to be defective."]

The Fourth Amendment contains no provision expressly precluding the use of evidence obtained in violation of its commands, and an examination of its origin and purposes makes clear that the use of fruits of a past unlawful search or seizure "work[s] no new Fourth Amendment wrong." United States v. Calandra, 414 U.S. 338, 354, 94 S.Ct. 613, 623, 38 L.Ed.2d 561 (1974). The wrong condemned by the Amendment is "fully accomplished" by the unlawful search or seizure itself, ibid., and the exclusionary rule is neither intended nor able to "cure the invasion of the defendant's rights which he has already suffered." Stone v. Powell, [428 U.S. 465, 96 S.Ct. 3037, 49 L.Ed.2d 1067 (1976)] at 540 (White, J., dissenting). The rule thus operates as "a judicially created remedy designed to safeguard Fourth Amendment rights generally through its deterrent effect, rather than a personal constitutional right of the person aggrieved." United States v. Calandra, supra, 414 U.S. at 348, 94 S.Ct. at 620.

Whether the exclusionary sanction is appropriately imposed in a particular case, our decisions make clear, is "an issue separate from the question whether the Fourth Amendment rights of the party seeking to invoke the rule were violated by police conduct." Illinois v. Gates, [462 U.S. 213, 103 S.Ct. 2317, 76 L.Ed.2d 527 (1983)]. Only the former question is currently before us, and it must be resolved by weighing the costs and benefits of preventing the use in the prosecution's case-in-chief of inherently trustworthy tangible evidence obtained in reliance on a search warrant issued by a detached and neutral magistrate that ultimately is found to be defective.

The substantial social costs exacted by the exclusionary rule for the vindication of Fourth Amendment rights have long been a source of concern. "Our cases have consistently recognized that unbending application of the exclusionary sanction to enforce ideals of governmental rectitude would impede unacceptably the truth-finding functions of judge and jury." United States v. Payner, 447 U.S. 727, 734, 100 S.Ct. 2439, 2445, 65 L.Ed.2d 468 (1980). An objectionable collateral consequence of this interference with the criminal justice system's truth-finding function is that some guilty defendants may go free or receive reduced sentences as a result of favorable plea bargains.[6] Particularly when law enforcement officers have acted in objective good faith or their transgressions have been minor, the magnitude of the benefit conferred on such guilty defendants offends basic concepts of the criminal justice system. Stone v. Powell, supra, at 490, 96 S.Ct. at 3050. Indiscriminate application of the exclusionary rule, therefore, may well "generat[e] disrespect for the law and the administration of justice." Id. at 491. Accordingly, "[a]s with any remedial device, the application of the rule has been restricted to those areas where its remedial objectives are thought most efficaciously served." United States v. Calandra, supra, 414 U.S. at 348, 94 S.Ct. at 670.

6. Researchers have only recently begun to study extensively the effects of the exclusionary rule on the disposition of felony arrests. One study suggests that the rule results in the nonprosecution or nonconviction of between 0.6% and 2.35% of individuals arrested for felonies. Davies, A Hard Look at What We Know (and Still Need to Learn) About the "Costs" of the Exclusionary Rule: The NIJ Study and Other Studies of "Lost" Arrests, 1983 A.B.F.Res.J. 611, 621. The estimates are higher for particular crimes the prosecution of which depends heavily on physical evidence. Thus, the cumulative loss due to nonprosecution or nonconviction of individuals arrested on felony drug charges is probably in the range of 2.8% to 7.1%. Id. at 680. Davies' analysis of California data suggests that screening by police and prosecutors results in the release because of illegal searches or seizures of as many as 1.4% of all felony arrestees, Id. at 650, that 0.9% of felony arrestees are released because of illegal searches or seizures at the preliminary hearing or after trial, id. at 653, and that roughly 0.5% of all felony arrestees benefit from reversals on appeal because of illegal searches. Id. at 654. See also K. Brosi, A Cross–City Comparison of Felony Case Processing 16, 18–19 (1979); Report of the Comptroller General of the United States, Impact of the Exclusionary Rule on Federal Criminal Prosecutions 10–11, 14 (1979); F. Feeney, F. Dill & A. Weir, Arrests Without Convictions:

How Often They Occur and Why 203–206 (1983); National Institute of Justice, The Effects of the Exclusionary Rule: A Study in California 1–2 (1982); Nardulli, The Societal Cost of the Exclusionary Rule: An Empirical Assessment, 1983 A.B.F.Res.J. 585, 600. The exclusionary rule also has been found to affect the plea-bargaining process. S. Schlesinger, Exclusionary Injustice: The Problem of Illegally Obtained Evidence 63 (1977). But see Davies, supra, at 668–669; Nardulli, supra, at 604–606.

Many of these researchers have concluded that the impact of the exclusionary rule is insubstantial, but the small percentages with which they deal mask a large absolute number of felons who are released because the cases against them were based in part on illegal searches or seizures. "[A]ny rule of evidence that denies the jury access to clearly probative and reliable evidence must bear a heavy burden of justification, and must be carefully limited to the circumstances in which it will pay its way by deterring official unlawlessness." Illinois v. Gates, 462 U.S., at 257–258, 103 S.Ct., at 2342 (White, J., concurring in the judgment). Because we find that the rule can have no substantial deterrent effect in the sorts of situations under consideration in this case, we conclude that it cannot pay its way in those situations.

[W]e have frequently questioned whether the exclusionary rule can have any deterrent effect when the offending officers acted in the objectively reasonable belief that their conduct did not violate the Fourth Amendment. "No empirical researcher, proponent or opponent of the rule, has yet been able to establish with any assurance whether the rule has a deterrent effect...." United States v. Janis, 428 U.S. at 452, n. 22, 96 S.Ct. at 3031, n. 22. But even assuming that the rule effectively deters some police misconduct and provides incentives for the law enforcement profession as a whole to conduct itself in accord with the Fourth Amendment, it cannot be expected, and should not be applied, to deter objectively reasonable law enforcement activity.

[T]his is particularly true, we believe, when an officer acting with objective good faith has obtained a search warrant from a judge or magistrate and acted within its scope. In most such cases, there is no police illegality and thus nothing to deter. It is the magistrate's responsibility to determine whether the officer's allegations establish probable cause and, if so, to issue a warrant comporting in form with the requirements of the Fourth Amendment. In the ordinary case, an officer cannot be expected to question the magistrate's probable-cause determination or his judgment that the form of the warrant is technically sufficient. "[O]nce the warrant issues, there is literally nothing more the policeman can do in seeking to comply with the law." Id. at 498, 96 S.Ct. at 3054 (Burger, C.J., concurring). Penalizing the officer for the magistrate's error, rather than his own, cannot logically contribute to the deterrence of Fourth Amendment violations.

We conclude that the marginal or nonexistent benefits produced by suppressing evidence obtained in objectively reasonable reliance on a subsequently invalidated search warrant cannot justify the substantial costs of exclusion.

[A]ccordingly, the judgment of the Court of Appeals is Reversed.

■ JUSTICE BLACKMUN, concurring.

I write separately, [t]o underscore what I regard as the unavoidably provisional nature of today's decisions.

As the Court's opinion in this case makes clear, the Court has narrowed the scope of the exclusionary rule because of an empirical judgment that the rule has little appreciable effect in cases where officers act in objectively reasonable reliance on search warrants. Because I share the view that the exclusionary rule is not a constitutionally compelled corollary of the Fourth Amendment itself, I see no way to avoid making an empirical judgment of this sort, and I am satisfied that the Court has made the correct one on the information before it. Like all courts, we face institutional limitations on our ability to gather information about "legislative facts," and the exclusionary rule itself has exacerbated the shortage of hard data concerning the behavior of police officers in the absence of such a rule. See United States v. Janis, 428 U.S. 433, 448–453, 96 S.Ct. 3021, 3029–3031, 49 L.Ed.2d 1046 (1976). Nonetheless, we cannot escape the responsibility to decide the question before us, however imperfect our information may be, and I am prepared to join the Court on the information now at hand.

What must be stressed, however, is that any empirical judgment about the effect of the exclusionary rule in a particular class of cases necessarily is a provisional one. By their very nature, the assumptions on which we proceed today cannot be cast in stone. To the contrary, they now will be tested in the real world of state and federal law enforcement, and this Court will attend to the results. If it should emerge from experience that, contrary to our expectations, the good faith exception to the exclusionary rule results in a material change in police compliance with the Fourth Amendment, we shall have to reconsider what we have undertaken here. The logic of a decision that rests on untested predictions about police conduct demands no less.

If a single principle may be drawn from this Court's exclusionary rule decisions, from *Weeks* through Mapp v. Ohio, 367 U.S. 643, 81 S.Ct. 1684, 6 L.Ed.2d 1081 (1961), to the decisions handed down today, it is that the scope of the exclusionary rule is subject to change in light of changing judicial understanding about the effects of the rule outside the confines of the courtroom.

■ JUSTICE BRENNAN, with whom JUSTICE MARSHALL joins, dissenting.

[T]he Court seeks to justify this result on the ground that the "costs" of adhering to the exclusionary rule in cases like those before us exceed the "benefits." But the language of deterrence and of cost/benefit analysis, if used indiscriminately, can have a narcotic effect. It creates an illusion of technical precision and ineluctability. It suggests that not only constitutional principle but also empirical data supports the majority's result. When the Court's analysis is examined carefully, however, it is clear that we have not been treated to an honest assessment of the merits of the exclusionary rule, but have instead been drawn into a curious world where the "costs" of excluding illegally obtained evidence loom to exaggerated heights and where the "benefits" of such exclusion are made to disappear with a mere wave of the hand.

[T]he Court's decisions over the past decade have made plain that the entire enterprise of attempting to assess the benefits and costs of the exclusionary rule in various contexts is a virtually impossible task for the judiciary to perform honestly or accurately. Although the Court's language in those cases suggests that some specific empirical basis may support its analyses, the reality is that the Court's opinions represent inherently unstable compounds of intuition, hunches, and occasional pieces of partial and often inconclusive data. In *Calandra,* for example, the Court, in considering whether the exclusionary rule should apply in grand jury proceedings, had before it no concrete evidence whatever concerning the impact that application of the rule in such proceedings would have either in terms of the long-term costs or the expected benefits. To the extent empirical data is available regarding the general costs and benefits of the exclusionary rule, it has shown, on the one hand, as the Court acknowledges today, that the costs are not as substantial as critics have asserted in the past, and, on the other hand, that while the exclusionary rule may well have certain deterrent effects, it is extremely difficult to determine with any degree of precision whether the incidence of unlawful conduct by police is now lower than it was prior to *Mapp*. See United States v. Janis, 428 U.S., at 449–453 and n. 22, 96 S.Ct., at 3029–3031 and n. 22; Stone v. Powell, 428 U.S., at 492, n. 32, 96 S.Ct., at 3051, n. 32.[9] The Court has sought to turn this uncertainty to its advantage by casting the burden of proof upon proponents of the rule, see e.g., United States v. Janis, 428 U.S., at 453–454, 96 S.Ct., at 3031–3032. "Obviously," however, "the assignment of the burden of proof on an issue where evidence does not exist and cannot be obtained is outcome determinative. [The] assignment of the burden is merely a way of announcing a predetermined conclusion."[10]

By remaining within its redoubt of empiricism and by basing the rule solely on the deterrence rationale, the Court has robbed the rule of legitimacy. A doctrine that is explained as if it were an empirical proposition but for which there is only limited empirical support is both inherently unstable and an easy mark for critics. The extent of this Court's fidelity to Fourth Amendment requirements, however, should not turn on such statistical uncertainties. I share the view, expressed by Justice Stewart for the Court in Faretta v. California, 422 U.S. 806, 95 S.Ct. 2525, 45 L.Ed.2d 562 (1975), that "[p]ersonal liberties are not based on the law of averages." Id. at 834, 95 S.Ct. at 2540. Rather than seeking to give effect to the liberties secured by the Fourth Amendment through guesswork about deterrence, the Court should restore to its proper place the principal framed 70 years ago in *Weeks* that an individual whose privacy has been invaded in violation of the Fourth Amendment has a right grounded in that Amendment to prevent the government from subsequently making use of any evidence so obtained.

[E]ven if I were to accept the Court's general approach to the exclusionary rule, I could not agree with today's result.

[A]t the outset, the Court suggests that society has been asked to pay a high price—in terms either of setting guilty persons free or of impeding the proper functioning of trials—as a result of excluding relevant physical evidence in cases where the police, in conducting searches and seizing evidence, have made only an "objectively reasonable" mistake concerning the constitutionality of their actions. But what evidence is there to support such a claim?

---

9. See generally on this point, Davies, A Hard Look at What We Know (and Still Need to Learn) About the "Costs" of the Exclusionary Rule: The NIJ Study and Other Studies of "Lost" Arrests, 1983 Am.Bar Found. Res.J. 611, 627–629; Canon, Ideology and Reality in the Debate over the Exclusionary Rule: A Conservative Argument for its Retention, 23 S.Tex.L.J. 559, 561–563 (1982); Critique, On the Limitation of the Empirical Evaluation of the Exclusionary Rule: A Critique of the Spiotto Research and United States v. Calandra, 69 N.W.U.L.Rev. 740 (1974).

10. Dworkin, Fact Style Adjudication and the Fourth Amendment: The Limits of Lawyering, 48 Ind.L.J. 329, 332–333 (1973).

Significantly, the Court points to none, and, indeed, as the Court acknowledges, recent studies have demonstrated that the "costs" of the exclusionary rule—calculated in terms of dropped prosecutions and lost convictions—are quite low. Contrary to the claims of the rule's critics that exclusion leads to "the release of countless guilty criminals," Bivens v. Six Unknown Federal Narcotics Officers, 403 U.S. 388, 416, 91 S.Ct. 1999, 2014, 29 L.Ed.2d 619 (Burger, C.J., dissenting), these studies have demonstrated that federal and state prosecutors very rarely drop cases because of potential search and seizure problems. For example, a 1979 study prepared at the request of Congress by the General Accounting Office reported that only 0.4% of all cases actually declined for prosecution by federal prosecutors were declined primarily because of illegal search problems. Report of the Comptroller General of the United States, Impact of the Exclusionary Rule on Federal Criminal Prosecutions 14 (1979). If the GAO data are restated as a percentage of *all* arrests, the study shows that only 0.2% of all felony arrests are declined for prosecution because of potential exclusionary rule problems. See Davies, A Hard Look at What We Know (and Still Need to Learn) About the "Costs" of the Exclusionary Rule: The NIJ Study and Other Studies of "Lost" Arrests, 1983 Am.Bar Found.Res.J. 611, 635.[11] Of course, these data describe only the costs attributable to the exclusion of evidence in all cases; the costs due to the exclusion of evidence in the narrower category of cases where police have made objectively reasonable mistakes must necessarily be even smaller. The Court, however, ignores this distinction and mistakenly weighs the aggregated costs of exclusion in *all* cases, irrespective of the circumstances that led to exclusion, against the

---

11. In a series of recent studies, researchers have attempted to quantify the actual costs of the rule. A recent National Institute of Justice study based on data for the four year period 1976–1979 gathered by the California Bureau of Criminal Statistics showed that 4.8% of all cases that were declined for prosecution by California prosecutors were rejected because of illegally seized evidence. National Institute of Justice, Criminal Justice Research Report—The Effects of the Exclusionary Rule: A Study in California 1 (1982). However, if these data are calculated as a percentage of all arrests that were declined for prosecution, they show that only 0.8% of all arrests were rejected for prosecution because of illegally seized evidence. See Davies, supra, at 619.

In another measure of the rule's impact—the number of prosecutions that are dismissed or result in acquittals in cases where evidence has been excluded—the available data again show that the Court's past assessment of the rule's costs has generally been exaggerated. For example, a study based on data from 9 mid-sized counties in Illinois, Michigan and Pennsylvania reveals that motions to suppress physical evidence were filed in approximately 5% of the 7,500 cases studied, but that such motions were successful in only 0.7% of all these cases. Nardulli, The Societal Cost of the Exclusionary Rule: An Empirical Assessment, 1983 Am.Bar Found. Res.J. 585, 596. The study also shows that only 0.6% of all cases resulted in acquittals because evidence had been excluded. Id. at 600. In the GAO study, suppression motions were filed in 10.5% of all federal criminal cases surveyed, but of the motions filed, approximately 80–90% were denied. GAO Report, supra, at 8, 10. Evidence was actually excluded in only 1.3% of the cases studied, and only 0.7% of all cases resulted in acquittals or dismissals after evidence was excluded. Id. at 9–11. See Davies, supra, at 660. And in another study based on data from cases during 1978 and 1979 in San Diego and Jacksonville, it was shown that only 1% of all cases resulting in nonconviction were caused by illegal searches. Feeney, Dill & Weir, Arrests Without Conviction: How Often They Occur and Why (1983). See generally Davies, supra, at 663.

potential benefits associated with only those cases in which evidence is excluded because police reasonably but mistakenly believe that their conduct does not violate the Fourth Amendment. When such faulty scales are used, it is little wonder that the balance tips in favor of restricting the application of the rule.

What then supports the Court's insistence that this evidence be admitted? Apparently, the Court's only answer is that even though the costs of exclusion are not very substantial, the potential deterrent effect in these circumstances is so marginal that exclusion cannot be justified. The key to the Court's conclusion in this respect is its belief that the prospective deterrent effect of the exclusionary rule operates only in those situations in which police officers, when deciding whether to go forward with some particular search, have reason to know that their planned conduct will violate the requirements of the Fourth Amendment. If these officers in fact understand (or reasonably should understand because the law is well-settled) that their proposed conduct will offend the Fourth Amendment and that, consequently, any evidence they seize will be suppressed in court, they will refrain from conducting the planned search. In those circumstances, the incentive system created by the exclusionary rule will have the hoped-for deterrent effect. But in situations where police officers reasonably (but mistakenly) believe that their planned conduct satisfies Fourth Amendment requirements—presumably either (a) because they are acting on the basis of an apparently valid warrant, or (b) because their conduct is only later determined to be invalid as a result of a subsequent change in the law or the resolution of an unsettled question of law—then such officers will have no reason to refrain from conducting the search and the exclusionary rule will have no effect.

[T]he flaw in the Court's argument, however, is that its logic captures only one comparatively minor element of the generally acknowledged deterrent purposes of the exclusionary rule. To be sure, the rule operates to some extent to deter future misconduct by individual officers who have had evidence suppressed in their own cases. But what the Court overlooks is that the deterrence rationale for the rule is not designed to be, nor should it be thought of as, a form of "punishment" of individual police officers for their failures to obey the restraints imposed by the Fourth Amendment. Instead, the chief deterrent function of the rule is its tendency to promote institutional compliance with Fourth Amendment requirements on the part of law enforcement agencies generally. Thus, as the Court has previously recognized, "over the long term, [the] demonstration [provided by the exclusionary rule] that our society attaches serious consequences to violation of constitutional rights is thought to encourage those who formulate law enforcement policies, and the officers who implement them, to incorporate Fourth Amendment ideals into their value system." Stone v. Powell, 428 U.S. at 492, 96 S.Ct. at 3051. It is only through such an institution-wide mechanism that information concerning Fourth Amendment standards can be effectively communicated to rank and file officers.[13]

---

13. Although specific empirical data on the systemic deterrent effect of the rule is not conclusive, the testimony of those actually involved in law enforcement suggests that,

If the overall educational effect of the exclusionary rule is considered, application of the rule to even those situations in which individual police officers have acted on the basis of a reasonable but mistaken belief that their conduct was authorized can still be expected to have a considerable long-term deterrent effect. If evidence is consistently excluded in these circumstances, police departments will surely be prompted to instruct their officers to devote greater care and attention to providing sufficient information to establish probable cause when applying for a warrant, and to review with some attention the form of the warrant that they have been issued, rather than automatically assuming that whatever document the magistrate has signed will necessarily comport with Fourth Amendment requirements.

After today's decision, however, that institutional incentive will be lost. Indeed, the Court's "reasonable mistake" exception to the exclusionary rule will tend to put a premium on police ignorance of the law.

STATE v. NOVEMBRINO

Supreme Court of New Jersey, 1987.
105 N.J. 95, 519 A.2d 820.

■ Stein, J.

Defendant, Ottavio Novembrino, was indicted for possession of controlled dangerous substances [a]nd possession of controlled dangerous substances with intent to distribute. [A] motion to suppress evidence was filed.

[T]he Appellate Division concluded that the affidavit failed to establish probable cause:

at the very least, the *Mapp* decision had the effect of increasing police awareness of Fourth Amendment requirements and of prompting prosecutors and police commanders to work towards educating rank and file officers. For example, as former New York Police Commissioner Murphy explained the impact of the *Mapp* decision: "I can think of no decision in recent times in the field of law enforcement which had such a dramatic and traumatic effect. . . . I was immediately caught up in the entire program of reevaluating our procedures, which had followed the *Defore* rule, and modifying, amending, and creating new policies and new instructions for implementing *Mapp*. . . . Retraining sessions had to be held from the very top administrators down to each of the thousands of foot patrolmen." Murphy, Judicial Review of Police Methods in Law Enforcement: The Problem of Compliance by Police Departments, 44 Tex.L.Rev. 939, 941 (1966).

Further testimony about the impact of the *Mapp* decision can be found in the statement of Deputy Commissioner Reisman: "The *Mapp* case was a shock to us. We had to reorganize our thinking, frankly. Before this, nobody bothered to take out search warrants. Although the U.S. Constitution requires warrants in most cases, the U.S. Supreme Court had ruled that evidence obtained without a warrant—illegally, if you will—was admissible in state courts. So the feeling was, why bother? Well, once that rule was changed we knew we had better start teaching our men about it." N.Y. Times, April 28, 1965, at 50, col. 1.

The affidavit here involved simply revealed that a police informant concluded for unknown reasons that defendant was a drug dealer, that a person previously arrested for possession of cocaine was seen at defendant's gas station engaged in some unspecified activities which caused a detective, whose education, training and experiences are unknown, to conclude that criminal activities in the form of violations of Title 24 were taking place at the gas station. The totality of the circumstances spelled out in the affidavit failed to contain a single objective fact tending to engender a "well grounded suspicion" that a crime was being committed. * * * We conclude, therefore, that probable cause was not established. [State v. Novembrino, 200 N.J.Super. 229, 236, 491 A.2d 37 (1985) (citation omitted).]

The State also argued that if probable cause was not established, the evidence should nevertheless be admissible on the basis of the good-faith exception recognized by the United States Supreme Court in *Leon*. The Appellate Division acknowledged that if *Leon* were followed in New Jersey, it would apply retroactively and thereby determine the admissibility of the evidence obtained at defendant's station. A majority of the Appellate Division was also satisfied that Detective Higgins had objectively and reasonably relied upon the warrant, which had been issued by a detached and neutral judge. Accordingly, the Appellate Division majority found that the record adequately raised the issue whether the good-faith exception should be applied under our State Constitution.

A majority of the Appellate Division panel determined that New Jersey should not recognize the good-faith exception because it would undermine the constitutional requirement of probable cause. [W]e granted the State's motion for leave to appeal.

[I]t is an established principle of our federalist system that state constitutions may be a source of "individual liberties more expansive than those conferred by the Federal Constitution." PruneYard Shopping Center v. Robins, 447 U.S. 74, 81, 100 S.Ct. 2035, 2040, 64 L.Ed.2d 741, 752 (1980).

[T]his Court has frequently resorted to our own State Constitution in order to afford our citizens broader protection of certain personal rights than that afforded by analogous or identical provisions of the federal Constitution. Although the language of article I, paragraph 7 of the New Jersey Constitution is virtually identical with that of the fourth amendment, we have held in other contexts that it affords our citizens greater protection against unreasonable searches and seizures than does the fourth amendment.

In this case, defendant urges that we construe our state-constitutional protection against unreasonable searches and seizures to preclude recognition of the good-faith exception to the exclusionary rule established in *Leon*. The Attorney General and the Hudson County Prosecutor argue that we should follow the Supreme Court's modification of the exclusionary rule and construe article I, paragraph 7 of our Constitution in a manner consistent with the good-faith exception. Our conclusion as to which of these courses to follow is strongly influenced by what we perceive to be the likely impact of our decision on the privacy rights of our citizens and the enforcement of our criminal laws, matters of "particular state interest" that afford an appropriate basis for resolving this issue on independent state grounds.

[T]he Attorney General and the County Prosecutors Association adopted in February 1985 a joint policy statement intended to achieve the "institutionalization of a systematic search warrant review procedure in New Jersey." The policy statement, which applies to all State, County, and municipal officers, requires that "[a]ll applications for search warrants shall be reviewed by the Attorney General or his designees, or the appropriate County Prosecutor, or his designees, prior to their submission to the Courts for authorization." The Court has been informed, in response to its direct inquiry, that this policy statement has been implemented without exception in every county in the State. We are also cognizant of the significant and recurring search warrant training programs offered regularly to municipal court judges throughout the state. We assume that the likely effect of such a statewide policy requiring competent legal review of search warrant applications, combined with the training programs for municipal judges, would be to enhance the extent of compliance with the probable-cause standard and minimize the incidents of suppression of evidence because of defectively-issued warrants.[33]

---

33. In his dissenting opinion in *Leon*, Justice Brennan emphasized that statistical studies on a national basis also suggest that the "costs" of the exclusionary rule are minimal:

[I]ndeed, as the Court acknowledges, recent studies have demonstrated that the "costs" of the exclusionary rule—calculated in terms of dropped prosecutions and lost convictions—are quite low. Contrary to the claims of the rule's critics that exclusion leads to "the release of countless guilty criminals," Bivens v. Six Unknown Federal Narcotics Agents, 403 U.S. 388, 416, 29 L.Ed.2d 619, 91 S.Ct 1999 [2014] (Burger, C.J., dissenting), these studies have demonstrated that federal and state prosecutors very rarely drop cases because of potential search and seizure problems. For example, a 1979 study prepared at the request of Congress by the General Accounting Office reported that only 0.4% of all cases actually declined for prosecution by federal prosecutors were declined primarily because of illegal search problems. Report of the Comptroller General of the United States, Impact of the Exclusionary Rule on Federal Criminal Prosecutions 14 (1979). If the GAO data are restated as a percentage of *all* arrests, the study shows

that only 0.2% of all felony arrests are declined for prosecution because of potential exclusionary rule problems. See Davies, A Hard Look at What We Know (and Still Need to Learn) About the "Costs" of the Exclusionary Rule: The NIJ Study and Other Studies of "Lost" Arrests, 1983 Am.Bar Found. Res.J. 611, 635. Of course, these data describe only the costs attributable to the exclusion of evidence in all cases; the costs due to the exclusion of evidence in the narrower category of cases where police have made objectively reasonable mistakes must necessarily be even smaller. The Court, however, ignores this distinction and mistakenly weighs the aggregated costs of exclusion in *all* cases, irrespective of the circumstances that led to exclusion against the potential benefits associated with only those cases in which evidence is excluded because police reasonably but mistakenly believe that their conduct does not violate the Fourth Amendment. When such faulty scales are used, it is little wonder that the balance tips in favor of restricting the application of the rule. [United States v. Leon, supra, 468 U.S. at 950–51, 104 S.Ct. at 3441–42, 82 L.Ed.2d at 716–17 (Brennan, J., dissenting).]

In this connection, a survey performed by the Administrative Office of the Courts with respect to suppression motions in ten counties during the six-month period of December 1, 1985, to May 31, 1986, reveals that of the 1082 motions filed, 540 motions have been resolved. Of these, 38 were granted and all of the granted motions involved warrantless searches. In addition, the study examined all of the granted suppression motions in three of the ten counties for an additional six-month period and in two additional counties during a twelve-month period. Out of 44 granted motions, only one suppression order involved a search warrant defective for lack of probable cause. Administrative Office of the Courts, Report on Suppression Motions, July 30, 1986. This survey was not statewide and examined a limited sample of suppression motions. Nevertheless, its results suggest that currently in New Jersey the grant of motions to suppress evidence obtained pursuant to defective search warrants is relatively uncommon and apparently poses no significant obstacle to law-enforcement efforts.

[O]ne obvious consequence of the application of the exclusionary rule in New Jersey has been the encouragement of law-enforcement officials to comply with the constitutionally-mandated probable-cause standard in order to avoid the suppression of evidence. The *Leon* rule avoids suppression of evidence even if the constitutional standard is violated, requiring only that the officer executing the defective warrant have an objectively reasonable basis for relying on it. Whatever else may be said for or against the *Leon* rule, the good-faith exception will inevitably and inexorably diminish the quality of evidence presented in search-warrant applications. By eliminating any cost for noncompliance with the constitutional requirement of probable cause, the good-faith exception assures us that the constitutional standard will be diluted.

[U]ltimately, we focus on the inevitable tension between the proposed good-faith exception and the guarantee contained in our State Constitution that search warrants "shall not issue except upon probable cause." In the twenty-five years during which we have applied the exclusionary rule in New Jersey, we have perceived no dilution of our probable-cause standard; rather, efforts to comply with the constitutional mandate have been enhanced. Nor do we perceive that application of the exclusionary rule has in any significant way impaired the ability of law-enforcement officials to enforce the criminal laws. The statistical evidence is to the contrary.

[J]ustice Blackmun, concurring in Leon, cautioned us as to the "unavoidably provisional nature" of the decision, 468 U.S. at 927, 104 S.Ct. at 3424, 82 L.Ed.2d at 701, and warned that if "the good faith exception to the exclusionary rule results in a material change in police compliance with the Fourth Amendment, we shall have to reconsider what we have undertaken here," id. at 928, 104 S.Ct. at 3424, 82 L.Ed.2d at 702. We suspect that Justice Blackmun's forebodings may be prophetic indeed. In our view, erosion of the probable-cause guarantee will be a corollary to the good-faith exception. We think it quite possible that the damage to the constitutional guarantee may reach such a level as to cause the Court to reconsider its experiment with the fourth amendment.

We see no need in New Jersey to experiment with the fundamental rights protected by the fourth-amendment counterpart of our State Constitution. We will not subject the procedures that vindicate the fundamental rights guaranteed by article 1, paragraph 7 of our State Constitution— procedures that have not diluted the effectiveness of our criminal justice system—to the uncertain effects that we believe will inevitably accompany the good-faith exception to the federal exclusionary rule.

The judgment of the Appellate Division is affirmed.

———

NOTES

1. Special Masters. In an article cited by both the majority and the dissent in *Leon*, Davies, A Hard Look at What We Know (and Still Need to Learn) About the "Costs" of the Exclusionary Rule: The NIJ Study and Other Studies of "Lost" Arrests, 1983 American Bar Foundation Research Journal 611, 688 n. 447 (1983), made the following suggestion:

> If an empirical question appears to be central to an appellate decision, perhaps it would be appropriate for an appellate court to appoint a master to take expert testimony to provide the court with a more fully developed record on the empirical data and the quality and completeness of the research relied on.

2. Tort Remedies. When the United States Supreme Court in Wolf v. Colorado declined to apply the federal exclusionary rule to state prosecutions, it noted that states could choose instead to rely on "the remedies of private action," i.e., to allow tort suits against police officers who violate a citizen's Fourth Amendment rights. When it overturned the *Wolf* decision in Mapp v. Ohio, however, the Court noted the "obvious futility" of remedies such as tort action to secure the Fourth Amendment.

Opponents of the exclusionary rule continue to promote tort suits against police officers alleged to have engaged in illegal searches as an alternative to excluding evidence from criminal proceedings. Casper, Benedict, and Perry, The Tort Remedy in Search and Seizure Cases: A Case Study in Juror Decision Making, 13 Law and Social Inquiry 279 (1988), reviewed the empirical literature on such suits and conclude that defendant police officers prevail about three-quarters of the time and that, when plaintiffs win, the damages awarded are relatively minor (e.g., about a third of the plaintiffs who won received less than $1,000, and 85% received less than $10,000). In a simulation study with persons called for jury service in Cook County, Illinois, Casper and his colleagues found that substituting the municipality (i.e., the city that employed the police officer) as the defendant, or substituting the federal government as the plaintiff, did not affect the incidence or size of damage awards. Denying jurors information about the outcome of the search, however—that is, not telling jurors whether the allegedly illegal search uncovered evidence of crime—increased both the incidence and the size of damages awarded.

2.   IMPEACHMENT OF A WITNESS

When a witness testifies at trial, his or her credibility is often contested. One way that an attorney cross-examining a witness may try to impeach the witness' testimony—to raise doubts in jurors' minds about the witness' credibility—is to introduce evidence that the witness has been convicted of a crime in the past. The rationale for this form of impeachment is the proposition that a person who has been convicted of crime is less worthy of belief than a person who has not been convicted. In a criminal case, when the witness is also the defendant, the risk of allowing the admission of such evidence is that the jury may use it for purposes other than the assessment of credibility, such as to support an inference that the witness must be guilty of the crime charged, since he or she has been found guilty before.

PEOPLE v. ALLEN

Supreme Court of Michigan, 1988.
429 Mich. 558, 420 N.W.2d 499.

■ BRICKLEY, JUSTICE.

[Five criminal cases in which the defendants were convicted by a jury were appealed. In each case, the defendant had testified in his own behalf, and the state had impeached the testimony by telling the jury of the defendant's prior criminal convictions.]

These cases were consolidated in order to resolve differing interpretations of the application of MRE [Michigan Rule of Evidence] 609(a) to the practice of impeaching criminal defendants by prior conviction.[1] [W]e also take this opportunity to promulgate an amendment to MRE 609(a) which will apply to all cases tried after March 1, 1988. (See appendix A.) It provides for bright-line rules that recognize and exclude certain prior convictions which are inherently more prejudicial than probative and allows admission of those convictions which are inherently more probative than prejudicial.

[A] jury should not be allowed to consider the defendant's guilt of the crime before it on the basis of evidence of his propensity for crime. Finding

---

1.   MRE 609 reads in pertinent part:

"(a) General rule. For the purpose of attacking the credibility of a witness, evidence that he has been convicted of a crime shall be admitted if elicited from him or established by public record during cross-examination but only if

"(1) the crime was punishable by death or imprisonment in excess of one year under the law under which he was convicted, or the crime involved theft, dishonesty or false statement, regardless of the punishment, and

"(2) the court determines that the probative value of admitting this evidence on the issue of credibility outweighs its prejudicial effect and articulates on the record the factors considered in making the determination."

a person guilty of a crime is not a pleasant or easy assignment for a representative group of twelve people. It is much easier to conclude that a person is bad than that he did something bad. Hence the appetite for more knowledge of the defendant's background and the slippery slope toward general "bad man" evidence.

This appetite presents three types of impropriety. First, that jurors may determine that although defendant's guilt in the case before them is in doubt, he is a bad man and should therefore be punished. Second, the character evidence may lead the jury to lower the burden of proof against the defendant, since, even if the guilty verdict is incorrect, no "innocent" man will be forced to endure punishment. Third, the jury may determine that on the basis of his prior actions, the defendant has a propensity to commit crimes, and therefore he probably is guilty of the crime with which he is charged. All three of these dimensions suggest a likelihood that innocent persons may be convicted.

The danger then is that a jury will misuse prior conviction evidence by focusing on the defendant's general bad character, rather than solely on his character for truthtelling.

[I]n spite of the likelihood of prejudice, it can be argued, and indeed the dissent does so eloquently, that a limiting instruction will suffice.

[T]he notion that a limiting instruction can prevent misuse of prior conviction evidence is simply mistaken, as it asks the jury to do what it cannot. This view is supported by a number of empirical studies. A Canadian study concluded that

"present research leaves little doubt that knowledge of a previous conviction biases a case against the defendant. The likelihood that a jury will convict the defendant is significantly higher if the defendant's record is made known to the jury. *The fact that the defendant has a record permeates the entire discussion of the case,* and appears to affect the juror's perception and interpretation of the evidence in the case.

" *. . . These effects are present in spite of the fact that jurors were given specific instructions to ignore the fact of record while assessing the defendant's guilt.*" Hans & Doob, *Section 12 of the Canada Evidence Act and the deliberations of simulated juries,* 18 Crim.L.Q. 235, 251 (1976) (emphasis added).

Perhaps most disturbing was the study's conclusion that

"jurors used [prior conviction evidence] only minimally in considering the issue of credibility." *Id.* at 247.

Thus, the intended use of the evidence was of little actual importance.

Another study observed that the notion of a successful limiting instruction, with respect to character evidence, runs counter to the basic evaluative mechanisms discussed above.

"The assumption that people can differentiate the use of information goes directly against what is known as the 'halo' effect: the phenomenon by which a person will infer positive characteristics about a person where favourable information has been received and will infer negative characteristics about someone where unfavourable information has been received. As Rosenberg and Olshan (1970) [citing Rosenberg & Olshan, *Evaluative and descriptive aspects in personality perception,* J of Personality and Soc Psyc, 16, 619–626 (1970)] have pointed out, 'Studies using [the technique by which a subject is asked to infer characteristics about an individual on the basis of information about other characteristics] ... have consistently shown that subjects infer favourable traits from one or more favourable stimulus traits and infer unfavourable traits from unfavourable stimulus traits' (p. 619). Thus, if a person is told one negative thing about another person, he is going to assume other negative things. With respect to s. 12 of the Canada Evidence Act, it follows that we would expect that if a juror hears that an accused has one unfavourable characteristic (e.g., that he has a criminal record) he will then think of that accused as a generally bad person. If this same juror is then asked to judge the guilt of the accused, he will be likely to infer that the accused is guilty of the crime in question." Doob & Kirshenbaum, *Some empirical evidence on the effect of s. 12 of the Canada Evidence Act upon an accused,* 15 Crim.L.Q. 88, 89–90 (1972–1973).

One of the researchers in the University of Chicago report leading to publication of *The American Jury* stated that the jury examinations revealed

" 'almost universal inability and/or unwillingness either to understand or follow the court's instruction on the use of defendant's prior criminal record for impeachment purposes. The jurors almost universally used defendant's record to conclude that he was a bad man and hence was more likely than not guilty of the crime for which he was then standing trial.' "

"Letter from Dale W. Broeder, Associate Professor, the University of Nebraska College of Law, who conducted intensive jury interviews, to Yale Law Journal, dated March 14, 1960, on file in Yale Law Library." Note, *Other crimes evidence at trial: Of balancing and other matters,* 70 Yale L J 763, 777, n 89 (1961).

In a far less scientific study, the Columbia Journal of Law and Social Problems conducted a random national survey of trial judges and criminal defense attorneys. When asked whether they believed jurors were able to follow limiting instructions concerning the use of prior conviction evidence, ninety-eight percent of the responding attorneys answered negatively, and, even more disturbingly, forty-three percent of the responding judges agreed. Note, *To take the stand or not to take the stand: The dilemma of the defendant with a criminal record,* 4 Colum J of Law & Social Problems 215, 218 (1968).

The most recent study of this problem concluded that mock jurors used prior conviction evidence to "help them judge the likelihood that the defendant committed the crime charged" in spite of limiting instructions. Wissler & Saks, *On the inefficacy of limiting instructions: When jurors use prior conviction evidence to decide on guilt,* 9 Law & Human Behavior 37, 44 (1985). Most telling was the fact that a higher conviction rate was found where, all else being the same, the impeaching crime was murder than where the impeaching crime was perjury. Id. at 43. The only explanation for this last result is that the prior conviction evidence was not used exclusively to evaluate credibility. This is emphasized by the fact that the researchers found that there was no significant difference between the mock jurors' ratings of defendant's credibility when a prior conviction was introduced and when one was not. Id. at 41. They concluded that "[t]he credibility ratings of defendant did not vary as a function of prior conviction," while "[c]onviction rates [did vary] as a function of prior conviction...." Id.

[I]n light of the overwhelming tendency for jurors, and even trial and appellate judges to misuse prior conviction evidence, it is our view that there is an "overwhelming probability" that most prior conviction evidence introduced for the purpose of impeachment will be considered as if it had been introduced to show that the defendant acted in conformity with his criminal past. See *Richardson v. Marsh,* 481 U.S. 200, 107 S.Ct. 1702, 95 L.Ed.2d 176 (1987).

The dissenters criticize us for making behavioral judgments and relying on studies in reaching this determination. They critique at length the conclusions and methodologies of the studies we have cited. We do not agree with their conclusions, but welcome their critique of these materials as social science experiments cannot serve as the primary basis for judicial decision. Many fundamental principles of our jurisprudence are based on assumptions of human behavior that have never been, and in most cases cannot be, scientifically tested. We also note that the rule we modify today, and that the dissent urges us to leave as is, was the result of assumptions about jury behavior and the effectiveness of limiting instructions that were accompanied by relatively little analysis or study.

The studies cited are nevertheless relevant, support our view, and deserve consideration. In citing them, however, we do not suggest that the amendment of MRE 609 is based solely upon them. The rule change is instead based upon the underlying principles of our legal system and our perception that these principles are not served by the scope of prior-conviction impeachment which is presently permitted.

Some of the most cherished and well-accepted of these principles have been defined by jurists who were willing to state the obvious. The obvious in this area is that criminal defendants are prejudiced by prior conviction evidence as presently allowed and that leaving the question to trial judges has not been successful.

[W]e, therefore, in the words of the dissent, act not on the basis of studies, but on the "common-sense premise" that some prior convictions are more probative than others, that some are inherently more prejudicial, and that it is absurd to suggest that jurors will be able to avoid improper consideration of a defendant's criminal character once it has become known to them.

APPENDIX A
REVISED MRE 609
IMPEACHMENT BY EVIDENCE OF CONVICTION OF CRIME

(a) General rule. For the purpose of attacking the credibility of a witness, evidence that the witness has been convicted of a crime shall not be admitted unless the evidence has been elicited from the witness or established by public record during cross-examination, and

(1) the crime contained an element of dishonesty or false statement, or

(2) the crime contained an element of theft, and

(A) the crime was punishable by imprisonment in excess of one year or death under the law under which the witness was convicted, and

(B) the court determines that the evidence has significant probative value on the issue of credibility and, if the witness is the defendant in a criminal trial, the court further determines that the probative value of the evidence outweighs its prejudicial effect.

(b) Determining probative value and prejudicial effect. For purposes of the probative value determination required by subrule (a)(2)(B), the court shall consider only the age of the conviction and the degree to which a conviction of the crime is indicative of veracity. If a determination of prejudicial effect is required, the court shall consider only the conviction's similarity to the charged offense and the possible effects on the decisional process if admitting the evidence causes the defendant to elect not to testify. The court must articulate, on the record, the analysis of each factor.

■ BOYLE, JUSTICE (dissenting).

The majority has today replaced the trial judge's discretionary authority to advance the truth-seeking process with its own view of the proper use of impeachment evidence.

[T]he majority has looked to empirical studies of mock jurors by behavioral psychologists to design these new rules. The very use of the concept that jurors "mediate" their conclusions through other perceptions bespeaks the majority's application of behavioral decision theory to the jury system. The majority fails to acknowledge, however, that simulations of the jury process are conceded even by proponents of "psycholegal" research to be "imperfect tools for answering empirical questions," Kerr & Bray, *The Psychology of the Courtroom* (New York: Academic Press, 1982), p 318. Notwithstanding such reservations and ignoring the fact that the prosecution must introduce sufficient evidence in the case in chief to support guilt beyond a reasonable doubt, the majority states that it is much easier for a jury to conclude that "a person is bad than that he did something bad," and then flatly asserts that the limiting instructions do not accomplish their purpose.

One study the majority believes deserves consideration involves forty-eight mock jurors being advised of seven prior similar convictions, Doob & Kirshenbaum, *Some empirical evidence on the effect of § 12 of the Canada Evidence Act upon an accused,* 15 Crim.L.Q. 88, 93 (1972–73). It is this study which provides the "halo effect" explanation in the majority opinion.[18]

The most recent study cited by the majority is based on observations of 160 persons approached in Laundromats, supermarkets, bus terminals, and private homes who were asked to determine guilt or innocence of a hypothetical defendant from a two-page case summation. This study concludes that mock jurors are more likely to convict a defendant when advised of conviction of a prior *similar* crime, not, as the majority implies, of any prior conviction—a result that supports the current approach of our jurisprudence to this category of case. Similarly, the study's observation that the participants' rating of the hypothetical defendant's credibility did not vary as a function of prior conviction is used by the majority to support its conclusion that a limiting instruction has no effect on how jurors use prior conviction evidence. It is obvious even to the untutored, however, that the fact that there was no significant variation in the mock jurors' evaluation of the "defendant's" credibility is equally explained by the fact that there was no real defendant to evaluate. As the authors of this study themselves note:

> "One should be cautious in generalizing from the results of this study to jurors in a real trial. First, the ratio of trial evidence to prior conviction information is much lower in simulations than in actual trials. In an actual trial, the greater richness of evidence and actors probably provides jurors with more bases for forming credibility judg-

---

18. The majority quotes at length from this study. Forty-eight persons were individually approached in and around various public buildings. Each was read a four-hundred-word description of a case of breaking and entering. Each was asked, "How likely do you think it is that he is guilty?" Each was asked to respond on a scale that ran from one (definitely guilty) to seven (definitely not guilty). Points three and five were labeled as "probably guilty" and "probably not guilty," respectively.

Twelve persons read the case and rated (Group 1); twelve persons read, in addition, that the defense attorney decided not to put his client on the stand because there was no purpose (Group 2); twelve persons were told that the defendant testified "but did not give any important evidence" and that the defendant was impeached with five prior felonies for breaking and entering an occupied dwelling and twice for possession of stolen property (Group 3); and twelve persons were told,

in addition to the convictions, the limiting instruction of the judge (Group 4). The results were:

The study concludes on the basis of the data that the presence of a record has a dramatic effect. I would expect that random disagreement in so small a sample could account for all of the difference, but, regardless, this study can hardly be urged as support for the majority's result.

There is simply no real basis for comparison between the methodology of this study and that of the courtroom. These are forty-eight individual ratings without a trial, evidence, voir dire, argument, witnesses, instructions, or deliberation, and the prior conviction evidence is overwhelming and unrepresentative.

Average Ratings of Guilt

Group 1	4.00
Group 2	4.33
Group 3	3.25
Group 4	3.00

ments than the subjects in our simulation had." Wissler & Saks, *On the inefficacy of limiting instructions: When jurors use prior conviction evidence to decide on guilt,* 9 Law & Human Behavior 37, 46 (1985).

Finally, not only was there no real defendant, no actual deliberation or explanation of the limiting instruction, the most telling indication of the absence of persuasive weight in this study is the fact that the observation the majority finds most important, that is, that all else being the same, the "conviction" rate was higher where the impeaching crime was murder, is a conclusion drawn from a survey of *twenty* people, fourteen of whom opined that the defendant was guilty.

[T]he fact is that there is no demonstrable evidence that juries resolve doubtful cases on the basis that the defendant is a "bad man" and should be punished, that juries lower the burden of proof even if a guilty verdict would be incorrect, that juries convict because of a belief that the defendant's convictions indicate that he is probably guilty of the crime charged, or that juries incorrectly convict where a defendant does not take the stand because of fear of impeachment. Thus, there is no basis other than the majority's preference for its own rules for the statements that there is an "overwhelming tendency for jurors ... to misuse prior conviction evidence," or that MRE 609 presents a "likelihood that innocent persons may be convicted."

NOTES

1. Taking Notes on Witness Testimony. Judge Henry F. Greene of the District of Columbia Superior Court adopted a note taking option for jurors. One of the parties in a case objected and Judge Greene filed a Memorandum and Order denying those objections. The Court of Appeals refused to intervene, allowing the innovation to continue. The Court of Appeals printed Judge Greene's Memorandum and Order in Yeager v. Greene, 502 A.2d 980, 986 (D.C.App.1985):

> In the most recent edition of its *Standards for Criminal Justice,* the American Bar Association reflected what it acknowledged to be the "trend toward permitting notetaking [by jurors]" in "Trial By Jury" Standard 15–3.2, which provides:

> Jurors may take notes regarding the evidence presented to them and keep these notes with them when they retire for their deliberations. Such notes should be treated as confidential between the juror making them and other jurors. American Bar Association, *Standards for Criminal Justice* (2nd ed. 1978), "Trial By Jury", 15–3.2.

[T]he reasons which favor permitting jurors to take notes during criminal and civil trials seem to this court both obvious and compelling. Notes assist jurors in recalling the evidence and the instructions, help some jurors to better understand and to focus attention on the testimony and evidence, aid jurors in organizing their thoughts during deliberations, and probably clarify issues during jury deliberations. Moreover, it seems likely that permitting jurors to take notes may insure a fuller discussion of relevant issues during jury deliberations.[5]

[D]efendants have been unable to assert any credible ground upon which to conclude that they will be prejudiced or their interests in any way impaired by permitting jurors to take notes during their trials. Consequently, their requests that note taking by jurors not be permitted during their trials will be denied.

B.   TORT LIABILITY

A second example of social science research being used to shape the common law can be found in the area of tort liability. The principal issue in the development of tort law on which social science has been brought to bear has been "foreseeability," that is, the degree to which a defendant should have known that his or her behavior could result in harm to another.

ZINCK v. WHELAN

Superior Court of New Jersey, Appellate Division, 1972.
120 N.J.Super. 432, 294 A.2d 727.

■ CONFORD, P.J.A.D.

[Patrick Schoudt, the defendant, parked his father's car on a residential street in front of their house on the evening of June 24, 1970. The car was unlocked and the key left in the ignition. During the night, a group of teenagers stole the car and later crashed into a car driven by the plaintiffs,

---

5. Over a period of several months in the spring of 1982, this court sent letters and accompanying questionnaires to nearly 200 jurors who had sat during the previous five months on misdemeanor cases in which note taking was permitted. The survey was intended to ascertain, *inter alia*, whether the jurors had found it helpful to be able to take notes during trials. 94 responses were received to 196 mailed questionnaires, the vast majority of which indicated a strong preference by jurors to be able to take notes. Moreover, the responses included comments reflecting each of the reasons indicated in the text in support of the jurors' views.

[T]here is empirical support for what would seem to be the self-evident propositions that (1) left only with their memories to rely upon, jurors' ability to accurately recall courtroom testimony is highly problematical, (2) note taking enhances recall even where the note taker does not retain his or her notes at the time recall is tested, (3) notes are a form of "external storage" available for review and reference at a later time, and (4) subjects who take notes and are provided with an opportunity to review them prior to a test of recall perform better than those who take notes and are not permitted to review them before such a test. *A fortiori*, it would appear that note takers who are able to retain their notes during a test of recall (e.g., jurors during jury deliberations after a trial) will be better able to remember what transpired than non-note takers. *See* Harris, Teske and Ginns, "Memory for Pragmatic Implications from Courtroom Testimony", 6 *Bulletin of the Psychonomic Society*, 494, 496 (1975) ("The results of this study offer discouraging reflections of jurors' memories of courtroom testimony"); DiVesta and Gray, "Listening and Note Taking", 63 *Journal of Educational Psychology* 8 (1972); Carter and Van Matre, "Note Taking vs. Note Having", 67 *Journal of Educational Psychology* 900 (1975).

who were severely injured. The plaintiffs sued Schoudt for negligently leaving his key in the ignition of the unlocked car, but the trial judge granted summary judgment in favor of Schoudt.]

Basically the key to duty, negligence and proximate cause in the fact-pattern under review is the foreseeability *vel non* to a reasonable man of an unreasonable *enhanced hazard,* when a motor vehicle is left unlocked in a public place with key in the ignition, of both the theft or misappropriation of the vehicle and an ensuing mishandling of it by the taker with death, injury or destruction of property of others lawfully using the highways as the result.

[C]ommon-law courts having evolved the law of negligence, they are obviously free to and should mold its application as developing experience and sound judgment counsel in the broad public interest and in the interests of justice. The fact that New Jersey has no pertinent legislation in the field under consideration is no bar against our courts performing their traditional common-law function in this regard. In undertaking to do so, however, courts should inform themselves on the basis of such reliable empirical data as are available. Such data were not available in 1951 when we decided Saracco v. Lyttle [78 A.2d 288 (App.Div.1951)]. However, the data now at hand, taken in conjunction with social trends which are commonly known, indicate that the hazard of car theft is rapidly growing and that both its relationship to keys being left in the ignitions of unlocked vehicles and the extraordinary correlation between thefts and disastrous incidental accidents are far clearer now than in the days when the doctrine of no-proximate-cause in this area was getting its foothold in judicial thought.

Some of the data is mentioned in [t]he recent District of Columbia Circuit Court of Appeals opinion in Gaither v. Myers, 404 F.2d at 222, particularly the allusion therein to the estimated accident rate for stolen cars being 200 times the normal accident rate. But there is much other concordant, convincing data from sources supplied us by appellants which we deem reliable.

In 1950 the national rate of stolen vehicles per 100,000 population was about 100. President's Commission on Law Enforcement and Administration of Justice, Task Force Report: Crime and its Impact—An Assessment, at 27 (1967). In 1970 the rate was 453.5, an increase of over 350%. United Crime Reports: Crime in the United States (1970) (promulgated by F.B.I.) ("Uniform Crime Reports"). The 1964 rate was 242. Since 1960 the rate increased 149.7%. That increase has been four times greater than both the percentage increase in automobile registrations generally and that of persons aged 15–24 years. 1970 Uniform Crime Reports, at 28.

As of 1964 50% of the thefts involved minors under 18. Uniform Crime Reports, at 19. 42% of the cars stolen had the keys left in the ignition or the ignition unlocked. Id. at 20. "Most auto thefts, two-thirds, occur at night, and over one-half of the thefts are from private residences, apartments and/or from streets in residential areas." Id. at 20.

In 1966 the Department of Justice conducted a survey of this subject. See Hearings on H.R. 15215 before Subcommittee No. 5 of the House Committee on the Judiciary, 90th Congress, 2d Session, at 31–39 (1968) ("Justice Department Survey"). This was based upon questionnaires returned by 1,659 convicted car thieves involved in 4,077 offenses. The survey showed that 59% of the cars stolen had the keys left in the ignition or the switch unlocked. Justice Department Survey, at 32. 18.2% of the cars taken were subsequently involved in accidents. Id. at 33.

Since 1967 the Attorney General of New Jersey has promulgated an annual statistical crime summary. Uniform Crime Reports of New Jersey. The 1969 report (at 57) indicates a rise in auto theft of 25% from 1967 to 1969. 48% of the thefts were by persons under 18. Ibid. Over 45% of the thefts were from the streets of residential areas and more than 70% occurred at night. Id. at 59. Inquiries of owners of cars stolen indicated that 34% professed to be unable to inform the police as to whether the key was in the ignition or whether the car was locked; but of those who purported to remember, the key was left in the ignition or elsewhere in the vehicle in 17% of the cases. Id. at 59. In any event, the same report (at 59) observes:

> The degree of negligence of motor vehicle operator in most cases dictates whether or not the theft will occur. The portion of thefts attributed to the professional car thief is relatively small when compared to that portion perpetrated by the non-professional whose actions depend chiefly on the opportunities afforded by careless operators who fail to take normal safeguards when leaving a motor vehicle unattended.

We think the reasonably prudent motor car operator can today justly be held to an awareness of the gravamen of the foregoing data, if not of the specific figures, which may vary from time to time, locality to locality or from one study to another. As noted above, on March 1, 1967 the United States Attorney General publicly announced the start of the Justice Department's National Auto Theft Prevention Campaign, a drive against the very problem here of concern. The campaign has continued since, abetted by wide media and other publicity. Automobile owners are continuously warned to remove the key and lock the vehicle when parking. [A]s to the question of Patrick's negligence in leaving the key in the ignition, a fact issue for the jury was clearly presented. The cover of darkness and absence of surveillance was an inviting setting for the taking. The car was inferably left in the street for the night. And the statistical data cited above indicate that thefts from residential streets, or after nightfall, are of relatively high incidence.

Judgment reversed.

————

HILL v. YASKIN

Supreme Court of New Jersey, 1977.
75 N.J. 139, 380 A.2d 1107.

■ CLIFFORD, J.

Plaintiff William E. Hill, a Camden police officer, was injured on October 8, 1971 when his police car collided with a vehicle which he was pursuing. The vehicle, owned by defendant Judith A. Yaskin, had been stolen the previous day from a parking lot operated by defendant Camden Parking Services, Inc. (Camden Parking). Suit was commenced against Yaskin and Camden Parking bottomed on the admitted fact that the ignition key had been left in the vehicle while it was parked in the lot. Specifically, the Complaint charged that defendant Yaskin "so negligently and carelessly allowed her motor vehicle to be * * * unattended, so as to allow the unknown driver to take and use the same." As to defendant Camden Parking the charge was that the Yaskin vehicle had been left unattended, with the keys placed in the ignition, on the specific instructions of the lot owner, and that this conduct on the part of Camden Parking constituted negligence.

The trial court granted summary judgment in favor of both defendants and the Appellate Division affirmed.

[W]hat the issue before us comes down to is whether there was a duty owed to plaintiff by either defendant or both of them.

[T]his "duty" aspect of foreseeability was concisely set forth by Judge Conford, in the stolen vehicle context, in Zinck v. Whelan, [294 A.2d 727 at 734 (1972)] wherein he noted:

> [B]asically the key to duty, negligence and proximate cause in the fact-pattern under review is the foreseeability *vel non* to a reasonable man of an unreasonably *enhanced hazard,* when a motor vehicle is left unlocked in a public place with key in the ignition, of both the theft or misappropriation of the vehicle and an ensuing mishandling of it by the taker with death, injury or destruction of property of others lawfully using the highways as the result.

The *Zinck* court fortified its "enhanced hazard" approach by reference to empirical data indicating the danger involved in leaving ignition keys in unattended vehicles. 120 N.J.Super. at 446–49, 294 A.2d 727. The continuing validity of such data may be recognized by reference to a recent study conducted by the Law Enforcement Assistance Administration [L.E.A.A.]. A report entitled Preliminary Study of the Effectiveness of Auto Anti-Theft Devices (Nat'l Inst. of Law Enforcement and Crim. Justice, L.E.A.A., U.S. Dept. of Justice 1975) [hereinafter *LEAA Study*] indicates that in at least 24% of the cases considered, the means used by a thief to mobilize a stolen car was a key. *LEAA Study* at 4–5. The study's conclusion on this point was that

> a significant number of the stolen and recovered cars involved keys left in the ignition lock or concealed in the car (under a mat or above the sun visor, for example). It would thus appear that owner/operator action may have directly contributed to a very large proportion of these thefts. [Id. at 4.]

This same study further concluded that the accident rate for stolen cars is 47 times greater than the rate for the general public. Id. at 29.

With this impressive array of statistical information as a backdrop, we have no hesitancy in concluding that summary judgment should not have been entered in favor of either defendant.

[I]t should be acknowledged that our search here is essentially one for desirable policy. In this area, the issue being whether the plaintiff William Hill's injured interest is one which falls within the protection of the rule he invokes, our function is "altogether an excursion into the domain of policy." Or, as put more succinctly by Chief Justice Weintraub, "[w]hether a duty exists is ultimately a question of fairness." Goldberg v. Housing Auth. of Newark, 186 A.2d at 293. As we view the matter, there is nothing unfair in requiring defendants to go to trial on the question of whether they should have foreseen that the leaving of Yaskin's automobile unattended under the circumstances recited above unreasonably increased the hazard of its theft and subsequent mishandling—particularly where that hazard could have so easily been substantially reduced.

[J]udgment reversed. The cause is remanded to the Law Division for trial as to both defendants.

————

McCLENAHAN v. COOLEY

Supreme Court of Tennessee, 1991.
806 S.W.2d 767.

■ DROWOTA, JUSTICE.

In this action for the wrongful death of his wife and two children and personal injuries to another child, William McClenahan, Plaintiff-Appellant, appeals the dismissal of his lawsuit against Glenn Cooley, Defendant-Appellee, by the Circuit Court of Bradley County. The central issue presented in this litigation is whether a jury should be permitted to determine the issue of proximate causation in cases where the keys are left in the ignition of a parked automobile that is subsequently stolen and thereafter involved in an accident.

[T]he facts to be taken as true in this case reveal that on May 20, 1988, at approximately 11 a.m., the Defendant, Glenn Cooley, drove his 1981 Pontiac Bonneville automobile to a bank located in the public parking lot of a shopping center in Athens. The Defendant left the keys in the ignition to his parked automobile while he went inside of the bank to transact business. While the Defendant was in the bank, a thief spotted the keys in the ignition of the vehicle, started the engine, and began driving down the interstate where he was spotted by a state trooper. When the thief exited the interstate a short time later, a high speed chase ensued on the busiest stretch of highway in Cleveland at the lunchtime hour. The thief was pursued by police officers approximately 80 miles per hour approaching the most dangerous intersection in the city. When the vehicles reached the intersection, the thief ran a red light traveling in excess of 80 miles per hour and slammed into another vehicle broadside.

[T]he Plaintiff brought an action predicated upon negligence per se and common law negligence for the wrongful death of his wife and the two children, and for injuries to the child who survived. The complaint alleges that the Defendant knew or should have known that it was unlawful to leave the keys in the ignition of an unattended vehicle; that he knew or should have known that it was unsafe to do so; and that he knew or should have known that the place where he had parked the vehicle, complete with keys in the ignition, created a foreseeable likelihood that the vehicle would be stolen. The claim is made by the Plaintiff that the actions of the thief are a foreseeable and/or expected result of the Defendant's purported negligence.

[G]iving foremost consideration to the established principles of common law negligence, we conclude, as many other jurisdictions have, that leaving a key in the ignition of an unattended automobile in an area where the public has access, be it public or private property, could be found by a reasonable jury to be negligent, whether or not a prohibitory statute is involved. The mere fact that an automobile is parked on private property and no statute is violated should not in all cases dictate a determination of absolute non-liability. The basic issue is foreseeability, both as to proximate causation and superseding intervening cause, and that is a question of fact rather than of law upon which reasonable minds can and do differ, at least where the accident has occurred during the flight of the thief relatively close thereto in time and distance.[8] [W]e thus expressly reject the contention that an intervening criminal act under the circumstances presented here automatically breaks the chain of causation as a matter of law, concluding instead that reasonable minds can differ as to whether a person of ordinary prudence and intelligence through the exercise of reasonable diligence could foresee, or should have foreseen, the theft of an unattended automobile with the keys in the ignition left in an area where the public has access, and could likewise foresee the increased risk to the public should a theft occur.

[F]or the foregoing reasons, the judgment of the trial court is reversed and the case remanded for proceedings consistent with this opinion.

NOTE

1. "Dramshop" Liability. The extension of tort liability to liquor stores—"dramshops"—when minors or intoxicated persons who purchase alcohol are later involved in car crashes has also invoked empirical research findings. For example, in McClellan v. Tottenhoff, 666 P.2d 408 (Wyo. 1983), the Supreme Court of Wyoming overturned a precedent to hold that a liquor store could be sued for selling alcohol to a minor who later became

---

8. A study conducted by the United States Department of Justice reveals that 42.3 percent of all automobiles stolen during the period covered by the study were left unattended with the keys in the ignition and that the rate of accidents involving such stolen vehicles was 200 times the normal accident rate. See 45 A.L.R.3d at 797.

intoxicated and caused a fatal collision. The court stated that "[t]he fact that the risk to the traveling public may readily be recognized and foreseen is supported by disturbing statistics," id. at 415, and recited data that over half of all fatal crashes in Wyoming involved alcohol, and in nearly one-fourth of these, the driver was a minor. On the further extension of tort liability, citing similar empirical data, to "social hosts," see Conaway, The Continuing Search for Solutions to the Drinking Driver Tragedy and the Problem of Social Host Liability, 82 Northwestern University Law Review 403 (1988).

SELECTED BIBLIOGRAPHY

A.   Rules of Evidence

Alschuler, "Close Enough for Government Work": The Exclusionary Rule After *Leon,* 1984 Supreme Court Review 309 (1984).

Davies, A Hard Look at What We Know (And Still Need to Learn) about the "Costs" of the Exclusionary Rule: The NIJ Study and Other Studies of "Lost" Arrests, 1983 American Bar Foundation Research Journal 611 (1983).

Dripps, Living with *Leon,* 95 Yale Law Journal 906 (1986).

Heffernan and Lovely, Evaluating the Fourth Amendment Exclusionary Rule: The Problem of Police Compliance With the Law, 24 University of Michigan Journal of Law Reform 311 (1991).

Perrin, Caldwell, Chase, and Fagan, If It's Broken, Fix It: Moving Beyond the Exclusionary Rule, 83 Iowa Law Review 669 (1998).

Uchida and Bynum, Search Warrants, Motions to Suppress and "Lost Cases:" The Effects of the Exclusionary Rule in Seven Jurisdictions, 81 Journal of Criminal Law and Criminology 1034 (1991).

B.   Tort Liability

Casper, Benedict, and Perry, The Tort Remedy in Search and Seizure Cases: A Case Study in Juror Decision Making, 13 Law and Social Inquiry 279 (1988).

Conaway, The Continuing Search for Solutions to the Drinking Driver Tragedy and the Problem of Social Host Liability, 82 Northwestern Law Review 403 (1988).

SECTION IV. SOCIAL AUTHORITY

In both constitutional and common law, courts have relied heavily upon Davis's concept of "legislative fact" for theoretical guidance in dealing with social science research. In our own work on the lawmaking uses of social science, however, we have become increasingly disenchanted with "legislative fact" and increasingly frustrated with the lack of direction—illustrated in the cases presented above—that it provides courts confronted with empirical questions. We have developed an alternative theoretical concept that we believe brings more coherence to the task of incorporating social science research in the judicial lawmaking process. We call our perspective "social authority."

SOCIAL AUTHORITY: OBTAINING, EVALUATING, AND ESTABLISHING SOCIAL SCIENCE IN LAW

John Monahan and Laurens Walker.
134 University of Pennsylvania Law Review 477 (1986).

It is difficult to gainsay the recent conclusion that "a viable formulation of rules ... with regard to legislative facts has not proven feasible."[37] [R]ather, improvement in the use of social science information in the courts may be possible only "within the perimeters of a new concept,"[39] a concept that would fundamentally alter the way in which courts view social science materials.

We propose *social authority* as such a concept. We argue that courts should treat social science research relevant to creating a rule of law as a source of authority rather than as a source of facts. More specifically we propose that courts treat social science research as they would legal precedent under the common law.

[O]ur initial case for the jurisprudential plausibility of viewing social science as a form of authority takes this observation as its point of departure: while empirical research has some of the characteristics of fact, it has some of the characteristics of law as well. Until now, courts and commentators have attended to the similarity between social science and fact, and have largely ignored the similarity between social science and law.

[I]   A.   *Similarity Between Social Science and Fact*

The principal similarity between social science research and fact is that both are *positive*—both concern the way the world *is,* with no necessary implications for the way the world *ought* to be. Both refer to the empirical reality that we infer from our senses, rather than to the value we impute to that reality. Law, in contrast, is *normative.* It does not describe how people *do* behave, but rather prescribes how they *should* behave.

B.   *Similarity Between Social Science and Law*

The principal similarity between social science research and law is that both are *general*—both produce principles applicable beyond particular instances. Facts, in contrast, are specific to particular instances. Social science research, though derived from specific empirical data, typically addresses persons, situations, and time periods beyond those present in a

---

37. E. Cleary, K. Broun, G. Dix, E. Gelhorn, D. Kaye, R. Meisenholder, E. Roberts & J. Strong, McCormick on Evidence 937 (3d ed. 1984).

39. Id. at 938.

particular investigation. Indeed, the purpose of most scientific research is to obtain knowledge that, while surely not immutable, holds true for many people over considerable time and in a variety of places. Because of this generality, the conclusions of empirical research are sometimes metaphorically described as scientific laws.

Like social science, law, particularly court decisions in a commonlaw system, derives from specific empirical events (the facts of a case), but speaks more broadly. It is this attribute of generality that is described as the "precedential effect" or authoritative nature of a court decision. A decision takes on the mantle of legal authority in subsequent litigation precisely to the extent that the decision transcends the people, situation, and time present in the original case. Indeed, the way to deny legal authority to a court decision is to deny its generality by claiming that the decision is limited to its own facts.

[C.] *The Criterion for Classification*

[I]f we have made our threshold case that it is jurisprudentially possible for social science research to be classified as either law or fact, the next question concerns the nature of the argument that is to decide which classification should be used. Of two plausible classification schemes, how does one choose between them? How, in other words, does one decide which similarities—the similarities to law or the similarities to fact—are the most important? The question is taxonomic, and the extensive literature in the field of classification yields a clear answer: the better classification is the one that is most useful.

[T]he adequacy of our proposal—that social science research be treated by the courts as courts treat legal precedent rather than as fact—depends, therefore, upon the quality of the judicial management procedures that flow from this social authority classification, as compared with the existing procedures that result from the fact classification.

[W]hat implications flow from conceiving of social science as more akin to law than to fact? We offer a series of proposals addressed to the three questions that have proved most vexing to American courts when empirical studies appear relevant to rendering a decision: (1) how should courts obtain information from the social sciences?; (2) how should they evaluate it?; and (3) how should they treat the empirical conclusions established by other courts?

The heuristic presumption with which we approach each question is that courts should treat social science data the same way they treat legal precedent.

[II] A. *Obtaining Social Authority*

From a theory that posits social science as a source of authority in the law flow two corollary propositions regarding how a court should obtain empirical research: the parties should present empirical research to the court in briefs rather than by testimony; and the court may locate social science studies through its own research.

1. Written Briefs From the Parties

[I]f the research is more analogous to law than to fact, the parties should present the research to the court in the same manner that they would offer legal precedents, that is, in written briefs rather than by oral testimony. Parties wishing to argue that a prior legal decision should be taken as precedent for the present case do not do so by introducing as a witness the judge who wrote the prior opinion. Similarly, the oral testimony of the authors of social science research should not be the vehicle by which the research is introduced in court.

[2.] Independent Judicial Investigation

[T]reating empirical research as a source of authority rather than as a type of fact can provide the principled direction now lacking on the issue of whether judges should locate research independently. The analogy is plain: as courts are free to find legal precedents that the parties have not presented, they should also have the power to locate social science research through independent investigation. Courts are not limited to the case precedents contained in the parties' briefs and are not required to remand for further hearings to develop a record in which case precedents can be introduced. Likewise, they should not be limited to the briefs or required to remand to obtain scientific research.

[B.] *Evaluating Social Authority*

[C]ourts assign precedential value to prior judicial decisions by a process that is neither clear nor simple. One need not unpack the whole jurisprudence of precedent, however, to arrive at an appreciation of the factors on which courts rely in evaluating prior cases. At least four indices of precedential persuasiveness can be easily abstracted from the jurisprudential literature: (1) cases decided by courts higher in the appellate structure have more weight than lower court decisions; (2) better reasoned cases have more weight than poorly reasoned cases; (3) cases involving facts closely analogous to those in the case at issue have more weight than cases involving easily distinguished facts; and (4) cases followed by other courts have more weight than isolated cases.

We realize that these indicia of precedential value cannot be applied literally to the evaluation of social science research. Scientific studies themselves, for example, are not "decided" by or "appealed" to varying levels of the judiciary. Yet, as we hope to demonstrate, the principles courts use to distinguish cases in terms of their precedential worth bear a striking similarity to the principles used by social scientists to distinguish research studies in terms of their scientific worth. We propose, therefore, that courts evaluate scientific research studies along four dimensions analogous to the four dimensions used to evaluate case precedent. Courts should place confidence in a piece of scientific research to the extent that the research (1) has survived the critical review of the scientific community; (2) has employed valid research methods; (3) is generalizable to the case at issue; and (4) is supported by a body of other research.

[C.]   *Establishing Social Authority*

Finally, we must consider a special issue in evaluating social science research: How should a court evaluate a study that another court has already evaluated? Studies of first impression may be evaluated as we propose, but additional considerations arise when another court previously has relied upon, or rejected, a particular piece of research. If the research has been evaluated by a court in another jurisdiction, the evaluation of the former court may be treated much as its conclusions of law are treated. That is, its value as precedent could be determined according to the guidelines we have developed. Yet, what of research that has been evaluated by a court in the same jurisdiction as the court presently reviewing it? The issue arises often, and in two legally distinct situations.

1.   The Effect of Lower Court Evaluation of Social Science Research upon Appellate Courts

If empirical studies are considered to be matters of fact, appellate courts would appear to be bound by lower court evaluations of the studies, at least if the lower court evaluations were not "clearly erroneous." [A]ppellate courts commonly resort to the distinction between legislative facts and adjudicative facts to avoid the untenable result of being bound by two inconsistent lower court evaluations of the same research, neither of which is "clearly erroneous." Lower court findings of adjudicative facts, according to this view, are not reviewable on appeal (unless clearly erroneous), but lower court findings of legislative facts are reviewable.

We reach the same result, but by a more parsimonious route. Since appellate courts are not bound by lower courts' conclusions of law, they should not be bound by lower courts' conclusions regarding empirical research. A reviewing court is completely free to evaluate *de novo* any precedent used in a lower court decision. Similarly, the court should be unconstrained in its ability to reevaluate any social science research upon which a lower court relied in creating a rule of law.

[2.]   The Effect of Appellate Court Evaluation of Social Science Research upon Lower Courts

[C]onsistent with our position on social authority, we suggest that appellate courts' evaluation of social science research should affect lower courts to the same extent that their evaluation of case precedent affects lower courts.

To say that lower courts should be influenced by the conclusions that appellate courts have derived from social science research in the same way that they are influenced by the rules that the courts abstract from prior cases, however, does not mean that lower courts need be merely passive recipients of the empirical judgments issued above. Just as new legal cases and commentary can develop and recast a given rule of law, so too new research and analysis—not previously considered by an appellate court—can change the empirical conclusions upon which a rule of law rests.

[W]e believe that if courts treat social science research as social authority, fewer judicial opinions will rely upon social science material, but the material that is used will be of much higher quality. Poor studies will be screened out, and exemplary research will become more apparent. In this way, the development of fair and efficient rules of law that rely in part upon empirical propositions will be facilitated.

THE SEARCH FOR THE TRUTH IN CONSTITUTIONAL CRIMINAL PROCEDURE

Tom Stacy.
91 Columbia Law Review 1369 (1991).

The notion that it is not for the [Supreme] Court to resolve debatable empirical questions has considerable surface appeal. The Court, it would seem, should interpret constitutional rights in light of constitutional values rather than the results of statistical experiments or, worse, its own empirical speculations. The problem with this view, though, is that in this and many other situations, constitutional values are inextricably intertwined with empirical questions. Constitutional values do not exist in a vacuum; they must be implemented in the real world. Questions about what the Constitution does and does not require thus have an inescapable empirical component. For the Court to allow others to resolve empirical questions inextricably linked with the maintenance of constitutional values is to abdicate its distinctive role as ultimate arbiter of the Constitution's meaning.

[I]n [a]reas where important constitutional values are inseparably linked with "empirical" questions, the Court has decided those questions for itself. Examples can be found in doctrines involving each of the Constitution's three basic functions: the separation of powers, federalism, and individual rights. In the separation of powers context, the Court has made empirical judgments in deciding the existence and scope of the President's implied Article II privilege to withhold confidential communications from the judicial process. In particular, the Court has premised its understanding of this privilege on empirical judgments regarding the effect that disclosure of confidential communications will likely have on the candor of the President and his aides. The making of empirical judgments is also endemic to the federalism doctrine defining the so-called "negative implications" of the Commerce Clause. In deciding the validity of state regulation adversely affecting the flow of interstate commerce, the Court often balances the regulation's adverse effect on interstate commerce against its contribution to the public health and safety. Both aspects of this balancing test—the regulation's effect on interstate commerce and its effect on public health—require empirical conclusions. Finally, the Court frequently makes empirical judgments in interpreting constitutional civil liberties. It has created a fairly elaborate set of First Amendment limits on the law of defamation, based in part on its predictions of the "chilling effect" that various common law rules have on the willingness of persons to criticize public officials. It also makes rough empirical judgments in assessing the deterrent effect of the Fourth Amendment exclusionary rule on the behavior of law enforcement officers. In each of these disparate areas, then, the Court must itself resolve empirical questions to safeguard important constitutional values. So-called judicial conservatives and liberals alike make such judgments, demonstrating their inevitability in implementing constitutional values thought important.

EMPIRICAL QUESTIONS WITHOUT EMPIRICAL ANSWERS

John Monahan and Laurens Walker.
1991 Wisconsin Law Review 569 (1991).

The issue here is how courts are to proceed when they acknowledge that an empirical proposition is a predicate for a rule of law, but lack "social authority" bearing on that proposition. Since the course of action courts take might differ depending upon whether the empirical assumption arises in the context of the common law or in the context of judicial review of state action, we consider each situation separately.

A. Empirical Assumptions in the Common Law

[C]onceiving of social science research, when used to create a legal rule, as more analogous to law itself than to fact (i.e., as a form of "social authority"), suggests the following heuristic: how do courts decide legal issues in the absence of precedent? That is, how do courts proceed in cases of "first impression"?

The predominant answer is that courts, faced with the necessity of deciding a novel case, often proceed by articulating the competing interests at stake and then formulating a rule that balances those interests to promote a desirable public policy. Empirical questions about the nature of those competing interests, and about the consequences of a policy giving priority to one of them may weigh heavily in the balancing process. When empirical assumptions are supported by "social authority" in the form of social science research, that research is often cited and relied upon in balancing interests and formulating a legal rule. When no research, or inadequate research, exists to support empirical assumptions, however, the courts fulfill their obligation to render a decision by relying upon those empirical assumptions that seem most *plausible*. Based on their experience and intuition, along with whatever information may be available, judges will *speculate* on what would be the likely impact of valid social science research on the empirical assumptions at issue.

[T]he great advantage of judicial candor about the role of empirical assumptions and the speculative nature of their resolution, then, is that the common law is left open to change as new social authority bearing on those assumptions becomes available. A corollary of this candor is that it clearly signals to the social science research community, and the government agencies that fund their research, the importance of empirical assumptions in the law (the judiciary's "working hypotheses"), and the receptiveness of courts to obtaining social authority bearing on them.

In the making of common law, therefore, courts often cannot avoid basing legal rules on empirical assumptions. Frequently, those assumptions will lack support in the form of social authority provided by the parties, or otherwise found by the court through its own independent research. In such cases, courts should rely upon the most plausible assumptions available at the time of the decision and allow future developments in experience or in research to modify these assumptions. This, of course, is how the common law always evolves.

B. Empirical Assumptions in Judicial Review of State Action

Judicial review of the decisions of other branches of government is a vast topic. We shall simplify our analysis by focusing on judicial review under the Equal Protection Clause of the fourteenth amendment and, specifically, on two sharply divergent tests for reviewing legislation.

[1]. THE RATIONALITY STANDARD

[T]wo concepts have been articulated as being central to judicial review under the standard of rationality: the "presumption" that the legislature acted rationally to pursue legitimate ends in enacting the statute, and the "burden of proof" to the contrary being placed on those challenging the statute. We believe, however, that both "presumption" and "burden of proof" are inapposite extrapolations; they are concepts developed in the arena of social facts and cannot properly be applied to the realm occupied by social authority.

[R]ather than employing the evidentiary concepts of case-specific social facts in judicial decisionmaking, we believe that concepts more appropriate to the "legislative" or "authoritative" nature of the inquiry should be adopted. Instead of stating that there is a "presumption of constitutionality" under the rationality standard, it would be more helpful to state that there was an "assumption of constitutionality." That is, under the "rationality" standard, *courts normally will accept as plausible the empirical assumptions made by the legislature in enacting a statute.* The challenger's burden is to demonstrate that these empirical assumptions are implausible. This is not a burden of "proof," however, since "proof" can be provided only by "evidence." Rather, the responsibility is one of "argument:" under the rationality standard, *it is the challenger's responsibility to convince the court to reject as implausible the empirical assumptions made by the legislature in enacting a statute.* This responsibility is met by providing the court with empirical research—"social authority"—the results of which so contradict the assumptions made by the legislature that it would be implausible ("irrational") to maintain them.

[W]hen courts consider a statute under the rationality standard and determine that the statute is based on empirical assumptions for which no adequate empirical support exists, the statute will normally be upheld. Only when the challenger presents—or the court finds through its own efforts—social authority sufficient to convince the court that the assumptions made by the legislature are implausible should the statute fail rationality review. Just as the common law judge is permitted to proceed by plausible speculation in a case of first impression, courts initially accept as plausible the empirical assumptions of the legislature. By such deference, courts acknowledge the legislature's primacy as a lawmaking institution. An empirical challenge to this deference, we believe, should be treated much as a legal argument challenging legislation is treated. It should be evaluated by criteria designed to test law-like social authority—rather than by criteria for reviewing factual evidence.

2. The Strict Scrutiny Standard

[T]he same two concepts traditionally employed for judicial review under the rationality standard, "presumption" and "burden of proof," appear central to judicial review under the strict scrutiny standard as well. Under the strict scrutiny standard, however, the presumption and burden are shifted. The presumption here is of unconstitutionality and the burden is on the state to prove otherwise. In addition, the strict scrutiny standard changes the nature of what is to be proven. The state must prove not merely that the ends it sought were "legitimate" and the means it chose were "rationally related" to achieving those ends—that is, that the legislature had a "plausible" justification for the statute. Rather, the state must prove that the ends it sought were "compelling" and the means it chose were "necessary" to their achievement—that is, that the legislature had a "valid" justification for the statute.

[W]e believe that both "presumption" and "burden of proof" are inappropriate extrapolations of social facts to the realm properly occupied by social authority. As with the rationality basis test, clarity would be brought to the strict scrutiny standard by adopting concepts more appropriate to the "legislative" or "authoritative" nature of the inquiry. Instead of stating that there is a "presumption of unconstitutionality" under the strict scrutiny standard, it would be more helpful to state that there is an "assumption of unconstitutionality." That is, under the "strict scrutiny" standard, *courts normally will reject as invalid the empirical assumptions made by the legislature in enacting a statute.* The "burden" is on the state to demonstrate that these assumptions are valid. As in the rationality standard, this is not a burden of "proof," since "proof" can be provided only by "evidence." Rather, the responsibility is again one of "argument": *it is the state's responsibility to convince the court to accept as valid the empirical assumptions made by the legislature in enacting a statute.* This responsibility is met by providing the court with empirical research— "social authority"—the results of which support the assumptions made by the legislature. Thus, strict scrutiny of a statute based on empirical assumptions for which no adequate empirical support exists should result in invalidation of the statute. Only when the state presents—or the court finds through its own research—sufficient social authority to convince the court that the assumptions made by the legislature are valid should a statute pass the strict scrutiny test. For statutes that impinge on fundamental interests or that classify on suspect bases, the respect ordinarily accorded by courts to the empirical assumptions of the legislature is much less. These special cases constitute an exception to the typical judicial deference to the legislature's primacy as a lawmaking institution. As with rationality review, however, casting the issue in terms of law-like "social authority" rather than in terms of factual evidence clarifies for courts the process of obtaining and evaluating research, and therefore, assists substantially in determining whether the state's responsibility has been met.

SELECTED BIBLIOGRAPHY

Acker, Social Science in Supreme Court Criminal Cases and Briefs: The Actual and Potential Contribution of Social Scientists as Amici Curiae, 14 Law and Human Behavior 25 (1990).

Faigman, To Have and Have Not: Assessing the Value of Social Science to the Law as Science and Policy, 38 Emory Law Journal 1005 (1989).

Faigman, "Normative Constitutional Fact Finding": Exploring the Empirical Component of Constitutional Interpretation, 139 University of Pennsylvania Law Review 541 (1991).

Grisso and Saks, Psychology's Influence on Constitutional Interpretation: A Comment on How to Succeed, 15 Law and Human Behavior 205 (1991).

Hafemeister and Melton, The Impact of Social Science Research on the Judiciary, in Reforming the Law: Impact of Child Development Research (G. Melton ed. 1987).

Keeton, Legislative Facts and Similar Things: Deciding Disputed Premise Facts, 73 Minnesota Law Review 1 (1988).

Korn, Law, Fact, and Science in the Courts, 66 Columbia Law Review 1080 (1966).

T. Marvell, Appellate Courts and Lawyers: Information Gathering in the Adversary System (1978).

Meares and Harcourt, Transparent Adjudication and Social Science Research in Constitutional Criminal Procedure, 90 Journal of Criminal Law and Criminology 733 (2000).

Monahan and Walker, Social Science Research in Law: A New Paradigm, 43 American Psychologist 465 (1988).

Roesch, Creating Change in the Legal System: Contributions from Community Psychology, 19 Law and Human Behavior 325 (1995)

Roesch, Golding, Hans, and Reppucci, Social Science and the Courts: The Role of Amicus Curiae Briefs, 15 Law and Human Behavior 1 (1991).

Saks, Judicial Attention to the Way the World Works, 75 Iowa Law Review 1011 (1990).

SOCIAL SCIENCE USED TO PROVIDE CONTEXT

It is commonplace to distinguish two fundamental uses of social science research in deciding legal cases. The first is to determine facts—what Kenneth Culp Davis called "adjudicative facts" and what we called "social facts" in Chapter 1. The second is to assist in making law—what Davis called "legislative facts" and what we called "social authority" in Chapter 2. Yet a reading of recent cases reveals a great number that seem anomalous by this method of classification. In these cases, social science is used neither as case-specific fact nor as authority for lawmaking. Instead, a new, third use of social science in deciding cases appears to be emerging, one that combines elements of each of the two conventional applications to provide judges and juries with a general context for determining factual issues in particular cases.

In this chapter, we first identify and define this maturing use of social science research, which we call "social framework". We then examine a variety of ways in which social science is employed to provide decision makers with frameworks for determining future, present, and past facts.

SECTION I.   SOCIAL SCIENCE AS CONTEXT

In the typical case in which social science research is used to determine facts, such as the trademark and obscenity cases described in Chapter 1, the research is done by one or both parties to the lawsuit and involves the actual items whose attributes—e.g., "likelihood of confusion" or "patent offensiveness"—are in dispute. In the typical case in which social science is used to make law, such as the constitutional or common law cases described in Chapter 2, the research is broadly-based and involves the parties only as exemplars of more general findings—e.g., the effects of segregated education on the self-esteem of all African-American children, or the deterrent value of the exclusionary rule on police officers as a class. In this third, hybrid, use of social science, however, research that appears to have the general, broadly-based characteristics usually associated with lawmaking is used to determine case-specific issues, a function usually conceived as fact-finding.

SOCIAL FRAMEWORKS: A NEW USE OF SOCIAL SCIENCE IN LAW

Laurens Walker and John Monahan.
73 Virginia Law Review 559 (1987).

Most of the uses of social science in court fall into either the "legislative fact" or "adjudicative fact" categories. Within the past several years, however, courts have increasingly begun to use research in ways that do not correspond to either of the traditional classifications. There are strong indications that a new, third use of social science in law is emerging. Notable examples can be found in cases concerning eyewitness identification, assessments of dangerousness, battered women, and sexual victimization.

Social Framework as an Organizing Concept

[In these cases] social science was not being used to provide "legislative facts." [N]either party contemplated a change in any rule of law. Rather, accepting the rules of law governing his or her respective case, the party introducing the research was attempting to demonstrate that the findings would assist the jury to decide the specific factual issues being litigated.

At the same time, [s]ocial science was not being used [in these cases] to provide "adjudicative facts" either. [In] none of the [cases] were the parties to the case involved in the research at all. The expert witnesses relied heavily—and in some of the cases, exclusively—on "off the rack" research studies published before the events that gave rise to the litigation took place, studies performed by researchers and using subjects with no knowledge of the case at bar.

Yet the way social science was used in these cases—while neither legislative nor adjudicative fact—does have some of the hallmarks of each. In each case, the research being introduced shared the critical characteristic of legislative fact—generality. The studies bore on issues at trial only as those issues were particular instances of larger empirical relationships that had been uncovered.

[H]owever, as in cases involving the use of social research to determine adjudicative facts, the studies here were introduced solely to help resolve specific factual issues disputed by the immediate parties to the case, issues whose resolution had no substantive significance beyond the case at hand.

[T]he research used in these [cases], then, is not pure legislative or adjudicative fact but rather incorporates the essential aspects of both of the established categories. We therefore propose a new category, which we term social framework, to refer to *the use of general*[31] conclusions from social science research in determining factual issues in a specific case.

[M]easuring social frameworks according to broad evidentiary policy reveals no general bar to this third use of social science in law. Social frameworks can make the existence of a fact at issue in a legal proceeding

---

31. The conclusions of social science research are "general" to the extent that they are informed by a theory of some aspect of human behavior.

more probable or less probable than it would otherwise appear. Frameworks run little risk of inflaming a juror's emotions or taking advantage of a juror's credulity. They can, with careful presentation, clarify rather than confuse the issues to be decided at trial. Frameworks often tell jurors something they do not already know, or disabuse them of common but erroneous perceptions. And while the use of frameworks should be constrained by the concerns expressed in the rule against character evidence, numerous exceptions to that rule suggest ample opportunity for the application of frameworks.

SELECTED BIBLIOGRAPHY

Fraher, Adjudicative Facts, Non-Evidence Facts, and Permissible Jury Background Information, 62 Indiana Law Journal 333 (1987).

Mansfield, Jury Notice, 74 Georgia Law Journal 395 (1985).

Meadow and Sunstein, Statistics, Not Experts, 51 Duke Law Journal 629 (2001).

Mosteller, Syndromes and Politics in Criminal Trials and Evidence Law, 46 Duke Law Journal 461 (1996).

Tanford, Thinking About Elephants: Admonitions, Empirical Research and Legal Policy, 60 University of Missouri-Kansas City Law Review 645 (1992).

SECTION II. CONTEXTS FOR DETERMINING FUTURE FACTS

At many junctures, the law calls for an estimation of what will happen in the future. The likelihood of future criminality, for example, is frequently treated as an issue of fact in bail, parole, and death penalty statutes. Increasingly, the foreseeable likelihood of harm is a central fact in determining tort liability when the harm is realized. The following cases examine the use of social science to provide decision makers with empirical contexts for determining each of these "facts."

A. BAIL

The prediction of one type of behavior, failure to appear at trial, has long played a central role in determining the pretrial release of criminal defendants. More recently, the prediction of another type of behavior, crime while awaiting trial, has been included among the factors to be considered in making pretrial release decisions.

REPORT OF THE COMMITTEE ON THE JUDICIARY UNITED STATES SENATE, 1983

Senate Report 98–225.

Comprehensive Crime Control Act of 1983: Title I-Bail Reform

The concept of permitting an assessment of defendant dangerousness in the pretrial release decision has been widely supported, and has been specifically endorsed by such diverse groups as the American Bar Association, the National Conference of Commissioners on Uniform State Laws, the National District Attorneys Association, and the National Association of Pretrial Service Agencies. In addition, the laws of several States recognize the validity of weighing the issue of the risk a released defendant may pose to community safety, and the release provisions of District of Columbia Code, passed by the Congress in 1970, specifically recognize that defendant dangerousness is an appropriate consideration in setting conditions of pretrial release and may also serve as a basis for pretrial detention.

This broad base of support for giving judges the authority to weigh risks to community safety in pretrial release decisions is a reflection of the deep public concern, which the Committee shares, about the growing problem of crimes committed by persons on release. In a recent study of release practices in eight jurisdictions, approximately one out of every six defendants in the sample studied were rearrested during the pretrial period—one-third of these defendants were rearrested more than once, and some were rearrested as many as four times.[14] Similar levels of pretrial criminality were reported in a study of release practices in the District of Columbia, where thirteen percent of all felony defendants released were rearrested. Among defendants released on surety bond, which under the District of Columbia Code, like the Bail Reform Act, is the form of release reserved for those defendants who are the most serious bail risks, pretrial rearrest occurred at the alarming rate of twenty-five percent.[15] The disturbing rate of recidivism among released defendants requires the law to recognize that the danger a defendant may pose to others should receive at least as much consideration in the pretrial release determination as the likelihood that he will not appear for trial.

In facing the problem of how to change current bail laws to provide appropriate authority to deal with dangerous defendants seeking release, the Committee concluded that while such measures as permitting consideration of community safety in setting release conditions and providing for revocation of release upon the commission of a crime during the pretrial period may serve to reduce the rate of pretrial recidivism, and that these measures therefore should be incorporated in this chapter, there is a small but identifiable group of particularly dangerous defendants as to whom neither the imposition of stringent release conditions nor the prospect of revocation of release can reasonably assure the safety of the community or other persons. It is with respect to this limited group of offenders that the courts must be given the power to deny release pending trial.

------

14. Lazar Institute, Pretrial Release: An Evaluation of Defendant Outcomes and Program Impact 48 (Washington, D.C., August 1981).

15. Institute for Law and Social Research, Pretrial Release and Misconduct in the District of Columbia 41 (April 1980).

BAIL REFORM ACT OF 1984

18 U.S.C.A. § 3142.

(f) Detention hearing

The judicial officer shall hold a hearing to determine whether any condition or combination of conditions [w]ill reasonably assure the appearance of [a criminal defendant at trial] as required and the safety of any other person and the community—

(1) upon motion of the attorney for the Government, in a case that involves—

(A) a crime of violence;

(B) an offense for which the maximum sentence is life imprisonment or death;

(C) an offense for which a maximum term of imprisonment of ten years or more is prescribed in the Controlled Substances Act (21 U.S.C.A. 801 et seq.), the Controlled Substances Import and Export Act (21 U.S.C.A. 951 et seq.), or section 1 of the Act of September 15, 1980 (21 U.S.C.A. 955a); or

(D) any felony if such person has been convicted of two or more offenses described in subparagraphs (A) through (C) of this paragraph, or two or more State or local offenses that would have been offenses described in subparagraphs (A) through (C) of this paragraph if a circumstance giving rise to Federal jurisdiction had existed, or a combination of such offenses; or

(2) upon motion of the attorney for the Government or upon the judicial officer's own motion in a case, that involves—

(A) a serious risk that such person will flee; or

(B) a serious risk that such person will obstruct or attempt to obstruct justice, or threaten, injure, or intimidate, or attempt to threaten, injure, or intimidate, a prospective witness or juror.

[(g)] Factors to be considered

The judicial officer shall, in determining whether there are conditions of release that will reasonably assure the appearance of the person as required and the safety of any other person and the community, take into account the available information concerning:

(1) the nature and circumstances of the offense charged, including whether the offense is a crime of violence or involves a narcotic drug;

(2) the weight of the evidence against the person;

(3) the history and characteristics of the person, including:

(A) the person's character, physical and mental condition, family ties, employment, financial resources, length of residence in the community, community ties, past conduct, history relating to drug or alcohol abuse, criminal history, and record concerning appearance at court proceedings; and

(B) whether, at the time of the current offense or arrest, the person was on probation, on parole, or on other release pending trial, sentencing, appeal, or completion of sentence for an offense under Federal, State, or local law; and

(4) the nature and seriousness of the danger to any person or the community that would be posed by the person's release.

UNITED STATES v. SALERNO

Supreme Court of the United States, 1987.
481 U.S. 739, 107 S.Ct. 2095, 95 L.Ed.2d 697.

■ CHIEF JUSTICE REHNQUIST delivered the opinion of the Court.

The Bail Reform Act of 1984 allows a federal court to detain an arrestee pending trial if the government demonstrates by clear and convincing evidence after an adversary hearing that no release conditions "will reasonably assure ... the safety of any other person and the community." The United States Court of Appeals for the Second Circuit struck down this provision of the Act as facially unconstitutional, because, in that court's words, this type of pretrial detention violates "substantive due process."

[T]he Court of Appeals concluded that "the Due Process Clause prohibits pretrial detention on the ground of danger to the community as a regulatory measure, without regard to the duration of the detention." 794 F.2d, at 71. Respondents characterize the Due Process Clause as erecting an impenetrable "wall" in this area that "no governmental interest—rational, important, compelling or otherwise—may surmount." Brief for Respondents 16.

We do not think the Clause lays down any such categorical imperative. We have repeatedly held that the government's regulatory interest in community safety can, in appropriate circumstances, outweigh an individual's liberty interest. For example, in times of war or insurrection, when society's interest is at its peak, the government may detain individuals whom the government believes to be dangerous. See Ludecke v. Watkins, 335 U.S. 160, 68 S.Ct. 1429, 92 L.Ed. 1881 (1948) (approving unreviewable Executive power to detain enemy aliens in time of war); Moyer v. Peabody, 212 U.S. 78, 84–85, 29 S.Ct. 235, 236–237, 53 L.Ed. 410 (1909) (rejecting due process claim of individual jailed without probable cause by Governor in time of insurrection). Even outside the exigencies of war, we have found that sufficiently compelling governmental interests can justify detention of dangerous persons. Thus, we have found no absolute constitutional barrier to detention of potentially dangerous resident aliens pending deportation proceedings. Carlson v. Landon, 342 U.S. 524, 537–542, 72 S.Ct. 525, 532–535, 96 L.Ed. 547 (1952); Wong Wing v. United States, 163 U.S. 228, 16 S.Ct. 977, 41 L.Ed. 140 (1896). We have also held that the government may detain mentally unstable individuals who present a danger to the public, Addington v. Texas, 441 U.S. 418, 99 S.Ct. 1804, 60 L.Ed.2d 323 (1979), and dangerous defendants who become incompetent to stand trial, Jackson v. Indiana, 406 U.S. 715, 731–739, 92 S.Ct. 1845, 1854–1858, 32 L.Ed.2d 435 (1972); Greenwood v. United States, 350 U.S. 366, 76 S.Ct. 410, 100 L.Ed. 412 (1956). We have approved of postarrest regulatory detention of juveniles when they present a continuing danger to the community. Schall v. Martin [467 U.S. 253 (1984)]. Even competent adults may face substantial liberty restrictions as a result of the operation of our criminal justice system. If the police suspect an individual of a crime, they may arrest and hold him until a neutral magistrate determines whether probable cause exists. Gerstein v. Pugh, 420 U.S. 103, 95 S.Ct. 854, 43 L.Ed.2d 54 (1975). Finally, respondents concede and the Court of Appeals noted that an arrestee may be incarcerated until trial if he presents a risk of flight, see Bell v. Wolfish, 441 U.S., at 534, 99 S.Ct., at 1871, or a danger to witnesses.

Respondents characterize all of these cases as exceptions to the "general rule" of substantive due process that the government may not detain a person prior to a judgment of guilt in a criminal trial. Such a "general rule" may freely be conceded, but we think that these cases show a sufficient number of exceptions to the rule that the congressional action challenged here can hardly be characterized as totally novel. Given the well-established authority of the government, in special circumstances, to restrain individuals' liberty prior to or even without criminal trial and conviction, we think that the present statute providing for pretrial detention on the basis of dangerousness must be evaluated in precisely the same manner that we evaluated the laws in the cases discussed above.

The government's interest in preventing crime by arrestees is both legitimate and compelling. De Veau v. Braisted, 363 U.S. 144, 155, 80 S.Ct. 1146, 1152, 4 L.Ed.2d 1109 (1960). In *Schall,* supra, we recognized the strength of the State's interest in preventing juvenile crime. This general concern with crime prevention is no less compelling when the suspects are adults. Indeed, "[t]he harm suffered by the victim of a crime is not dependent upon the age of the perpetrator." Schall v. Martin, 467 U.S., at 264–265, 104 S.Ct., at 2410. The Bail Reform Act of 1984 responds to an even more particularized governmental interest than the interest we sustained in *Schall.* The statute we upheld in *Schall* permitted pretrial detention of any juvenile arrested on any charge after a showing that the individual might commit some undefined further crimes. The Bail Reform Act, in contrast, narrowly focuses on a particularly acute problem in which the government interests are overwhelming. The Act operates only on individuals who have been arrested for a specific category of extremely serious offenses. 18 U.S.C.A. § 3142(f). Congress specifically found that these individuals are far more likely to be responsible for dangerous acts in the community after arrest. See S.Rep. No. 98–225, pp. 6–7. Nor is the Act by any means a scattershot attempt to incapacitate those who are merely suspected of these serious crimes. The government must first of all demonstrate probable cause to believe that the charged crime has been committed by the arrestee, but that is not enough. In a full-blown adversary hearing, the government must convince a neutral decisionmaker by clear and convincing evidence that no conditions of release can reasonably assure the safety of the community or any person. 18 U.S.C.A. § 3142(f). While the government's general interest in preventing crime is compelling, even this interest is heightened when the government musters convincing proof that the arrestee, already indicted or held to answer for a serious crime, presents a demonstrable danger to the community. Under these narrow circumstances, society's interest in crime prevention is at its greatest.

[A]s we stated in *Schall,* "there is nothing inherently unattainable about a prediction of future criminal conduct." Id., (at 278, 104 S.Ct., at 2417).

[T]he judgment of the Court of Appeals is therefore *reversed.*

NOTE

1. **Bail Guidelines in Operation.** J. Goldkamp, M. Gottfredson, P. Jones, and D. Weiland, Personal Liberty and Community Safety: Pretrial Release in the Criminal Court (1995), describe the development and implementation of bail guidelines in several cities. In Maricopa County (Phoenix), Arizona, for example, the researchers gathered data on a large number of variables from 2,200 felony cases. Defendants were followed for 90 days following pretrial release to determine the extent of failure to appear at trial or rearrest for a new crime. Statistical analyses identified eight factors that were predictive of failure to appear (FTA) or recidivism. These factors were combined in a "Classification Worksheet," that is completed by the local Pretrial Services Agency on all defendants in jail. The worksheet is reproduced below.

Risk Group Calculations			
Check the Applicable Categories Below			Enter Below
Beginning Score of....		1	1
☐ Prior FTAs	☐ One .... ☐ Two or more	36 40	
☐ Police: Flight Risk Facts	☐ Police note facts defendant might flee	67	
☐ Property Offense	☐ Charges involve Property........................	34	
☐ Defendant Lives Alone	☐ Lives alone	37	
☐ Robbery Offense	☐ Charges involve robbery........................	45	

☐	Police Risk with FTAs	☐ ☐	With one prior FTA.............. With two or more...............	8 17	
☐	Police Risk and Lives Alone	☐	Police: flight risk and lives alone	28	
	TOTAL COLUMN IN SPACE AT RIGHT				

Points	Risk Group
1 to 34	Group 1 [ ]
35 to 67	Group 2 [ ]
68 to 107	Group 3 [ ]
108 or more	Group 4 [ ]

"Police" refers to a notation on the police arrest report that the arresting officer believes that the defendant poses a risk of flight.

The follow-up revealed the following rates of "failure" (FTA or rearrest) while on pretrial release:

Risk Group	Percent Failure
1	7
2	15
3	20
4	53

The total failure rate was 17 percent. Approximately two-thirds of the failures were rearrests and one-third were FTA.

Based on this research, courts in Maricopa County now rely on the risk group classification, along with a ranking of the severity of the pending charges, as "guidelines" in making bail decisions. Courts now accept the guideline suggestions in 78 percent of the cases. For example, a low score on the seriousness of the charges (e.g., assault, drug possession) and placement in Risk Group 1 or 2 results in a presumptive guideline decision of release on the defendant's own recognizance. A high score on the seriousness of the charges (e.g., murder, sexual assault) and a placement in Risk Group 4 results in a guideline suggestion for bail being set for $10,000 to $20,000, which often results in pretrial detention. Initial evaluation of the use of guidelines in Maricopa County showed that when courts deviate from the guidelines, they almost always impose higher bail than the guidelines recommend.

B.   PAROLE

In many states, the role of the judge in criminal sentencing is simply to set the upper bound of time that a convicted offender can spend in prison, within the constraints of the applicable sentencing statute. The actual time spent incarcerated—up to the court-imposed maximum—is determined by an administrative agency, often called a parole board. These agencies are created by statute or, in a few states, are incorporated in the state constitution. Some parole boards, in setting the length of time an offender spends in prison, make explicit reference to social science estimates of the likelihood that he or she will offend again.

[GEORGIA] STATE BOARD OF PARDONS AND PAROLES
Parole Decision Guidelines (1998)

Parole Decision Guidelines help the Board make a more consistent, soundly based, prompt, and explainable parole decision. Guidelines help the Board decide on a tentative parole month for the inmate or decide that the inmate will complete his sentence without parole. When making decisions, the Board may depart from the Guidelines recommendation and make an independent decision using the full discretion given it under Georgia Law. The length of the prison sentence imposed by the court will be considered in establishing a tentative parole month.

[GEORGIA] STATE BOARD OF PARDONS AND PAROLES
Crime Severity Levels (1998)

The Crime Severity Level is selected from the table of offenses listed below. [I]f the inmate is serving a sentence for multiple offenses, the most serious offense will determine the Crime Severity Level.

LEVEL I

Bad Checks—Under $2,000

Credit Card Theft

Theft of Vehicle—not to sell; 1st offense

LEVEL II

Bad Checks—$2,000 or more

Theft—$1,000 to $4,999

Theft of Vehicle—not to sell; 2nd offense

LEVEL III

Terroristic Threats

Theft—$5,000 to $10,000

Theft of Vehicle to sell

LEVEL IV

Arson—over $2,000

Non-residential Burglary—over $5,000

Theft—over $10,000

LEVEL V

Aggravated Assault

Residential Burglary

Homicide by Vehicle While DUI

LEVEL VI

Kidnapping—no ransom, no injury

Opiate-related Violations, 14 to 27 grams

Voluntary Manslaughter

LEVEL VII

Armed Robbery—Sentence not Life

Kidnapping—for ransom or with injury, sentence not Life

Rape—sentence not Life

————

[GEORGIA] STATE BOARD OF PARDONS AND PAROLES
Parole Success Factors (1998)

ITEM A.　AGE AT FIRST COMMITMENT　　　　　　　　　　———
　　　　　(26 or over = 5)
　　　　　(22–25 = 3)
　　　　　(18–21 = 2)
　　　　　(17 or less = 0)

ITEM B.　PRIOR FELONY CONVICTIONS (JUVENILE AND　———
　　　　　ADULT)
　　　　　(None = 3)
　　　　　(1 = 2)
　　　　　(2–3 = 1)
　　　　　(4 or more = 0)

ITEM C.　PRIOR FELONY INCARCERATIONS SINCE AGE　———
　　　　　17
　　　　　(None = 2)
　　　　　(1 = 1)
　　　　　(2 or more = 0)

ITEM D.　PROBATION AND PAROLE FAILURE　　　　　　———
　　　　　(No Failures = 4)
　　　　　(Probation Only = 2)
　　　　　(Parole Only = 1)
　　　　　(Both = 0)

ITEM E.　NO USE, POSSESSION OR ATTEMPT TO OBTAIN　———
　　　　　HEROIN, OPIATE DRUGS, OR COCAINE
　　　　　(No = 1)
　　　　　(Yes = 0)

ITEM F.　COMMITMENT OFFENSE DID NOT INVOLVE　———
　　　　　BURGLARY OR FORGERY
　　　　　(No = 2)
　　　　　(Yes = 0)

ITEM G.　FULLY EMPLOYED DURING 6 MONTHS PRIOR　———
　　　　　TO CURRENT OFFENSE
　　　　　(Yes = 1)
　　　　　(No = 0)

ITEM H.   HAD WRAT SCORE OF 8 OR HIGHER AT TIME   _____
OF DIAGNOSTIC TESTING
(Yes = 2)
(No = 0)
PAROLE SUCCESS LIKELIHOOD SCORE (TOTAL)   _____

_____

[GEORGIA] STATE BOARD OF PARDONS AND PAROLES
Guidelines Recommended Months to Serve (1998)

Read across the Crime Severity Level and down from the Parole Success Likelihood score to find the Guidelines recommended months to serve. For certain Crime Severity Level V, VI, and VII offenses, the Guidelines recommendation will be one-third of the court-imposed sentence length or the grid recommendation, *whichever is greater*. For inmates serving for non-violent offenses with prior incarcerations, the recommendation will be one-third of the court imposed sentence or the Grid recommendation, whichever is greater. For inmates serving for a violent offense with no prior incarceration for a violent offense, the recommendation will be fifty percent of the court imposed sentence or the Grid recommendation, whichever is greater. For inmates serving for a violent offense with prior incarceration for a violent offense, the recommendation will be seventy-five percent of the court imposed sentence or the Grid recommendation, whichever is greater. The Board, using its discretion in specific cases, may depart from the Guidelines recommendation.

Parole Success Likelihood Score

CRIME SEVERITY LEVEL	EXCELLENT 14–20	AVERAGE 9–13	POOR 0–8
I	10	16	22
II	12	18	24
III	14	20	26
IV	16	22	28
V	34	40	52
VI	52	62	78
VII	72	84	102

NOTES

1. Achievement Test. The WRAT Score of 8 mentioned in Item H of the Parole Success Factors refers to a score on the Wide Range Achievement Test equivalent to that earned by the average eighth grader in a national sample. The test measures abilities at reading, spelling, and arithmetic. J. Salvia and J. Ysseldyke, Assessment (8th ed. 2001).

2. Validation Research. The Parole Success Likelihood Score was developed by the Georgia State Board of Pardons and Paroles by studying the behavior of large samples of parolees before the Guidelines project was first implemented in 1979. The Likelihood Score was re-validated in 2001 on 37,455 persons released from Georgia prisons between 1992 and 1997. "Failure" was defined as a return to prison (for the commission of any new crime or violation of the conditions of parole) during the first one, two, or three years after release. (Data provided by Division of Clemency and Parole Selection, Georgia State Board of Pardons and Paroles, July 2001; confirmed July 2005).

PAROLE SUCCESS LIKELIHOOD SCORE

% Failure by Follow-up Period	Excellent 14–20	Average 9–13	Poor 0–8
1 Year	1.9	11.1	22.0
2 Years	6.1	26.5	45.1
3 Years	9.7	36.1	57.6

3.   Constitutionality. The constitutionality of Georgia's use of the Parole Success Likelihood Score in setting "Guidelines Recommended Months to Serve" was upheld against an inmate's Fourteenth Amendment challenge in Sultenfuss v. Snow, 35 F.3d 1494 (11th Cir.1994).

4.   Other States. The Michigan Department of Corrections developed an Assaultive Risk Screening Sheet to aid in parole decision making. Information on 350 variables was collected on each of 1200 male inmates released on parole. The dependent measure was arrest and return to prison for the commission of a new *violent* crime during the first 14 months on parole. Statistical analyses were then performed to ascertain which combination of the 350 variables was associated with recidivism. The flow chart below emerged.

This flow chart was then applied to a new group of male prisoners released on parole. The following results were obtained:

Assaultive Risk Screening Scores

	Very Low	Low	Middle	High	Very High
Percent Failure	3	7	12	21	40

A male prisoner's score on the Assaultive Risk Screening Sheet figures heavily in the Parole Board's determination of the length of time he will spend in prison. For example, 71 percent of those who score Very Low, but only 17 percent of those who score Very High, are paroled at their earliest release date. (Research Division, Michigan Department of Corrections, June 2001; confirmed June 2005).

An attempt to generalize the Assaultive Risk Screening Sheet to female parolees was not successful. Both because of the small number of female prisoners (approximately 4 percent of the prison population) and because of the low rate of violent recidivism among these women (less than one-third of the male rate), it was not possible to obtain reliable data. For example, between 1974 and 1978, a total of only 10 female prisoners in the state scored in the Very High range of the Assaultive Risk Screening Sheet, and only one of these ("10 percent") committed a new violent crime on parole. Murphy, Final Report: Michigan Female Risk Prediction Study (1988). In light of this research, the Michigan Department of Corrections issued Policy Directive Number 05.01.135 in 1998. Section II (B) of this Directive reads: "All newly committed female prisoners shall be automatically designated very low risk without being screened."

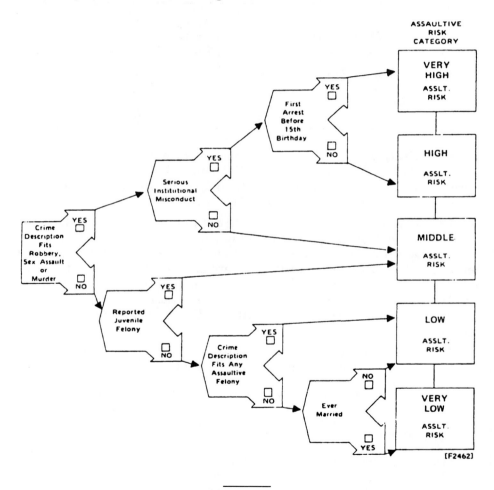

KANSAS v. HENDRICKS

Supreme Court of the United States, 1997.
521 U.S. 346, 117 S.Ct. 2072, 138 L.Ed.2d 501.

■ JUSTICE THOMAS delivered the opinion of the Court.

In 1994, Kansas enacted the Sexually Violent Predator Act, which establishes procedures for the civil commitment of persons who, due to a "mental abnormality" or a "personality disorder," are likely to engage in "predatory acts of sexual violence." Kan. Stat. Ann. § 59–29a01 et seq. (1994). The State invoked the Act for the first time to commit Leroy Hendricks, an inmate who had a long history of sexually molesting children, and who was scheduled for release from prison shortly after the Act became law. Hendricks challenged his commitment on, inter alia, "substantive" due process, double jeopardy, and ex post facto grounds. The Kansas Supreme Court invalidated the Act, holding that its precommitment condition of a "mental abnormality" did not satisfy what the court perceived to be the "substantive" due process requirement that involuntary civil commitment must be predicated on a finding of "mental illness." In re Hendricks, 259 Kan. 246, 261, 912 P.2d 129, 138 (1996).

[T]he Act defined a "sexually violent predator" as:

"any person who has been convicted of or charged with a sexually violent offense and who suffers from a mental abnormality or personality disorder which makes the person likely to engage in the predatory acts of sexual violence." § 59–29a02(a).

A "mental abnormality" was defined, in turn, as a "congenital or acquired condition affecting the emotional or volitional capacity which predisposes the person to commit sexually violent offenses in a degree constituting such person a menace to the health and safety of others." § 59–29a02(b).

[T]he statute thus requires proof of more than a mere predisposition to violence; rather, it requires evidence of past sexually violent behavior and a present mental condition that creates a likelihood of such conduct in the future if the person is not incapacitated. As we have recognized, "[p]revious instances of violent behavior are an important indicator of future violent tendencies." Heller v. Doe, 509 U.S. 312, 323 (1993); see also Schall v. Martin, 467 U.S. 253, 278 (1984) (explaining that "from a legal point of view there is nothing inherently unattainable about a prediction of future criminal conduct").

A finding of dangerousness, standing alone, is ordinarily not a sufficient ground upon which to justify indefinite involuntary commitment. We have sustained civil commitment statutes when they have coupled proof of dangerousness with the proof of some additional factor, such as a "mental illness" or "mental abnormality." See, e.g., Heller, supra, at 314–315 (Kentucky statute permitting commitment of "mentally retarded" or "mentally ill" and dangerous individual). These added statutory requirements serve to limit involuntary civil confinement to those who suffer from a volitional impairment rendering them dangerous beyond their control. The Kansas Act is plainly of a kind with these other civil commitment statutes: It requires a finding of future dangerousness, and then links that finding to the existence of a "mental abnormality" or "personality disorder" that makes it difficult, if not impossible, for the person to control his dangerous behavior. The precommitment requirement of a "mental abnormality" or "personality disorder" is consistent with the requirements of these other statutes that we have upheld in that it narrows the class of persons eligible for confinement to those who are unable to control their dangerousness.

Hendricks nonetheless argues that our earlier cases dictate a finding of "mental illness" as a prerequisite for civil commitment. He then asserts that a "mental abnormality" is not equivalent to a "mental illness" because it is a term coined by the Kansas Legislature, rather than by the psychiatric community. Contrary to Hendricks' assertion, the term "mental illness" is devoid of any talismanic significance. [W]e have never required state legislatures to adopt any particular nomenclature in drafting civil commitment statutes. [T]o the extent that the civil commitment statutes we have considered set forth criteria relating to an individual's inability to control his dangerousness, the Kansas Act sets forth comparable criteria and Hendricks' condition doubtless satisfies those criteria. The mental health professionals who evaluated Hendricks diagnosed him as suffering from pedophilia, a condition the psychiatric profession itself classifies as a serious mental disorder. See, e.g., [American Psychiatric Association, Diagnostic and Statistical Manual of Mental Disorders (4th ed. 1994)], at 524–525, 527–528. Hendricks even conceded that, when he becomes "stressed out," he cannot "control the urge" to molest children. This admitted lack of volitional control, coupled with a prediction of future dangerousness, adequately distinguishes Hendricks from other dangerous persons who are perhaps more properly dealt with exclusively through criminal proceedings. Hendricks' diagnosis as a pedophile, which qualifies as a "mental abnormality" under the Act, thus plainly suffices for due process purposes.

We granted Hendricks' cross-petition to determine whether the Act violates the Constitution's double jeopardy prohibition or its ban on ex post facto lawmaking. The thrust of Hendricks' argument is that the Act establishes criminal proceedings; hence confinement under it necessarily constitutes punishment. He contends that where, as here, newly enacted "punishment" is predicated upon past conduct for which he has already been convicted and forced to serve a prison sentence, the Constitution's Double Jeopardy and Ex Post Facto Clauses are violated.

[A]s a threshold matter, commitment under the Act does not implicate either of the two primary objectives of criminal punishment: retribution or deterrence. The Act's purpose is not retributive because it does not affix culpability for prior criminal conduct. Instead, such conduct is used solely for evidentiary purposes, either to demonstrate that a "mental abnormality" exists or to support a finding of future dangerousness. [N]or can it be said that the legislature intended the Act to function as a deterrent. Those persons committed under the Act are, by definition, suffering from a "mental abnormality" or a "personality disorder" that prevents them from exercising adequate control over their behavior. Such persons are therefore unlikely to be deterred by the threat of confinement.

[W]here the State has "disavowed any punitive intent"; limited confinement to a small segment of particularly dangerous individuals; provided strict procedural safeguards; directed that confined persons be segregated from the general prison population and afforded the same status as others who have been civilly committed; recommended treatment if such is possible; and permitted immediate release upon a showing that the individual is no longer dangerous or mentally impaired, we cannot say that it acted with punitive intent. We therefore hold that the Act does not establish criminal proceedings and that involuntary confinement pursuant to the Act is not punitive. Our conclusion that the Act is nonpunitive thus removes an essential prerequisite for both Hendricks' double jeopardy and ex post facto claims.

[W]e hold that the Kansas Sexually Violent Predator Act comports with due process requirements and neither runs afoul of double jeopardy principles nor constitutes an exercise in impermissible ex post facto law-making. Accordingly, the judgment of the Kansas Supreme Court is reversed.

SEXUALLY VIOLENT PREDATORS ACT

Virginia Acts, Chapter 989, 2003.

"Sexually violent predator" means any person who (i) has been convicted of a sexually violent offense or has been charged with a sexually violent offense and is unrestorably incompetent to stand trial [a]nd (ii) because of a mental abnormality or personality disorder, finds it difficult to control his predatory behavior which makes him likely to engage in sexually violent acts.

[T]he CRC [Commitment Review Committee] shall consist of seven members to be appointed as follows: (i) three full-time employees of the Department of Corrections, appointed by the Director of the Department of Corrections; (ii) three full-time employees of the Department of Mental Health, Mental Retardation and Substance Abuse Services, appointed by the Commissioner, at least one of whom shall be a psychiatrist or psychologist licensed to practice in the Commonwealth of Virginia who is skilled in the diagnosis of mental abnormalities and personality disorders associated with violent sex offenders; and (iii) one assistant or deputy attorney general, appointed by the Attorney General.

[E]ach month, the Director [of the Department of Corrections] shall review the database of prisoners incarcerated for sexually violent offenses and identify all such prisoners who are scheduled for release from prison within 10 months from the date of such review who receive a score of four or more on the Rapid Risk Assessment for Sexual Offender Recidivism or a like score on a comparable, scientifically validated instrument as designated by the Commissioner [of the Department of Mental Health, Mental Retardation and Substance Abuse Services].

[F]ollowing the examination and review of a prisoner, [t]he CRC shall recommend that such prisoner (i) be committed as a sexually violent predator pursuant to this article; (ii) not be committed, but be placed in a conditional release program as a less restrictive alternative; or (iii) not be committed because he does not meet the definition of a sexually violent predator. [I]n determining whether to file a petition to civilly commit a prisoner under this article, [t]he CRC recommendation is not binding on the Attorney General.

[T]he Attorney General or the person who is the subject of the petition shall have the right to a trial by jury. [I]f a jury determines a person to be a sexually violent predator, a unanimous verdict shall be required. If no demand is made by either party for a trial by jury, the trial shall be before the court. [T]he court or jury shall determine whether, by clear and convincing evidence, the person who is the subject of the petition is a sexually violent predator.

[T]he committing court shall conduct a hearing 12 months after the date of commitment to assess each committed person's need for inpatient hospitalization. A hearing for assessment shall be conducted at yearly intervals for five years and at biennial intervals thereafter.

[A]ll proceedings conducted hereunder are civil proceedings.

––––––––

NOTE

1. Actuarial Prediction. The Rapid Risk Assessment for Sex Offense Recidivism (RRASOR) mentioned in the Act is an actuarial risk assessment instrument consisting of four items, scored as follows:

		Score
1.	Prior Sex Offenses (not including index offense)	
	None	0
	1 conviction or 1–2 charges	1
	2–3 convictions or 3–5 charges	2
	4+ convictions or 6+ charges	3
2.	Age at Release (current age)	
	more than 25	0
	less than 25	1
3.	Victim Gender	
	only females	0
	any males	1
4.	Relationship to Victim	
	only related	0
	any non-related	1

A person's score on the RRASOR is the sum of his scores on these four items. The RRASOR was empirically developed by studying large samples of male offenders in Canadian prisons and forensic hospitals. R. Hanson, The Development of a Brief Actuarial Risk Scale for Sexual Offense Recidivism (1997). A score of 4 or more on the RRASOR was associated with a 5–year sex offense recidivism rate of 37 percent and a 10–year sex offense recidivism rate of 55 percent. Subsequent to the development of the

RRASOR, a new actuarial instrument, called the Static–99, has been created. This instrument includes the four items on the RRASOR plus six additional items (e.g., never married, noncontact sex offenses [such as obscene telephone calls]) and has somewhat higher predictive validity than the RRASOR. Hanson and Thornton, Improving Risk Assessment for Sex Offenders: A Comparison of Three Actuarial Scales, 24 Law and Human Behavior 119 (2000).

C. CAPITAL PUNISHMENT

The death penalty statutes of several states specify that execution of first-degree murderers is contingent upon the jury making the factual finding that the defendant is likely to repeat his or her violent acts. Some social scientists have served as expert witnesses for the prosecution and some for the defense in capital sentencing hearings to provide estimates of the risk that defendants pose. Other social scientists have participated in writing briefs and as expert witnesses at hearings, challenging the empirical basis of the estimates of risk that their colleagues offer.

BAREFOOT v. ESTELLE

Supreme Court of the United States, 1983.
463 U.S. 880, 103 S.Ct. 3383, 77 L.Ed.2d 1090.

■ JUSTICE WHITE delivered the opinion of the Court.

[Thomas Barefoot was convicted of the capital murder of a police officer. At a separate sentencing hearing, the same jury considered the two questions put to it under the Texas death penalty statute: whether the conduct causing the death was "committed deliberately and with reasonable expectation that the death of the deceased or another would result," and whether "there is a probability that the defendant would commit criminal acts of violence that would constitute a continuing threat to society." The jury's affirmative answer to both questions required the imposition of the death penalty.]

Petitioner's merits submission is that his death sentence must be set aside because the Constitution of the United States barred the testimony of the two psychiatrists who testified against him at the punishment hearing. [I]t is urged that psychiatrists, individually and as a group, are incompetent to predict with an acceptable degree of reliability that a particular criminal will commit other crimes in the future and so represent a danger to the community.

[T]he suggestion that no psychiatrist's testimony may be presented with respect to a defendant's future dangerousness is somewhat like asking us to disinvent the wheel. In the first place, it is contrary to our cases. If the likelihood of a defendant committing further crimes is a constitutionally acceptable criterion for imposing the death penalty, which it is, Jurek v. Texas, 428 U.S. 262, 96 S.Ct. 2950, 49 L.Ed.2d 929 (1976), and if it is not impossible for even a lay person sensibly to arrive at that conclusion, it makes little sense, if any, to submit that psychiatrists, out of the entire universe of persons who might have an opinion on the issue, would know so little about the subject that they should not be permitted to testify. In *Jurek,* seven Justices rejected the claim that it was impossible to predict future behavior and that dangerousness was therefore an invalid consideration in imposing the death penalty.

[A]cceptance of petitioner's position that expert testimony about future dangerousness is far too unreliable to be admissible would immediately call into question those other contexts in which predictions of future behavior are constantly made [such as the civil commitment of the mentally ill.]

[I]n the second place, the rules of evidence generally extant at the federal and state levels anticipate that relevant, unprivileged evidence should be admitted and its weight left to the factfinder, who would have the benefit of cross examination and contrary evidence by the opposing party. Psychiatric testimony predicting dangerousness may be countered not only as erroneous in a particular case but as generally so unreliable that it should be ignored. If the jury may make up its mind about future dangerousness unaided by psychiatric testimony, jurors should not be barred from hearing the views of the State's psychiatrists along with opposing views of the defendant's doctors.

Third, petitioner's view mirrors the position expressed in the *amicus* brief of the American Psychiatric Association (APA). [H]owever, the same view was presented and rejected in Estelle v. Smith, [451 U.S. 454, 101 S.Ct. 1866, 68 L.Ed.2d 359 (1981).] We are no more convinced now that the view of the APA should be converted into a constitutional rule barring an entire category of expert testimony. We are not persuaded that such testimony is almost entirely unreliable and that the factfinder and the adversary system will not be competent to uncover, recognize, and take due account of its shortcomings.

The *amicus* does not suggest that there are not other views held by members of the Association or of the profession generally. Indeed, as this case and others indicate, there are those doctors who are quite willing to testify at the sentencing hearing, who think, and will say, that they know what they are talking about, and who expressly disagree with the Association's point of view.[7] Furthermore, their qualifications as experts are regularly accepted by the courts. If they are so obviously wrong and should be discredited, there should be no insuperable problem in doing so by calling members of the Association who are of that view and who confidently assert that opinion in their *amicus* brief. Neither petitioner nor the Association suggests that psychiatrists are always wrong with respect to

---

7. [W]e are aware that many mental health professionals have questioned the usefulness of psychiatric predictions of future dangerousness in light of studies indicating that such predictions are often inaccurate.

[A]ll of these professional doubts about the usefulness of psychiatric predictions can be called to the attention of the jury. Petitioner's entire argument, as well as that of Justice Blackmun's dissent, is founded on the premise that a jury will not be able to separate the wheat from the chaff. We do not share in this low evaluation of the adversary process.

future dangerousness, only most of the time. Yet the submission is that this category of testimony should be excised entirely from all trials. We are unconvinced, however, at least as of now, that the adversary process cannot be trusted to sort out the reliable from the unreliable evidence and opinion about future dangerousness, particularly when the convicted felon has the opportunity to present his own side of the case.

[T]he judgment of the District Court is affirmed.

■ JUSTICE BLACKMUN, with whom JUSTICE BRENNAN and JUSTICE MARSHALL join, [d]issenting.

[T]he Court holds that psychiatric testimony about a defendant's future dangerousness is admissible, despite the fact that such testimony is wrong two times out of three. The Court reaches this result—even in a capital case—because, it is said, the testimony is subject to cross-examination and impeachment. In the present state of psychiatric knowledge, this is too much for me.

[At the sentencing hearing, Dr. Grigson, a prosecution psychiatrist, testified on the basis of a hypothetical question, without having examined Barefoot, that] he could diagnose Barefoot "within reasonable psychiatric certainty" as an individual with "a fairly classical, typical, sociopathic personality disorder." He placed Barefoot in the "most severe category" of sociopaths (on a scale of one to ten, Barefoot was "above ten"), and stated that there was no known cure for the condition. Finally, Doctor Grigson testified that whether Barefoot was in society at large or in a prison society there was a *"one hundred percent and absolute"* chance that Barefoot would commit future acts of criminal violence that would constitute a continuing threat to society.

[T]he American Psychiatric Association (APA), participating in this case as *amicus curiae,* informs us that "[t]he unreliability of psychiatric predictions of long-term future dangerousness is by now an established fact within the profession." The APA's best estimate is that *two out of three* predictions of long-term future violence made by psychiatrists are wrong. The Court does not dispute this proposition, and indeed it could not do so; the evidence is overwhelming. For example, [J]ohn Monahan, recognized as "the leading thinker on this issue" even by the State's expert witness at Barefoot's federal habeas corpus hearing, concludes that "the 'best' clinical research currently in existence indicates that psychiatrists and psychologists are accurate in no more than one out of three predictions of violent behavior," even among populations of individuals who are mentally ill and have committed violence in the past. J. Monahan, The Clinical Prediction of Violent Behavior 47–49 (1981). [N]either the Court nor the State of Texas has cited a single reputable scientific source contradicting the unanimous conclusion of professionals in this field that psychiatric predictions of long-term future violence are wrong more often than they are right.[2]

2. Among the many other studies reaching this conclusion are APA Task Force Report. Clinical Aspects of the Violent Individual 28 (1974) (90% error rate "[u]nfortu-

[T]hus, the Court's remarkable observation that "[n]either petitioner nor the [APA] suggests that psychiatrists are *always wrong* with respect to future dangerousness, *only most of the time,*" misses the point completely, and its claim that this testimony was no more problematic than "other relevant evidence against any defendant in a criminal case," is simply incredible. Surely, this Court's commitment to ensuring that death sentences are imposed reliably and reasonably requires that nonprobative and highly prejudicial testimony on the ultimate question of life or death be excluded from a capital sentencing hearing.

Despite its recognition that the testimony at issue was probably wrong and certainly prejudicial, the Court holds this testimony admissible because the Court is "unconvinced ... that the adversary process cannot be trusted to sort out the reliable from the unreliable evidence and opinion about future dangerousness." One can only wonder how juries are to separate valid from invalid expert opinions when the "experts" themselves are so obviously unable to do so. Indeed, the evidence suggests that juries are not effective at assessing the validity of scientific evidence. Gianelli, Scientific Evidence, 80 Colum.L.Rev., at 1239–1240, and n. 319.

[U]ltimately, when the Court knows full well that psychiatrists' predictions of dangerousness are specious, there can be no excuse for imposing on the defendant, on pain of his life, the heavy burden of convincing a jury of laymen of the fraud.

––––––

NOTES

1. Social Framework and Social Authority. There are two distinct uses of social science in *Barefoot*. Dr. Grigson, the psychiatrist testifying as expert witness for the prosecution, presented a clinically-oriented version of what we would call a social framework: given the high risk of recidivism characteristic of sociopaths as a group, Grigson predicted that the defen-

nately ... is the state of the art") (APA, Clinical Aspects); Steadman & Morrissey, The Statistical Prediction of Violent Behavior, 5 Law & Human Behavior 263, 271–273 (1981); Dix, Expert Prediction Testimony in Capital Sentencing; Evidentiary and Constitutional Considerations, 19 Am.Crim.L.Rev. 1, 16 (1981); Schwitzgebel, Prediction of Dangerousness and Its Implications for Treatment, in W. Curran, A. McGarry & C. Petty, Modern Legal Medicine, Psychiatry, and Forensic Science 783, 784–786 (1980); Cocozza & Steadman, Prediction in Psychiatry: An Example of Misplaced Confidence in Experts, 25 Soc.Probs. 265, 272–273 (1978); Report of the [American Psychological Association's] Task Force on the Role of Psychology in the Criminal Justice System, 33 Am.Psychologist 1099, 1110 (1978); Steadman & Cocozza, Psychiatry, Dangerousness and the Repetitively Violent Offender, 69 J. Crim.L. & Criminology 226, 227, 230 (1978); Cocozza & Steadman, The Failure of Psychiatric Predictions of Dangerousness: Clear and Convincing Evidence, 29 Rutgers L.Rev. 1084, 1101 (1976); Diamond, The Psychiatric Prediction of Dangerousness, 123 U.Pa.L.Rev. 439, 451–452 (1974); Ennis & Litwak, Psychiatry and the Presumption of Expertise: Flipping Coins in the Courtroom, 62 Calif.L.Rev. 693, 711–716 (1974). A relatively early study making this point is Rome, Identification of the Dangerous Offender, 42 F.R.D. 185 (1968).

dant—whom he saw as a member of this group—would offend again. The American Psychiatric Association as *amicus,* however, filed a brief claiming that expert testimony such as Grigson's was specious as a matter of legislative fact or social authority. The Association, based on a review of available social science research, argued that there was no empirical basis for the kind of risk assessment demanded by death penalty statutes.

2. New Developments. The dissent in *Barefoot* quoted one researcher as concluding that "psychiatrists and psychologists are accurate in no more than one out of three predictions of violent behavior." While that may have been a valid summary of the empirical evidence in the mid-1980's, a recent study has reported accuracy rates for violence risk assessment far higher than previously obtained. J. Monahan, H. Steadman, E. Silver, P. Appelbaum, P. Robbins, E. Mulvey. L. Roth, T. Grisso, and S. Banks, Rethinking Risk Assessment: The MacArthur Study of Mental Disorder and Violence (2001) assessed over 1,000 people in psychiatric facilities on over 100 risk factors for future violence to others. Patients were followed in the community for several months after discharge from the hospital. The researchers were able to combine the risk factors statistically—rather than clinically—in such a way as to place all subjects into one of five groups, with rates of serious violence in the next several months of 1, 8, 26, 56, and 76 percent, respectively. That is, in the highest group, three-out-of-four people predicted in the hospital to be violent were later found to commit a violent act in the community, rather than the one-out-of-three accuracy rate for clinical prediction quoted in *Barefoot*. Among the risk factors that predicted violence in different groups of patients were prior arrests, substance abuse, having been abused as a child, one's father having abused drugs, having fantasies about being violent, male gender, and young age. Violence risk assessment software based on these data has recently been released. J. Monahan, H. Steadman, P. Appelbaum, T. Grisso, E. Mulvey, L. Roth, P. Robbins, S. Banks, and E. Silver, The Classification of Violence Risk (2005).

STATE v. DAVIS

Supreme Court of New Jersey, 1984.
96 N.J. 611, 477 A.2d 308.

■ PER CURIAM

On April 12, 1983, defendant, Steven Raymond Davis, was indicted for murder. Defendant subsequently pled guilty, and, pursuant to the provisions of N.J.S.A. 2C:11–3c, a penalty trial was scheduled.

[O]n February 8, 1984, defense counsel advised the State that he intended to proffer, in mitigation of a death penalty verdict pursuant to N.J.S.A. 2C:11–3c(5)(h), the expert testimony of Professor Marvin E. Wolfgang, Ph.D. Dr. Wolfgang would testify as to the contents of a report prepared by him on February 7, 1984, that asserted that defendant was a likely candidate "for a thirty year sentence instead of a death sentence" because empirical studies demonstrate that a defendant sharing Mr. Davis' statistical profile "would never again commit another serious crime of any kind" after serving the mandatory minimum thirty year term. The statute provides that if the jury does not determine to impose the death penalty, the defendant shall be sentenced to a term of life imprisonment in which he shall not be eligible for release on parole until he has served a minimum term of thirty years.

Dr. Wolfgang holds a doctorate in sociology and is a member of the faculty of the department of sociology at the University of Pennsylvania. A review of his *curriculum vitae* and published works reveals that for more than twenty-five years a principal focus of Dr. Wolfgang's research has been the study of criminal violence, with specific emphasis upon the psychological and sociological determinants of violent crime. Dr. Wolfgang is described by defendant and *amicus* as an "eminent criminologist" who is an "expert in statistics." He holds no degrees in psychology or psychiatry, and has had no formal training in those fields.

Dr. Wolfgang's report on behalf of Mr. Davis was not based on any personal evaluation of defendant. (In fact, Dr. Wolfgang has never met Mr. Davis.) Rather, the professor relied upon demographic "features" that defendant possessed, and then selectively drew upon statistical research that demonstrates a low rate of recidivism among offenders sharing these demographic features.

His four-page report notes Mr. Davis' present age and that "he will be 57 years old were he sentenced to 30 years without parole as a minimum sentence." Dr. Wolfgang then cites his own research findings and "national statistics" to demonstrate that males aged 55–59 are highly unlikely to commit homicide. Moreover, "after age 29, as age increases crime rates decrease." Next, Dr. Wolfgang notes that according to statistics presented in a 1980 report of the U.S. Department of Justice and in a 1969 study by the New York Division of Parole, murderers are the least likely to commit subsequent offenses of any sort upon release from prison. Thus, according to Dr. Wolfgang, "the best available research shows that persons convicted of first degree murder * * * have the lowest rates of future offending among all types of offenders." The report proceeds to assert that

> [t]aking these factors into account, and recognizing that Mr. Davis has no previous crime record, that he would have served a minimum of 30 years in prison, and were he given this sentence, that he would minimally be 57 years old at the time of release, our conclusion is that Mr. Davis would never again commit another serious crime of any kind.

The State moved to exclude Dr. Wolfgang's testimony on the ground that it is irrelevant to any mitigating factor properly before the jury. The trial court ruled that the proffered testimony would be excluded during the penalty phase since the statement in no way pertained to Mr. Davis' individual character. The court concluded that while "the question of potential for rehabilitation" may be testified to as part of the indicia of a defendant's character, "the statistical approach doesn't tell us anything at all about a given defendant."

[N]J.S.A. 2C:11–3c(5) provides, in pertinent part:

The mitigating factors which may be found by the jury or the court are:

* * *

(h) Any other factor which is relevant to the defendant's character or record or to the circumstances of the offense.

The parties to this action do not dispute that a defendant's potential for rehabilitation is an aspect of his character, and therefore may be considered as a factor militating in favor of a sentence less than death in the penalty phase of a capital proceeding. It is the means by which this defendant seeks to make the showing—through the introduction of statistical evidence of the rehabilitative potential of similarly situated defendants—that has prompted this appeal.

We determine that evidence consisting of statistical data based upon empirical studies can assist the jury in the penalty phase of a capital proceeding in evaluating an individual defendant's potential for rehabilitation as an aspect of his character presented as a mitigating factor under N.J.S.A. 2C:11–3c(5)(h). Accordingly, we hold that, subject to appropriate standards concerning its competency (such as its scientific reliability and the qualifications of the expert witness), evidence of this nature is relevant and admissible.

Evidence of empirical studies and findings, including the statistical presentation and analysis of data, may under appropriate circumstances be sufficiently related to a defendant's rehabilitative potential to satisfy the statutory threshold of relevancy. Such evidence may, in effect, encapsulate ordinary human experience and provide an appropriate frame of reference for a jury's consideration of a defendant's character. For example, insofar as the proffered report in this case focuses primarily on defendant's present age and his age at the time of his earliest possible release, it can be noted that age, as a demographic variable, has consistently been found to be strongly related to subsequent criminal activity. See, e.g., Cocozza & Steadman, "Some Refinements in the Prediction of Dangerous Behavior," 131 Am.J. of Psychiatry 1012 (1974) (examination of possible importance of variables other than those having to do with prior criminal activity, including variety of social and demographic factors, reveals that only one, age, is highly related to predictions of future violence).

Moreover, this kind of information, when presented by experts, can supplement or explain ordinary human experience and can assist laypersons in the deliberative process to reach sound determinations concerning an individual's character. Indeed, it has been observed that a layperson with access to relevant statistics can assess a defendant's rehabilitative potential at least as well as, and possibly better than, those with psychiatric training in this area. Barefoot v. Estelle, 463 U.S. 880, 103 S.Ct. 3383, 77

L.Ed.2d 1090, 1122 (1983) (Blackmun, J., dissenting) (citing American Psychiatric Association Task Force Report, Clinical Aspects of the Violent Individual 28 (1974)); see also J. Monahan, The Clinical Prediction of Violent Behavior, 47–49 (1981) ("the 'best' clinical research currently in existence indicates that psychiatrists and psychologists are accurate in no more than one out of three predictions of violent behavior"); Steadman & Morrissey, "The Statistical Prediction of Violent Behavior," 5 Law & Human Behavior 263, 271–73 (1981); Cocozza & Steadman, "The Failure of Psychiatric Predictions of Dangerousness: Clear and Convincing Evidence," 29 Rutgers L.Rev. 1084, 1101 (1976).

[A]ccordingly, it is our ruling that the proposed testimony of the defendant's expert, reflected in the report proffered in this case, generally satisfies broad standards of relevancy and is therefore admissible as a mitigating factor in the penalty phase of a capital proceeding, pursuant to N.J.S.A. 2C:11–3c(5)(h).

We do not, and, indeed, on this record cannot, determine that the report, in the form presented, is admissible in respects other than relevancy. We consider the report merely as a proffer, sufficient to pose the legal question as to whether the type of evidence it represents satisfies standards of relevancy under N.J.S.A. 2C:11–3c(5)(h). We nonetheless deem it appropriate to comment generally on other aspects of admissibility that will undoubtedly arise in the penalty phase of the trial upon defendant's attempt to introduce this evidence.

The evidence as proffered relates to a subject matter that is appropriately within the competence of experts or specialists. Consequently, the testifying expert witness, Dr. Wolfgang, must be qualified. Further, the subject matter of his testimony must be established as scientifically reliable. We stress, however, that the conventional standards of competency, relating to both the expert's qualifications and the scientific reliability of the subject matter, are not to be strictly applied in this context—the penalty phase of a capital proceeding—in which the choice before the jury is between life and death.

[T]o the extent that evidence of the type sought to be proffered in the case at bar arguably may suffer shortcomings when measured by strict rules of evidential relevance and competence, such deficits will go to the weight of the testimony, properly relegating to the adversarial process the task of "separating the wheat from the chaff." Barefoot v. Estelle, supra, 463 U.S. at ___, 103 S.Ct. at 3398, 77 L.Ed.2d at 1109 (psychiatric testimony concerning defendant's future dangerousness offered pursuant to specific provision in Texas death penalty statute held admissible despite fact that such testimony is not based on personal examination of defendant).

However, relaxed standards for admissibility are not to be equated with automatic admissibility. Judicial tolerance is not judicial license. For example, in this case the court may, upon a persuasive showing, consider the report, or any of its component parts, incomplete and therefore unhelpful. Arguably, the report could, upon countervailing proofs presented by the prosecutor through cross-examination or rebuttal evidence, be considered untrustworthy because of its failure to consider the educational background, employment history, familial status, criminal record, or some other important demographic factor relating to the potential for rehabilitation. It might also be considered flawed because of its use of, or its undifferentiated emphasis upon, statistical data based upon race, gender, or some other suspect characteristic.[2] The court must retain discretion to exclude the evidence, in whole or in part, if its probative value is substantially outweighed by its unfounded or speculative character and the risk of confusion of the essential issues.

———

SALDANO v. TEXAS

Supreme Court of the United States, 2000.
530 U.S. 1212, 120 S.Ct. 2214, 147 L.Ed.2d 246.

Brief in Opposition to Petition for Writ of Certiorari

Saldano's Crime

In 1996, the Petitioner, Victor Hugo Saldano, was convicted of capital murder in Collin County, Texas, for the murder of Paul King. [N]either Saldano nor his accomplice knew Mr. King, and the crime appears to have been random. [P]rior to his trial, Saldano told the jailer that he had shot Mr. King four times, and then once in the head just to make sure he was dead. Saldano said he felt nothing when he shot Mr. King.

The Admittance of Race as a Factor in Determining Future Dangerousness

In the penalty phase of Saldano's trial, the jury [w]as charged with finding beyond a reasonable doubt the probability that Saldano would commit criminal acts of violence that would constitute a continuing threat to society. The jury was instructed that the burden of proving this "future dangerousness" lay solely on the prosecution.

The jury was presented with more than enough evidence to warrant its finding of "future dangerousness." [T]his evidence includes the facts that: (1) the circumstances of Saldano's capital offense demonstrate that it was particularly random, callous, cruel, and bold; (2) Saldano expressed no remorse for the slaying of his victim and has even stated that he felt nothing at the time of the killing; (3) Saldano was engaged in an escalating

---

2. In this regard we note that Dr. Wolfgang's proffered report refers to race—i.e., that defendant is a "white male"—as a demographic factor. The use of such a variable may have unacceptably invidious implications, bearing upon the ultimate admissibility of the expert's testimony. We mention this circumstance, but do not further consider the issue because it has not been raised or addressed in the present appeal and, further, it has not been shown to what extent Dr. Wolfgang's proposed testimony will coincide with his report in all of its present detail. We assume that the parties and trial court will be alert to this issue in the sentencing proceeding.

series of criminal activities prior to the killing of his victim; and (4) Saldano's relatively young age.

During the sentencing phase of Saldano's trial, the prosecution presented testimony on the issue of Saldano's future dangerousness, including evidence that there were twenty-four factors to be weighed in determining future dangerousness, one of which was Saldano's race. The witness testified that African-Americans and Hispanics are over-represented in prison compared to their percentage of the general population. He explained that "race itself may not explain the over-representation, so there are other subrealities that may have to be considered." Further, the witness testified that because Saldano was from Argentina, he would be considered Hispanic. As the Texas Court of Criminal Appeals recognized, the prosecution's witness "testified that because [Saldano] is Hispanic, this was a factor weighing in the favor of future dangerousness." At the conclusion of the witness's direct testimony, the State admitted into evidence a series of exhibits consisting of flip-charts that listed each of the factors the jury was to weigh in determining future dangerousness. The charts had marks next to each factor that was said to apply to Saldano, including race.

Counsel for Saldano did not object to the introduction of testimony regarding race. Instead, defense counsel cross-examined regarding the reliability of the data and whether Saldano, as a Argentinian, fit within the category of Hispanic.

[W]hile not mentioning race specifically, in closing argument the prosecution told the jury to rely on the twenty-four factors provided by its witness. The jury was told to take the formula of twenty-four factors and "plug it in." The jury found that Saldano was a future danger to society and that there were not sufficient mitigating factors to warrant life imprisonment. Accordingly, the trial court sentenced Saldano to the death penalty.

ARGUMENT

[T]he sole issue raised by Saldano is whether the Texas Court of Criminal Appeals erred in upholding his death sentence, despite the improper introduction of testimony inviting the use of race as a factor in determining future dangerousness, due to his counsel's failure to object. Because the use of race in Saldano's sentencing seriously undermined the fairness, integrity, or public reputation of the judicial process, Texas confesses error and agrees that Saldano is entitled to a new sentencing hearing.

[D]espite the fact that sufficient proper evidence was submitted to the jury to justify the finding of Saldano's future dangerousness, the infusion of race as a factor for the jury to weigh in making its determination violated his constitutional right to be sentenced without regard to the color of his skin.

Conclusion

For the reasons stated, Texas respectfully requests that the Court grant the petition, vacate the trial court's imposition of sentence on Saldano, and remand the case to the trial court with instructions that Saldano receive a new sentencing hearing in which race is not considered.

––––––

SALDANO v. TEXAS

Supreme Court of the United States, 2000.
530 U.S. 1212, 120 S.Ct. 2214, 147 L.Ed.2d 246.

The motion of petitioner for leave to proceed in forma pauperis and the petition for a writ of certiorari are granted. The judgment is vacated and the case is remanded to the Court of Criminal Appeals of Texas for further consideration in light of the confession of error by the Solicitor General of Texas.

––––––

TEXAS CODE OF CRIMINAL PROCEDURE, 2001

Article 37.07(3)(a)(2): Admissibility in a Criminal Trial of Race or Ethnicity As a Predictor of Future Criminal Behavior

Evidence may not be offered by the state to establish that the race or ethnicity of the defendant makes it likely that the defendant will engage in future criminal conduct.

––––––

LAW AND THE CRYSTAL BALL: PREDICTING BEHAVIOR WITH STATISTICAL INFERENCE AND INDIVIDUALIZED JUDGMENT

Barbara D. Underwood.
88 Yale Law Journal 1408 (1979).

Important benefits and burdens are distributed in American society on the basis of predictions about individual behavior. Release from prison, places in schools, jobs, and retail credit are among the benefits distributed to those applicants who are found most likely to succeed. The effort to predict an applicant's behavior can be made in a variety of ways: by professional experts or ordinary laymen, by use of individualized judgment or formulas that assign fixed weights to predetermined characteristics of the applicant. No matter what method is used, it typically generates controversy.

[T]wo main themes dominate the controversy over predictive techniques of selection: questions of accuracy and questions of legitimacy. Critics contend that the techniques are not sufficiently accurate to justify their use, and that in any event their use is not legitimate in some particular context because it is inconsistent with respect for the autonomous individual.

One example of this controversy arises over the use of prediction to fix the period of imprisonment for a convicted criminal. The prevailing system for sentencing criminals relies on prediction at two different points. First, the sentencing judge typically fixes a period of imprisonment based partly on a judgment about the chance that the offender will commit further crimes. This criterion is seldom made explicit in the statutes, but it rests on the common understanding that one important function of imprisonment is incapacitation: the prevention of those crimes that would have been committed during the period of imprisonment. An offender who is thought likely to commit further crimes will for that reason be sentenced to a longer term than a similar offender who is thought less likely to do so. The effort at prediction enters the process again when the prisoner is considered for release to the supervised status of parole. Typically one of the most important prerequisites for parole is a finding that the prisoner is likely to avoid further crimes while at liberty.

Critics have challenged both the accuracy and the legitimacy of prediction in the context of sentencing and parole. Most critics contend that predictions of criminal behavior are not accurate enough to use as a basis for a decision about a matter as important as liberty.

[O]ne reason to reject efforts to improve prediction may be grounded in the view that the limitations in existing techniques are inherent in the nature of prediction. The argument is that a prediction of future behavior is necessarily less accurate than any other determination that might be the basis for decision. Some may trace this inherent limitation to a distinction between future fact and present or past fact: the claim would be that for a question of past or present fact there is in principle a true answer, and any errors in factfinding are attributable only to inadequacies of evidence or of judgment. For a question of future fact, however, it may be that no amount of evidence or judgment can make the answer accessible.

As a practical matter, however, the distinction between future facts and past or present facts is unsound. Some past or present facts are as elusive as any prediction, and some predictions can be made with as much confidence as most determinations of past fact. If accuracy is the chief concern, it should be possible to specify the level of error that is tolerable in the decision to imprison an offender, and hold all factfinding to that standard, whether it involves matters of past or future fact. Perhaps no available predictive method is sufficiently accurate to satisfy the high standard of accuracy appropriate for the decision to incarcerate, but it may still be possible to develop one.

Moreover, in contexts other than parole, the requisite standard of accuracy may be more easily met. For example, the attempt to predict school success or failure from test scores is notoriously limited in accuracy. Nevertheless, the decision to reject applicants from school demands a lower standard of accuracy than the decision to deny prisoners parole, and the limited accuracy of test predictions may satisfy that standard.

The use of predictive criteria for selection is subject to challenge not only on grounds of accuracy, however, but also on the ground that it conflicts with other important social values, involving respect for individual autonomy. The attempt to predict an individual's behavior seems to reduce him to a predictable object rather than treating him as an autonomous person. It is this apparent conflict, between predicting behavior and respecting autonomy, that leads some critics to argue that a prediction of individual behavior, however small the risk of error, is an inappropriate criterion for the selection of individuals for imprisonment, and for various other benefits and burdens as well. To imprison a person because of the crimes he is expected to commit denies him the opportunity to choose to avoid those crimes. Similarly, to reject a job applicant on the basis of a test score that predicts poor performance denies him the opportunity to outperform the prediction. The argument is that respect for individual autonomy requires recognition of the possibility that an individual can choose to refute any prediction about himself.

[I]n spite of the persuasiveness of these criticisms of selection by prediction, the tension between predictive selection and respect for individual autonomy cannot be resolved in the abstract. It must be considered in light of the nature of the behavior that is being predicted, and the nature of the benefits or burdens to be distributed. Moreover the assessment of predictive selection must take into account the nature of the plausible alternatives to predictive selection.

Criteria that purport to punish fault and reward merit frequently provide the chief alternative to predictive criteria for selection. In admitting students to school, the chief alternative to predicting future performance is rewarding past effort and industry. In selecting criminals for release from prison, the chief alternative to predicting future crime is punishing past crime in proportion to its seriousness.

But these alternatives have their own limitations with respect to both accuracy and legitimacy. [T]hus, despite substantial questions about the legitimacy and accuracy of predicting individual behavior, predictive selection will sometimes be preferable to any other available means of selection. For this reason, the various methods of making predictions must be considered more carefully.

The Choice Between Statistical and Clinical Methods

Techniques for predicting individual behavior generally use one of two competing approaches to the problem. One approach relies on the subjective judgment of experienced decision makers, who evaluate each applicant on an individual basis in light of the experience accumulated by the decisionmaker and his profession. Psychiatrists use this method to predict violent behavior for purposes of involuntary hospitalization, and in that context it is often called the exercise of clinical judgment, or clinical prediction. The term clinical prediction can be generalized to refer to the subjective evaluations performed in other fields as well. For example, sentencing judges and some parole boards evaluate individuals in a subjective manner in order to predict future crime, and similar methods are sometimes used by admissions officers to predict academic success, by personnel officers to predict job success, and by loan officers to predict loan repayment. In all these fields, clinical prediction occurs when a decision-maker attempts to assess applicants as individuals, taking into account the characteristics that distinguish each applicant.

The alternative method for making predictions evaluates each applicant according to a predetermined rule for counting and weighting key characteristics. The relevant characteristics are specified in advance, and so is the rule for combining them to produce a score for each applicant. This score must be convertible into an estimate of the applicant's expected performance. This method of making predictions is often called statistical prediction, because statistical techniques are generally used to generate the rule from an analysis of prior cases to measure the accuracy of the rule in describing those prior cases, and to decide whether the rule should be used to predict results in future cases.

Statistical scoring schemes have been used to predict parole success from such items as number of prior convictions, type of crime, employment history, and family ties. They have been used to predict the repayment of loans from such items as age, marital status, location of residence, income, and assets. Educational testing is a more elaborate version of the same technique. Instead of a small number of predictive items, a test used to select applicants for a school typically rests on a large number of items— the answers to the questions that constitute the test. These answers are scored and weighted according to a predetermined rule, and applicants are then ranked on the basis of their scores.

[O]ne way to describe the difference between clinical and statistical methods is to say that clinical methods pay more attention to individual applicants, and statistical methods pay more attention to the rules for selecting them. Thus the tension between clinical and statistical methods mirrors in large part the familiar tension between discretion and rules. Clinical methods have the advantages of individualized discretionary decisionmaking, while statistical methods have the advantages of a system that depends on the uniform application of well-defined rules. Thus, clinical methods protect most effectively against failure to consider unanticipated individual differences, and statistical methods protect most effectively against the implicit use of illegal or otherwise unacceptable criteria for decision. The choice of a method must depend in part on which of these dangers seems most threatening. It must also depend on the extent to which there is available a group of clinical judges who command respect and confidence. A decisionmaker using a statistical rule will be perceived as less legitimate than a highly respected clinical decisionmaker, but more legitimate than a clinical decisionmaker who commands less community respect.

———

NOTE

1. Group Statistics and Individual Cases. Dawes, Faust, and Meehl, Clinical Versus Actuarial Judgment, 243 Science 1668 (1989) reviewed the social science literature on the relative accuracy of clinical and statistical prediction. They located nearly 100 comparative studies. "In virtually every one of these studies, the actuarial method has equalled or surpassed the clinical method, sometimes slightly and sometimes substantially." Id. at 1669.

> A common anti-actuarial argument, or misconception, is that group statistics do not apply to single individuals or events. The argument abuses basic principles of probability. Although individuals and events may exhibit unique features, they typically share common features with other persons or events that permit tallied observations or generalizations to achieve predictive power. An advocate of this anti-actuarial position would have to maintain, for the sake of logical consistency, that if one is forced to play Russian roulette a single time and is allowed to select a gun with one or five bullets in the chamber, the uniqueness of the event makes the choice arbitrary.

Id. at 1672.

D. TORT LIABILITY

The determination of bail and prison sentences and the imposition of capital punishment, as well as other legal interventions, such as involuntary mental hospitalization, are often premised on assessments of risk that are provided by social scientists. Among the goals of these interventions is the prevention of the forecasted behavior. Social scientists have also been involved in cases assigning tort liability when "foreseeable" harmful conduct has not been prevented. By the way it assigns tort liability, many believe that the law induces greater care in assessing risk on the part of those charged with the duty to do so.

TARASOFF v. REGENTS OF THE UNIVERSITY OF CALIFORNIA

Supreme Court of California, 1976.
17 Cal.3d 425, 131 Cal.Rptr. 14, 551 P.2d 334.

■ TOBRINER, JUSTICE.

On October 27, 1969, Prosenjit Poddar killed Tatiana Tarasoff. Plaintiffs, Tatiana's parents, allege that two months earlier Poddar confided his intention to kill Tatiana to Dr. Lawrence Moore, a psychologist employed by the Cowell Memorial Hospital at the University of California at Berkeley. They allege that on Moore's request, the campus police briefly detained Poddar, but released him when he appeared rational. They further claim that Dr. Harvey Powelson, Moore's superior, then directed that no further action be taken to detain Poddar. No one warned plaintiffs of Tatiana's peril.

[P]laintiffs' complaints predicate liability on two grounds: defendants' failure to warn plaintiffs of the impending danger and their failure to bring about Poddar's confinement pursuant to the Lanterman-Petris-Short Act (Welf. & Inst.Code, § 5000ff.) Defendants, in turn, assert that they owed no duty of reasonable care to Tatiana and that they are immune from suit under the California Tort Claims Act of 1963 (Gov.Code, § 810ff.).

We shall explain that defendant therapists cannot escape liability merely because Tatiana herself was not their patient. When a therapist determines, or pursuant to the standards of his profession should determine, that his patient presents a serious danger of violence to another, he incurs an obligation to use reasonable care to protect the intended victim against such danger. The discharge of this duty may require the therapist to take one or more of various steps, depending upon the nature of the case. Thus it may call for him to warn the intended victim or others likely to apprise the victim of the danger, to notify the police, or to take whatever other steps are reasonably necessary under the circumstances.

[T]he second cause of action can be amended to allege that Tatiana's death proximately resulted from defendants' negligent failure to warn Tatiana or others likely to apprise her of her danger. Plaintiffs contend that as amended, such allegations of negligence and proximate causation, with resulting damages, establish a cause of action. Defendants, however, contend that in the circumstances of the present case they owed no duty of care to Tatiana or her parents and that, in the absence of such duty, they were free to act in careless disregard of Tatiana's life and safety.

In analyzing this issue, we bear in mind that legal duties are not discoverable facts of nature, but merely conclusory expressions that, in cases of a particular type, liability should be imposed for damage done.

[T]he most important of these considerations in establishing duty is foreseeability. [W]hen the avoidance of foreseeable harm requires a defendant to control the conduct of another person, or to warn of such conduct, the common law has traditionally imposed liability only if the defendant bears some special relationship to the dangerous person or to the potential victim. Since the relationship between a therapist and his patient satisfies this requirement, we need not here decide whether foreseeability alone is sufficient to create a duty to exercise reasonable care to protect a potential victim of another's conduct.

[A]lthough plaintiffs' pleadings assert no special relation between Tatiana and defendant therapists, they establish as between Poddar and defendant therapists the special relation that arises between a patient and his doctor or psychotherapist. Such a relationship may support affirmative duties for the benefit of third persons. Thus, for example, a hospital must exercise reasonable care to control the behavior of a patient which may endanger other persons. A doctor must also warn a patient if the patient's condition or medication renders certain conduct, such as driving a car, dangerous to others.

[D]efendants contend, however, that imposition of a duty to exercise reasonable care to protect third persons is unworkable because therapists cannot accurately predict whether or not a patient will resort to violence. In support of this argument amicus representing the American Psychiatric Association and other professional societies cites numerous articles which indicate that therapists, in the present state of the art, are unable reliably to predict violent acts; their forecasts, amicus claims, tend consistently to overpredict violence, and indeed are more often wrong than right.[10] Since predictions of violence are often erroneous, amicus concludes, the courts should not render rulings that predicate the liability of therapists upon the validity of such predictions.

The role of the psychiatrist, who is indeed a practitioner of medicine, and that of the psychologist who performs an allied function, are like that of the physician who must conform to the standards of the profession and who must often make diagnoses and predictions based upon such evaluations. Thus the judgment of the therapist in diagnosing emotional disorders and in predicting whether a patient presents a serious danger of violence is comparable to the judgment which doctors and professionals must regularly render under accepted rules of responsibility.

We recognize the difficulty that a therapist encounters in attempting to forecast whether a patient presents a serious danger of violence. Obviously we do not require that the therapist, in making that determination, render a perfect performance; the therapist need only exercise "that reasonable degree of skill, knowledge, and care ordinarily possessed and exercised by members of [that professional specialty] under similar circumstances." Bardessono v. Michels (1970) 3 Cal.3d 780, 788, 91 Cal.Rptr. 760, 764, 478 P.2d 480, 484. Within the broad range of reasonable practice and treatment in which professional opinion and judgment may differ, the therapist is free to exercise his or her own best judgment without liability; proof, aided by hindsight, that he or she judged wrongly is insufficient to establish negligence.

In the instant case, however, the pleadings do not raise any question as to failure of defendant therapists to predict that Poddar presented a serious danger of violence. On the contrary, the present complaints allege that defendant therapists did in fact predict that Poddar would kill, but were negligent in failing to warn. Amicus contends, however, that even when a therapist does in fact predict that a patient poses a serious danger of violence to others, the therapist should be absolved of any responsibility for failing to act to protect the potential victim. In our view, however once a therapist does in fact determine, or under applicable professional standards

---

10. See, e.g., People v. Burnick (1975) 14 Cal.3d 306, 325–328, 121 Cal.Rptr. 488, 535 P.2d 352; Monahan, The Prevention of Violence, in Community Mental Health in the Criminal Justice System (Monahan ed. 1975); Diamond, The Psychiatric Prediction of Dangerousness (1975) 123 U.Pa.L.Rev. 439; Ennis & Litwack, Psychiatry and the Presumption of Expertise: Flipping Coins in the Courtroom (1974) 62 Cal.L.Rev. 693.

reasonably should have determined, that a patient poses a serious danger of violence to others, he bears a duty to exercise reasonable care to protect the foreseeable victim of that danger. While the discharge of this duty of due care will necessarily vary with the facts of each case, in each instance the adequacy of the therapist's conduct must be measured against the traditional negligence standard of the rendition of reasonable care under the circumstances.

[T]he risk that unnecessary warnings may be given is a reasonable price to pay for the lives of possible victims that may be saved. We would hesitate to hold that the therapist who is aware that his patient expects to attempt to assassinate the President of the United States would not be obligated to warn the authorities because the therapist cannot predict with accuracy that his patient will commit the crime.

Defendants further argue that free and open communication is essential to psychotherapy. [T]he giving of a warning, defendants contend, constitutes a breach of trust which entails the revelation of confidential communications. We recognize the public interest in supporting effective treatment of mental illness and in protecting the rights of patients to privacy, and the consequent public importance of safeguarding the confidential character of psychotherapeutic communication. Against this interest, however, we must weigh the public interest in safety from violent assault.

[W]e conclude that the public policy favoring protection of the confidential character of patient-psychotherapist communications must yield to the extent to which disclosure is essential to avert danger to others. The protective privilege ends where the public peril begins.

Our current crowded and computerized society compels the interdependence of its members. In this risk-infested society we can hardly tolerate the further exposure to danger that would result from a concealed knowledge of the therapist that his patient was lethal. If the exercise of reasonable care to protect the threatened victim requires the therapist to warn the endangered party or those who can reasonably be expected to notify him, we see no sufficient societal interest that would protect and justify concealment.

■ CLARK, JUSTICE (dissenting).

[B]y imposing a duty to warn, the majority contributes to the danger to society of violence by the mentally ill and greatly increases the risk of civil commitment—the total deprivation of liberty—of those who should not be confined. The impairment of treatment and risk of improper commitment resulting from the new duty to warn will not be limited to a few patients but will extend to a large number of the mentally ill. Although under existing psychiatric procedures only a relatively few receiving treatment will ever present a risk of violence, the number making threats is huge, and it is the latter group—not just the former—whose treatment will be impaired and whose risk of commitment will be increased.

Both the legal and psychiatric communities recognize that the process of determining potential violence in a patient is far from exact, being fraught with complexity and uncertainty. In fact precision has not even been attained in predicting who of those having already committed violent acts will again become violent, a task recognized to be of much simpler proportions.

This predictive uncertainty means that the number of disclosures will necessarily be large. [P]sychiatric patients are encouraged to discuss all thoughts of violence, and they often express such thoughts. However, unlike this court, the psychiatrist does not enjoy the benefit of overwhelming hindsight in seeing which few, if any, of his patients will ultimately become violent. Now, confronted by the majority's new duty, the psychiatrist must instantaneously calculate potential violence from each patient on each visit. The difficulties researchers have encountered in accurately predicting violence will be heightened for the practicing psychiatrist dealing for brief periods in his office with heretofore nonviolent patients. And, given the decision not to warn or commit must always be made at the psychiatrist's civil peril, one can expect most doubts will be resolved in favor of the psychiatrist protecting himself. [T]he warning itself is an impairment of the psychiatrist's ability to treat, depriving many patients of adequate treatment. It is to be expected that after disclosing their threats, a significant number of patients, who would not become violent if treated according to existing practices, will engage in violent conduct as a result of unsuccessful treatment. In short, the majority's duty to warn will not only impair treatment of many who would never become violent but worse, will result in a net increase in violence.

NOTES

1. The Impact of Tarasoff on Psychotherapists. To evaluate the effects of the *Tarasoff* decision on the practice of psychotherapy, the Stanford Law Review surveyed 1,200 California psychologists and psychiatrists. The respondents indicated that they saw an average of more than one case per month that they believed to be "potentially dangerous."

One-quarter of those responding to the survey said that they now gave more attention in their therapy sessions to the possibility of their patients' violent behavior. One-third of the psychiatrists and psychologists surveyed had increased the frequency with which they consulted colleagues concerning cases in which violence was an issue. Over half reported an increase in their own anxiety concerning the entire topic of "dangerousness" as a result of the *Tarasoff* decision. The survey also revealed that, as a result of *Tarasoff,* almost one-fifth of the respondents had decided to avoid asking questions that could yield information bearing on the likelihood of violent behavior by their patients. Even more reported that they had changed their recordkeeping procedures in an effort to avoid legal liability they might otherwise incur as a result of *Tarasoff.* "Some therapists ceased keeping detailed records; others began keeping *more* detailed records, including information that might justify any decisions they made and thereby trying to create a favorable evidentiary record for future litigation." Note, Where the Peril Begins: A Survey of Psychotherapists to Determine the Effects of *Tarasoff,* 31 Stanford Law Review 165, 182, n. 88 (1978).

Givelber, Bowers, and Blitch, *Tarasoff:* Myth and Reality: An Empirical Study of Private Law In Action, 1984 Wisconsin Law Review 443 (1984), surveyed the effects of the *Tarasoff* decision on a representative sample of psychiatrists, psychologists, and social workers in the eight largest standard metropolitan statistical areas in the United States. Virtually all therapists in California, and the great majority outside California, had heard of *Tarasoff* or "a case like it." The researchers stated that "it is a fair guess that there is no other legal decision, with the possible exception of controversial cases such as *Brown v. Board of Education,* which could command this level of recognition among a subgroup of lay persons." Id. at 457–458.

Further, the survey found that more than half of the therapists *outside* California believed that they were "legally bound" by the California Supreme Court's decision in *Tarasoff* because they mistakenly thought that the decision "applied to their professions." As the authors noted, "The proponents of the *Tarasoff* duty, having won an initial battle in California, have, in essence, won the entire war without firing another shot." Id. at 485.

2. The Impact of Tarasoff on Patients. Buckner and Firestone, "Where the Peril Begins": 25 Years After *Tarasoff,* 21 Journal of Legal Medicine 187 (2000) reviewed the literature on the effects of the *Tarasoff* decision on persons undergoing psychotherapy. They concluded:

> Based upon the case law and surveys over the past 25 years, even if confidentiality must be breached, the earlier anticipated negative effects have not materialized. There is just no evidence thus far that patients have been discouraged from coming to therapy, or discouraged from speaking freely once there, for fear that their confidentiality will be breached. Id at 221.

THOMPSON v. COUNTY OF ALAMEDA

Supreme Court of California, 1980.
27 Cal.3d 741, 167 Cal.Rptr. 70, 614 P.2d 728.

■ RICHARDSON, JUSTICE.

We recite the gravamen of plaintiffs' causes of action as contained in their amended complaint. Plaintiffs, husband and wife, and their minor son lived in the City of Piedmont, a few doors from the residence of the mother of James F. (James), a juvenile offender. Prior to the incident in question, James had been in the custody and under the control of County and had been confined in a county institution under court order. County knew that James had "latent, extremely dangerous and violent propensities regarding young children and that sexual assaults upon young children and violence connected therewith were a likely result of releasing [him] into the community." County also knew that James had "indicated that he would, if released, take the life of a young child residing in the neighborhood." (James gave no indication of which, if any, young child he intended as his victim.) County released James on temporary leave into his mother's custody at her home, and "[a]t no time did [County] advise and/or warn [James' mother], the local police and/or parents of young children within the immediate vicinity of [James' mother's] house of the known facts...." Within 24 hours of his release on temporary leave, James murdered plaintiffs' son in the garage of James' mother's home.

[D]UTY TO WARN THE LOCAL POLICE, THE NEIGHBORHOOD PARENTS, OR THE JUVENILE'S CUSTODIAN

We now examine the principal and most troublesome contentions of plaintiffs, namely, that County is liable for its failure to warn the local police and the parents of neighborhood children that James was being released or, alternatively, to warn James' mother of his expressed threat.

[B]y their very nature parole and probation decisions are inherently imprecise. According to a recent study by the California Probation Parole and Correction Association, during 1977 in California a total of 315,143 persons (225,331 adults and 89,912 juveniles) were supervised on probation. (The Future of Probation, A Report of the CPPCA Committee on the Future of Probation (Jul. 1979) p. 15.) During the same year, cases removed from probation because of violations totaled 13.4 percent in the superior courts, 14.8 percent in the lower courts, and 11.5 percent in the juvenile courts. (*Id.*, at pp. 27–28.) Additionally, a large number of parole violations occur. National parole violation rates reflect that 18–20 percent of parolees fail on one-year follow-up, 25 percent on two-year follow-up, and 26 percent on three-year follow-up. (*Id.*, at p. 35.) Although we fully recognize that not all violations involve new or violent offenses, a significant proportion do.

[B]earing in mind the ever present danger of parole violations, we nonetheless conclude that public entities and employees have no affirmative duty to warn of the release of an inmate with a violent history who has made *nonspecific threats of harm directed at nonspecific victims.* Obviously aware of the risk of failure of probation and parole programs the Legislature has nonetheless as a matter of public policy elected to continue those programs even though such risks must be borne by the public.

Similar general public policy considerations were described in a recent analysis of the *Tarasoff* issue. The author reasoned: "Assume that one person out of a thousand will kill. Assume also that an exceptionally accurate test is created which differentiates with 95% effectiveness those who will kill from those who will not. If 100,000 people were tested, out of the 100 who would kill 95 would be isolated. Unfortunately, out of the 99,900 who would not kill, 4,995 people would also be isolated as potential killers. In these circumstances, it is clear that we could not justify incarcerating all 5,090 people. If, in the criminal law, it is better that ten guilty men go free than that one innocent man suffer, how can we say in the civil commitment area that it is better that fifty-four harmless people be incarcerated lest one dangerous man be free? [Citation.]" (Comment, *Tarasoff* and the Psychotherapist's Duty to Warn (1975) 12 San Diego L.Rev. 932, 942–943, fn. 75.)

Furthermore, we foresee significant practical obstacles in the imposition of a duty in the form that plaintiffs seek, concluding that it would be unwieldy and of little practical value. As previously indicated a large number of persons are released and supervised on probation and parole each year in this state. Notification to the public at large of the release of each offender who has a history of violence and who has made a generalized threat at some time during incarceration or while under supervision would, in our view, produce a cacophony of warnings that by reason of their sheer volume would add little to the effective protection of the public.

[I]n summary, whenever a potentially dangerous offender is released and thereafter commits a crime, the possibility of the commission of that crime is statistically foreseeable. Yet the Legislature has concluded that the benefits to society from rehabilitative release programs mandate their continuance. Within this context and for policy reasons the duty to warn depends upon and arises from the existence of a prior threat to a specific identifiable victim. In those instances in which the released offender poses a predictable threat of harm to a named or readily identifiable victim or group of victims who can be effectively warned of the danger, a releasing agent may well be liable for failure to warn such persons. Despite the tragic events underlying the present complaint, plaintiffs' decedent was not a known, identifiable victim, but rather a member of large amorphous public group of potential targets. Under these circumstances we hold that County had no affirmative duty to warn plaintiffs, the police, the mother of the juvenile offender, or other local parents.

BRADY v. HOPPER

United States District Court, District of Colorado, 1983.
570 F.Supp. 1333.

■ John P. Moore, District Judge.

This matter comes before the Court on defendant's motion to dismiss. Consequently, the well-pleaded allegations of fact must be accepted as true, and the facts must be construed in a light most favorable to the pleader.

[P]laintiffs James Scott Brady, Timothy John McCarthy, and Thomas K. Delahanty were all shot and seriously injured by John W. Hinckley, Jr. ("Hinckley") in his attempt to assassinate President Reagan on March 30, 1981, in Washington, D.C. The defendant, Dr. John J. Hopper, Jr., is the psychiatrist who had been treating Hinckley from late October, 1980, until March, 1981.

Plaintiffs' complaint alleges that Dr. Hopper was negligent in examining, diagnosing, and treating Hinckley in conformity with reasonable standards of psychiatric care.

[T]he complaint alleges that Dr. Hopper knew or should have known that Hinckley was a danger to himself or others, and that Dr. Hopper either possessed or had access to, information which would have indicated that Hinckley identified with the assassin in the movie "Taxi Driver"; that he was collecting books and articles on political assassination; and that Hinckley possessed guns and ammunition. (Complaint ¶ 28). According to the complaint, Hinckley's parents were aware of and concerned about their son's worsening condition, and contacted Dr. Hopper and recommended that their son be hospitalized. (Complaint ¶¶ 13–17). Despite the possibility Hinckley might have been amenable to that idea, Dr. Hopper recommended that Hinckley not be hospitalized, and that treatment continue on an outpatient basis. (Complaint ¶ 18).

The rest of Hinckley's strange story is well known. In March, 1981, Hinckley left Denver and traveled across the country to Washington, D.C. On March 30, 1981, he attempted to assassinate President Reagan, and, in the process, shot and injured plaintiffs. Hinckley was subsequently tried for these crimes and found not guilty by reason of insanity. He is currently confined to St. Elizabeth's Hospital where he is receiving medical and psychiatric care.

The gravamen of plaintiffs' complaint is that if Dr. Hopper had properly performed his professional duties, he would have controlled Hinckley's behavior; therefore, Hinckley would not have made the presidential assassination attempt.

[S]ummary of the Arguments

The primary issue raised by defendant's motion is whether the relationship between therapist and patient gives rise to a legal duty such that Dr. Hopper can be held liable for the injuries caused to plaintiffs by Hinckley. The Restatement (Second) of Torts ¶ 315 states as follows:

> There is no duty so to control the conduct of a third person as to prevent him from causing physical harm to another unless
>
> (a) a special relation exists between the actor and the third person which imposes a duty upon the actor to control the third person's conduct, or
>
> (b) a special relation exists between the actor and the other which gives to the other a right to protection.

The thrust of defendant's argument is that the relationship between Dr. Hopper and Hinckley, that of a therapist and outpatient, is not a "special relationship" which gives rise to a duty on the part of the therapist to control the actions of the patient. In other words, defendant asserts that the therapist-outpatient relationship lacks sufficient elements of control required to bring the therapist within the language of ¶ 315.

[D]efendant next argues that the duty to control the violent acts of another does not arise absent specific threats directed to a reasonably identifiable victim. The leading case on a therapist's liability for the violent actions of a patient is Tarasoff v. Regents of University of California, 17 Cal.3d 425, 131 Cal.Rptr. 14, 551 P.2d 334 (1976). In Tarasoff, the patient communicated to the therapist specific threats and his intention to kill an unnamed—although readily identifiable—girl. The therapist informed law enforcement authorities of these threats, but failed to warn the girl or her parents. The California Supreme Court held that when a therapist determines (or pursuant to the standards of his profession should determine) that his patient presents a serious danger of violence to another, he is then obligated to take reasonable care to protect the intended victim against such danger. The court further held in such cases reasonable care may include the duty to warn the intended victim.

In Thompson v. County of Alameda, 27 Cal.3d 741, 167 Cal.Rptr. 70, 614 P.2d 728 (1980), the California Supreme Court again faced the question of the extent of liability to a third party for the dangerous acts of another. In *Thompson,* a juvenile offender known to have dangerous propensities was confined in a county institution. This patient had made generalized threats regarding his intention to kill, but had made no specific threats regarding any identifiable person. The county institution released the patient on temporary leave, and, within a day, the patient killed a young boy in his neighborhood. The court refused to extend *Tarasoff* to a setting where there was no identifiable victim. Instead, it took a more limited approach to the duty to warn, and concluded that even in the case of a person with a history of violence, no duty existed when the person had made only nonspecific threats of harm directed at nonspecific victims. Id. at 614 P.2d 735.

In essence, defendant argues that the instant case presents an even clearer basis than *Thompson* for a finding of no duty. It is argued that even according to the allegations in the complaint, Hinckley had no history of violence directed to persons other than himself; he had no history of arrests; no previous hospitalizations arising from any violent episodes; and in fact, he did not appear to be a danger to others. Thus, defendant asserts, this case involves, and plaintiffs have pled, none of the "warning signs" by which Hinckley's conduct or mental state would give rise to a duty on the part of Dr. Hopper.

[P]laintiffs have responded to each of the arguments. First plaintiffs assert that the therapist-outpatient relationship between Dr. Hopper and Hinckley was a "special relationship" within the meaning of Restatement (Second) of Torts ¶ 315. Plaintiffs argue that the duty to warn imposed in Tarasoff was premised on the assumption that such a special relationship exists between psychotherapist and patient.

[P]laintiffs further argue the duty to control is not limited to those situations where the patient makes specific threats to specific persons. According to plaintiffs, a duty on the part of the therapist arises whenever violence by the patient is foreseeable. In other words, depending on the nature of the patient's behavior, the therapist's duty is multifaceted: it may be to warn the potential victim or law enforcement authorities; it may be to take steps to have the patient confined; it may be to warn the patient's family or guardian of the potential danger; or it may be to take whatever action seems appropriate under the circumstances.

[D]iscussion

In my opinion, the main issue raised by the pleadings and briefs is not simply whether the therapist-outpatient relationship is a "special relationship" which gives rise to a legal duty on the part of the therapist; rather the key issue is to what extent was Dr. Hopper obligated to protect these particular plaintiffs from this particular harm? It is implicit in the majority of cases in this area that the therapist-patient relationship is one which under certain circumstances will give rise to a duty on the part of the therapist to protect third persons from harm. Tarasoff v. Regents of University of California, supra. However, the existence of a special relationship does not necessarily mean that the duties created by that relationship are owed to the world at large. It is fundamental that the duty owed be measured by the foreseeability of the risk and whether the danger created is sufficiently large to embrace the specific harm. Palsgraf v. Long Island R. Co., 248 N.Y. 339, 162 N.E. 99 (1928).

[A]ccepting as true the facts alleged in the complaint and viewing them in a light most favorable to plaintiffs, it is my conclusion that plaintiffs' injuries were not foreseeable; therefore, the plaintiffs fall outside of the scope of defendant's duty. Nowhere in the complaint are there allegations that Hinckley made any threats regarding President Reagan, or indeed that he ever threatened anyone. At most, the complaint states that if Dr. Hopper had interviewed Hinckley more carefully, he would have discovered that Hinckley was obsessed with Jody Foster and the movie "Taxi Driver", that he collected books on Ronald Reagan and political assassination, and that he practiced with guns. According to plaintiffs, if Dr. Hopper had properly performed his professional duties, he would have learned that Hinckley suffered from delusions and severe mental illness, as opposed to being merely maladjusted. Even assuming all of these facts and many of plaintiffs' conclusions to be true, the allegations are still insufficient to create a legal duty on the part of Dr. Hopper to protect these plaintiffs from the specific harm.

The parties have for the most part cast their arguments in terms of whether the relationship between Dr. Hopper and *Hinckley* gave rise to a particular duty on the part of Dr. Hopper. However, the legal obstacle to the maintenance of this suit is that there is no relationship between Dr. Hopper and *plaintiffs* which creates any legal obligation from Dr. Hopper to these plaintiffs. As explained by Justice Cardozo, negligence is a matter of relation between the parties, and must be founded upon the foreseeability of harm to the person in fact injured. Palsgraf v. Long Island R. Co., 162 N.E. at 101.

The question of whether a legal duty should be imposed necessarily involves social policy considerations. See Prosser, Law of Torts § 43, 257 (4th Ed.1971). In the present case, there are cogent policy reasons for limiting the scope of the therapist's liability. To impose upon those in the counseling professions an ill-defined "duty to control" would require therapists to be ultimately responsible for the actions of their patients. Such a rule would closely approximate a strict liability standard of care, and therapists would be potentially liable for all harm inflicted by persons presently or formerly under psychiatric treatment. Human behavior is simply too unpredictable, and the field of psychotherapy presently too inexact, to so greatly expand the scope of therapists' liability. In my opinion, the "specific threats to specific victims" rule states a workable, reasonable, and fair boundary upon the sphere of a therapist's liability to third persons for the acts of their patients.

The present case is one which makes application of the previously stated rules and policy considerations particularly difficult. Plaintiffs' injuries are severe and their damages extensive. Their plight as innocent bystanders to a bizarre and sensational assassination attempt is tragic and evokes great sympathy. Nevertheless, the question before the Court is whether Dr. Hopper can be subjected to liability as a matter of law for the injuries inflicted upon plaintiffs by Hinckley. I conclude that under the facts pleaded in the complaint, the question must be answered in the negative.

Accordingly, it is ordered that defendant's motion to dismiss is granted.

————

NOTE

1. Negligent Warning. In Hopewell v. Adebimpe, Court of Common Pleas of Allegheny County, Pennsylvania, Civil Case No. G.D. 78–28756, 130 Pittsburgh Legal Journal 107 (1982), a patient sued her psychiatrist for breaching the confidentiality provisions of the state Mental Health Procedures Act. The psychiatrist had sent the following letter to the patient's employer, without the patient's consent, Id. at 108.

RE: Rebecca Hopewell

Dear Sir:

In the course of a psychiatric interview which took place in my office on October 2, the above-named reported feelings of being so enraged about her work situation that she "will blow up and hurt somebody very seriously if the harassment does not stop".

This information is being relayed to you because there is a legal precedent requiring it and is not to be taken as an estimate of the probability that the threat will actually be carried out. It is, however, important that the person or persons at risk be notified. In this case I believe that her immediate supervisor should know of this letter.

Yours sincerely,

/s/VICTOR R. ADEBIMPE, M.D.

The court granted summary judgment for the plaintiff, commenting, Id. at 108–109, as follows:

> In [cases such as this], the psychologist, psychiatrist or psychotherapist is generally confronted with the dilemma of having to choose between the patient or his potential victim. On the one hand the professional must seek to protect the confidentiality of the privileged psychotherapist-patient communication while on the other hand he is faced with the possible imposition of tort liability for failure to disclose and warn third persons of the threatened harm.

> While certain jurisdictions such as the State of California in the landmark decision of Tarasoff v. Regents of the University of California have specifically recognized the duty of the psychotherapist to warn the person potentially harmed of the pending danger where the therapist either in fact had determined that the patient presented a serious danger of violence to the third person, or pursuant to the standard of the profession should have so determined, the Commonwealth of Pennsylvania has effectively eliminated the psychotherapist enigma by striking the balance in favor of confidentiality through the passage of appropriate statutory law.

> Section 111 of the "Mental Health Procedures Act", Act of July 9, 1976, P.L. 817, No. 143, 50 P.S. Section 7111, entitled "Confidentiality of records" provides in pertinent part:

> *"In no event [s]hall privileged communication, whether written or oral, be disclosed to anyone without [w]ritten consent."* (Emphasis added)

> When, as in the case at hand, the words of a statute are clear and free from all ambiguity, the letter of it is not to be disregarded under the pretext of pursuing its spirit. The Court does not have the slightest doubt that the disclosure by Dr. Adebimpe of the confidential and privileged communication as set forth in this letter of October 3, 1978, without the prior written consent of the Plaintiff, Rebecca Hopewell, violated Section 111 of the Act.

In light of the great publicity the *Tarasoff* decision received in national mental health publications, Dr. Adebimpe evidently believed that it was a "legal precedent" in Pennsylvania as well as in California. In 1998, the Pennsylvania Supreme Court adopted a version of *"Tarasoff* liability." See Emerich v. Philadelphia Center for Human Development, Inc., 554 Pa. 209, 720 A.2d 1032 (1998).

————

CIVIL CODE OF CALIFORNIA, 1985

§ 43.92. Psychotherapists; duty to warn of threatened violent behavior of patient; immunity from monetary liability

(a) There shall be no monetary liability on the part of, and no cause of action shall arise against, any person who is a psychotherapist as defined in Section 1010 of the Evidence Code in failing to warn of and protect from a patient's threatened violent behavior or failing to predict and warn of and protect from a patient's violent behavior except where the patient has communicated to the psychotherapist a serious threat of physical violence against a reasonably identifiable victim or victims.

(b) If there is a duty to warn and protect under the limited circumstances specified above, the duty shall be discharged by the psychotherapist making reasonable efforts to communicate the threat to the victim or victims and to a law enforcement agency.

SELECTED BIBLIOGRAPHY

A. Bail

Ewing, *Shall v. Martin:* Preventive Detention and Dangerousness Through the Looking Glass, 34 Buffalo Law Review 173 (1985).

Goldkamp, Prediction in Criminal Justice Policy Development, in Prediction and Classification: Criminal Justice Decision Making (D. Gottfredson and M. Tonry eds. 1987).

Note, The Trial of Pretrial Dangerousness: Preventive Detention After *United States v. Salerno,* 75 Virginia Law Review 639 (1989).

B. Parole

Carson, A Risk Management Approach to Legal Decision–Making About "Dangerous" People, in Law and Uncertainty (R. Baldwin ed. 1997).

R. Hood, Race and Sentencing (1992).

Monahan, The Case for Prediction in the Modified Desert Model of Criminal Sentencing, 5 International Journal of Law and Psychiatry 103 (1982).

Rice, Violent Offender Research and Implications for the Criminal Justice System, 52 American Psychologist 414 (1997).

Rice and Harris, Sexual Aggressors, in Modern Scientific Evidence: The Law and Science of Expert Testimony, 2d ed. (D. Faigman, D. Kaye, M. Kaks, and J. Sanders eds. 2002).

Zimring and Hawkins, Dangerousness and Criminal Justice, 85 Michigan Law Review 481 (1986).

C. Capital Punishment

Goodman, Demographic Evidence in Capital Sentencing, 39 Stanford Law Review 499 (1987).

Grisso and Appelbaum, Is It Unethical To Offer Predictions of Future Violence?, 16 Law and Human Behavior 621 (1992).

Grove and Meehl, Comparative Efficiency of Informal (Subjective, Impressionistic) and Formal (Mechanical, Algorithmic) Prediction Procedures: The Clinical-Statistical Controversy, 2 Psychology, Public Policy, and Law 293 (1996).

Hoge and Grisso, Accuracy and Expert Testimony, 20 Bulletin of the American Academy of Psychiatry and the Law 67 (1992).

Slobogin, Dangerousness and Expertise, 133 University of Pennsylvania Law Review 97 (1984).

Sorensen and Pilgrim, An Actuarial Risk Assessment of Violence Posed By Capital Murder Defendants, 90 Journal of Criminal Law and Criminology 1251 (2000).

D. Tort Liability

Appelbaum, Zonana, Bonnie, and Roth, Statutory Approaches to Limiting Psychiatrists' Liability for Their Patients' Violent Acts, 146 American Journal of Psychiatry 821 (1989).

Backstrom, Unveiling the Truth When It Matters Most: Implementing the *Tarasoff* Duty for California's Attorneys, 73 Southern California Law Review 139 (1999).

Dvoskin and Heilbrun, Risk Assessment and Release Decision-Making: Toward Resolving the Great Debate, 29 Journal of the American Academy of Psychiatry and the Law 6 (2001).

Grisso and Appelbaum, Structuring the Debate About Ethical Predictions of Future Violence, 17 Law and Human Behavior 482 (1993).

T. Gutheil and P. Appelbaum, Clinical Handbook of Psychiatry and the Law 3d (2000).

Heilbrun, Prediction Versus Management Models Relevant to Risk Assessment: The Importance of Legal Decision-Making Context, 21 Law and Human Behavior 347 (1997).

Kachigian and Felthous, Court Responses to *Tarasoff* Statutes, 32 Journal of the American Academy of Psychiatry and Law 263 (2004).

McNiel, Binder, and Fulton, Management of Threats of Violence Under California's Duty-to-Protect Statute, 155 American Journal of Psychiatry 1097 (1998).

Monahan, Limiting Therapist Exposure to *Tarasoff* Liability: Guidelines for Risk Containment, 48 American Psychologist 242 (1993).

Monahan, Clinical and Actuarial Predictions of Violence, in Modern Scientific Evidence: The Law and Science of Expert Testimony 2d ed (D. Faigman, D. Kaye, M. Saks, and J. Sanders, eds. 2002).

Monahan, Violence Risk Assessment: Scientific Validity and Evidentiary Admissibility, 57 Washington and Lee Law Review 901 (2000).

Monahan, Steadman, Robbins, Appelbaum, Banks, Grisso, Heilbrun, Mulvey, Roth, and Silver, An Actuarial Model of Violence Risk Assessment for Persons with Mental Disorders. 56 Psychiatric Services 810 (2005).

Section III.   Contexts for Determining Present Facts

Unlike the use of social science to provide contexts for determining facts that will occur in the future—a use that educates the decisions of judges or jurors—the use of social science to supply contexts for determining facts that are in the process of occurring informs the decisions of law enforcement officers. Many law enforcement situations are characterized by (a) the clear knowledge that violations of the law are occurring; (b) the presence of large numbers of persons ("suspects") who could be the ones violating the law; and (c) a lack of resources to investigate each of these persons. In some of these situations, the police have found it useful to rely upon social science characterizations of potential violators to assist in giving priority to their investigations.

The typical case in this area concerns a person who "fit" or "matched" the behavioral characteristics of known groups of persons who have engaged in given criminal acts, and who therefore was stopped and questioned. The ensuing investigation uncovered contraband, and the person was arrested. At trial, the defendant attempts to have the evidence suppressed, arguing that the initial investigation violated the Fourth Amendment, since social science data do not give rise to probable cause needed for a search or even to the reasonable suspicion needed for a brief investigatory "stop" according to Terry v. Ohio, 392 U.S. 1, 88 S.Ct. 1868, 20 L.Ed.2d 889 (1968).

We consider here the use of social science to provide contexts for determining "present" facts relating to illegal weapons, illegal automobiles, illegal aliens, and illegal drugs.

A.   Illegal Weapons

Metal detectors and "skyjacker profiles" are forms of screening airline passengers for the presence of illegal weapons. The "skyjacker profile" is the one use of social science to provide a context for determining an ongoing fact—whether a given passenger is carrying a weapon—that occasions little controversy.

UNITED STATES v. LOPEZ

United States District Court, Eastern District of New York, 1971.
328 F.Supp. 1077.

■ Weinstein, District Judge.

[Two Deputy United States Marshals questioned Lopez and a companion at Kennedy Airport after an employee of Pan American Airlines "pointed out the two passengers as 'selectees'—persons whose 'profile' suggested a substantial likelihood that they were potential hijackers; who had activated a magnetometer, a metal detection device; and who, upon request, had failed to produce identification." When the marshals frisked Lopez for a weapon, they found heroin, arrested him, and charged him with concealing and facilitating the transportation of heroin. He moved to suppress the evidence taken from his person.]

Presented is the question of whether the anti-hijacking system used at our airports is constitutional. For the reasons indicated below, we hold the system valid.

[I]n October 1968 a Task Force was appointed to consider methods of combating the increasing number of airline hijackings. A number of interested agencies including the Federal Aeronautics Administration, the Department of Justice and the Department of Commerce were represented. This Task Force included individuals trained in several disciplines including psychology, law, engineering and administration. Dr. John T. Dailey, a well-trained psychologist with a broad practical background in education and government personnel, took a leading role in developing and testing the Task Force ideas. At the hearing he testified at length and impressed the Court with his skill and honesty.

One of the serious problems faced by the Task Force was that many millions of passengers use air transportation. Any practical procedure would have to permit maximum access to aircraft with minimal inconvenience and embarrassment to passengers and almost no delay in the operations of the airlines.

Among the investigations undertaken by this group were a detailed study of the characteristics of all the then known hijackers and of the air traveling public. Background investigations of hijackers as well as visual and photographic studies of boarding air passengers were relied upon. Among the findings were (1) hijackers were generally not highly motivated and resourceful and (2) they shared certain characteristics markedly distinguishing them from the general traveling public.

[O]ne sample consisting of 500,000 screened passengers showed that only 1,406 satisfied the profile—.28%. Approximately one-half of those were nevertheless permitted to board immediately after failing to activate the magnetometer, leaving 712, or .14% to be interviewed. Of those interviewed, 283, approximately one-third, were actually searched. Therefore, only .05% of the sample were ultimately subjected to a preventive weapons frisk. Twenty persons were denied boarding—approximately $\frac{1}{15}$ of those searched and of these, 16 were arrested. In sum, almost everyone (99.86%) of the one-half million persons passed swiftly through the boarding process without even being asked a question and 99.95% boarded without being searched.

In another sample of 226,000 screened passengers .57% were selected as meeting the profile; .28% were interviewed; and .13% were searched. It was reported that none were searched "involuntarily" and only 24 were denied boarding.

[T]hat the risk of hijacking is greatly increased when a passenger possesses weapons can hardly be doubted. In the 80 hijacking incidents involving planes of United States registry up to June of 1970, there were 55 firearms, 20 knives, 14 alleged bombs, 3 razors or razor blades, 1 BB gun, 1 tear gas pen, and 1 broken bottle.

In camera testimony was persuasive that the characteristics of the potential hijackers chosen for the profile were well calculated to eliminate safe persons while isolating those likely to be dangerous. No one can be certain, of course, that anyone failing all the tests of the system will be a hijacker. In fact, approximately 14 out of every 15 people who were searched proved to have no weapons and were then permitted to proceed. Moreover, as the facts detailed below indicate, there is always the risk that a soundly designed process will be abused by ignorant, careless or malevolent personnel. As one commentator pointed out

> "permitting *any* use of certain mathematical methods entails a sufficiently high risk of misuse, or a risk of misuse sufficiently costly to avoid, that it would be irrational not to take such misuse into account when deciding whether to permit the methods to be employed at all." Tribe, Trial by Mathematics: Precision and Ritual in the Legal Process, 84 Harv.L.Rev. 1329, 1331 (1971) (emphasis in original).

Measured against the air traveling population as a whole, the method is highly effective in narrowing the group which needs particular attention. Where the risks of hijacking to passengers and crew and to the viability of the entire industry are so great we cannot say on balance that use of the system is imprudent. Whether it meets the reasonableness test of the Constitution is an issue dealt with below.

[T]he testimony revealed that studies underlying the profile were thorough. Procedures followed in developing it were adequate. Appropriate statistical, sociological and psychological data and techniques were utilized. The profile is a highly effective procedure for isolating potential hijackers.

After studying known hijackers, the task force compiled twenty-five to thirty characteristics in which hijackers differed significantly from the air-traveling public. By putting only a few of them together they could obtain a reliable combination sharply differentiating potential hijackers from non-hijackers.

During the testing period and shortly thereafter in 1969 the task force studied an additional sample of 30 new hijackers and found that over 90% of that group would have met the profile. There has been a continuous process of reevaluation in light of new hijackings and changes in trends of hijacking. Thus far the original profile has retained validity.

[T]he anti-hijacking system is unusual in that it provides statistics showing the precise probabilities involved. Based upon the surveys available, out of every approximately 15 persons who are frisked one person is found with a weapon. Thus the probability that any person who is selected to be frisked has a weapon is approximately 6%. We know that the frisk is conducted in private with as much courtesy as the circumstances permit and that those who are frisked and allowed to go on their way generally welcome the protective measures taken in their behalf rather than resent them. The substantial interest in preserving the integrity and safety of air travel by preventing hijacking is obvious. In light of the circumstances, a 6% danger of arms suffices to justify a frisk.

The statistics discussed earlier indicate that only somewhere on the order of $\frac{1}{10}$ of 1% of all passengers screened are actually frisked and that included in that .1% are practically all of the potential hijackers. The procedure, as designed, operates on purely objective criteria independent of race, color, or creed. It is well calculated to winnow out potential hijackers while occasioning a bare minimum of inconvenience to a very small percentage of the flying public—an inconvenience which most subjects seem, in fact, to accept. A United States Marshal would be imprudent were he to refuse to heed the warning given to him by the system. A narrowly circumscribed protective weapons "pat-down" or "frisk" is constitutionally permissible under these circumstances.

[W]e reach this conclusion recognizing that the system used is disquieting. Employing a combination of psychological, sociological, and physical sciences to screen, inspect and categorize unsuspecting citizens raises visions of abuse in our increasingly technological society. Proposals based upon statistical research designed to predict who might commit crimes and giving them the special attention of law enforcement agencies is particularly disturbing. There is a basis for

" … what anti-utopians like Huxley and Orwell have forecast— though … these dismal despotisms will be far more stable and effective than their prophets have foreseen. For they will be equipped with techniques of inner-manipulation as unobtrusively fine as gossamer." T. Roszak, The Making of a Counter Culture xiii (1969).

Undoubtedly there are persons with objectively observable characteristics who provide a higher statistical probability of danger than the population as a whole. But our criminal law is based on the theory that we do not condemn people because they are potentially dangerous. We only prosecute illegal acts. Putting a group of potential violators in custody on the ground that this group contained all or nearly all of the people who would commit crimes in the future would raise the most serious constitutional issues. The procedure before us accomplishes no such result and raising such specters does not assist in a rational evaluation of the anti-hijacking program. This system does not constitute a first step along the road to preventive detention of potentially dangerous classes of persons.

[W]hile candidly recognizing the disquieting possibilities suggested by the techniques of the anti-hijacking campaign, we are unpersuaded that the rights of air travellers generally have been or will be violated by the proper application of this system. We ought not be frightened out of taking sensible protective steps by the possibilities of misuse so long as our courts are in a position to prevent abuse should it arise.

SUPPRESSION IN THIS CASE

While evidence discovered during a frisk pursuant to this anti-hijacking procedure would normally be admissible, the special circumstances of the instant case require suppression. The Pan American Passenger Service Manager issued a memorandum on July 22, 1970 purporting to "update" the "profile" to be applied in the anti-hijacking screening procedure. This action was not authorized by Pan American Security Services, the United States Marshal Service, or the Federal Aeronautics Administration. It eliminated one criterion included in the official profile established by the F.A.A. and added two additional categories.

Both the government and Pan American disowned the memorandum and indicated that it had been withdrawn. Neither were able, however, to assure the Court that the boarding area personnel responsible for applying the profile to passengers on November 14, 1970 had not read the memorandum and were not following it. Under the circumstances, the Court must assume that the "updated" profile was, in fact, employed in selecting the defendant.

The one characteristic eliminated by this supplemental memorandum effectively excised from the screening procedure one of the fundamental characteristics of hijackers as described by Dr. Dailey during *in camera* testimony. One of the characteristics added introduced an ethnic element for which there is no experimental basis, thus raising serious equal protection problems. The second added criterion called for an act of individual judgment on the part of airline employees. The effect of these changes was to destroy the essential neutrality and objectivity of the approved profile.

In evaluating the constitutionality of the system that was actually in operation on the day in question we cannot now rely on the statistics presented to the Court since the properly conducted samplings utilized the official Task Force profile. These statistics were critical in our determination that this system was an appropriate method of protecting air travellers.

The procedure instituted to detect hijackers becomes unacceptable when abused in the manner described in this case. The approved system survives constitutional scrutiny only by its careful adherence to absolute objectivity and neutrality. When elements of discretion and prejudice are interjected it becomes constitutionally impermissible.

[T]he anti-hijacking system can be a valuable and effective method of protecting millions of air travellers from the threat of violence and sudden death in the air. Properly supervised it is also constitutional. Abuses such as the one which occurred in this case must, however, be eliminated if evidence obtained in its operation is to be used in our Courts.

CONCLUSION

Defendant's motion to suppress evidence must be granted. Since without this evidence the government has no case, the indictment is dismissed.

———

NOTE

1. Use of the "Profile." Lopez was sent through a magnetometer only after he was noticed to fit the hijacker profile. It was FAA policy in 1971 to use the magnetometer only on those persons who "fit the profile." In 1973, the policy changed to the currently existing one, whereby all airline passengers, not just specially selected ones, pass through a magnetometer. There was then no need for a behavioral "profile" to identify persons likely to be in the possession of weapons, since the magnetometer accomplished this task by screening everyone. The FAA therefore discontinued the use of the hijacker profile in 1973.

In 1980, however, there was a series of plane hijackings in which the hijacker had boarded the plane in the possession of a plastic flask filled with gasoline, and a cigarette lighter. The plastic flask had not activated the magnetometer. As of 1980, the FAA began to deploy the hijacker profile again in order to identify persons who would hijack a plane with the use of a nonmetallic weapon.

FINAL REPORT TO PRESIDENT CLINTON

White House Commission on Aviation Safety and Security, 1997.

[Recommendation:] Complement technology with automated passenger profiling.

Profiling can leverage an investment in technology and trained people. Based on information that is already in computer databases, passengers could be separated into a very large majority who present little or no risk, and a small minority who merit additional attention. Such systems are employed successfully by other agencies, including the Customs Service. By utilizing this process Customs is better able to focus its resources and attention. As a result, many legitimate travelers never see a customs agent anymore—and drug busts are way up. The FAA and Northwest Airlines are developing an automated profiling system tailored to aviation security, and the Commission supports the continued development and implementation of such a system.

To improve and promote passenger profiling, the Commission recommends three steps. First, FBI, CIA, and ATF should evaluate and expand the research into known terrorists, hijackers, and bombers needed to develop the best possible profiling system. They should keep in mind that such a profile would be most useful to the airlines if it could be matched against automated passenger information which the airlines maintain.

Second, the FBI and CIA should develop a system that would allow important intelligence information on known or suspected terrorists to be used in passenger profiling without compromising the integrity of the intelligence or its sources. Similar systems have been developed to give environmental scientists access to sensitive data collected by satellites.

Third, the Commission will establish an advisory board on civil liberties questions that arise from the development and use of profiling systems.

[A]ugmenting Recommendation

[T]he Commission supports the development and implementation of manual and automated profiling systems, such as the one under development by the FAA and Northwest Airlines. The Commission strongly believes the civil liberties that are so fundamentally American should not, and need not, be compromised by a profiling system. Consistent with this viewpoint, the Commission sought the counsel of leading experts in the civil liberties field. The Commission recommends the following safeguards:

1. No profile should contain or be based on material of a constitutionally suspect nature—e.g., race, religion, national origin of U.S. citizens. The Commission recommends that the elements of a profiling system be developed in consultation with the Department of Justice and other appropriate experts to ensure that selection is not impermissibly based on national origin, racial, ethnic, religious or gender characteristics.

2. Factors to be considered for elements of the profile should be based on measurable, verifiable data indicating that the factors chosen are reasonable predictors of risk, not stereotypes or generalizations. A relationship must be demonstrated between the factors chosen and the risk of illegal activity.

3. Passengers should be informed of airlines security procedures and of their right to avoid any search of their person or luggage by electing not to board the aircraft.

4. Searches arising from the use of an automated profiling system should be no more intrusive than search procedures that could be applied to all passengers. Procedures for searching the person or luggage of, or for questioning, a person who is selected by the automated profiling system should be premised on insuring respectful, non-stigmatizing, and efficient treatment of all passengers.

5. Neither the airlines or the government should maintain permanent databases on selectees. Reasonable restrictions on the maintenance of records and strict limitations on the dissemination of records should be developed.

6. Periodic independent reviews of profiling procedures should be made. The Commission considered whether an independent panel be appointed to monitor implementation and recommends at a minimum that the DOJ, in consultation with the DOT and FAA, periodically review the profiling standards and create an outside panel should that, in their judgment, be necessary.

———

NOTE

1. Subsequent Developments. The "automated profiling system" recommended in the above 1997 report was called the Computer Assisted Passenger Prescreening System (CAPPS I). After the events of September 11, 2001, the newly-created Transportation Security Agency (TSA) commissioned the development of the Computer Assisted Passenger Prescreening System, Second Version (CAPPS II), a program that would use commercial and government databases in addition to airline data. CAPPS II was cancelled by TSA in 2004 before being implemented, however, due to widespread privacy concerns. In its place, a third system, called Secure Flight, was developed and scheduled to be implemented in late 2005. A recent Government Accountability Office report, "Secure Flight Development and Testing Under Way, but Risks Should Be Managed as System Is Further Developed" (March 2005), stated

> TSA [has] initiated a number of actions designed to improve the ability of Secure Flight to identify passengers who should undergo additional security scrutiny, in place of the prescreening currently conducted by air carriers [i.e., CAPPS I]. Specifically, TSA officials stated that recently completed initial testing identified improvements over the current prescreening system, and TSA plans to use intelligence analysts to increase the accuracy of data matches. However, the effectiveness of Secure Flight in identifying passengers who should undergo additional security scrutiny has not been fully determined. For example, TSA has not resolved how passenger data will be transmitted from air carriers to TSA to support Secure Flight operations. Further, the ability of Secure Flight to make accurate matches between passenger data and data contained in the terrorist screening database is dependent on the quality of the data used, which has not been determined. [A]dditionally, TSA has taken steps to minimize potential impacts on passengers and to protect passenger rights during Secure Flight testing. However, TSA has not yet clearly defined the privacy impacts of the operational system or all of the actions TSA plans to take to mitigate potential impacts.

B.   ILLEGAL AUTOMOBILES

To increase the number of arrests of persons driving stolen vehicles, some law enforcement agencies have attempted to target certain types of cars, certain types of drivers, and certain roads for increased investigatory attention. Empirical research has been used to assist in selecting their targets.

STATE v. OCHOA

Supreme Court of Arizona, 1976.
112 Ariz. 582, 544 P.2d 1097.

■ STRUCKMEYER, VICE CHIEF JUSTICE.

Appellee, Raymond Arcadio Ochoa, was indicted for the theft of a 1973 Ford pickup truck. From an order suppressing all evidence obtained from the asserted wrongful stopping of the Ford truck which Ochoa was driving, the State has appealed.

[A]t about six o'clock A.M. on July 27, 1974, Ochoa was driving south on U.S. 89 between Tucson and Nogales, near Milepost 26, when he was stopped by Patrolman Luis Chaboya of the Department of Public Safety, Highway Patrol. Ochoa was stopped because he and the truck he was driving fitted a profile developed for the detection of stolen motor vehicles.

[I]t was Ochoa's position in the court below that there was no probable cause to stop him or the vehicle he was driving and that consequently everything which followed the stop was contaminated by the wrongful action of the officers in the first instance.

[T]he State, while recognizing that peace officers cannot constitutionally stop the drivers of motor vehicles at random on the chance of discovering something illegal, see United States v. Mallides, 473 F.2d 859 (9th Cir. 1973), urges [that] a police task force developed a profile, by the use of which there was a founded suspicion that Ochoa was driving a stolen vehicle. The Supreme Court of the United States has laid down the test that:

> " * * * in justifying the particular intrusion the police officer must be able to point to specific and articulable facts which, taken together with rational inferences from those facts, reasonably warrant the intrusion." Terry v. Ohio, supra, 392 U.S. at 21, 88 S.Ct. at 1880, 20 L.Ed.2d at 906.

[T]he profile pursuant to which Ochoa and his vehicle were stopped was developed at a meeting of peace officers in Phoenix on May 15, 1974. This meeting was called specifically to discuss the problem of stolen vehicles being taken to Mexico where they were either sold or traded for narcotics. [A]t the meeting, a profile was developed from an analysis of the 6,000 thefts in Phoenix in 1973 and 4,000 thefts in the first five months of 1974. In the Phoenix area, Fords and Chevrolets constituted at least 75% of the stolen vehicles, 90% of which were not recovered. It was ascertained through pooled information that vehicles which were particularly in demand for sale in Mexico were 1972 through 1974 Ford and Chevrolet sedans and 1972 through 1974 Ford, Chevrolet, GMC and Dodge pickups.

[I]n addition, these factors were found to be significant: The driver would probably be between 17 and 27 years of age; he would usually be alone; he would have no apparent luggage; if there was a passenger, there would be no children; and the car's license plate would show a registration to either Pima or Maricopa County. There was no testimony as to the number of vehicles and persons which fit this profile, but the evidence did indicate that this profile fit only a small percentage of those people driving between Tucson and Nogales.

After this meeting, a task force was organized. [T]eams were put together to work the highway between Tucson and Nogales, Arizona. A two-man unit was used as spotters, whose job was to watch approaching traffic and alert by radio a unit called the "marked unit" which then halted suspicious vehicles and investigated them as possibly stolen. Whether there was a reasonable suspicion that the vehicle was stolen was to be determined from the driver's license and the vehicle registration.

This task force operation was carried on approximately 30 miles north of the border town of Nogales, Arizona. In the first 14 days of June before the task force went into operation, there were 26 profile vehicles stolen, of which only four were recovered, for a percentage of recovered vehicles of 15.38%. After June 14, while the task force was in operation, there were nine profile vehicles stolen and three recovered, for a percentage of 33⅓%. The team operated for a three-day period in July and recovered vehicles of the approximate value of $25,000. We do not consider it significant that the recoveries were for but a small percentage of the entire body of stolen vehicles. One person who was apprehended admitted to stealing over 100 trucks and cars and taking them to Mexico, and another person apprehended admitted to stealing approximately 150 vehicles. The justification for the use of the profile lies in the fact that apprehension of one such person might stop the future theft of many vehicles and thus significantly reduce criminal activities in this area.

We therefore hold that the stop here questioned is warranted by specific and articulable facts taken together with rational inferences therefrom and satisfies the test laid down in Terry v. Ohio, supra.

[T]he judgment of the Superior Court is reversed.

————

STATE v. GRACIANO

Supreme Court of Arizona, 1982.
134 Ariz. 35, 653 P.2d 683.

■ FELDMAN, JUSTICE.

On March 7, 1981, appellant was driving a four-by-four Ford pickup truck on Interstate 19, approximately 18 miles north of the Arizona–Mexico border, near Nogales, Arizona. When first seen by Highway Patrol Officer Gordon Hopke, appellant was headed south toward the border; Officer Hopke was northbound. As soon as he saw appellant's vehicle, the officer made a U-turn in the median, switched on his red, flashing light, and stopped appellant. After the stop, the officer learned that the vehicle was stolen and appellant was then arrested.

[T]he only issue presented by this appeal is whether the officer's stop violated appellant's fourth amendment rights.

[O]fficer Hopke [k]new that in 1980 the Arizona Department of Public Safety had compiled statistics concerning vehicles registered in Arizona which were most often stolen. The statistics revealed that the four types of vehicles in Arizona with the highest probability of being stolen were, in descending order, Ford four-by-four pickups, Ford four-by-four Broncos, Chevrolet Camaros, and Ford Vans.

Officer Hopke [t]estified about the stop of appellant. [T]he vehicle was not being driven in any suspicious or unlawful manner. The pickup was, however, a Ford four-by-four and the license plate indicated that the vehicle came from a point farther north than Tucson. Furthermore, Officer Hopke testified that the driver "appeared" to be "Mexican." It is clear from cross-examination, however, that the officer saw very little of the driver. Hopke could not tell whether the driver was young or old, male or female. When asked how he knew whether the driver was Mexican "rather than Armenian or Syrian," he admitted that he did not know. All he was sure of was that the driver had dark skin. Based upon only this information, the officer stopped appellant.

Therefore, the totality of knowledge the officer had before the stop of this driver was that some dark-skinned person, male or female, old or young, was driving toward the Mexican border in a lawful and unremarkable manner, in a vehicle of a type most desired by thieves, with license plates from farther north in Arizona. We hold that this is not sufficient to raise a justifiable suspicion that appellant was involved in criminal activity. These are certainly not the "specific and articulable facts" which will warrant an investigatory stop. Terry v. Ohio, 392 U.S. at 21, 88 S.Ct. at 1880. Further, these circumstances apply to a large group of presumably innocent travelers. To uphold the stop in question on the basis of these observed circumstances would subject many innocent individuals to just the type of intrusions prohibited by the fourth amendment.

Most importantly, we cannot agree that in these circumstances the color of the skin of the driver could raise a reasonable suspicion that the appellant was engaged in wrongdoing. There was no information in the officer's possession to indicate that the particular vehicle had been stolen which would have justified him in assuming that whoever was in possession of the truck might be a thief. We know of no statistics which would indicate that dark-skinned Mexican-Americans are more likely to be automobile thieves than light-skinned ones, nor that Mexican-Americans are more likely to be automobile thieves than Irish-Americans, Polish-Americans, or any other subdivision of Americans.

The State argues that the statistics from the Department of Public Safety, along with the information Officer Hopke said he had received from meetings and discussions with other highway patrol officers, constitute a "profile" similar to that used in State v. Ochoa, 112 Ariz. 582, 544 P.2d 1097 (1976). The formal profile examined in *Ochoa* is clearly distinguishable from the information used by Hopke in this case.

In *Ochoa,* we upheld a vehicle stop on the basis of a written profile developed at a meeting of peace officers in May of 1974. That profile was compiled on the basis of information received from 40 representatives of various state and federal law enforcement agencies and an analysis of 10,000 vehicle thefts in the Phoenix area. We held that stops made because a driver and vehicle fit that profile were "warranted by specific and articulable facts taken together with rational inferences therefrom." Id. at 586, 544 P.2d at 1101.

In this case, however, there is no written profile. It is not even clear what the elements of this so-called profile are. This became clear when the court questioned Hopke about the elements of the "profile."

THE COURT: What was the profile?

THE WITNESS: It was Ford pickups, young Mexican male drivers, single driver, young individual. The majority of the profiles was young Mexican drivers, Mexican males. Four-by-fours were the main item that they, we were interested in.

THE COURT: Was there some agreement established as to how many of these items they had to fit before you would decide to stop them?

THE WITNESS: I believe it was mainly the type of driver, the type of vehicle, whether the driver more or less fit the described vehicles [sic].

The statistics which the State submitted and which were part of the record below concerned only the type of vehicle "preferred" by thieves and contained no information with regard to the type of thief likely to be found with such a vehicle. Aside from the officer's unsupported statement, no facts in the record establish the other elements of the profile. The stop in this case was not the result of the formal statistical analysis used in *Ochoa*. We can only conclude that this is not a true profile case and the State's reliance on *Ochoa* is misplaced.

The circumstances here make it clear that there was no justified, founded suspicion that appellant was engaged in criminal activity. As a result, the stop and subsequent arrest of appellant violated his fourth amendment rights.

Accordingly, the judgment of conviction is reversed.

C.   ILLEGAL ALIENS

In an effort to control illegal immigration to the United States, the Border Patrol operates permanent "checkpoints" away from the border where all motorists are observed as they drive through. On the basis of this observation, some of the motorists are stopped for questioning and inspection. The empirical foundation for the decision to select certain motorists for closer scrutiny has been the subject of much judicial dispute.

UNITED STATES v. MARTINEZ-FUERTE

Supreme Court of the United States, 1976.
428 U.S. 543, 96 S.Ct. 3074, 49 L.Ed.2d 1116.

■ MR. JUSTICE POWELL delivered the opinion of the Court.

These cases involve criminal prosecutions for offenses relating to the transportation of illegal Mexican aliens. Each defendant was arrested at a permanent checkpoint operated by the Border Patrol away from the international border with Mexico, and each sought the exclusion of certain evidence on the ground that the operation of the checkpoint was incompatible with the Fourth Amendment. In each instance whether the Fourth Amendment was violated turns primarily on whether a vehicle may be stopped at a fixed checkpoint for brief questioning of its occupants even though there is no reason to believe the particular vehicle contains illegal aliens.

[I]n *Brignoni-Ponce,* we recognized that Fourth Amendment analysis in this context also must take into account the overall degree of interference with legitimate traffic. 422 U.S., at 822–883, 95 S.Ct., at 2580–2581. We concluded there that random roving-patrol stops could not be tolerated because they "would subject the residents of . . . [border] areas to potentially unlimited interference with their use of the highways, solely at the discretion of Border Patrol officers." [I]bid. There also was a grave danger that such unreviewable discretion would be abused by some officers in the field.

Routine checkpoint stops do not intrude similarly on the motoring public. First, the potential interference with legitimate traffic is minimal. Motorists using these highways are not taken by surprise as they know, or may obtain knowledge of, the location of the checkpoints and will not be stopped elsewhere. Second, checkpoint operations both appear to and actually involve less discretionary enforcement activity. The regularized manner in which established checkpoints are operated is visible evidence, reassuring to law-abiding motorists, that the stops are duly authorized and believed to serve the public interest. [A]nd since field officers may stop only those cars passing the checkpoint, there is less room for abusive or harassing stops of individuals than there was in the case of roving-patrol stops. Moreover, a claim that a particular exercise of discretion in locating or operating a checkpoint is unreasonable is subject to post-stop judicial review.

The defendants arrested at the San Clemente checkpoint suggest that its operation involves a significant extra element of intrusiveness in that only a small percentage of cars are referred to the secondary inspection area, thereby "stigmatizing" those diverted and reducing the assurances provided by equal treatment of all motorists. We think defendants overstate the consequences. Referrals are made for the sole purpose of conducting a routine and limited inquiry into residence status that cannot feasibly be made of every motorist where the traffic is heavy. The objective intrusion of the stop and inquiry thus remains minimal. Selective referral may involve some annoyance, but it remains true that the stops should not be frightening or offensive because of their public and relatively routine nature. Moreover, selective referrals—rather than questioning the occupants of every car—tend to advance some Fourth Amendment interests by minimizing the intrusion on the general motoring public.

[W]e further believe that it is constitutional to refer motorists selectively to the secondary inspection area at the San Clemente checkpoint on the basis of criteria that would not sustain a roving-patrol stop. Thus, even if it be assumed that such referrals are made largely on the basis of apparent Mexican ancestry,[16] we perceive no constitutional violation. As the intrusion here is sufficiently minimal that no particularized reason need exist to justify it, we think it follows that the Border Patrol officers must have wide discretion in selecting the motorists to be diverted for the brief questioning involved.[17]

[I]n summary, we hold that stops for brief questioning routinely conducted at permanent checkpoints are consistent with the Fourth Amendment and need not be authorized by warrant. The principal protection of Fourth Amendment rights at checkpoints lies in appropriate limitations on the scope of the stop. We have held that checkpoint searches are constitutional only if justified by consent or probable cause to search. And our holding today is limited to the type of stops described in this opinion. "[A]ny further detention ... must be based on consent or probable cause." *United States v. Brignoni-Ponce,* supra, at 882.

■ MR. JUSTICE BRENNAN, with whom MR. JUSTICE MARSHALL joins, dissenting.

[I]n abandoning any requirement of a minimum of reasonable suspicion, or even articulable suspicion, the Court in every practical sense renders meaningless, as applied to checkpoint stops, the *Brignoni-Ponce* holding that "standing alone [Mexican appearance] does not justify stopping all Mexican-Americans to ask if they are aliens."[1] 422 U.S., at 887, 95

---

16. The Government suggests that trained Border Patrol agents rely on factors in addition to apparent Mexican ancestry when selectively diverting motorists. This assertion finds support in the record. Less than 1% of the motorists passing the checkpoint are stopped for questioning, whereas American citizens of Mexican ancestry and legally resident Mexican citizens constitute a significantly larger proportion of the population of southern California. The 1970 census figures, which may not fully reflect illegal aliens, show the population of California to be approximately 19,958,000 of whom some 3,102,000, or 16%, are Spanish-speaking or of Spanish surname. The equivalent percentages for metropolitan San Diego and Los Angeles are 13% and 18% respectively. If the statewide population ratio is applied to the approximately 146,000 vehicles passing through the checkpoint during the eight days surrounding the arrests in No. 74–1560, roughly 23,400 would be expected to contain persons of Spanish or Mexican ancestry, yet only 820 were referred to the secondary area. This appears to refute any suggestion that the Border Patrol relies extensively on apparent Mexican ancestry standing alone in referring motorists to the secondary area.

17. Of the 820 vehicles referred to the secondary inspection area during the eight days surrounding the arrests involved in No. 74–1560, roughly 20% contained illegal aliens. Thus, to the extent that the Border Patrol relies on apparent Mexican ancestry at this checkpoint, see n. 16, supra, that reliance clearly is relevant to the law enforcement need to be reserved. Cf. United States v. Brignoni-Ponce, supra, at 886–887, 95 S.Ct., at 2583, where we noted that "[t]he likelihood that any given person of Mexican ancestry is an alien is high enough to make Mexican appearance a relevant factor ...," although we held that apparent Mexican ancestry by itself could not create the reasonable suspicion required for a roving-patrol stop. Different considerations would arise if, for example, reliance were put on apparent Mexican ancestry at a checkpoint operated near the Canadian border.

1. *Brignoni-Ponce,* which involved roving-patrol stops, said:

"[Mexican ancestry] alone would justify neither a reasonable belief that they were aliens, nor a reasonable belief that the car concealed other aliens who were illegally in the country. Large numbers of native-born and naturalized citizens have the physical

S.Ct., at 2583. Since the objective is almost entirely the Mexican illegally in the country, checkpoint officials, uninhibited by any objective standards and therefore free to stop any or all motorists without explanation or excuse, wholly on whim, will perforce target motorists of Mexican appearance. The process will then inescapably discriminate against citizens of Mexican ancestry and Mexican aliens lawfully in this country for no other reason than that they unavoidably possess the same "suspicious" physical and grooming characteristics of illegal Mexican aliens.

Every American citizen of Mexican ancestry and every Mexican alien lawfully in this country must know after today's decision that he travels the fixed checkpoint highways at the risk of being subjected not only to a stop, but also to detention and interrogation, both prolonged and to an extent far more than for non-Mexican appearing motorists. To be singled out for referral and to be detained and interrogated must be upsetting to any motorist. One wonders what actual experience supports my Brethren's conclusion that referrals "should not be frightening or offensive because of their public and relatively routine nature." In point of fact, referrals, viewed in context, are not relatively routine; thousands are otherwise permitted to pass. But for the arbitrarily selected motorists who must suffer the delay and humiliation of detention and interrogation, the experience can obviously be upsetting. And that experience is particularly vexing for the motorist of Mexican ancestry who is selectively referred, knowing that the officers' target is the Mexican alien. That deep resentment will be stirred by a sense of unfair discrimination is not difficult to foresee.[4]

---

characteristics identified with Mexican ancestry, and even in the border area a relatively small proportion of them are aliens. The likelihood that any given person of Mexican ancestry is an alien is high enough to make Mexican appearance a relevant factor, but standing alone it does not justify stopping all Mexican-Americans to ask if they are aliens." 422 U.S., at 886–887, 95 S.Ct., at 2583 (footnote omitted).

Today we are told that secondary referrals may be based on criteria that would not sustain a roving-patrol stop, and specifically that such referrals may be based largely on Mexican ancestry. Even if the difference between *Brignoni-Ponce* and this decision is only a matter of degree, we are not told what justifies the different treatment of Mexican appearance or why greater emphasis is permitted in the less demanding circumstances of a checkpoint. That law in this country should tolerate use of one's ancestry as probative of possible criminal conduct is repugnant under any circumstances.

4. [E]ven if good faith is assumed, the affront to the dignity of American citizens of Mexican ancestry and Mexican aliens lawfully within the country is in no way diminished. The fact still remains that people of Mexican ancestry are targeted for examination at checkpoints and that the burden of checkpoint intrusions will lie heaviest on them. That, as the Court observes, "[l]ess than 1% of the motorists passing the checkpoint are stopped for questioning," whereas approximately 16% of the population of California is Spanish-speaking or of Spanish surname, has little bearing on this point—or, for that matter, on the integrity of Border Patrol practices. There is no indication how many of the 16% have physical and grooming characteristics identifiable as Mexican. There is no indication what portion of the motoring public in California is of Spanish or Mexican ancestry. Given the socioeconomic status of this portion, it is likely that the figure is significantly less than 16%. Neither is there any indication that those of Mexican ancestry are not subjected to lengthier initial stops than others,

NOTES

1. Further Developments. In United States v. Montero-Camargo (208 F.3d 1122, 2000), Border Patrol agents arrested two individuals driving cars with Mexacali license plates, who had made a U-turn just before a permanent stationary checkpoint in El Centro, California, fifty miles north of the Mexican border. Defendants filed a pre-trial motion to suppress evidence on the ground that the vehicle stop was not based on reasonable suspicion. The district court denied the motion based on several factors, including the fact that the occupants of the car "appeared to be of Hispanic descent." On appeal, the Ninth Circuit upheld the district court's finding of reasonable suspicion, but the Ninth Circuit based its finding on factors other than apparent ethnicity. Concerning the use of apparent ethnicity, the court stated:

> The likelihood that in an area in which the majority-or even a substantial part-of the population is Hispanic, any given person of Hispanic ancestry is in fact an alien, let alone an illegal alien, is not high enough to make Hispanic appearance a relevant factor in the reasonable suspicion calculus. [T]he population of Imperial County, in which El Centro is located, is 73% Hispanic. [A]ccordingly, Hispanic appearance is of little or no use in determining which particular individuals among the vast Hispanic populace should be stopped by law enforcement officials on the lookout for illegal aliens. Reasonable suspicion requires *particularized* suspicion, and in an area in which a large number of people share a specific characteristic, that characteristic casts too wide a net to play any part in a particularized reasonable suspicion determination. [S]tops based on race or ethnic appearance send the underlying message to all our citizens that those who are not white are judged by the color of their skin alone. Such stops also send a clear message that those who are not white enjoy a lesser degree of constitutional protection-that they are in effect assumed to be potential criminals first and individuals second. Id at 1132–35.

2. Other Highway Checkpoints. In Michigan Department of State Police v. Sitz, 496 U.S. 444, 110 S.Ct. 2481, 110 L.Ed.2d 412 (1990), the United States Supreme Court upheld the constitutionality of highway sobriety checkpoint stops. The court relied on a study finding that "approximately 1.5 percent of the drivers passing through the checkpoint were arrested for alcohol impairment. [B]y way of comparison, the record from one of the consolidated cases in *Martinez-Fuerte* showed that in the associated checkpoint, illegal aliens were found in only 0.12 percent of the vehicles passing through the checkpoint." 496 U.S. at 453–455, 110 S.Ct. at 2487–2488.

even if they are not secondarily detained. Finally, there is no indication of the ancestral makeup of the 1% who are referred for secondary detention. If, as is quite likely the case, it is overwhelmingly Mexican, the sense of discrimination which will be felt is only enhanced.

In Indianapolis v. Edmond, 531 U.S. 32, 121 S.Ct. 447, 148 L.Ed.2d 333 (2000), however, the Supreme Court, by a vote of 5–4, invalidated highway vehicle checkpoints set up to interdict illegal drugs. "Because the primary purpose of the Indianapolis checkpoint program is ultimately indistinguishable from the general interest in crime control, the checkpoints violate the Fourth Amendment." Id.

D. ILLEGAL DRUGS

By far the most controversial use of social science to provide a context for making law enforcement decisions is the "drug courier profile." At many major American airports, agents of the Drug Enforcement Administration use this screening device to determine which travellers are most likely to be transporting drugs, and thus should receive a disproportionate share of investigatory attention.

UNITED STATES v. MENDENHALL

Supreme Court of the United States, 1980.
446 U.S. 544, 100 S.Ct. 1870, 64 L.Ed.2d 497.

■ MR. JUSTICE STEWART announced the judgment of the Court and delivered an opinion in which MR. JUSTICE REHNQUIST joined.

The respondent was brought to trial in the United States District Court for the Eastern District of Michigan on a charge of possessing heroin with intent to distribute it. She moved to suppress the introduction at trial of the heroin as evidence against her on the ground that it had been acquired from her through an unconstitutional search and seizure by agents of the Drug Enforcement Administration (DEA).

[T]he respondent arrived at the Detroit Metropolitan Airport on a commercial airline flight from Los Angeles early on the morning of February 10, 1976. As she disembarked from the airplane, she was observed by two agents of the DEA, who were present at the airport for the purpose of detecting unlawful traffic in narcotics. After observing the respondent's conduct, which appeared to the agents to be characteristic of persons unlawfully carrying narcotics,[1] the agents approached her as she was walking through the concourse, identified themselves as federal agents, and asked to see her identification and airline ticket. The respondent produced her driver's license, which was in the name of Sylvia Mendenhall, and, in answer to a question of one of the agents, stated that she resided at the

---

1. The agent testified that the respondent's behavior fit the so-called "drug courier profile"—an informally compiled abstract of characteristics thought typical of persons carrying illicit drugs. In this case the agents thought it relevant that (1) the respondent was arriving on a flight from Los Angeles, a city believed by the agents to be the place of origin for much of the heroin brought to Detroit; (2) the respondent was the last person to leave the plane, "appeared to be very nervous," and "completely scanned the whole area where [the agents] were standing"; (3) after leaving the plane the respondent proceeded past the baggage area without claiming any luggage; and (4) the respondent changed airlines for her flight out of Detroit.

address appearing on the license. The airline ticket was issued in the name of "Annette Ford." When asked why the ticket bore a name different from her own, the respondent stated that she "just felt like using that name." In response to a further question, the respondent indicated that she had been in California only two days. Agent Anderson then specifically identified himself as a federal narcotics agent and, according to his testimony, the respondent "became quite shaken, extremely nervous. She had a hard time speaking."

After returning the airline ticket and driver's license to her, Agent Anderson asked the respondent if she would accompany him to the airport DEA office for further questions. She did so. [A]t the office the agent asked the respondent if she would allow a search of her person and handbag and told her that she had the right to decline the search if she desired. She responded: "Go ahead."

[A] female police officer then arrived to conduct the search of the respondent's person. [T]he policewoman again asked the respondent if she consented to the search, and the respondent replied that she did. [A]s the respondent removed her clothing, she took from her undergarments two small packages, one of which appeared to contain heroin, and handed both to the policewoman. The agents then arrested the respondent for possessing heroin.

[T]he Court of Appeals reversed the respondent's subsequent conviction, stating only that "the court concludes that this case is indistinguishable from United States v. McCaleb," 552 F.2d 717 (C.A.6 1977). In *McCaleb* the Court of Appeals had suppressed heroin seized by DEA agents at the Detroit Airport in circumstances substantially similar to those in the present case. The Court of Appeals there disapproved the Government's reliance on the so-called "drug courier profile," and held that the agents could not reasonably have suspected criminal activity in that case, for the reason that "the activities of the [persons] observed by DEA agents, were consistent with innocent behavior," id., at 720.

[W]e conclude that a person has been "seized" within the meaning of the Fourth Amendment only if, in view of all of the circumstances surrounding the incident, a reasonable person would have believed that he was not free to leave. Examples of circumstances that might indicate a seizure, even where the person did not attempt to leave, would be the threatening presence of several officers, the display of a weapon by an officer, some physical touching of the person of the citizen, or the use of language or tone of voice indicating that compliance with the officer's request might be compelled.

[B]ecause the search of the respondent's person was not preceded by an impermissible seizure of her person, it cannot be contended that her apparent consent to the subsequent search was infected by an unlawful detention. There remains to be considered whether the respondent's consent to the search was for any other reason invalid. The District Court explicitly credited the officers' testimony and found that the "consent was freely and voluntarily given." There was more than enough evidence in this case to sustain that view. First, we note that the respondent, who was 22 years old and had an 11th-grade education, was plainly capable of a knowing consent. Second, it is especially significant that the respondent was twice expressly told that she was free to decline to consent to the search, and only thereafter explicitly consented to it.

[W]e conclude that the District Court's determination that the respondent consented to the search of her person "freely and voluntarily" was sustained by the evidence and that the Court of Appeals was, therefore, in error in setting it aside. Accordingly, the judgment of the Court of Appeals is reversed, and the case is remanded to that court for further proceedings.

It is so ordered.

■ MR. JUSTICE POWELL, with whom THE CHIEF JUSTICE and MR. JUSTICE BLACKMUN join, concurring in part and concurring in the judgment.

[B]ecause neither of the courts below considered the question, I do not reach the Government's contention that the agents did not "seize" the respondent within the meaning of the Fourth Amendment. In my view, we may assume for present purposes that the stop did constitute a seizure. I would hold—as did the District Court—that the federal agents had reasonable suspicion that the respondent was engaging in criminal activity, and, therefore, that they did not violate the Fourth Amendment by stopping the respondent for routine questioning.

[T]he public has a compelling interest in detecting those who would traffic in deadly drugs for personal profit. Few problems affecting the health and welfare of our population, particularly our young, cause greater concern than the escalating use of controlled substances. Much of the drug traffic is highly organized and conducted by sophisticated criminal syndicates. The profits are enormous. And many drugs, including heroin, may be easily concealed. As a result, the obstacles to detection of illegal conduct may be unmatched in any other area of law enforcement.

To meet this pressing concern, the Drug Enforcement Administration since 1974 has assigned highly skilled agents to the Detroit Airport as part of a nationwide program to intercept drug couriers transporting narcotics between major drug sources and distribution centers in the United States. Federal agents have developed "drug courier profiles," that describe the characteristics generally associated with narcotics traffickers. For example, because the Drug Enforcement Administration believes that most drugs enter Detroit from one of four "source" cities (Los Angeles, San Diego, Miami, or New York), agents pay particular attention to passengers who arrive from those places.

During the first 18 months of the program, agents watching the Detroit Airport searched 141 persons in 96 encounters. They found controlled substances in 77 of the encounters and arrested 122 persons. 409 F.Supp., at 539. When two of these agents stopped the respondent in February 1976, they were carrying out a highly specialized law enforcement operation designed to combat the serious societal threat posed by narcotics distribution.

[I]n reviewing the factors that led the agents to stop and question the respondent, it is important to recall that a trained law enforcement agent may be "able to perceive and articulate meaning in given conduct which would be wholly innocent to the untrained observer." Brown v. Texas, [443 U.S. 47, 99 S.Ct. 2637, 61 L.Ed.2d 357 (1979)] at 52, n. 2, 99 S.Ct., at 2641, n. 2. Among the circumstances that can give rise to reasonable suspicion are the agent's knowledge of the methods used in recent criminal activity and the characteristics of persons engaged in such illegal practices. Law enforcement officers may rely on the "characteristics of the area," and the behavior of a suspect who appears to be evading police contact. United States v. Brignoni-Ponce, 422 U.S., at 884–885, 95 S.Ct., at 2581–2582. "In all situations the officer is entitled to assess the facts in light of his experience." Id., at 885, 95 S.Ct., at 2582.

The two officers who stopped the respondent were federal agents assigned to the Drug Enforcement Administration. Agent Anderson, who initiated the stop and questioned the respondent, had 10 years of experience and special training in drug enforcement. He had been assigned to the Detroit Airport, known to be a crossroads for illicit narcotics traffic, for over a year and he had been involved in approximately 100 drug-related arrests.

The agents observed respondent as she arrived in Detroit from Los Angeles. The respondent, who appeared very nervous, engaged in behavior that the agents believed was designed to evade detection. She deplaned only after all other passengers had left the aircraft. Agent Anderson testified that drug couriers often disembark last in order to have a clear view of the terminal so that they more easily can detect government agents. Once inside the terminal respondent scanned the entire gate area and walked "very, very slowly" toward the baggage area. When she arrived there, she claimed no baggage. Instead, she asked a skycap for directions to the Eastern Airlines ticket counter located in a different terminal. Agent Anderson stood in line immediately behind the respondent at the ticket counter. Although she carried an American Airlines ticket for a flight from Detroit to Pittsburgh, she asked for an Eastern Airlines ticket. An airline employee gave her an Eastern Airlines boarding pass. Agent Anderson testified that drug couriers frequently travel without baggage and change flights en route to avoid surveillance. Ibid. On the basis of these observations, the agents stopped and questioned the respondent.

The District Court, which had an opportunity to hear Agent Anderson's testimony and judge his credibility, concluded that the decision to stop the respondent was reasonable. I agree. The public interest in preventing drug traffic is great, and the intrusion upon respondent's privacy was minimal. The specially trained agents acted pursuant to a well-planned, and effective, federal law enforcement program. They observed respondent engaging in conduct that they reasonably associated with criminal activity. Furthermore, the events occurred in an airport known to be frequented by drug couriers.[6] In light of all of the circumstances, I would hold that the agents possessed reasonable and articulable suspicion of criminal activity when they stopped the respondent in a public place and asked her for identification.

The jurisprudence of the Fourth Amendment demands consideration of the public's interest in effective law enforcement as well as each person's constitutionally secured right to be free from unreasonable searches and seizures. In applying a test of "reasonableness," courts need not ignore the considerable expertise that law enforcement officials have gained from their special training and experience. The careful and commendable police work that led to the criminal conviction at issue in this case satisfies the requirements of the Fourth Amendment.

■ Mr. Justice White, with whom Mr. Justice Brennan, Mr. Justice Marshall, and Mr. Justice Stevens join, dissenting.

[A]t the time they stopped Ms. Mendenhall, the DEA agents' suspicion that she was engaged in criminal activity was based solely on their brief observations of her conduct at the airport. The officers had no advance information that Ms. Mendenhall, or anyone on her flight, would be carrying drugs. What the agents observed Ms. Mendenhall do in the airport was not "unusual conduct" which would lead an experienced officer reasonably to conclude that criminal activity was afoot, id., at 30, 88 S.Ct. at 1884, but rather the kind of behavior that could reasonably be expected of anyone changing planes in an airport terminal.

None of the aspects of Ms. Mendenhall's conduct, either alone or in combination, were sufficient to provide reasonable suspicion that she was engaged in criminal activity. The fact that Ms. Mendenhall was the last person to alight from a flight originating in Los Angeles was plainly insufficient to provide a basis for stopping her. Nor was the fact that her flight originated from a "major source city," for the mere proximity of a person to areas with a high incidence of drug activity or to persons known to be drug addicts, does not provide the necessary reasonable suspicion for an investigatory stop.

Under the circumstances of this case, the DEA agents' observations that Ms. Mendenhall claimed no luggage and changed airlines were also insufficient to provide reasonable suspicion. Unlike the situation in Terry v. Ohio, 392 U.S., at 28, 88 S.Ct., at 1883, where "nothing in [the suspects'] conduct from the time [the officer] first noticed them until the time he confronted them and identified himself as a police officer gave him sufficient reason to negate [his] hypothesis" of criminal behavior, Ms. Mendenhall's subsequent conduct negated any reasonable inference that she was traveling a long distance without luggage or changing her ticket to a

---

6. The results of the Drug Enforcement Agency's efforts at the Detroit Airport support the conclusion that considerable drug traffic flows through the Detroit Airport. Contrary to Mr. Justice White's apparent impression, post at n. 11, I do not believe that these statistics establish by themselves the reasonableness of this search. Nor would reliance upon the "drug courier profile" necessarily demonstrate reasonable suspicion. Each case raising a Fourth Amendment issue must be judged on its own facts.

different airline to avoid detection. Agent Anderson testified that he heard the ticket agent tell Ms. Mendenhall that her ticket to Pittsburgh already was in order and that all she needed was a boarding pass for the flight. Thus it should have been plain to an experienced observer that Ms. Mendenhall's failure to claim luggage was attributable to the fact that she was already ticketed through to Pittsburgh on a different airline. Because Agent Anderson's suspicion that Ms. Mendenhall was transporting narcotics could be based only on "his inchoate and unparticularized suspicion or 'hunch,'" rather than "specific reasonable inferences which he is entitled to draw from the facts in light of his experience," id., at 27, 88 S.Ct., at 1883, he was not justified in "seizing" Ms. Mendenhall.[11]

NOTES

1.   Experience as "Data." The Supreme Court's original "stop and frisk" case, Terry v. Ohio, 392 U.S. 1, 88 S.Ct. 1868, 20 L.Ed.2d 889 (1968) is an early example of the use of impressionistic data to identify persons in the process of committing crime. Chief Justice Earl Warren described in detail the experience of Officer McFadden, who had stopped and frisked the defendant. "[H]e had been a policeman for 39 years and a detective for 35 and [h]e had been assigned to patrol his vicinity of downtown Cleveland for shoplifters and pickpockets for 30 years. He explained that he had developed routine habits of observation over the years." 392 U.S. at 5, 88 S.Ct. at 1871. Officer McFadden testified that when he noticed Terry, the defendant, and a companion, "they didn't look right to me." He observed the two men standing on a street corner for a lengthy period, taking turns walking down the street to stare into a store window 24 times, and conferring with each other after each trip. The Chief Justice stated that "It would have been poor police work indeed for an officer of 30 years' experience in the detection of thievery from stores in this same neighborhood to have failed to investigate this behavior." Id. at 23, 88 S.Ct. at 1881. Officer McFadden approached the suspects, frisked them for weapons, and found two guns. The Supreme Court ruled that it was constitutionally permissible for Officer McFadden to rely upon his own experience in

---

11. Mr. Justice Powell's conclusion that there were reasonable grounds for suspecting Ms. Mendenhall of criminal activity relies heavily on the assertion that the DEA agents "acted pursuant to a well-planned, and effective, federal law enforcement program." Yet there is no indication that the asserted successes of the "drug courier program" have been obtained by reliance on the kind of nearly random stop involved in this case. Indeed, the statistics Mr. Justice Powell cites on the success of the program at the Detroit Airport refer to the results of searches following stops "based upon information acquired from the airline ticket agents, from [the agents'] independent police work," and occasional tips, as well as observations of behavior at the airport. United States v. Van Lewis, 409 F.Supp. 535, 538 (E.D.Mich.1976), aff'd, 556 F.2d 385 (C.A.6 1977). Here, however, it is undisputed that the DEA agents' suspicion that Ms. Mendenhall was engaged in criminal activity was based solely on their observations of her conduct in the airport terminal.

forming the "reasonable suspicion" necessary to make what is now referred to as a "*Terry*-stop."

2.   Competence to Consent. Justice Stewart thought it relevant to "note that the respondent, who was 22 years old and had an 11th-grade education, was plainly capable of a knowing consent" to be searched. While he did not cite it, there is a growing body of social science research on "competence" to waive rights. These studies have focused on the competence of children to waive *Miranda* rights. T. Grisso, Juvenile's Waiver of Rights: Legal and Psychological Competence (1981) found that over half of a large sample of incarcerated juveniles aged 11–16 did not comprehend at least one of their *Miranda* rights. The two most common misunderstandings concerned the warning that statements made to the police "can and will be used against you in a court of law" (often understood to mean that disrespect to a police officer would be punished) and the warning of a right to consult an attorney before and during an interrogation (often understood to apply only to future court appearances). Comprehension of rights increased with age through age 13, and by age 14 was equivalent to that of adults.

3.   Subsequent Research on the Validity of the Drug Courier Profile. The National Institute of Justice conducted an empirical study of the validity of the Drug Enforcement Administration's efforts to identify drug couriers. Zedlewski, The DEA Airport Surveillance Program: An Analysis of Agent Activities (1984). For an 8-week period in the summer of 1982, DEA agents completed an Encounter Report on all passengers they contacted in airports in the United States. In addition, they kept a log on the number of passengers observed on each arriving and departing flight. Of approximately 107,000 passengers observed during this period, 146 were approached by DEA agents, a "contact rate" of 1.3 per thousand passengers. The report stated, id. at 2:

> A preponderance (120 of 146) of the encounters [82 percent] resulted from a combination of behavioral and demographic peculiarities exhibited by the subject which made the agent suspicious (e.g., ___,[1] etc.). In the opinions of the agents filling out the reports, these behaviors were suspicious but not sufficient to detain the subject.

In 42 of the 146 contacts (29 percent), the agents permitted the passengers to proceed after questioning without searching them. In 81 contacts (55 percent) the passengers consented to being searched. In 15 cases (10 percent) the agents conducted a search either after obtaining a warrant or incident to arrest. There were "other" outcomes, such as "an

---

1. Ed. Note: Examples of these "profile" characteristics presented in the original report were "deleted in the interest of safeguarding surveillance techniques" in the version that became public information. We would like to thank Charles J. Fanning, Special Assistant to the Assistant Administrator for Operations of the Drug Enforcement Administration, for obtaining the release of this report to the Editors pursuant to the Freedom of Information Act, and Edwin W. Zedlewski, Office of Research and Evaluation Methods, National Institute of Justice, for clarifying several points in the report.

alert call to the subjects' destination [or] referral to local police" in 8 cases (5 percent).

The study noted that "of the 103 searches conducted, 49 uncovered either contraband or evidence of some other crime. Thus the agent's suspicions were confirmed in nearly half [48 percent] of the occasions in which they sought a search."[2] Id. at 2. In 33 of these 49 cases (67 percent) the evidence discovered consisted of illegal drugs—heroin, cocaine, amphetamines, or "large quantities" of hashish. One case uncovered illegal weapons (and two of the drug discoveries also uncovered firearms). In 25 searches (31 percent) the evidence consisted of "coded payment ledgers," the identification of "known dealers," "large sums of currency" (from $30,000 to $196,000), or "other contraband."

Of the 49 persons whose search uncovered evidence of illegal behavior, 17 (35 percent) had refused a request to consent to the search. The report commented upon this finding, id. at 2:

> The consent to search granted by the other 65 percent has two interpretations: either they were unaware of their rights or they felt that denial was futile. Support for the latter hypothesis can be found in an analysis of those 11 cases[3] where a consent search was denied: agents either obtained a warrant or made an arrest in 9 of those cases. [I]t appears that in certain cases the agent stands ready to arrest or to seek a search warrant if consent is denied.

———

UNITED STATES v. SOKOLOW

Supreme Court of the United States, 1989.
490 U.S. 1, 109 S.Ct. 1581, 104 L.Ed.2d 1.

■ CHIEF JUSTICE REHNQUIST delivered the opinion of the Court.

Respondent Andrew Sokolow was stopped by Drug Enforcement Administration (DEA) agents upon his arrival at Honolulu International Airport. The agents found 1,063 grams of cocaine in his carry-on luggage. When respondent was stopped, the agents knew, *inter alia,* that (1) he paid $2,100 for two airplane tickets from a roll of $20 bills; (2) he traveled under a name that did not match the name under which his telephone number was listed; (3) his original destination was Miami, a source city for illicit drugs; (4) he stayed in Miami for only 48 hours, even though a round-trip

2. Ed. Note: The "103 searches" consisted of 81 persons who consented to be searched, 15 persons who were searched with a warrant or incident to arrest and 7 of the persons who experienced "other" outcomes.

3. Ed. Note: The discrepancy between the 17 subjects mentioned as refusing a request to consent to being searched and the 11 subjects analyzed here appears to lie in the fact that in 6 of the "other outcomes" cases a search was made, but not by the DEA. For example, the local police may have been called and may have arrested a subject for disorderly conduct and performed a search incident to the arrest.

flight from Honolulu to Miami takes 20 hours; (5) he appeared nervous during his trip; and (6) he checked none of his luggage.

[T]his case involves a typical attempt to smuggle drugs through one of the Nation's airports. On a Sunday in July 1984, respondent went to the United Airlines ticket counter at Honolulu Airport, where he purchased two round-trip tickets for a flight to Miami leaving later that day. The tickets were purchased in the names of "Andrew Kray" and "Janet Norian," and had open return dates. Respondent paid $2,100 for the tickets from a large roll of $20 bills, which appeared to contain a total of $4,000. He also gave the ticket agent his home telephone number. The ticket agent noticed that respondent seemed nervous; he was about 25 years old; he was dressed in a black jumpsuit and wore gold jewelry; and he was accompanied by a woman, who turned out to be Janet Norian. Neither respondent nor his companion checked any of their four pieces of luggage.

After the couple left for their flight, the ticket agent informed Officer John McCarthy of the Honolulu Police Department of respondent's cash purchase of tickets to Miami. Officer McCarthy determined that the telephone number respondent gave to the ticket agent was subscribed to a "Karl Herman," who resided at 348A Royal Hawaiian Avenue in Honolulu. Unbeknownst to McCarthy (and later to the DEA agents), respondent was Herman's roommate. The ticket agent identified respondent's voice on the answering machine at Herman's number. Officer McCarthy was unable to find any listing under the name "Andrew Kray" in Hawaii. McCarthy subsequently learned that return reservations from Miami to Honolulu had been made in the names of Kray and Norian, with their arrival scheduled for July 25, three days after respondent and his companion had left. He also learned that Kray and Norian were scheduled to make stopovers in Denver and Los Angeles.

On July 25, during the stopover in Los Angeles, DEA agents identified respondent. He "appeared to be very nervous and was looking all around the waiting area." App. 43–44. Later that day, at 6:30 p.m., respondent and Norian arrived in Honolulu. As before, they had not checked their luggage. Respondent was still wearing a black jumpsuit and gold jewelry. The couple proceeded directly to the street and tried to hail a cab, where Agent Richard Kempshall and three other DEA agents approached them. Kempshall displayed his credentials, grabbed respondent by the arm and moved him back onto the sidewalk. Kempshall asked respondent for his airline ticket and identification; respondent said that he had neither. He told the agents that his name was "Sokolow," but that he was traveling under his mother's maiden name, "Kray."

Respondent and Norian were escorted to the DEA office at the airport. There, the couple's luggage was examined by "Donker," a narcotics detector dog, which alerted to respondent's brown shoulder bag. The agents arrested respondent. He was advised of his constitutional rights and declined to make any statements. The agents obtained a warrant to search the shoulder bag. They found no illicit drugs, but the bag did contain several suspicious documents indicating respondent's involvement in drug trafficking. The agents had Donker reexamine the remaining luggage, and this time the dog alerted to a medium sized Louis Vuitton bag. By now, it was 9:30 p.m., too late for the agents to obtain a second warrant. They allowed respondent to leave for the night, but kept his luggage. The next morning, after a second dog confirmed Donker's alert, the agents obtained a warrant and found 1,063 grams of cocaine inside the bag.

Respondent was indicted for possession with the intent to distribute cocaine in violation of 21 U.S.C.A. § 841(a)(1). The United States District Court for Hawaii denied his motion to suppress the cocaine and other evidence seized from his luggage, finding that the DEA agents had a reasonable suspicion that he was involved in drug trafficking when they stopped him at the airport. Respondent then entered a conditional plea of guilty to the offense charged.

The United States Court of Appeals for the Ninth Circuit reversed respondent's conviction by a divided vote, holding that the DEA agents did not have a reasonable suspicion to justify the stop. 831 F.2d, at 1423. The majority divided the facts bearing on reasonable suspicion into two categories. In the first category, the majority placed facts describing "ongoing criminal activity," such as the use of an alias or evasive movement through an airport; the majority believed that at least one such factor was always needed to support a finding of reasonable suspicion. Id., at 1419. In the second category, it placed facts describing "personal characteristics" of drug couriers, such as the cash payment for tickets, a short trip to a major source city for drugs, nervousness, type of attire, and unchecked luggage. Id., at 1420. The majority believed that such facts, "shared by drug couriers and the public at large," were only relevant if there was evidence of ongoing criminal behavior and the Government offered "[e]mpirical documentation" that the combination of facts at issue did not describe the behavior of "significant numbers of innocent persons." Ibid. Applying this two-part test to the facts of this case, the majority found that there was no evidence of ongoing criminal behavior, and thus that the agents' stop was impermissible.

[T]he Court of Appeals held that the DEA agents seized respondent when they grabbed him by the arm and moved him back onto the sidewalk. 831 F.2d, at 1416. The Government does not challenge that conclusion, and we assume—without deciding—that a stop occurred here. Our decision, then, turns on whether the agents had a reasonable suspicion that respondent was engaged in wrongdoing when they encountered him on the sidewalk. In Terry v. Ohio, 392 U.S. 1, 30, 88 S.Ct. 1868, 1884–85, 20 L.Ed.2d 889 (1968), we held that the police can stop and briefly detain a person for investigative purposes if the officer has a reasonable suspicion supported by articulable facts that criminal activity "may be afoot," even if the officer lacks probable cause.

The officer, of course, must be able to articulate something more than an "inchoate and unparticularized suspicion or 'hunch'." Id., at 27, 88 S.Ct., at 1883. The Fourth Amendment requires "some minimal level of objective justification" for making the stop. INS v. Delgado, 466 U.S. 210,

217, 104 S.Ct. 1758, 1763, 80 L.Ed.2d 247 (1984). That level of suspicion is considerably less than proof of wrongdoing by a preponderance of the evidence. We have held that probable cause means "a fair probability that contraband or evidence of a crime will be found," Illinois v. Gates, 462 U.S. 213, 238, 103 S.Ct. 2317, 2332, 76 L.Ed.2d 527 (1983), and the level of suspicion required for a *Terry* stop is obviously less demanding than that for probable cause.

The concept of reasonable suspicion, like probable cause, is not "readily, or even usefully, reduced to a neat set of legal rules." Gates, supra, 462 U.S., at 232, 103 S.Ct., at 2329. We think the Court of Appeals' effort to refine and elaborate the requirements of "reasonable suspicion" in this case create unnecessary difficulty in dealing with one of the relatively simple concepts embodied in the Fourth Amendment. In evaluating the validity of a stop such as this, we must consider "the totality of the circumstances—the whole picture." United States v. Cortez, 449 U.S. 411, 417, 101 S.Ct. 690, 695, 66 L.Ed.2d 621 (1981). As we said in *Cortez:*

> "The process does not deal with hard certainties, but with probabilities. Long before the law of probabilities was articulated as such, practical people formulated certain common-sense conclusions about human behavior; jurors as factfinders are permitted to do the same— and so are law enforcement officers." Id., at 418, 101 S.Ct., at 695.

The rule enunciated by the Court of Appeals, in which evidence available to an officer is divided into evidence of "ongoing criminal behavior," on the one hand, and "probabilistic" evidence, on the other, is not in keeping with the quoted statements from our decisions. It also seems to us to draw a sharp line between types of evidence, the probative value of which varies only in degree. The Court of Appeals classified evidence of traveling under an alias, or evidence that the suspect took an evasive or erratic path through an airport, as meeting the test for showing "ongoing criminal activity." But certainly instances are conceivable in which traveling under an alias would not reflect ongoing criminal activity: for example, a person who wished to travel to a hospital or clinic for an operation and wished to conceal that fact. One taking an evasive path through an airport might be seeking to avoid a confrontation with an angry acquaintance or with a creditor. This is not to say that each of these types of evidence is not highly probative, but they do not have the sort of ironclad significance attributed to them by the Court of Appeals.

On the other hand, the factors in this case that the Court of Appeals treated as merely "probabilistic" also have probative significance. Paying $2,100 in cash for two airplane tickets is out of the ordinary, and it is even more out of the ordinary to pay that sum from a roll of $20 bills containing nearly twice that amount of cash. Most business travelers, we feel confident, purchase airline tickets by credit card or check so as to have a record for tax or business purposes, and few vacationers carry with them thousands of dollars in $20 bills. We also think the agents had a reasonable ground to believe that respondent was traveling under an alias; the evidence was by no means conclusive, but it was sufficient to warrant consideration. While a trip from Honolulu to Miami, standing alone, is not a cause for any sort of suspicion, here there was more: surely few residents of Honolulu travel from that city for 20 hours to spend 48 hours in Miami during the month of July.

Any one of these factors is not by itself proof of any illegal conduct and is quite consistent with innocent travel. But we think taken together they amount to reasonable suspicion. We said in Reid v. Georgia, 448 U.S. 438, 100 S.Ct. 2752, 65 L.Ed.2d 890 (1980) (*per curiam*), "there could, of course, be circumstances in which wholly lawful conduct might justify the suspicion that criminal activity was afoot." Id., at 441, 100 S.Ct., at 2754. Indeed, *Terry* itself involved "a series of acts, each of them perhaps innocent" if viewed separately, "but which taken together warranted further investigation." 392 U.S., at 22, 88 S.Ct., at 1881; see also *Cortez*, 449 U.S., at 417–419, 101 S.Ct., at 694–696. We noted in *Gates*, 462 U.S., at 243–244, n. 13, 103 S.Ct., at 2335 n. 13 (1983), that "innocent behavior will frequently provide the basis for a showing of probable cause," and that "[i]n making a determination of probable cause the relevant inquiry is not whether particular conduct is 'innocent' or 'guilty,' but the degree of suspicion that attaches to particular types of noncriminal acts." That principle applies equally well to the reasonable suspicion inquiry.

We do not agree with respondent that our analysis is somehow changed by the agents' belief that his behavior was consistent with one of the DEA's "drug courier profiles."[6] A court sitting to determine the existence of reasonable suspicion must require the agent to articulate the factors leading to that conclusion, but the fact that these factors may be set forth in a "profile" does not somehow detract from their evidentiary significance as seen by a trained agent.

[W]e hold that the agents had a reasonable basis to suspect that respondent was transporting illegal drugs on these facts. The judgment of the Court of Appeals is therefore reversed and the case remanded for further proceedings consistent with our decision.

———

NEW JERSEY v. SOTO ET AL

Superior Court of New Jersey, Law Division, 1996.
324 N.J.Super. 66, 734 A.2d 350.

■ ROBERT E. FRANCIS, J.S.C.

These are consolidated motions to suppress under the equal protection and due process clauses of the Fourteenth Amendment. Seventeen defendants of African ancestry claim that their arrests on the New Jersey Turnpike south of exit 3 between 1988 and 1991 result from discriminatory enforcement of the traffic laws by the New Jersey State Police. After a

---

6. Agent Kempshall testified that respondent's behavior "had all the classic aspects of a drug courier." App. 59. Since 1974, the DEA has trained narcotics officers to identify drug smugglers on the basis of the sort of circumstantial evidence at issue here.

lengthy hearing, I find defendants have established a *prima facie* case of selective enforcement which the State has failed to rebut requiring suppression of all contraband and evidence seized.

Defendants base their claim of institutional racism primarily on statistics. During discovery, each side created a database of all stops and arrests by State Police members patrolling the Turnpike between exits 1 and 7A out of the Moorestown Station for thirty-five randomly selected days between April 1988 and May 1991 from arrest reports, patrol charts, radio logs and traffic tickets.

[T]o establish a standard against which to compare the stop data, the defense conducted a traffic survey and a violator survey. Dr. John Lamberth, Chairman of the Psychology Department at Temple University who I found is qualified as an expert in statistics and social psychology, designed both surveys.

The traffic survey was conducted over twenty-one randomly selected two and one-half hour sessions between June 11 and June 24, 1993 and between 8:00 a.m. and 8:00 p.m. at four sites, two northbound and two southbound, between exits 1 and 3 of the Turnpike. Teams supervised by Fred Last, Esq., of the Office of the Public Defender observed and recorded the number of vehicles that passed them except for large trucks, tractor-trailers, buses and government vehicles, how many contained a ''black'' occupant and the state of origin of each vehicle. Of the 42,706 vehicles counted, 13.5% had a black occupant. Dr. Lamberth testified that this percentage is consistent with the 1990 Census figures.

[T]he violator survey was conducted over ten sessions in four days in July 1993 by Mr. Last traveling between exits 1 and 3 in his vehicle at sixty miles per hour on cruise control after the speedometer had been calibrated and observing and recording the number of vehicles that passed him, the number of vehicles he passed and how many had a black occupant. Mr. Last counted a total of 2096 vehicles other than large trucks, tractortrailers, buses and government vehicles of which 2062 or 98.1% passed him going in excess of sixty miles per hour including 306 with a black occupant equaling about 15% of those vehicles clearly speeding. Multiple violators, that is those violating the speed limit and committing some other moving violation like tailgating, also equaled about 15% black. Dr. Lamberth testified that the difference between the percentage of black violators and the percentage of black travelers from the surveys is statistically insignificant and that there is no evidence traffic patterns changed between the period April 1988 to May 1991 in the databases and June–July 1993 when the surveys were done.

Using 13.5% as the standard or benchmark against which to compare the stop data, Dr. Lamberth found that 127 or 46.2% of the race identified stops between exits 1 and 3 were of blacks constituting an absolute disparity of 32.7%, a comparative disparity of 242% (32.7% divided by 13.5%) and 16.35 standard deviations. By convention, something is considered statistically significant if it would occur by chance fewer than five times in a hundred (over two standard deviations).[3]

[T]he State presented the testimony of Dr. Leonard Cupingood to challenge or refute the statistical evidence offered by the defense. I found Dr. Cupingood is qualified to give expert testimony in the field of statistics. [D]r. Cupingood had no genuine criticism of the defense traffic survey. Rather, he centered his criticism of the defense statistical evidence on the violator survey. Throughout his testimony he maintained that the violator survey failed to capture the relevant data which he opined was the racial mix of those speeders most likely to be stopped or the "tail of the distribution." He even recommended the State authorize him to design a study to collect this data, but the State declined. [I]n any event, his supposition that maybe blacks drive faster than whites above the speed limit was repudiated by all State Police members called by the State who were questioned about it. [M]oreover, Dr. Cupingood acknowledged that he knew of no study indicating that blacks drive worse than whites.

[C]onvinced in his belief that the defense 15% standard or benchmark was open to question, Dr. Cupingood attempted to find the appropriate benchmark to compare with the databases. He did [several] studies of presumedly race-blind stops: night stops versus day stops; [and] radar stops versus non-radar stops.

[I]n his study of night stops versus day stops, he compared the percentage of stops of blacks at night between exits 1 and 7A in the databases with the percentage of stops of blacks during daytime and found that night stops were 37.3% black versus 30.2% for daytime stops. Since he presumed the State Police generally cannot tell race at night, he concluded the higher percentage for night stops of blacks supported a standard well above 15%. His premise that the State Police generally cannot recognize race at night, however, is belied by the evidence. On July 16, 1994 between 9:40 p.m. and 11:00 p.m. Ahmad S. Corbitt, now an assistant deputy public defender, together with Investigator Minor of the Office of the Public Defender drove on the Turnpike at 55 miles per hour for a while and parked perpendicular to the Turnpike at a rest stop for a while to see if they could make out the races of the occupants of the vehicles they observed. Mr. Corbitt testified that the two could identify blacks versus whites about 80% of the time in the moving mode and close to 100% in the stationary mode.

[N]ext, in his study of radar stops versus non-radar stops, Dr. Cupingood focused on the race identified tickets where radar was used in the databases and found that 28.5% of them were issued to blacks. Since he assumed that radar is race neutral, he suggested 28.5% might be the

---

3. Dr. Lamberth erred in using 13.5% as the standard for comparison with the stop data. The violator survey indicates that 14 .8%, rounded to 15%, of those observed speeding were black. This percentage is the percentage Dr. Lamberth should have used in making statistical comparisons with the stop data in the databases. Nonetheless, it would appear that whatever the correctly calculated disparities and standard deviations are, they would be nearly equal to those calculated by Dr. Lamberth.

correct standard. As Dr. Kadane said in rebuttal, this study is fundamentally flawed because it assumes what is in question or that the people stopped are the best measure of who is eligible to be stopped. If racial prejudice were afoot, the standard would be tainted. In addition, although a radar device is race-blind, the operator may not be. Of far more significance is the defense study comparing the traffic tickets issued by the Radar [U]nit which shows again that where radar is used by a unit concerned primarily with speeders [rather than drugs] and acting with little or no discretion like the Radar Unit, the percentage of tickets issued to blacks is consistent with their percentage on the highway.

[T]he right to be free from discrimination is firmly supported by the Fourteenth Amendment to the United States Constitution and the protections of *Article I, paragraphs 1* and *5 of the New Jersey Constitution of 1947*. To be sure, "[t]he eradication of the 'cancer of discrimination' has long been one of our State's highest priorities." *Dixon v. Rutgers, The State University of N.J., 110 N.J. 432, 451, 541 A.2d 1046 (1988)*. It is indisputable, therefore, that the police may not stop a motorist based on race or any other invidious classification. See *State v. Kuhn, 213 N.J.Super. 275, 517 A.2d 162 (1986)*.

[W]here objective evidence establishes "that a police agency has embarked upon an officially sanctioned or *de facto* policy of targeting minorities for investigation and arrest," any evidence seized will be suppressed to deter future insolence in office by those charged with enforcement of the law and to maintain judicial integrity. *State v. Kennedy, 247 N.J.Super. 21, 588 A.2d 834 (App.Div.1991)*.

Statistics may be used to make out a case of targeting minorities for prosecution of traffic offenses provided the comparison is between the racial composition of the motorist population violating the traffic laws and the racial composition of those arrested for traffic infractions on the relevant roadway patrolled by the police agency. *Wards Cove Packing Co. v. Atonio,* [490 U.S. 642 (1989)]. While defendants have the burden of proving "the existence of purposeful discrimination," discriminatory intent may be inferred from statistical proof presenting a stark pattern or an even less extreme pattern in certain limited contexts. *McCleskey v. Kemp, 481 U.S. 279* (1987).

[O]nce defendants expose a *prima facie* case of selective enforcement, the State generally cannot rebut it by merely calling attention to possible flaws or unmeasured variables in defendants' statistics. Rather, the State must introduce specific evidence showing that either there actually are defects which bias the results or the missing factors, when properly organized and accounted for, eliminate or explain the disparity.

[H]ere, defendants have proven at least a *de facto* policy on the part of the State Police out of the Moorestown Station of targeting blacks for investigation and arrest between April 1988 and May 1991 both south of exit 3 and between exits 1 and 7A of the Turnpike. Their surveys satisfy *Wards Cove, supra.* The statistical disparities and standard deviations revealed are indeed stark. The discretion devolved upon general road troopers to stop any car they want [e]vinces a selection process that is susceptible of abuse. The utter failure of the State Police hierarchy to monitor and control [its officers] or investigate the many claims of institutional discrimination manifests its indifference if not acceptance. Against all this, the State submits only denials and the conjecture and flawed studies of Dr. Cupingood.

The eradication of illegal drugs from our State is an obviously worthy goal, but not at the expense of individual rights. As Justice Brandeis so wisely said dissenting in *Olmstead v. United States, 277 U.S. 438, 479, 48 S.Ct. 564, 72 L.Ed. 944 (1928)*:

> "Experience should teach us to be most on our guard to protect liberty when the government's purposes are beneficent. Men born to freedom are naturally alert to repel invasion of their liberty by evil-minded rulers. The greatest dangers to liberty lurk in insidious encroachment by men of zeal, well-meaning but without understanding."

Motions granted.

———

UNITED STATES v. NEW JERSEY

United States District Court for the District of New Jersey, 1999.
CIVIL NO. 99-5970(MLC)

JOINT APPLICATION FOR ENTRY OF CONSENT DECREE

Plaintiff, the United States, and Defendants, the State of New Jersey and the Division of State Police of the New Jersey Department of Law and Public Safety, respectfully move this Court for entry of [this] Consent Decree.

The United States has simultaneously filed its Complaint against the Defendants alleging violations of 42 U.S.C. § 14141 and 42 U.S.C. § 3789d(c). The Complaint alleges a pattern or practice of conduct by troopers of the New Jersey State Police that deprives persons of rights, privileges, or immunities secured or protected by the Constitution and the laws of the United States. Defendants deny that the State Police has engaged in a pattern or practice of conduct that deprives persons of rights, privileges,or immunities secured or protected by the Constitution and laws of the United States.

The parties seek to enter into this Decree jointly for the purpose of avoiding the risks and burdens of litigation, and to support vigorous, lawful, and nondiscriminatory traffic enforcement that promotes traffic safety and assists law enforcement to interdict drugs and other contraband, arrest fugitives, and enforce firearms and other criminal statutes.

The United States and the State of New Jersey have agreed upon a proposed Consent Decree that would resolve all claims in the United States' Complaint. The proposed Decree would address the claims in the United States' Complaint by amending certain policies, practices, and procedures relating to the manner in which the State of New Jersey manages and operates the New Jersey State Police.

[T]he proposed Decree includes the following provisions:

1) *Policy Requirements*: State troopers may not rely to any degree on the race or national or ethnic origin of motorists in selecting vehicles for traffic stops and in deciding upon the scope and substance of post-stop actions, except where state troopers are on the look-out for a specific suspect who has been identified in part by his or her race or national or ethnic origin.

[2] *Traffic Stop Documentation*: State troopers engaged in patrol activities will document the race, ethnic origin, and gender of all motor vehicle drivers who are the subject of a traffic stop, and also will record information about the reason for each stop and any post-stop action that is taken (including the issuance of a ticket or warning, asking the vehicle occupants to exit the vehicle and frisking them, consensual and non-consensual vehicle searches, uses of force, and arrests).

3) *Supervisory Review of Individual Traffic Stops*: Supervisors regularly will review trooper reports concerning post-stop enforcement actions and procedures, and patrol car video tapes of traffic stops, to ensure that troopers are employing appropriate practices and procedures.

[4] *Supervisory Review of Patterns of Conduct*: The State will develop and implement an early warning system, called the "Management Awareness Program," that uses computerized information on traffic stops, misconduct investigations, and other matters to assist State Police supervisors to identify and modify potentially problematic behavior.

[5] *Misconduct Allegations*: The State Police will make complaint forms and informational materials available at a variety of locations, will institute a 24-hour toll-free telephone hotline, and will publicize the State Police toll-free number at all State-operated rest stops located on limited access highways.

[6] *Training*: The State Police will continue to implement measures to improve training for recruits and incumbent troopers. The training will address such matters as supervisory issues, communication skills, cultural diversity, and the nondiscrimination requirements of the Decree.

[7] *Auditing by the New Jersey Attorney General's Office*: The State Attorney General's Office will have special responsibility for ensuring implementation of the Decree. The Office will conduct various audits of State Police performance, which will include contacting samples of persons who were the subject of a State Police traffic stop to evaluate whether the stops were appropriately conducted and documented.

[8] *State Police Public Reports*: The State Police will issue semiannual public reports containing aggregate statistics on certain law enforcement activities, including traffic stop statistics.

9) *Independent Monitor*: An Independent Monitor, who will be an agent of the court, will be selected by the United States and the State of

New Jersey to monitor and report on the State's implementation of the Decree.

[10] *Decree Term*: The basic term of the Decree will be five years, however, based on the State's record of compliance, the United States and the Independent Monitor may agree to a request by the State to shorten the term of the Decree if the State has been in substantial compliance for at least two years.

Joint entry of this Decree is in the public interest since it provides for expeditious remedial activity and avoids the diversion of federal and State resources to adversarial actions by the parties.

[F]or the reasons discussed above, entry of the Decree is lawful and appropriate. Therefore, the United States and the State jointly move for entry of the Consent Decree.

SO ORDERED this 30th day of December 30, 1999.

MARY L. COOPER, UNITED
STATES DISTRICT JUDGE

SELECTED BIBLIOGRAPHY

Acker, Social Sciences and the Criminal Law: The Fourth Amendment, Probable Cause, and Reasonable Suspicion, 23 Criminal Law Bulletin 49 (1987).

Baker, Flying While Arab–Racial Profiling and Air Travel Security, 67 Journal of Air Law and Commerce 1375 (2002).

Kadish, The Drug Courier Profile: In Planes, Trains, and Automobiles; And Now in the Jury Box, 46 American University Law Review 747 (1997).

Harcourt, Rethinking Racial Profiling: A Critique of the Economics, Civil Liberties, and Constitutional Literature, and of Criminal Profiling More Generally, 71 University of Chicago Law Review 1275 (2004).

Harris, The Stories, the Statistics, and the Law: Why "Driving While Black" Matters, 84 Minnesota Law Review 265 (1999).

Knowles, Persico, and Todd, Racial Bias in Motor Vehicle Searches; Theory and Evidence, 109 Journal of Political Economy 203 (2001).

K. Meeks, Driving While Black: What To Do If You Are a Victim of Racial Profiling (2000).

Michelson, Driving While Black: A Skeptical Note, 44 Jurimetrics 161 (2004).

Slobogin, The World Without a Fourth Amendment, 39 U.C.L.A. Law Review 1 (1991).

Slobogin and Schumacher, Rating the Intrusiveness of Law Enforcement Searches and Seizures, 17 Law and Human Behavior 183 (1993).

Slobogin and Schumacher, Reasonable Expectations of Privacy and Autonomy in Fourth Amendment Cases: An Empirical Look at "Understandings Recognized and Permitted by Society." 42 Duke Law Journal 727 (1993).

Thompson, Stopping the Usual Suspects: Race and the Fourth Amendment, 74 New York University Law Review 956 (1999).

SECTION IV.   CONTEXTS FOR DETERMINING PAST FACTS

The most frequent use of social science to provide a context for determining facts occurs when a fact is alleged to have happened in the past. This use takes place only at trial, the setting in which the legal system formally adjudicates past events. Social science has been used at trial to provide contexts for determining facts concerning defendants, victims, and witnesses.

A.   DEFENDANTS

In criminal law, a number of social factors have been brought to bear upon the determination of whether the defendant committed the act in question, and, if so, committed it with the state of mind required by the statute. We here consider the effect of a defendant's culture, subculture, personality, and a variety of what might be called "life events."

1.   CULTURE

The question of whether "cultural difference" is a factor that may legitimately be taken into account in reaching decisions about criminal liability and punishment is one that evokes strong opinions. In cases involving recent immigrants to the United States as defendants, anthropologists are increasingly being called as expert witnesses to provide decision makers with a cultural context for making a determination about the defendants' state of mind.

PEOPLE v. PODDAR

California Court of Appeal, 1972.
26 Cal.App.3d 438, 103 Cal.Rptr. 84.

■ DEVINE, PRESIDING JUSTICE.

Appellant, who was a student at the University of California at Berkeley, killed a young woman, Tanya Tarasoff, with whom he had a romantic interest which, while temporarily and partly reciprocated, later was rejected. He called at her home, asked to speak with her. She refused to converse, and screamed. Thereupon, appellant shot her with a pellet gun, pursued her as she ran from the house, grabbed her and stabbed her many times with a kitchen knife which, with the gun, he had brought with him. He called the police, told them he had stabbed the woman, and asked that he be handcuffed. He was found guilty of second degree murder, and on his plea of not guilty by reason of insanity, he was found sane. On appeal he does not contend that the judgment on the insanity plea should be set aside.

[A]t the trial, appellant offered to present as witness an anthropologist, possessor of a Ph.D. degree in social sciences, who had lived more than twenty years in India. She had particularly studied adjustment and difficulties of Indian students who had come to American universities. Appellant offered to prove that the expert would testify to cultural stresses which would affect the adjustment of appellant in shifting from the simple culture in which he had lived (he was of the Harijan caste, the untouchables) to the sophisticated milieu of an American university. More particularly, she would testify that the cultural strain becomes acute in relationships between men and women because the normal marriage in India is arranged for the parties. Altogether, according to the offer of proof, her testimony would give evidence of diminished capacity.

The judge was of the opinion that the witness was not qualified to testify on the direct consequences to appellant of cultural stresses, but the judge did offer to allow the witness to testify to facts of cross-cultural difficulties, and to allow counsel to ask hypothetical questions of psychiatric experts, the questions to include factual data supplied by the anthropologist. Appellant's counsel declined, on the ground that he wished to use the anthropologist as an independent expert witness on the issue of diminished capacity so that the jury could draw whatever inferences it found proper from this testimony itself and not as filtered through the testimony of psychiatrists.

[W]e conclude that it was proper to exclude the testimony in the form in which it was offered. Diminished capacity is a mental infirmity. To the extent that it is to be evaluated by experts, the experts should be those qualified in the mental sciences. The effect, therefore, of such matters as cultural stress should be assessed by experts in the fields of psychiatry and psychology, and ultimately by the jury with the assistance of the testimony of such experts. We need not consider whether it would have been proper to exclude the anthropologist's testimony completely, because the court was willing, as we have said above, to allow the testimony as furnishing material for the opinions of the psychiatrists. It is desirable to give direction and control to the presentation of expert testimony of such delicate matters as the capacity of a person to deliberate or to entertain malice. To allow independent testimony on sociological, ethnic or like influences, not as reviewed by experts in psychological sciences, but as directly presented to the jury, would be to open the door to a vast amount of argument from various sources, the result of which would often be distraction of the jury and the removing of their deliberation from the essential element of the mental capacity of the accused.

———

NOTES

1. Diminished Capacity. Poddar argued that expert evidence of "cultural stresses" should have been admitted on the issue of diminished capacity.

"Diminished capacity" had been explained to the jury as follows: "if you find that [Poddar's] mental capacity was diminished to the extent that you have a reasonable doubt whether he did harbor malice aforethought, you cannot find him guilty of murder of either the first or second degree." 111 Cal.Rptr. at 913 n. 3, 518 P.2d at 345 n. 3.

The California Supreme Court overturned the court of appeal's *Poddar* decision, 10 Cal.3d 750, 111 Cal.Rptr. 910, 518 P.2d 342 (1974), but not on the ground that the anthropologist's testimony was excluded. Rather, the court held that the above jury instructions had been defective because the jurors had not been "specifically told that the evidence of diminished capacity was directly applicable to the questions of whether defendant was both aware that he must act within the law, and that he acted despite such awareness." 111 Cal.Rptr. at 917, 518 P.2d at 349.

The California legislature abolished diminished capacity as a defense to crime in 1982, largely on the basis of the arguments of Professor Stephen Morse in Diminished Capacity: A Moral and Legal Conundrum, 2 International Journal of Law and Psychiatry 271 (1979).

2.   The Anthropology of "Wrongful" Conduct. An instance in which a court completely barred an anthropologist from testifying at trial occurred in Chase v. United States, 468 F.2d 141 (7th Cir.1972). On May 25, 1969, Chase and numerous others broke into a Selective Service office in Chicago, removed draft records, and burned them to protest the Vietnam War. They were tried on four counts related to destroying government property. Several of the defendants pleaded not guilty by reason of insanity, but were convicted. Among the issues on appeal was whether the trial judge had improperly excluded evidence supporting this claim. The Seventh Circuit, Id. at 147–149, stated why it did not find the exclusion improper:

> There is virtually nothing in the record to suggest that any of the defendants was suffering from any legally cognizable mental illness on May 24 or May 25, 1969, or that they did not fully understand that their conduct was "wrong" as measured by the standards prescribed by society. Their evidence of "insanity" merely tended to prove that their moral judgment as to whether certain conduct—specifically their own deliberate violations of law—was "right" or "wrong" was at odds with the judgment expressed by society at large.

> [T]he trial judge properly excluded certain evidence which [w]ould have provided no support for the claim that these defendants could not comprehend the criminal character of their conduct. Thus, an anthropologist was not allowed to testify that the defendants believed their conduct was morally correct, and further, that the same conduct might be considered sane in one culture and insane in another.

> [T]he judge's evidentiary rulings were well within the scope of his discretion. We find absolutely no merit in the contention that these four dedicated intellectuals were not given an adequate opportunity to present their defense of "insanity."

———

PEOPLE v. APHAYLATH

Court of Appeals of New York, 1986.
68 N.Y.2d 945, 510 N.Y.S.2d 83, 502 N.E.2d 998.

MEMORANDUM

Defendant, a Laotian refugee living in this country for approximately two years, was indicted and tried for the intentional murder of his Laotian wife of one month. At trial, defendant attempted to establish the affirmative defense of extreme emotional disturbance to mitigate the homicide (Penal Law § 125.25[1][a]) on the theory that the stresses resulting from his status of a refugee caused a significant mental trauma, affecting his mind for a substantial period of time, simmering in the unknowing subconscious and then inexplicably coming to the fore. Although the immediate cause for the defendant's loss of control was his jealousy over his wife's apparent preference for an ex-boyfriend, the defense argued that under Laotian culture the conduct of the victim wife in displaying affection for another man and receiving phone calls from an unattached man brought shame on defendant and his family sufficient to trigger defendant's loss of control.

The defense was able to present some evidence of the Laotian culture through the cross-examination of two prosecution witnesses and through the testimony of defendant himself, although he was hampered by his illiteracy in both his native tongue and English. Defendant's ability to adequately establish his defense was impermissibly curtailed by the trial court's exclusion of the proffered testimony of two expert witnesses concerning the stress and disorientation encountered by Laotian refugees in attempting to assimilate into the American culture. It appears from the record before us that the sole basis on which the court excluded the expert testimony was because "neither one * * * was going to be able to testify as to anything specifically relating to this defendant". It is unclear from this ruling whether the Trial Judge determined that she had no discretion to allow the testimony because the experts had no knowledge of this particular defendant or that she declined to exercise her discretion because of the experts' lack of knowledge of the defendant or his individual background and characteristics. Under either interpretation, however, the exclusion of this expert testimony as a matter of law was erroneous because the admissibility of expert testimony that is probative of a fact in issue does not depend on whether the witness has personal knowledge of a defendant or a defendant's particular characteristics. Whether or not such testimony is sufficiently relevant to have probative value is a determination to be made by the Trial Judge in the exercise of her sound discretion.

Accordingly, because the court's ruling was not predicated on the appropriate standard and the defendant may have been deprived of an opportunity to put before the jury information relevant to his defense, a new trial must be ordered.

———

DANG VANG v. VANG XIONG X. TOYED

United States Court of Appeals, Ninth Circuit, 1991.
944 F.2d 476.

■ Brunetti, Circuit Judge:

Vang Xiong Toyed ("Xiong") appeals from a judgment entered after a jury verdict against him in a suit pursuant to 42 U.S.C.A. § 1983 (§ 1983). Plaintiffs, along with their spouses, brought this action against Xiong, a Washington State employee, asserting he raped them during the course of his employment.

[T]he parties in this case are Hmong refugees from Laos. Appellee Yia Moua ("Moua") moved with her family to Spokane, Washington in 1979. In 1981 she sought employment and was referred to Xiong who was employed by the Washington State Employment Security office. Xiong was responsible for interviewing and finding refugees suitable employment.

[I]n 1983 Moua contacted Xiong to assist her in learning to drive and in passing the Washington driver's license test. Moua alleged that sometime between January and March 1983 Xiong picked her up and told her he was going to take her some place where she could study for the driver's exam. The two drove to a motel where, Moua charges, Xiong raped her.

In 1983 appellee Maichao Vang ("Vang") moved with her family to the Spokane area from a refugee camp in Thailand. Vang testified she eventually contacted Xiong to assist her in obtaining employment. [O]n one occasion Xiong insisted that she accompany him to Idaho to deliver a letter to a Hmong family. Instead, Xiong drove Vang to a motel where he raped her twice.

[E]ventually each plaintiff revealed the rape to her husband and the couples filed a complaint under § 1983 against Xiong. [T]he trial resulted in a verdict in favor of the plaintiffs for $300,000. [P]rior to trial, Xiong challenged the testimony of Marshall Hurlich, an epidemiologist with the Seattle Department of Public Health. Hurlich described Hmong culture and explained the behavior of the plaintiffs in this case within that cultural context. The trial court granted Xiong's motion in limine in part and denied it in part. Hurlich was permitted to testify "generally as to the Hmong culture, but [he was precluded from testifying] as to his opinion regarding the specifics of this case, such as whether there was a rape or why these particular plaintiffs did not report the rape."

At trial, Hurlich explained that Hmong women are generally submissive, and are raised to respect and obey men. He described the role of Hmong women in marriage; their attitudes towards sex, discussion of sex, and extramarital affairs. Most significantly, Hurlich explained that upon fleeing from Laos, Hmong refugees were reliant on government officials for their needs and would not survive in the United States without government assistance. Because of this reliance on government assistance, the Hmong have developed an awe of persons in government positions.

[T]he district court in this case did not abuse its discretion in deciding that Hurlich's testimony, which the court limited to a general explanation of Hmong culture and the role of women in that culture, was relevant. In a hearing that preceded the evidentiary ruling the court said "Hurlich is . . . the only expert that either side has located who can explain to the trier of fact who these people are, where they came from, and *why they have responded the way they have in these various functions and various relationships.*" The testimony was relevant to assist the trier of fact to understand certain behavior of the parties here that might otherwise be confusing,[3] and to explain the cause, effect and nature of long term Hmong reliance on governmental agencies for support. The testimony was prejudicial to Xiong because it supported plaintiffs assertions that he raped them. It was not, however, *unduly prejudicial* because of its limited scope and its direct relevance to the issues in the case.

[T]he judgment of the district court is AFFIRMED.

PEOPLE v. WU

California Court of Appeal, Fourth District, 1991.
286 Cal.Rptr. 868.*

■ TIMLIN, ACTING PRESIDING JUDGE.

[The defendant, Helen Wu, was convicted by a jury of the second degree murder of her eight year old son, Sidney. Ms. Wu was born and raised in China, where she resided. Sidney lived with his father in the United States. On a visit to California, Ms. Wu learned that her mother-in-law, who had been kind to her son, was dying of cancer. Ms. Wu was also told by Sidney that his father—Ms. Wu's estranged husband—was having an affair with another woman. Upon hearing this, Ms. Wu cut the cord off a window blind and strangled Sidney to death, and then slashed her own wrists. She was discovered several hours later by Sidney's father and revived by paramedics.]

The prosecution's theory seems to have been that defendant killed Sidney because of anger at Sidney's father, and to get revenge. The defense's theory was that defendant believed that Sidney [w]as looked down upon and was ill-treated by everyone except his paternal grandmother because he had been borne out of wedlock, and that when she learned that the grandmother was dying of cancer, she felt trapped and, in an intense emotional upheaval, strangled Sidney and then attempted to kill herself so that she could take care of Sidney in the afterlife.

---

3. For example, plaintiffs continued to have contact with Xiong after he raped them. Hurlich's testimony regarding the place of Hmong women in that culture was helpful in understanding plaintiffs' actions after Xiong's attacks.

* [Ed. Note: In denying review, the California Supreme Court ordered that this decision be not officially published. See Wu, 286 Cal. Rptr. at 868 n.*. California Rule of Court 977 prohibits its citation as precedent.]

[D]efendant contends that the trial court erred by refusing to give an instruction which pinpointed a significant aspect of her theory of the case, i.e., an instruction which told the jury it could choose to consider the evidence of defendant's cultural background in determining the presence or absence of the various mental states which were elements of the crimes with which she was charged.

[D]efendant requested the following instruction:

"You have received evidence of defendant's cultural background and the relationship of her culture to her mental state. You may, but are not required to, consider that the [sic] evidence in determining the presence or absence of the essential mental states of the crimes defined in these instructions, or in determining any other issue in this case."

At trial, the prosecutor objected to this instruction. ["]I just think we are making law that we simply are not in a position to make. There is no guidance in the appellate courts as far as I know on the issue of cultural jury instructions or cultural defense."

[U]ltimately, the court refused to give the instruction, commenting that it did not want to put the "stamp of approval on [defendant's] actions in the United States, which would have been acceptable in China."

The experts on transcultural psychology specifically testified that, in their opinion, defendant was acting while in an emotional crisis during the time that she obtained the knife and cord, strangled Sidney and then slashed her own wrist, and that her emotional state was intertwined with, and explainable by reference to, her cultural background. Specifically, the following testimony was given:

Dr. Chien testified:

["]It was very—in my expertise as a transcultural psychiatry, in my familiarity, with my familiarity with the Chinese culture translate and from the information interview I obtain from Helen, she thought she was doing that out from the mother's love, mother's responsibility to bring a child together with her when she realized that there was no hope for her or a way for her to survive in this country or in this earth.

"Q Well, are you telling us that the death of Sidney was her act of love?

"A Yes. It's a mother's altruism. This may be very difficult for the Westerner to understand because I have dealt with many other so-called children who are sent to me from the children bureau. Children can be easily taken away from the mother in our agencies' mind. Social worker, when they discovered child abuse case or whatever case, children can be easily taken away from the parents.

"But in the Asian culture when the mother commits suicide and leave the children alone, usually they'll be considered to be a totally irresponsible behavior, and the mother will usually worry what would happen if she died, 'Who is going to take care of the children?' "[B]ecause the requested instruction was, for the most part, a correct statement of the law,[6] and because it was applicable to the evidence and one of defendant's [b]asic defenses in this case, upon retrial defendant is entitled to have the jury instructed that it may consider evidence of defendant's cultural background in determining the existence or nonexistence of the relevant mental states.

Because we have already decided that the judgment must be reversed [on other grounds] and because we only considered defendant's assertion that it was error not to give the cultural background instruction for purposes of guiding the trial court on retrial, we need not consider whether defendant was prejudiced by the failure to give the cultural background instruction.

———

STATE v. KARGAR

Supreme Judicial Court of Maine, 1996.
679 A.2d 81.

■ DANA, JUSTICE.

Mohammad Kargar, an Afghani refugee, appeals from the judgments entered in the Superior Court convicting him of two counts of gross sexual assault. Kargar contends on appeal that the court erred in denying his motion to dismiss pursuant to the de minimis statute, 17–A M.R.S.A. § 12 (1983).

[O]n June 25, 1993, Kargar and his family, refugees since approximately 1990, were babysitting a young neighbor. While the neighbor was there, she witnessed Kargar kissing his eighteen-month-old son's penis. When she was picked up by her mother, the girl told her mother what she had seen. The mother had previously seen a picture of Kargar kissing his son's penis in the Kargar family photo album. After her daughter told her what she had seen, the mother notified the police.

Peter Wentworth, a sergeant with the Portland Police Department, went to Kargar's apartment to execute a search warrant. [T]he picture of Kargar kissing his son's penis was found in the photograph album. Kargar admitted that it was him in the photograph and that he was kissing his son's penis. Kargar told Wentworth that kissing a young son's penis is accepted as common practice in his culture. Kargar also said it was very possible that his neighbor had seen him kissing his son's penis. Kargar was arrested and taken to the police station.

Prior to the jury-waived trial Kargar moved for a dismissal of the case pursuant to the de minimis statute. With the consent of the parties, the

---

6. The jury should not be instructed that the evidence of defendant's cultural background may be considered in connection with "any issue" in the case as stated in the last portion of the subject instruction; evidence may only be considered if it is relevant, and the evidence of defendant's cultural background was not necessarily relevant to "any issue" in the case. However, upon retrial, the trial court should correct such defects and give the requested instruction as so corrected.

court held the trial phase of the proceedings first, followed by a hearing on the de minimis motion. The de minimis hearing consisted of testimony from many Afghani people who were familiar with the Afghani practice and custom of kissing a young son on all parts of his body.[2] Kargar's witnesses, all relatively recent emigrants from Afghanistan, testified that kissing a son's penis is common in Afghanistan, that it is done to show love for the child, and that it is the same whether the penis is kissed or entirely put into the mouth because there are no sexual feelings involved.[3] The witnesses also testified that pursuant to Islamic law any sexual activity between an adult and a child results in the death penalty for the adult. Kargar also submitted statements from Professor Ludwig Adamec of the University of Arizona's Center for Near Eastern Studies and Saifur Halimi, a religious teacher and Director of the Afghan Mujahideen Information Bureau in New York. Both statements support the testimony of the live witnesses. The State did not present any witnesses during the de minimis hearing. Following the presentation of witnesses the court denied Kargar's motion and found him guilty of two counts of gross sexual assault.

Maine's de minimis statute [Section 12(1)] provides, in pertinent part:

1.   The court may dismiss a prosecution if, . . . having regard to the nature of the conduct alleged and the nature of the attendant circumstances, it finds the defendant's conduct:

> A.   Was within a customary license or tolerance, which was not expressly refused by the person whose interest was infringed and which is not inconsistent with the purpose of the law defining the crime; or
>
> B.   Did not actually cause or threaten the harm sought to be prevented by the law defining the crime or did so only to an extent too trivial to warrant the condemnation of conviction; or
>
> C.   Presents such other extenuations that it cannot reasonably be regarded as envisaged by the Legislature in defining the crime.

[O]ur review of the record in the instant case reveals that the court, in its analysis of section 12(1)(C), denied Kargar's motion without considering the full range of relevant factors. The court's interpretation of the subsection, which focused on whether the conduct met the definition of the gross sexual assault statute, operated to nullify the effect of the de minimis analysis called for by the statute. The focus is not on whether the conduct falls within the reach of the statute criminalizing it. If it did not, there would be no need to perform a de minimis analysis. The focus is on whether the admittedly criminal conduct was envisioned by the Legislature when it defined the crime. If the Legislature did not intend that there be an

---

2.   Kargar testified during the de minimis hearing that the practice was acceptable until the child was three, four, or five years old.

3.   Kargar testified during the de minimis hearing that his culture views the penis of a child as not the holiest or cleanest part of the body because it is from where the child urinates. Kargar testified that kissing his son there shows how much he loves his child precisely because it is not the holiest or cleanest part of the body.

individual, case-specific analysis then there would be no point to the de minimis statute. Subsection 1(C) provides a safety valve for circumstances that could not have been envisioned by the Legislature. It is meant to be applied on a case-by-case basis to unanticipated "extenuations," when application of the criminal code would lead to an "ordered but intolerable" result.

[A]ll of the evidence presented at the de minimis hearing supports the conclusion that there was nothing "sexual" about Kargar's conduct. There is no real dispute that what Kargar did is accepted practice in his culture. The testimony of every witness at the de minimis hearing confirmed that kissing a young son on every part of his body is considered a sign only of love and affection for the child. This is true whether the parent kisses, or as the trial court found, "engulfs" a son's penis. There is nothing sexual about this practice. In fact, the trial justice expressly recognized that if the State were required to prove a purpose of sexual gratification it "wouldn't have been able to have done so."

During its sentencing of Kargar, the court stated: "There is no sexual gratification. There is no victim impact." The court additionally recognized that the conduct for which Kargar was convicted occurred in the open, with his wife present, and noted that the photograph was displayed in the family photo album, available for all to see.[4] The court concluded its sentencing by recognizing that this case is "not at all typical [but instead is] fully the exception.... The conduct was unequivocally criminal, but the circumstances of that conduct and the circumstances of this defendant call for leniency." Although the court responded to this call for leniency by imposing an entirely suspended sentence, the two convictions expose Kargar to severe consequences independent of any period of incarceration, including his required registration as a sex offender [a]nd the possibility of deportation. [T]hese additional consequences emphasize why the factors recognized by the court during the sentencing hearing were also relevant to the de minimis analysis.

Although it may be difficult for us as a society to separate Kargar's conduct from our notions of sexual abuse, that difficulty should not result in a felony conviction in this case. The State concedes that dismissing this case pursuant to the de minimis statute would pose little harm to the community.

[I]n virtually every case the assumption that a physical touching of the mouth of an adult with the genitals of a child under the age of fourteen is inherently harmful is correct. This case, however, is the exception that proves the rule. Precisely because the Legislature did not envision the extenuating circumstances present in this case, to avoid an injustice the de minimis analysis set forth in section 12(1)(C) requires that Kargar's convictions be vacated.

----

4. Kargar's wife, Shamayel, testified during the sentencing hearing that she took the picture to send to Kargar's mother to show her how much he loved his son.

NOTES

1. Man Bites Dog. Haldane, Culture Clash or Animal Cruelty?, Los Angeles Times, March 13, 1989, Part 2, p. 1, reports the case of two Cambodian refugees who lived in Long Beach, California. A co-worker had given the men a German Shepherd puppy as a pet. Once in their apartment, however, the refugees slashed the dog's throat and began skinning it. Neighbors who heard the dog's yelps called the police, and the two men were arrested for cruelty to animals, an offense that carries a penalty of up to a year in jail.

> The defense [claimed] that the dog was killed humanely in a manner consistent with contemporary slaughterhouse practices, and that the two recent immigrants were following their own national customs with no idea they were offending American sensibilities.

> The trial judge ruled that killing a dog for food is not illegal unless done in a cruel way, and that cruelty had not been proven. Accordingly, all charges in the case were dismissed. In the wake of this decision, the Los Angeles Society for the Prevention of Cruelty to Animals began an educational campaign to teach immigrants that American culture does not condone the consumption of domestic pets. The Society began to distribute recipes which substituted other ingredients for dog and cat meat. McMillan, Pets Are Not Food in U.S., SPCA Will Advise Immigrants. Los Angeles Times, March 28, 1989, Part 2, p. 3.

2. "Female Circumcision." A Gambian immigrant to Paris was convicted of child mutilation and sentenced to one year in jail for arranging the clitorectomy of her two infants. The practice of "female circumcision" is prevalent in more than 20 African nations. "French doctors and social workers described with horror how midwives perform the ritual without anesthetic. Infections and complications that hinder intercourse and childbirth often follow." Simons, Crime or Custom? French Court Jails Mother For Girls' Ritual Mutilation, New York Times, January 17, 1993, p. E-2. One French anthropologist, however, denounced the verdict. "People practice it because they say the mutilation makes a girl more beautiful and cleaner. Girls who are not cut have trouble finding a husband. Parents are under heavy social pressure to do it. They mean no harm to their children. To make this a crime is excessive." Id.

> In Mohammed v. Gonzales, 400 F.3d 785 (9th Cir. 2005), a case concerning a Somalian woman's application for asylum, the Ninth Circuit held that "the extremely painful, physically invasive, psychologically damaging and permanently disfiguring process of genital mutilation undoubtedly rises to the level of persecution." Id. at 796. The court "reject[ed] the government's suggestion that female genital mutilation cannot be a basis for a claim of past persecution because it is 'widely-accepted and widely-practiced.'" Id.

3. Assimilation or Coercion? In England, a Yoruban immigrant was convicted of child abuse for scarring her child's face with a razor. She argued that she was initiating her child into her ethnic group, and that it would have been abusive *not* to have practiced this ritual. The British trial judge refused to recognize a cultural defense, but discharged the mother upon conviction. DeBenedictis, Judges Debate Cultural Defense, American Bar Association Journal, December 1992, p. 28. Professor Alison Dunes Renteln criticized this decision at a meeting of the U.S. National Association of Women Judges.

> A pluralistic society like the United States is "only pretending to accept cultural diversity if it rejects it when it really matters," she said. [R]enteln questioned that judge's assumption that the mother and other Yorubans must assimilate into English society. Requiring or expecting assimilation of minorities into the dominant culture is "potentially coercive," she said. Accommodation of other world views would be better, Renteln argued. Id.

> Others at the conference argued that any cultural defense for immigrants be time-limited, perhaps to be available only during the defendant's first ten years in the new country. It was also argued by a Native American judge that if any cultural defense became available to modern immigrants to the U.S., it should also be made available to Native American ethnic groups. Id. at 29.

2. SUBCULTURE

Not only foreign cultures, but subcultures within the United States as well have been argued to influence a criminal defendant's state of mind. The "subculture of poverty" has been the prototypic illustration of this form of social influence.

UNITED STATES v. ALEXANDER AND MURDOCK

United States Court of Appeals, District of Columbia Circuit, 1972.
471 F.2d 923.

■ BAZELON, CHIEF JUDGE, dissenting.

[Alexander and Murdock, both African-American males, were at a hamburger restaurant when a group of five white male Marine lieutenants and a woman friend of one of the Marines entered and sat at the counter. The two groups exchanged stares. Alexander verbally challenged the Marines, one of whom responded with a racial epithet. Alexander and Murdock then drew guns and began shooting. Two Marines were killed and one other Marine and the woman were wounded. Murdock raised the insanity defense, but was convicted of second-degree murder. Alexander was found guilty of assault with a dangerous weapon.

Numerous issues were raised on appeal, including the claim by Murdock that the instructions given by the trial judge unfairly prejudiced his insanity claim. The instructions included the statement:

> We are not concerned with a question of whether or not a man had a rotten social background. We are concerned with the question of his criminal responsibility. That is to say, whether he had an abnormal

condition of the mind that affected his emotional and behavioral processes at the time of the offense.

The majority of the court of appeals did not find this instruction to constitute reversible error.]

The thrust of Murdock's defense was that the environment in which he was raised—his "rotten social background"—conditioned him to respond to certain stimuli in a manner most of us would consider flagrantly inappropriate. Because of his early conditioning, he argued, he was denied any meaningful choice when the racial insult triggered the explosion in the restaurant. He asked the jury to conclude that his "rotten social background," and the resulting impairment of mental or emotional processes and behavior controls, ruled his violent reaction in the same manner that the behavior of a paranoid schizophrenic may be ruled by his "mental condition." Whether this impairment amounted to an "abnormal condition of the mind" is, in my opinion, at best an academic question. But the consequences we predicate on the answer may be very meaningful indeed.

We have never said that an exculpatory mental illness must be reflected in some organic or pathological condition. Nor have we enshrined psychosis as a prerequisite of the defense. But our experience has made it clear that the terms we use—"mental disease or defect" and "abnormal condition of the mind"—carry a distinct flavor of pathology. And they deflect attention from the crucial, functional question—did the defendant lack the ability to make any meaningful choice of action—to an artificial and misleading excursion into the thicket of psychiatric diagnosis and nomenclature.

It does not necessarily follow, however, that we should push the responsibility defense to its logical limits and abandon all of the trappings of the medical or disease model. However illogical and disingenuous, that model arguably serves important interests. Primarily, by offering a rationale for detention of persons who are found not guilty by reason of "insanity," it offers us shelter from a downpour of troublesome questions. If we were to facilitate Murdock's defense, as logic and morality would seem to command, so that a jury might acquit him because of his "rotten social background" rather than any treatable mental illness, the community would have to decide what to do with him.

We are left [w]ith an obligation to choose among four unattractive alternatives:

A.   We can impose narrow and admittedly illogical limitations on the responsibility defense to insure that a defendant like Murdock will not be acquitted on the theory that he lacked responsibility. By confining such a defendant in a penitentiary, we can avoid the difficult questions presented by the effort to hold him in confinement following a successful use of the responsibility defense.

B.   If we remove the practical impediments to Murdock's defense and he is, in fact, acquitted for lack of responsibility, he could be released from custody in spite of his apparent dangerousness. That result would conform with the principle that civil commitment is ordinarily barred where a defendant is dangerous but not mentally ill. And there are even precedents for the acquittal and release of dangerous defendants who have been brought to trial on a criminal charge. The fourth amendment exclusionary rule, for example, effectively precludes conviction of some defendants who appear to be dangerous. But that rule has been subjected to heavy assault even though it serves important, extrinsic interests—the redress and deterrence of unconstitutional action and the preservation of judicial integrity. Acquitting a defendant like Murdock and returning him to the street might also protect our integrity. But it would probably be more difficult to obtain public support for, or even unfriendly acquiescence in, Murdock's release than to defend the operation of the exclusionary rule. It could be said, after all, that acquittal would result not in spite of Murdock's dangerousness, but precisely because of it. Thus, while there may be no reason in logic why Murdock could not be returned to the street, as a practical matter that is probably an unfeasible result.

C. If the community will not tolerate Murdock's release we can strive to find a vaguely therapeutic purpose for hospitalization. Skinnerian-like techniques may be available to re-program his behavior. We might conclude that they should be used and that their use justifies his confinement. But that will require us to stretch the medical model substantially so that new techniques can be applied to many persons not conventionally considered "sick."

[D.] Finally, if there are no known or foreseeable techniques for "curing" someone like Murdock (or if we are unwilling to utilize the techniques that may be available), and if the incapacitation of the defendant is a practical imperative, we will have to confine him in exclusive reliance on a prediction of dangerousness. That confinement would be nothing more or less than unadorned preventive detention.

The options that would permit us to acquit Murdock but hold him in custody nonetheless—preventive detention and a stretching of the medical model to permit the use of new techniques—raise profound moral and legal questions. Resolution of those questions would require a prolonged and thorough public debate. But however they are resolved, it is at least clear that each of these options requires an expansion of the boundaries of the civil commitment doctrine. We could strive to limit the expansion by applying the new rationale only to persons who have undergone a criminal trial and been acquitted for lack of responsibility. But as a practical matter it seems very unlikely that the expansion could be so confined. The new rationale would permit—perhaps demand—that all persons who are rendered dangerous by a "rotten social background" should be preventively detained. Or that all persons who exhibit antisocial behavior patterns should have their behavior re-conditioned. We cannot escape the probability, if not absolute certainty, that every effort to diminish the class of persons who can be found criminally responsible will produce a concomitant expansion in the class of persons who can be subjected to involuntary civil commitment. The implications in this context are staggering. The price of permitting Murdock to claim the benefit of a logical aspect of the responsibility doctrine may be the unleashing of a detention device that operates, by hypothesis, at the exclusive expense of the lowest social and economic class.

That result can certainly be avoided—even if we are unwilling to return the defendant to the street—by reading the responsibility doctrine so narrowly that the issue of post-acquittal custody rarely arises. We could, for example, redefine the concept of responsibility so that it would approximate the concept of self-defense. All civil and criminal sanctions on the nonresponsible defendant would be barred, and the test would be reformulated to ask explicitly, which defendants should escape all state-imposed sanctions. Alternatively, we could retain the medical model and acknowledge its illogic as a significant virtue. Psychosis may be an irrational test of criminal responsibility, but it does have a recognizable symptomatology. In the civil commitment context it may provide the only manageable stopping point short of a fullfledged scheme of preventive detention. These limitations on the responsibility defense permit an avoidance—perhaps to the good—of a confrontation with the difficult questions posed by preventive detention and the various forms of behavior control.

On the other hand, we sacrifice a great deal by discouraging Murdock's responsibility defense. If we could remove the practical impediments to the free flow of information we might begin to learn something about the causes of crime. We might discover, for example, that there is a significant causal relationship between violent criminal behavior and a "rotten social background."[122] That realization would require us to consider, for example, whether income redistribution and social reconstruction are indispensable first steps toward solving the problem of violent crime.

THE TWILIGHT OF WELFARE CRIMINOLOGY

Stephen J. Morse.
49 Southern California Law Review 1247 (1976).

It is helpful to begin this analysis by noting that the probable source of Judge Bazelon's views is "liberal" social science orthodoxy. With the ascent of the social sciences to a position of intellectual respect, it was assumed generally that behavior was "caused" and that the causes of and the cures of crime would be discovered. Sociological thinkers saw the causes of crime in the social order; psychological and psychiatric thinkers saw the causes of crime in the personality disturbances of the criminal—which were usually hypothesized to have been produced by disordered family law. Sick societies and sick individuals were the causes of crime. The traditional criminal

---

122. We already know, of course, that there is an enormous *coincidental* relationship between violent street crime and "rotten social backgrounds." And the data plainly suggests that there is a strong *causal* rela-

tionship as well. See, e.g., Staff Report to the Nat'l Comm. on the Causes and Prevention of Violence, Vol. 12, Chapter 11: Sociological and Cultural Explanations (1969).

justice system was characterized as a band-aid and an ineffective "home remedy." The new scientific approach, however, would cure the underlying causes of crime (e.g., poverty, crowding, slum life, racism, mental illness, broken families) rather than concentrating on the symptom: criminal behavior. [A]s a follower of the liberal social science tradition, Judge Bazelon similarly believes that poverty causes crime and poverty must therefore be eliminated in order to prevent crime.

But does poverty cause crime? It is certainly true that there is a very strong correlation between low socioeconomic status and the sort of violent street crime that worries urban America so much. Further, we must agree with Judge Bazelon that persons of low socioeconomic status probably find it easier than others to turn to violent street crime for money, excitement, or release. Yet it is also true that the majority of poor people are not violent criminals. Judge Bazelon is simply wrong in his belief that poverty "causes" crime. Poverty is neither a sufficient nor a necessary cause of crime. Poverty may make the choice to obey the law more difficult, but the majority choose to obey the law.

Will eradicating poverty eradicate crime? Improvement in the economic conditions of poor persons does not reduce the level of violent crime. Rather, the opposite occurs—there is a rise in crime that accompanies most periods of rising wealth. The "poverty cure" does not work.

THE MORALITY OF THE CRIMINAL LAW: A REJOINDER TO PROFESSOR MORSE

David L. Bazelon.
49 Southern California Law Review 1269 (1976).

The crux of his disagreement seems to come in his answer to the question, "Does poverty cause crime?" Professor Morse correctly notes, as I did, that "a rise in crime ... accompanies most periods of rising wealth." From this he concludes that "the 'poverty cure' does not work." But the Professor offers no evidence—and I know of none—suggesting that the increase in crime in periods of economic growth is produced by persons who are no longer poor suddenly turning violent. Rather, it is persons *who remain poor*—who essentially do *not* benefit from the economic growth—who become more violent. The data Professor Morse cites is simply evidence of what de Tocqueville observed long ago, and of what social psychologists have gone to great lengths to explain: violence is born of hope—of rising expectations—not despair. Thus, Professor Morse is simply wrong. For all practical purposes, poverty *is* a necessary cause of violent street crime.

MALIGN NEGLECT—RACE, CRIME, AND PUNISHMENT IN AMERICA (1995)*

Michael Tonry.

The practical objections [to Judge Bazelon's proposal in *Alexander and Murdock*] involve the mechanics of a social adversity defense. Would it apply to all offenses committed by an offender to which it applies? That seems doubly wrong because it would eliminate all incentives to be law-abiding and, as Stephen Morse argues, public safety concerns would inevitably lead to a system of preventive detention to protect the rest of us from offenders who cannot be held legally accountable for crimes.

[T]he overriding objection to a social adversity defense is that there are no groups for which the base expectancy rate for first offenses is 100 percent. No matter how conducive to criminality the circumstances are, there always are people who live law-abiding lives. The reason may be remarkable strength of character, religious convictions, nurturing parents, a friend or coach or employer who provides a positive role model, or sheer good luck. Whatever the reason, the general interests in public safety and in encouraging the development of law-abiding people argue powerfully against a social adversity defense.

The analogy between insanity and social adversity is only partial. In the paradigm case to which the insanity defense applies, there is little question that the defendant is not morally responsible. If we accept that the knife-wielding killer believed that he was slicing bread, [f]ew would argue that he was morally responsible for his actions. He may be dangerous, and we may want to take steps to assess that danger and to prevent future dangerous acts, but he is not responsible.

[T]here are no paradigm cases in which most people agree that a particular disadvantaged offender could not have done otherwise. And if we believe that there are individuals who in specific circumstances may or may not commit an offense, the idea of removing all threat of consequences for making the wrong choice is perverse. As James Fitzjames Stephen, the leading Nineteenth Century scholar of the English criminal law, observed, "it is at the moment when temptation is strongest that the law should speak most clearly and emphatically to the contrary." Put provocatively, a social adversity defense would authorize one or more "free crimes," a policy that public opinion would not tolerate.

———

NOTE

1. Abolition of the Volitional Prong. The test of insanity used in Murdock's trial was that found in the Model Penal Code of the American Law Institute, Section 4.01 (1962):

A person is not responsible for criminal conduct if at the time of such conduct as a result of mental disease or defect he lacks substantial capacity either to appreciate the criminality [wrongfulness] of his conduct or to conform his conduct to the requirements of the law.

Judge Bazelon stated in *Alexander and Murdock* that "the crucial functional question" in insanity cases is "did the defendant lack the ability to make any meaningful choice of action?," i.e., could he "conform his conduct to the requirements of law?" This is frequently referred to as the "irresistible impulse" or "volitional" prong of the Model Penal Code test.

In the wake of the public outcry over the verdict of not guilty by reason of insanity in the case of John W. Hinckley, Jr., for the attempted assassination of then-President Ronald Reagan, the American Psychiatric Association issued a Statement on the Insanity Defense, 140 American Journal of Psychiatry 681 (1983). The statement noted that "[s]anity is, of course, a legal issue not a medical one." Id. at 683. It went on to observe, id. at 685, that psychiatry did not have much to offer regarding the assessment of "volition":

> The line between an irresistible impulse and an impulse not resisted is probably no sharper than that between twilight and dusk. Psychiatry is a deterministic discipline that views all human behavior as, to a good extent, "caused." The concept of volition is the subject of some disagreement among psychiatrists. Many psychiatrists therefore believe that psychiatric testimony (particularly that of a conclusory nature) about volition is more likely to produce confusion for jurors than is psychiatric testimony relevant to a defendant's appreciation or understanding [of the wrongfulness of his or her conduct].

The Association then endorsed a proposal by Professor Richard Bonnie for a test of insanity that eliminated the volitional prong of the Model Penal Code. See Bonnie, The Moral Basis of the Insanity Defense, 69 American Bar Association Journal 194 (1983). The American Bar Association also endorsed this test as its official position on the insanity defense. Standing Committee on Association Standards for Criminal Justice, Criminal Justice Mental Health Standards (1984).

In 1984, the "Insanity Defense Reform Act" eliminated the volitional prong of the insanity defense in federal courts. The new federal test (18 U.S.C.A. § 17) reads:

> It is an affirmative defense to a prosecution under any Federal statute that, at the time of the commission of the acts constituting the offense, the defendant, as a result of a severe mental disease or defect, was unable to appreciate the nature and quality or the wrongfulness of his acts. Mental disease or defect does not otherwise constitute a defense.

The act placed the burden of proving insanity on the defendant, by clear and convincing evidence.

3. PERSONALITY

Evidence of an individual's "personality" or "character" is sometimes offered to demonstrate that he or she acted in conformity with established patterns of behavior in the criminal incident at issue. The prosecution attempts to introduce evidence of the defendant's crime-prone personality, and the defense attempts to introduce evidence of the defendant's non-aggressive nature.

NEW JERSEY v. CAVALLO

Supreme Court of New Jersey, 1982.
88 N.J. 508, 443 A.2d 1020.

■ PASHMAN, J.

Defendants Michael Cavallo and David Murro were indicted by the Hunterdon County grand jury for abduction, sodomy, private lewdness, and rape. The indictments arose out of an incident on June 16, 1977 involving defendants and S.T., the alleged victim, a married woman who was two months pregnant. S.T. states that she was abducted from a Hunterdon bar and raped by defendants who in turn assert that she willingly accompanied them from the bar to engage in consensual sexual activity. Since there were no witnesses, the trial necessarily focused on the credibility of the conflicting descriptions of those events.

At trial, defendant Cavallo sought to offer the expert testimony of Dr. Kuris, a psychiatrist from the Hunterdon Medical Center. This witness was offered as an expert character witness who would testify that Cavallo does not have the psychological traits of a rapist. The offer of proof, as it appears in the transcript, is as follows:

> MR. SKOWRONEK: Your Honor, he is going to testify as to Mr. Cavallo's character which is that he knows right from wrong, that he is a well-meaning individual, he would not wilfully do a wrong, he recognizes the force and violence of rape are wrongful acts, he is a non-violent, non-aggressive person and he will also testify to the fact [that] the characteristics exhibited by rapists in his experience as a psychiatrist are these people are aggressive, violent people and that Mr. Cavallo does not fit within this mold.

The trial judge refused to allow the expert testimony. The sole issue on this appeal is the correctness of that ruling under Evidence Rules 47 and 56.

[D]r. Kuris' testimony is offered as expert opinion evidence of Cavallo's character under Rule 47, which provides:

> Subject to Rules 48 and 55, a trait of character offered for the purpose of drawing inferences as to the conduct of a person on a specified occasion may be proved only by: (a) testimony in the form of opinion, (b) evidence of reputation, or (c) evidence of conviction of a crime which tends to prove the trait. Specific instances of conduct not the subject of a conviction of a crime shall be inadmissible. In a

criminal proceeding, evidence offered by the prosecution of a trait of character of the defendant on trial may be admitted only if the judge has admitted evidence of good character offered by the defendant. Character evidence offered by the defendant may not be excluded under Rule 4. The credibility of a character witness testifying on behalf of the defendant may not be impaired by an inquiry into his knowledge of the defendant's alleged criminal conduct not evidenced by a conviction.

This rule, adopted in 1967, amended the prior New Jersey practice by allowing a trait of character to be proved by opinion as well as reputation evidence. This amendment permits both lay and expert opinions. The rule does not exclude expert opinions and the comment explicitly includes them. However, while allowing expert character evidence, Rule 47 clearly contemplates that such testimony must qualify as proper expert evidence:

> This type of evidence is now admissible provided that a proper foundation is laid for the expert's testimony. If the court feels that a witness does not have sufficient expertise to give expert testimony as to character or that the opinion offered does not satisfy the requirements of Rule 56(2), the opinion evidence may be excluded. [State Rules of Court Review Commission, New Jersey Rules of Evidence, Rule 47, comment 4]

[T]he State argues that the proffered evidence is irrelevant, since regardless of whether Cavallo has the characteristics of a "rapist," he may indeed have committed rape on this particular occasion. However, this is not the standard for relevance under our rules. The State's argument would render virtually all character testimony, lay or expert, irrelevant and inadmissible. That argument addresses the weight to be accorded the testimony rather than its relevance.

Rule 1(2) defines relevant evidence as "evidence having any tendency in reason to prove any material fact." New Jersey case law both before and after the promulgation of the rule defines the test to be whether the evidence "renders the desired inference more probable than it would be without the evidence." State v. Deatore, 70 N.J. 100, 116, 358 A.2d 163 (1976). The inquiry is whether knowledge that Cavallo does not possess the traits commonly found in "rapists" increases the likelihood that Cavallo did not commit a rape on the occasion in question. For purposes of determining relevance, we treat the proffered testimony as reliable. Obviously, inaccurate testimony, lay or expert, has no tendency to prove any material fact.

Viewed from that standpoint, the testimony is clearly relevant for the same reason that all character testimony is relevant: favorable evidence of the defendant's character has some tendency to create doubts as to whether the defendant committed the offense charged. Rule 47 assumes the relevance of character evidence "offered for the purpose of drawing inferences as to the conduct of a person on a specified occasion." [T]hat is precisely the inference for which Dr. Kuris' testimony is proffered: the fact that Cavallo has the character of a non-rapist is used to draw an inference that he did not commit rape on this occasion. Assuming the reliability of Dr. Kuris' conclusions, his testimony makes it more likely than otherwise that Cavallo did not rape S.T. Consequently, the proffered evidence is relevant.

Having concluded that the testimony offered is relevant and that expert character testimony is generally permitted under Rule 47, we now determine whether Dr. Kuris' expert testimony satisfies the special limitations placed on expert evidence by Rule 56(2) and by New Jersey case law. Rule 56(2) provides:

> If the witness is testifying as an expert, testimony of the witness in the form of opinions or inferences is limited to such opinions as the judge finds are (a) based primarily on facts, data or other expert opinion established by evidence at the trial and (b) within the scope of the special knowledge, skill, experience or training possessed by the witness.

Under Rule 56(2)(b), expert testimony is admissible only if the expert has sufficient expertise to offer the intended testimony and the testimony itself is sufficiently reliable. No question has been raised as to the general qualification of Dr. Kuris as a psychiatrist. The relevant inquiry therefore is whether the testimony satisfies New Jersey's "standard of acceptability for scientific evidence." State v. Hurd, 86 N.J. 525, 536, 432 A.2d 86 (1981).

Scientific evidence is admissible if the proposed technique or mode of analysis has "sufficient scientific basis to produce uniform and *reasonably reliable* results and will contribute materially to the ascertainment of the truth." State v. Cary, 49 N.J. 343, 352, 230 A.2d 384 (1967), quoted in *Hurd,* 86 N.J. at 536, 432 A.2d 86 (emphasis added). See Frye v. United States, 293 F. 1013 (D.C.Cir.1923) (generally viewed as the seminal case on scientific evidence).

Applying this test to the testimony offered here, the issue becomes whether there exists a "special knowledge, skill, experience or training" by which any expert can determine, with reasonable reliability, whether an individual has a mental makeup rendering him unlikely to have committed rape on a specific occasion.

[I]n this case the psychiatrist sought to testify that Cavallo did not have the characteristics common to all or most rapists. Two assumptions underlie this testimony: (1) there exist particular mental characteristics peculiar to rapists, and (2) psychiatrists, by examining an individual, can determine whether or not he possesses those characteristics. The policy that scientific evidence be reasonably accurate requires us to apply the standards for admission of scientific evidence to Dr. Kuris' testimony. Defendants must therefore demonstrate that these two assumptions satisfy the Rule 56 standard of reliability.

Defendants argue that considerations of reliability should determine the weight accorded to scientific testimony, not its admissibility. Such evidence should be placed before the jury, which can evaluate the evidence as it deems proper, as it traditionally evaluates all evidence before it. However, this Court has previously pointed to substantial countervailing considerations that mandate that there be some assurance of reliability before scientific evidence is admitted.

In *Hurd,* we alluded to the problems of "prejudice, jury confusion, and consumption of time and trial resources." Id. 86 N.J. at 536, 432 A.2d 86. The danger of prejudice through introduction of unreliable expert evidence is clear. While juries would not always accord excessive weight to unreliable expert testimony, there is substantial danger that they would do so, precisely because the evidence is labeled "scientific" and "expert."

Further, if defendants are permitted to introduce psychiatric testimony on their character, "the State will not stand idly by without producing psychiatrists favorable to its cause." State v. Sinnott, 24 N.J. 408, 429, 132 A.2d 298 (1957). The result must necessarily be a "battle of experts" concerning the validity of the expert evidence. This would consume substantial court time and cost both parties much time and expense. Much of the trial would focus on the tangential issue of the reliability of the expert evidence rather than the central issue of what the defendants did or did not do.

The inevitability of a "battle of the experts" in this type of case is clear. In so subjective a field as psychiatry, the experts are bound to differ. The parties will spend untold time and money locating experts and preparing to cross-examine opposing experts. Court time will then be spent presenting the experts. With so much attention paid to the expert testimony, it is likely that the attention of the jury will be similarly diverted. As a result, there is the danger that the trial will turn not on the facts of the case, not on whether the defendant committed the crime of rape, but rather on whether the defendant manifests the characteristics of a "rapist."

[W]here expert testimony is sufficiently reliable to be of assistance to the jury, it should be admitted despite the dangers discussed above. It will then be for the opposing party to discredit the evidence and for the jury ultimately to determine its proper weight. Scientific testimony can be quite useful at trial. However, expert testimony is admissible only if it meets the threshold of reliability required by Rule 56.

[U]nder *Hurd,* scientific evidence is admissible if it possesses a "sufficient scientific basis to produce uniform and reasonably reliable results and will contribute materially to the ascertainment of the truth." 86 N.J. at 536, 432 A.2d 86, quoting *Cary,* 49 N.J. at 352, 230 A.2d 384.

What constitutes reasonable reliability depends in part on the context of the proceedings involved. The policy underlying Rule 56 is to exclude expert evidence when the danger it poses of prejudice, confusion and diversion of attention exceeds its helpfulness to the factfinder because the expertise is not sufficiently reliable. In part, the Rule entails a weighing of reliability against prejudice in light of the context in which the evidence is offered. Expert evidence that poses too great a danger of prejudice in some situations, and for some purposes, may be admissible in other circumstances where it will be more helpful and less prejudicial.

The *Hurd* formulation differs somewhat from the traditional standard set forth in *Frye,* supra, where the D.C.Circuit Court held:

> Just when a scientific principle or discovery crosses the line between the experimental and demonstrable stages is difficult to define. Somewhere in this twilight zone the evidential force of the principle must be recognized, and while courts will go a long way in admitting expert testimony deduced from a well-recognized scientific principle or discovery, *the thing from which the deduction is made must be sufficiently established to have gained general acceptance in the particular field in which it belongs.* [Id. at 1014 (emphasis supplied)]

The *Frye* test recognizes that most judges are experts in few, if any, fields of scientific endeavor. Judges are not well suited to determine the inherent reliability of expert evidence, but they can decide whether the proffered evidence has gained "general acceptance" in the scientific community. The proponent of expert evidence can therefore meet his burden by demonstrating that the testimony has achieved enough acceptance in the scientific community to convince the court that it is reasonably reliable. We need not at this time conclude that this is the only permissible means of demonstrating reliability.

[W]e turn now to the difficult question of how the proponent of scientific evidence can prove its "general acceptance" and thereby its reliability. "Three methods of proof have been recognized by the courts: (1) expert testimony, (2) scientific and legal writings, and (3) judicial opinions." Giannelli, "The Admissibility of Novel Scientific Evidence: Frye v. United States, a Half-Century Later," 80 Colum.L.Rev. 1197, 1215 (1980). All three present problems, but all three may be used in appropriate circumstances. [H]ere, defendants have offered no expert testimony as to the general acceptance, by psychiatrists or any other medical community, of the scientific premises upon which Dr. Kuris based his analysis.[4]

Evidence of scientific reliability may also be reflected in authoritative scientific and legal writings. [D]efendants did not cite any articles on which we could rely in taking judicial notice of scientific acceptance.

Defendants therefore must rely on precedent from other courts that have considered the matter and have admitted similar evidence. They urge in addition that similar scientific evidence is generally relied on in the law for other purposes.

[T]here is substantial support for the general acceptance of psychiatric witnesses in court. But the issue here is not the reliability of psychiatric testimony relating to an individual's psychiatric condition. Rather, the question is the reliability of psychiatric testimony on the likelihood that an individual behaved in a particular manner on a specific occasion. We must decide here (1) whether psychiatrists agree that rapists share particular

---

4. At oral argument before this Court, counsel for defendants was asked several times whether he was prepared, at trial, to demonstrate the acceptance of those premises in the scientific community. His answers indicated that he was not so prepared.

mental characteristics and (2) whether psychiatrists can ascertain if an individual possesses those characteristics by examining him.

A review of cases in other jurisdictions does not persuade us that it is generally accepted in the medical or legal communities that psychiatrists possess such knowledge or capabilities.

[S]imilarly, the other areas in which psychiatric or psychological testimony is generally admitted in evidence are inapposite because such evidence there is admitted for different purposes and in different contexts. [For example,] the expert evidence in parole determinations is offered in a quite different context to establish whether there is substantial likelihood that the inmate will commit future crimes. Unlike a jury trial in the parole context, the evidence is heard by the Parole Board, which routinely makes predictions of the sort required and which has substantial experience evaluating psychiatric testimony. Therefore, such testing can be of reasonable assistance to the factfinder there without the concomitant risk of serious confusion, prejudice and diversion of attention that is likely to result from its admission in a jury trial.

Defendants have thus failed to persuade us that the proffered evidence has been accepted as reliable by other jurisdictions, or for other purposes in the New Jersey legal system. Defendants therefore have not met their burden under Rule 56 of showing that Dr. Kuris' testimony is based on reasonably reliable scientific premises.

[W]e conclude that defendants have not met their burden of showing that the scientific community generally accepts the existence of identifiable character traits common to rapists. They also have not demonstrated that psychiatrists possess any special ability to discern whether an individual is likely to be a rapist. Until the scientific reliability of this type of evidence is established, it is not admissible.

The judgment of the Appellate Division excluding the evidence is affirmed.

––––––––

STATE v. HICKMAN

Supreme Court of Iowa, 1983.
337 N.W.2d 512.

■ ULENHOPP, JUSTICE.

[The defendant was charged with first degree murder. The state alleged that he killed a woman after raping her. The defendant admitted stabbing the victim to death, but claimed that the intercourse that preceded the killing had been consensual. This claim, if accepted, would mean that the murder was not in the first degree.]

[R]ebuttal evidence. One of the bases of the State's charge of first-degree murder was murder in the perpetration of sexual abuse. In his

defense, defendant testified in substance that the sexual intercourse was consensual.

The State relied of course on its evidence of violence to disprove that the intercourse was consensual. To reinforce that evidence, the State introduced testimony by a psychiatrist who had made a study of the psychology of rapists and had examined defendant and his medical history. The psychiatrist described various kinds of rapists and characterized defendant as of the class of aggressive, antisocial or sociopathic, hatred rapists.

Defendant objected to this testimony as not rebuttal and argues that the trial court should not have admitted it. We agree with the trial court, however, that this testimony was admissible as rebutting defendant's claim of consensual intercourse. See State v. Nelson, 261 Iowa 204, 209, 153 N.W.2d 711, 714 (1967) ("Rebutting evidence is that which explains, repels, controverts, or disproves evidence produced by the other side.").

NOTE

1. Character Evidence. The Iowa rules on character evidence are similar to Federal Rule of Evidence 404. There, it is stated that "[e]vidence of a person's character or a trait of character is not admissible for the purpose of proving action in conformity therewith on a particular occasion," but an exception is listed for "[e]vidence of a pertinent trait of character offered by an accused, or by the prosecution to rebut the same." See Appendix A. Given this definition of character evidence, *Hickman* would seem erroneously decided.

SKINNER v. STATE

Supreme Court of Wyoming, 2001
33 P.3d 758.

■ Kite, Justice.

This is an appeal from Brad Skinner's conviction of aggravated assault and battery. [M]r. Skinner was sentenced to life in prison pursuant to Wyo. Stat. Ann. § 6–10–201, the habitual criminal law.

[I]n its case-in-chief, the state called an expert witness to testify regarding the battered woman syndrome. Mr. Skinner argues a portion of the testimony was inadmissible because the expert referenced patterns in domestic violence situations and how a batterer's anger and violence often escalates. Mr. Skinner complains this testimony implied to the jury that he had acted in conformity with the profile of a batterer and, in fact, held a knife to his wife's throat.

[A]lthough battered-woman-syndrome testimony is admissible and helpful to the jury, it must not run afoul of W.R.E. 404(a) which provides in pertinent part: "Evidence of a person's character or a trait of his character is not admissible for the purpose of proving that he acted in conformity therewith on a particular occasion." When battered-woman-syndrome testimony is raised by the state in its case-in-chief and relates to a defendant, as it did in the instant case, the "testimony 'draws close to commenting directly on what likely happened' and 'looks like character evidence after all.' "*Ryan* [*v. State*], 988 P.2d [46] at 55 [Wyo. 1990] (quoting Christopher B. Mueller & Laird C. Kirkpatrick, 3 Federal Evidence § 637 (2d ed.1994)).

[T]he expert in the instant case did not directly reference the particular character traits of Mr. Skinner. He did, however, explore the general cycle of violence, the shortened period of remorse, the escalation of violence, and the patterns of control. The use of profile testimony has been examined in the following way:

> Strictly speaking, the data offered to create a social framework are not "character evidence," since they do not pertain to "*a person's* character or a trait of *his* character." Rather, the research describes the behavior of *groups* or *other* persons. Yet the purpose of offering character evidence is similar to the purpose of introducing social frameworks: to prove—that is, to make "more probable or less probable"—that an individual acted in conformity with an established pattern. By definition, knowledge of the general pattern of an individual's behavior (i.e., his or her character)—like knowledge of the general pattern of behavior in persons in the groups to which he or she belongs—allows one to recalculate the probabilities that the person acted in a certain way on a given occasion. The policy concern that gave rise to a rule barring the admissibility of evidence of an individual's "characteristic" behavior applies with equal force to the use of information on behavior characteristic of the groups to which he or she belongs: individuals should be accountable for their specific acts and not for their general proclivities.

Laurens Walker & John Monahan, *Social Frameworks: A New Use of Social Science in Law,* 73 Va. L.Rev. 559, 581 (1987). The following aptly describes the most appropriate guideline:

> However firm the libertarian values barring the admission of character evidence, modern evidence law, as exemplified by the Federal Rules, contains several important exceptions allowing the introduction of character evidence. In criminal proceedings, the defendant may offer evidence of his or her own character and, if this occurs, the prosecution may offer character evidence in rebuttal. The defendant also may offer evidence of the victim's character, and if this occurs, the prosecution again may offer character evidence in rebuttal. In either civil or criminal proceedings, any party may offer evidence of the character of a witness. In addition, the prohibition against character evidence operates only when that evidence is used to prove that a person "acted" in conformity with his or her character on a particular occasion. Character evidence may be admissible for many other purposes such as proof of knowledge, intent, or preparation.

The rule against character evidence, therefore, suggests a bar to some, but by no means all, applications of social frameworks. Where traditional forms of character evidence are prohibited, social frameworks also should be barred; where traditional forms of character evidence are allowed, there is no reason to prohibit social frameworks.

Id. at 581–82. The introduction of the battered woman syndrome should not be a prosecutorial tool to covertly allow expert testimony regarding the dynamics and propensities of batterers intended to show a defendant acted in conformity therewith during the incident at issue.

In this case, the assault itself was undisputed. Mr. Skinner did not first open the door to character testimony, and the testimony did not have an alternate proper evidentiary purpose such as intent or motive. Mr. Skinner argues the only purpose of the expert testimony regarding the behavior of a batterer was to leave the implication that, because he had a history of battering his wife, he had, in fact, threatened his wife with a knife, thus constituting aggravated assault. Under these circumstances, the profile testimony is inadmissible.

Applying the harmless error analysis, we cannot discern from the record a reasonable possibility that the verdict might have been more favorable to Mr. Skinner if the error had never occurred. The expert's testimony, while discussing the pattern of escalating violence, did not suggest the escalation would typically include the use of a deadly weapon, such as a knife. The victim ultimately testified, confirming her initial statement to the police at the time of the assault, that Mr. Skinner had threatened her with a knife. The jury also heard about Mr. Skinner's additional assault on his wife after his arrest and the threats he made against her if she testified at trial that he had used a knife—a fact that most likely persuaded the jury he had done so. The knife was also found in his pocket. There was ample evidence from which the jury could conclude the knife was used without drawing any indirect inference from the expert's profile testimony which covered only seven pages of the more than 530 pages of transcript. In closing argument, the state did not unduly reference the objectionable testimony. [W]e conclude the error did not affect Mr. Skinner's substantial rights and, therefore, was harmless.

4.   LIFE EVENTS

Discrete types of "life events"—experiences more circumscribed than culture, subculture, or personality—have also been claimed to influence a criminal defendant's behavior and state of mind in legally relevant ways. Social science research has been used to provide a context for allowing decision makers to better understand the effect on the defendant of having been assaulted, having served in combat, having been kidnapped, and having frequently watched violent television programs.

(a) Assault

The defendant's prior history of having been the victim of assault has been offered by both the prosecution and the defense in a large number of recent cases. The prosecution has attempted to introduce evidence that the defendant fit the "battering parent profile," and the defense has attempted to introduce evidence that the defendant fit the "battered spouse syndrome."

MINNESOTA v. LOEBACH

Supreme Court of Minnesota, 1981.
310 N.W.2d 58.

■ YETKA, JUSTICE.

[Appellant Robert Loebach was convicted of the third degree murder of his three-month old son. He was sentenced to a maximum prison term of 15 years. The principal issue raised on appeal was "Whether the trial court erred in admitting testimony as to appellant's background and personality traits used to prove he fit the diagnosis of a 'battering parent.' "]

Dr. Robert ten Bensel, an expert on child abuse, testified concerning the so-called "battered child syndrome." He concluded that it fit this case almost perfectly. [T]he multiple injuries were clearly not caused by accidents of the kind the defendant stated and were not self-inflicted. Dr. ten Bensel was firmly convinced that the baby's death was the final result of nonaccidental physical abuse of the baby over a period of time.

Dr. ten Bensel also was permitted to testify, over a general objection by defense counsel, that battering parents tend to have similar personality traits and personal histories.

Defense counsel objected generally to the state's calling of two witnesses from appellant's past in an attempt to prove appellant fit the pattern of a "battering parent." Judith Carpenter is a former case worker who was assigned to appellant when he was a juvenile in Illinois. She testified that appellant's mother, who raised appellant alone, had abused him until he was old enough to fight back, that his mother expected too much of him, and that appellant was not good at controlling his anger. Charles Nelson, an employee of a school for disturbed adolescent boys which appellant attended for 3 years until he reached age 18, testified that appellant often withdrew from others, had a low frustration level, and was adolescent in behavior. Testimony from other witnesses also aided in showing that appellant fit the "battering parent" profile. There was testimony that appellant and Anna [appellant's wife] were isolated and did not have contact with many people and that in April 1978, appellant had slapped her and broken her nose. Defense counsel did not object to the testimony concerning the broken nose.

The defense strategy for countering this testimony was partly to show that the "battering parent" profile also fit Anna and that it did not necessarily fit appellant. In cross-examining Anna's sister, defense counsel elicited testimony that appellant was proud, confident and not lacking in self-esteem, whereas Anna was hypertense, unable to cope, unable to handle liquor, and was herself a victim of child abuse. Appellant's direct testimony, however, tended to corroborate the state's evidence that he fit the profile. He testified that his mother called him the man of the family and that he developed a bad temper.

Appellant denied abusing the baby. He testified that he did not see anyone else abuse the baby and that he had no explanation for the injuries the doctor found in the autopsy, although he thought he might have broken the baby's ribs when he accidently dropped the baby one day. He also testified that for a period of time, until warned [t]hat it was dangerous, he had playfully thrown the baby high in the air and caught it. He testified that he stopped doing this 1 to 2 months before the baby died. He also testified that while he admitted slapping the baby once, the slap was more like a love pat.

Appellant contends that the state's use of evidence of his character constitutes prejudicial error and warrants reversal. The specific testimony objected to concerns that given by the state's expert, Dr. ten Bensel, and the two prosecution witnesses who knew appellant as an adolescent.

On direct examination, Dr. ten Bensel was asked to state the characteristics of a "battering parent." According to Dr. ten Bensel, the "battering parent" syndrome is an "inner [sic] generational phenomena" in that adults who abuse their children were often abused themselves. The doctor testified that abusing parents frequently experience role reversal and often expect their children to care for them. He also stated that battering parents often exhibit similar characteristics such as low empathy, a short fuse, low temper, short temper, low boiling point, high blood pressure, strict authoritarianism, uncommunicativeness, low self-esteem, isolation and lack of trust. Dr. ten Bensel did not testify that appellant possessed any of these characteristics, but the state's witnesses, Judith Carpenter and Charles Nelson, suggested that he did.

The obvious purpose for the introduction of the Carpenter and Nelson testimony and other character evidence was to demonstrate that appellant fit within the "battering parent" profile. The general rule as to the admission of such character evidence is contained in Minn.R.Evid. 404(a) which provides in relevant part as follows:

> (a) *Character evidence generally.* Evidence of a person's character or a trait of his character is not admissible for the purpose of proving that he acted in conformity therewith on a particular occasion, except:
>
> > (1) *Character of accused.* Evidence of a pertinent trait of his character offered by an accused, or by the prosecution to rebut the same;

* * *

Appellant did not put his character in evidence in this case so the cited exception to the rule's general prohibition does not apply.

[T]here are three basic reasons for the exclusion of character evidence used to prove a criminal defendant acted in conformity with such character. First, there is the possibility that the jury will convict a defendant in order to penalize him for his past misdeeds or simply because he is an undesirable person. Second, there is the danger that a jury will overvalue the character evidence in assessing the guilt for the crime charged. Finally, it is unfair to require an accused to be prepared not only to defend against immediate charges, but also to disprove or explain his personality or prior actions.

[T]he state argues that the potential for prejudice to defendants that justifies the rule excluding character evidence is outweighed by the public interest in assuring conviction of persons who batter children. The state's position is that the difficulties involved in prosecuting those who abuse children warrant an exception to the general rule. The victim, as the state's expert testified, is usually an infant and therefore particularly defenseless. Children who are abused are also almost wholly dependent on those who inflict the abuse. The victims' age and dependence act to prevent them from testifying against abusing caretakers. Finally, abuse almost always occurs when the child is in the exclusive care of a battering caretaker. These features of abuse cases make it very difficult to establish a defendant's guilt by means of direct evidence. The state contends, therefore, that an exception to the general rule is necessary to offset these obstacles to the prosecution of battering individuals.

[W]e now hold that in future cases the prosecution will not be permitted to introduce evidence of "battering parent" syndrome or to establish the character of the defendant as a "battering parent" unless the defendant first raises that issue. We feel this finding is required until further evidence of the scientific accuracy and reliability of syndrome or profile diagnoses can be established.

Our determination that the "battering parent" evidence should not have been admitted does not affect the result of this case in the court below. A defendant claiming error in the trial court's reception of evidence has the burden of showing both the error and the prejudice resulting from the error. A reversal is warranted only when the error substantially influences the jury to convict.

The record in this case indicates that the "battering parent" testimony consisted of only a small percentage of the evidence. The record also reveals that there was overwhelming evidence of appellant's guilt even without the "battering parent" testimony.

[I]n light of this substantial evidence to support appellant's conviction, the error in admitting "battering parent" testimony was not prejudicial.

––––––

NOTE

1. The Effects of Child Abuse. Research on the effects of child abuse on later violent behavior toward one's own children was reviewed in Kaufman and Zigler, Do Abused Children Become Abusive Parents?, 57 American Journal of Orthopsychiatry 186, 190 (1987):

[T]he best estimate of intergenerational transmission [of abuse] appears to be 30% ± 5%. This suggests that approximately one-third of all individuals who were physically abused, sexually abused, or extremely neglected will subject their offspring to one of these forms of maltreatment, while the remaining two-thirds will provide adequate care for their children. [T]he rate of abuse among individuals with a history of abuse [i]s approximately six times higher than the base rate for abuse in the general population (5%).

In terms of the effects of being victimized as a child on later crime in general (i.e, not limited to crimes victimizing one's own children), Widom and Maxfield, An Update on the "Cycle of Violence," National Institute of Justice Research in Brief, February 2001, recently reported data following children processed by the courts for having been abused or neglected, and a comparison group of children who had not been abused or neglected. At the time of the follow-up, the subjects' mean age was 32 years.

Of primary interest was the question, "Would arrest histories of those who had been abused or neglected be worse than those with no reported abuse?" The answer [w]as evident: Those who had been abused or neglected as children were more likely to be arrested as juveniles (27 percent versus 17 percent), adults (42 percent versus 33 percent), and for violent crime (18 percent versus 14 percent). Id at 3.

————

IBN-TAMAS v. UNITED STATES

District of Columbia, Court of Appeals, 1979.
407 A.2d 626.

■ Ferren, Associate Judge:

[Dr. and Mrs. Ibn-Tamas had been married for three and a half years. The marriage "was marred by recurring violent episodes separated by periods of relative harmony." On the morning of his death, Dr. Ibn-Tamas beat his wife. He threatened her with a gun and told her to leave the house. In the ensuing argument, Mrs. Ibn-Tamas picked up the gun and shot him three times, killing him in what she testified was self-defense.

Dr. Ibn-Tamas' secretary, however, testified that between the shots Dr. Ibn-Tamas yelled "don't shoot me any more" and Mrs. Ibn-Tamas said, "I am not going to leave you, I mean it." The prosecution suggested in its closing argument that "Mrs. Ibn-Tamas, threatened with the prospect of being thrown out of her home [h]ad simply decided that she had endured enough of her husband's abuse [and] ambushed him."

Mrs. Ibn-Tamas was convicted of second-degree murder and sentenced to prison for a period of one-to-five years. She raised several issues on appeal, including "the trial court's exclusion of expert testimony offered by the defense on the subject of battered women."]

Appellant claims the trial court erred in excluding the testimony of Dr. Lenore Walker, a clinical psychologist, proffered as a defense expert on the subject of "battered women." Specifically, the defense proffered Dr. Walker for two purposes: to describe the phenomenon of "wife battering," and to give her opinion of the extent to which appellant's personality and behavior corresponded to those of 110 battered women Dr. Walker had studied. The defense claimed the testimony was relevant because it would help the jury appraise the credibility of appellant's contention that she had perceived herself in such imminent danger from her husband that she shot him in self-defense.

The trial court refused to permit this expert testimony on three grounds. First, it would "go [ ] beyond those [prior violent] acts which a jury is entitled to hear about, sift, and try to understand the circumstances under which they arose, and draw conclusions therefrom." Second, it would "invade [ ] the province of the jury, who are the sole judges of the facts and triers of the credibility of the witnesses, including the defendant." Third, Dr. Walker, "of necessity, concludes that the decedent was a batterer. And that is not being tried in this case. It is the defendant who is on trial."

[O]ver the years, appellate courts have applied two levels of analysis to a trial court's ruling on expert testimony. First, there is the question of admissibility, for which a three-fold test is applied. Second, the probative value of the testimony must outweigh its prejudicial impact.

A. *Admissibility*

Of the three grounds given by the trial court for excluding Dr. Walker's testimony, only the second (it would "invade[ ] the province of the jury . . .") goes to admissibility. There are two ways in which an expert can preempt the jury's function. The expert either can speak too directly to the ultimate issue (i.e., guilt or innocence), or can speak to matters in which "the jury is just as competent as the expert to consider and weigh the evidence and draw the necessary conclusions."

1. Here, the expert would not preempt in either fashion. As to the first—the "ultimate facts" or "ultimate issue" rule—Dr. Walker was not going to express an opinion on the ultimate question whether Mrs. Ibn-Tamas actually and reasonably believed she was in danger when she shot her husband. Rather, this expert would have merely supplied background data to help the jury make that crucial determination. In any event, the ultimate issue rule has, over time, been reduced to a prohibition only against questions to an expert "which, in effect, submit the whole case to an expert witness for decision." There is no such risk here.

2. Even when an expert is not speaking to the ultimate facts or issue, he or she cannot testify to matters which "the jury itself is just as competent" to consider. In order to evaluate this concern, we have adopted a three-fold test for admissibility:

> (1) the subject matter "must be so distinctively related to some science, profession, business or occupation as to be beyond the ken of the

average layman"; (2) "the witness must have sufficient skill, knowledge, or experience in that field or calling as to make it appear that his opinion or inference will probably aid the trier in his search for truth"; and (3) expert testimony is inadmissible if "the state of the pertinent art or scientific knowledge does not permit a reasonable opinion to be asserted even by an expert." [Dyas v. United States, [D.C.App., 376 A.2d 827 (1977)] at 832 (quoting McCormick on Evidence ? 13 (2d ed. E. Cleary (1972)) (emphasis omitted)).]

Thus, the subject of the testimony must lend itself to expertise, the proffered expert must be qualified to give it, and experts must have studied the subject in a manner that will justify an expert opinion.

The substantive element of this test, whether the expert witness' subject matter is "beyond the ken of the average layman," means that Dr. Walker's testimony, to be admissible, must provide a relevant insight which the jury otherwise could not gain in evaluating appellant's self-defense testimony about her relationship with her husband. More specifically, Dr. Walker must purport to shed light on a relevant aspect of their relationship which a layperson, without expert assistance, would not perceive from the evidence itself.

On direct examination, Mrs. Ibn-Tamas had testified that immediately before the shooting Dr. Ibn-Tamas had told her to pack and leave home by 10:00 a.m. When she replied that she could not, he hit her in the head, under the arms, and in the thighs, and kicked her in the stomach even though she was pregnant.

[O]n cross-examination the government attempted to discredit this testimony by suggesting to the jury, through its questions, that Mrs. Ibn-Tamas' account of the relationship with her husband over the years had been greatly overdrawn, and that her testimony about perceiving herself in imminent danger on February 23, was therefore implausible. For example, the government implied to the jury that the logical reaction of a woman who was truly frightened by her husband (let alone regularly brutalized by him) would have been to call the police from time to time or to leave him. In an effort to rebut this line of attack by the government, the defense proffered Dr. Walker's testimony to (1) inform the jury that there is an identifiable class of persons who can be characterized as "battered women," (2) explain why the mentality and behavior of such women are at variance with the ordinary lay perception of how someone would be likely to react to a spouse who is a batterer, and thus (3) provide a basis from which the jury could understand why Mrs. Ibn-Tamas perceived herself in imminent danger at the time of the shooting.

More specifically, Dr. Walker told the trial court, out of the presence of the jury, that she had studied 110 women who had been beaten by their husbands. Her studies revealed three consecutive phases in the relationships: "tension building," when there are small incidents of battering; "acute battering incident," when beatings are severe; and "loving-contrite," when the husband becomes very sorry and caring. Dr. Walker then testified that women in this situation typically are low in self-esteem, feel powerless, and have few close friends, since their husbands commonly "accuse [ ] them of all kinds of things with friends, and they are embarrassed. They don't want to cause their friends problems too." Because there are periods of harmony, battered women tend to believe their husbands are basically loving, caring men; the women assume that they, themselves, are somehow responsible for their husbands' violent behavior. They also believe, however, that their husbands are capable of killing them, and they feel there is no escape. Unless a shelter is available, these women stay with their husbands, not only because they typically lack a means of self-support but also because they fear that if they leave they will be found and hurt even more.

[W]hen asked about appellant, whom she had interviewed, Dr. Walker replied that Mrs. Ibn-Tamas was a "classic case" of the battered wife. Dr. Walker added her belief that on the day of the killing, when Dr. Ibn-Tamas had been beating his wife despite protests that she was pregnant, Mrs. Ibn-Tamas' pregnancy had had a "major impact on the situation. . . . [T]hat is a particularly crucial time."

Dr. Walker's testimony, therefore, arguably would have served at least two basic functions: (1) it would have enhanced Mrs. Ibn-Tamas' general credibility in responding to cross-examination designed to show that her testimony about the relationship with her husband was implausible; and (2) it would have supported her testimony that on the day of the shooting her husband's actions had provoked a state of fear which led her to believe she was in imminent danger ("I just knew he was going to kill me"), and thus responded in self-defense. Dr. Walker's contribution, accordingly, would have been akin to the psychiatric testimony admitted in the case of Patricia Hearst "to explain the effects kidnapping, prolonged incarceration, and psychological and physical abuse may have had on the defendant's mental state at the time of the robbery, insofar as such mental state is relevant to the asserted defense of coercion or duress." [United States v. Hearst, 412 F.Supp. 889 (N.D.Cal.1976)] at 890. Dr. Walker's testimony would have supplied an interpretation of the facts which differed from the ordinary lay perception ("she could have gotten out, you know") advocated by the government. The substantive element of the *Dyas,* supra, test— "beyond the ken of the average layman"—is accordingly met here.

We conclude, therefore, that as to either substantive basis for ruling that Dr. Walker's testimony would "invade[ ] the province of the jury"— either the "ultimate issue" or the "beyond the ken" basis—the trial court erred as a matter of law.

3. Because *Dyas,* supra, provides a three-fold test, we must consider, next, whether the trial court can be said to have ruled, implicitly, that the expert testimony was inadmissible for failure to meet either the second or third elements of that test.

[W]e therefore confront the question whether the record clearly manifests a trial court ruling that Dr. Walker did not have "sufficient skill, knowledge, or experience" in the field (second *Dyas* criterion), or that "the state of the pertinent art or scientific knowledge" was insufficient for an expert opinion (third *Dyas* criterion).

Dr. Walker testified as to her credentials, her study of battered women, and her diagnosis of Mrs. Ibn-Tamas. The court then inquired whether Dr. Walker was offering a "medical diagnosis" and asked several questions about the 110 women she had interviewed. After reviewing the record, we cannot say that the trial court's ruling was meant to encompass the second or third *Dyas* criterion.

[4.] The question thus becomes whether the trial court, despite its failure to rule on the second or third *Dyas* criterion, had "but one option," [United States v. Green, 548 F.2d 1261, 1268 (6th Cir.1977)]—i.e., whether Dr. Walker's testimony is inadmissible as a matter of law.

[5.] The most we can say from this record is that the second *Dyas* criterion—sufficient skill, knowledge, or experience in the expert's field—may or may not have been satisfied. Although no one has questioned Dr. Walker's qualifications as a clinical psychologist, the expert's credentials must be sufficient for the type of psychological testimony proffered.

[O]n this record, we cannot resolve the question of Dr. Walker's qualifications; but we can say on the basis of her background, that she cannot be disqualified as a matter of law.

6. We turn, finally, to the third *Dyas* criterion: whether "the state of the pertinent art or scientific knowledge" is sufficient to permit an expert opinion. The government argues that the "battered woman" concept is not sufficiently developed, as a matter of commonly accepted scientific knowledge, to warrant testimony under the guise of expertise. The government relies substantially on Frye v. United States, 54 App.D.C. 46, 293 F. 1013 (1923):

> Just when a scientific principle or discovery crosses the line between the experimental and demonstrable stages is difficult to define. Somewhere in this twilight zone the evidential force of the principle must be recognized, and while courts will go a long way in admitting expert testimony deduced from a well-recognized scientific principle or discovery, the thing from which the deduction is made *must be sufficiently established to have gained general acceptance in the particular field in which it belongs.* [Id. at 47, 293 F. at 1014 (emphasis added).]

The government is mistaken. [I]t is important to note that the third criterion focuses on the general acceptance of a particular methodology in the field, not (as the government would have it) on the subject matter studied. The United States Court of Appeals for the District of Columbia Circuit recently emphasized that *Frye,* supra—which rejected admissibility of lie detector results—dealt with "admissibility of expert testimony based on new methods of scientific measurement." United States v. Addison, 162 U.S.App.D.C. 199, 201, 498 F.2d 741, 743 (1974). Thus, the third criterion is directed to the general acceptance of generic categories of scientific inquiry, such as use of the polygraph, spectrographic identification, psycholinguistics, tests for marijuana, and even neutron activation analysis, as well as the variety of analyses used by psychiatrists and clinical psychologists.

[I]n summary, satisfaction of the third *Dyas* criterion begins—and ends—with a determination of whether there is general acceptance of a particular scientific methodology, not an acceptance, beyond that, of particular study results based on that methodology. Thus, the relevant question here is whether Dr. Walker's methodology for identifying and studying battered women has such general acceptance—not whether there is, in addition, a general acceptance of the battered woman concept derived from that methodology. Again, on this record, we cannot say, as a matter of law, that Dr. Walker's methodology falls short.

7. We conclude, therefore, that the trial court erred in ruling Dr. Walker's testimony inadmissible on the ground that it would invade the province of the jury; and, on the record to date, we cannot exclude that testimony as inadmissible on any other ground.

B.   *Probative Value v. Prejudicial Impact*

Because "admissibility" remains an open question, we turn to the second level of inquiry: probative value versus prejudicial impact. The trial court's first and third grounds for excluding Dr. Walker's testimony related to the prejudicial character of the evidence. Specifically, the court stated that the evidence would "go[ ] beyond those [prior violent] acts" which a jury should consider and that, in effect, the testimony put the decedent on trial as "a batterer, [a]nd that is not being tried in this case."

We have stated, apropos of this first ground, that prior acts of violence are admissible in "homicide cases where the defendant raises the claim of self-defense against the decedent as the alleged first aggressor." United States v. Akers, D.C.App., 374 A.2d 874, 877 (1977) (emphasis omitted). The trial court, in fact, admitted a substantial amount of evidence relating to the decedent's earlier attacks on the appellant and other persons. In light of the admission of this evidence, it is apparent that the incremental, prejudicial impact of Dr. Walker's testimony on battered wives, including the labeling of Dr. Ibn-Tamas as a batterer, would have been minimal.

In contrast, as we have previously observed, the testimony on battered wives was highly probative. Because Mrs. Ibn-Tamas' identity as a "battered wife," if established, may have had a substantial bearing on her perceptions and behavior at the time of the killing, it was central to her claim of self-defense. We conclude, accordingly, as a matter of law, that the probative value of this expert testimony would outweigh the risk of "engender[ing] vindictive passions within the jury or . . . confus[ing] the issues." [United States v. Green, 548 F.2d 1261, 1268 (6th Cir.1977)]

[A]ccordingly, we must remand the case for a trial court determination of admissibility consistent with this opinion.

■ Nebeker, Associate Judge, dissenting:

[A]s to her method for examining or interviewing Mrs. Ibn-Tamas and analyzing her situation, the record reveals only that the expert "had contact" with her. No other indication is made. We learned from the witness that her opinion was going to be based upon a paltry universe of 110 other women who were "researched" by her. We know nothing of these few women other than their apparent claim of being abused. Nothing was said of the techniques for "interviewing," the duration of the interview, the number of times each woman was interviewed or any follow-up. The expert interviewed only the abused women and not their husbands, physicians or family. She even testified that "*we* have talked to" some 60 percent of the abused women referred by others (emphasis added). When questioned by the court, the witness candidly acknowledged that 40 percent of the women apparently were prompted to seek an interview by newspapers, television or radio. No estimated potential margin for error was expressed. The foundation for the testimony is patently inadequate, as there was no indication in the record of what method the expert employed or that the expert's method was generally accepted in the field.

I would affirm the conviction.

————

IBN-TAMAS v. UNITED STATES

District of Columbia Court of Appeals, 1983.
455 A.2d 893.

JUDGMENT

This is an appeal from an order entered after remand proceedings. We earlier ordered those proceedings, with discretion whether to hold an evidentiary hearing, for clarification because "we cannot be certain that the record otherwise supports the ruling as a matter of law." Ibn-Tamas v. United States, 407 A.2d 626, 640 n. 29 (D.C.1979). The trial court has stated on remand that it did consider the relevant factors as outlined by this court in its original ruling. It concluded, *inter alia,* "that defendant failed to establish a general acceptance by the expert's colleagues of the methodology used in the expert's study of 'battered women.' "Since the expert's testimony could have been excluded "for failure to meet either the second or third elements of the test," id. at 635, and the trial court did exclude that testimony on one such basis, we are left with deciding whether "the evidence, despite our inability to observe the witness, permits but one interpretation." Id. at 636 n. 17. As the court said in its earlier decision in this case, our scope of review on this issue is "narrow" to the point where manifest error must appear for reversal. Id. at 632. We hold that the trial judge was not compelled, as a matter of law, to admit the evidence. He had discretion whether to admit it and "this court should not substitute its judgment in [such] a discretionary ruling...." Id. at 636 n. 17.

Accordingly, the order appealed from is affirmed.

■ GALLAGHER, ASSOCIATE JUDGE, Retired, concurring:

I believe this proffered testimony on "battered women" is properly considered to be within the category of novel scientific evidence. Consequently, it falls within the underlying doctrine of Frye v. United States, 54 App.D.C. 46, 293 F. 1013 (1923). The essence of *Frye* is that there must be a reliable body of scientific opinion supporting a *novel scientific theory* before it is admissible in evidence.

Subsequent to the decision of this court in its first opinion, Ibn-Tamas v. United States, 407 A.2d 626 (D.C.1979), a book authored by Dr. Lenore E. Walker, whose expert testimony on "battered women" was proffered in Ibn-Tamas, supra, and which testimony is at the core of the issue on this appeal, was published, entitled, The Battered Woman (Harper & Rowe, 1979). In the introduction of that book, Dr. Walker made this statement:

> I think this research has raised more questions for me than it has answered. As a trained researcher, I felt uneasy about stating some of the conclusions in this book. They seemed too tentative to write down in the positive manner which I have used. Yet they are confirmed repeatedly by all the available data so far. (p. XV–XVI).

Dr. Walker went on to define the term: "A battered woman is a woman who is repeatedly subjected to any forceful physical *or psychological behavior* by a man in order to coerce her to do something he wants her to do without any concern for her rights." (p. XV) [emphasis added].

In discussing the viewpoint from which she wrote The Battered Woman, Dr. Walker said: "[I] view women as victims in order to understand what the toll of such domestic violence is like for them. Unfortunately, in doing so *I tend to place all men in an especially negative light,* instead of just those men who do commit such crimes." (p. XVII) [emphasis added].

Initially, I must say that though there may be good reason for the light in which, for the sake of the study, Dr. Walker feels she must place "all men," it does give one a bit of a start. While it may be that "all men" are victims of the male role in society, it would seem one must establish the necessity for Dr. Walker's premise, which at first glance is a trifle disconcerting. It appears that the Doctor's approach would require tracing the man-woman relationship back to the roots of civilization—a subject which would require a little pondering, I should think.

In a case subsequent to *Ibn-Tamas I,* supra, the Supreme Court of Wyoming had misgivings about the "state of the art" on this subject. Buhrle v. State of Wyoming, 627 P.2d 1374 (1981). During the trial in that case, Dr. Walker was questioned on voir dire concerning the statement in her book that she felt uneasy about some of its conclusions and felt they were too tentative to write in the positive manner she had used. In explaining the statement, Dr. Walker testified she had received a research grant "to study the matter in a much more scientific way" and that her research was ongoing with completion to be in the future. Id. at 1370–77. For these and other reasons, the court went on to conclude that "research in 'the battered woman syndrome' is in its infancy." Id. at 1377. In so doing, the court did not rule out admissibility in the future if by then an adequate foundation is laid.

I agree. *Frye* requires the profferor of the expert on a new scientific theory to show that the evidence is not still in the experimental stage but has gained a scientific acceptance substantial enough to warrant an exercise of judicial discretion in favor of admissibility. The *Buhrle* opinion demonstrates the fundamental soundness of *Frye*. As the court in *Frye* pointed out, scientific evidence by its nature necessarily has a special impact on a jury. This is why the judiciary should proceed with reasonable caution, where the evidence comes as a new scientific theory, as distinguished from a well established field, e.g., fingerprint evidence.

I do not mean to imply I believe that expert testimony on the "battered woman" will not lend itself to a recognition with sufficient scientific underpinning to warrant its admission into evidence in court. What I do say is that, as *Frye* soundly requires, more needs to be known by the court initially in the specific area of the science before its admissibility will be warranted.

————

NOTE

1.   Right to an Expert Witness. In Dunn v. Roberts, 963 F.2d 308 (10th Cir.1992), the Tenth Circuit overturned a conviction of aiding and abetting felony-murder because the trial court denied the request of an indigent defendant for $1,800 to retain a psychologist to evaluate her for battered woman's syndrome.

> The mystery in this case, as in all battered woman cases, is why Petitioner remained with [her batterer] despite repeated abuse. An expert could have explained to the jury the nature of battered woman's syndrome and given an opinion on whether Petitioner suffered from the syndrome. This is an area where expert opinion is particularly useful and oftentimes necessary to interpret for the jury a situation beyond average experience and common understanding. [W]e agree with the District Court that this evidence should have been "considered by the jury in evaluating whether Petitioner had the requisite intent to participate in the crimes of which she was charged." [B]y refusing Petitioner the funds for expert assistance, the state trial court effectively prohibited Petitioner from presenting relevant information directly bearing on an essential element of the crime of which she was convicted. Without that assistance, Petitioner was deprived of the fair trial due process demands. Id. at 314.

————

NIXON v. UNITED STATES

District of Columbia Court of Appeals, 1999.
728 A.2d 582

■ SCHWELB, ASSOCIATE JUDGE:

The principal question presented in this domestic violence case is whether the trial judge committed reversible error by permitting the prosecution to introduce expert testimony on the subject of the battered woman syndrome in order to explain, *inter alia,* the conduct of the complaining witness in response to the alleged battering.

[F]ollowing a lengthy jury trial, [G]regory E. Nixon was convicted of assault with a dangerous weapon, possession of a firearm during a crime of violence, [and] simple assault. [N]ixon's prosecution arose from his relationship with the complainant, Kelita Boyd, who was his live-in girlfriend, and who became the mother of his son, Amore. The evidence against Nixon consisted primarily of the testimony of Ms. Boyd (which was corroborated in part by Ms. Boyd's mother and by several other witnesses) and the expert evidence of Dr. Mary Ann Dutton, a board-certified clinical psychologist. Nixon appeared as a witness on his own behalf and generally denied Ms. Boyd's allegations.

[A]. *The expert testimony.*

Following an *in limine* hearing outside the presence of the jury, the trial judge ruled that Dr. Dutton, the government's expert witness, would be permitted to testify regarding the following topics:

1. myths about domestic violence;

2. common patterns of battering; and

3. common behavior of victims of battering.

At trial, Dr. Dutton addressed these subjects in some detail. She described as a "common myth" regarding domestic violence the widespread belief that the victim can easily leave her abuser. This belief is unfounded, according to Dr. Dutton, because a battered woman will often fear that the batterer will use violence against her or her family if she does attempt to leave. Dr. Dutton also explained that many battered women are economically dependent on their abusers and lack the financial resources to set up households of their own. Moreover, women are often inhibited by personal shame or embarrassment. Dr. Dutton also testified that there is no empirical basis for the notion that battered women stay in abusive relationships because they "enjoy" the abuse.

Focusing on the batterer, Dr. Dutton identified several common patterns of domestic abuse, including, *inter alia:*

1. coercion and threats;

2. emotional abuse, such as degrading or humiliating the victim;

3. intimidation;

4. isolation (*e.g.,* restricting the victim's access to the telephone or to the car, or monitoring her comings and goings); and

5. minimizing the injury, or blaming the victim for being hit.

Dr. Dutton testified that by downplaying the victim's injuries and by isolating her from friends and family, the batterer often reinforces her feelings of helplessness and her tendency to blame herself for her situation.

Dr. Dutton then addressed common patterns of behavior on the part of victims of abuse. According to Dr. Dutton, the relevant studies show that approximately fifty percent of battered women do not report the abuse to the police, and that "[t]here are many women who unfortunately put on one front or one view for the world, even their family and friends, and in private experience the violence." Dr. Dutton stated that the term "cycle of violence" is used to describe the three stages of domestic violence—attention building, acute battering, and contrition. When the abuser appears to be contrite—when there are "apologies, flowers, I'm sorry, it was a mistake, it won't happen again"—and when he pleads for forgiveness, his victim often allows herself to be persuaded that the abuse will not recur. Moreover, abuse is not necessarily constant, for "most abusers aren't battering and mean and abusive one hundred percent of the time." Therefore, according to Dr. Dutton, it is more common than uncommon for a victim to leave the relationship, only to return. In particular, pregnancy and children can intensify the victim's attachment to the abuser and her reluctance to leave or to stay away.

Finally, Dr. Dutton testified that she had not examined either Nixon or Ms. Boyd. She did not know whether Ms. Boyd had been abused at all, or whether Nixon had abused her. Dr. Dutton therefore made it clear that she was not rendering an opinion as to the guilt or innocence of the defendant.

LEGAL DISCUSSION

On appeal from his convictions, Nixon challenges the admission of Dr. Dutton's testimony on several grounds. [B]efore addressing each of Nixon's specific contentions, we first identify the applicable legal standard and the scope of appellate review.

A. *The standard of review.*

The criteria for the admission of expert testimony in the District of Columbia are set forth in a three-part test which was adopted by this court in *Dyas v. United States*, 376 A.2d 827 (D.C.), *cert. denied*, 434 U.S. 973, 98 S.Ct. 529, 54 L.Ed.2d 464 (1977):

> (1) the subject matter must be so distinctively related to some science, profession, business or occupation as to be beyond the ken of the average [juror], (2) the witness must have sufficient skill, knowledge, or experience in that field or calling as to make it appear that his opinion or inference will probably aid the trier in his search for truth, and (3) expert testimony is inadmissible if the state of the pertinent art or scientific knowledge does not permit a reasonable opinion to be asserted even by an expert

Id. at 832. Where an issue is raised for the first time on appeal, we review only for plain error.

[B]. *"General acceptance."*

Nixon [c]ontends that "the admission of Dr. Dutton's expert testimony was reversible error because the methodology behind 'battered woman syndrome' is not generally accepted." He relies on *United States v. Porter,* 618 A.2d 629 (D.C.1992), in which this court reiterated and expanded upon the seminal decision in *Frye v. United States,* 54 App.D.C. 46, 293 F. 1013 (1923):

> [U]nder *Frye,* the proponent of a new technology must demonstrate by a preponderance of the evidence that th[e] technology has been generally accepted in the relevant scientific community.... Given the requirement in *Frye* of general acceptance, [t]he issue is consensus versus controversy over a particular technique, not its validity.... If scientists significant either in number or expertise publicly oppose [a new technique] as unreliable, then that technique does not pass muster under *Frye.*

Porter, 618 A.2d at 633–34.

According to Nixon's appellate counsel, "battered woman syndrome is nothing more than radical political feminism wrapped in the veneer of science, and as such, fails to satisfy the *Frye* test." Counsel cites a number of articles criticizing the methodology used by Dr. Lenore Walker, the author of THE BATTERED WOMAN SYNDROME and by other proponents of BWS, and contends that the consensus contemplated by *Frye* and *Porter* therefore does not exist.

[N]ixon's attorney made no claim in the trial court that there are scientists who dissent from BWS methodology, and the theory on which Nixon now relies is being presented for the first time on appeal. If, under these circumstances, we may consider the contention at all, our review must be for plain error.

The trial judge was not "obviously" wrong in concluding that Dr. Dutton's testimony satisfied the third prong of *Dyas.* Contrary to Nixon's thesis, Dr. Dutton's testimony was not "junk science." A decade ago, the Supreme Court of Washington held that the methodology in the diagnosis and treatment of battered women utilized by an expert witness who relied primarily on Dr. Lenore Walker's work "has received general acceptance in the community of mental health experts." *State v. Ciskie,* 110 Wash.2d 263, 751 P.2d 1165, 1170 (1988). As of 1992, the courts of thirty-two states had allowed the use of expert testimony on the subject of BWS. *See Bechtel [v State],* 840 P.2d at 7 & n. 5. "The American Psychological Association, representing more than 55,000 psychologists, endorsed expert testimony on the syndrome in its amicus brief [in] *Hawthorne v. State,* 408 So.2d 801 (Fla.Dist.Ct.App.1982).... "*Id.* n. 4.

More recently, the Supreme Court of Michigan has recognized that "the majority of jurisdictions favor the admissibility of expert testimony regarding the battered woman syndrome." *People v. Christel,* 449 Mich. 578, 537 N.W.2d 194, 202 n. 26 (1995). The court further stated that "Dr. Walker's premise and understanding of a battering relationship has been widely accepted throughout the United States, and we now join the majority of jurisdictions recognizing the discipline." *Id.* The Supreme Court of Minnesota has likewise stated that "battered woman syndrome has gained sufficient scientific acceptance to warrant admissibility as expert testimony." *State v. Grecinger,* 569 N.W.2d 189, 194 (Minn.1997) (citation omitted). [A]t the very least, in light of [t]he authorities relied on by the courts in those cases, the admission of Dr. Dutton's testimony was not plainly wrong.

[C].   *"Beyond the ken."*

Nixon next contends that "the admission of Dr. Dutton's expert testimony was reversible error because battered woman syndrome is not beyond the ken of the average layperson."

[D]uring the course of the trial, the defense repeatedly attempted to persuade the jury that Ms. Boyd's testimony was not credible. Nixon's counsel argued that for a long period, Ms. Boyd did not report, and even denied, the alleged abuse, and that her allegations were therefore belied by her own conduct. In his opening statement, Nixon's attorney told the jurors that there would be "no medical records . . . no pictures . . . no police reports of my client beating up Miss Boyd." Counsel asked the jurors to ponder why. During his cross-examination of the complainant, Nixon's attorney focused on her failure to report or disclose the abuse. Subsequently, in closing argument, counsel suggested that the failure of Ms. Boyd (or her family) to report the alleged battering to the police "doesn't make sense."

[A]ctions sometimes speak louder than words, and a lay juror might well wonder whether Ms. Boyd's actions (and inaction) at the time of the alleged abuse were consistent with the narrative which she provided in the courtroom long after the events occurred. Dr. Dutton's testimony was designed to apprise the jurors of certain repeated patterns of behavior on the part of many battered women. With that information, the jurors were in a better position to determine whether these patterns of behavior might explain any perceived discrepancy between Ms. Boyd's words and her deeds.

This court and other courts have held that testimony of the type provided by Dr. Dutton may assist the jury in understanding the evidence and is "beyond the ken" of the average lay juror within the meaning of *Dyas. See, e.g., Ibn–Tamas [v United States],* 407 A.2d at 635. In *[State v.] Borrelli,* the Supreme Court of Connecticut held that the testimony of the prosecution's expert on battered woman syndrome was "beyond the knowledge and experience of the average juror." 629 A.2d at 1112. The court relied on empirical research indicating that

> potential jurors may hold beliefs and attitudes about abused women at variance with the views of experts who have studied or had experience with abused women. In particular, males are likely to be skeptical about the fear the woman feels in an abusive relationship and about her inability to leave a setting in which abuse is threatened.

Id. (quoting N. Vidmar & R. Schuller, *Juries and Expert Evidence: Social Framework Testimony,* 52 Law & Contemp.Probs. 133, 154 (1989)).

[I]n this case, too, the judge could reasonably conclude, without abusing his discretion, that Dr. Dutton's testimony was beyond the ken of a lay trier of fact and would be helpful to the jurors in their consideration of the evidence.

[D].   *Relevance.*

Nixon also asserts on appeal, as he did in the trial court, that because "Dr. Dutton failed to examine or specifically diagnose Miss Boyd, her opinion regarding 'battered women' generally was irrelevant." The authorities on this issue, however, are uniformly to the contrary. [N]umerous other courts have [h]eld that expert testimony regarding BWS and other aspects of domestic violence is admissible where the expert has not examined the complaining witness and has not testified that she is a battered woman or suffers from BWS. *See, e.g.,* Cynthia Lynn Barnes, J.D., Annotation, *Admissibility of Expert Testimony Concerning Domestic-Violence Syndromes to Assist Jury in Evaluating Victim's Testimony or Behavior,* 57 A.L.R.5th 315 (1998). Indeed, in most of these cases, the courts have held or suggested that testimony by the expert to the effect that the complainant was a battered woman should be excluded as unduly prejudicial and because it would invade the province of the jury. In light of these decisions, any attempt by the prosecution to adduce expert testimony to the effect that Ms. Boyd was a battered woman would have injected into the record a significant possibility of undue prejudice.

[I]n this case, we conclude, as did the trial judge, that Dr. Dutton's testimony was relevant and that the prosecution had laid a sufficient foundation for its admission.

[E].   *Limiting instruction.*

Nixon claims that reversal is required because the trial court failed to give the jury a limiting instruction regarding the purpose for which Dr. Dutton's testimony was received in evidence. [N]ixon argues that in the absence of such an instruction, "the jury may easily mistake the expert's 'general' case-specific testimony as a case-specific diagnosis or as substantive evidence that the defendant is a 'batterer.' "Although a limiting instruction might have been appropriate, Nixon's claim of reversible error is without merit. In the present case, as we have noted, Dr. Dutton testified on direct examination that she had met neither the defendant nor Ms. Boyd and that she therefore had no opinion regarding Nixon's guilt. On cross-examination, Nixon's attorney elicited from Dr. Dutton, even more forcefully, exactly what testimony she did *not* give:

Q.   Dr. Dutton, you don't know whether Ms. Kelita Boyd is an abused person, do you?

A.   No, I do not.

Q. And, Dr. Dutton, you don't know that my client has ever abused or threatened Ms. Kelita Boyd, do you?

A. No, I do not.

* * *

Q. So, just to conclude, you don't know anything about the specifics of this case; is that correct?

A. That's correct.

Q. Thank you. I have no further questions.

In light of these unequivocal statements on the part of the witness, the jury could not reasonably have understood Dr. Dutton to be testifying that Ms. Boyd was a battered woman or that Nixon was her batterer.

[F]. *Probative value and prejudice.*

Finally, Nixon claims that Dr. Dutton's testimony was more prejudicial than probative, and that it should have been excluded on that ground.

[A] party seeking to override the trial judge's exercise of discretion must show that the probative value of the evidence is *substantially* outweighed by its potential prejudicial effect. Particularly where expert testimony is concerned, reversals on this ground do not abound

In *Ibn-Tamas I,* this court recognized the centrality of Dr. Lenore Walker's testimony regarding BWS when such evidence was offered by a homicide defendant who claimed to have been battered by her late husband, the decedent, whom she was alleged to have murdered. 407 A.2d at 639. The court held, as a matter of law, that the probative value of the proposed testimony outweighed its potential prejudice. *Id.* The issue in the present case is somewhat different, for Ms. Boyd was a prosecution witness, and not the accused. Nevertheless, as the court explained in *Arcoren [v United States],*

[i]t would seem anomalous to allow a battered woman, where she is a criminal defendant, to offer this type of expert testimony in order to help the jury understand the actions she took, yet deny her that same opportunity when she is the complaining witness and/or victim and her abuser is the criminal defendant.

929 F.2d at 1241 (quoting *State v. Frost,* 242 N.J.Super. 601, 577 A.2d 1282, 1287 (App.Div.1990)).

CONCLUSION

For the foregoing reasons, Nixon's convictions are hereby *Affirmed.*

———

STATE v. YUSUF

Appellate Court of Connecticut, 2002.
70 Conn.App. 594, 800 A.2d 590.

■ HEALEY, J.

The defendant, Asheek Yusuf, appeals from the judgment of conviction, rendered after a jury trial, of kidnapping in the second degree, assault in the second degree, unlawful restraint in the first degree, and cruelty to persons. On appeal, the defendant [c]laims that the court improperly allowed Stark, a sociologist, to testify as an expert witness on battered woman syndrome.

[D]uring his testimony, Stark [w]as asked a number of hypothetical questions that tracked the facts that gave rise to the charges against the defendant.[12] Generally, with respect to each hypothetical question, Stark

---

12. The state's questions and Stark's responses in relevant part were:

"[Prosecutor]: Assume the following facts: A fifteen year old woman becomes romantically involved with a twenty-four year old man who is physically larger and stronger than her. The relationship continues for about a year. During that relationship, the woman is assaulted, punched with fists, kicked with feet, assaulted with inanimate objects, burned with a lighter, verbally degraded with obscenities, all by that same man who's in the relationship with her. She's seriously assaulted perhaps five or six times over the course of this relationship. She never calls the police. She never reports this. She remains in the relationship. Is this behavior on the part of the woman consistent with behavior of a woman suffering from battered woman syndrome?

"[Witness]: Certainly."

[Prosecutor]: Is it consistent with battered women that a woman in that situation, in a relationship wherein she suffered assaults five or six times over the course of that relationship, is it consistent that she may not report these assaults to the police?

"[Witness]: Yes.

"[Prosecutor]: And is there—what role, if any, do minor assaults play based upon your study of women in such situations?

"[Witness]: In our experience ... the vast majority of assaults and battering situations tend to be minor rather than significant in the criminal justice and medical sense. And the effect of those assaults, in addition to the severe assaults which punctuate the history of ongoing minor assaults, is a level of physical intimidation that can create the learned helplessness that we described earlier. There are a variety of reasons why women don't report, but the data is pretty clear that in only a very small minority of instances where

history of battering is established are women able or do they call the police or visit the hospital.

"[Prosecutor]: Doctor, assume further that this particular man instructs a woman that she must call or page him before she goes anywhere, tell him who she'll be seeing, where she'll be going, when she'll return, she has to get [his] permission before she goes out before leaving work, she complies with this order. Is this consistent with a woman suffering battered woman syndrome?

"[Witness]: Yes.

"[Prosecutor]: And why is that?

"[Witness]: In situations—first of all, let me say that the beeper is being used ... more and more frequently in my experience in this area as a way of reporting in and as a form of control. So, that particular thing is certainly consistent in the hypothetical that you offered with what we know about battering, in this area at least.... [I]n addition, because of the isolation and because of the intimidation, the victim often concludes that what is right for her is following the rules. You can get almost a hostage-like situation which creates almost like childlike dependence on the batterer. It's maybe hard for people to understand this....

"The question of why women don't leave in situations like that, or why they don't report, is probably the most perplexing to people who work in the area. And what we've learned ... is that they don't leave because it's more dangerous to leave often than to stay. They don't leave because they love the guy and they hope that things will change even though they fear it won't, and a variety of other reasons associated with that, economic reasons and other dependence. But the main reason they don't leave, seems to be because of the level of control that is not was asked to give his expert opinion whether the hypothetical victim's conduct was consistent with that of a woman suffering from battered woman syndrome. In each case, Stark concluded that the victim's conduct as set out in the hypothetical question was indeed consistent with a woman suffering from battered woman syndrome.

[B]efore expert testimony about battered woman syndrome becomes relevant, an evidentiary foundation must first be established that the victim is a battered woman and that her conduct is such that the jury would be aided by expert testimony providing an explanation therefor. Here, contrary to the defendant's assertions, we conclude that the state presented sufficient evidence of an abusive relationship warranting the testimony on battered woman syndrome.

The state presented evidence that the defendant battered LeJeune [the woman he was living with] on a number of occasions during the course of their relationship. Stark's testimony was offered to assist the jury in understanding whether LeJeune's conduct was consistent with the pattern and profile of a battered woman. His expert testimony provided the jury with a relevant insight into LeJeune's behavior that it might not otherwise bring to its evaluation of her credibility. That insight was made more

easily observed by people who are outsiders, that he exercises over her every movement and everyday life, in her mind, if not in fact, but usually a combination of both.

"[Prosecutor]: Specifically relating to—continuing from that answer, assume these facts: A man becomes enraged over something because the woman has disobeyed or lied to him. He orders her into his car . . . [h]e beats her, assaults her. He then leaves the car momentarily later on, he threatens to kill the woman if she leaves the vehicle, the woman remains in the car. Is it consistent with battered woman syndrome for a woman to comply in this type of situation with a man's orders even though she may have an opportunity to escape?

"[Witness]: Yeah. I mean, unfortunately it is. What we may think is an opportunity to escape, in her mind may not be. Or she may think, and this is very commonly the case, that if she escapes and she's found, and she believes . . . that he can find her anywhere . . . that she's even going to be hurt worse; again, as strange as it may sound, there are many women who believe [that] getting the beating over with is better than living with the fear and anxiety and stress of what will happen to them if he does find them and she does escape. . . . [E]ven people who are mature in years can be reduced to almost childlike dependence in this situation and be para-

lyzed by the fear of what will happen to them even when to an outsider it seems perfectly reasonable they should open the door, and in the hypothetical you offer, of a car and simply run away." [Prosecutor]: Assume further that the man returns to the car and drives the woman to their apartment, drags her into the apartment, he orders her to remove clothing, orders her to a specific area of the apartment, assaults her . . . mandates that she remain there, eats his dinner, goes to sleep, allows her to go to sleep . . . the woman sleeps next to him, the man wakes, tells the woman if she leaves the apartment he will kill her, he leaves, the woman falls asleep. Is that a similar situation, similarly consistent with what you just described?

"[Witness]: Yes, it is.

"[Prosecutor]: Despite having a possible method or means or opportunity to escape, does not?

"[Witness]: Well, what you're describing in the hypothetical is what I would call a hostage-like situation, almost. Where, at least, in her mind, these opportunities to escape are not available even though they may be, again, to an outsider. . . .

"[Prosecutor]: The scenario I painted in the last hypothetical . . . is it consistent type of behaviors with a woman who is suffering battered woman syndrome?

significant in light of the defendant's extensive cross-examination of Le-Jeune, which focused on her failure to escape from the defendant when she had the opportunity to do so.

Moreover, Stark's testimony was particularly crucial to the jury's determination because although battered woman syndrome has become known to the public more widely than it was in the past, much of the subject still remains beyond the ken of the average juror. Indeed, "[c]ommentators have noted that the research data indicates that potential jurors may hold beliefs and attitudes about abused women at variance with the views of experts who have studied or had experience with abused women. In particular, males are likely to be skeptical about the fear the woman feels in an abusive relationship and about her inability to leave a setting in which abuse is threatened." [State v. Borrelli, 629 A.2d 1105 (1993)]. Reliance, therefore, on an expert such as Stark in a case such as this one was well warranted.

[W]e therefore are not persuaded that the court abused its discretion in admitting Stark's testimony, especially in light of the court's limiting instruction to the jury.[13] [A]ccordingly, the court did not abuse its discretion in admitting Stark's testimony.

[T]he judgment is affirmed.

CALIFORNIA EVIDENCE CODE (1991)

§ 1107. Battered women's syndrome; expert testimony in criminal actions; exception; sufficiency of foundation.

(a) In a criminal action, expert testimony is admissible by either the prosecution or the defense regarding the battered women's syndrome, including the physical, emotional, or mental effects upon the beliefs, perceptions, or behavior of victims of domestic violence, except when offered against a criminal defendant to prove the occurrence of the act or acts of abuse which form the basis of the criminal charge.

"[Witness]: It is."

13. In its final charge to the jury, the court instructed in relevant part:

"Dr. Stark's testimony presented a general description of battered woman syndrome, and he then testified as to certain characteristics that are commonly found in relationships involving domestic violence and on general or typical behavior patterns of victims of domestic violence. Dr. Stark, however, did not testify about whether Carissa LeJeune was in fact battered or whether her testimony here in court was truthful and accurate. His testimony was offered instead to help you understand whether Ms. Le-Jeune's conduct was consistent with the pattern and profile of a battered woman to help explain her conduct and thus to aid you in evaluating the credibility of her testimony.

"Expert testimony is presented to you to assist you in your deliberations. No such testimony is binding upon you, however, and you may disregard such testimony either in whole or in part. It's up to you as triers of the facts to determine whether such testimony was credible and whether and how it applies to the case. It's for you to consider the testimony with the other circumstances in the case and using your best judgment determine whether you will give it any weight and, if so, what weight you will give to it."

(b) The foundation shall be sufficient for admission of this expert testimony if the proponent of the evidence establishes its relevancy and the proper qualifications of the expert witness. Expert opinion testimony on battered women's syndrome shall not be considered a new scientific technique whose reliability is unproven.

JAHNKE v. WYOMING

Supreme Court of Wyoming, 1984.
682 P.2d 991.

■ Thomas, Justice.

[On November 16, 1982, Richard John Jahnke, then 16 years old, killed his father with a shotgun as the father was returning home after dinner at a restaurant. Jahnke had prepared for the shooting for an hour and a half. He was charged with first-degree murder. The state did not seek the death penalty. Jahnke pleaded self-defense, arguing that his father had repeatedly beaten him, his sister, and his mother over the course of many years. He was convicted by a jury of the lesser included offense of voluntary manslaughter and sentenced by the trial judge to 5 to 15 years in the state prison. Among the issues raised by the defendant on appeal was the trial judge's exclusion of psychiatric testimony on the issue of "battered youth."]

The essential questions presented in this case arise out of a notion that a victim of abuse has some special justification for patricide.

[P]rior to dealing with the specific issues raised by the appellant his theory of defense should be put in perspective. Appellant has cited to us the case of Buhrle v. State, 627 P.2d 1374 (Wyo.1981), which involved a homicide by a wife who claimed to be a victim of abuse. The cases which are cited in Burhle v. State, supra, lead into a series of cases involving homicides committed by women who were perceived as being victims of the "battered-wife syndrome." While those cases deal with wives as victims of abuse, conceptually there is no reason to distinguish a child who is a victim of abuse. A perusal of those cases leads to a conclusion that the effort which is made on behalf of the defendants is to secure the recognition of a special defense in a homicide case for victims of family abuse. Succinctly stated, the attempt that is made is to establish the concept that one who is a victim of family abuse is justified in killing the abuser.

The departure of this theory from the usual requirements of self-defense is patent. In Garcia v. State, 667 P.2d 1148 (Wyo.1983), the prior decisions of this court with respect to the defense of self-defense were collected. There we said:

> "[T]hat to justify the taking of human life in self-defense, it must appear from the evidence that the defendant not only really, and in good faith, endeavored to decline any conflict with the deceased, and to escape from his assailant, if he had the opportunity to do so, if he was

assailed, before he fired the shot in question, but it must also appear that the circumstances were such as to excite the fears of a reasonable person that the deceased intended to take his life, or to inflict upon him great bodily harm, and that the defendant really acted under the influence of such fears, and not in a spirit of revenge.... Ross v. State, supra [8 Wyo. 351, 57 P. 924 (1899)], 8 Wyo. at 383, 57 P. at 931."

It is clear that self-defense is circumscribed by circumstances involving a confrontation, usually encompassing some overt act or acts by the deceased, which would induce a reasonable person to fear that his life was in danger or that at least he was threatened with great bodily harm.

This same circumstantial circumscription is discernible in the line of cases involving abused or battered wives. See Ibn-Tamas v. United States, 407 A.2d 626 (D.C.App.1979); People v. White, 90 Ill.App.3d 1067, 46 Ill.Dec. 474, 414 N.E.2d 196 (1980); and State v. Thomas, 66 Ohio St.2d 518, 20 Ohio Op.3d 424, 423 N.E.2d 137 (1981). [A]lthough many people, and the public media, seem to be prepared to espouse the notion that a victim of abuse is entitled to kill the abuser, that special justification defense is antithetical to the mores of modern civilized society. It is difficult enough to justify capital punishment as an appropriate response of society to criminal acts even after the circumstances have been carefully evaluated by a number of people. To permit capital punishment to be imposed upon the subjective conclusion of the individual that prior acts and conduct of the deceased justified the killing would amount to a leap into the abyss of anarchy.

In People v. White, supra, and State v. Thomas, supra, the courts suggest that the true role of any evidence with respect to family abuse is to assist the jury to determine whether the defendant's belief that he was in danger of his life or serious bodily injury was reasonable under the circumstances. In those cases the courts indicate that expert testimony with respect to such an issue is neither necessary nor relevant and for that reason is best eschewed.

[C]ounsel for the appellant [described] the overall purpose of the testimony of the forensic psychiatrist. It is clear that the psychiatrist had interviewed the appellant on seven separate occasions for a total of twelve hours in preparation for the trial. He also had visited with other people about the appellant. At the trial appellant's counsel advised the court that the psychiatrist would express an opinion as to the appellant's mental or emotional condition, and the assertion was made that the appellant had a right to establish the facts which formed the basis for that opinion. The counter-argument of the State was premised upon Smith v. State, 564 P.2d 1194 (Wyo.1977), and was to the effect that such an opinion was not admissible in the absence of a plea of not guilty by reason of mental illness or deficiency. Reference was made to the psychiatrist's testimony at the time of the hearing on the appellant's motion to transfer the case to the juvenile court. On that occasion the psychiatrist had testified that in his opinion the appellant was a battered youth suffering from a mental disorder which was not defined or recognized under the accepted standards of diagnosis of mental and personality disorders in his field of expertise. At that hearing he related the history of the appellant's abuse at the hands of his father as the appellant had given it to him. He said that the appellant was very much afraid of his father.

[A]s noted, the appellant invokes the theory discussed in Buhrle v. State, supra, and the other cases involving the "battered-wife syndrome." We do not perceive how the offer of proof presented by the appellant was sufficient to satisfy the criteria for admissibility of expert testimony quoted in Buhrle v. State, supra, 627 P.2d 1374 (Wyo.1981) from Dyas v. United States, 376 A.2d 827, 832 (D.C.App.1977), cert. denied 434 U.S. 973, 98 S.Ct. 529, 54 L.Ed.2d 464 (1977). We particularly note that there was no offer to prove that the state of the pertinent art of scientific knowledge permitted a reasonable opinion to be asserted by the expert, and the suggestion of his earlier testimony on the occasion of the motion hearing is to the contrary.

[S]ince there is no error in these proceedings such as that claimed by the appellant, the judgment and sentence of the district court is affirmed.

■ Rose, Justice, dissenting, with whom Cardine, Justice, joins.

This case concerns itself with what happens—or can happen—and did happen when a cruel, ill-tempered, insensitive man roams, gun in hand, through his years of family life as a battering bully—a bully who, since his two children were babies, beat both of them and his wife regularly and unmercifully. Particularly, this appeal has to do with a 16–year-old boy who could stand his father's abuse no longer—who could not find solace or friendship in the public services which had been established for the purpose of providing aid, comfort and advice to abused family members—and who had no place to go or friends to help either him or his sister for whose protection he felt responsible and so—in fear and fright, and with fragmented emotion, Richard Jahnke shot and killed his father one night in November of 1982. In these courts, Richard pleads self-defense and, since the jury was given a self-defense instruction, it must be conceded that the trial judge recognized this as a viable defense theory under the evidence adduced at trial.

In this dissenting opinion, [I] find error in the majority opinion's conclusion that the trial court properly excluded the proffered expert psychiatric witness' testimony from the jury's consideration.

[D]enied the explanatory assistance of a qualified expert witness, it is as though Richard Jahnke had not been permitted to defend himself at all. [H]ow could this young boy structure an understandable defense when—even though the record discloses that since age two he had been bullied, battered, frightened and emotionally traumatized—he was, nevertheless, denied the opportunity to have explained to his jury how abused people reasonably handle their fears and anxieties—what their apprehensions are—how, in the dark moments of their aloneness, they perceive the imminence of danger—and how, in response, they undertake to assert their right of self-defense?

It is my conception that Richard Jahnke properly came to the courts of Wyoming asking—not that he be judged as one who, at the time and place in question, was insanely unreasonable—but that his 14 years of beatings and uncivilized emotional abuse be explained by a qualified expert in order that judgment be passed on the question which asks whether or not his behavior was sanely reasonable. One might wonder why—since our courts admit expert testimony with commendable regularity upon the issue of sanity when that is the ultimate fact—and the plea is insanity—it is not acceptable that a psychiatrist testify about whether behavior such as that with which this case is concerned and which is unlike that which lay jurors would understand to be the expected, is, nevertheless, sanely typical of the behavior of a reasonable person acting in the same or similar circumstances. Richard was not, however, permitted to have the impact of 14 years of abuse upon his alleged self-defensive behavior explained to the jury through the testimony of a psychiatrist even though this is the only way the fallout from brutality can be communicated.

[I]n contemplating the overall problem which brings on my dissent, it is initially necessary to be aware of at least these following facts:

Richard Jahnke, a sensitive boy who had never been in any sort of trouble in his life, had been beaten regularly and unmercifully by his father since he was two years old. On the night of the homicide he had received a severe beating, and when his father and mother left the house to go to dinner that night, his father said:

> "I'm disgusted with the shit you turned out to be. I don't want you to be here when I get back."

The father also said:

> "I don't care what I have to do, I'm going to get rid of you. I don't know how but I'm going to get rid of you, you bastard."

The boy felt he had to protect his sister who was hysterical when the mother and father left for dinner. He did not believe that there was any place or anyone where or to whom they could go for safety. The mother testified that the elder Jahnke always carried a gun, and Richard believed he had one with him that night. Mrs. Jahnke said that when the father said to Richard, "I'm going to get rid of you"?

> "He was trying to frighten him and maybe do something else besides just throwing him out of the house."

When Richard was in the garage after having stationed his father's guns around the house for "backup," he reflected upon past confrontations with his father and he was afraid the father would kill him when he returned and found what Richard had done with the guns. Even as he contemplated these things, the father drove the car into the driveway. Richard said he wanted to go and hug him and tell him he loved him, but he remembered when he had done this before, he had received a beating for his efforts. He knew from past experience that when his father "stomped" after him that he was in for a beating. He testified about how his father approached the garage door that night:

"A. Yes. I remember he was stomping. When he stomped down the hall when he was really mad and really prepared to beat someone up, beat on one of us. I remember being a little kid, just sitting in my room. My dad stomping after me to hit me, that I could never stop him.

"This time I stopped him."

[I]n this appeal [w]e do not have defensive behavior with which the lay juror is naturally familiar, and yet a doctor of psychiatric medicine was denied the opportunity to testify that Richard Jahnke's behavior was that of a battered individual whose consequent perception of the imminence of danger is different than the perception of the nonbrutalized person and who would have explained how the battered person responds to danger. Here, the victim was "stomping" up the driveway in a familiarly menacing way into the face of the fears and anxieties of his son whom he had beaten for 14 years and who recognized the "stomping" as a preface to violence. Here, we have a boy who, from long experience, had come to know what to expect from this confrontation—who believed he would be beaten or would be killed by gun—who did not try to escape because he did not believe that he had any place to go and who did not feel that he could leave his sister unprotected—who taught his sister to fire the gun in case his father should kill him—all in what he believed to be his only defense against further savagery which he knew from past experience would surely come. Could a jury understand this behavior as falling within the requirements of the self-defense instruction without help from an expert psychiatric witness? The asking of the question is to answer it.

Therefore, in the ordinary self-defense situation where there are no psychiatric implications and where the jury is permitted to know what the accused knew about the violent character of his victim, there need be no expert testimony touching upon the reasonableness of the defendant's behavior. In normal circumstances, these are things that jurors can fathom for themselves. However, when the beatings of 14 years have—or may have—caused the accused to harbor types of fear, anxiety and apprehension with which the nonbrutalized juror is unfamiliar and which result in the taking of unusual defensive measures which, in the ordinary circumstances, might be thought about as premature, excessive or lacking in escape efforts by those who are uninformed about the fear and anxiety that permeate the world of the brutalized—then expert testimony is necessary to explain the battered-person syndrome and the way these people respond to what they understand to be the imminence of danger and to explain their propensity to employ deadly force in their self-defensive conduct. Given this information, the jury is then qualified to decide the reasonableness of a self-defense defendant's acts at the time and place in question.

[T]HE PROFFERED TESTIMONY OF THE FORENSIC PSYCHIATRIST

Dr. McDonald, a forensic psychiatrist, was offered by the defendant for the purpose of testifying about the behavior of battered children—that Richard was a battered child—all as an aid to the triers of fact with respect to their obligation to decide whether or not this defendant—as a battered person—behaved reasonably on the night of November 16, 1982, but the court would not permit the jury to hear the testimony.

The defendant suggests that his offer of proof represented that Dr. McDonald would testify that:

1. The doctor had diagnosed Richard Jahnke as a battered child, based on interviews with him and upon other information.

2. Battered children behave differently from other children, and perceive things differently from other children.

3. Because he was a battered child, Jahnke reasonably believed himself to be in immediate danger on the night he shot his father, and perceived himself as acting in self-defense.

[T]his offer says to me that the doctor's testimony would have supplied such underlying psychiatric information as would have permitted the jury to resolve the issue of reasonableness in an intelligent and informed manner. Even if the offer is read to say that the testimony would have touched on the ultimate issue of the reasonableness of the defendant's behavior at the time and place in question, this is no longer prohibited—at least within the context of the law of this case. In Ibn-Tamas v. United States, 407 A.2d 626, 628 (D.C.App.1979), a battered-person self-defense case, the court said:

" . . . As to the first—the 'ultimate facts' or 'ultimate issue' rule— Dr. Walker was not going to express an opinion on the ultimate question whether Mrs. Ibn-Tamas actually and reasonably believed she was in danger when she shot her husband. Rather, this expert would have merely supplied background data to help the jury make that crucial determination. See United States v. Hearst, 412 F.Supp. 889 (N.D.Cal.1976) (Hearst I). In any event, the ultimate issue rule has, over time, been reduced to a prohibition only against questions to an expert 'which, in effect, submit the whole case to an expert witness for decision.' n14 Id. There is no such risk here."

[L]astly, the majority opinion takes issue with the fact that the offer of proof does not meet the state-of-the-art criteria for the reception of battered-person expert testimony as set out in Dyas v. United States, 376 A.2d 827, 832 (D.C.App.1977), cert. denied 434 U.S. 973, 98 S.Ct. 529, 54 L.Ed.2d 464 (1977) and adopted by our Buhrle v. State, 627 P.2d 1374 (Wyo.1981). It is urged by the majority that it was not shown by Dr. McDonald's testimony that the battered-person theory had progressed to that place in the scientific scheme of things where a reasonable opinion can be asserted by an expert as to how a battered person perceives the imminence of danger and responds thereto.

[W]ith respect to the state-of-the-art issue, I would hold that the testimony in question is being recognized and admitted in a majority of jurisdictions in this country because it is central to the defense of the battered person who pleads self-defense—as is shown by the numerous citations of authority in this opinion—and therefore it was error as a matter of law to have excluded the testimony for the reason that there was inadequate foundation proof on this subject.

Even if we were to assign the same importance to this issue that the majority does, this court is obligated, in my opinion, to remand the case to the trial court for the purpose of supplementing the record in this regard. Ibn-Tamas v. United States, supra.

———

NOTE

1.   Commutation of Sentence. On June 15, 1984, one week after the Wyoming Supreme Court upheld Richard Jahnke's 5–15 year prison sentence, Governor Ed Herschler commuted the sentence to three years at a state reform school. The Governor stated, "I guess I have some compassion for this young individual. I think it's something I had to do." Youth Who Killed Abusive Father Has Term Cut, New York Times, June 16, 1984 at A6. Deborah Jahnke, Richard Jahnke's younger sister, was convicted at a separate trial and sentenced to 3–8 years in prison, a sentence that was also upheld by the Wyoming Supreme Court. One week after that decision, the Governor commuted her sentence to one year at a home for "troubled women."

———

STATE v. NEMETH

Supreme Court of Ohio, 1998.
82 Ohio St.3d 202, 694 N.E.2d 1332.

■ [MOYER, CHIEF JUSTICE]

In the early morning hours of January 7, 1995, sixteen-year-old Brian Nemeth took a compound bow and arrows from his room and shot his mother, Suzanne Nemeth, five times in the head and neck. She died eight days later. Brian was tried for aggravated murder.

[A]t his trial, Brian testified that his mother had been abusive toward him for several years. She drank to excess several nights a week and when she was drinking she would become very angry with him—hitting, slapping, and psychologically abusing him.

Brian testified that [on the evening before the killing, his] mother started screaming and cursing at him and threw a full beer can at him, cutting his lip. He ran to his room and locked the door. He testified that his mother's tone had changed and she was cursing him and threatening to beat his face in. He believed that he was in serious danger. She had removed the phone from his room, so he could not call for help. [H]e was crying and shaking. She pounded on his door for several hours. [A]round 4:00 a.m., after hours of sitting there listening to his mother's threats and attempts to get into his room, Brian heard her walk away.

Brian testified, "[S]he walked—I don't know, [s]he kind of—she must have gave up or something. All of a sudden, I just—everything just started coming back to me and I just—the bow was in my room. * * * It was laying on my chair and the way I was facing, I was facing the chair and I was like a robot. I just picked it up and walked out in the hall. * * * I don't even—I don't even know where I was walking to. * * * I just kept on walking out towards the living room and I got to the end of the hall and my mom, she was laying there on the couch. I just started shooting. * * * I only remember the first shot. I blacked out. I found myself on the floor. I went back to my room."

After shooting his mother, Brian called the police and told them what happened. When they did not arrive immediately, he called back and begged the dispatcher to hurry. He cooperated with the paramedics and confessed to the police. His mother had a blood-alcohol level of 0.20 when she was killed.

The Juvenile Court of Jefferson County bound Brian over to the Jefferson County Court of Common Pleas and he was subsequently tried as an adult and convicted of murder. Prior to the bindover hearing, Brian was examined by Dr. James R. Eisenberg, Ph.D. Dr. Eisenberg diagnosed Brian as suffering from "battered child syndrome" and as having "very compatible symptoms as do women in abusive relationships."

[A]t the close of its case, the defense proffered the testimony of Dr. Eisenberg as an expert on battered child syndrome. The proffered testimony would have explained the psychological effects of long-term child abuse, including the effect on a child's perception of danger. The testimony was proffered in support of a self-defense theory. [T]he proffered testimony was not admitted into evidence.

[T]he court of appeals reversed Brian's conviction and remanded the cause for a new trial. The court of appeals held that the defense had put forth sufficient evidence to warrant the admission of expert testimony regarding battered child syndrome, in support of a claim of self-defense, and that preclusion of such testimony was prejudicial.

[T]he defense in this case did not ask that battered child syndrome be recognized as a new defense or an independent justification for the killing of an abusive parent. The proffer made at trial was limited to expert testimony that would explain the psychological effects of long-term child abuse, and was proffered in support of a self-defense theory as well as a charge on voluntary manslaughter. As such, the issue before us is an evidentiary matter and is governed by the Ohio Rules of Evidence.

[I]n this case, the testimony on battered child syndrome, which was proffered by the defense, is relevant for at least four separate purposes, including the determination of whether Brian (1) had acted with prior calculation and design as charged in the indictment, (2) had acted with purpose as required for the lesser included offense of murder, (3) had created the confrontation or initiated the aggression, and (4) had an honest belief that he was in imminent danger, a necessary element in the affirmative defense of self-defense.

[E]xpert testimony on battered child syndrome would, in this case, tend to enhance the probability that Brian's account of the facts leading up to the killing was truthful and would lend credibility to his assertion that he was in a state of rage and dissociation at the time of the killing. A diagnosis of battered child syndrome and an explanation of its effects would therefore be relevant in determining whether the case warranted a jury charge on voluntary manslaughter.

In addition to the requirement of relevancy, expert testimony must meet the criteria of *Evid.R. 702*. *Rule 702* provides that a witness may testify as an expert if all of the following apply:

> "(A) The witness' testimony either relates to matters beyond the knowledge or experience possessed by lay persons or dispels a misconception common among lay persons;

> "(B) The witness is qualified as an expert by specialized knowledge, skill, experience, training, or education regarding the subject matter of the testimony;

> "(C) The witness' testimony is based on reliable scientific, technical, or other specialized information. * * * "

The first prong of the rule is satisfied in this case. This trial presents precisely the kind of situation in which expert testimony is most necessary. [N]onconfrontational killings do not fit the general pattern of self-defense. Without expert testimony, a trier of fact may not be able to understand that the defendant at the time of the killing could have had an honest belief that he was in imminent danger of death or great bodily harm. Further, it is difficult for the average person to understand the degree of helplessness an abused child may feel.

[E]xpert testimony as to the effects of abuse may also help to counter popular misconceptions about the nonreporting of abuse. Prolonged exposure to abuse results in feelings of powerlessness, embarrassment, fear of reprisal, isolation, and low self-esteem. These effects often prevent a child from seeking help from third parties. The abusive parent also generally becomes adept at concealing the abuse from outsiders. Note, Toffel, Crazy Women, Unharmed Men, and Evil Children: Confronting Myths About Battered People Who Kill Their Abusers, and the Argument for Extending Battering Syndrome Self-Defenses to all Victims of Domestic Violence (1996), *70 S.Cal.L.Rev. 337, 364*. The effects of abuse thereby diminish the likelihood that the defense will be able to present corroborating testimony of third parties.

Absent corroborating evidence, a trier of fact is likely to believe that the abuse allegations are fabricated in response to the charges levied against the child-defendant. The existence and prevalence of such misconceptions are evident in the transcript of this trial. The prosecution repeatedly stressed that Brian could have left the house again, that he could have gone to his father or grandparents, that he was not in actual imminent danger at the time of the killing, and implying that he must have created the allegations of abuse after the fact because, otherwise, more people would have known about it. Even the trial court judge questioned whether there was corroborating evidence of abuse before granting the state's motion *in limine,* excluding testimony on battered child syndrome in connection with a claim of self-defense.

[T]he second prong of the test has not been challenged. The trial court disallowed any testimony as to battered child syndrome and did not specifically challenge the qualifications of Dr. Eisenberg.

The final requirement for the admission of testimony by experts is whether the testimony is based on reliable scientific, technical, or other specialized information. Dr. Eisenberg's testimony was based on scientific, technical, or otherwise specialized information. He is a trained psychologist who has specialized training in the behavioral and psychological effects of child abuse. The only question remaining is whether the information supporting his opinion is sufficiently reliable.

[I]n *Miller [v. Bike Athletic Co., 687 N.E.2d 735 (1998)],* the court designated the following four factors to be considered in evaluating the reliability of scientific evidence: (1) whether the theory or technique has been tested, (2) whether it has been subjected to peer review, (3) whether there is a known or potential rate of error, and (4) whether the methodology has gained general acceptance. These factors were adopted from *Daubert v. Merrell Dow Pharmaceuticals, Inc. (1993), 509 U.S. 579, 593–594, 113 S.Ct. 2786, 2797, 125 L.Ed.2d 469, 482–483.* Both the United States Supreme Court in *Daubert* and this court in *Miller* were careful to emphasize that none of these factors is a determinative prerequisite to admissibility. *Miller at 612–613, 687 N.E.2d at 741; Daubert at 593, 113 S.Ct. at 2797, 125 L.Ed.2d at 483.*

[T]hough it is not necessary to show general acceptance to pass the threshold of reliability for the admission of expert testimony, the behavioral and psychological effects of prolonged child abuse on the child have been generally accepted in the medical and psychiatric communities and therefore unquestionably meet the requisite level of reliability for admission as the subject of expert testimony.

[T]he behavioral and psychological effects of child abuse, or battered child syndrome, are most often discussed as a form of posttraumatic stress disorder ("PTSD"). PTSD is an anxiety disorder listed in the DSM-IV, which categorizes universally recognized mental disorders. This specific disorder has been recognized in children at least since 1987 when the DSM-III-R was published. The fourth and most recent edition of the manual specifically notes that PTSD can manifest in children. The triggering event for posttraumatic stress disorder can be any traumatic event that involved "actual or threatened death or serious injury, or a threat to the physical integrity of self or others" and where the person's response involved "intense fear, helplessness, or horror." DSM-IV at 427–428.

[T]he psychological effects of abuse suffered by battered children are equivalent to the effects of prolonged abuse experienced by abused women and have been recognized as appropriate for expert testimony in the context of battered women. The psychiatric and legal communities have clearly accepted that despite any minor differences in the degree of power differentials between the batterer and the abused, the psychological effects of family violence are legally indistinguishable whether suffered by children or adults.

Several states have allowed the defendant to present expert testimony of a "battered child" or "battered person" syndrome where a child has killed or attempted to kill an abusive family member. See, *e.g., State v. Janes (1993), 121 Wash.2d 220, 850 P.2d 495 (en banc)*. Still others, while not faced with the issue of expert testimony, have recognized that abused children may exhibit identifiable psychological characteristics that point to a causal connection between the abuse and the killing of the abuser. See, *e.g., People v. Cruickshank (1985), 105 A.D.2d 325, 484 N.Y.S.2d 328*. Six states have enacted statutes that allow the presentation of testimony regarding the psychological effects on victims of domestic violence, including children, in cases where the victim of abuse is on trial for acts of violence against the abuser. [See, e.g.,] *Tex.Code Crim. Pro. Art. 38.36(b)(2) (1997)*.

While specific legislation may be helpful in defining the parameters of a new defense, such legislative action is not necessary in order for us to determine whether expert testimony concerning battered child syndrome meets the evidentiary requirements of *Evid.R. 702* and whether it should therefore be admissible in appropriate cases. Battered child syndrome is not a new defense or justification for murder. We are making no new law with this opinion. Pursuant to well-established Rules of Evidence and case law dealing with the admission of expert testimony, we hold that the proffered expert testimony on battered child syndrome was both relevant and reliable and that the trial court in this case erred in granting the motion prohibiting the testimony. Because the preclusion of such testimony was prejudicial, we affirm the holding of the court of appeals, which vacated the defendant's conviction and remanded the cause for a new trial.

BATTERED CHILD SYNDROME AND OTHER PSYCHOLOGICAL EFFECTS OF SEXUAL AND PHYSICAL ABUSE OF CHILDREN

Regina Schuller and Patricia A. Hastings.
In Modern Scientific Evidence: The Law and Science of Expert Testimony, 2d ed. (D. L. Faigman, D. H. Kaye, M. J. Saks, and J. Sanders eds. 2002).

Some agreement in the area is found regarding the psychological impact that abuse can have on a child, but as to the existence of a specific syndrome or profile, the literature remains silent. Therefore, attempting to identify agreement and disagreement regarding battered child syndrome in the scientific literature is premature. The parallel between battered child syndrome and battered woman syndrome that has been drawn is, at this point, not based on an empirical body of work. There is a small body of research documenting the existence of some of the symptoms associated with battered woman syndrome in a proportion of abused children, but [t]hese areas are not yet well developed. Further, no studies have attempted to assess what group of symptoms constitute a reliable and valid battered child syndrome and how well it captures the impact of abuse in this population. The heterogeneity of children's responses to abuse suggests, however, that, as is the case with battered women, a single profile is unlikely to adequately capture the impact of abuse on a child.

In summary, the applicability of the research findings on battered women to battered children still needs to be demonstrated. Certainly the impact of the violence on these two populations will result in some similar effects, but generalizing from battered women to battered children, two very different populations, is only speculative until the effects can be demonstrated in the latter population. While there is evidence to suggest that PTSD [post-traumatic stress disorder] is associated with abuse (sexual and physical), there is also considerable variability in children's responses.

(b) Combat

The strain of combat, once known as "shell shock," has long been known to affect human behavior. Only with the advent of the Vietnam War, however, was "post-traumatic stress disorder," with combat being the "stressor," argued as a defense to crime.

STATE v. FELDE

Supreme Court of Louisiana, 1982.
422 So.2d 370.

■ WATSON, JUSTICE.

Defendant, Wayne Robert Felde, was convicted of first degree murder. The jury unanimously recommended a death sentence on the ground of one aggravating circumstance: the victim was a peace officer engaged in his lawful duties. The defendant has appealed.

[F]elde, convicted of manslaughter and assault in Maryland, was serving a twelve year sentence when he escaped from a minimum security job and hitchhiked to his mother's home in Grand Cane, Louisiana. [He] returned to Louisiana because of his mother's terminal cancer. [H]is mother died on October 13, 1978.

On October 20, 1978, Felde's sister, Florence McDonald, told him the police were looking for him. She drove Felde [to] Shreveport where Felde purchased a .357 Magnum gun and a box of shells. [Felde then went] to the Dragon Lounge [where he] drank enough beer to get "pretty loaded." [B]ecause a customer reported there was someone at the Lounge with a gun, two officers arrived. [A]fter being told Felde was the man with the gun, officers Norwood and Thompkins searched him but did not discover the pistol.

[O]fficer Thompkins arrested him as a simple drunk. Felde's hands were handcuffed behind his back and he was placed in the rear seat of Thompkins' police car. While Felde was being driven in the police car, William David Sweet, in another car, observed Felde up close behind the front seat. Felde was leaning forward on the right hand side of the driver. The officer put on his brakes and simultaneously made a motion to push Felde back in the seat. Felde said he was trying to shoot himself when he was pulled forward and pushed back. A shot was fired. There was testimony that the car filled with smoke. Felde did not remember anything after the first explosion. There were three other shots, leaving Felde with at least one bullet in his gun. The vehicle swerved against a guard rail and stopped. Thompkins staggered out of the car across the road before collapsing dead in a ditch.

[T]he defense was insanity at the time of the crime; defendant allegedly suffered a post-traumatic stress syndrome as the result of combat in Vietnam.

[T]here was lay testimony that there was a noticeable difference in Felde's behavior before and after his military duty in Vietnam. Before his service, he was a jovial, happy-go-lucky kid. Afterward, he was moody, depressed, and irritable, with erratic sleeping habits and a low tolerance for alcohol. One of Wayne Felde's sisters, Maria Kristine Krebsbach, testified that she had sent one brother to Vietnam and a different one, a stranger, had returned. This sister, a nurse, and her mother, also a nurse, attempted to get psychiatric help for Felde but were unable to do so.

[D]r. John P. Wilson testified for the defense as an expert psychologist and professor of psychology who has made special studies of the post-traumatic stress disorder in Vietnam veterans. Dr. Wilson examined Felde on August 30, 1979, at the Caddo Parish Jail for four and a half hours. Dr. Wilson concluded unequivocally that Wayne Felde had a chronic form of post-traumatic stress disorder. This is a recognized behavioral disorder or mental defect which is recognized by the American Psychiatric Association. The symptoms are also shared by survivors of atomic attacks, holocausts or natural disasters. Post-traumatic stress response symptoms include: depression; flashbacks to the trauma; inability to control one's impulses; violent, explosive behavior; frequent suicidal thoughts and recurring nightmares. There is often memory impairment and inability to feel close to people, an emotional numbing. There is a great deal of survivor guilt with this disorder. Because of the type of combat required in Vietnam, veterans of that conflict also have moral guilt. The disorder is not new but was only recently recognized by the American Psychiatric Association as a bonafide mental disorder. Sixty percent of Vietnam combat veterans experience post-traumatic stress, a very high percentage. This is because units did not stay together, there was no real war objective, the soldiers were quite young, and drugs were freely available at a low price. Vietnam soldiers averaged 19.2 years, whereas those in World War II and Korea averaged 26½. The units in World War II stayed intact and came home together whereas in Vietnam each veteran came home alone. Vietnam veterans with P.T.S.D., or post-traumatic stress disorder, tend to move from one job to another. Felde's military record showed three AWOLs and a drunk charge, the first AWOL occurring one month after he returned from Vietnam. On one of these occasions, Felde wrecked a brand new car; his behavior was erratic and irrational. These episodes were consistent with his post-traumatic stress syndrome as were his marital difficulties. Part of the syndrome is a hyper alertness, where the person becomes easily irritated and agitated and startles easily. Sleep disturbances are part of the disorder. Twenty-five percent of all men in prison are Vietnam era veterans. The suicide rate of Vietnam veterans is thirty-three to forty percent higher than that of others the same age. The alcoholism rate among Vietnam veterans is sixty percent higher than it was for veterans of World War II or Korea. The Veterans' Administration now recognizes post-traumatic stress disorder as a service connected disability for which treatment can be received. Stress in a person's emotional life, such as the death of a mother, can trigger disassociative reactions. Dr. Wilson said that Felde's Maryland killing sounded like a classic disassociative reaction in which a person uses survival contact tactics because he is not fully aware of what is happening. Many Vietnam veterans suffering from post-traumatic stress disorder are being misdiagnosed as being alcoholics or having other disorders. Felde's prison record in Maryland was exemplary, which is characteristic of Vietnam veterans. The confined, controlled environment helps the post-traumatic stress disorder. Although they suffer tremendously, such inmates tend to behave well while incarcerated. Dr. Wilson testified that, since his father died when Wayne Felde was twelve, he was particularly close to his mother, the most significant support person in his life. After losing his mother and then learning that the police were coming for him, he felt helpless, trapped and scared. He bought the gun as a form of security against an impending threat. Many Vietnam veterans even sleep with their weapons. In the doctor's opinion, Felde bought the gun as part of a decision to kill himself. When Felde pulled the gun in the car, it was Dr. Wilson's opinion that he wanted to kill himself rather than Officer Thompkins. Dr. Wilson recounted Felde's account of the situation beginning at the Dragon Lounge, "they asked me where, where I had the, where the gun was, then they handcuffed me and put me in the police car. I was in the back of the car and I thought I'd blow my brains out. I tried to turn the barrel around towards my face. I remember the jerk going forward then I saw flashes, flashes like incoming round hits, like firecrackers, hearing machine guns, I heard machine guns, I heard rifle fire, I heard more explosions and I couldn't move. I was happy because I knew I was going to die." According to Dr. Wilson, this fragmented memory is totally consistent with a disassociated state and flashback typical of post-traumatic stress disorder. In Dr. Wilson's opinion, "At that time, in that disassociated state, he couldn't discriminate right from wrong and he couldn't conform his conduct to the law. I think he was totally disoriented." (Tr.1806) Dr. Wilson said that Felde needed long term group psychotherapy with other veterans and, if he were put on the street, he would either kill himself or kill someone else.

[I]t is contended that the jury erred in finding Felde guilty of first degree murder and rejecting his defense of insanity at the time of the crime on the basis of the evidence presented.

Defendant is correct in his contention that the expert testimony about Felde's post-traumatic stress syndrome by Dr. Wilson, [and other defense experts], as well as the lay testimony about the effect of the Vietnam combat on Felde, is very persuasive. However, [t]he three members of the sanity commission all testified that defendant was sane at the time of the offense. [Two of these government witnesses] are psychiatrists and a rational jury could have adopted their testimony over that of the defense witnesses.

[T]he conviction and sentence of defendant, Wayne Robert Felde, are affirmed.

————

NOTE

1. Legal uses of PTSD with combat as the stressor. The defense sometimes has introduced Post Traumatic Stress Disorder as part of the affirmative defense of insanity. It has been suggested by Erlinder, Post-Traumatic Stress Disorder: Vietnam Veterans and the Law: A Challenge to Effective Representation, 1 Behavioral Sciences and the Law 25, 43 (1983), however, that self-defense may be a more appropriate defense strategy in these situations:

> The Model Penal Code would allow the defendant to demonstrate that his or her responses were subjectively reasonable [Section 3.04(1)]. The use of PTSD in this context might parallel that of the "battered spouse syndrome" that has been used to explain a female defendant's violent acts. It may be possible to show that a particular type of provocation caused a PTSD-type reaction in which the defendant felt attacked and responded involuntarily or even reasonably given his or her experiences. In this circumstance, the existence of PTSD would again make the whole of a defendant's life relevant to show his state of mind at the time of the occurrence.

Erlinder also cited cases where combat-induced Post Traumatic Stress Disorder had been used in plea bargaining and in pre-sentence reports, often with the defendant receiving treatment as a condition of probation, in addition to its use to establish insanity, diminished capacity, and self-defense.

————

DIAGNOSTIC AND STATISTICAL MANUAL OF MENTAL DISORDERS*

(4th ed., Text Revision, 2000).
American Psychiatric Association.

Diagnostic criteria for 309.81 Posttraumatic Stress Disorder

A. The person has been exposed to a traumatic event in which both of the following were present:

   (1) the person experienced, witnessed, or was confronted with an event or events that involved actual or threatened death or serious injury, or a threat to the physical integrity of self or others

   (2) the person's response involved intense fear, helplessness, or horror. **Note**: In children, this may be expressed instead by disorganized or agitated behavior.

B. The traumatic event is persistently reexperienced in one (or more) of the following ways:

   (1) recurrent and intrusive distressing recollections of the event, including images, thoughts, or perceptions. **Note**: In young children, repetitive play may occur in which themes or aspects of the trauma are expressed.

   (2) recurrent distressing dreams of the event. **Note**: In children, there may be frightening dreams without recognizable content.

   (3) acting or feeling as if the traumatic event were recurring (includes a sense of reliving the experience, illusions, hallucinations, and dissociative flashback episodes, including those that occur on awakening or when intoxicated). **Note**: In young children, trauma-specific reenactment may occur.

   (4) intense psychological distress at exposure to internal or external cues that symbolize or resemble an aspect of the traumatic event

   (5) physiological reactivity on exposure to internal or external cues that symbolize or resemble an aspect of the traumatic event

C. Persistent avoidance of stimuli associated with the trauma and numbing of general responsiveness (not present before the trauma), as indicated by three (or more) of the following:

   (1) efforts to avoid thoughts, feelings, or conversations associated with the trauma

   (2) efforts to avoid activities, places, or people that arouse recollections of the trauma

   (3) inability to recall an important aspect of the trauma

   (4) markedly diminished interest or participation in significant activities

* Reprinted with permission from the Diagnostic and Statistical Manual of Mental Disorders, Fourth Edition, Copyright 2000, American Psychiatric Association.

(5) feeling of detachment or estrangement from others

(6) restricted range of affect (e.g., unable to have loving feelings)

(7) sense of a foreshortened future (e.g., does not expect to have a career, marriage, children, or a normal life span)

D. Persistent symptoms of increased arousal (not present before the trauma), as indicated by two (or more) of the following:

(1) difficulty falling or staying asleep

(2) irritability or outbursts of anger

(3) difficulty concentrating

(4) hypervigilance

(5) exaggerated startle response

E. Duration of the disturbance (symptoms in Criteria B, C, and D) is more than 1 month.

F. The disturbance causes clinically significant distress or impairment in social, occupational, or other important areas of functioning.

————

NOTES

1. Prevalence of the disorder. One study of a random sample of veterans from the Vietnam War found that "20 to 30 percent would be formally diagnosable" as experiencing a Post Traumatic Stress Disorder. Egendorf, The Postwar Healing of Vietnam Veterans: Recent Research, 33 Hospital and Community Psychiatry 901 (1981).

A research project using a volunteer sample of 111 veterans participating in a Veterans' Administration Operation Outreach program found a statistically significant correlation of .27 between the number of weeks in combat in Vietnam and later being convicted for manslaughter. The number of combat roles performed in Vietnam (e.g., infantry, demolition) correlated .43 with later conviction for assault. Wilson and Ziegelbaum, The Vietnam Veteran on Trial, 1 Behavioral Sciences and the Law 69 (1983).

The first post-September 11, 2001, study of the mental health effects of combat has recently been published. Hoge, Castro, Messer, McGurk, Cotting, and Koffman, Combat Duty in Iraq and Afghanistan, Mental Health Problems, and Barriers to Care, 351 New England Journal of Medicine 13 (2004). The researchers evaluated members of three Army units and one Marine Corps unit either before their deployment to Iraq (n=2,530) or three to four months after their return from combat duty in Iraq or Afghanistan (n=3,671). Exposure to combat was significantly greater among those who were deployed to Iraq than among those deployed to Afghanistan. The percentage of subjects whose responses met the screening criteria for major depression, generalized anxiety disorder, or PTSD was significantly higher after duty in Iraq (15.6 to 17.1 percent) than after duty in Afghanistan (11.2 percent) or before deployment to Iraq (9.3 percent). Of those whose responses were positive for a mental disorder, only 23 to 40 percent sought mental health care.

2. Next edition. The Fifth Edition of the Diagnostic and Statistical Manual of Mental Disorders (DSM–V) is scheduled to be published by the American Psychiatric Association in 2011. Updates on the progress of DSM–V can be found at http://www.dsm5.org

(c) Kidnapping

While many people have been assaulted and many have served in combat, relatively few have been the victims of kidnappers. In one notorious case, social science research was used to provide an empirical context for decision makers to assess the effects of being kidnapped and held hostage upon the state of mind of the kidnap victim, who later became a criminal defendant.

UNITED STATES v. HEARST

United States District Court, Northern District of California, 1976.
Trial Transcript, Criminal Case 74–374.

[Patricia Hearst was tried for the crimes of armed bank robbery and use of a weapon during the commission of a felony. She pleaded duress as a defense, premised on the fact that approximately 10 weeks prior to the alleged crimes, she had been kidnapped from her apartment in Berkeley, California, by members of a group calling itself the Symbionese Liberation Army and held captive. In support of her defense, Dr. Louis West, a psychiatrist, was called as an expert witness to testify regarding, among other things, the nature of "coercive persuasion."]

Direct Examination by Mr. Bailey:

Q. [Have] you worked together in the past fifteen or twenty years with others who are recognized experts in the field of coercive persuasion?

A. [I] would say that I've joined with others in consulting. Some of the more specific types of laboratory studies to try to reproduce these results, I haven't actually carried out myself. But, when, for example, the Zimbardo experiments at Stanford were published and broadcast last year, they came as no surprise to those of us who were familiar with the old coercive persuasion research, because it was exactly what you would expect. That study done at Stanford University, you may recall, took a group of normal young men, divided them in half, and half of them were assigned the role of prisoners and the other half were assigned the role of captors. And, it was a game. And, they were being paid for this and it was supposed to run two weeks. And, Doctor Zimbardo and his group had to stop the experiment after six days, because by that time fifty percent of those who were supposed to be prisoners in this artificial laboratory game at the university had broken down one way or another and had shown such psychological disturbances that they had to take them out so they couldn't continue it past six days.

[C]ross-Examination by Mr. Bancroft

Q. Doctor, in your direct testimony, you spoke of some studies done by a gentleman down here in Palo Alto by the name of Zimbardo. Do you remember that?

A. Yes.

Q. Those studies, I think to refresh the jury's recollection, had to do with prisoner—a prisoner situation in which students were solicited as volunteers to act as guards and some as prisoners; is that right?

A. Young men were solicited to act as volunteers. I don't think they were students.

Q. And in that study, the volunteers were solicited by a newspaper ad, were they not, calling for them to participate in a psychological study of prison life? Do you remember that?

A. I don't remember the newspaper ad, but I know that Dr. Zimbardo solicited volunteers.

Q. Well, as a matter of fact, you called him down at Stanford a short time ago to ask about his research; didn't you?

A. To ask him about whether there were any other publications on it beyond those that I had already read.

Q. And—

A. Fascinating experiment.

Q. Why?

A. The Zimbardo Study?

Q. Yes.

A. It shows how tremendously people can be caught up in a role even to the point of getting sick in it in a very short period of time.

Q. Do you think that that's what that study represents, Doctor?

A. That's a very important part of what it represents.

Q. Well, real prison guards and real prisoners aren't sick, are they, and they are assigned their roles in a prison?

A. [I]t's been my observation that people commonly do get sick in prisons, especially under conditions of the type that were simulated in the Zimbardo experiment.

[Q.] Doctor, does the Zimbardo study really prove anything more than when people are assigned certain tasks, they tend to solidify themselves and do it with some vigor?

A. They weren't assigned the task of having nervous breakdowns.

Q. No, and therefore, isn't that study peculiar for that very reason?

A. Well, I didn't consider it peculiar. The thing that differentiated the Zimbardo study and made it especially interesting was that it was done under such relatively benign conditions and results were so disastrous so fast; in six days, 50 percent of the prisoners were sick. Now, that's a significant result.

Q. Do you think comparing that to the general prison situation, real prisoners put in real prisons, 50 percent of them get mentally sick?

A. No, I wouldn't say that.

[Q.] Wasn't it—don't you think, Doctor, it was because they thought it was a game and not even though they thought it was a game [that the subjects became sick]?

A. Mr. Bancroft, I assure you people do not deliberately develop the kind of psychiatric disturbances that these young men did in the course of a game.

UNITED STATES v. HEARST

United States District Court, Northern District of California, 1976.
412 F.Supp. 889.

MEMORANDUM AND ORDER DENYING PLAINTIFF'S MOTIONS TO BAR DEFENDANT'S PROFFERED PSYCHIATRIC TESTIMONY AND MOTION TO STRIKE EXPERT TESTIMONY

■ OLIVER J. CARTER, CHIEF JUDGE.

The Government has filed extensive points and authorities in support of its motion to bar the introduction of testimony by expert witnesses on the defendant's mental state at the time of the bank robbery for which she is now on trial.

[A]s the Court understands the purpose of psychiatric expert testimony offered here by the defense, it is to explain the effects kidnapping, prolonged incarceration, and psychological and physical abuse may have had on the defendant's mental state at the time of the robbery, insofar as such mental state is relevant to the asserted defense of coercion or duress. The jury, of course, are free to accept or reject the defendant's own account of her experiences with her captors. If they choose, however, to believe her testimony, then they may be served by the testimony of the experts called by both sides in determining whether or not the defendant was coerced into committing the offenses charged in the indictment.

[T]he Court is of the opinion that the peculiar question to which the experts here will address themselves—whether the defendant's initial status as a kidnap victim and the subsequent treatment of her by her captors could have deprived her of the requisite general intent to commit the offense charged—is not only relevant to the asserted defense of coercion but also beyond the common experience of most jurors and within the special competence of the experts. The jury need not concur with the expert opinions expressed on this matter, but this Court will not deprive them of the opportunity to consider the testimony that will be offered and make whatever use of it they deem advisable.

Accordingly, IT IS ORDERED that plaintiff's motion to bar admission of expert psychiatric testimony on the issue of coercion and general intent be, and the same is hereby, denied.

IT IS FURTHER ORDERED that plaintiff's motion to strike the testimony of Dr. Louis J. West be, and the same is hereby, denied.

INTERPERSONAL DYNAMICS IN A SIMULATED PRISON

Craig Haney, Curtis Banks, and Philip Zimbardo.
1 International Journal of Criminology and Penology 69 (1973).

The effects of playing the role of "guard" or "prisoner" were studied in the context of an experimental simulation of a prison environment. The research design was a relatively simple one, involving as it did only a single treatment variable, the random assignment to either a "guard" or "prisoner" condition. These roles were enacted over an extended period of time (nearly one week) within an environment which was physically constructed to resemble a prison. Central to the methodology of creating and maintaining a psychological state of imprisonment was the functional simulation of significant properties of "real prison life" (established through information from former inmates, correctional personnel and texts).

The "guards" were free with certain limits to implement the procedures of induction into the prison setting and maintenance of custodial retention of the "prisoners". These inmates, having voluntarily submitted to the conditions of this total institution in which they now lived, coped in various ways with its stresses and its challenges. The behaviour of both groups of subjects was observed, recorded and analyzed. The dependent measures were of two general types: transactions between and within each group of subjects, recorded on video and audio tape as well as directly observed; individual reactions on questionnaires, mood inventories, personality tests, daily guard shift reports, and post experimental interviews.

Subjects

The 21 subjects who participated in the experiment were selected from an initial pool of 75 respondents, who answered a newspaper advertisement asking for male volunteers to participate in a psychological study of "prison life" in return for payment of $15 per day. Those who responded to the notice completed an extensive questionnaire concerning their family background, physical and mental health history, prior experience and attitudinal propensities with respect to sources of psychopathology (including their involvement in crime). Each respondent who completed the background questionnaire was interviewed by one of two experimenters. Finally, the 24 subjects who were judged to be most stable (physically and mentally), most mature, and least involved in anti-social behaviour were selected to participate in the study. On a random basis, half of the subjects were assigned the role of "guard", half to the role of "prisoner".

The subjects were normal, healthy males attending colleges throughout the United States who were in the Stanford area during the summer. They were largely of middle class socio-economic status, Caucasians (with the exception of one Oriental subject). Initially they were strangers to each other, a selection precaution taken to avoid the disruption of any pre-existing friendship patterns and to mitigate against any transfer into the experimental situation of previously established relationships or patterns of behaviour.

[P]rocedure

Physical aspects of the prison

The prison was built in a 35-ft section of a basement corridor in the psychology building at Stanford University. It was partitioned by two fabricated walls, one of which was fitted with the only entrance door to the cell block, the other contained a small observation screen. Three small cells (6 H 9 ft) were made from converted laboratory rooms by replacing the usual doors with steel barred, black painted ones, and removing all furniture.

A cot (with mattress, sheet and pillow) for each prisoner was the only furniture in the cells. A small closet across from the cells served as a solitary confinement facility; its dimensions were extremely small (2 H 2 H 7 ft) and it was unlit.

[R]ole instruction

All subjects had been told that they would be assigned either the guard or the prisoner role on a completely random basis and all had voluntarily agreed to play either role for $15.00 per day for up to two weeks. They signed a contract guaranteeing a minimally adequate diet, clothing, housing and medical care as well as the financial remuneration in return for their stated "intention" of serving in the assigned role for the duration of the study.

It was made explicit in the contract that those assigned to be prisoners should expect to be under surveillance (have little or no privacy) and to have some of their basic civil rights suspended during their imprisonment, excluding physical abuse. They were given no other information about what to expect nor instructions about behaviour appropriate for a prisoner role. Those actually assigned to this treatment were informed by phone to be available at their place of residence on a given Sunday when we would start the experiment.

The subjects assigned to be guards attended an orientation meeting on the day prior to the induction of the prisoners. At this time they were introduced to the principal investigators, the "Superintendent" of the prison (P.G.Z.) and an undergraduate research assistant who assumed the administrative role of "Warden". They were told that we wanted to try to simulate a prison environment within the limits imposed by pragmatic and ethical considerations. Their assigned task was to "maintain the reasonable degree of order within the prison necessary for its effective functioning", although the specifics of how this duty might be implemented were not explicitly detailed.

[U]pon arrival at our experimental prison, each prisoner was stripped, sprayed with a delousing preparation (a deodorant spray) and made to stand alone naked for a while in the cell yard. After being given the uniform described previously and having an I.D. picture taken ("mug shot"), the prisoner was put in his cell and ordered to remain silent.

Administrative routine

When all the cells were occupied, the warden greeted the prisoners and read them the rules of the institution (developed by the guards and the warden). They were to be memorized and to be followed. Prisoners were to be referred to only by the number on their uniforms, also in an effort to depersonalize them.

The prisoners were to be served three bland meals per day, were allowed three supervised toilet visits, and given two hours daily for the privilege of reading or letterwriting. Work assignments were issued for which the prisoners were to receive an hourly wage to constitute their $15 daily payment. Two visiting periods per week were scheduled, as were movie rights and exercise periods. Three times a day all prisoners were lined up for a "count" (one on each guard work-shift). The initial purpose of the "count" was to ascertain that all prisoners were present, and to test them on their knowledge of the rules and their I.D. numbers. The first perfunctory counts lasted only about 10 minutes, but on each successive day (or night) they were spontaneously increased in duration until some lasted several hours. Many of the pre-established features of administrative routine were modified or abandoned by the guards, and some were forgotten by the staff over the course of the study.

[R]esults

Although it is difficult to anticipate exactly what the influence of incarceration will be upon the individuals who are subjected to it and those charged with its maintenance (especially in a simulated reproduction), the results of the present experiment support many commonly held conceptions of prison life and validate anecdotal evidence supplied by articulate ex-convicts. The environment of arbitrary custody had great impact upon the affective states of both guards and prisoners as well as upon the interpersonal processes taking place between and within those role-groups.

In general, guards and prisoners showed a marked tendency toward increased negativity of affect and their overall outlook became increasingly negative. As the experiment progressed, prisoners expressed intentions to do harm to others more frequently. For both prisoners and guards, self-evaluations were more deprecating as the experience of the prison environment became internalized.

Overt behaviour was generally consistent with the subjective self-reports and affective expressions of the subjects. Despite the fact that guards and prisoners were essentially free to engage in any form of interaction (positive or negative, supportive or affrontive, etc.), the characteristic nature of their encounters tended to be negative, hostile, affrontive and dehumanising. Prisoners immediately adopted a generally passive response mode while guards assumed a very active initiating role in all interactions. Throughout the experiment commands were the most frequent form of verbal behaviour and, generally verbal exchanges were strikingly impersonal, with few references to individual identity. Although it was clear to all subjects that the experimenters would not permit physical violence to take place, varieties of less direct aggressive behaviour were observed frequently (especially on the part of guards). In lieu of physical violence, verbal affronts were used as one of the most frequent forms of interpersonal contact between guards and prisoners.

The most dramatic evidence of the impact of this situation upon the participants was seen in the gross reactions of five prisoners who had to be released because of extreme emotional depression, crying, rage and acute anxiety. The pattern of symptoms was quite similar in four of the subjects and began as early as the second day of imprisonment. The fifth subject was released after being treated for a psychosomatic rash which covered portions of his body. Of the remaining prisoners, only two said they were not willing to forfeit the money they had earned in return for being "paroled". When the experiment was terminated prematurely after only six days, all the remaining prisoners were delighted by their unexpected good fortune. In contrast, most of the guards seemed to be distressed by the decision to stop the experiment and it appeared to us they had become sufficiently involved in their roles so that they now enjoyed the extreme control and power which they exercised and were reluctant to give it up. One guard did report being personally upset at the suffering of the prisoners and claimed to have considered asking to change his role to become one of them—but never did so. None of the guards ever failed to come to work on time for their shift, and indeed, on several occasions guards remained on duty voluntarily and uncomplaining for extra hours—without additional pay.

The extremely pathological reactions which emerged in both groups of subjects testify to the power of the social forces operating, but still there were individual differences seen in styles of coping with this novel experience and in degrees of successful adaptation to it. Half the prisoners did endure the oppressive atmosphere, and not all the guards resorted to hostility. Some guards were tough but fair ("played by the rules"), some went far beyond their roles to engage in creative cruelty and harassment, while a few were passive and rarely instigated any coercive control over the prisoners.

[C]onclusions and Discussion

It should be apparent that the elaborate procedures (and staging) employed by the experimenters to insure a high degree of mundane realism in this mock prison contributed to its effective functional simulation of the psychological dynamics operating in "real" prisons. We observed empirical relationships in the simulated prison environment which were strikingly isomorphic to the internal relations of real prisons, corroborating many of the documented reports of what occurs behind prison walls.

The conferring of differential power on the status of "guard" and "prisoner" constituted, in effect, the institutional validation of those roles. But further, many of the subjects ceased distinguishing between prison role and their prior self-identities. When this occurred, within what was a surprisingly short period of time, we witnessed a sample of normal, healthy American college students fractionate into a group of prison guards who seemed to derive pleasure from insulting, threatening, humiliating and dehumanizing their peers—those who by chance selection had been assigned to the "prisoner" role. The typical prisoner syndrome was one of passivity, dependency, depression, helplessness and self-deprecation. Prisoner participation in the social reality which the guards had structured for them lent increasing validity to it and, as the prisoners became resigned to their treatment over time, many acted in ways to justify their fate at the hands of the guards, adopting attitudes and behaviour which helped to sanction their victimization. Most dramatic and distressing to us was the observation of the ease with which sadistic behaviour could be elicited in individuals who were not "sadistic types" and the frequency with which acute emotional breakdowns could occur in men selected precisely for their emotional stability.

––––––

NOTES

1.   External validity. The most frequent criticism of this study is that it lacked external validity, i.e., that its findings cannot be generalized to "real" prisoners and guards. This was the contention of the prosecution in *Hearst* and also of Banuazizi and Movahedi, Interpersonal Dynamics in a Simulated Prison: A Methodological Analysis, 30 American Psychologist 151, 156 (1975), who offered the following alternative explanation to account for the findings of the Haney et al. study:

> (a) The subjects entered the experiment carrying strong social stereotypes of how guards and prisoners act and relate to one another in a real prison; (b) in the experimental context itself, there were numerous cues pointing to the experimental hypothesis, the experimenters' expectations, and possibly, the experimenter's ideological commitment; and thus (c) complying with the actual or perceived demands in the experimental situation, and acting on the basis of their own role-related expectancies, the subjects produced data highly in accord with the experimental hypothesis.

To evaluate whether Haney, Banks, and Zimbardo's subjects had pre-existing stereotypic expectations of the prisoner and guard roles, Banuazizi and Movahedi sent a questionnaire to 185 undergraduate students in the Boston area (who had not heard of the Stanford study) describing its methodology. They asked their respondents to identify the purpose of the Stanford study and to predict the subjects' behavior. "[T]he overwhelming majority of the respondents (81%) were able to articulate quite accurately the intent of the experiment [and] 89.9% predicted that the behavior of guards toward prisoners would be oppressive, hostile, aggressive, etc." Id. at 157–8.

2. Website. Material related to the Stanford Prison Experiment, including a slide show, can be found at http://www.prisonexp.org

————

Final Report of the Independent Panel to Review Department of Defense Detention Operations, 2004.

James R. Schlesinger, Chair

The potential for abusive treatment of detainees during the Global War on Terrorism was entirely predictable based on a fundamental understanding of the principle of social psychology principles coupled with an awareness of numerous known environmental risk factors. Most leaders were unacquainted with these known risk factors, and therefore failed to take steps to mitigate the likelihood that abuses of some type would occur during detainee operations. While certain conditions heightened the possibility of abusive treatment, such conditions neither excuse nor absolve the individuals who engaged in deliberate immoral or illegal behaviors.

The abuse the detainees endured at various places and times raises a number of questions about the likely psychological aspects of inflicting such abuses. Findings from the field of social psychology suggest that the conditions of war and the dynamics of detainee operations carry inherent risks for human mistreatment, and therefore must be approached with great caution and careful planning and training.

The Stanford Prison Experiment

In 1973, Haney, Banks and Zimbardo published their landmark Stanford study, "Interpersonal Dynamics in a Simulated Prison." Their study provides a cautionary tale for all military detention operations. The Stanford Experiment used a set of tested, psychologically sound college students in a benign environment. In contrast, in military detention operations, soldiers work under stressful combat conditions that are far from benign.

The Stanford Prison Experiment attempted to "create a prison-like situation" and then observe the behavior of those involved. The researchers randomly assigned 24 young men to either the "prison" or "guard" group. Psychological testing was used to eliminate participants with overt psychopathology, and extensive efforts were made to simulate actual prison conditions. The experiment, scheduled to last two weeks, was cancelled after only six days due to the ethical concerns raised by the behaviors of the participants. The study notes that while guards and prisoners were free to engage in any form of interpersonal interactions, the "characteristic nature of their encounters tended to be negative, hostile, affrontive and dehumanizing."

The researchers found that both prisoners and guards exhibited "pathological reactions" during the course of the experiment. Guards fell into three categories: (1) those who were "tough but fair," (2) those who were passive and reluctant to use coercive control and, of special interests, (3) those who "went far beyond their roles to engage in creative cruelty and harassment." With each passing day, guards "were observed to generally escalate their harassment of the prisoners." The researchers reported: "We witnessed a sample of normal, healthy American college students fractionate into a group of prison guards who seemed to derive pleasure from insulting, threatening, humiliating, and dehumanizing their peers."

Because of the random assignment of subjects, the study concluded the observed behaviors were the result of situational rather than personality factors:

> The negative, anti-social reactions observed were not the product of an environment created by combining a collection of deviant personalities, but rather, the result of an intrinsically pathological situation which could distort and rechannel the behaviour of essentially normal individuals. The abnormality here resided in the psychological nature of the situation and not in those who passed through it.

The authors discussed how prisoner-guard interactions shaped the evolution of power use by the guards:

> The use of power was self-aggrandizing and self-perpetuating. The guard power, derived initially from an arbitrary label, was intensified whenever there was any perceived threat by the prisoners and this new level subsequently became the baseline from which further hostility and harassment would begin. The most hostile guards on each shift moved spontaneously into the leadership roles of giving orders and deciding on punishments. They became role models whose behaviour was emulated by other members of the shift. Despite minimal contact between the three separate guard shifts and nearly 16 hours a day spent away from the prison, the absolute level of aggression as well as the more subtle and "creative" forms of aggression manifested, increased in a spiraling function. Not to be tough and arrogant was to be seen as a sign of weakness by the guards and even those "good" guards who did not get as drawn into the power syndrome as the others respected the implicit norm of never contradicting or even interfering with an action of a more hostile guard on their shift.

In an article published 25 years after the Stanford Prison Experiment, Haney and Zimbardo noted their initial study "underscored the degree to which institutional settings can develop a life of their own, independent of the wishes, intentions, and purposes of those who run them." They highlighted the need for those outside the culture to offer external perspectives on process and procedures. [Haney and Zimbardo, The Past and Future of U.S. Prison Policy, Twenty–Five Years After the Stanford Prison Study, 53 American Psychologist 709 (1998).]

(d) Television

The effects of televised violence on the behavior of children and adolescents has been the subject of a great deal of research. In one case, that research was brought to bear on the criminal responsibility of an adolescent for murder.

FLORIDA v. ZAMORA

Circuit Court, Dade County, Florida, 1977.
Trial Transcript, Case No. 77–2566.

[Ronney Albert Zamora was tried for the first degree murder of Elinor Haggart, his next door neighbor in Miami Beach. Zamora was 15. Mrs. Haggart was 82. Zamora admitted that he shot her with a pistol he found in her house when she returned home and found him in the process of burglary. Zamora and an accomplice stole $400 after having shot Mrs. Haggart. Due to Zamora's age, the state did not ask for the death penalty.

Zamora's attorney, Ellis Rubin, pleaded him not guilty by reason of insanity. Rubin argued that Zamora was a "television addict," that he was "a sociopathic personality who could not refrain from doing wrong," and that because of the "thousands and thousands and thousands of murders that he has seen [on television], this was a reaction that he imitated or a conditioned reflex."

Rubin attempted to introduce expert witnesses to present empirical studies on the association between watching violent television programs and later violent behavior.

The first such witness was Dr. Margaret Thomas. The prosecutor was Thomas Headley. The trial judge was H. Paul Baker. In an innovative program, the trial was videotaped and shown on public television in the Miami area for nine nights.]

ELLIS RUBIN: Your Honor, this witness is a Doctor of Psychology, currently the Assistant Dean of Academic Affairs of Florida Technological University, Orlando, Florida. She has a B.A. from Vanderbilt, an M.A. from Vanderbilt, a Ph.D. from Tulane. She has fellowships and awards, several teaching positions, psychological testing and evaluation experience, and she has had published—how many papers, round figures?

DR. THOMAS: Around fifteen. I'm not sure.

RUBIN: Around fifteen.

JUDGE BAKER: Okay, Now, that qualifies her as an expert in something. Now, what's she going to testify to?

RUBIN: Well, here are some of the titles of some of the papers that she has published: "Does Media Violence Increase Children's Toleration of Real Life Aggression?" "Toleration of Real Life Aggression as a Function of Exposure to Televised Violence and Age of Subject;" "Desensitization to Portrayals of Real Life Aggression as a Function of Exposure to Television Violence;" "Effects of Television Violence on Expectation of Other's Aggressions."

Doctor Thomas is an expert on behavior and the social ramifications of certain types of behavior. Since 1969, she has specialized in the field of what effect, if any, does television violence have on the viewer, and, specifically, young children, adolescents, and adults. We will confine her testimony to adolescents. She is. . . .

JUDGE BAKER: That goes beyond the scope of what the Court's instructions were at the pretrial conference.

RUBIN: No, Your Honor . . .

JUDGE BAKER: She will have to be confined to Ronney Zamora.

RUBIN: It *is* confined to Ronney Zamora. Your Honor, if I may, I would like to make this presentation.

JUDGE BAKER: All right. Go ahead.

RUBIN: It's the heart of my defense. Your Honor, this is similar to a defense of intoxication by alcohol, intoxication by hypnosis, or any other defense. The jury has nothing to compare Ronney Zamora's conduct with, if they do not hear that there have been studies on children his age, relating what the effect of X amount of hours of violence on television has shown by experiments with children. It's the same as if I brought an expert in here, if I were defending on the grounds of not guilty by involuntary intoxication. I certainly would have a right to bring in an expert on what are the properties of alcohol, how much alcohol is required to give a 1.0 reading on the drunkometer, unless the Court wished to take judicial notice that 1.0 is drunk. Your Honor, how can the jury understand what the effect of television is on Ronney Zamora if there is no one from the defense to show, through expert experiments and testimony, what the effect has been on other youngsters his age? All that we're doing is establishing a standard. The defense of involuntary television intoxication is new, but so was insanity at one time a new defense. So was involuntary intoxication by alcohol at some stage in our civilization, a new defense. But there are expert. . . .

JUDGE BAKER: But let's stop right there. The first word you've mentioned to me is "involuntary." I haven't heard one bit of testimony throughout this trial that anything that happened to this defendant was involuntary.

RUBIN: Well, here we . . .

JUDGE BAKER: Now how do we get over that hurdle?

RUBIN: Right. This is the lady who's going to get over that hurdle.

JUDGE BAKER: How can she do that? She's never seen the defendant.

RUBIN: She doesn't have to see the defendant, Your Honor. If I may make myself . . .

JUDGE BAKER: Go ahead.

RUBIN: I'm trying to make myself understood. And I realize that it may be a difficult premise.

This expert on the effects of television violence is prepared to testify, and we have others who will testify likewise, that what comes out of television on the programs that are produced by the networks and the sponsors contain an inordinate amount of violence. Young children— but especially, Your Honor, the studies will show that sociopaths and emotionally disturbed children are more affected by violence on television than any other category of human beings. And that what comes out of that television tube is not controlled by the viewer and the viewer doesn't realize that he is being desensitized to violence by seeing so much of it. Involuntarily, he is seeing all of these heroes and bad guys, the black hats and the white hats using guns, stabbing people, abnormal behavior, bizarre situations, robberies, burglaries, killings of old ladies. And this is coming to him and going into his brain and is desensitizing this child to the normal regard for violence, the normal standards of right and wrong for killing, because this boy is a classic example. And we have laid the predicate that he is an addict, that his viewing hours were more than ordinary, and his type of programs . . .

Your Honor, what's the difference in bringing in somebody who's an expert on alcohol, a chemist, and who can testify that by experiments over the years, we find that a certain amount of alcohol will cause a loss of control? Well, that's what I want to do with television. This witness is prepared to say that television does affect the viewer, did affect Ronney Zamora. She doesn't have to interview Ronney Zamora. I have other people who have interviewed Ronney Zamora. The jury has already heard the testimony of his mother. Certainly television, if the jury believes Mrs. Zamora—and that's a jury question. Not to allow me to present an expert who will say, well, there have been so many studies, and here is what has been found, and it's uncontradicted—and she has done papers that have been accepted for publication by the scientific journals, and she has to be quizzed on those, and there has to be verification of them, and that has been done.

Your Honor, don't deny me the right to present everything to the jury that they should have for this defense, and that is this doctor who is an expert on what are the effects of television on children. Then, let the jury say does it affect Ronney Zamora—and we will have other witnesses who will so say. This is the premise for our whole defense.

JUDGE BAKER: Mr. Headley?

THOMAS HEADLEY: Your Honor, I thought that we had argued this at the pretrial conference. Your Honor, the State's position is quite clearly that this testimony is completely irrelevant and immaterial.

Now, the example given of the alcohol—it doesn't apply here, Your Honor. When you come in with a machine reading of a certain amount of alcohol in your blood, then possibly, a doctor can come in and say what effect that has, because that has an organic or a biological effect on the body that influences or affects everyone the same way. This isn't true, Judge. We're not dealing with an intoxicant. There's been nothing to establish that television is an intoxicant. There's nothing to show that the viewing of television reacts or treats everyone the same way. This doesn't have anything to do with this defendant, Judge, and it would be totally irrelevant and immaterial.

RUBIN: Television does affect everybody the same way, when they are a sociopathic personality. Those are the studies—that these people copy and imitate what they see on television and it arouses them to unusual actions. That's just like—how did the alcohol expert establish that .10 was the point of drunkenness? There had to be tests made. There had to be scientific studies. We're giving that to the jury through this witness. What is the standard for television being too much or not enough? Somebody has to start from somewhere.

JUDGE BAKER: All right. The rule in Capelin, which is adopted in Rodriguez is very simple: where the evidence is based solely upon scientific tests and experiments, it is essential that the reliability of the tests and results thereof shall be recognized and accepted by scientists, or that the demonstration shall have passed from the stage of experimentation and uncertainty to that of reasonable demonstrability. And I do not see that in this defense.

HEADLEY: Judge, excuse me . . .

RUBIN: May I make the proffer, then? May I put the doctor through the testimony?

JUDGE BAKER: Yes.

RUBIN: And then we'll see. (to Dr. Thomas) What is your name and address?

DR. THOMAS: Margaret Hanratty Thomas. (She states her address)

RUBIN: What is your occupation or profession?

DR. THOMAS: Psychologist and college professor.

RUBIN: Are you prepared to say that an excessive amount of television viewing would have an effect on an emotionally disturbed fifteen-year-old male child from a middle class, poor economic background?

DR. THOMAS: It's very possible.

RUBIN: Very possible? Can you say it within a reasonable psychological certainty?

DR. THOMAS: I would feel fairly confident that, given that type of background, an excessive amount of television violence would—well, it has an effect on everyone. It would be much more likely to have an unusual or extreme effect on such a child, in my opinion.

RUBIN: (to Judge Baker) You may inquire.

JUDGE BAKER: Let me ask you this. Can you state, within reasonable psychological certainty, under the set of facts that Mr. Rubin just gave you, that such an amount of television on the type of child could produce . . .

RUBIN: Your Honor, I should have added six to eight hours a day, as has been testified. I'm sorry. I didn't put that in.

JUDGE BAKER: Whatever—could produce a state of mind where he did not know right from wrong and could not appreciate the nature and consequences of his acts?

DR. THOMAS: Watching that much television over a long period of time, in my opinion, is at least one of the important factors as to how a person acquires a sense of right and wrong.

JUDGE BAKER: That's not the question. The question is can you state, with reasonable psychological certainty, in any of the tests that you've conducted, in any of the tests that you have referred to, in any of the papers that you've published—not that it could—that it has—had that effect on any individual tested, to the extent that they did not know right from wrong?

DR. THOMAS: Would studies that show that children who tend to watch a lot of violent television tend to be more approving . . .

JUDGE BAKER: No. Not approving. Would they be so affected that they would not know right from wrong and appreciate the nature and consequences of their act—in other words, have absolutely no idea of right or wrong, couldn't appreciate the nature and consequences of their act? In other words, are you familiar with the rule of M'Naghten's case?

DR. THOMAS: Well, I learned of it last evening when Mr. Headley was taking my deposition, and I guess I'm a little confused.

HEADLEY: Judge, excuse me.

DR. THOMAS: What I'm saying is . . .

HEADLEY: May I ask a question, Your Honor?

JUDGE BAKER: Please.

RUBIN: Your Honor, she's answering your questions.

JUDGE BAKER: Let her answer mine. Then you can ask one. But just please let me finish. Go ahead.

HEADLEY: I'm sorry.

DR. THOMAS: The distinction that I'm having trouble with is that, yes, I would feel comfortable saying that exposure to television violence can shape a child's conceptions of what is right and wrong—that is such that a very heavy television viewer, perhaps, who comes up in an atmosphere where there are not other restraints built in can—could develop such an attitude that what society in general sees as right and wrong is not his reality, is not his sense of right and wrong. You see what I mean, that it's all—for example, there are studies that show that children tend to think of aggression as more ordinary, more commonplace, and approve of it more as a result of exposure to television violence. Their sense of right and wrong then, is a little different than that of a child who watches very little television. They do have it, I mean, I guess those values are different.

JUDGE BAKER: I'll accept that values are different. But we're talking about the legal definition of insanity, which—go ahead, Mr. Headley. Ask your question. Maybe it'll clear it up.

HEADLEY: Dr. Thomas, can you advise the Court of one study or one experiment or any number that have linked the viewing of television violence with insanity?

DR. THOMAS: You mean use the term "insanity"?

HEADLEY: Yes.

DR. THOMAS: Legal insanity—of course not.

HEADLEY: I think that's all we're resolving here, Your Honor.

JUDGE BAKER: That's it.

RUBIN: One more chance. They're comparing apples and oranges. How can you relate, Your Honor, psychological, medical, scientific experiments of proof with the legal definition of the word "insanity"? This is not her field. Our field is the legal definition of a defense. Her field is what are the effects of television violence on children. Your Honor will instruct the jury on the law of insanity. I want to show the jury the facts that went into this child's concept of right and wrong. Your Honor, she's prepared to—I have psychiatrists who will use this testimony, subject to cross examination, who will testify as to what you asked this young doctor. She can't testify that there's ever been a case where insanity has been found to result from too much television, because they don't have the word "insanity" in her field. They don't have it even in the field of psychiatry, as you know.

JUDGE BAKER: I understand that.

RUBIN: Let the scientists come—let the psychiatrists, Your Honor, come in. And let Your Honor voir dire the psychiatrists and say, "Has there ever been a case where too much television has caused insanity?" And they will answer, "Yes." And the victim is Ronney Zamora. And let the jury hear that. Please.

JUDGE BAKER: Let me ask you this, Ma'am. Let's forget the word "insanity." In any of your tests, in any scientific journal that you have read, have you ever conclusively linked any particular television program or amount of television violence directly to a homicide?

DR. THOMAS: Well, those are not scientific studies. There are cases . . .

JUDGE BAKER: Or any crime?

DR. THOMAS: No, because they're always after the fact. You can't . . .

JUDGE BAKER: Thank you. The testimony is excluded.

ZAMORA v. STATE

District Court of Appeal of Florida, Third District, 1978.
361 So.2d 776.

■ HENDRY, JUDGE:

At trial, Zamora's insanity defense was based upon "involuntary subliminal television intoxication." On appeal, Zamora contends that certain rulings of the trial judge limiting the scope of defense counsel's inquiry into the area of television's effect upon sociopathic children effectively frustrated his insanity defense. In particular, appellant argues that the trial judge committed reversible error by failing to allow psychologist Dr. Margaret Hanratty Thomas to testify at trial on the effect of television violence upon adolescent viewers. We are not of the opinion that the court erred in granting the state's motion in limine thereby limiting inquiry into television and its effects on children.

[B]ased upon the law of insanity, as established in this state, the trial judge correctly limited the evidence of insanity to the M'Naghten standard. *Sub judice,* as brought out through proffer, Dr. Thomas' testimony would have been directed to the effect of television on adolescents, generally. She would have been, however, unable to testify that watching violent television programs to excess affects an individual to the extent that said individual would not be able to distinguish between right and wrong under the M'Naghten test. Her testimony, therefore, would not have been relevant to the proceedings. [A]s Dr. Thomas' testimony was not relevant as to the issue of insanity, it was properly excluded.

[O]ne final comment need be made. In the concluding pages of defense counsel's lengthy brief the following language appears: "In the case at bar, television was on trial . . . and the trial was on television." Such was simply not the case. While the proceedings were televised (and much covered by the media, generally), television was not on trial; Ronney Zamora was on trial. Zamora was on trial for the senseless slaying of an elderly woman. His defense was not guilty by reason of insanity induced by "involuntary subliminal television intoxication" and a jury, failing to accept that defense, found Zamora guilty on all charges. The proceedings below in no way represented a forum for the discussion of the relative pros and cons of the television media. Stated simply, this was a murder trial, and it is to the trial judge's credit that he confined the testimony and evidence to the relevant issues. Anyone failing to comprehend the true nature and purpose of these proceedings suffers from a total misconception of our criminal justice system.

ZAMORA v. COLUMBIA BROADCASTING SYSTEM

United States District Court, Southern District of Florida, 1979.
480 F.Supp. 199.

■ HOEVELER, DISTRICT JUDGE.

Ronny Zamora, a minor, together with his father and mother sued the National Broadcasting Company, Columbia Broadcasting System and the American Broadcasting Company for damages. [I]n brief, the plaintiffs alleged that Ronney Zamora, from the age of five years (he was 15 when this action was filed) has become involuntarily addicted to and "completely subliminally intoxicated" by the extensive viewing of television violence offered by the three defendants. The defendants are charged with breaching their duty to plaintiffs by failing to use ordinary care to prevent Ronny Zamora from being "impermissibly stimulated, incited and instigated" to duplicate the atrocities he viewed on television.

[R]educed to basics, the plaintiffs ask the Court to determine that unspecified "violence" projected periodically over television (presumably in any form) can provide the support for a claim for damages where a susceptible minor has viewed such violence and where he has reacted unlawfully. [T]o permit such a claim by the person committing the act [w]ould [g]ive birth to a legal morass through which broadcasting would have difficulty finding its way.

At the risk of overdeveloping the apparent, I suggest that the liability sought by plaintiffs would place broadcasters in jeopardy for televising Hamlet, Julius Caesar, Grimm's Fairy Tales, more contemporary offerings such as All Quiet on the Western Front, and even the Holocaust, and indeed would render John Wayne a risk not acceptable to any but the boldest broadcasters.

[W]ithout question, television programming presents problems and the study of these continues. One day, medical or other sciences with or without the cooperation of programmers may convince the F.C.C. or the Courts that the delicate balance of First Amendment rights should be altered to permit some additional limitations in programming. The complaint before the Court in no way justifies such a pursuit.

ZAMORA v. DUGGER

United States Court of Appeals, Eleventh Circuit, 1987.
834 F.2d 956.

■ JOHNSON, CIRCUIT JUDGE.

This case involves an appeal from the district court's denial of Appellant's petition for a writ of habeas corpus.

[Z]amora contends that his trial counsel was ineffective. [Z]amora argues that Rubin made a mockery of his insanity defense by alleging that it was caused by "television intoxication" even though the cause of insanity is irrelevant to the defense itself. [However,] Rubin's attempt to explain Zamora's alleged insanity by claiming it was caused by subliminal "television intoxication" does not render his assistance ineffective.

On the issue of preparation for trial, Rubin testified [t]hat he read many studies linking violence to television viewing. He also interviewed many psychologists regarding television violence, but he was unsuccessful in attempting to introduce their testimony. The evidence suggests that counsel was prepared and that he attempted to develop a defense in a weak case. In addition, the magistrate and district court determined that by focusing on television violence Rubin was able to introduce evidence of Zamora's unfortunate background, to the defendant's advantage.

[A]ccordingly, we affirm the district court's denial of habeas corpus.

––––––––

NOTE

1. The Status of Research on Television Violence. In 1972, the Scientific Advisory Committee on Television and Social Behavior, appointed by the Surgeon General at the request of Congress, issued a report, Television and Growing Up: The Impact of Televised Violence. The major conclusion of that report was:

> There is a convergence of the fairly substantial experimental evidence for a short-run causation of aggression among some children by viewing violence on the screen and much less certain evidence from field studies that extensive violence viewing precedes some long-run manifestations of aggressive behavior. The convergence of the two types of evidence constitutes some preliminary indication of a causal relationship, but a good deal of research remains to be done before one can have confidence in these conclusions.

In the years following the publication of the Surgeon General's report, more than 2,500 additional research publications on the influence of television upon behavior appeared. A committee appointed by the National Institute of Mental Health evaluated these newer research findings in a report titled Television and Behavior (1982). The report concluded, Id. at 37:

> Most of the researchers [since 1972] look at the totality of evidence and conclude, as did the Surgeon General's advisory committee, that the convergence of findings supports the conclusion of a causal relationship between televised violence and later aggressive behavior. The evidence now is drawn from a large body of literature. Adherents to this convergence approach agree that the conclusions reached in the

Surgeon General's program have been significantly strengthened by more recent research.

A more recent review in this area, Felson, Mass Media Effects on Violent Behavior, 22 Annual Review of Sociology 103 (1996), concluded that "exposure to television violence probably does have a small effect on violent behavior for some viewers, possibly because the media directs viewer's attention to novel forms of violent behavior that they would not otherwise consider." Id. at 103.

B.   VICTIMS

In addition to providing a context for decision makers to reach judgments on facts that pertain to criminal defendants, social science research has also been used to provide decision makers with a context for determining facts relating to victims. The principal application of victim-oriented frameworks has been in the "rape trauma syndrome."

STATE v. MARKS

Supreme Court of Kansas, 1982.
231 Kan. 645, 647 P.2d 1292.

■ HERD, JUSTICE.

[The defendant was convicted of rape and aggravated sodomy. He admitted that sexual acts had taken place, but claimed that they were consensual.]

Appellant [a]ttacks the admission of the expert testimony of Dr. Herbert Modlin, a board certified psychiatrist and neurologist who practices psychiatry and teaches at the Menninger Foundation. He is also one of a small number of doctors to be certified in the field of forensic psychiatry.

[D]uring his testimony Dr. Modlin discussed the diagnosis and treatment of "post traumatic stress disorders." The condition is caused when a person experiences a "very frightening, stressful event" and manifests itself in a kind of "psychological hangover." According to Dr. Modlin a type of post traumatic stress disorder labeled "rape trauma syndrome" is the result of a sexual assault. Symptoms of rape trauma syndrome include fear of offender retaliation, fear of being raped again, fear of being home alone, fear of men in general, fear of being out alone, sleep disturbance, change in eating habits and sense of shame.

Dr. Modlin examined the victim two weeks after the rape. Based upon his psychiatric evaluation Dr. Modlin testified he was of the opinion she had been the victim of "a frightening assault, an attack" and that she was suffering from the post-traumatic stress disorder known as rape trauma syndrome.

[A]ppellant does not contend Dr. Modlin lacks the requisite "special knowledge, skill, experience or training," to testify as an expert in this area. He argues that expert testimony regarding rape trauma syndrome should be per se inadmissible in a case where consent is the defense because it invades the province of the jury.

The identification of rape trauma syndrome is a relatively new psychiatric development. Even so, if the presence of rape trauma syndrome is detectable and reliable as evidence that a forcible assault did take place, it is relevant when a defendant argues the victim consented to sexual intercourse. As such an expert's opinion does not invade the province of the jury. It is merely offered as any other evidence, with the expert subject to cross-examination and the jury left to determine its weight.

In State v. Washington, 229 Kan. 47, 53, 622 P.2d 986 (1981), we stated "before a scientific opinion may be received in evidence at trial, the basis of that opinion must be shown to be generally accepted as reliable within the expert's particular scientific field." See also Frye v. United States, 293 F. 1013 (D.C.Cir.1923). Although *Washington* involved physical scientific evidence, the same test is applicable to the admission of testimony regarding a psychiatric diagnosis.

An examination of the literature clearly demonstrates that the so-called "rape trauma syndrome" is generally accepted to be a common reaction to sexual assault. See McCombie, The Rape Crisis Intervention Handbook, pp. 124–26 (1980); Comprehensive Textbook of Psychiatry ?_ 21.1d, 24.15, pp. 1519, 1804–05 (Kaplan, Freedman and Sadock 3rd ed.1980); Warner, Rape & Sexual Assault, pp. 145–49 (1980); Burgess & Holmstrom, Rape: Crisis & Recovery, pp. 35–47 (1979); Katz & Mazur, Understanding the Rape Victim, pp. 215–31 (1979); E. Hilberman, The Rape Victim, p. 36 (1976); Burgess & Holmstrom, Rape: Victims of Crisis, pp. 37–51 (1974). As such, qualified expert psychiatric testimony regarding the existence of rape trauma syndrome is relevant and admissible in a case such as this where the defense is consent.

————

STATE v. SALDANA

Supreme Court of Minnesota, 1982.
324 N.W.2d 227.

■ SCOTT, JUSTICE.

[The defendant was convicted of criminal sexual conduct. He admitted that intercourse had occurred, but claimed that it was with the complainant's consent.]

Our concern is directed toward the testimony of Lynn Dreyer, a counselor for sexual assault victims, who testified for the state. Dreyer, the director of the Victim Assistance Program in Mankato, holds a bachelor's degree in psychology and social work. Dreyer testified that she met Martha Fuller, the complainant, 10 days after the alleged rape and that she counseled Fuller for approximately a 10–week period. In her testimony, Dreyer explained the stages that a rape victim typically goes through and discussed typical behavior of victims after a rape. She then described

Fuller's reactions as she had observed them. In response to a question, Dreyer testified that it was not unusual that Fuller did not report the incident until the following day and that many rape victims never report a rape. Dreyer stated that Fuller was the victim of "acquaintance rape," that she definitely believed Fuller was a victim of sexual assault and rape, and that she did not think Fuller fantasized or "made it up."

The issue is whether admission of testimony concerning typical post-rape symptoms and behavior of rape victims, opinions that Fuller was a victim of rape, and an opinion that Fuller did not fantasize the rape was reversible error.

To be admissible, expert testimony must be helpful to the jury in reaching its decision:

> The basic requirement of Rule 702 is the helpfulness requirement. If the subject of the testimony is within the knowledge and experience of a lay jury and the testimony of the expert will not add precision or depth to the jury's ability to reach conclusions about that subject which is within their experience, then the testimony does not meet the helpfulness test.

State v. Helterbridle, 301 N.W.2d 545, 547 (Minn.1980). If the jury is in as good a position to reach a decision as the expert, expert testimony would be of little assistance to the jury and should not be admitted. Expert testimony may also be excluded if its probative value is substantially outweighed by the danger of unfair prejudice, confusion, or misleading the jury. Minn. R.Evid. 403. Under this test of admissibility, we must examine each segment of Dreyer's testimony.

Dreyer's discussion of the stages a rape victim typically goes through was essentially an explanation of "rape trauma syndrome,"[1] although she did not so label it. On the facts of the case before us, such testimony is of no help to the jury and produces an extreme danger of unfair prejudice. The factual question to be decided by the jury is whether the alleged criminal conduct occurred. It is not necessary that Fuller react in a typical manner to the incident. Fuller need not display the typical post-rape symptoms and behavior of rape victims to convince the jury that her view of the facts is the truth.

Rape trauma syndrome is not the type of scientific test that accurately and reliably determines whether a rape has occurred. The characteristic symptoms may follow *any* psychologically traumatic event. American Psychiatric Association, Diagnostic and Statistical Manual of Mental Disorders 236 (3d ed.1980). At best, the syndrome describes only symptoms that occur with some frequency, but makes no pretense of describing every single case. C. Warner, Rape and Sexual Assault 145 (1980). The jury must

---

1. Ann Burgess and Lynda Holmstrom coined the term in their seminal 1974 article to describe the recurring pattern of post-rape symptoms. Burgess & Holmstrom, Rape Trauma Syndrome, 131 Am.J.Psychiatry 981 (1974). For a discussion of rape trauma syndrome, see In re Pittsburgh Action Against Rape, 494 Pa. 15, 428 A.2d 126, 138–40 (1981) (Larsen, J., dissenting).

not decide this case on the basis of how most people react to rape or on whether Fuller's reactions were the typical reactions of a person who has been a victim of rape. Rather, the jury must decide what happened in *this case*, and whether the elements of the alleged crime have been proved beyond a reasonable doubt.

The scientific evaluation of rape trauma syndrome has not reached a level of reliability that surpasses the quality of common sense evaluation present in jury deliberations. As we stated in refusing to permit introduction of "battering parent" syndrome, the evidence may not be introduced "until further evidence of the scientific accuracy and reliability of syndrome or profile diagnoses can be established." State v. Loebach, 310 N.W.2d 58, 64 (Minn.1981). Permitting a person in the role of an expert to suggest that because the complainant exhibits some of the symptoms of rape trauma syndrome, the complainant was therefore raped, unfairly prejudices the appellant by creating an aura of special reliability and trustworthiness. Since jurors of ordinary abilities are competent to consider the evidence and determine whether the alleged crime occurred, the danger of unfair prejudice outweighs any probative value. To allow such testimony would inevitably lead to a battle of experts that would invade the jury's province of fact-finding and add confusion rather than clarity.

Rape trauma syndrome is not a fact-finding tool, but a therapeutic tool useful in counseling. Because the jury need be concerned only with determining the facts and applying the law, and because evidence of reactions of other people does not assist the jury in its fact-finding function, we find the admission of expert testimony on rape trauma syndrome to be error.

[W]e hold that in this prosecution for criminal sexual conduct where the defendant claimed consent it was reversible error for an expert to testify concerning typical post-rape symptoms and behavior of rape victims and give opinions that the complainant was a victim of rape and had not fantasized the rape. Our holding is necessary to ensure accuracy in the truth-seeking process and to guarantee fairness to the accused.

[W]e reverse appellant's conviction and remand for a new trial.

––––––––

NOTE

1. Probabilistic Versus Particularistic Evidence. Justice Scott, in *Saldana,* wrote that the jury "must not decide this case on the basis of how most people respond to rape." Rather, the jury "must decide what happened in *this* case." In the context of responding to Tribe, Trial by Mathematics: Precision and Ritual in the Legal Process, 84 Harvard Law Review 1329 (1971), Saks and Kidd addressed the distinction between statistical or base-rate information on "how most people respond" and information that is believed to be particular to a given case. In Human Information Processing and Adjudication: Trial by Heuristics, 15 Law and Society Review 123, 151–52 (1980), they state:

[I]t seems obvious that background base-rate information is about other cases while particularistic information is about *this* case. Whatever meaning the distinction may have, it is not one that pertains to the probability of an accurate decision on the facts. Much of the testimony that is commonly thought of as particularistic only seems so. It is far more probabilistic than we normally allow jurors (or judges) to realize. [A]ll identification techniques place the identified object in a class with others. There is little if any, pin-pointed, one-person-only evidence in this world. In fairness to Tribe, he notes this non-distinction, then promptly ignores its implications by saying, "I am, of course, aware that *all* factual evidence is ultimately statistical, and all legal proof ultimately probabilistic, in the epistemological sense that no conclusion can ever be drawn from empirical data without some step of inductive inference—even if only an inference that things are usually what they are perceived to be ... My concern however, is only with types of evidence and modes of proof that bring this 'probabilistic' element of inference to explicit attention in a quantified way. As I hope to show, much turns on whether such explicit quantification is attempted" [Tribe, at 1330 n. 2]. The problems of probability do not come into existence only when we become aware of them. Making them explicit does not create the problems, it only forces us to recognize them and enables us to begin dealing with them. Burying them in implicitness is no solution; revealing their existence is not the problem.

———

PEOPLE v. TAYLOR

Court of Appeals of New York, 1990.
75 N.Y.2d 277, 552 N.Y.S.2d 883, 552 N.E.2d 131.

■ WACHTLER, CHIEF JUDGE.

In these two cases, we consider whether expert testimony that a complaining witness has exhibited behavior consistent with "rape trauma syndrome" is admissible at the criminal trial of the person accused of the rape.

[I.]   *People v. Taylor*

On July 29, 1984, the complainant, a 19–year-old Long Island resident, reported to the town police that she had been raped and sodomized at gunpoint on a deserted beach near her home.

[T]he complainant arrived home around 11:00 P.M., woke her mother and told her about the attack. Her mother then called the police. Sometime between 11:30 P.M. and midnight, the police arrived at the complainant's house. At that time, the complainant told the police she did not know who her attacker was. She was taken to the police station where she described the events leading up to the attack and again repeated that she did not know who her attacker was. At the conclusion of the interview, the complainant was asked to step into a private room to remove the clothes that she had been wearing at the time of the attack so that they could be examined for forensic evidence. While she was alone with her mother, the complainant told her that the defendant John Taylor, had been her attacker. The time was approximately 1:15 A.M. The complainant had known the defendant for years.

[H]er mother summoned one of the detectives and the complainant repeated that the defendant had been the person who attacked her.

[T]he defendant's first trial ended without the jury being able to reach a verdict. At his second trial, the Judge permitted Eileen Treacy, an instructor at the City University of New York, Herbert Lehman College, with experience in counseling sexual assault victims, to testify about rape trauma syndrome. The prosecutor introduced this testimony for two separate purposes. First, Treacy's testimony on the specifics of rape trauma syndrome explained why the complainant might have been unwilling during the first few hours after the attack to name the defendant as her attacker where she had known the defendant prior to the incident. Second, Treacy's testimony that it was common for a rape victim to appear quiet and controlled following an attack, responded to evidence that the complainant had appeared calm after the attack and tended to rebut the inference that because she was not excited and upset after the attack, it had not been a rape. At the close of the second trial, the defendant was convicted.

[II.] *People v. Banks*

On July 7, 1986, the defendant Ronnie Banks approached the 11-year-old complainant, who was playing with her friends in the City of Rochester. The complainant testified that the defendant told her to come to him and when she did not, he grabbed her by the arm and pulled her down the street. According to the complainant, the defendant took her into a neighborhood garage where he sexually assaulted her. The complainant returned to her grandmother's house, where she was living at the time. The next morning, she told her grandmother about the incident and the police were contacted. The defendant was arrested and charged with [several sex offenses].

At trial, the complainant testified that the defendant had raped and sodomized her. In addition, she and her grandmother both testified about the complainant's behavior following the attack. Their testimony revealed that the complainant had been suffering from nightmares, had been waking up in the middle of the night in a cold sweat, had been afraid to return to school in the fall, had become generally more fearful and had been running and staying away from home. Following the introduction of this evidence, the prosecution sought to introduce expert testimony about the symptoms associated with rape trauma syndrome.

Clearly, the prosecution, in an effort to establish that forcible sexual contact had in fact occurred, wanted to introduce this evidence to show that the complainant was demonstrating behavior that was consistent with patterns of response exhibited by rape victims. The prosecutor does not appear to have introduced this evidence to counter the inference that the complainant consented to the incident, since the 11-year-old complainant is legally incapable of consent (Penal Law § 130.05[3][a]). Unlike *Taylor,* the evidence was not offered to explain behavior exhibited by the victim that the jury might not understand; instead, it was offered to show that the behavior that the complainant had exhibited after the incident was consistent with a set of symptoms commonly associated with women who had been forcibly attacked. The clear implication of such testimony would be that because the complainant exhibited these symptoms, it was more likely than not that she had been forcibly raped.

The Judge permitted David Gandell, an obstetrician-gynecologist on the faculty of the University of Rochester, Strong Memorial Hospital, with special training in treating victims of sexual assault, to testify as to the symptoms commonly associated with rape trauma syndrome. After Gandell had described rape trauma syndrome he testified hypothetically that the kind of symptoms demonstrated by the complainant were consistent with a diagnosis of rape trauma syndrome. At the close of the trial, the defendant was [c]onvicted.

[III.]   *Rape Trauma Syndrome*

In a 1974 study rape trauma syndrome was described as "the acute phase and long-term reorganization process that occurs as a result of forcible rape or attempted forcible rape. This syndrome of behavioral, somatic, and psychological reactions is an acute stress reaction to a life-threatening situation" (Burgess & Holmstrom, *Rape Trauma Syndrome,* 131 Am.J.Psychiatry 981, 982 [1974]). Although others had studied the reactions of rape victims prior to this publication (see, e.g., Sutherland & Scherl, *Patterns of Response Among Victims of Rape,* 40 Am.J.Orthopsychiatry 503 [1970]), the Burgess and Holmstrom identification of two separate phases in a rape victim's recovery has proven enormously influential.

According to Burgess and Holmstrom, the rape victim will go through an acute phase immediately following the incident. The behavior exhibited by a rape victim after the attack can vary. While some women will express their fear, anger and anxiety openly, an equal number of women will appear controlled, calm, and subdued (Burgess & Holmstrom, op. cit., at 982). Women in the acute phase will also experience a number of physical reactions. These reactions include the actual physical trauma that resulted from the attack, muscle tension that could manifest itself in tension headaches, fatigue, or disturbed sleep patterns, gastrointestinal irritability and genitourinary disturbance (id.). Emotional reactions in the acute phase generally take the form of fear, humiliation, embarrassment, fear of violence and death, and self-blame (id., at 983).

As part of the long-term reorganizational phase, the victim will often decide to make a change in her life, such as a change of residence. At this point, the woman will often turn to her family for support (id.). Other symptoms that are seen in this phase are the occurrence of nightmares and the development of phobias that relate to the circumstances of the rape (id., at 984). For instance, women attacked in their beds will often develop a fear of being indoors, while women attacked on the street will develop a fear of being outdoors (id.).

While some researchers have criticized the methodology of the early studies of rape trauma syndrome, Burgess and Holmstrom's model has nonetheless generated considerable interest in the response and recovery of rape victims and has contributed to the emergence of a substantial body of scholarship in this area (see, e.g., Nadelson, Notman, Zackson & Gornick, *A Follow-up Study of Rape Victims*, 139 Am.J.Psychiatry 1266 [1982]; Ruch, Chandler & Harter, *Life Change and Rape Impact*, 21 J.Health & Social Behavior 248 [1980]; Kilpatrick, Veronen & Resick, *The Aftermath of Rape: Recent Empirical Findings*, 49 Am.J.Orthopsychiatry 658 [1979]; Notman & Nadelson, *The Rape Victim: Psychodynamic Considerations*, 133 Am.J.Psychiatry 408 [1976]; *see generally,* Symonds, *Victims of Violence: Psychological Effects and Aftereffects,* 35 Am.J.Psychoanalysis 19 [1975]; Note, *Checking the Allure of Increased Conviction Rates: The Admissibility of Expert Testimony on Rape Trauma Syndrome in Criminal Proceedings,* 70 Va.L.Rev. 1657, 1667–1680 [summarizing the research in the field and criticizing the reliability of rape trauma syndrome studies]). The question before us today, then, is whether the syndrome, which has been the subject of study and discussion for the past 16 years, can be introduced before a lay jury as relevant evidence in these two rape trials.

We realize that rape trauma syndrome encompasses a broad range of symptoms and varied patterns of recovery. Some women are better able to cope with the aftermath of sexual assault than other women (see, e.g., Ruch, Chandler & Harter, op. cit., at 253). It is also apparent that there is no single typical profile of a rape victim and that different victims express themselves and come to terms with the experience of rape in different ways. We are satisfied, however, that the relevant scientific community has generally accepted that rape is a highly traumatic event that will in many women trigger the onset of certain identifiable symptoms (see, Frye v. United States, 293 F. 1013 (D.C.Cir.); People v. Hughes, 59 N.Y.2d 523, 537, 466 N.Y.S.2d 255, 453 N.E.2d 484).

We note that the American Psychiatric Association has listed rape as one of the stressors that can lead to posttraumatic stress disorder (American Psychiatric Association, Diagnostic & Statistical Manual of Mental Disorders 247, 248 [3d ed rev 1987] [DSM III-R]). According to DSM III-R, there is an identifiable pattern of responses that can follow an intensely stressful event. The victim who suffers from posttraumatic stress disorder will persistently reexperience the traumatic event in a number of ways, as through dreams, flashbacks, hallucinations, or intense distress at exposure to events that resemble or symbolize the traumatic event (id., at 250). The victim will also avoid stimuli that he or she associates with the trauma (id.). Finally, the victim will experience "persistent symptoms of increased arousal," which could include difficulty in falling or staying asleep, sudden outbursts of anger, or difficulty concentrating (id.). While the diagnostic criteria for posttraumatic stress disorder that are contained in DSM III-R have convinced us that the scientific community has accepted that rape as a stressor can have marked, identifiable effects on a victim's behavior, we would further note that although rape trauma syndrome can be conceptualized as a posttraumatic stress disorder (see, Nadelson, Notman, Zackson & Gornick, *op. cit.,* at 1267), victims of rape will often exhibit peculiar symptoms—like a fear of men—that are not commonly exhibited by victims of other sorts of trauma (see generally, Massaro, *Experts, Psychology, Credibility, and Rape: The Rape Trauma Syndrome Issue and Its Implications for Expert Psychological Testimony,* 69 Minn.L.Rev. 395, 447).

We are aware that rape trauma syndrome is a therapeutic and not a legal concept. Physicians and rape counselors who treat victims of sexual assault are not charged with the responsibility of ascertaining whether the victim is telling the truth when she says that a rape occurred. That is part of the truth-finding process implicated in a criminal trial. We do not believe, however, that the therapeutic origin of the syndrome renders it unreliable for trial purposes. Thus, although we acknowledge that evidence of rape trauma syndrome does not by itself prove that the complainant was raped, we believe that this should not preclude its admissibility into evidence at trial when relevance to a particular disputed issue has been demonstrated.

IV. *The Law*

Having concluded that evidence of rape trauma syndrome is generally accepted within the relevant scientific community, we must now decide whether expert testimony in this area would aid a lay jury in reaching a verdict. "[E]xpert opinion is proper when it would help to clarify an issue calling for professional or technical knowledge, possessed by the expert and beyond the ken of the typical juror" (De Long v. County of Erie, 60 N.Y.2d 296, 307, 469 N.Y.S.2d 611, 457 N.E.2d 717). [R]ape is a crime that is permeated by misconceptions (*see generally,* Brownmiller, Against Our Will: Men, Women and Rape, at 343–350; Estrich, *Rape,* 95 Yale L.J. 1087). [S]tudies have shown that one of the most popular misconceptions about rape is that the victim by behaving in a certain way brought it on herself (see, Massaro, op. cit., at 404). For that reason, studies have demonstrated that jurors will under certain circumstances blame the victim for the attack and will refuse to convict the man accused (id.). Studies have also shown that jurors will infer consent where the victim has engaged in certain types of behavior prior to the incident (id., at 405–406).

[B]ecause cultural myths still affect common understanding of rape and rape victims and because experts have been studying the effects of rape upon its victims only since the 1970's, we believe that patterns of response among rape victims are not within the ordinary understanding of the lay juror. For that reason, we conclude that introduction of expert testimony describing rape trauma syndrome may under certain circumstances assist a lay jury in deciding issues in a rape trial.

In reaching our conclusions in this area, we note that an extensive body of case law has developed concerning the admissibility of this type of evidence. There is no uniform approach to the admission of evidence of rape trauma syndrome among the States that have considered the question. The Minnesota Supreme Court in one of the earliest rape trauma syndrome cases held such evidence inadmissible (State v. Saldana, 324 N.W.2d 227).

[C]alifornia has similarly held that evidence of rape trauma syndrome is inadmissible to prove that a rape occurred (People v. Bledsoe, 36 Cal.3d 236, 203 Cal.Rptr. 450, 681 P.2d 291). The court noted in dicta, however, that where evidence of rape trauma syndrome was offered not to prove that a rape had occurred, but to explain conduct of the victim after the incident that may appear inconsistent with a claim of rape, "expert testimony on rape trauma syndrome may play a particularly useful role by disabusing the jury of some widely held misconceptions about rape and rape victims, so that it may evaluate the evidence free of the constraints of popular myths" (36 Cal.3d at 247–48, 203 Cal.Rptr. at 457, 681 P.2d at 298).

Among those States that have allowed such testimony to be admitted, the purpose for which the testimony was offered has proven crucial.

In the two cases now before us, testimony regarding rape trauma syndrome was offered for entirely different purposes. We conclude that its admission at the trial of John Taylor was proper, but that its admission at the trial of Ronnie Banks was not.

As noted above, the complaining witness in *Taylor* had initially told the police that she could not identify her assailant. Approximately two hours after she first told her mother that she had been raped and sodomized, she told her mother that she knew the defendant had done it. The complainant had known the defendant for years and had seen him the night before the assault. We hold that under the circumstances present in this case, expert testimony explaining that a rape victim who knows her assailant is more fearful of disclosing his name to the police and is in fact less likely to report the rape at all was relevant to explain why the complainant may have been initially unwilling to report that the defendant had been the man who attacked her. Behavior of this type is not within the ordinary understanding of the jury and testimony explaining this behavior assists the jury in determining what effect to give to the complainant's initial failure to identify the defendant. This evidence provides a possible explanation for the complainant's behavior that is consistent with her claim that she was raped. As such, it is relevant.

Rape trauma syndrome evidence was also introduced in *Taylor* in response to evidence that revealed the complainant had not seemed upset following the attack. We note again in this context that the reaction of a rape victim in the hours following her attack is not something within the common understanding of the average lay juror. Indeed, the defense would clearly want the jury to infer that because the victim was not upset following the attack, she must not have been raped. This inference runs contrary to the studies cited earlier, which suggest that half of all women who have been forcibly raped are controlled and subdued following the attack (Burgess & Holmstrom, op. cit., at 982). Thus, we conclude that evidence of this type is relevant to dispel misconceptions that jurors might possess regarding the ordinary responses of rape victims in the first hours after their attack. We do not believe that evidence of rape trauma syndrome, when admitted for that express purpose, is unduly prejudicial.

The admission of expert testimony describing rape trauma syndrome in *Banks,* however, was clearly error. As we noted earlier, this evidence was not offered to explain behavior that might appear unusual to a lay juror not ordinarily familiar with the patterns of response exhibited by rape victims. We conclude that evidence of rape trauma syndrome is inadmissible when it inescapably bears solely on proving that a rape occurred, as was the case here.

Although we have accepted that rape produces identifiable symptoms in rape victims, we do not believe that evidence of the presence, or indeed of the absence, of those symptoms necessarily indicates that the incident did or did not occur. Because introduction of rape trauma syndrome evidence by an expert might create such an inference in the minds of lay jurors, we find that the defendant would be unacceptably prejudiced by the introduction of rape trauma syndrome evidence for that purpose alone. We emphasize again that the therapeutic nature of the syndrome does not preclude its admission into evidence under all circumstances. We believe, however, that its usefulness as a fact-finding device is limited and that where it is introduced to prove the crime took place, its helpfulness is outweighed by the possibility of undue prejudice. Therefore, the trial court erred in permitting the admission of expert testimony regarding rape trauma syndrome under the facts present in *Banks.*

On this record, we cannot conclude that the introduction of the evidence of rape trauma syndrome evidence in *People v. Banks* was harmless error. Accordingly, in *People v. Banks,* the order of the Appellate Division should be reversed and a new trial ordered.

We have considered defendant John Taylor's other arguments and we conclude that they are without merit. The order of the Appellate Division in *People v. Taylor* should therefore be affirmed.

————

STATE v. KINNEY

Supreme Court of Vermont, 2000.
171 Vt. 239, 762 A.2d 833.

■ DOOLEY, J.

Defendant Steven Kinney was convicted by a jury on charges of kidnapping, aggravated sexual assault, and lewd and lascivious behavior. He was sentenced to two concurrent terms of forty-years-to-life imprisonment and one concurrent term of four-to-five-years imprisonment. On appeal he argues that the trial court erred [i]n admitting expert testimony about rape trauma syndrome.

[A]ccording to defendant's testimony, [h]e and the victim got into bed, where "one thing led to another," and they had consensual sex. The victim, on the other hand, testified that when they got to defendant's house, he took her to his room and raped her. Afterwards, she fell asleep. In the morning when she woke up, she asked to be taken home, and he arranged for a friend to give her a ride.

[T]he State called Dr. Jan Tyler to testify about rape trauma syndrome and the characteristics and conduct of rape victims. The admissibility of this testimony was first contested in pretrial proceedings when the State made an offer of proof indicating Dr. Tyler would testify about rape trauma syndrome and "the behavioral patterns of victims of sexual assault." The State noted that the expert witness would have no contact with the victim and would not offer an opinion on whether the victim was raped by defendant. Defendant challenged the evidence as inadmissible under *Daubert v. Merrell Dow Pharmaceuticals, Inc., 509 U.S. 579, 113 S.Ct. 2786, 125 L.Ed.2d 469 (1993).*

Dr. Tyler testified that rape trauma syndrome is associated with post-traumatic stress disorder—that is, it is a set of behaviors and symptoms experienced by victims of trauma. She explained that victims of severe trauma commonly experience symptoms such as nightmares, anxiety, and fear as a result of the trauma. Victims of rape, in particular, may experience symptoms such as difficulty in interpersonal relationships, guilt, shame, and sexual dysfunction. [F]urthermore, she said that it is not unusual for victims to delay in reporting a rape, especially if the attacker is an acquaintance, and that a rape victim may be more likely to report to a friend first, rather than to someone with whom she is having an intimate relationship. This delay in reporting is related to the feelings of guilt and shame experienced due to the trauma of the rape. Dr. Tyler then testified to statistics regarding the rate of false reporting of rape. Finally, she testified that, although she had no statistics, she thought it would not be unusual for a victim of rape to fall asleep immediately after the assault, due to the physical exertion and psychological responses to the trauma such as denial and withdrawal.

[I]n this Court, defendant makes three arguments: (1) the court failed to conduct a proper *Daubert* inquiry; (2) the expert's evidence was not admissible under *Daubert*; and (3) the expert's testimony on the rate of false reporting improperly bolstered the credibility of the victim.

[W]e recognize that *Daubert,* and the more recent decision in *Kumho Tire Co. v. Carmichael, 526 U.S. 137, 119 S.Ct. 1167, 143 L.Ed.2d 238 (1999),* emphasized the gatekeeper function of the trial court to determine that novel scientific or technical evidence is sufficiently reliable and relevant before it is admissible. [T]he gatekeeper can perform this function in a number of ways. In many cases, like this one, [t]he issue is whether a certain category of evidence is admissible, often in particular types of cases that are recurring. In some cases, both the trial court and this Court can fully evaluate the reliability and relevance of the evidence generally based on the decisions of other appellate courts. In this way, we can avoid conducting our own lengthy and expensive evidentiary hearing aimed at establishing, or attacking, the foundation for the disputed expert testimony.

We are not suggesting that the new standard for admissibility has somehow become general acceptance among appellate courts. Irrespective of the decisions of other courts, the responsibility for determining the admissibility of evidence in Vermont courts remains with our trial judges, and on appeal with this Court. However, scientific or technical evidence which is novel to us is frequently not novel to many other state and federal courts. To the extent the evaluation of these courts is complete and persuasive, we can affirmatively rely upon it in reaching our own decision.

[M]uch of defendant's argument is that the trial court in this case failed to comply with the procedural requirements of *Daubert*—that is, that it failed to exercise its gatekeeping function by determining the reliability and relevance of Dr. Tyler's testimony based on foundational evidence presented to the court in this case. We acknowledge that we have never explicitly ruled upon the admissibility of evidence of rape trauma syndrome and the common behavior of adult rape victims. [T]hus, the trial court was required to evaluate the admissibility of Dr. Tyler's testimony, beyond her qualifications to provide such testimony, and the result of this evaluation was not clearly dictated by a decision of this Court. This does not mean, however, that the State was obligated in this case to present independent evidence that Dr. Tyler's methodology could be tested, was subject to peer review and publication, had a known and measurable error rate, and was generally accepted in the relevant scientific community, the factors suggested in *Daubert*. Nor was the trial court required to make findings on each of these factors. It could find the evidence admissible because its reliability equals that of other technical evidence we have given trial courts the discretion to admit and the evaluation of other courts allowing admission of the evidence is complete and persuasive.

We concur with the trial court that expert evidence of rape trauma syndrome and the associated typical behavior of adult rape victims is admissible to assist the jury in evaluating the evidence, and frequently to respond to defense claims that the victim's behavior after the alleged rape was inconsistent with the claim that the rape occurred. [F]or example, the defense made much of the fact [t]hat the victim appeared to be sleeping peacefully in defendant's bed the next morning, and that she failed to immediately tell her boyfriend she had been raped. Dr. Tyler's testimony explained why a rape victim might exhibit these behaviors. [A]s the trial court noted in this case, Dr. Tyler was prepared to address some of the studies that formed the bases for her opinions if the defendant raised them in cross-examination.

We note that the evidence here was of a type that the danger of improper usage or excessive prejudice was at a minimum. The expert never interviewed the victim and offered no opinion whether the victim suffered from rape trauma syndrome or exhibited any of the behavior of a rape victim. Thus, there was little risk that Dr. Tyler would be seen as a truth detector

We do not, however, have the same view of the expert's testimony about the incidence of false reporting by rape victims. The prosecutor asked Dr. Tyler whether "there are any data on the issue of false reporting that you are aware of?" She answered:

> False reporting, the percentages are very low. About two percent. That's about the same as any other crime that's committed. In other words, the number of people who would report a burglary that didn't happen is about the same as people who would report a rape, with one difference. The statistics for the rape include those reports that are made and then either withdrawn by the victim for whatever reason, either they were false or there's a fear of going through the legal system, or they're being pressured by other persons. Those also include reports that the police will not arrest on because they don't feel they have enough evidence. And they also include those that don't get to trial because the prosecutor feels it's not a winnable case. So when you get down to literal false reporting of this really never happened, it's very small.

In short, Dr. Tyler testified that at least 98% of the rapes reported actually occurred.

[D]r. Tyler's testimony on the rate of false reporting clearly went over the line. [T]he jury could infer from her testimony that scientific studies have shown that almost no woman falsely claims to have been raped and convict defendant on that basis.

[A]lthough the evidence of the incidence of false reporting of rape accusations was inadmissible and prejudicial, the State argues that its admission is not grounds for reversal. [D]r. Tyler never testified about the story or credibility of the victim because she had never interviewed, or even met, the victim. Her testimony was entirely theoretical. Further, defense counsel was able to reduce the prejudicial effect of the testimony of the low incidence of false reporting by cross-examination. Finally, the prosecutor did not highlight this testimony in closing argument.

We cannot conclude that failure to exclude the inadmissible expert testimony caused a miscarriage of justice in this case. Accordingly, we find no plain error. Affirmed.

––––––

RAPE TRAUMA SYNDROME

Patricia A. Frazier.
In Modern Scientific Evidence: The Law and Science of Expert Testimony, 2d ed. (D. L. Faigman, D. H. Kaye, M. J. Saks, and J. Sanders eds. 2002).

[I]t is important to acknowledge some of the difficulties of doing research in this area. One such difficulty concerns recruiting victims to participate in the research. Several different methods have been used and each has its strengths and limitations. One method is to recruit participants from clients seen at rape crisis centers. Investigators that recruit victims through rape crisis centers are able to assess immediate reactions and assess symptoms longitudinally over time. However, because many women do not seek help at such centers, those that do may not be representative of most victims.[5] To further compound the problem, of the minority that do report, often a small percentage participate in the research. Another recruitment method is to advertise for research participants who have been sexually assaulted. Sample representativeness also is a concern in studies that rely on this method because research volunteers may differ in various ways from other victims. A third method is to identify rape victims through screening questions in surveys of larger samples. The validity of studies that identify victims in this manner depends in large part on the screening questions used to assess sexual assault. Because many women do not define experiences as "rape," even if they meet the legal definition, many victims will be undetected if that terminology is used. Questions that describe rape in behavioral terms are much more likely to identify victimization experiences.

NOTE

1. Rape and Posttraumatic Stress Disorder. Breslau, Davis, Andreski, and Peterson, Traumatic Events and Posttraumatic Stress Disorder in an Urban Population of Young Adults, 48 Archives of General Psychiatry 216 (1991), conducted a study of 1,200 randomly selected 21–30 year old members of a health maintenance organization. The researchers reported that, except under one condition, less than 25 percent of the people exposed to a traumatic event (e.g., physical assault, serious accident, fire, or flood) developed full-fledged Posttraumatic Stress Disorder. The one exception was when rape was the traumatic event: 80 percent of women who reported being raped also reported subsequent symptoms that qualified for a diagnosis of Posttraumatic Stress Disorder.

CHECKING THE ALLURE OF INCREASED CONVICTION RATES: THE ADMISSIBILITY OF EXPERT TESTIMONY ON RAPE TRAUMA SYNDROME IN CRIMINAL PROCEEDINGS

Robert Lawrence.
70 Virginia Law Review 1657 (1984).

The systematic use of RTS [Rape Trauma Syndrome] in the criminal process may [e]ventually undermine important accomplishments of the

---

5. Women who seek help at rape crisis centers may, however, be representative of victims whose cases go to trial because both groups have sought help.

rape law reform movement. If courts consistently permit the introduction of expert testimony on RTS, defendants will seek, under their sixth amendment rights, to introduce this evidence on their own behalf. The confrontation and compulsory process clauses of the sixth amendment are read together to guarantee the criminal defendant the right to present all probative evidence in his defense. If the RTS evidence is admitted to assist the state in making its case, the defendant must be allowed to introduce it to the extent that it may demonstrate innocence.

In exercising this right, the defendant may seek to have a court appointed psychiatrist examine the complainant. If the doctor concludes that the complainant does not suffer from RTS, the defendant may introduce testimony to that effect as evidence of consent. Although rape reform advocates have denounced compulsory psychiatric examinations of rape victims, the admissibility of expert testimony on RTS could reinstitute that practice. Rape trials once again would focus not on the defendant's conduct but on the psychological state of the victim. The dispositive issue in most rape trials could become whether the alleged victim exhibited symptoms of RTS. Unless the complainant suffered clinically observable signs of a PTSD, the state would be unable to secure a conviction. Because not all rape victims experience RTS as a result of the attack, the defendant's use of RTS testimony might lead to acquittals of guilty defendants.

[E]xpert testimony on RTS would also have implications with respect to the rape shield statutes. Most rape shield statutes allow inquiries into the complainant's sexual history only when it is relevant to an issue in controversy. For example, if the victim is pregnant or has venereal disease and claims this resulted from the alleged rape, the defendant may offer evidence that the pregnancy or venereal disease resulted from sexual intercourse with another. The sixth amendment guarantees the defendant this right. Similarly, if the state introduces evidence that the victim suffers from RTS, the door is open for the defendant to probe the complainant's sexual or psychological history in attempting to establish another cause of the PTSD. Courts once again would focus on the victim's character and conduct rather than the defendant's. This focus would eviscerate the goal of the rape reform movement of treating rape like other violent crimes.

––––––

HENSON v. STATE

Supreme Court of Indiana, 1989.
535 N.E.2d 1189.

■ DeBruler, Justice.

Defendant Rickey J. Henson was convicted in a jury trial of Rape as a Class B Felony, Criminal Deviate Conduct as a Class A Felony, Criminal Confinement, and Battery in Howard Circuit Court. He was sentenced to [sixty five years in prison.]

[O]n appeal, Henson argues that [t]he trial court erred by not allowing the testimony of an expert witness that the victim's conduct after the alleged rape was inconsistent with that of a person who had suffered a traumatic forcible rape.

[T]he facts which tend to support the conviction are as follows: Henson was at a crowded bar in Kokomo and asked J.O., who was sitting alone, if he could join her. She consented and the two exchanged names, but otherwise did not speak. Two other men joined them at the table and J.O. danced with them during the course of the evening but not with Henson. J.O. stayed at the bar until it closed and then left to have more drinks at the home of one of the bar's waitresses. After she got in her car, but before she could shut the door, Henson approached her with a knife, pushed her over to the passenger's seat, got in the car and drove to a secluded place. He then forced her to have sexual intercourse with him as well as oral sex. He also attempted to cut her blouse off with the knife and J.O. received superficial lacerations as a result. The next evening, J.O. returned to the same bar where she stayed for two hours and drank.

At trial, one witness testified that J.O. was drinking as well as dancing on the evening after the rape allegedly occurred. Defendant then called a psychologist, Dr. David Gover, and established that the witness was an expert in the study and treatment of post-traumatic stress syndrome. Defendant's counsel then asked the following question:

Q.   Doctor, in your professional opinion, a person who has allegedly suffered a traumatic, forcible rape, would it be consistent in your experience that a person who had gone through a situation such as that would go back to the same place the act allegedly occurred and socialize, drink, dance, on the same day of the alleged act?

After establishing that Dr. Gover had never consulted with J.O. personally and that he had no firsthand knowledge of the incident in question, the prosecution objected to the question. The objection was sustained on the grounds that the testimony was not relevant and that a proper foundation had not been laid. There followed a lengthy offer to prove, out of the jury's presence, in which the objection was again sustained on the grounds that the testimony was too speculative.

The testimony of Dr. Gover would clearly have been relevant to the issues at trial. Evidence is relevant if it is material and has probative value. Evidence is material if it is offered to prove a matter in issue. Evidence has probative value if it has any tendency to make the existence of any fact that is of consequence to the determination of the action (i.e., any material fact) more or less probable than it would be without the evidence. Here, Dr. Gover's testimony would have tended to prove that J.O.'s behavior after the incident was inconsistent with that of a victim who had suffered a traumatic rape such as that which J.O. recounted. The evidence therefore would have a tendency to make it less probable that a rape in fact occurred, clearly a matter in issue at trial, and was therefore relevant.

Still, where an expert is to give opinion testimony in the form of an answer to a hypothetical question, more than mere relevance is required to make the evidence admissible. A proper foundation must be laid which is two-fold. First, the expert's ability to give such an opinion must be established through testimony showing he has the requisite knowledge, skill, education or experience on which to base the opinion. However, firsthand knowledge of the facts are not required. It is well established in our state that an expert may give opinion testimony even though he does not have personal knowledge of the facts on which his opinion is based.

Second, there must be a proper evidentiary foundation supporting the facts that are included in the hypothetical question. That is to say, a hypothetical question is proper if it embraces facts that have been placed into evidence. However, it is not necessary that a hypothetical question include all pertinent facts that are in evidence. If the opposing counsel feels the facts included do not fairly include all the pertinent facts as presented in the record, the remedy is not exclusion of the expert's testimony but to include such facts in questions on cross-examination.

[H]ere both foundations were met. The record indicates that, once counsel for the defendant had fully explored Dr. Gover's credentials, the trial court was fully satisfied with the psychologist's ability to testify. The evidence shows Dr. Gover had worked extensively with patients who had suffered from post-traumatic stress syndrome and these included patients with rape in their backgrounds. Moreover, there was ample evidence to support the facts embraced by the hypothetical question posed to Dr. Gover by defendant's counsel. One witness for the prosecution had testified that J.O. had returned to the bar on the evening after the alleged rape and was drinking and dancing; and J.O. herself admitted she was drinking at the same bar that evening. If the State did not think the hypothetical embraced facts favorable to its version of the events, its remedy was to bring these inconsistencies out on cross-examination of the witness.

[T]he State also argues that the testimony was too speculative.

[However,] the record clearly reflects Dr. Gover's competence to give an opinion as to behavior of the victim without having interviewed her. On cross-examination, he stated that it would not have been particularly helpful to talk with the victim since he was merely making a general observation that certain behavior, of which there was evidence from previous testimony, was inconsistent with post-traumatic stress syndrome. To argue that evidence is too speculative is to say merely that it is lacking in probative value. There is little doubt that an alleged rape victim's conduct after the fact is probative of whether a rape in fact occurred. The prosecution in this case was clearly aware of this as they introduced testimony regarding J.O.'s behavior after the rape was reported: she was upset, had difficulty sleeping and was shaking when she identified the defendant in a photo lineup. It cannot be said, therefore, that the testimony of Dr. Gover was lacking in probative value. That the expert did not personally interview the victim bears on the weight of the evidence not on its admissibility; and such facts may be brought out by opposing counsel on cross-examination just as any perceived deficiencies in the facts underlying the hypothetical question are brought out.

[M]oreover, this Court has already recognized the admissibility of rape trauma syndrome evidence in *Simmons*. It would be fundamentally unfair to allow the use of such testimony by the State, as was the case in *Simmons,* and then deny its use by a defendant here. In so holding, we are not unmindful of the considerable body of literature in this area and recent case law in other jurisdictions. See, e.g., State v. Marks (1982), 231 Kan. 645, 647 P.2d 1292; People v. Bledsoe (1984), 36 Cal.3d 236, 203 Cal.Rptr. 450, 681 P.2d 291; Kruse v. State (Fla.App.1986), 483 So.2d 1383; Massaro, Experts, Psychology, Credibility, and Rape; The Rape Trauma Syndrome Issue and Its Implications for Expert Psychological Testimony, 69 Minn. L.R. 395 (1985); McCord, The Admissibility of Expert Testimony Regarding Rape Trauma Syndrome in Rape Prosecutions, 26 B.C.L.Rev. 1143 (1985); Annot., 42 A.L.R.4th 879 (1985). The commentators and case law address, for the most part, whether evidence of post-traumatic stress syndrome in the form of rape trauma syndrome should be admissible at all. A large part of the discussion has centered on the reliability of such evidence under the familiar *Frye* rule that expert scientific testimony is only admissible if the phenomenon testified to is generally accepted in the relevant scientific community. Frye v. United States, 293 F. 1013 (D.C.Cir.1923). Since we have already crossed that hurdle in *Simmons,* our decision here is focused more on the issue above: whether, having allowed a trial court to admit such testimony when offered by the State to prove a rape was committed, we can say it is not an abuse of discretion to exclude it when offered by a defendant to prove that one was not. We conclude, in light of our decision in *Simmons,* that to bar the defendant from presenting such evidence exceeds the discretion of the trial court; and, in this case, the trial court's ruling impinged upon the substantial rights of appellant to present a defense and was reversible error.

[T]he judgment of the trial court is accordingly vacated and this case is remanded for a new trial.

RAPE TRAUMA SYNDROME

In Modern Scientific Evidence: The Law and Science of Expert Testimony, 2d ed. (D. L. Faigman, D. H. Kaye, M. J. Saks, and J. Sanders eds. 2002).

[T]he legal framework [presented in Henson v. State, above] is somewhat more complicated than any simple *quid pro quo* approach would suggest. Most evidence codes today provide special protection for alleged victims of sexual assault in what are commonly called "rape shield statutes." These provisions, enacted to remedy the historical abuses surrounding the examination of complainants, severely restrict defense inquiries into the personal histories of alleged victims. To the extent that defense use of RTS raises the possibility that the alleged victim's personal history will be put in issue, contrary to a rape shield statute, some control over defense use should be exerted. Otherwise, unrestricted defense use of RTS could lead to the evisceration of the safeguards enacted in rape shield statutes.

How courts strike the balance regarding defense use of RTS depends on both the values embodied in evidence codes and the Constitution, together with the validity of the science associated with testimony on RTS. Unrestricted prosecutorial use of this evidence while, at the same time, complete foreclosure of defense use, would violate basic precepts of fairness. This is particularly true given the criminal justice system's commitment to guaranteeing defendants due process. At the same time, most jurisdictions are committed to protecting alleged victims from the kinds of abuse that were commonplace prior to enactment of protective legislation. These considerations might lead courts to strike a balance whereby defense use of RTS is limited to rebuttal of prosecution use of this evidence. In particular cases, therefore, if the state opens the door to the "psychological state" of the alleged victim, the defense would be permitted to rigorously test and rebut this claim.

————

NOTES

1. Prosecution Use of Defense Expert. In State v. Jackson, 97 N.M. 467, 641 P.2d 498 (1982), a defendant charged with rape requested a mental health examination of the complainant to ascertain whether she experienced the rape trauma syndrome. The prosecution had not first raised the issue of rape trauma. The trial judge ordered the complainant to submit to the examination. Contrary to the expectations of the defense, however, the examining psychologist "reported that this was one of the worst cases of rape trauma syndrome he had ever seen." Id. at 499. Accordingly, the defense did not seek to introduce the expert. The prosecution then attempted to call the psychologist as an expert witness of its own, and the defense objected. The New Mexico Supreme Court held that the prosecution could make use of the expert witness originally retained by the defense.

2. Male victims. In People v. Yates, 168 Misc.2d 101, 637 N.Y.S.2d 625 (Sup.1995), the issue arose as to whether expert testimony on the rape trauma syndrome was admissible when applied to male complainants alleging homosexual assault. The Court concluded as follows:

> [L]egal authorities, scientific writings, constitutional doctrine and logic all favor acceptance of the principle that expert testimony concerning rape trauma syndrome as applied to male victims is scientifically reliable and may, when appropriate, be admitted to aid a jury in understanding the sequelae of sexual assault against a man. Id at 630.

C. WITNESSES

Finally, in addition to its use in determining facts pertaining to defendants and victims, social science research is often offered to provide a context for decisionmakers in evaluating the testimony of witnesses. Research on eyewitness identification has been the primary witness-oriented framework that has been offered at trial.

ARIZONA v. CHAPPLE

Supreme Court of Arizona, 1983.
135 Ariz. 281, 660 P.2d 1208.

■ FELDMAN, JUSTICE.

[Three persons were murdered in the process of transacting the sale of 300 pounds of marijuana. Malcolm Scott and his sister, Pamela Buck, both of whom were parties to the transaction, identified Dolan Chapple as the murderer in a police photo line-up and in the courtroom. Chapple was convicted of first degree murder and sentenced to life imprisonment without the possibility of parole for twenty-five years.]

With identification the one issue on which the guilt or innocence of [the] defendant hinged, [d]efense counsel offered the testimony of an expert on eyewitness identification in order to rebut the testimony of Malcolm Scott and his sister, Pamela Buck. The witness called by the defense was Dr. Elizabeth Loftus, a professor of psychology at the University of Washington. Dr. Loftus specializes in an area of experimental and clinical psychology dealing with perception, memory retention and recall. Her qualifications are unquestioned, and it may fairly be said that she "wrote the book" on the subject. The trial court granted the State's motion to suppress Dr. Loftus' testimony. Acknowledging that rulings on admissibility of expert testimony are within the discretion of the trial court, defendant contends that the court erred and abused its discretion in granting the motion to suppress Dr. Loftus' testimony.

The admissibility of expert testimony is governed by Rule 702, Ariz.R. of Evid. That rule states:

> If scientific, technical, or other specialized knowledge will assist the trier of fact to understand the evidence or to determine a fact in issue, a witness qualified as an expert by knowledge, skill, experience, training, or education, may testify thereto in the form of an opinion or otherwise.

In what is probably the leading case on the subject, the Ninth Circuit affirmed the trial court's preclusion of expert evidence on eyewitness identification in United States v. Amaral, 488 F.2d 1148 (9th Cir.1973). In its analysis, however, the court set out four criteria which should be applied in order to determine the admissibility of such testimony. These are: (1) qualified expert; (2) proper subject; (3) conformity to a generally accepted explanatory theory; and (4) probative value compared to prejudicial effect. Id. at 1153. We approve this test and find that the case at bar meets these criteria.

We recognize that the cases that have considered the subject have uniformly affirmed trial court rulings denying admission of this type of testimony. However, a careful reading of these cases reveals that many of them contain fact situations which fail to meet the *Amaral* criteria or are decided on legal principles which differ from those we follow in Arizona.

[A]pplying the *Amaral* test to the case at bench, we find from the record that the State has conceded that the expert was qualified and that the question of conformity to generally accepted explanatory theory is not raised and appears not to be a question in this case. The two criteria which must therefore be considered are (1) determination of whether the probative value of the testimony outweighs its possible prejudicial effect and (2) determination of whether the testimony was a proper subject.

(1) PROBATIVE VALUE vs. PREJUDICE

The State argues that there would have been little probative value to the witness' testimony and great danger of unfair prejudice. The latter problem is claimed to arise from the fact that Loftus' qualifications were so impressive that the jury might have given improper weight to her testimony. We do not believe that this raises the issue of *unfair* prejudice. The contention of lack of probative value is based on the premise that the offer of proof showed that the witness would testify to general factors which were applicable to this case and affect the reliability of identification, but would not express any opinion with regard to the accuracy of the specific identification made by Scott and Buck and would not express an opinion regarding the accuracy percentage of eyewitness identification in general.

We believe that the "generality" of the testimony is a factor which favors admission. Witnesses are permitted to express opinions on ultimate issues but are not required to testify to an opinion on the precise questions before the trier of fact.

(2) PROPER SUBJECT

[T]he remaining criterion at issue is whether the offered evidence was a proper subject for expert testimony. Ariz.R. of Evid. 702 allows expert testimony if it "will assist the trier of fact to understand the evidence or to determine a fact in issue." Put conversely, the test "is whether the subject of inquiry is one of such common knowledge that people of ordinary education could reach a conclusion as intelligently as the witness. . . . "State v. Owens, 112 Ariz. 223, 227, 540 P.2d 695, 699 (1975). Furthermore, the test is not whether the jury could reach some conclusion in the absence of the expert evidence, but whether the jury is qualified without such testimony "to determine intelligently and to the best possible degree the particular issue without enlightenment from those having a specialized understanding of the subject. . . ." Fed.R.Evid. 702 advisory committee note (quoting Ladd, Expert Testimony, 5 Vand.L.Rev. 414, 418 (1952)).

In excluding the evidence in the case at bench, the trial judge stated:

> I don't find anything that's been presented in the extensive discussions that I have read in your memorandum with regard to the fact that this expert is going to testify to anything that isn't within the

common experience of the people on the jury, that couldn't really be covered in cross-examination of the witnesses who made the identification, and probably will be excessively argued in closing arguments to the jury.

This basis for the view that eyewitness identification is not a proper subject for expert testimony is the same as that adopted in United States v. Amaral, supra, and in the great majority of cases which have routinely followed *Amaral*.

However, after a careful review of these cases and the record before us, we have concluded that although the reasons cited by the trial judge would correctly permit preclusion of such testimony in the great majority of cases, it was error to refuse the testimony in the case at bench. In reaching this conclusion, we have carefully considered the offer of proof made by the defense in light of the basic concept of "proper subject" underlying Rule 702.

We note at the outset that the law has long recognized the inherent danger in eyewitness testimony. Of course, it is difficult to tell whether the ordinary juror shares the law's inherent caution of eyewitness identification. Experimental data indicates that many jurors "may reach intuitive conclusions about the reliability of [such] testimony that psychological research would show are misguided." Note, Did Your Eyes Deceive You? Expert Psychological Testimony on the Unreliability of Eyewitness Identification, 29 Stan.L.Rev. 969, 1017 (1977).

Even assuming that jurors of ordinary education need no expert testimony to enlighten them to the danger of eyewitness identification, the offer of proof indicated that Dr. Loftus' testimony would have informed the jury that there are many specific variables which affect the accuracy of identification and which apply to the facts of this case. For instance, while most jurors would no doubt realize that memory dims as time passes, Dr. Loftus presented data from experiments which showed that the "forgetting curve" is not uniform. Forgetting occurs very rapidly and then tends to level out; immediate identification is much more trustworthy than long-delayed identification. Thus, Scott's recognition [of another suspect as the murderer when the other suspect's photograph was shown] at the inception of the investigation is probably a more reliable identification than Scott's identification of Chapple's photograph in the photographic lineup thirteen months later. By the same token, Scott's failure to identify Chapple's photograph when it was first shown to him on March 26, 1978 (four months after the crime) and when Scott's ability to identify would have been far greater, is of key importance.

Another variable in the case is the effect of stress upon perception. Dr. Loftus indicated that research shows that most laymen believe that stressful events cause people to remember "better" so that what is seen in periods of stress is more accurately related later. However, experimental evidence indicates that stress causes inaccuracy of perception with subsequent distortion of recall.

Dr. Loftus would also have testified about the problems of "unconscious transfer," a phenomenon which occurs when the witness confuses a person seen in one situation with a person seen in a different situation. Dr. Loftus would have pointed out that a witness who takes part in a photo identification session without identifying any of the photographs and who then later sees a photograph of one of those persons may relate his or her familiarity with the picture to the crime rather than to the previous identification session.

Another variable involves assimilation of post-event information. Experimental evidence, shown by Dr. Loftus, confirms that witnesses frequently incorporate into their identifications inaccurate information gained subsequent to the event and confused with the event. An additional problem is the "feedback factor." We deal here with two witnesses who were related and who, according to Loftus' interview, engaged in discussions with each other about the identification of [the defendant]. Dr. Loftus, who interviewed them, emphasized that their independent descriptions of [the defendant] at times utilized identical language. Dr. Loftus would have explained that through such discussions identification witnesses can reinforce their individual identifications. Such reinforcement will often tend to heighten the certainty of identification. The same may be said of the continual sessions that each witness had with the police in poring over large groups of photographs.

The last variable in this case concerns the question of confidence and its relationship to accuracy. Dr. Loftus' testimony and some experimental data indicate that there is no relationship between the confidence which a witness has in his or her identification and the actual accuracy of that identification. Again, this factor was specifically tied to the evidence in the case before us since both Scott and Buck indicated in their testimony that they were absolutely sure of their identification. Evidently their demeanor on the witness stand showed absolute confidence.

We cannot assume that the average juror would be aware of the variables concerning identification and memory about which Dr. Loftus was qualified to testify. [T]hus, considering the standard of Rule 702, supra,—whether the expert testimony will assist the jury in determining an issue before them—and the unusual facts in this case, we believe that Dr. Loftus' offered evidence was a proper subject for expert testimony and should have been admitted. [T]here were a number of substantive issues of ultimate fact on which the expert's testimony would have been of significant assistance. Accordingly, we hold that the order precluding the testimony was legally incorrect and was unsupported by the record. It was, therefore, an abuse of discretion.

In reaching this conclusion, we do not intend to "open the gates" to a flood of expert evidence on the subject. We reach the conclusion that Dr. Loftus should have been permitted to testify on the peculiar facts of this case and have no quarrel with the result reached in the vast majority of cases which we have cited above. The rule in Arizona will continue to be that in the usual case we will support the trial court's discretionary ruling on admissibility of expert testimony on eyewitness identification. Nor do we invite opinion testimony in even the most extraordinary case on the likelihood that a particular witness is correct or mistaken in identification or that eyewitness identification in general has a certain percentage of accuracy or inaccuracy.

[T]he judgment below is reversed and the case remanded for a new trial.

■ HAYS, JUSTICE, concurring in part and dissenting in part.

I cannot agree with the majority's position that the trial court abused its discretion in excluding the testimony of an expert witness on eyewitness identification. With a view to preserving the integrity of the jury as finders of fact, I dissent in part.

[M]y concern here goes beyond the borders of this case. Once we have opened the door to this sort of impeaching testimony, what is to prevent experts from attacking any real or supposed deficiency in every other mental faculty? The peculiar risk of expert testimony with its scientific aura of trustworthiness and the possibility of undue prejudice should be respected. I have great reluctance to permit academia to take over the fact-finding function of the jury. Although clothed in other guise, that will be the practical effect. With little to distinguish this case from the general rule against admitting expert testimony on eyewitness identification, we are left with no guidelines to decide the deluge of similar issues which are sure to result.

––––––––––

NOTES

1. Common Experience. It was the position of the trial court in *Chapple* that the subject of eyewitness identification is within the "common experience"—that is, it is not "beyond the ken"—of the jury and therefore not a proper subject for expert testimony about empirical research. However, a survey of a random sample of jury-eligible persons in one jurisdiction described the methodology of several published eyewitness identification studies and asked the prospective jurors to estimate the percentage of accurate identifications that were made in the studies described. For one study, in which the actual percent of correct identification was 12.5, the prospective jurors estimated the accuracy rate at 70.6 percent. For another study, in which the actual accuracy rate was 31.3 percent, the prospective jurors estimated that 68.9 percent of the subjects made an accurate identification. According to the authors, "the present data refute the claim that expert psychological testimony on eyewitness identifications would not tell the jury members anything they do not already know. [The] data indicate that the testimony of an expert on these matters would not invade the province of the jury." Brigham and Bothwell, The Ability of Prospective Jurors to Estimate the Accuracy of Eyewitness Identification, 7 Law and Human Behavior 19, 29 (1983).

2. Widespread Consensus. Kassin, Tubb, Hosch, and Memon, On the "General Acceptance" of Eyewitness Testimony Research: A New Survey of the Experts, 56 American Psychologist 4–5 (2001) surveyed a "blue-ribbon" sample of 64 psychological experts on the topic of eyewitness testimony. They summarized their conclusions as follows:

> By an agreement rate of at least 80%, there was a strong consensus that the following phenomena are sufficiently reliable to present in court: the wording of questions, lineup instructions, confidence malleability, mug-shot-induced bias, postevent information, child witness suggestibility, alcohol intoxication, the cross-race bias, weapon focus, the accuracy-confidence correlation, the forgetting curve, exposure time, presentation format, and unconscious transference. Id at 405.

3. The Whole Truth. At a conference on eyewitness identification, Professor Loftus described an expert testimony issue that she "felt a little uneasy about": "What if the psychologist [testifying for the defense] is quite sure that the prosecuting attorney doesn't know enough about the research to raise damaging questions? Should the psychologist mention the one or two studies whose results contradict the gist of numerous other studies? Should she mention how the length of time since the crime can affect memory, but leave out that the length of time with the assailant is also a factor? The current ethical standards that govern psychologists, such as the [American Psychological Association's] Ethical Principals of Psychologists, offer little guidance in defining the degree of advocacy to be taken in court." Cunningham, Scientific Expert Witnesses Cross-Examine Own Value, 14 American Psychological Association Monitor 6 (1983).

WEATHERRED v. STATE

Court of Appeals of Texas, Beaumont, 1998.
963 S.W.2d 115.

■ WALKER, CHIEF JUSTICE.

A jury convicted appellant of Capital Murder. [Appellant] complains of the trial court's refusal to allow appellant to call Dr. Kenneth Deffenbacher as an expert witness on the issue of photo bias and eyewitness misidentification.

[T]he State contends that appellant failed to carry his burden to show that the testimony was admissible by failing to show that the testimony was reliable and that it was relevant. The leading Texas cases on the issue at present are Kelly v. State, *824 S.W.2d 568 (Tex.Crim.App.1992)*, which was available at the time of the trial of the instant case, and Jordan v. State, *928 S.W.2d 550 (Tex.Crim.App.1996)*, which was not available. Both cases discuss, and rely heavily upon, the United States Supreme Court case of Daubert v. Merrell Dow Pharmaceuticals, Inc., *509 U.S. 579, 113 S.Ct. 2786, 125 L.Ed.2d 469 (1993)*.

We [present] pertinent portions of the testimony of Dr. Deffenbacher as it appears in the record:

[Q]. Are there specific variables that can, at least according to your research, alter or vary the reliability of eyewitness identification?

A. Yes.

[Q]. What do these variables do or what effect do they have upon the credibility of eyewitness identification?

A. [Y]ou [h]ave to be concerned about the fidelity or faithfulness of human memory. That's the most important factor. But one thing—well, one of the variables I mentioned is forgetting. We all have common sense intuitions about forgetting and these are approximately true. The strength of a trace or a representation in our brain of whatever circumstances we have been exposed to rarely gets stronger over time and it ordinarily over time and circumstances gets weaker.

[I]f you ask most laypersons, and studies have done this, they will agree that memory gets worse over time, memory traces get weaker. What is not always—in fact, frequently isn't clear to the layperson is just how fast they get weaker over time. And that is where cognitive psychologists with the aid of mathematics and a lot of research on live human subjects are able to provide some more specificity as to how strong a memory representation might be in hours, days, weeks after a person's been exposed to a situation.

[Q]. Okay. And I believe you also, when you were talking to me, mentioned something about the relationship of eyewitness confidence to eyewitness accuracy?

A. Yes. This was a somewhat surprising finding. I don't think I was the first to find it, but there was one previous finding out there. The finding I am referring to is a somewhat counter-intuitive one. We all have the common sense intuition that the more confident that somebody appears to be, the more likely they are accurate in what they are representing to us. The less confident they appear to be, the less accurate they are.

That had been my assumption prior to conducting a study that was published in 1977. And it isn't—this particular finding is not one we set out to find, but we had the data. We not only asked people are—is—are each of these people in these photographs or in this live line-up, are they the person that you saw in a particular situation or doing a particular thing. And we also asked them on a five-point rating scale how confident are you when they made their decision, yes or no. And we decided we had this information so we would just check to see how closely the ratings, their own ratings of how confident they felt, how well those related or correlated with their accuracy.

And we were somewhat startled to find out in several different calculations we did in this series of studies that the relationship was virtually zero, that is, given the one piece of information confidence, the subjective ratings that they made of their confidence, an observer could not use that information to predict at all the actual accuracy. In other words, a highly confident person could just as easily be inaccurate. A low confidence, a person who did not feel very confident could just as likely be making the correct decision in each case.

[Q]. One other area that we have touched on just briefly a few minutes ago and that is a variable that you have labeled, called photo bias; is that correct?

A. Yes.

Q. And, in your opinion, having reviewed this testimony and seen the pictures and so forth that have been admitted into evidence, is this a variable that you feel would be significant in this particular case?

A. Yes.

Q. [W]ould you tell the Judge just a little short summary or synopsis of what photo biases is as you view it or as you use it in connection with your research?

A. Well, this is the situation where an eyewitness confronts some kind of situation that involves them encountering a stranger and sometime later prior to them viewing any sort of [live] line-up or photo line-up, they are exposed to one or more photographs that also include the presence of an image of a person who later turns out to be a suspect and at that time or at those times, they don't make a positive identification, but later at a line-up they do make a positive identification of the suspect who turns out to have been in one or more previous photo viewings. Sometimes these can be photo spreads and/or they may be a picture somebody saw in the paper, on TV or whatever. But these represent additional encounterings of an image of a person in different circumstances than the presumably original circumstances.

[Q]. The principles that we have been discussing the last 15 or 20 minutes and the findings that have resulted from your scientific studies and review of other scientific data, do you feel that they apply to the specific facts of this case?

A. Yes.

Q. Would you tell us how they apply to the facts of this case?

A. Taking each of those three factors I mentioned?

Q. Yes.

A. Well, starting with the forgetting of a stranger's face, as I have been given to understand the facts in this case, the time between the ultimate memory test and that—and the original exposure to the incident or the circumstances of their encountering, of the witness encountering the stranger was, I understand, on the order of 12 to 13 weeks. And our studies and those of others show that if one has, let's say, a five to ten-second glimpse of a stranger, that on average, it depends on how distinctive the face is and there are some individual differences in how good—we don't understand how they exist, but there are some individual differences on how good people are at recognition memory of stranger faces.

[But] in general the degree of strength of a person's memory representation after around 90 days or three months could easily been down to maybe 30 percent accuracy.

Q.   There was [another] area you said applied in this specific case?

A.   Well, [o]ne was the operation of photo biasing of line-ups.

[Q].   How does it apply specifically to this case?

A.   Well, you have the circumstances of eyewitnesses getting a brief look at the face of a stranger or no look at the face of a stranger and then subsequently days or a few weeks later they are shown two different—well, two different sets of photographic images that both contain the image of the suspect. And then I believe in the case of one witness whose testimony I heard this morning that witness apparently was exposed to a newspaper photo as well which included the image also of the suspect.

So what we have here then are two or three subsequent encounters with, presumably under good viewing circumstances when you get to look at the photograph of the image or the suspect. So the question then becomes can an eyewitness base their identification only on the image of the face of the stranger they saw at the scene of the crime or is their memory based wholly or in part on the subsequent images they have seen.

And from what cognitive psychologists [know] about human memory, it especially—when the glimpse wasn't that long or the viewing circumstances weren't that good, the possibility of photo bias becomes stronger and there is no way for the individual involved or for any of us to know for certain how much the identification would be based on the subsequent images.

Q.   The third area, the third variable you mentioned a little earlier that you felt would apply to this case, I believe you called it eyewitness confidence to eyewitness accuracy?

A.   Yes.

Q.   And how would that variable apply to the specific facts of this case?

A.   Well, given, as I mentioned earlier, that it is common sense intuition that highly confident people ought to be accurate and less confident people are less likely to be accurate, the assumption of most laypersons including triers of fact would be that that is what is operating in the case of human [eyewitnesses].

[But] what tends to happen over time is as a person goes over their memory for an event, as they tell others about it, they get more confident, and sometimes more confident for reasons that have little to do with accuracy.

Meanwhile, the memory representation that is the only basis for an eyewitness' accuracy of report, that never gets stronger and generally over time and circumstances gets weaker. So what you have is individuals who are moderate to highly confident and that may increase over time for reasons unrelated to accuracy and you have accuracy going the other way. And in that way confidence, an eyewitness' confidence and their actual accuracy can kind of get unhinged or unhooked and that may explain why confidence is typically not all that highly related to actual accuracy.

[I]n addition to the above testimony, appellant included in his bill of exceptions articles taken from a variety of publications describing scientifically-conducted experiments and the results of said experiments; all related to the accuracy of eyewitness identification.

[T]he testimony of Dr. Deffenbacher taken together with the scientific articles lead us to conclude that appellant proved, by clear and convincing evidence, the reliability prong of Daubert and Kelly. [T]he trial court abused its discretion in refusing to admit said evidence before the jury. [T]he erroneous refusal to permit Dr. Deffenbacher's evidence, which would have called into question the accuracy of the State's only *direct,* as opposed to circumstantial, witnesses, in the light of the entire record before us, affected appellant's substantial rights to the extent that had the evidence in question been admitted, it could have had a substantial influence on the jury.

[T]he judgment of the trial court is reversed, and the cause remanded to said court for a new trial on the merits.

––––––––

NOTE

1. Information Necessary to Determine What Constitutes "Scientific Knowledge." In United States v. Kime, 99 F.3d 870 (8th Cir.1996), the defendants proffered Dr. Gary Wells as an expert witness on eyewitness identification. In the proffer, defense counsel submitted to the court Dr. Wells' vitae and two articles that Dr. Wells had written. The trial judge excluded the expert under *Daubert*, and the defendants appealed their conviction. The Eighth Circuit upheld the exclusion of the expert, commenting as follows:

While the articles admirably articulate Dr. Wells' theories and hypotheses regarding how to conduct a non-misleading pretrial lineup, they are utterly deficient in regard to determining whether his views constitute "scientific knowledge" within the meaning of *Daubert*. [T]heir reference to the research and/or studies upon which Dr. Wells' propositions and corollaries are based consist of nothing more than the name of the researcher followed by the date of the study (i.e. "Wells, 1978."). Whereas this shorthand may communicate volumes to those in the field of psychology, it says nothing whatsoever to the district judge attempting to assess the credibility of the research underlying Dr. Wells' opinions. We are left in a situation analogous to that of the Ninth Circuit in *United States v. Rincon*, 28 F.3d 921, 923–25 (9th Cir.) (affirming the district court's exclusion of proffered expert eyewitness identification testimony under *Daubert*), *cert. denied*, 513 U.S. 1029, 115 S.Ct. 605, 130 L.Ed.2d 516 (1994): "[W]hile the article identified the research on some of the topics, it did not discuss the research in sufficient detail that the district court could determine if the research was scientifically valid." *Id.* at 924.

STATE v. CROMEDY

Supreme Court of New Jersey, 1999.
158 N.J. 112, 727 A.2d 457.

■ COLEMAN, J.

On the night of August 28, 1992, D.S., a white female student then enrolled at Rutgers University in New Brunswick, was watching television in her basement apartment. While she was relaxing on the couch, an African-American male entered the brightly-lit apartment and [robbed and raped her]. D.S. immediately called the New Brunswick Police Department after the intruder left the apartment.

[T]hree days later, a composite sketch was drawn by an artist with her assistance. The following day at police headquarters, D.S. was shown many slides and photographs, including a photograph of defendant, in an unsuccessful attempt to identify her assailant.

On April 7, 1993, almost eight months after the crimes were committed, D.S. saw an African-American male across the street from her who she thought was her attacker. [D].S. ran home and telephoned the police, giving them a description of the man she had just seen. Defendant was picked up by the New Brunswick police and taken to headquarters almost immediately.

[B]ecause of the nature of the crimes, the races of the victim and defendant, and the inability of the victim to identify defendant from his photograph, and because defendant was not positively identified until almost eight months after the date of the offenses, defense counsel sought a cross-racial identification jury charge. [I]n support of that request, defendant cited the June 1992 *New Jersey Supreme Court Task Force on Minority Concerns Final Report*, 131 *N.J.L.J.* 1145 (1992) (Task Force Report). The trial court denied the request.

[A] cross-racial identification occurs when an eyewitness is asked to identify a person of another race. The reliability of such an identification, though discussed in many cases throughout the country, is an issue of first impression in New Jersey. Because defendant requested a cross-racial identification jury charge, he bore the burden of showing that a reliable basis existed to support the requested charge. Defendant relied on common knowledge, the Task Force Report, and judicial notice to support his request. Rather than calling an expert to testify regarding the factors that may make some cross-racial eyewitness identifications unreliable, defendant maintained that an expert would not aid the jury. In this context, we must decide whether a cross-racial jury instruction should be required where scientific evidence demonstrating the need for a specific instruction has not been presented.

For more than forty years, empirical studies concerning the psychological factors affecting eyewitness cross-racial or cross-ethnic identifications have appeared with increasing frequency in professional literature of the behavioral and social sciences. One study finds that jurors tend to place great weight on eyewitness identifications, often ignoring other exculpatory evidence. *See* R.C.L. Lindsay et al., *Can People Detect Eyewitness-Identification Accuracy Within and Across Situations?*, 66 *J. Applied Psychol.* 79, 79–89 (1981). Others have concluded that eyewitnesses are superior at identifying persons of their own race and have difficulty identifying members of another race. *See generally* Gary L. Wells & Elizabeth F. Loftus, *Eyewitness Testimony: Psychological Perspectives* 1 (1984). See also Sheri Lynn Johnson, Cross-Racial Identification Errors in Criminal Cases, 69 Cornell L. Rev. 934 (1984). This phenomenon has been dubbed the "own-race" effect or "own-race" bias. Its corollary is that eyewitnesses experience a "cross-racial impairment" when identifying members of another race. Studies have consistently shown that the "own-race effect" is "strongest when white witnesses attempt to recognize black subjects." [People v.] McDonald, 690 P.*2d at 720.*

Although researchers generally agree that some eyewitnesses exhibit an own-race bias, they disagree about the degree to which own-race bias affects identification. In one study, African-American and white "customers" browsed in a convenience store for a few minutes and then went to the register to pay. Researchers asked the convenience store clerks to identify the "customers" from a photo array. The white clerks were able to identify 53.2% of the white customers but only 40.4% of the African-American subjects. Platz & Hosch, [Cross-Racial/Ethnic Eyewitness Identification: A Field Study], 18 *J. Applied Soc. Psychol.* at 977–78. The overall accuracy rate for all participants was only 44.2%. Similar studies have found that own-race bias exists to a lesser degree. *See* John C. Brigham et al., *Accuracy of Eyewitness Identifications in a Field Setting*, 42 *J. Personality & Soc. Psychol.* 673, 681 (1982) (finding white clerks misidentified white "customers" 45% of the time and African-American "customers" 50% of the time). A snap-shot of the literature reveals that although many scientists agree that witnesses are better at identifying suspects of their own race, they cannot agree on the extent to which cross-racial impairment affects identification.

[M]any studies on cross-racial impairment involve subjects observing photographs for a few seconds. [T]here is disagreement over whether the results of some of the tests can be generalized to real-world situations in which a victim or witness confronts an assailant face-to-face and experiences the full range of emotions that accompany such a traumatic event.

The debate among researchers did not prevent the Supreme Court of the United States, in the famous school desegregation case of Brown v. Board of Education of Topeka, *347* U.S. *483, 494 n. 11, 74* S.Ct. *686, 692 n. 11, 98* L.Ed. *873 (1954),* from using behavioral and social sciences to support legal conclusions without requiring that the methodology employed by those scientists have general acceptance in the scientific community. The ultimate holding in Brown that segregation is harmful "was not only a nomological statement but a sociological observation as well." Paul L. Rosen, *The Supreme Court and Social Science* ix (1972). The Court's finding that segregation was harmful "was not based simply on [intuition] or common-sense, ... [but] was attributed to ... seven social science studies." *Id.* at x. The extralegal facts contained in the social science studies conducted by Dr. Kenneth B. Clark and others were presented to the Court in the form of a "Brandeis Brief." That characterization is derived from a brief first submitted by Louis D. Brandeis (later Justice Brandeis) in the case of Muller v. Oregon, *208* U.S. *412, 419–20, 28* S.Ct. *324, 325–26, 52* L.Ed. *551 (1908).* Thus, Brown v. Board of Education is the prototypical example of an appellate court using modern social and behavioral sciences as legislative evidence to support its choice of a rule of law. John Monahan & Laurens Walker, Social Authority: Obtaining, Evaluating and Establishing Social Science in Law, *134* U. Pa. L.Rev. *477, 484 (1986).*

[T]he Court-appointed Task Force discussed and debated the issue of the need for a cross-racial and cross-ethnic identification jury instruction for more than five years. That Task Force was comprised of an appellate judge, trial judges, lawyers representing both the prosecution and defense, social scientists, and ordinary citizens. Professional consultants to the Task Force included Dr. Howard F. Taylor, Professor, Princeton University; Dr. William J. Chambliss, Professor, George Washington University; and Dr. Kenneth B. Clark, Distinguished Professor of Psychology Emeritus, City University of New York, who was prominently associated with the behavioral science studies submitted to the Supreme Court in Brown v. Board of Education.

Task Force sessions were conducted in much the same way as legislative committees conduct hearings on proposed legislation. The Task Force consulted a substantial body of professional literature in the behavioral and social sciences concerning the reliability of cross-racial identifications. Except for the view expressed by a county prosecutor, the Task Force was unanimously convinced that a problem exists respecting cross-racial identifications and that the Court should take corrective action. Ultimately, in 1992 the Task Force submitted its final report to the Court in which it recommended, among other things, that the Court develop a special jury charge regarding the unreliability of cross-racial identifications.

The Court referred that recommendation to the Criminal Practice Committee. The Criminal Practice Committee reviewed the recommendation and created a subcommittee to draft a cross-racial identification charge for consideration by the full Committee. The subcommittee drafted and submitted to the Criminal Practice Committee the following proposed charge:

> You know that the identifying witness is of a different race than the defendant. When a witness, who is a member of one race, identifies a defendant, who is a member of another race, we say that there has been a cross-racial identification. You may consider, if you think it is appropriate to do so, whether the cross-racial nature of the identification has affected the accuracy of the witness' [sic] original perception and/or the accuracy of the subsequent identification(s).

The Criminal Practice Committee, however, decided against recommending a charge to the Court. Development of a cross-racial charge was deemed to be premature because the issue of admissibility of evidence to support the charge had not been decided by case law. Thereafter, the Committee on Minority Concerns submitted to the Model Criminal Jury Charge Committee for its consideration a revised model jury charge on identification that included cross-racial eyewitness identification as a factor to be considered by the jury. As revised, the proposed cross-racial factor reads: "The fact that the witness is not of the same race as the perpetrator and/or defendant and whether that fact might have had an impact on the witness' [sic] ability to make an accurate identification." The Model Criminal Jury Charge Committee is withholding further consideration of a cross-racial identification charge pending the Court's decision in the present case.

[C]onsistent with [t]he Task Force Report and our review of the professional literature of the behavioral and social sciences, we hold that a cross-racial identification, as a subset of eyewitness identification, requires a special jury instruction in an appropriate case.

[W]e embrace the California rule requiring a cross-racial identification charge under the circumstances of this case despite some differences of opinion among the researchers. Notwithstanding those differences, there is an impressive consistency in results showing that problems exist with cross-racial eyewitness identification. McDonald, *208* Cal.Rptr. *236, 690 P.2d at 718.* We conclude that the empirical data encapsulate much of the ordinary human experience and provide an appropriate frame of reference for requiring a cross-racial identification jury instruction.

[A]t the same time, we recognize that unrestricted use of cross-racial identification instructions could be counter-productive. Consequently, care must be taken to insulate criminal trials from base appeals to racial prejudice. An appropriate jury instruction should carefully delineate the context in which the jury is permitted to consider racial differences. The simple fact pattern of a white victim of a violent crime at the hands of a black assailant would not automatically give rise to the need for a cross-racial identification charge. More is required.

A cross-racial instruction should be given only when, as in the present case, identification is a critical issue in the case, and an eyewitness's cross-

racial identification is not corroborated by other evidence giving it independent reliability. Here, the eyewitness identification was critical; yet it was
not corroborated by any forensic evidence or other eyewitness account. The
circumstances of the case raise some doubt concerning the reliability of the
victim's identification in that no positive identification was made for nearly
eight months despite attempts within the first five days following the
commission of the offenses. Under those circumstances, turning over to the
jury the vital question of the reliability of that identification without
acquainting the jury with the potential risks associated with such identifications could have affected the jurors' ability to evaluate the reliability of
the identification. We conclude, therefore, that it was reversible error not
to have given an instruction that informed the jury about the possible
significance of the cross-racial identification factor, a factor the jury can
observe in many cases with its own eyes, in determining the critical issue—
the accuracy of the identification.

For the sake of clarity, we repeat that the purpose of a cross-racial
instruction is to alert the jury through a cautionary instruction that it
should pay close attention to a possible influence of race. Because of the
"widely held commonsense view that members of one race have greater
difficulty in accurately identifying members of a different race," [United
States v.] Telfaire, *469* F.*2d at 559* (Bazelon, C.J., concurring) expert
testimony on this issue would not assist a jury, N.J.R.E. *702,* and for that
reason would be inadmissible. We request the Criminal Practice Committee
and the Model Jury Charge Committee to revise the current charge on
identification to include an appropriate statement on cross-racial eyewitness identification that is consistent with this opinion.

The judgment of the Appellate Division is reversed. The case is
remanded to the Law Division for a new trial.

————

NOTE

1. Historic Precedent. While the use of empirical data at trial to
question the accuracy of an eyewitness' identification has become frequent
only in recent years, the practice has a distinguished precedent. Shortly
after his debate with Stephen Douglas, Abraham Lincoln was asked by a
friend to assist in defending her son against the charge of having murdered
a man during a fight on the evening of August 29, 1857. According to F.
Hill, Lincoln the Lawyer, 232–233 (1906):

> [At trial] no very damaging testimony was elicited until a man by
> the name of Allen took the stand. This witness, however, swore that he
> actually saw the defendant strike the fatal blow with a slungshot [sic]
> or some such weapon; and Lincoln, pressing him closely, forced him to
> locate the hour of the assault as about eleven at night, and then
> demanded that he inform the jury how he had managed to see so
> clearly at that time of night. "By the moonlight," answered the witness
> promptly. "Well, was there light enough to see everything that hap-

pened?'' persisted the examiner. The witness responded that ''the moon was about in the same place that the sun would be at ten o'clock in the morning and was almost full,'' and the moment the words were out of his mouth the cross-examiner confronted him with a calendar showing that the moon, which at its best was only slightly past its first quarter on August 29, had afforded practically no light at eleven o'clock and that it had absolutely set at seven minutes after midnight. This was the turning-point in the case, and from that moment Lincoln carried everything before him, securing an acquittal of the defendant after a powerful address to the jury.

STATE v. VIA

Supreme Court of Arizona, 1985.
146 Ariz. 108, 704 P.2d 238.

■ CAMERON, JUSTICE.

Defendant, William Dabney Via, Jr., was convicted by a jury of first degree murder. [D]efendant raises [an issue] on appeal:

> [W]as the testimony of an expert witness on eyewitness identification improperly limited?

[D]efendant presented the testimony of an authority on eyewitness identification, Dr. Elizabeth Loftus. She testified as to the variables affecting the accuracy of eyewitness identifications and to the empirical studies done in the field. The trial court, however, precluded her from testifying as to an informal test she had conducted. She performed the test at airports and on board a plane en route to Phoenix to testify. The test involved providing fifteen persons with a photograph of the live lineup and a description of defendant. Dr. Loftus would have testified that fourteen of those tested picked defendant as the person described to them.

Defendant maintains that the trial court's ruling violated our holding in State v. Chapple, 135 Ariz. 281, 660 P.2d 1208 (1983). [O]n the contrary, one of the factors we emphasized in *Chapple* was that:

> The testimony offered was carefully limited to an exposition of the factors affecting reliability, with experimental data supporting the witness' testimony and *no attempt was made to have the witness render opinions on the actual credibility or accuracy of the identification witnesses. Issues of ultimate fact may be the subject of expert testimony, but witnesses are not ''permitted as experts on how juries should decide cases.''* Ariz.R. of Evid. 704 comment.

Id. at 295, 660 P.2d at 1222 (emphasis added).

We have also examined the progeny of *Chapple* and have been unable to find a case mandating admissibility of the type of testimony proffered by defendant. Rather, these cases stand for the proposition that general testimony as to the variables affecting eyewitness identification is permissible, but within the discretion of the trial court.

FORENSIC PSYCHOLOGY (1981)

L. Haward.

Following complaints that indecent behaviour was taking place in a public convenience, two [British] police officers were given the duty of keeping a watch on the interior. To do this effectively, they secreted themselves in a narrow broom cupboard, standing upon a wooden box and peering through a zinc gauze screen partially obscured on the inside by old sacking. After many days of gross discomfort on shift duty in this cubicle, the officers observed two men acting in a manner they regarded as improper, and bursting out of the broom cupboard, arrested both "*in flagrante delicto*", and charged them with committing an act of gross indecency. One of the men, a local citizen of some substance and considerable reputation in the town, denied the charge vehemently and said the policemen were mistaken in what they thought they had seen. The barrister called in for the defense asked for a psychological opinion on the probability that the two policemen could be mistaken, and if so, how. Using volunteer actors, photographs were taken on the site, the positions of the two men having been described in detail in the police statements. The toilet was a subterranean one whose only illumination during daytime was from the daylight which filtered through the glass grill set in the pavement above, lighting conditions at the time and date in question were again obtained from the Meteorological Office. An experiment was set up using students who saw the pictures projected in a range of lighting conditions approximating to those obtaining at the time, and under three levels of expectancy of "set". The police statements said that everyone entering the convenience was viewed with suspicion; that is, the police observers had a high degree of expectancy that they would see an offense committed. Moreover, they had a high degree of desire to make an arrest and so gain release from their own uncomfortable confinement in the cupboard. The psychological conditions were thus favourable to perceptual error. So too were the physical factors, for the lighting was extremely poor, being eight times darker than the dull day outside, the men were more than ten feet from the policemen, at an angle to them and therefore partly obscured, and the police admitted contact was no more than "a few seconds" before they burst from their hiding place. Reproducing these factors experimentally provided conditions in which one picture in every eight was "seen" as indicating an indecent act. A report was prepared detailing the various factors involved, listing relevant studies showing perceptual error from the literature and experimental psychology, and describing the present experimental work. Rather than put this evidence in court directly, the counsel used it as a basis for invalidating the police evidence and so obtained an acquittal.

————

NEWSOME v. McCABE

United States Court of Appeals, Seventh Circuit, 2003.
319 F.3d 301.

■ EASTERBROOK, CIRCUIT JUDGE.

Fifteen years after his conviction for killing Edward Cohen, James Newsome was pardoned on the ground of innocence: fingerprints and other information strongly imply that Dennis Emerson committed the crime. Newsome filed this suit under 42 U.S.C. § 1983, seeking damages from police officers who, he contends, induced three witnesses to identify him as the killer. Two years ago we held that officers McCabe and McNally are not entitled to qualified immunity if, as Newsome alleges, they not only induced witnesses to accuse him falsely but also concealed their improper activities. *Newsome v. McCabe,* 256 F.3d 747, rehearing denied, 260 F.3d 824 (7th Cir.2001). On remand the City of Chicago, which has a financial stake in the outcome as a potential indemnitor of the officers, intervened to protect its interests. A jury found that, by concealing evidence favorable to the defense, McCabe and McNally had violated Newsome's constitutional right to due process of law and awarded him $15 million in damages, to which the district judge (after denying all post-trial motions) added some $850,000 in attorneys' fees and costs. In this appeal Chicago [c]ontests some of the district judge's evidentiary decisions at trial.

[A]nthony Rounds, Josie Nash, and John Williams supplied the principal evidence at Newsome's criminal trial. Rounds and Nash, who had been in Cohen's grocery store when the murder occurred, positively identified Newsome as the killer; Williams, who had been outside, testified that he saw Newsome flee.

[M]ost persons have difficulty remembering or describing the features of strangers. A person who sees a criminal for only a brief time takes away a vague sense of appearance and behavior—and that sense may be focused by a sketch, photograph, showup, or lineup after the events. Sometimes the witness zeroes in on the correct person, sometimes not; there is an element of chance and an opportunity for manipulation. Once the witness decides that "X is it" the view may be unshakable. Psychological research has established that the witness's faith is equally strong whether or not the identification is correct. We described these findings in *Krist v. Eli Lilly & Co.,* 897 F.2d 293 (7th Cir.1990): "An important body of psychological research undermines the lay intuition that confident memories of salient experiences ... are accurate and do not fade with time unless a person's memory has some pathological impairment.... The basic problem about testimony from memory is that most of our recollections are not verifiable. The only warrant for them is our certitude, and certitude is not a reliable test of certainty.... [T]he mere fact that we remember something with great confidence is not a powerful warrant for thinking it true." 897 F.2d at 296–97 (citations to the scholarly literature omitted). See Elizabeth F. Loftus & James M. Doyle, *Eyewitness Testimony: Civil and Criminal* (3d ed.1997); Elizabeth F. Loftus, *Eyewitness Testimony* (1979; rev. ed.1996); Daniel L. Schacter, *The Seven Sins of Memory: How the Mind Forgets and Remembers* 112–37 (2001). Jurors, however, tend to think that witnesses' memories are reliable (because jurors are confident of their own), and this gap between the actual error rate and the jurors' heavy reliance on eyewitness testimony sets the stage for erroneous convictions when (as in Newsome's prosecution) everything depends on uncorroborated eyewitness testimony by people who do not know the accused.

[B]ecause recollection is suggestive, it was important in this civil case to explore the question whether the testimony of Rounds, Nash, and Williams identifying Newsome at the criminal trial was attributable to deliberate manipulation or instead to chance. For if chance errors are to blame, and the witnesses would have identified Newsome no matter how the officers prompted them during the lineups, then defendants' conduct did not cause the wrongful conviction and an award of damages would be improper. To explore this issue Newsome presented the testimony of Gary Wells, a professor of psychology who has performed experiments and written scholarly works in this field. See, e.g., Gary L. Wells & Elizabeth A. Olson, *Eyewitness Identification,* 54 Ann. Rev. Psych. 277 (2003); Gary L. Wells, *Eyewitness Identification: A System Handbook* (1988). Wells conducted an experiment to determine the likelihood that three persons who saw Emerson nonetheless would identify Newsome. He showed two panels of subjects different pictures of Emerson for 15 seconds then, after some time had passed, showed them pictures of the men in the lineup and asked them to choose the one they had seen in the initial photograph. Of 50 members on the first panel, none selected Newsome's photo; of 500 members on the second panel (which was shown a different photo of Emerson), 15 chose Newsome's photo. Performing a chi-square test, Wells calculated that the probability of all three eyewitnesses independently picking Newsome out of a lineup by chance error was substantially less than one in 1,000, implying that the officers must have manipulated their identifications.

Chicago asked the district judge to exclude Wells' testimony under Fed.R.Evid. 702, which as amended in 2000 codifies (with some variation) the holding of *Daubert v. Merrell Dow Pharmaceuticals, Inc.,* 509 U.S. 579, 113 S.Ct. 2786, 125 L.Ed.2d 469 (1993). The district judge concluded that Wells is an expert on the subject of identification, that his testimony was based on sufficient data, that his methods were reliable by the standards of the field, and that he applied these methods reliably to the facts of Newsome's case. Experiments of the kind that Wells performed are the norm in this branch of science and have met the standard for scholarly publication and acceptance. There were of course potential problems. For example, Wells assumed that Emerson is the killer, so that the witnesses saw him; if anyone other than Emerson committed the murder, the test is invalid. Wells was candid about this vital assumption, which was open to probing and argument by the defendants. Wells also assumed that two-dimensional images (pictures) yield the same effects on memory as three-dimensional views (live action in the victim's grocery store; lineups in the police station; identifications in open court). This may or may not hold, but the claim of equivalence was open to exploration at trial, and it is hard to see what else Wells could have done. Even if he could have conscripted Emerson and the lineup participants for an experiment, time has so altered their appearance since the events of October 1979 that the results would have been unreliable. Chicago does not contend that there was a better way to find out whether Rounds, Nash, and Williams would have identified Newsome without the coaching. Instead it insists that Wells' testimony was irrelevant because he did not determine *how* the witnesses had been induced to believe that they saw Newsome commit the murder. Yet testimony need not prove everything in order to be useful. As we have said, the jury had to consider the possibility that unhappy chance rather than malfeasance led to the mistaken conviction. Wells provided information valuable in this endeavor. Appellate review of the district judge's decision is deferential, *General Electric Co. v. Joiner,* 522 U.S. 136, 118 S.Ct. 512, 139 L.Ed.2d 508 (1997), and there was no abuse here; indeed, we would have acted precisely as did the district judge.

————

Eyewitness Identification Procedures: Recommendations for Lineups and Photospreads*

Gary Wells, Mark Small, Steven Penrod, Roy Malpass, Solomon Fulero, and C. Brimacombe
22 Law and Human Behavior 603 (1998).

The evidence [from psychological research] makes a strong case that some lineup identification procedures lead to increased risk of false identification or inflated confidence. These procedures are under the control of the criminal justice system. Hence, any role of these procedures in contributing to false identification or false confidence could be eliminated by controlling the procedures in critical ways. In the present section, we describe four simple rules of procedure that follow from the scientific literature that we argue could largely relieve the criminal justice system of its role in contributing to eyewitness identification problems.

[R]ule 1. Who Conducts the Lineup

The person who conducts the lineup or photospread should not be aware of which member of the lineup or photospread is the suspect.

[R]ule 2. Instructions on Viewing

Eyewitnesses should be told explicitly that the person in question might not be in the lineup or photospread and therefore should not feel that they must make an identification. They should also be told that the person

* With kind permission of Springer Science and Business Media.

administering the lineup does not know which person is the suspect in the case.

[R]ule 3. Structure of Lineup or Photospread

The suspect should not stand out in the lineup or photospread as being different from the distractors based on the eyewitness's previous description of the culprit or based on other factors that would draw extra attention to the suspect.

[R]ule 4. Obtaining Confidence Statements

A clear statement should be taken from the eyewitness at the time of the identification and prior to any feedback as to his or her confidence that the identified person is the actual culprit.

[A] main reason why we are proposing only these four rules at this time is [b]ecause we think that proposing too many rules would produce resistance by police and legal policy makers and perhaps dilute the import of the four primary rules. There are, however, two potential recommendations that are particularly important, [n]amely a recommendation that lineups be sequential rather than simultaneous and a recommendation that lineups be videotaped. We recognize that there are many eyewitness scholars who believe that the sequential idea and the videotaping idea should be among the rules recommended in this article.

[T]he extensive scientific literature in eyewitness identification has led to a good understanding of the fact that eyewitness identification errors can arise out of the procedures that are used for obtaining those identifications. The psychological processes involved in eyewitness identifications from lineups and photospreads, especially the relative judgment process, require that eyewitnesses be warned that the actual culprit might not be in the lineup and that all members of the lineup fit the verbal description that the eyewitness had given of the perpetrator. The dynamic interaction between the person administering the lineup and the eyewitness, in conjunction with what we know about interpersonal influence, necessitates that the administering agent not know which person in the lineup is the suspect. In addition, the primary role played by eyewitness confidence in the legal system's assessment of the credibility of the identification, in conjunction with clear empirical evidence of confidence malleability, demands that confidence statements be obtained at the time of the identification (before other variables begin to exert their influence on the eyewitness). The adoption of these four rules into lineup practices can remove a great deal of the contribution that the justice system itself contributes to the problem of mistaken identification.

―――――

EYEWITNESS EVIDENCE: A GUIDE FOR LAW ENFORCEMENT

National Institute of Justice, 1999.

In an effort to bring together the perspectives of law enforcement, lawyers, and researchers, the National Institute of Justice convened the

Technical Working Group for Eyewitness Evidence. The purpose of this group was to recommend uniform practices for the collection and preservation of eyewitness evidence. [T]his *Guide* is supported by social science research. During the past 20 years, research psychologists have produced a substantial body of findings regarding eyewitness evidence. These findings offer the legal system a valuable body of empirical knowledge in the area of eyewitness evidence. This *Guide* makes use of psychological findings, either by including them in the procedures themselves or by using them to point the way to the design and development of further improvements in procedures and practices for possible inclusion in future amendments or revision to this document.

[A]dvances in social science and technology will, over time, affect procedures used to gather and preserve eyewitness evidence. The following examples illustrate areas of potential change. Scientific research indicates that identification procedures such as lineups and photo arrays produce more reliable evidence when the individual lineup members or photographs are shown to the witness sequentially—one at a time—rather than simultaneously. Although some police agencies currently use sequential methods of presentation, there is not a consensus on any particular method or methods of sequential presentation that can be recommended as a *preferred* procedure; although sequential procedures are included in the *Guide*, it does not indicate a preference for sequential procedures.

Similarly, investigators' unintentional cues (e.g., body language, tone of voice) may negatively impact the reliability of eyewitness evidence. Psychology researchers have noted that such influences could be avoided if "blind" identification procedures were employed (i.e., procedures conducted by investigators who do not know the identity of the actual suspect). However, blind procedures, which are used in science to prevent inadvertent contamination of research results, may be impractical for some jurisdictions to implement. Blind procedures are not included in the *Guide* but are identified as a direction for future exploration and field testing. In the interim, an enhanced awareness on the part of investigators of the subtle impact they may have on witnesses will result in more professional identification procedures.

Procedures for Eyewitness Identification of Suspects

A. Composing Lineups

Live Lineup: In composing a live lineup, the investigator should:

1. Include only one suspect in each identification procedure.

2. Select fillers who generally fit the witness' description of the perpetrator. When there is a limited/inadequate description of the perpetrator provided by the witness, or when the description of the perpetrator differs significantly from the appearance of the suspect, fillers should resemble the suspect in significant features.

3. Consider placing suspects in different positions in each lineup, both across cases and with multiple witnesses in the same case. Position the

suspect randomly unless, where local practice allows, the suspect or the suspect's attorney requests a particular position.

4. Include a *minimum* of four fillers (nonsuspects) per identification procedure.

5. When showing a new suspect, avoid reusing fillers in lineups shown to the same witness.

6. Consider that complete uniformity of features is not required. Avoid using fillers who so closely resemble the suspect that a person familiar with the suspect might find it difficult to distinguish the suspect from the fillers.

7. Create a consistent appearance between the suspect and fillers with respect to any unique or unusual feature (e.g., scars, tattoos) used to describe the perpetrator by artificially adding or concealing that feature.

B.   Instructing the Witness Prior to Viewing a Lineup

Live Lineup: Prior to presenting a live lineup, the investigator should:

1. Instruct the witness that he/she will be asked to view a group of individuals.

2. Instruct the witness that it is just as important to clear innocent persons from suspicion as to identify guilty parties.

3. Instruct the witness that individuals present in the lineup may not appear exactly as they did on the date of the incident because features such as head and facial hair are subject to change.

4. Instruct the witness that the person who committed the crime may or may not be present in the group of individuals.

5. Assure the witness that regardless of whether an identification is made, the police will continue to investigate the incident.

6. Instruct the witness that the procedure requires the investigator to ask the witness to state, in his/her own words, how certain he/she is of any identification.

C.   Conducting the Identification Procedure

Live Lineup: When presenting a sequential live lineup, the lineup administrator/investigator should:

1. Provide viewing instructions to the witness as outlined in subsection B, "Instructing the Witness Prior to Viewing a Lineup."

2. Provide the following *additional* viewing instructions to the witness:

   a.   Individuals will be viewed *one at a time*.

   b.   The individuals will be presented in random order.

   c.   Take as much time as needed in making a decision about each individual before moving to the next one.

   d.   If the person who committed the crime is present, identify him/her.

e. All individuals will be presented, even if an identification is made; *or* the procedure will be stopped at the point of an identification (consistent with jurisdictional/departmental procedures).

3. Begin with all lineup participants out of the view of the witness.

4. Instruct all those present at the lineup not to suggest in any way the position or identity of the suspect in the lineup.

5. Present each individual to the witness separately, in a previously determined order, removing those previously shown.

6. Ensure that any identification actions (e.g., speaking, moving) are performed by all members of the lineup.

7. Avoid saying anything to the witness that may influence the witness' selection.

8. If an identification is made, avoid reporting to the witness any information regarding the individual he/she has selected prior to obtaining the witness' statement of certainty.

9. Record any identification results and witness' statement of certainty.

[F]urther Reading: Wells, Small, Penrod, Malpass, Fulero, and Brimacombe, Eyewitness Identification Procedures: Recommendations for Lineups and Photospreads, 22 Law and Human Behavior 603 (1998).

———

Report of the Task Force on Eyewitness Evidence

Office of the Suffolk County District Attorney and the Boston Police Commissioner, 2004.

On March 8, 2004, the Suffolk County District Attorney, Daniel F. Conley and the Boston Police Commissioner, Kathleen M. O'Toole, announced the formation of a Task Force on Eyewitness Evidence. The Task Force was charged with reviewing the investigative process for cases in which eyewitness identification was a significant issue, and recommending any appropriate changes in the means and manner of investigation. The Task Force was born of the concern, as evidenced by a series of recently overturned convictions, that better practices in such cases would yield more reliable results and significantly reduce the potential for error.

The Task Force offers 25 separate recommendations. A number of these are, to our knowledge, without precedent in any major city police department and prosecutor's office. Taken together, these 25 recommendations represent a dramatic leap forward in the manner in which police and prosecutors investigate and prosecute cases and would place Boston and Suffolk County in the forefront in comprehensively addressing an issue of both local and national concern.

[I]dentification Procedures.

The Task Force recommends adoption of the identification protocols described in the Department of Justice's Eyewitness Evidence Guide [excerpted above]. Using the DOJ protocols is an important step forward for fair and reliable identification procedures, but the Task Force concluded that there were significant steps that go beyond the DOJ Guide that need to be taken to insure the highest standards for Boston. Scientific research strongly supports sequential identification procedures and blind administration procedures as the best tools available to combat misidentifications. Historically, law enforcement in this country has not used either sequential or blind administration procedures. Research conducted in the 1980s and 1990s built academic support among psychological scientists for these new procedures. Despite the best efforts of some of its members, the DOJ national working group that produced the DOJ Guide could not agree to recommend the two biggest changes: sequential and blind administration procedures. After reviewing the scientific evidence, the Task Force concluded that sequential and blind administration procedures should, in conjunction with the DOJ protocols, be used in Boston as the most effective way to reduce misidentifications.

The following list [i]ncludes each specific recommendation made by the Task Force.

1. Adopt in full the recommendations on eyewitness evidence set forth by the United States Department of Justice.

2. Use sequential presentation of photographs in photo lineups.

3. Use sequential presentation of persons in live lineups.

4. Blind administration of photo lineups, which requires that the photo lineup be shown by an investigator who has no knowledge of which photograph is the suspect's.

5. Blind administration of live lineups, which requires that the live lineup be administered by an investigator who does not know which person is the suspect.

6. Use a standard printed form which provides eyewitnesses essential instructions for viewing a photo lineup or a live lineup.

7. Require detailed documentation, by means of a separate report, of every identification procedure conducted by the Boston Police.

8. Adopt as policy that every photo lineup shall consist of 8 photographs (7 fillers and 1 suspect) and that every live lineup shall consist of 6 persons (5 fillers and 1 suspect).

9. Use a live lineup subsequent to a photographic array in certain cases where testing the witness' ability to make an in-person identification could be of significant evidentiary value.

10. Use booking photograph compilations ("mug books") of scores of people as a possible source of identification only when all other investigative leads have been exhausted.

[T]he Scientific Approach to Eyewitness Evidence

In studying eyewitness evidence, Professor [Gary] Wells [, a member of the Task Force] uses an analogy that assisted the Task Force in its analysis and recommendations. Professor Wells likens eyewitness evidence to physical trace evidence. Physical trace evidence, such as fingerprints, fibers or blood, can help determine the facts of a crime and the identity of the perpetrator. The observations of an eyewitness are items of trace evidence contained in the witness' memory. Like physical evidence, memory trace evidence can be contaminated, lost, destroyed or otherwise made to produce inaccurate results. Like physical trace evidence, the manner in which memory trace evidence is collected can have important consequences for the accuracy of the results. The Task Force concluded that a more scientific approach to collecting and analyzing eyewitness evidence should be the guiding principle for our recommendations.

SELECTED BIBLIOGRAPHY

A. Defendants

Anderson, Berkowitz, Donnerstein, Huesmann, Johnson, Linz, Malamuth, and Wartella, The Influence of Media Violence on Youth, 4 Psychological Science in the Public Interest 81 (2003).

D. Carson, Professionals and the Courts: A Handbook for Expert Witnesses (1990).

Chiu, The Cultural Defense: Beyond Exclusion, Assimilation, and Guilty Liberalism, 82 California Law Review 1053 (1994).

Coughlin, Excusing Women, 82 California Law Review 1 (1994).

Dixon and Dixon, Gender–Specific Clinical Syndromes and their Admissibility Under the Federal Rules of Evidence, 27 American Journal of Trial Advocacy 25 (2003).

Edens, Buffington–Vollum, Keilen, Roskamp, and Anthony, Predictions of Future Dangerousness in Capital Murder Trials: Is it Time to "Disinvent the Wheel?", 29 Law and Human Behavior 55 (2005).

Faigman, Struggling to Stop the Flood of Unreliable Expert Testimony, 76 Minnesota Law Review 877 (1992).

Faigman, The Battered Woman Syndrome and Self-Defense: A Legal and Empirical Dissent, 72 Virginia Law Review 619 (1986).

Faigman, Discerning Justice When Battered Women Kill, 39 Hastings Law Journal 207 (1987).

Faigman and Wright, The Battered Woman Syndrome in the Age of Science, 39 Arizona Law Review 67 (1997).

Falk, Novel Theories of Criminal Defense Based on the Toxicity of the Social Environment: Urban Psychosis, Television Intoxication, and Black Rage, 74 North Carolina Law Review 731 (1996).

Fiske, Bersoff, Borgida, Deaux, and Heilman, Social Scientific Research on Trial: The Use of Sex Stereotyping Research in *Price Waterhouse v. Hopkins,* 46 American Psychologist 1049 (1991).

Follingstad, Forensic Evaluations of Battered Women Defendants: Relevant Data to be Applied to Elements of Self-Defense, 5 Applied and Preventive Psychology 165 (1996).

Gatowski, Dobbin, Richardson, and Ginsburg, The Globalization of Behavioral Science Evidence About Battered Women: A Theory of Production and Diffusion, 15 Behavioral Sciences and the Law 285 (1997).

T. Grisso and R. Schwartz, Youth on Trial: A Developmental Perspective on Juvenile Justice (2000).

Heilbrun, DeMatteo, Marczyk, Finello, Smith, and Mack–Allen, Applying Principles of Forensic Mental Health Assessment to Capital Sentencing, 11 Widener Law Review 93 (2005).

K. Heilbrun, G. Marczyk, and D. Dematteo, Forensic Mental Health Assessment: A Casebook (2002).

Jayaraman, Rotten Social Background Revisited, 14 Capital Defense Journal 327 (2002).

Johnson, Cohen, Smailes, Kasen, and Brook, Television Viewing and Aggressive Behavior During Adolescence and Adulthood, 295 Science 2468 (2002).

Koch, O'Neill, Douglas, Empirical Limits for the Forensic Assessment of PTSD Litigants, 29 Law and Human Behavior 121 (2005).

Lam, Culture as Defense: Preventing Judicial Bias Against Asians and Pacific Islanders, 1 UCLA Asian American Pacific Islands Law Journal 49 (1993).

Levine, Negotiating the Boundaries of Crime and Culture: A Sociolegal Perspective on Cultural Defense Strategies, 28 Law and Social Inquiry 39 (2003).

Maguigan, Cultural Evidence and Male Violence: Are Feminist and Multiculturalist Reformers on a Collision Course in Criminal Courts?, 70 New York University Law Review 36 (1995).

G. Melton, J. Petrila, N. Poythress, and C. Slobogin, Psychological Evaluations for the Courts (2d ed. 1997).

Morse, Blame and Danger: An Essay on Preventive Detention, 76 Boston University Law Review 113 (1996).

Morse, Brain and Blame, 84 Georgetown Law Journal 527 (1996).

Morse, Excusing and the "New" Excuses, In Crime and Justice: An Annual Review of Research (M. Tonry, ed. 1997).

Morse, Deprivation and Desert, in From Social Justice to Criminal Justice: Poverty and the Administration of Criminal Law (W. Heffernan and J. Kleinig eds. 2000).

Morse, Rationality and Responsibility, 74 Southern California Law Review 251 (2000).

Note, The Cultural Defense in the Criminal Law, 99 Harvard Law Review 1293 (1986).

Note, A Place for Consideration of Culture in the American Criminal Justice System: Japanese Law and the *Kimura* case, 4 Journal of International Law and Practice 507 (1995).

Poythress and Slobogin, Insanity and Diminished Capacity, in Modern Scientific Evidence: The Law and Science of Expert Testimony 2d ed (D. L. Faigman, D. H. Kaye, M. J. Saks, and J. Sanders eds., 2002).

A. Renteln, The Cultural Defense (2004).

Saks and Kidd, Human Information Processing and Adjudication: Trial by Heuristics, 15 Law and Society Review 123 (1980).

Savage, Does Viewing Violent Media Really Cause Criminal Violence? A Methodological Review, 10 Aggression and Violent Behavior 99 (2004).

Schopp, Sturgis, and Sullivan, Battered Woman Syndrome, Expert Testimony, and the Distinction Between Justification and Excuse, 1994 University of Illinois Law Review 45 (1994).

Schuller and Cripps, Expert Evidence Pertaining to Battered Women: The Impact of Gender of Expert and Timing of Testimony, 22 Law and Human Behavior 17 (1998).

Schuller and Hastings, Trials of Battered Women Who Kill: The Impact of Alternative Forms of Expert Evidence, 20 Law and Human Behavior 167 (1996).

Schuller and Rzepa, Expert Testimony Pertaining to Battered Woman Syndrome: Its Impact on Jurors' Decisions, 26 Law and Human Behavior 655 (2002).

Scott, Reppucci and Woolard, Evaluating Adolescent Decision Making in Legal Contexts, 19 Law and Human Behavior 221 (1995).

D. Shuman, Psychiatric and Psychological Evidence (2d. 1995).

R. Shweder, Why Do Men Barbecue? Recipes for Cultural Psychology (2003).

Slobogin, A Jurisprudence of Dangerousness, 98 Northwestern University Law Review 1 (2003).

Slobogin, The Structure of Expertise in Criminal Cases, 34 Seton Hall Law Review 105 (2003).

Sing, Culture as Sameness: Toward a Synthetic View of Provocation and Culture in the Criminal Law, 108 Yale Law Journal 1845 (1999).

Veinsreideris, The Prospective Effects of Modifying Existing Law to Accommodate Preemptive Self-defense by Battered Women, 149 University of Pennsylvania Law Review 613 (2000).

Vuoso, Background, Responsibility, and Excuse, 96 Yale Law Journal 1661 (1987).

Wanderer and Connors, Culture and Crime: *Kargar* and the Existing Framework for a Cultural Defense, 47 Buffalo Law Review 829 (1999).

Wang, Battered Asian American Women: Community Responses from the Battered Women's Movement and the Asian American Community, 3 Asian Law Journal 151 (1996).

Widom, The Cycle of Violence, 244 Science 160 (1989).

Wilson, J. (1997). Moral Judgment: Does the Abuse Excuse Threaten Our Legal System?

B. Victims

Dobbin and Gatowski, The Social Production of Rape Trauma Syndrome as Science and as Evidence, in Science in Court (M. Freeman and H. Reece eds. 1998).

Frazier and Borgida, Rape Trauma Syndrome: A Review of Case Law and Psychological Research, 16 Law and Human Behavior 293 (1992).

Goodman, Taub, Jones, England, Port, Rudy, and Prado, Testifying in Criminal Court: Emotional Effects on Child Sexual Assault Victims, 57 Monographs of the Society for Research in Child Development 1 (1992).

Orenstein, No Bad Men! A Feminist Analysis of Character Evidence in Rape Trials, 49 Hastings Law Journal 663 (1998).

Posttraumatic Stress Disorder: Acute and Long-Term Responses to Trauma and Disaster (C. Fullerton and R. Ursano eds. 1997).

Posttraumatic Stress Disorder in Litigation: Guidelines for Forensic Assessment (R. Simon, ed. 1995).

Stefan, The Protection Racket: Rape Trauma Syndrome, Psychiatric Labeling, and the Law, 88 Northwestern University Law Review 1271 (1994).

C. Witnesses

Abshire and Bornstein, Juror Sensitivity to the Cross–Race Effect, 27 Law and Human Behavior 471 (2003).

Cutler and Penrod, Mistaken Identification: The Eyewitness, Psychology, and the Law (1995).

Deffenbacher, Bornstein, Penrod and McGorty, A Meta–Analytic Review of the Effects of High Stress on Eyewitness Memory, 28 Law and Human Behavior 687 (2004).

Devenport and Cutler, Impact of Defense–Only and Opposing Eyewitness Experts on Juror Judgments, 28 Law and Human Behavior 569 (2004).

Egeth, What Do We *Not* Know About Eyewitness Identification?, 48 American Psychologist 577 (1993).

Gerrie, Garry, and Loftus, False Memories, In Psychology and Law: An Empirical Perspective (N. Brewer and K. Williams, eds. 2005).

Goodman, Bottoms, Rudy, Davis, Schwartz–Kenney, Effects of Past Abuse Experiences on Children's Eyewitness Memory, 25 Law and Human Behavior 269 (2001).

Gonzalez, Davis, and Ellsworth, Who Should Stand Next to the Suspect? Problems in the Assessment of Lineup Fairness, 80 Journal of Applied Psychology 525 (1995).

E. Loftus, Eyewitness Testimony (1979; reissued 1996).

Loftus, Psychologists in the Eyewitness World, 48 American Psychologist 550 (1993).

Loftus, Experimental Psychologist as Advocate or Impartial Educator, 10 Law and Human Behavior 63 (1986).

McCloskey and Egeth, Eyewitness Identification: What Can a Psychologist Tell a Jury?, 38 American Psychologist 550 (1983).

Meissner and Brigham, Thirty Years of Investigating the Own—Race Bias in Memory for Faces, 7 Psychology, Public Policy, and Law 3 (2001).

Psychological Issues in Eyewitness Identification (S. Sporer, R. Malpass, and G. Koehnken eds. 1996).

D. Schacter, The Seven Sins of Memory: How the Mind Forgets and Remembers (2001).

Sporer, Penrod, Read, and Cutler, Choosing, Confidence, and Accuracy: A Meta-Analysis of the Confidence—Accuracy Relation in Eyewitness Identification Studies, 118 Psychological Bulletin 315 (1995).

Steblay, Dysart, Fulero, and Lindsay, Eyewitness Accuracy Rates in Police Showup and Lineup Presentations: A Meta–Analytic Comparison, 27 Law and Human Behavior 523 (2003).

Wells, Eyewitness Identifications, in Modern Scientific Evidence: The Law and Science of Expert Testimony 2d (D. Faigman, D. Kaye, M. Saks, and J. Sanders eds., 2002).

Wells, and Loftus, Eyewitness Memory for People and Events, In 11 Handbook of Psychology: Forensic Psychology (A. Goldstein, ed. 2003).

Wells and Olson, Eyewitness Testimony, 54 Annual Review of Psychology 277 (2003).

Yarmey, Yarmey and Yarmey, Accuracy of Eyewitness Identifications in Showups and Lineups, 20 Law and Human Behavior 459 (1996)

Section V. Social Frameworks

We began this chapter by stating that social frameworks have some of the characteristics of social facts and some of the characteristics of social authority. We end it by drawing upon both of these primary uses of social science to develop a heuristic theory for providing decision makers with frameworks for determining facts in court.

SOCIAL FRAMEWORKS: A NEW USE OF SOCIAL SCIENCE IN LAW

Laurens Walker and John Monahan.
73 Virginia Law Review 559 (1987).

PROCEDURES FOR USING SOCIAL FRAMEWORKS IN COURT

A. The Traditional "Fact" Perspective

Social science used as a social framework is now almost always introduced in court precisely as is social science used as an "adjudicative fact"— by expert testimony before a jury or other factfinder. This customary procedure has two significant liabilities. First, it is an inefficient use of court time. The same testimony about the same research studies must be heard in case after case, whenever a framework for a given type of factual determination is sought. Second, the current method of introducing empirical frameworks is expensive. The pool of expert witnesses is limited to a small group of basic researchers in each topical area and these researchers must be transported and paid to repeat their testimony in each new case. Access to expert testimony on empirical research is effectively precluded in a large number of cases in which the introduction of a framework would seem justified.

One source of proposals for improving the introduction of social frameworks might derive from the recognition that frameworks resemble legislative facts as much as they resemble adjudicative facts. Social frameworks possess a legislative fact "generality" based on the research from which they are derived and an adjudicative fact "specificity" which currently controls the procedures for their introduction. Pursuing this insight, one might consider formulating a two-stage process for introducing social frameworks: first, attention should focus on the legislative fact "generality" of the framework; and then, attention should shift to the adjudicative fact "specificity" of its application to the given case.

The practical difficulty of this seemingly plausible tack, however, [is that] recognizing the legislative fact aspect of social frameworks does not yield a coherent set of procedural ideas for introducing those frameworks in court.

B. The Social Authority Perspective

A heuristic concept is needed that reflects the generality of the basic research data used in a framework and at the same time provides a richer source of procedural ideas than the concept of legislative fact. One such concept may be "social authority." Under this view, courts would treat social science research, when used to create a rule of law, as a source of authority rather than as a type of act. Accordingly, courts would deal with empirical research much as they now deal with legal precedent in a common-law system.

[C.]   Social Frameworks as a Mix of Social Authority and Fact

Reconceptualizing social frameworks as a mix of social authority and fact yields a two-stage process with clear procedural ramifications. First we consider how courts should obtain and evaluate frameworks, recognizing the dominance of the social authority classification at this stage; then we specify communication techniques that follow from the factual aspect of social frameworks.

1.   Obtaining and Evaluating Social Frameworks

The social authority aspect of frameworks suggests two corollary propositions regarding how a court should obtain empirical research: parties should present empirical research to the court in briefs rather than by testimony; and the court may locate social science studies through its own research.

Under this view, when the attorney for one of the parties determines that providing an empirical context or framework for a factual issue in the case would be useful [t]he attorney would begin a search for relevant empirical information. If such information were found, it would be presented to the court in a written brief, the purpose of which, as described below, would be to propose and justify a set of jury instructions incorporating a social framework.

[2.]   Communicating Social Frameworks

Considering social frameworks as part social authority and part fact leads to radically different roles for the jury and the court than exist under current practice. [W]hat we call social frameworks are now presented to the jury by expert testimony, and it is the jury's responsibility to evaluate what they have heard and to apply it to the facts of the case at bar. The court's role is a passive one, limited to ruling on whether given expert testimony is admissible as evidence for the jury's consideration. Under the mixed social authority-fact view, in contrast, the court is much more active. The research is presented directly to the court by brief, or the court may independently locate the research. Most importantly, just as it is the responsibility of the court, rather than the jury, to evaluate case precedent, so it is the responsibility of the court, rather than the jury, to evaluate the social science research.

If the evaluating judge finds both that the research supports the introduction of a social framework and that no policy issues—for example, the prohibition against some forms of character evidence—bar a framework's application, then the final procedural implication of the social authority view is clear: the result of the court's evaluation of the applicable research should be communicated to the jury in the same manner that the court's evaluation of the applicable statutes and case law is communicated to the jury, that is, by instruction. The role of the jury is thus limited to applying the social framework given by the court to the specific facts of the case, just as the role of the jury is traditionally limited to applying the law given by the court to the specific facts of the case.

[A]s social science is repeatedly brought to bear in framing a given type of factual determination, attention should be given to establishing standard instructions on a variety of topics. This could be done either through the common law process of taking instructions from prior cases, or by an appellate court using its supervisory powers to endorse "pattern" instructions, perhaps drafted by a committee composed of lawyers and social scientists. Whichever the means of their creation, establishing pattern instructions and providing for their periodic review and revisions hold great promise for standardizing the third use of social science in law.

———

STATE v. ALGER

Court of Appeals of Idaho, 1988.
115 Idaho 42, 764 P.2d 119.

■ Burnett, Judge.

On a wintry evening in 1984, an Albertson's supermarket in Boise was robbed at gunpoint. Law enforcement officers throughout Idaho began searching for two suspects, Timothy Alger and an alleged accomplice. Several days later, Alger and his partner were spotted in Twin Falls. After a lengthy pursuit and intense manhunt, both individuals were apprehended. A jury eventually found Alger guilty of armed robbery. The judge imposed a ten-year indeterminate sentence for the robbery and a fifteen-year indeterminate enhancement for use of a firearm during commission of the crime. On appeal, Alger has presented a potpourri of issues [including the] admission and sufficiency of evidence at trial.

[A]lger's [e]videntiary issue focuses upon the trial judge's refusal to admit an article entitled "Eyewitness Testimony," which had appeared in the December, 1974, issue of *Scientific American* magazine. The article discussed social science research disclosing problems of reliability in eyewitness identification testimony. The trial judge ruled that the article was inadmissible hearsay.

Alger argues that the article should have been admitted, despite a lack of live testimony by the author, because an article culled from a well-known periodical is a self-authenticating document. See I.R.E. 902(6). We think this argument misses the point. The issue is not whether the document was authentic; it is whether the document contained hearsay and, if so, whether any exception to the hearsay rule was applicable. Underlying this issue is a broader question of policy: whether juries should be allowed to consider as "facts" the data and conclusions generated by social science research.

We first discuss the hearsay question. Although a research article may be hearsay, it is admissible at trial if it is introduced in compliance with the "learned treatise" exception to the hearsay rule. See I.R.E. 803(18). The state has argued that this exception is available only when an expert witness relies upon the treatise or when the treatise is used by counsel to cross-examine the expert.

[However,] we believe that a broad interpretation of the learned treatise exception is consonant with the general policy underlying the Idaho Rules of Evidence. Rather than encouraging rigid formalism, the rules seek to promote justice through a flexible approach to truth-seeking. Where, as a matter of economic or practical necessity, a party seeks to introduce evidence in the form of a learned treatise, we discern no principled reason for precluding its admission merely because the treatise is unaccompanied by an in court witness. Accordingly, we conclude in this case that admission of the *Scientific American* article was not barred by Idaho's version of the hearsay rule.

Of course, this conclusion does not end our discussion. The learned treatise exception does not mandate admission of all published works. We still must determine, as a matter of policy, whether scientific research material on eyewitness identification should be allowed in court where identity is an issue at trial. As noted above, this type of evidence normally is presented in conjunction with the testimony of an expert who takes the witness stand. However, the policy issue does not turn on the method of presentation. The real question is whether research data and conclusions are appropriate aids for the triers of fact in evaluating eyewitness testimony.

In State v. Hoisington, 104 Idaho 153, 657 P.2d 17 (1983), a majority of our Supreme Court offered an answer to this question. Citing cases from other jurisdictions, the Court upheld a trial judge's exclusion of psychiatric testimony about the trustworthiness of eyewitness observations. The majority declared that the subject did not require elucidation by an expert because it was not "beyond the ken" of ordinary jurors. Id. at 165, 657 P.2d at 29. Implicit in the Court's holding was an assumption that use of experts in this manner would invade the fact-finding function of the jury.

Faced with this same issue today, we think that our Supreme Court would follow a different approach. *Hoisington* was decided prior to adoption of the Idaho Rules of Evidence. These rules have expanded significantly the permissible scope of expert testimony. I.R.E. 702 broadly allows an expert witness to testify "[i]f scientific, technical, or other specialized knowledge will assist the trier of fact to understand the evidence or to determine a fact in issue...." Rule 704 further provides that otherwise admissible opinion testimony "is not objectionable because it embraces an ultimate issue to be decided by the trier of fact." The wide reach of the rules governing expert testimony is derived from a fundamental policy favoring admissibility of all relevant evidence. See I.R.E. 401.

The current rules substantially undercut the justifications listed by the *Hoisington* court for precluding expert testimony on eyewitness identification. General research data pertaining to this topic is relevant under the rules. Where a scientist's research casts doubt upon the ability of eyewitnesses to perceive accurately—or to memorize and recall fully—certain observed events, such research clearly has a "tendency to make the existence of any fact of consequence to the determination of the action [i.e. the reliability of the eyewitness identification in the instant case] more probable *or less probable* than it would be without the evidence." I.R.E. 401 (emphasis added). Moreover, any concern for invasion of the jury's fact-finding mission is obviated by Rule 704, which permits experts to render opinions on ultimate issues. Accordingly, we conclude that expert testimony concerning eyewitness identification is admissible under appropriate circumstances. See I.R.E. 403.

Our conclusion is consistent with recent decisions of other state courts that have considered this question. In State v. Chapple, 660 P.2d 1208 (Ariz.1983) (en banc), the Arizona Supreme Court held that even if jurors of ordinary education need no expert testimony to enlighten them on the dangers inherent in eyewitness identification, expert testimony on the issue nonetheless would be admissible to support a defense of misidentification. The Court reasoned that the concepts developed through the expert's research would be of substantial assistance to the jury. This trend is reflected by decisions of other courts mandating the use of jury instructions warning the jury of the dangers inherent in eyewitness identification. See, e.g., State v. Warren, 230 Kan. 385, 635 P.2d 1236 (1981); Commonwealth v. Bowden, 379 Mass. 472, 399 N.E.2d 482 (1980); State v. Long, 721 P.2d 483 (Utah 1986); State v. Payne, 167 W.Va. 252, 280 S.E.2d 72 (1981).

We recognize that the eyewitness identification issue illustrates a fundamental question regarding the use of social science research by the courts. The question is one of intense interest to legal scholars. Authors of the most highly developed thesis on the subject have identified three roles that such research can play in court. See Walker and Monahan, Social Frameworks: A New Use of Social Science in Law, 73 U.Va.L.Rev. 559 (1987). At one end of the spectrum are data obtained specifically to aid in the determination of facts at issue in a single case. These case-specific or "adjudicative" facts usually answer the questions of who did what, where, when, how, why, and with what motive or intent. At the other end of the spectrum are data germane to determinations of law and policy. These have been termed "legislative" facts. Such types of research data traditionally have been admissible as substantive evidence. See I.R.E. 201.

In the middle of the spectrum is an emerging new category of data: findings of researchers which provide insight into the likelihood that certain events or behavior will occur under given conditions. This category includes research on eyewitness perception and recollection. Walker and Monahan describe this third category as a "social framework," and they define it as "the use of general conclusions from social science research in determining factual issues in a specific case." Id. at 570. Walker and Monahan note that social frameworks often are presented through the oral testimony of an expert witness. However, they argue that because social framework research provides a general guide for evaluating evidence, the research is more akin to law than to fact. Accordingly, they propose that the research be offered directly to the trial judge, who will evaluate it and, upon finding it to be apparently reliable and likely to assist the jury, will convey it to the jurors by special instruction. Id. at 560. In this manner, Walker and Monahan assert, the level of social science research used by courts will be refined in much the same way that legal precedent evolves through continuous application.

The Walker and Monahan procedural scheme may not be universally accepted, and we do not mandate it in today's decision. But we agree with the authors' underlying thesis: "A novel role for empirical research is emerging: a use of general research conclusions to set a background context for deciding crucial factual issues at trial." Id. at 598. The courts should not categorically bar this new contribution of social science to the law. Rather, each introduction of a social framework—such as eyewitness observation research—should be evaluated carefully on its own empirical and legal merits. This evaluation requires trial judges to exercise a sound and informed discretion.

In the present case, the trial judge did not undertake such an exercise of discretion. He perceived the issue narrowly as whether the *Scientific American* article was excludible as hearsay. He held that it was. In doing so he erred, as we have explained. The question, then, is whether this error warrants reversal or?like the evidence of the police chase near Twin Falls?is harmless under I.C.R. 52. We conclude that it is.

As we have detailed above, there was abundant evidence, in addition to eyewitness testimony, implicating Alger in the robbery. Alger was explicitly linked to the clothing and weapons used in the crime. His own statements were incriminating. Furthermore, the accomplice, having been convicted himself, stated that Alger participated in the robbery. Finally, there has been no showing of any unusually significant nexus between the eyewitness identifications in this case and the general problems identified in the *Scientific American* article. Thus, even if the article had been admitted, we remain convinced beyond a reasonable doubt that the verdict would have been the same.

––––––

NOTE

1. Judicial Research. In United States v. Shonubi, 895 F.Supp. 460 (E.D.N.Y.1995), the defendant was convicted of entering the United States with 427.4 grams of heroin in his digestive tract. At sentencing, the trial judge, Jack B. Weinstein, found that the defendant had made seven prior drug-smuggling trips. Under the federal Sentencing Guidelines, the judge is required to estimate the total amount of heroin imported. The judge multiplied 427.4 by eight and arrived at a total of 3419.2 grams of heroin, which translated into a sentence of 151 months in prison. The defense argued that the trial judge "failed to account for the likelihood that smugglers carry more heroin with each successive trip, a putative learning curve it termed the 'trip effect.'" The judge rejected this hypothesis as follows. Id. at 468.

The judges of this district—which once contained a great port and now contains a great international airport—have had wide experience with the importation of drugs, in all its variations. To draw upon this institutional experience, a questionnaire was sent to members of the Eastern District bench. The judges were asked to rate, "based on their trial and sentencing experience," their confidence in five hypotheses about heroin swallowers, using a scale of 1 (unlikely) to 5 (likely). Nearly all the judges responded. Their replies, with names redacted, are on file with the court. The hypotheses, and the average "scores" received, were:

1. They start with smaller amounts and increase the amounts on later trips.

   2.4

2. They start with an amount close to the maximum amount they can carry and keep carrying that amount until caught.

   4.3

3. There is no relation between trip number and amount.

   2.2

[P]roposition 2, which suggests that the trip effect, if it exists, is minimal, received the highest "rating." Proposition 1, a "strong" version of the trip effect, received a significantly lower score. These results parallel the sentencing judge's assumption about the behavior of heroin swallowers.

Judge Weinstein's opinion in this case was vacated by the Court of Appeals, United States v. Shonubi, 103 F.3d 1085 (2d Cir.1997). Chief Judge Newman wrote:

> Though his comprehensive opinion is a valuable addition to the legal literature on the subject of evidence in particular and judicial decision-making in general, we conclude that he relied on evidence beyond the category of "specific evidence" that our prior opinion ruled was required for determination of a "relevant conduct" drug quantity for purposes of imposing a criminal sentence. Id. at 1092.

EMPIRICAL QUESTIONS WITHOUT EMPIRICAL ANSWERS

John Monahan and Laurens Walker.
1991 Wisconsin Law Review 569 (1991).

The question [i]s what courts should do when a party requests "social framework" instructions but presents no social science research, or only inadequate social science research, to support the request. The answer is to be found by turning to the standard for framing jury instructions. That standard is clear: courts must give only instructions that state the law "correctly" or "accurately." As was the case with judicial review of state legislation, general principles for obtaining and evaluating research can be employed: correctness, accuracy, or what a social scientist would term "validity"—rather than the "relevancy" or "Frye" rules used to test scientific evidence of social facts. If the research comprising the framework is valid in the court's estimation, and relevant to the facts of the case, the instruction should be given. If the research is invalid, or nonexistent, it would follow from the law regarding jury instructions that no instruction would be forthcoming. An instruction would be unnecessary to decide the case: lacking valid research, a jury is as well equipped as a judge to speculate on the effect of social context in determining the facts at issue in the case.

SELECTED BIBLIOGRAPHY

Goodman and Croyle, Social Framework Testimony in Employment Discrimination Cases, 7 Behavioral Sciences and the Law 227 (1989).

Mosteller, Legal Doctrines Governing the Admissibility of Expert Testimony Concerning Social Framework Evidence, 52 Law and Contemporary Problems 85 (Autumn 1989).

Vidmar & Schuller, Social Framework Evidence and Jury Decision Making Processes, 52 Law and Contemporary Problems 133 (Autumn 1989).

CHAPTER FOUR

SOCIAL SCIENCE USED TO PLAN THE LITIGATION OF A CASE

It is now common for attorneys to employ social scientists to assist in the preparation of a case for trial and during trial. The contributions of these social scientists have been quite varied, but issues involving the place of trial, the selection of jurors, and the instruction of jurors have dominated. This work began during the early 1970s when conditions of social unrest generated much controversial criminal litigation. Recently, the techniques have been increasingly applied in important civil cases.

SECTION I. CHOOSING A VENUE

Both state and federal courts recognize the occasional need to change the place of trial because local public opinion may render a fair jury unlikely. For example, Federal Rule of Criminal Procedure 21(a) provides that "The court upon motion of the defendant shall transfer the proceeding ... if the court is satisfied that there exists in the district where the prosecution is pending so great a prejudice against the defendant that the defendant cannot obtain a fair and impartial trial." Proof that this situation exists is made to the trial judge, and now often involves the use of social science research.

PRETRIAL PUBLICITY, CHANGE OF VENUE, PUBLIC OPINION POLLS—A THEORY OF PROCEDURAL JUSTICE

Peter D. O'Connell.*
65 University of Detroit Law Review 169 (1988).

The excitement that a sensational case causes in a small community is a phenomena that one must observe in order to fully understand its impact on the community. During morning coffee breaks, over backyard fences, while obtaining gas, while getting a haircut or purchasing a newspaper, each citizen becomes an expert on the facts of the case.

The existence of the news media has left only the hermit uninformed as to the details of the case. As a result of this publicity, most citizens

* [Judge, 76th District Court, Mt. Pleasant, Michigan].

512

consciously or subconsciously develop an attitude concerning defendant's guilt or innocence. This attitude is embedded into each juror's subconscious.

The court must determine if prospective jurors are capable of rendering a fair and impartial verdict when they are called for jury duty. This is an awesome responsibility. It is critical to the fair administration of justice. It is also an area where trial judges receive little formal education. In the interest of efficiency, some judges tend to qualify jurors who have expressed doubts about their biases and prejudices.

Bias and prejudice are attitudes. They are not something you can see, feel, or touch. They are discovered through the use of wisdom, knowledge, and an understanding of human nature. In this regard, they are similar to the concepts of truth, beauty, goodness, and justice. The senses cannot experience these notions. Only the mind can capture these concepts because they are incapable of absolute definition. They exist in degrees. The best we can do is to define the characteristics of bias and prejudice and search for a methodology that will facilitate discovery of these characteristics.

[T]he favorite tool of the trial judge is to ask the jurors a series of questions. The answers to the questions lead to the discovery of a juror's attitude on any given subject. This attitude can be discovered if the proper questions are asked. However, the answers can be suppressed if the wrong questions are asked or if the voir dire examination places too much pressure on the juror.

The pressure of the voir dire examination sometimes causes jurors to temporarily forget their own names. In fact, when novices attempt to probe a juror's psyche, some jurors are offended. The result is juror repression of the attitude rather than juror exposure of the attitude.

Generally, the last question the trial judge asks is whether the juror can render a fair and impartial verdict. If the juror answers "yes," he or she is usually qualified to sit as a juror:

This methodology is a little like asking a practicing alcoholic if he has his drinking under control; we are asking the person who has the prejudice to determine if the prejudice will affect his decision. This method of determining prejudice has been approved by the Supreme Court. No one can be certain that jurors will render a fair and impartial verdict and no better system has been developed.

[T]he public opinion poll is conducted in an atmosphere free from the pressure and regimentation of the jury selection process. The answers to the poll's questions are an indication of what the juror's attitudes may be on a given subject. Their answers may or may not be an accurate assessment of a juror's true feeling, but these answers combined with the responses of other individuals in the community create the atmosphere of the community. These responses assist the court in determining if the pretrial publicity is inherently prejudicial.

———

PENNSYLVANIA v. COHEN

Supreme Court of Pennsylvania, 1980.
489 Pa. 167, 413 A.2d 1066.

■ ROBERTS, JUSTICE.

On November 14, 1974, a man walking along a fire trail in Reading's Egelman Park discovered the body of Steven Warunek, a sixteen year-old Reading youth. Warunek had been shot to death. On November 18, police arrested three eighteen year-old suspects [a]nd charged all three with murder. Police also charged appellant with conspiracy to commit murder. Police investigation revealed that appellant hired the other two to kill Warunek in retaliation for threats Warunek made on appellant's life. Warunek allegedly told his fiancé, Kerry Young, he would kill appellant, Young's former boyfriend.

[A]ppellant filed a number of pre-trial applications, including [o]ne for a change of venue. [T]he trial court [h]eld a hearing on appellant's application for a change of venue. At the hearing, appellant presented copies of Berks County newspaper articles and transcripts of local radio broadcasts which discussed appellant's case. Appellant also presented Dr. Jay Schulman, a professor at Columbia University and member of the National Jury Project, who is an expert on the impact of publicized criminal proceedings on public opinion. Dr. Schulman testified on the results of a public opinion poll he conducted which tested Berks County residents' views on appellant's guilt. Dr. Schulman, four other expert witnesses, and six lay witnesses all expressed an opinion that appellant could not receive a fair trial in Berks County. The Commonwealth opposed the application for a change of venue, but offered no evidence. The court denied appellant's application without opinion or other explanation of record.

[O]n September 2, 1975, before the scheduled date of trial, appellant filed a "Re-Application For Change of Venue." In support of his "Re-Application," appellant presented the results of a second public opinion survey. This survey was conducted on August 22 and 23 by Dr. Robert Buckhout, another member of the National Jury Project. Once again, the Commonwealth, opposing the motion, presented no contrary evidence. The court denied appellant's "Re-Application," again without explanation. Appellant immediately applied for and was denied another continuance. Trial was set for September 8.

Voir dire began Monday, September 8 and lasted two full weeks, through Friday, September 19. In all, 180 persons were called in order to select a twelve-member jury and two alternates. The court ordered each juror immediately sequestered upon selection. At the close of voir dire, appellant for the third time requested a change of venue. The trial court denied this request, again without explanation. Trial began the following Monday, September 22.

[T]he case went to the jury on Wednesday, October 1. That Friday, October 3, the jury returned verdicts of guilty of murder of the third degree and conspiracy to commit murder.

Appellant then filed written post-verdict motions for a new trial and in arrest of judgment, which included appellant's claim that the trial court erred in denying a change of venue.

[J]udge Edenharter, however, denied all of appellant's post-verdict motions. In his accompanying opinion, Judge Edenharter for the first time sought to explain his orders denying appellant's three pre-trial applications for a change of venue. The court summarily dismissed appellant's principal contention that the pre-trial publicity was "inherently prejudicial," concluding that [t]here is insufficient evidence that any inflammatory information was widely disseminated at the time of trial. The court also concluded that the jury appellant did select was not affected by the pre-trial publicity.

On July 15, 1977, the court imposed sentence of ten to twenty years imprisonment, costs, and a fine of $15,000 on the murder conviction, as well as a concurrent sentence of five to ten years, costs, and a fine of $10,000 on the conspiracy conviction. These appeals followed.

[F]rom appellant's arrest in mid-November, 1974 until hearings in May of 1975 on appellant's first application for a change of venue, Reading's two newspapers the "Times" and the "Eagle," as well as Reading radio stations WRAW and WEEU, extensively covered every aspect of this case. The record contains thirty-seven newspaper articles, including sixteen front-page stories, and thirty-eight radio broadcasts which directly feature aspects of this case.

Most extensively publicized is the allegation of a "contract killing." The front page of the December 13 Eagle reported Assistant District Attorney Murphy's disclosure that the Commonwealth "may seek the death penalty which, he said, is allowed for premeditated contract killings." The December 14 Times and radio station WRAW also immediately gave similar coverage. Forty-one subsequent newspaper stories, reporting through the May hearings on appellant's application for a change of venue, carried what became standard-reference to the fact that a "contract killing" was involved.

[A]lso well-publicized were allegations that appellant and the co-conspirators made plans to kill Warunek while "high" on drugs and alcohol. A front-stage story of the January Times 25 entitled "Cohen murder hearing begun," accompanied by a 6½ inch by 6¾ inch photograph of appellant and his attorney, summarizes witnesses' allegations that

> "a conspiracy to 'mess up' the 16-year-old Steve E. Warunek was made during a dope and booze party in an apartment at 111 S. 8th St. when the alleged conspirators were 'high.' "

The same day the Eagle also carried a story entitled "Killing Linked To Lover's Spat." Accompanying this story, like the story in the Times, is a 5 inch by 6 inch photograph of appellant and his attorney. The story begins:

"The November slaying of 16-year-old Steve E. Warunek in Egelman Park was depicted Friday as a contract murder, carried out amidst fear of reprisal in a heated lovers' triangle with the conspirators discussing plans during smoke-filled pot and alcohol parties."

[B]erks County media also gave great attention to appellant's pre-trial application for a change of venue. The court began to hear testimony on appellant's application on May 1. The May 2 Times carried a lengthy story entitled "Court ponders trial site plea" which set forth testimony on the qualifications of appellant's expert witness Dr. Jay Schulman. The same day's Eagle carried another extensive story entitled "Survey Allowed in Cohen Case," which discussed the court's ruling allowing appellant to introduce Schulman's expert testimony. Both the May 3 Times and Eagle carried related, extensive stories.

Eight more stories appeared between May 5 to May 9, all of which discussed testimony at the hearing on appellant's application for a change of venue, including "Consultant Queried on Survey Errors," "Jury researcher calls Berks biased," " 'Prejudice' Is Probed At Hearing," "Prejudice Is Estimated," and "4 rule out fairness."

[T]he record clearly establishes that the repeatedly-disseminated prejudicial material was widespread throughout Berks County at the time of trial. Thus inapposite are those cases in which the allegedly objectionable reports were not particularly widespread. Equally distinguishable are those cases in which the claimed objectionable reports so long preceded jury selection as to allow for a period of "cooling off."

Here in the months between arrest and trial Berks County residents became increasingly aware of this case. So too an ever-growing number of residents formed an opinion on the merits. The public opinion poll conducted by Dr. Schulman in March and April of 1975 and admitted into evidence at the May hearing on appellant's first application for a change of venue revealed that, of 804 randomly-selected Berks County registered voters, 65% then were aware of the case. Of those polled, 30%, or 242 out of 804 people, expressly conceded they had prejudged appellant guilty. Dr. Buckhout's survey, conducted approximately four months later in late August, revealed a still greater public awareness of this case. Of the 250 people randomly interviewed, 79% were aware of this case, an increase of approximately 15% from the level of awareness found four months earlier. Dr. Buckhout's survey also revealed that 57% of all persons interviewed, or 143 out of 250 people, attributed guilt to appellant.[34] This figure is nearly twice as great as the figure found in the previous poll. These results, unchallenged and undisturbed by the trial court, demonstrate with unquestionable clarity the substantial extent to which pretrial publicity had reached the local population and had influenced its judgment.[35]

34. Dr. Buckhout asked persons polled to rate their belief of appellant's guilt on a scale of "zero" to "ten." One hundred forty-three ascribed more than "zero" guilt. One hundred thirty-eight of the 143, or 55% of all persons interviewed, ascribed to appellant guilt of "five" or greater.

35. The trial court here in no respect questioned the basic results of the surveys relied upon in text. Instead, the trial court

Voir dire, conducted in September, about two weeks after Dr. Buckhout's August survey, confirmed the results of Dr. Buckhout's poll. Of the 180 prospective jurors called, eleven were excused on various grounds of hardship and not questioned concerning the merits. Of the 169 persons questioned, 105 stated they held an opinion concerning the merits. Indeed, of these 105 prospective jurors, eighty-nine were excused on the ground that they admitted a "fixed," irrevocable opinion on guilt. Thus, 53% of the prospective jurors questioned were excused because of prejudgment.

These percentages of persons expressing an opinion on an accused's guilt are unprecedented in our cases.

[I]t therefore must be concluded that the prejudicial material was widespread at the time of trial and that the court abused its discretion in refusing on this record to grant a change of venue.

———

NOTE

1. Oklahoma City. In United States v. McVeigh, 918 F.Supp. 1467 (1996), the Court considered an application by defendants for a change of venue. The defendants, Timothy McVeigh and Terry Nichols, were charged with building a "truck bomb" and using the bomb on April 19, 1995 to destroy the Murrah Federal Building in Oklahoma City, Oklahoma, resulting in the deaths of 168 men, women, and children, injuries to hundreds, and costs estimated at $651,594,000. "Dramatic pictures of the Murrah Federal Building were shown nationwide immediately after the explosion. There was intensive coverage of the rescue efforts. The immediate reactions of the President, the Attorney General and an FBI spokesman were broadcast across the nation. There were extensive interviews with injured victims, members of the families of the dead and missing persons, rescue and relief workers, and residents of Oklahoma City." Id. at 1470–1471. After his arrest, McVeigh was shown on television "in restraints and clad in bright orange jail clothing being led into a van while surrounded by a very vocal and angry crowd. Some bystanders could be heard shouting 'murderer' and 'baby killer'." Id. at 1471. The question before the Court was whether trial could be held anywhere in Oklahoma. All parties had agreed that trial could not be held in Oklahoma City and Lawton had been designated by the Court as the trial site. The defendants supported their motion with a public opinion survey. The opinion poll showed that almost half of the respondents in the Lawton area had formed an opinion about the guilt of McVeigh and ninety six percent of those respondents believed McVeigh was guilty. Jones and Hillelman, McVeigh, McJustice, McMedia, 1998 University of Chicago Legal Forum 53. The Court ordered that the venue be changed to Denver, Colorado. Both McVeigh and Nichols were

merely questioned Dr. Schulman's estimation based upon the results of the survey that as many as 75% to 80% of Berks County residents prejudged appellant guilty. (Nowhere in its opinion does the trial court in any respect dispute either the evidence or conclusions of Dr. Buckhout.)

convicted in the Colorado trial which followed, and McVeigh was sentenced to death and executed June 11, 2001.

THE PSYCHOLOGY OF THE AMERICAN JURY (1987)

Jeffrey T. Frederick.

In view of the impact of prejudicial pretrial publicity, the question arises as to how one can assess the exposure of jurors to pretrial publicity and the detrimental effects produced, if any. Social sciences can provide valuable information regarding the possibility of prejudice in the community where a trial is to be held and, therefore, are of great assistance in determining the need for and/or the validity of change of venue motions. Such assistance can come in several areas. Expert evaluation can be provided regarding the impact of the content of the media coverage on community opinions. Affidavits from members of the community attesting to levels of prejudice present in the community can be presented to the court. Probably the best tool at the disposal of the social scientist is the use of surveys or polls of the community to reveal the *actual* level of prejudice, not simply the inferred level. At least 12 years ago the courts began to find this kind of information relevant and useful. It is therefore, worthwhile to look more closely at the methods used by social scientists to determine the presence or absence of prejudice.

In conducting an attitudinal survey for support of a change of venue motion, random samples of jury-eligible persons must be drawn from at least two communities or districts. The use of a random sample ensures a valid representation of the range and distribution of community attitudes and provides a basis for valid statistical tests. The use of two or more communities reflects the relative nature of social science statements, e.g., County "X" has a higher level of prejudice than County "Y." The use of a comparison community helps to eliminate the ambiguity in interpreting an absolute figure (a measurement of one county only). For example, suppose a community poll reveals that approximately 40% of the community believes that the defendant is guilty. Should the venue be changed? Obviously, the establishment of an acceptable absolute level of bias in the community is difficult, if not impossible. The question of change of venue is difficult to answer without a meaningful standard of comparison. If a poll of an adjacent community revealed that 15% of its population was biased, this fact would obviously make the need for a change of venue clear. This conclusion would be impossible to come to without comparative data. The use of comparison communities provides the necessary ground on which to make a decision about the need for a change of venue. That is, using one or more comparison communities or districts provides a way of assessing whether a fair trial could be gained by such a move. It is always possible that a move could place the trial in a more prejudiced community, thus worsening the plight of the defendant.

The questionnaire used in assessing a change of venue motion should contain questions concerning level of publicity, case-specific issues, and general attitudes. In support of a change of venue motion based upon prejudicial pretrial publicity, information is needed about how much exposure to publicity the residents have had. A question such as "How much have you heard about the _____ case?" with response categories of "none," "a little," "somewhat," and "a lot," is generally appropriate. In the event that a particular news story is at issue, it may be necessary to ask specifically how they have heard about the case in order to determine if they have been exposed to the prejudicial publicity.

Questions concerning case-specific issues are included in the venue questionnaire in order to determine the level of prejudice in the community. A question such as "Do you believe that the defendant, $\underline{X}$, is guilty?" is necessary to detect any preconceptions of the defendant's guilt in the community. However, additional questions regarding other issues (e.g., opinions about insanity defense or a defendant's prior criminal record) may be asked in order to support an assertion of a specific prejudice against the defendant. Finally, general attitudinal questions should be asked (e.g., about racial attitudes, attitudes toward crime, bias against defendants, or sex and political biases) in order to determine if a general prejudice against the defendant exists. While this latter information may not by itself support a change of venue motion, it can buttress the assertions of specific prejudice.

ABA STANDARDS FOR CRIMINAL JUSTICE (3D ED. 1992)

Standard 8–3.3. Change of venue or continuance

The following standards govern the consideration and disposition of a motion in a criminal case for change of venue or continuance based on a claim of threatened interference with the right to a fair trial:

(a) Except as federal or state constitutional or statutory provisions otherwise require, a change of venue or continuance may be granted on motion of either the prosecution or the defense.

(b) A motion for change of venue or continuance should be granted whenever it is determined that, because of the dissemination of potentially prejudicial material, there is a substantial likelihood that, in the absence of such relief, a fair trial by an impartial jury cannot be had. This determination may be based on such evidence as qualified public opinion surveys or opinion testimony offered by individuals, or on the court's own evaluation of the nature, frequency, and timing of the material involved. A showing of actual prejudice shall not be required.

NOTES

1. Prosecution Requests. The opportunity of the prosecution to request a change of venue is severely limited. In federal court, the language of Criminal Rule 21(a) does not permit a prosecution motion, and prosecution motions are also barred by the Sixth Amendment of the Constitution which guarantees to criminal defendants the right to trial in the district where the offense was committed. Of course, a defendant's request for change constitutes a waiver of this right. Changes within the district where the offense was committed are not barred by the Rule or the Constitution, so presumably the prosecution could request such a limited move. See Wright, 2 Federal Practice and Procedure 3d Sec. 341 (2000). In state courts, similar statutory and state constitutional limits would also constrain such requests. Thus, the use of social science to change venue in criminal trials is largely reserved for defendants.

2. Discovery. In federal court, and in states which have adopted the Federal Rules model, discovery of research materials produced in an effort to secure a change of venue motion would generally not be permitted. Criminal Rule 16(b)(1)(B), limits prosecution discovery of "scientific tests or experiments" to situations where the defendant has first requested discovery of similar materials from the government. Discovery by a defendant of prosecution research would likely be permitted by Criminal Rule 16(a)(1)(D). Of course, a defendant requesting prosecution research materials might be required to exchange similar materials. Contrary to this situation, Moskitis, The Constitutional Need for Discovery of Pre-Voir Dire Jury Studies, 49 Southern California Law Review 597 (1976) argues in favor of widespread discovery of juror studies as a solution for potential constitutional issues. Richardson, Swain, Codega and Bazzell, Forensic Sociology: Some Cautions and Recommendations, 18 The American Sociologist 385 (1987) report a successful prosecution effort to obtain research materials developed for a defendant's change of venue motion.

FIRESTONE v. CROWN CENTER REDEVELOPMENT CORP.

Supreme Court of Missouri, 1985.
693 S.W.2d 99.

■ HIGGINS, JUDGE.

Plaintiff obtained a jury verdict of $15,000,000 damages for injuries suffered when suspended balconies in the Hyatt Regency Kansas City Hotel fell on July 17, 1981.

[A]ppellants assert that the trial court erred in denying their application for a change of venue. The publicity surrounding the tragic collapse of the Hyatt Regency skyways, causing the deaths of 114 people and severe injuries to scores of others; the pretrial publicity about plaintiff's case; and publicity about the lawsuits of three other Hyatt Regency victims which had been tried in the three months preceding plaintiff's case, had, according to defendants' argument, caused the residents of Jackson County to be prejudiced against defendants so that they could not receive a fair trial there.

The granting of a change of venue in Jackson County, a county of over 75,000 population, is discretionary with the trial court, Rule 51.04, subject to review for abuse of discretion.

In an evidentiary hearing upon defendant's application, the defendants produced evidence of newspaper and television publicity about the Hyatt Regency disaster and the ensuing litigation over a period beginning with the disaster itself and continuing up to the time of trial. The Kansas City Star and the Kansas City Times, reaching half the households of Jackson County on a daily basis, published over 1,000 articles on the subject. The television coverage was no less intense.

The news media featured stories about the purported causes of the collapse, and the persons responsible. Another favorite topic was possible criminal penalties and disciplinary proceedings against persons participating in the design and construction of the hotel. There were newspaper articles and television pieces reporting on the commencement of investigations by the Jackson County Prosecutor, the U.S. District Attorney, a Jackson County Grand Jury, and the Missouri board licensing architects and engineers. Also reported and highlighted after the commencement of litigation were allegations (from whatever source) of misconduct on the part of defendants and their counsel in the conduct of litigation.

[A]ppellants do not claim that the publicity necessarily caused adverse community reaction, but acknowledge that they must show such prejudice. The disaster occurred July 17, 1981; this trial took place September 13, 1983. The intensity of the publicity had considerably abated several months before trial. If, as appellants argue, the publicity had incited public passion and prejudice against them, the passage of time had done its healing work. The trial judge noted in overruling the change of venue on September 6, 1983: "Generally speaking, in the past nine to twelve months the publicity involved has been substantially reduced and consisted mainly of reporting on the three trials that have been conducted."

To show the public hostility toward themselves, defendants produced the results of a telephone survey of 1,000 randomly selected Jackson County residents. The findings of this survey were conditionally admitted by the trial judge, but were ultimately excluded by him. The exclusion of this survey is said to be erroneous. Appellants say that if the survey had been admitted and been given proper weight, it would have supported their application for change of venue.

The survey consisted of two questions. The first question was: "Have you heard, or read or seen any news coverage about the Hyatt Hotel skywalk collapse?" Ninety-eight percent of the respondents said they had.

The next question was, to those who answered the first question in the affirmative: "Based on what you have heard, read or seen, do you believe that in the current compensatory damage trials, the defendants, such as the contractors, designers, owners, and operators of the Hyatt Hotel, should be punished?" Five hundred thirty-six of the respondents, or 54 percent, answered yes. One hundred thirty-five, or 14 percent, answered no. One hundred one, or 10 percent, refused to comment; and two hundred twelve, or 22 percent, were reported as unable to comment.

One of the requirements for the admissibility of a survey is that it be trustworthy. This does not mean merely that it be honestly conducted, but that it be designed to yield an accurate assessment of the relevant public opinion, belief or attitude under investigation.

[W]hat is the public opinion, belief or attitude being inquired into upon an application for change of venue? The reason for the change of venue provisions of Rule 51 is that a party is entitled to an impartial jury to hear and decide his case. If there is in the venue from which the jury is to be drawn a pervasive hostility toward a party, or a pervasive prejudgment of the case, it will be difficult or impossible to select an impartial jury. It is assumed that the jury panel members, and ultimately the jury, will reflect the prevailing opinion of the community from which they are drawn. In such a case the party is entitled to a change of venue.

The question becomes whether the survey rejected by the trial court gave a reliable reading of whether there was in Jackson County a pervasive hostility toward defendants or a pervasive prejudgment of Sally Firestone's case. On this question, this Court cannot condemn the trial court's rejection of the survey. The responses to the critical question were not an index to the true sentiments of the community. The fault is in the design of the question. A layman's answer to the critical question (i.e., "[D]o you believe that ... the defendants ... should be punished?"), having no more background than the generalized information gained from newspaper and television accounts, will reveal nothing at all about his ability to deal fairly with a specific case upon the basis of specific evidence, guided by the court's instructions and the argument of counsel. In admitting the results of a survey in Zippo Manufacturing Company v. Rogers Imports, Inc., 216 F.Supp. 670 (S.D.N.Y.1963), the court noted: "The developmental phase of the project involved preparation of questions that could be handled properly by an interviewer, correctly understood by respondents [i.e., those persons interviewed in the survey] and easily answered by them. This required several drafts of questionnaires and some pretesting." Id. at 681.

The question asked of the interviewees in this case did not measure up to the standard of the *Zippo* questions. The question used in this survey could neither be "correctly understood" nor "easily answered" by them. The phrase "compensatory damages" summons to the lawyer's mind a certain well-defined concept. The concept includes the idea of focusing upon the plaintiff's loss, and determining the amount of money which will make him whole; the concept excludes the idea of focusing upon the quality of defendant's fault to determine what if any penalty he should pay, above the amount which will make plaintiff whole, to make the defendant smart. All this is assumed by the lawyer, but not by the layman. The ideas of compensatory as opposed to punitive damages do not spring to his mind with the term "compensatory damages."

The word "punished" is another confusing word in this context. "Punished" how? Would the answers have been the same had the persons interviewed known (as the jury was instructed in the trial of this case) that defendants had paid $20,000,000 punitive damages to be distributed among the persons injured in the disaster?

It is doubtful whether any single "yes" or "no" question could be designed which could be relied upon to test the kind of prejudice which would disqualify a person as an impartial juror. This is not such a question. Among those who answered "yes," that the defendants should be "punished," was the belief a deep-seated one, one which could not be laid aside if he were selected as a juror, or was it shallow and tentative? Did it take into account the good will which some of the defendants enjoyed in the community? It is noted that none of the defendants was named in the survey.

Appellants say the survey, even with its deficiencies, should have been admitted by the court and given such weight as it deserved. This was, perhaps, an option for the court. If evidence is remotely relevant to prove an issue under investigation, an appellate court can approve the trial court's discretionary ruling in admitting it, saying that its weight is for the trier of fact.

[T]he defendants filed a motion to reconsider the court's denial of their motion for a change of venue, to which motion was appended a second survey. The second survey contained the following prefatory explanation: "Some of the cases resulting from the skywalk collapse are now coming to trial. The jurors are being asked to determine the amounts of money those bringing suit should receive as compensation for the injuries, pain incurred, medical costs and other losses they have suffered."

There followed the question: "Do you feel that the defendants such as the contractors, designers, owners and operators of the Hyatt Hotel should be required to pay damages to those bringing suit in addition to the compensation I have mentioned?"

Over one-half of the total number of interviewees answered in the affirmative.

This question, with the prefatory explanation, was more easily understood by the layman than the question submitted in the first survey; still, the survey could not really plumb the attitudes of the respondents. If the respondents had a fixed opinion that the defendants "should be required to pay damages to those bringing suit in addition to the compensation," that would not have disqualified them as jurors in this case. That the defendants would pay punitive damages was agreed, as the jurors in the trial were expressly told by the court's instructions.

[The jury verdict is affirmed.]

NOTES

1.   Federal Cases. The *Firestone* case shows that change of venue can be an issue in state court civil litigation. In federal civil cases similar issues would arise under a statute, 28 U.S.C.A. § 1404(a) which suggests that social science methods might be used to change the place of trial, based on a claim of local prejudice. The statute includes "in the interest of justice" as one reason for change, and some courts have cited this language in considering motions based on local prejudice. See Wright, Miller and Cooper, 15 Federal Practice and Procedure Sec. 3854 (1986). At least in federal court, the motion for change may be made by either plaintiff, defendant, or by a party added to the litigation after the beginning of suit. Id. at Sec. 3844. Of course plaintiffs, who choose the place to begin suit, will typically be satisfied with their choices. The availability of the motion in civil cases should be about the same in most state courts, though plaintiffs requesting a change might sometimes face the effective argument that the initial choice of a forum constituted a waiver of any request for change.

2.   Discovery. In federal court and in states following the federal model, discovery of research done to support a change of venue motion would likely be governed by Civil Rule 26(b)(4) which controls "discovery of facts known and opinions held by experts." In the case of an expert expected to be called at trial, as would ordinarily be the case in a change of venue situation, the rule permits discovery by interrogatory of the identity of the expert, the subject matter, and the substance of facts and opinions which the expert will discuss in court. The Rule provides that further discovery may be permitted by the trial judge. This permission is often granted, and usually results in the deposition of the trial expert being taken.

SELECTED BIBLIOGRAPHY

Brodsky, Change of Venue Assessments in Civil Litigation: Methodologies for a Comprehensive Evaluation, 28 Journal of Law and Psychiatry 335 (2000).

J. Frederick, The Psychology of the American Jury (1987).

Jones and Hillerman, McVeigh, McJustice, McMedia, 1998 University of Chicago Legal Forum 53.

Kovera, The Effects of General Pretrial Publicity on Juror Decisions: An Examination of Moderators and Mediating Mechanisms, 26 Law and Human Behavior 43 (2002).

Nietzel and Dillehay, Psychologists As Consultants for Change of Venue, 7 Law and Human Behavior 309 (1983).

M. Nietzel and R. Dillehay, Psychological Consultation in the Courtroom (1986).

O'Connell, Pretrial Publicity, Change of Venue, Public Opinion Polls—A Theory of Procedural Justice, 65 University of Detroit Law Review 169 (1988).

Ogloff and Vidmar, The Impact of Pretrial Publicity on Jurors: A Study to Compare the Relative Effects of Television and Print Media in a Child Sex Abuse Case, 18 Law and Human Behavior 507 (1994).

Otto, Penrod and Dexter, The Biasing Impact of Pretrial Publicity on Juror Judgments, 18 Law and Human Behavior 453 (1994).

Posey and Dahl, Beyond Pretrial Publicity: Legal and Ethical Issues Associated With Change of Venue Surveys, 26 Law and Human Behavior 107 (2002).

Richardson, Swain, Codega and Bazzell, Forensic Sociology: Some Cautions and Recommendations, 18 The American Sociologist 385 (1987).

Steblay, Besirevic, Fulero, and Jimenez-Lorente, The Effects of Pretrial Publicity on Juror Verdicts: A Meta-Analytic Review, 23 Law and Human Behavior 219 (1999).

Studebaker and Penrod, Pretrial Publicity: The Media, the Law and Common Sense, 3 Psychology, Public Policy and Law 428 (1997).

Studebaker, Robbennolt, Penrod, Pathak-Sharma, Groscup, and Devenport, Studying Pretrial Publicity Effects: New Methods for Improving Ecological Validity and Testing External Validity, 26 Law and Human Behavior 19 (2002).

Studebaker, Robbennolt, Pathak-Sharma, and Penrod, Assessing Pretrial Publicity Effects: Integrating Content Analytic Results, 24 Law and Human Behavior 317 (2000).

Zeisel and Diamond, The Jury Selection in the Mitchell-Stans Conspiracy Trial, 1976 American Bar Foundation Research Journal 151.

SECTION II.   CHOOSING A JURY

A traditional aspect of the jury trial is the opportunity, during the voir dire phase, for parties and their attorneys to participate in the selection of members of the jury. In recent years social scientists have been asked to assist in this part of the process. Typically, these social scientists have furnished advice concerning the best use of peremptory challenges to prospective jurors, the right to eliminate a limited number of prospective jurors without stating a reason. For example, in federal court, in criminal cases, Rule 24(b) provides that in capital cases each side has 20 peremptory challenges, and lesser numbers are provided to each side as the potential punishment diminishes. In federal civil cases 28 U.S.C.A. § 1870 provides that each side will have 3 peremptory challenges. According to that statute, if there are several plaintiffs or defendants the court may allow additional challenges. The same general pattern can be found in state courts.

From the beginning this use of social science has been controversial, in large part (and ironically) because lawyers and judges seem to believe these practices are highly effective. Even the title of an early description of this work, Schulman, Shaver, Coleman, Emrich and Christie, Recipe for a Jury,

7 Psychology Today 34 (1973), has evoked consternation. The image of social scientists concocting a "recipe" for a jury and passing that along to the lawyers that retain them has surely troubled many members of the legal community.

ATTORNEY FOR THE DEFENSE

Clarence Darrow.
5 Esquire Magazine 36 (May 1936).*

[L]et us assume that we represent one of "the underdogs" because of injuries received, or because of an indictment brought by what the prosecutors name themselves, "the state." Then what sort of men will we seek? An Irishman is called into the box for examination. There is no reason for asking about his religion; he is Irish; that is enough. We may not agree with his religion, but it matters not; his feelings go deeper than any religion. You should be aware that he is emotional, kindly and sympathetic. If he is chosen as a juror, his imagination will place him in the dock; really, he is trying himself. You would be guilty of malpractice if you got rid of him, except for the strongest reasons.

An Englishman is not so good as an Irishman, but still, he has come through a long tradition of individual rights, and is not afraid to stand alone; in fact, he is never sure that he is right unless the great majority is against him. The German is not so keen about individual rights except where they concern his own way of life; liberty is not a theory, it is a way of living. Still, he wants to do what is right, and he is not afraid. He has not been among us long, his ways are fixed by his race, his habits are still in the making. We need inquire no further. If he is a Catholic, then he loves music and art; he must be emotional, and will want to help you; give him a chance.

If a Presbyterian enters the jury box and carefully rolls up his umbrella, and calmly and critically sits down, let him go. He is cold as the grave; he knows right from wrong, although he seldom finds anything right. He believes in John Calvin and eternal punishment. Get rid of him with the fewest possible words before he contaminates the others.

[N]ever take a wealthy man on a jury. He will convict, unless the defendant is accused of violating the anti-trust law, selling worthless stocks or bonds, or something of that kind. Next to the Board of Trade, for him, the penitentiary is the most important of all public buildings. These imposing structures stand for capitalism. Civilization could not possibly exist without them. Don't take a man because he is a "good" man; this means nothing. You should find out what he is good *for*. Neither should a man be accepted because he is a bad sort. There are too many ways of being good or bad. If you are defending, you want imaginative individuals. You are not interested in the morals of the juror. If a man is instinctively kind and sympathetic, take him.

————

MODERN TRIALS (2D ED. 1982)

Melvin Belli, Sr.

CONSIDERATIONS IN SELECTING A JURY— RACIAL CONSIDERATIONS

[A]s a rule of thumb, if plaintiff is an Irishman or a Swede, prospective juror Olsen or O'Brien in the several cases will not be excused by plaintiff's lawyer. On the other hand, rule of thumb would lead to a plaintiff's peremptory challenge of an Italian juror when defendant is an Italian and particularly if a vigorous cross-examination is to be contemplated of the Italian defendant.

[C]ONSIDERATIONS IN SELECTING A JURY—ACCOUNTANTS, STATISTICIANS AND BANK CLERKS

The author believes that a plaintiff does better on the amount of verdict by peremptorily challenging the accountant, statistician and bank and insurance clerks. [H]e will be the first to think, and even argue, that "this amount of money that plaintiff is asking is more than he would ever have earned in his lifetime and certainly more than he would need presently."

[C]ONSIDERATIONS IN SELECTING A JURY—ARTISTS, MUSICIANS, WRITERS AND ACTORS

The rule of thumb here: artists, writers, musicians, actors and public figures generally make good plaintiff jurors on the civil side, and good defendant's jurors in the criminal case. As plaintiff's counsel and a criminal defendant's lawyer, I love this type of juror. They are philosophically tuned in to my side of the case and will vote for me substantively, and will usually give a substantial award.

[C]ONSIDERATIONS IN SELECTING A JURY—FARMERS

If I had my choice I would not want a jury of farmers. I do not mean to be disrespectful of those who make it possible for me to survive, but in the dealings I've had with farmers, their concept of law is different from mine as is their concept of the adequacy of awards—to others, not themselves.

What then do you do as a plaintiff's lawyer when you find yourself in a farming community? I think your time would be better spent picking corn than arguing to this type of jury!

————

THE EFFECT OF PEREMPTORY CHALLENGES ON JURY AND VERDICT: AN EXPERIMENT IN A FEDERAL DISTRICT COURT*

Hans Zeisel and Shari Seidman Diamond.
30 Stanford Law Review 491 (1978).

Trial lawyers tell us that they occasionally win their cases at voir dire by the shrewd use of their peremptory challenges. This is the report of an experiment designed to discover whether they really do. Normally, this question cannot be answered with precision: Because the excused jurors do not attend the trial, there is no way of knowing how they would have voted had they not been removed. Our experiment attempted to secure this missing information by asking the peremptorily excused jurors to remain as shadow jurors in the courtroom and to reveal at the end of the trial how they would have voted in the case. This allowed us to become retrospectively clairvoyant—to see how well the prosecutor and defense counsel performed in their attempts to eliminate hostile jurors. More important, by combining this knowledge with posttrial interviews of the real jurors, we reconstructed the vote of the jury that would have decided the case had there been no peremptory challenges—that is, if the first 12 jurors in the venire, not excused for cause, had formed the jury. By comparing what the reconstructed "jury without peremptory challenges" would have done with what the real jury did, we were able to gauge the effect, if any, of the peremptory challenges on the composition of the jury and its verdict.

[T]he experiment was conducted in 12 criminal trials before three judges of the United States District Court for the Northern District of Illinois. Financial considerations limited the number and size of the cases, and we selected only trials that were expected to last no longer than 2 weeks. Within these bounds, the willingness of the judge, prosecutor and defense attorney to cooperate in the experiment dictated the actual selection of cases. We initially planned to look at both criminal and civil cases, but while the parties to the criminal trials generally gave their consent to the experiment, we managed to obtain consent in only three civil cases, too small a sample to integrate into our experimental design. In retrospect, the overwhelming refusal rate in civil cases was a blessing, for it gave us a more homogeneous sample of exclusively criminal cases.

Because of these constraints on their selection, the 12 cases that formed the basis of our study are not a probability sample of anything: They are 12 modestly sized criminal jury cases. Therefore, our experiment should be regarded as only the first step toward an understanding of the effect of peremptory challenges on jury verdicts.

[O]ur data gave us some idea of how well the attorneys used their allotted challenges to excuse jurors who, had they been allowed to sit on the jury, would have voted against their side. We designed a rough performance index that evaluated the extent to which counsel employed peremptory challenges to dismiss hostile or friendly jurors. [The nature of the index is illustrated by calculating, as follows, the prosecutor's performance in one of the 12 cases.]

The original venire consisted of 28 potential jurors, of whom 22.2 would have voted guilty and 5.8 not guilty.[43] The prosecutor's "best performance," therefore, would have used the allotted 6 peremptory challenges to eliminate all 5.8 jurors voting not guilty; 100% of the remaining jurors would have voted guilty. In formulating our attorney performance index, we would have assigned this optimal performance a score of $+100$. The prosecutor's "worst performance" would have excluded 6 guilty-voting jurors, leaving the proportion of guilty votes at 16.2 out of 22, or 73.6%; this worst possible performance would have been assigned a score of -100. A zero score would represent a performance leaving unchanged the original distribution of the venire, estimated at 79% guilty votes.

In the actual case (Case 10), the prosecutor selected his jurors so as to leave a voting constellation of 91.1% guilty votes. We therefore computed this prosecutor's score as follows: (1) because the prosecutor increased the proportion of favorable jurors, the score was given a positive value; (2) the absolute value then was measured by calculating the difference between the percentage of guilty votes in the original venire (79) and the percentage of guilty votes after the prosecutor's challenges (91.1), a score of 12.1; (3) this value then was normalized by dividing by the maximum possible improvement (the difference between the guilty percentage at a zero score, 79, and the guilty percentage at a $+100$ score, 100). The resulting ratio, $+12.1/21$, expressed as a percentage, $+58$, became the prosecutor's performance score.

To complete the attorney performance index, we performed parallel computations for the prosecution and defense counsel in each of the 12 cases.

[T]he collective performance of the attorneys is not impressive. The prosecutors' average score is close to zero (0.5). Thus, in the aggregate, the prosecutors made about as many good challenges as bad ones. The defense counsel's average performance score ($+17.0$) is slightly better, which suggests that, on the average, defense attorneys shifted in their favor the proportion of not guilty votes in the venire. These averages are misleading, however, because the fluctuations around them are so large. The prosecutors' scores fluctuate between $+62$ (Case 11) and 61 (Cases 6 and 12); the defense counsel's scores fluctuate between $+48$ (Case 5) and 62 (Case 8). The average fluctuations around the mean scores are ±38 for the prosecutor and ±25 for the defense, suggesting that in this limited sample of 12 cases, attorney performance was highly erratic. As a result, even though

---

43. We established this distribution of first ballot votes in the standardized 28-person venire by determining the proportion of guilty votes among the potential jurors questioned during voir dire.

attorneys' scores on the average were around zero, in some cases the attorneys performed very poorly, and in others very well. And if, in a case, one side performs poorly while the other side performs well, such disparity may have interesting results.

THE USE OF SOCIAL SCIENCE IN TRIALS WITH POLITICAL AND RACIAL OVERTONES: THE TRIAL OF JOAN LITTLE

John B. McConahay, Courtney J. Mullin, and Jeffrey Frederick.
41 Law and Contemporary Problems 205 (Winter 1977).

The Joan Little case began in Washington, North Carolina. Early on the morning of August 27, 1974, Clarence Alligood, the night jailer for the Beaufort County jail, was found dead in a locked cell in the women's section of the jail. Alligood, a sixty-four-year-old white male, had ice pick punctures in his body and semen on his leg; and his pants and shoes were outside the cell. The person incarcerated in the cell during the preceding weeks was Joan Little, a twenty-year-old black female. Both Ms. Little and the keys to the cell and jail were missing. Over the next few days, there was an extensive search for Ms. Little in Beaufort and adjacent counties. She was on the verge of being declared an outlaw when, accompanied by her attorney, Jerry Paul, she turned herself in to the authorities in Raleigh. She was immediately charged with first degree murder. On April 28, 1975, her trial was moved from Beaufort to Wake County (Raleigh), North Carolina. And on August 15, after a trial of five weeks, she was acquitted of all charges.

[I]n the trial of Joan Little, the judge asked potential jurors, in groups of twelve, general questions—largely regarding their ability to serve for the expected four-to six-week period. Then they were examined individually out of the sight and hearing of other jurors. The prosecution questioned them first and, if they were not excused for cause, made a decision to accept or peremptorily challenge the juror. Once it had passed a juror, the prosecution could not change its decision. At this point, the potential juror was examined by the defense and, if the person was not excused for cause, the defense had to decide to accept or use one of its peremptory challenges. If the defense accepted a juror, he or she was immediately sequestered in the jury room. This process continued until sixteen jurors (twelve regular jurors and four alternates) were seated. The process of jury selection took ten working days during which over two hundred potential jurors were interviewed.

[S]treams of data were combined in the defense's decision to accept or reject a potential juror. First, on the basis of a random sample survey of Wake County, we had developed a mathematical model of the juror who would be ideal for the defense. Second, we observed the behavior of the potential juror during the voir dire and rated him or her on a psychological characteristic known as authoritarianism. Third, we observed the "body language" including both kinesic and paralinguistic behavior in order to determine the degree to which a potential juror was defense or prosecution oriented. Fourth, the attorneys drew upon their voir dire experience and common sense. [F]inally, Ms. Little was asked how she felt about any juror whom we were seriously considering accepting.

[A]   The Survey and Mathematical Model

Although it was expensive to construct (about $35 thousand), the most important scientific tool we had was the mathematical model of the defense's ideal juror based upon a random sample survey of Wake County. Its effectiveness rested upon two assumptions which, fortunately, proved to be justified. First, we assumed that the jury pool would be close to a random sample of the citizens of Wake County eligible for jury service. Second, we assumed that those characteristics of the survey respondents which enabled us to predict opinions regarding Joan Little's guilt or innocence in the sample survey would also enable us to predict them in the jury pool.

In order to facilitate a general understanding of the mathematical model by readers unfamiliar with statistical methods, it will be described in a brief, nontechnical fashion. The basic idea behind this approach is that individuals who are predisposed to believe that the defendant in question is guilty will differ from other individuals with respect to a number of observable characteristics. Once these characteristics have been identified for the population as a whole, they can be used to predict the predispositions of each potential juror.

Before the model can be employed, a survey of attitudes in the particular geographical area of interest must be undertaken. This provides an assessment of the attitudinal composition of that area from which the mathematical model will then generate its predictions. The mathematical model itself is a predictive hybrid of several statistical techniques. First, we chose an appropriate measure of the attitudes or opinions we wished to predict, i.e., belief in the guilt or innocence of the accused. Next, a series of statistical techniques was employed to determine what demographic characteristics of the respondents in the sample would act as predictors of these important opinions. Demographic characteristics might include age, race, sex, political and religious affiliations.

In the first phase of the procedure, an attempt was made to divide the sample into groups possessing similar opinions. That is, if those of higher ages and lower ages differed in their opinions regarding the guilt or innocence of the accused, it would be helpful to divide the sample into younger and older age groups before an attempt was made to formulate predictions of their important opinions. This was accomplished by using a modified version of a statistical computer program known as AID (Automatic Interaction Detection).

The AID program searched the survey data until it had successfully divided the sample into as many groups as possible based upon the homogeneity of the sample members' opinions. Membership in any one homogeneous group was often defined by several demographic characteristics—for example, young democrats with at least a college education. As a result of this first phase, our ability to predict opinions was increased by decreasing the variability of our sample.

After the sample was divided into groups of individuals with fairly similar opinions, each group was examined to establish which of their social and psychological characteristics were important with respect to our ability to predict a potential juror's opinions. In more technical terms, this phase was concerned with the formulation of predictive equations for jurors' opinions. In order to do this, we used a [statistical] technique [w]hich enabled us to develop a mathematical model of the opinions of potential jurors based upon a series of characteristics that differed from one demographic group to another. An example of this would be the case where one group produced by phase I consisted of young democrats with at least a college education. For members of this group we may need to know the sex, religious attitudes, and income characteristics of the individuals. In another group from phase I, e.g., democrats over forty-five years old with a high school education, the terms in the predictive equation might be the type of magazines read, sex, and preferred presidential candidate.

Though the social and psychological factors used to predict opinions varied from group to group, they combined to form the same thing: a prediction of the likelihood that a potential juror would be willing to vote Joan Little not guilty before hearing any of the evidence.

One of the advantages of this procedure is obvious. Regardless of what a juror might say during the voir dire, by observing or obtaining his or her demographic characteristics (age, education, etc.) and social-psychological characteristics (politics, reading habits, etc.), the mathematical model enabled us to predict how predisposed he or she was to side with the prosecution or defense. Potential jurors might lie about their preconceptions of guilt or innocence, but they were much less likely to lie about their age or education.

A second advantage is not so obvious. Because the judge permitted both prosecution and defense to send out with the jury summons a questionnaire concerning the jurors' demographic characteristics, we were able to get a preliminary estimate of what proportion of the jury pool would be predisposed to be "pro-defense" or "pro-defendant" before the voir dire began and before we had seen a single juror. The advantage here is that in the early part of the voir dire we could afford to let some promising jurors go because we knew that better potential jurors would appear later. Many of the news reporters failed to see how important this was. Informally, if not in print or on the air, they expressed the opinion that the mathematical model and the other scientific procedures were not necessary because anyone would have known we wanted health food waitresses (the final jury had two of them) and a former drama major turned record store manager. What they failed to notice was that we got these persons as jurors because we had not already filled the slots with secretaries and IBM engineers.

B. Authoritarianism

Although we expected the math model to be between 85 per cent and 95 per cent accurate, we supplemented it with courtroom observations of authoritarianism and body language. Our observations of authoritarianism were based upon the theory of the authoritarian personality developed in the 1950s by researchers at the University of California at Berkeley.

According to this theory, which is supported by mountains of empirical research, extreme authoritarians are rigid, racist, anti-semitic, sexually repressed, politically conservative, highly punitive individuals who will accept the word of an authority figure over that of a lesser person. The authoritarian is servile and obsequious in a subordinate position, but takes out all of his or her pent-up hostility and frustration upon those perceived to be in violation of the conventional norms of society.

It is obvious that no defense attorney would want a jury loaded with extreme authoritarians. However, people vary in the degree to which they exhibit authoritarian personality traits. To the extent that potential jurors are more or less authoritarian, we would expect them to be more or less desirable from the viewpoint of the defense as jurors in trials involving minority persons, political and social nonconformists, or other controversial defendants. It is possible that the juror's level of authoritarianism might be something of a factor in all criminal trials. In the adversary system, the juror must weigh the evidence and arguments presented by the prosecution on behalf of the state or society and by the defense attorney on behalf of someone accused of a crime and therefore of lower status than the prosecutor.

[T]he authoritarianism rating scale we used in the courtroom ranged from a low of zero which represented minimum authoritarianism to a high of thirty which represented maximum authoritarianism. The neutral point between high authoritarian and low authoritarian behavior was fifteen. [The psychologists believed] that the average American rated about twenty on this scale of authoritarianism. By observing the authoritarianism-related behavior of potential jurors—their rigidity, their sexual prudery, their introspectiveness, and so on—three social psychologists were able to rate reliably the person's level of authoritarianism. When a decision was made to accept or reject a potential juror, these independently made, written ratings were combined to feed an authoritarianism rating into the decision making process.

The average rating assigned by our observers to all persons who were interviewed for Ms. Little's jury was 21.02, which is not very different from the general American population. On the other hand, the average for the sixteen seated jurors was 14.03. For the twelve who made the final decision to acquit her, the average authoritarianism rating was 12.95. Thus, we were able to pick a jury which was significantly less authoritarian than the jury pool as a whole.

C. Body Language

In a highly publicized case such as Ms. Little's, there were some people who actively desired to be on the jury. These people might have said whatever was necessary to insure that they were picked for the jury. Some of them could be expected to be pro-defense, some to be pro-prosecution. It was crucial for the defense to determine in some way the truthfulness of the jurors being selected. To do this, we called upon the newly emerging science of kinesics and paralinguistics, i.e. body language.

Although people frequently communicate their true feelings in the words they speak, it is now clear that we can also communicate a great deal of information by means of our body movements, gestures, positions, vocal intonations, pauses and the like. In other words, it is not what we say but the way we say it. We are perfectly capable of expressing one type of attitude with our language and a diametrically opposed attitude with our body language, for example, by unduly long pauses when speaking or by loudness or softness of the voice.

Our approach was to measure the levels of anxiety expressed by the individuals being questioned. We employed five variables to determine the kinesic response (body movement, body orientation, body posture, eye contact, and hand movement). We also employed two paralinguistic measures (vocal intonation and vocal hesitancy).

No single kinesic or paralinguistic response determined the acceptance or rejection of any juror. We were looking for patterns of behavior. Human communication is extremely complex and one must look at the whole in order to make any determination as to the attitudes being expressed. Some popular writers on the subject would have one believe that a single gesture is indicative of an overall attitude. In truth, the single gesture must be deeply incorporated into a pattern of response expressed throughout the body and by the voice.

[O]bservers [n]oted each prospective juror's pattern of [b]ehavior [a]nd rated the juror on a scale ranging from one point, least favorable to the defense, to five points, most favorable to the defense. These preliminary ratings were written down independently by each observer and then combined to form a final five-point rating of the juror's attitude toward the defense (a high score indicating maximum favorableness).

To assess the relationship between the measures made on the basis of authoritarianism and body language, we correlated the two scales. The overall correlation was .79. This correlation was high and indicated that authoritarianism was associated with being least favorable toward the defense. The correlation was not so high, however, as to indicate that the two scales were simply measuring the same phenomena. Each measure both reinforced and added to the other. The use of both approaches insured more complete knowledge of the attitudes of the potential jurors than the use of either alone.

D.   The Final Decision

When, in the course of the voir dire, a member of the defense team thought that a decision should be made on the potential juror under consideration, a conference was called. At this point, the members of the team put their heads together in a fashion that resembled a football huddle. Each social scientist read to the team from a written estimate of the potential juror based upon the juror's demographic rating, authoritarianism, or body language. In this way we minimized the influence upon an estimate from one technique (e.g., body language) by another technique (e.g., authoritarianism). The attorneys [a]nd Ms. Little also indicated their opinions of the potential juror in this "huddle." One of three decisions was made: accept, reject, or obtain more information.

[A]t the close of the five week trial, the jury took seventy-eight minutes to find Ms. Little not guilty of all charges.

―――――

NOTES

1.   Prosecution Use. Virtually all of the reported instances of the use of social science research to choose a jury in criminal cases have involved use by defendants. Whether the prosecution could use these methods remains an open question, though apparently no specific statutory or constitutional provision seems, on its face, to bar such action. Indeed, in State v. Banks, 295 N.C. 399, 245 S.E.2d 743 (1978) the court refused to rule that the trial judge abused his discretion in permitting a student psychologist "to consult with the district attorney during the *voir dire* of the jury." Id. at 749. On the other hand, in United States v. Collins, 972 F.2d 1385 (5th Cir.1992), the prosecution commissioned a survey intended to aid in jury selection. The defendants found out about the survey and reported it to the trial judge, who ordered the government to terminate the survey and turn over the results to the court. For some, prosecution use of social science in choosing a jury would seem only prudent trial preparation by government attorneys; for others, it would seem an unfair advantage for an already advantaged party. The later view might be translated into arguments that a defendant's due process rights under the Fifth and Fourteenth Amendments of the United States Constitution would be infringed or that the Sixth Amendment right to trial by an impartial jury would be impaired. See Moskitis, The Constitutional Need for Discovery of Pre-Voir Dire Jury Studies, 49 Southern California Law Review 597, 607–621 (1976). Indeed, Moskitis even contends that constitutional principles might prevent defense use of scientific jury selection, a view not likely to be supported and contrary now to long practice. Id. at 621–24. These issues do not, of course, arise in civil cases where two private parties are typically involved and, presumably, either is free to use social science research in choosing a jury.

2.   Discrimination. In Batson v. Kentucky, 476 U.S. 79, 106 S.Ct. 1712, 90 L.Ed.2d 69 (1986), the Supreme Court, in an opinion by Justice Powell, held that the Constitution "forbids the prosecutor to challenge potential jurors solely on account of their race or on the assumption that black jurors as a group will be unable impartially to consider the State's case against a black defendant." 476 U.S. at 89, 106 S.Ct. at 1719. The Court listed several elements that defendants must show to establish a prima facie case of discrimination, then recognized the possibility that a prosecutor might "come forward with a neutral explanation for challenging black jurors." Id. at 97, 106 S.Ct. at 1723. The role, if any, of social science research in providing such a "neutral explanation" was not discussed by Justice Powell in his opinion.

3. Discovery. Where social science research is used to assist in jury selection the research would be generally protected from discovery in federal court and in states adopting federal rules. In criminal cases, the reciprocal limitation of Federal Rule 16(b)(1)(B) would protect defendant research unless defendant sought similar prosecution studies, an unlikely situation. In civil cases, Federal Rule 26(b)(4)(B) would permit discovery only upon a showing of "exceptional circumstances under which it is impracticable for the party seeking discovery to obtain facts or opinions on the same subject by other means." This very restrictive requirement applies to experts who are employed to prepare for trial but who will not testify, the invariable situation in scientific jury selection.

THE LIMITS OF SCIENTIFIC JURY SELECTION: ETHICAL AND EMPIRICAL

Michael Saks.
17 Jurimetrics Journal 3 (1976).

[T]he defense of scientific jury selection might begin by pointing out that it is thoroughly legal. Prospective jurors are not themselves approached or tampered with. They are merely compared to statistical profiles of the population from which they were drawn. They are questioned only during *voir dire,* and only to the extent permitted by the trial judge, as has been the way for generations. All that has changed is that lawyers can now know the hidden meaning of the answers and of jurors' background characteristics.

The practice of *voir dire* and of challenging jurors was not invented by [social scientists]. [I]t has been part of the jury system for centuries. And for those centuries lawyers have sought to impanel the most favorable possible juries for their clients. This has always been widely regarded as a proper goal for the lawyer. Why should the fact that he has finally been given the means to achieve that goal be so objectionable? If the goal was good, why has the ability to actually achieve it become bad?

[T]he goal of jury selection is not, I think, an unwise one. The intent is to impanel an impartial jury, that is, a jury whose members do not have biases that would make them unable to fairly weigh the evidence. Jurors are supposed to reach a verdict shaped by the weight of the evidence and not by the decision-makers' biases. The strategy for achieving that goal—allowing both advocates some opportunity to exclude from the jury persons thought to be biased against their side—also seems to me a wise and workable one. Scientific jury selection can add substantially to the achievement of that goal. Instead of guessing at who will be biased and will therefore not respond impartially to the evidence, lawyers can make informed judgments. If both sides have social science help, each will more effectively exclude jurors favorable to the other side, and the final panel will consist of the neutral jurors, the very ones who will be most able to do what a jury is intended to do. Thus, juror attitudes and personality would play a minimal role in determining the outcome of the trial. Evidence would be permitted to play the greatest possible role, which is how it was always supposed to be. Thus, scientific jury selection would make the goal of impartial jury decisions more attainable than has ever before been possible.

But, the critics would interject, the presence of such expertise on both sides is a fantasy which ignores the realities of justice in America. Today only the wealthy and celebrated have such help, and tomorrow the only additional people to have it will be prosecutors, and they will use it routinely. And this criticism is probably entirely true. But it does not demonstrate some evil inherent in scientific jury selection. It points instead to a fundamental inequity in our courts. *All* resources will be unevenly distributed in a system where those with wealth or the right friends can obtain services unavailable to the average citizen. This is not the fault of the resources or their inventors.

[E]very material and service commodity is systematically more available to one side than it is to the other. And every new invention of social scientists, legal service providers, or anyone else will be too. The problem lies not in each service and invention but in the system in which these things are used. The critics of scientific jury selection, to keep existing inequities from becoming more pronounced, would keep this new technology out of the courtroom or restructure court proceedings to minimize its potential impact. But next year or decade they will have to rally again to ban yet another innovation and then another and another after that. I suggest that these energies would be more efficiently directed at reforming the system which fosters all of these inequities. To do so would eliminate long standing inequities and make future innovations welcome for the benefits they may offer. The alternative is to live with existing imbalances and eternally eschew new developments.

[I] have saved for last what is perhaps the most interesting reason for not worrying excessively about scientific jury selection: the empirical reason. No evidence exists to support the apparently widely held belief that scientific jury selection is a powerful tool. What has most people upset about the technique is the fact that no one who has used it has lost a case. By the usual standards for evaluating empirical evidence, the same standards used by the social and behavioral scientists who developed the basic principles for the technique, this seemingly impressive evidence is really no evidence at all. The venerated scientific method usually calls for a control group, that is, a comparison group to tell you what an observation really means. To elucidate, suppose there were a control group. Suppose each of the cases had been tried before two juries—one selected the scientific way and one selected the old way. We could then compare the verdicts delivered by the scientific juries with those delivered by the conventional juries (the control juries.) We know that all of the scientifically selected juries refused to convict. What would the conventionally selected juries have done? The answer to this question is absolutely essential to an assessment of how effective scientific jury selection is or even whether it works at all. Without such comparisons it simply is impossible to know. If a significant number of control juries convicted we would know that the use of scientific jury selection techniques helped the defense effort.

If all of the conventional juries also refused to convict, we would know that scientific jury selection offered no help to the defense in those cases.

[A] balanced assessment of the effectiveness of scientific jury selection, based on what is generally known about human decision-making and on the data offered by the studies that have been done is, I believe, the following. It is safe to say that scientific jury selection "works;" juror characteristics do influence the decisions they make. But it is evidence that most determines the outcome of trials, rather than the characteristics of the jurors. If the evidence against a defendant is very strong or very weak, it isn't going to matter who is on the jury. If the evidence is close, then the jury selection could make the difference. One wouldn't be wasting money or time if he employed scientific jury selection, but if he did so at the expense of building a strong case out of evidence, he would be making a mistake. In cases where the evidence is close or ambiguous, scientific jury selection would be especially helpful.

———

SOCIAL SCIENCE INVOLVEMENT IN VOIR DIRE: PRELIMINARY DATA ON THE EFFECTIVENESS OF "SCIENTIFIC JURY SELECTION"*

Jeffrey T. Frederick.
2 Behavioral Sciences and the Law 375 (1984).

[The author examined data from an important civil case to answer the question whether the survey technique of scientific jury selection is an effective litigation device.]

This case involved a suit for breach of contract between Shell Oil Company and Newport News Shipbuilding, Inc., concerning the late delivery of Ultra Large Crude Carriers (large oil tankers) to Shell. The plaintiff claimed that the over two year delay in delivery had cost it approximately $100 million. The defendant claimed that the delays (allegedly resulting from facility construction delays, subcontractor delays, and governmental priorities on other projects, among others) were justified under the contract signed by the parties. In conjunction with its litigation efforts, the defendant sought assistance in evidence preparation and persuasion and jury selection. Two projects were conducted which have a bearing on the present discussion of systematic jury selection, community survey and mock jury projects.

Methods

The first project conducted was an attitudinal survey of the Fourth Federal Judicial District, the jurisdiction in which the trial was to be held. A random sample of 967 registered voters were interviewed by telephone.[8] The questionnaire employed in this survey explored a variety of content areas. These areas included items addressing contracts, delays in delivery of products, buyer mitigation of losses, and defense contractor issues, among others. The general perceptions of the two litigants outside the scope of the case were assessed. The questionnaire also examined attitudes regarding equity, victim compensation, and authoritarianism. In addition, over 15 demographic questions were asked.

A critical component of the questionnaire was the introduction of a hypothetical case (concerning an aircraft manufacturer) that mirrored the basic facts and issues in the case. Respondents were given the basic facts and asked to decide whether the plaintiff should be awarded full compensation, partial compensation, or no compensation at all. Following this decision, respondents were presented with a series of seven independent informational items.

[A]fter each informational item, respondents again decided whether to provide the plaintiff with full, partial, or no compensation.

A mock jury project was also conducted for the defendant. While this project was aimed at testing evidentiary and persuasive aspects of the case, data from this project are also relevant to jury selection. A one hour and 35 minute videotape of a mock trial involving the litigants was developed using attorneys and law faculty as the actors in the case.

[J]urors viewed the videotape, rendered a preliminary verdict, participated in deliberations, rendered a final verdict, and answered special interrogatories.

[Based on the survey results, a model or profile of juror favorability was constructed.] A four variable predictive equation consisting of belief concerning the responsibility of manufacturer for delays beyond its control, race of respondent, prior military service, and education of the respondent proved to be the best predictors of the dependent measure.

---

8. The total sample had an approxi-   present sample size.
mately 30% refusal rate which yielded the

[T]he question now becomes how effective was this model in predicting individual juror decisions in this case. The case settled the day before the trial was to begin and, therefore, any actual verdict data in this case do not exist. However, relevant data are available from the mock jury project. The voir dire for that project included all the questions necessary to fit these individuals to the profiles developed from the survey. Thus, a comparison can be made between jurors' predicted orientation and their preliminary verdicts.

The individual jurors were assigned a party specific orientation score by fitting these individuals to the predictive equation. Because of the complex nature of the verdict questionnaire, the preliminary verdicts were classified into four categories: $20 million to $50 million award for the plaintiff equals *1,* $1 million to $19 million award for the plaintiff equals *2,* no award for the plaintiff equals *3,* and $1 to $12 million award for the defendant equals *4.*[11] The party specific orientation score was then correlated with the verdict scale.

[T]o further examine how effective the party specific orientation scores were in predicting the verdicts of jurors these scores were used to classify jurors into one of three categories, pro-plaintiff, undifferentiated, and pro-defense. The classification was based on approximately equal representation in each of the groups. This yielded a distribution of the seven lowest scores classified as pro-plaintiff, the five middle scores classified as undifferentiated, and the seven highest scores classified as pro-defense. In view of the small sample size, verdict scores were classified as either a plaintiff's verdict (1 or 2) or a defense verdict (3 or 4). The overall distribution of verdicts was 42% favoring the plaintiff and 58% favoring the defense.

[A]nalysis of these classifications reveal that they tended to correctly predict verdict preference. Seventy-one percent of those classified as pro-plaintiff rendered verdicts in favor of the plaintiff. Of those classified as undifferentiated, 40% found for the plaintiff. Finally, only 14% of those classified as pro-defense returned a verdict for the plaintiff. In other words, 86% of those classified as pro-defense found for the defendant.

[T]hese results reveal several important points. First, they show that individual differences in party specific orientation could be established in survey respondents' decision preferences using a case relevant hypothetical situation. Second, this orientation could be estimated by the use of a predictive equation. Third, these estimates could accurately predict verdicts in an analogous trial situation using an independent sample (mock jurors).

SELECTED BIBLIOGRAPHY

Diamond, Scientific Jury Selection: What Social Scientists Know And Do Not Know, 73 Judicature 178 (1990).

11. The jurors could award money to the defendant because of a cross-claim in this case being brought by the defendant.

Frederick, Social Science Involvement in Voir Dire: Preliminary Data on the Effectiveness of "Scientific Jury Selection," 2 Behavioral Sciences and the Law 375 (1984).

J. Frederick, The Psychology of the American Jury (1987).

J. Frederick, Getting the Most Out of Voir Dire (1993).

J. Frederick, Mastering Voir Dire and Jury Selection: Gain an Edge in Questioning and Selecting Your Jury (2nd ed. 2005).

Saks, The Limits of Scientific Jury Selection: Ethical and Empirical, 17 Jurimetric Journal 3 (1976).

Saks, What Do Jury Experiments Tell Us About How Juries (Should) Make Decisions? 6 Southern California Interdisciplinary Law Journal 1 (1997).

Zeisel and Diamond, The Jury Selection in the Mitchell-Stans Conspiracy Trial, 1976 American Bar Foundation Research Journal 151.

SECTION III.   CHOOSING INSTRUCTIONS

A third use of social science has involved the preparation of jury instructions. In federal court, the instruction practice is controlled by Criminal Rule 30 and by Civil Rule 51. Both rules provide that the parties may request particular instructions to the jury. Commentators have long speculated that the traditional jargon-laden jury instruction is often little help to jurors, and sometimes is actually misleading, and researchers have demonstrated the truth of these speculations. Happily, they have also demonstrated that the effectiveness of a particular instruction can be enhanced by following a series of relatively simple drafting rules. This research has already been used in drafting "pattern instructions," standard suggestions for trial judges. Recently, courts have begun to use research about jury instructions to determine the adequacy of instructions.

PATTERN JURY INSTRUCTIONS: THE APPLICATION OF SOCIAL SCIENCE RESEARCH

Harvey S. Perlman.
65 Nebraska Law Review 520 (1986).

Since 1970 a series of empirical studies have documented first, that pattern jury instructions are not completely understood by the jurors to whom they are addressed, and second, that the use of certain techniques of drafting and organization improve juror comprehension.

In 1976 Strawn and Buchanan examined juror comprehension of Florida's criminal pattern jury instructions.[35] Randomly selected Florida

---

35. Strawn & Buchanan, Jury Confu-   (1976).
sion: A Threat to Justice, 59 Judicature 478

jurors were shown videotaped jury instructions and were then tested by a multiple choice, true/false test to measure their comprehension. A control group was given the test without viewing any instructions. Jurors who had received instructions knew more than those who had not, but the instructed jurors still missed thirty percent of the test items, and on four issues regarded by the study's authors as critical, including an understanding of the concept of "reasonable doubt," the instructed jurors showed no better understanding than the control group.[36]

In 1977, Elwork, Sales, and Alfini published the first results of a large study they conducted utilizing the Michigan civil pattern instructions.[37] Again, random subjects viewed videotaped instructions and were then compared against a control group that had been given no instructions. In one study the subjects watched an entire videotaped trial to provide a factual context. Again, the authors found that traditional pattern jury instructions did not provide a significant measure of comprehension beyond that of the control group. They found, in fact, a nearly forty-percent rate of misunderstanding among those who viewed the traditional pattern instructions.

However, Elwork, Sales, and Alfini went further. Utilizing psycholinguistic literature, and, I think they will admit, a substantial measure of common sense, they redrafted the traditional instructions to improve juror comprehension. The literature they employed and the techniques they adopted focused on vocabulary, grammar, and organization. They replaced legal jargon with common words, abstract words with concrete words, and negative words with positive words. Homonyms—words with multiple meanings—were avoided.

Their revised instructions were sensitive to grammatical construction that had been shown empirically to improve comprehension. They avoided, where possible, embedded and compound sentences and the passive voice. They adopted what some social scientists termed a hierarchical and algorithmic organization scheme which breaks down general concepts into component parts such that concepts flow from previously explained concepts. Empirical tests demonstrated that their revised instructions heightened comprehension by lay jurors.

In 1982 the same authors published a book-length treatment of the subject entitled *Making Jury Instructions Understandable,* which reports on a wider test sample, refines the linguistic rules that demonstrably improve comprehension, and then sets out a step-by-step process through

---

36. Id. at 480–83. Although I disclaim any expertise in empirical validity, as a lawyer I am uncomfortable with these findings. The jurors did not deliberate, they did not have a context within which to understand or apply the instructions as they did not see a trial, and they were not asked to apply the instructions. They were, in fact, given a test much like students in a classroom. Judged in that context a 73% on a test is by any normal measure a passing grade. This study, although not conclusive, did encourage more sophisticated efforts.

37. [Elwork, Sales & Alfini, Juridic Decisions: In Ignorance of the Law or In Light Of It, 1 L. & Human Behav. 167 (1977).]

which lawyers (or others) may both rewrite instructions to improve understanding and empirically test their efforts.

A similar project was conducted by Charrow and Charrow and published in the Columbia Law Review in 1979.[41] In their study subjects listened to instructions and were then asked to paraphrase what they had heard. Comparing the traditional to the linguistically revised instructions, they concluded again that much could be done to improve juror comprehension.

In two more recent studies,[44] Severance, Green, and Loftus carried the empirical observations a step further. To find sources of misunderstanding, they surveyed those cases in which juries had asked the judge questions during deliberations. They isolated three particularly bothersome instructions—those dealing with intent, reasonable doubt, and the use of evidence of prior convictions.

In the first study, jury-eligible college students viewed an hour-long videotape of a burglary trial and were then divided into six groups. One group received no instructions, one received a general instruction telling it what its duties were, and one received specific pattern instructions on the three areas to be studied. Half of each of these groups deliberated, the other half did not.

The authors examined the "jurors" through a questionnaire to determine whether they could distinguish between correct and incorrect expressions of the relevant law. In a separate test to determine whether jurors could apply the instructions to novel fact situations, the jurors were given ten hypothetical situations and asked to evaluate the outcome.

Comprehension measures replicated the earlier studies. Subjects receiving no instructions missed 35.6% of the questions on comprehension, subjects receiving the general instruction only missed 34.7%, and subjects receiving the specific instructions erred 29.6% of the time.

In measuring the subject's ability to apply the law to new situations, subjects receiving specific instructions did apply the law correctly more often, but the specific instruction on intent actually diminished that ability.

The authors then redrafted the specific instructions using the psycholinguistic techniques developed by the Charrows and Elwork groups and obtained consistently more accurate responses. Jurors receiving the redrafted specific instructions had an error in comprehension of 20.3%.[50]

In a second, more detailed study, the same authors used both ex-jurors and persons who had been called for jury duty. They discovered that the

41. Charrow & Charrow, Making Legal Language Understandable: A Psycholinguistic Study of Jury Instructions, 79 Col.L.Rev. 1306 (1979).

44. Severance, Greene & Loftus, Toward Criminal Jury Instructions that Jurors can Understand, 75 J.Crim.L. & Criminology 198 (1984); Severance & Loftus, Improving the Ability of Jurors to Comprehend and Apply Criminal Jury Instructions, 17 L. & Soc'y R. 153 (1982).

50. Id. at 213. By comparison, jurors receiving the pattern instruction had a 24.3% error rate, and jurors receiving no instruction had an error rate of 29.3%. The difference was statistically significant.

more experienced jurors had greater accuracy of comprehension. They also replicated the finding that their revised instructions aided comprehension, particularly when jurors were able to deliberate. They also used the Charrow technique of asking jurors to paraphrase instructions and again found their revised instructions were better understood.

The Severance group also surveyed trial judges throughout the country to determine whether the group's set of revised instructions were regarded as correct statements of the law. They concluded that judges would accept as accurate their revised instructions.

———

THE LAW AND PSYCHOLOGY OF JURY INSTRUCTIONS

J. Alexander Tanford.
69 Nebraska Law Review 71 (1990).

Much of the empirical research [about jury instructions] has focused on how to improve [c]omprehension. [P]sycholinguists suggest that comprehension would be improved if instructions were written along the following guidelines:

1.   Eliminate nominalizations (making nouns out of verbs) and substitute verb forms; e.g., changing "an *offer* of evidence" to "items *were offered* into evidence."

2.   Replace the prepositional phrase "as to" with "about;" e.g., changing "you must not speculate *as to* what the answer might have been" to "you must not speculate *about* what the answer might have been."

3.   Relocate prepositional phrases so they do not interrupt a sentence; e.g., avoiding sentences such as "proximate cause is a cause which, *in a natural and continuous sequence,* produces the injury."

4.   Replace words that are difficult to understand with simple ones; e.g., changing "agent's negligence is *imputed* to plaintiff" to "agent's negligence *transfers* to plaintiff."

5.   Avoid multiple negatives in a sentence; e.g., "innocent *mis*recollection is *not un*common."

6.   Use the active rather than passive voice; e.g., changing "no emphasis is intended by me" to "I do not intend to emphasize."

7.   Avoid "whiz" deletions (omitting words "which is"); e.g., by changing "statements of counsel" to "statements *which are* made by counsel."

8.   Reduce long lists of words with similar meanings to only one or two; e.g., shortening "knowledge, skill, experience, training, or education" to "training or experience."

9. Organize instructions into meaningful discourse structures that avoid connecting unrelated ideas in ways that make them seem related.[63]

10. Avoid embedding subordinate clauses in sentences; e.g., "you must not speculate *to be true* any insinuation *suggested by a question asked a witness.*"

MITCHELL v. GONZALES

Supreme Court of California, 1991.
54 Cal.3d 1041, 1 Cal.Rptr.2d 913, 819 P.2d 872.

■ Lucas, Chief Justice.

In this case we decide whether BAJI No. 3.75,[1] the so-called proximate cause instruction, which contains a "but for" test of cause in fact, should continue to be given in this state, or whether it should be disapproved in favor of BAJI No. 3.76, the so-called legal cause instruction, which employs the "substantial factor" test of cause in fact.[2]

Plaintiffs James and Joyce Mitchell, the parents of 12-year-old Damechie Mitchell, who drowned in Lake Gregory on July 4, 1985, sued defendants Jose L. Gonzales, Matilde Gonzales, and Mrs. Gonzales's son Luis (hereafter defendants) for damages, claiming defendants' negligence caused Damechie's death. By special verdict, the jury found that defendants were negligent, i.e., they had breached a duty, but that the negligence was not a proximate cause of the death.

The Court of Appeal concluded that, under the facts, the trial court erred when it denied plaintiffs' request to instruct the jury pursuant to BAJI No. 3.76 and instead instructed under BAJI No. 3.75. After reviewing both instructions, the Court of Appeal concluded that BAJI No. 3.75 is potentially misleading and should not have been given, and that the trial court committed prejudicial error when it refused to give BAJI No. 3.76.

---

63. ([E.]g., change "If in these instructions any rule is repeated, no emphasis thereon is intended; for that reason, you must consider these instructions as a whole; the order in which they are given has no significance" to "There are three things you must keep in mind: first, repetition of an instruction does not mean I am emphasizing it; second, you must consider all the instructions together; and third, the order has no significance.")

1. All BAJI [Book of Approved Jury Instructions] instructions referred to are from the bound volume of the seventh edition (1986) unless otherwise noted.

2. BAJI No. 3.75, requested by defendants and given by the trial court, provides:

"A proximate cause of [injury] [damage] [loss] [or] [harm] is a cause which, in natural and continuous sequence, produces the [injury] [damage] [loss] [or] [harm] and without which the [injury] [damage] [loss] [or] [harm] would not have occurred." Because of the "without which" language, courts often refer to this instruction as the "but for" instruction of causation.

BAJI No. 3.76, requested by plaintiffs and refused by the trial court, provides: "A legal cause of [injury] [damage] [loss] [or] [harm] is a cause which is a substantial factor in bringing about the [injury] [damage] [loss] [or] [harm]."

We granted review in this case to determine whether courts should continue to instruct juries on cause in fact using BAJI No. 3.75 in light of the frequent criticism of that instruction.

[A]lleged Instructional Error

As Dean Prosser observed over 40 years ago, "Proximate cause remains a tangle and a jungle, a palace of mirrors and a maze...." Cases "indicate that 'proximate cause' covers a multitude of sins, that it is a complex term of highly uncertain meaning under which other rules, doctrines and reasons lie buried...." (Prosser, Proximate Cause in California (1950) 38 Cal.L.Rev. 369, 375.)

[T]he misunderstanding engendered by the term "proximate cause" has been documented. In a scholarly study of 14 jury instructions, BAJI No. 3.75 produced proportionally the most misunderstanding among laypersons. (Charrow, *Making Legal Language Understandable: A Psycholinguistic Study of Jury Instructions* (1979) 79 Colum.L.Rev. 1306, 1353 (hereafter *Psycholinguistic Study*).) The study noted two significant problems with BAJI No. 3.75. First, because the phrase "natural and continuous sequence" precedes "the verb it is intended to modify, the construction leaves the listener with the impression that the cause itself is in a natural and continuous sequence. Inasmuch as a single 'cause' cannot be in a continuous sequence, the listener is befuddled." (*Psycholinguistic Study, supra,* 79 Colum.L.Rev. at p. 1323.) Second, in one experiment, "the term 'proximate cause' was misunderstood by 23% of the subjects.... They interpreted it as 'approximate cause,' 'estimated cause,' or some fabrication." (Id., at p. 1353.)

[W]e recognize that BAJI No. 3.76 is not perfectly phrased. The term "legal cause" may be confusing. As part of the psycholinguistic study referred to above, the experimenters rewrote BAJI No. 3.75 to include the term "legal cause."[8] The study found that "25% of the subjects who heard 'legal cause' misinterpreted it as the opposite of an 'illegal cause.' We would therefore recommend that the term 'legal cause' not be used in jury instructions; instead, the simple term 'cause' should be used, with the explanation that the law defines 'cause' in its own particular way."[9] (*Psycholinguistic Study, supra,* 79 Colum.L.Rev. at p. 1353.)

[T]he continued use of BAJI No. 3.75 as an instruction on cause in fact is unwise. The foregoing amply demonstrates that BAJI No. 3.75 is grammatically confusing and conceptually misleading. Continued use of this instruction will likely cause needless appellate litigation regarding the

---

8. The modified instruction read, "A legal cause of an injury is something that triggers a natural chain of events that ultimately produces the injury. [¶] Without the legal cause, the injury would not occur." (*Psycholinguistic Study, supra,* 79 Colum.L.Rev. at p. 1352.)

9. Although we need not decide whether BAJI No. 3.76 should be rewritten to eliminate the term "legal cause," we do suggest that the Committee on Standard Jury Instructions consider whether the instruction could be improved by adopting the suggestion of the *Psycholinguistic Study* or by otherwise modifying the instruction.

propriety of the instructions in particular cases. Use of BAJI No. 3.76 will avoid much of the confusion inherent in BAJI No. 3.75. It is intelligible and easily applied. We therefore conclude that BAJI No. 3.75, the so-called proximate cause instruction, should be disapproved and that the court erred when it refused to give BAJI No. 3.76 and instead gave BAJI No. 3.75. [A]ccordingly, the decision of the Court of Appeal reversing the judgment in favor of defendants is affirmed.

DECIDING ON DEATH: REVISING JURY INSTRUCTIONS TO IMPROVE JUROR COMPREHENSION OF THE LAW

7 Researching Law: An ABF Update 1 (1996).

In 1972 the Supreme Court, in *Furman v. Georgia*, invalidated the death penalty statutes of thirty-five states on the grounds that the broad discretion under which juries operated in imposing the death penalty was producing arbitrary and inconsistent decisions in violation of the Eighth and Fourteenth Amendments. In setting forth a new standard of guided discretion, the Court held in later cases that states could constitutionally execute offenders if jurors were told what factors to consider and how they should be weighed. But a study* conducted by [American Bar Foundation] Research Fellow Shari Diamond, in collaboration with Professor Judith Levi, has found that the instructions jurors receive in some capital cases do not provide sufficient guidance and that jury deliberations cannot be relied on to reduce the high level of miscomprehension. In an experiment with jury-eligible citizens, Diamond and Levi found that a revised set of instructions that addressed sources of juror confusion did increase comprehension substantially.

Incorrect Interpretations

It was not until 1991 that a court was persuaded by scientific evidence that jury instructions in a capital case were unconstitutional because "they failed to provide jurors with a clear understanding of the law," the researchers note. The issue arose in a hearing on the capital habeas corpus petition of James Free, an Illinois death row inmate. A magistrate judge recommended that the petition be granted on the ground that survey evidence had "raised serious questions about the ability of Illinois capital jury instructions to provide the constitutionally requisite guidance to the jury."

The survey had been conducted by the late Professor Hans Zeisel. Jurors in a Chicago courthouse were asked to hear and read both a description of the evidence from a trial and capital sentencing hearing and the jury instructions used in the sentencing hearing. They then read a

---

* [Ed note: Diamond and Levi, Improving Decisions on Death by Revising and Test-ing Jury Instructions, 79 Judicature 224 (1996)].

series of juror decisions and were asked whether the hypothetical juror had correctly followed the judge's instruction.

The sixteen questions on the survey were designed to test understanding of several key legal issues, including:

- Unenumerated Mitigators—whether jurors understand that they may consider any reason supported by the evidence as a possible mitigator, not just those enumerated in the instructions or comparable to them.

- Nonunanimity in Mitigation—whether jurors understand that one juror can identify a factor (like age) as a mitigator even if other jurors do not agree that it should be considered.

- Weighing—whether jurors understand that the law asks jurors to weigh the aggravating and mitigating factors, rather than to assume that death is the appropriate sentence unless mitigating factors are sufficient to overcome that presumption.

Respondents did not perform well on the Zeisel survey, the authors note. A majority of the respondents gave the correct answer on only three of the sixteen questions. On eleven of the sixteen questions, "the majority explicitly gave the incorrect answer (rather than the correct answer or 'do not know.')"

After extensive hearings on the quality of evidence, the magistrate judge concluded that the instructions were not "intelligible and definite enough to provide even a majority of jurors hearing them with a clear understanding of how they are to go about deciding whether the defendant lives or dies." He then found that the jury instructions violated the Eighth and Fourteenth amendments because they permitted arbitrary and unguided imposition of the death penalty. The Federal District Court judge accepted the magistrate's recommendation and vacated the death sentence pending a resentencing. But later, the Seventh Circuit voted two to one to reinstate Free's death sentence "on the ground that it was offered as the basis for a new rule and was produced after the judgment in *Free* had become final." However, Judge Posner, writing for the majority, did not reject the position "that an instruction in a death penalty case could be constitutionally defective if empirical evidence indicated that jurors were confused by it." But Posner had two concerns about the Zeisel survey. He noted first that "jurors simply might not be good test takers" but still might be able to perform effectively in the juryroom. Posner also considered the absence of a control group to be "fatal" because the study could not demonstrate that "performance would be better if the instructions were rewritten." Joining the opinion, Judge Bauer raised a third issue—the survey did not capture the effect of deliberations. That is, initial misunderstanding might be cured after a juror has a chance to discuss the instructions with fellow jurors.

Experimenting With Revised Instructions

Diamond and Levi designed their study to respond to some of the issues raised by the Seventh Circuit in *Free*. They preserved the basic format of the Zeisel study but made two changes in the research design:

- The jury instructions were rewritten so that "we could see whether the responses of jury-eligible citizens to the original and the revised instructions would differ." Adding a "control" group would test whether the revised instructions provided clear guidance to jurors and whether the poor juror performance in the original survey "was attributable merely to the test-taking ability of jurors."

- To test whether deliberations improved juror comprehension of instructions, half the participants in the new study were given the opportunity to deliberate as jurors.

Participants in the study were 170 jury-eligible persons. Of this number, 21 were excluded from the study because their responses to a questionnaire indicated either that they would always favor the death penalty for anyone convicted of a capital crime or that [their attitude against the death penalty would substantially impair their ability to find a defendant guilty or] to vote as a juror for the death penalty. The remaining 149 death-qualified jurors, in groups of 12 to 16, listened to an audiotaped description of the evidence in the guilt phase and the sentencing phase of James Free's trial, and to an audiotape of jury instructions, either the Illinois Pattern Jury Instructions for capital cases or the researchers' revised version of those instructions.

One group of six jurors from each session was then randomly selected to deliberate. The remaining jurors individually answered written questions "designed to elicit their understanding of what these instructions told them about how jurors should apply the law." At the end of the questions, the jurors were asked "whether they were leaning toward or against a death sentence." The deliberating jurors also answered the same set of questions when they finished their discussion.

The revised instructions addressed general linguistic problems, such as ambiguous vocabulary, but also attempted to clarify the three major legal points that appeared to confuse jurors in the Zeisel survey.

- Unenumerated mitigators, which were treated tersely in the pattern instructions, were placed in a more prominent position in the revised instructions, and the instruction was expanded considerably to provide "more detailed guidance on identifying mitigating factors beyond the enumerated ones."

- The text on mitigating factors in the pattern instructions "obscures or simply fails to express" the fact that decisions on mitigators need not be unanimous and that jurors have individual discretion. The revised instructions expanded the text and state explicitly, "Illinois law permits each juror to decide for himself or herself whether one or more mitigating factors exist.... [T]he jury does NOT need to reach a unanimous decision about what counts as a mitigating factor."

- The pattern instructions simply tell the jurors to consider the aggravating and mitigating factors. There is no mention of weighing or balancing. Further, the researchers note, "the wording of the pattern instructions suggested that the default sentence is death." The revised instructions have a more balanced vocabulary. "In references to the penalty ..., the word *death* occurs only 57% of the time (rather than 100%), while the word *imprisonment* appears 33% of the time (rather than never). The words *weigh, weight,* or *outweigh* appear seventeen times in the revised instructions but never in the pattern instructions." Further, a revised instructions include a section on weighing aggravating and mitigating factors that "explains in detail which decisions are to be made by individual jurors, which decisions by the jury as a whole, and the relation between those two kinds of decisions."

Improved Comprehension

In analyzing the responses, Diamond and Levi found that the revised jury instructions increased juror comprehension levels significantly. The percentage of correct responses increased on average from 50% to 65%; incorrect responses dropped from an average of 45% to 30%. The revised instructions also produced substantial improvement in comprehension of the three issues raised in *Free*:

- The greatest improvement occurred on the issue of Unenumerated Mitigators, moving from an average of 41% correct to an average of 58% correct. Percent correct on questions about Weighing increased from 51% to 66%. However, the opportunity to deliberate did not further increase comprehension levels on these two issues.

- Comprehension also increased significantly on questions related to Nonunamity on Mitigators with the revised instructions. Moreover, deliberation was found to increase comprehension on this issue: nondeliberators averaged 67% correct while jurors who deliberated averaged 79% correct. The isolated positive effect of deliberation on this issue also "suggests why earlier studies have shown little or no effect of deliberation on comprehension," the authors note. Their findings indicate, "that deliberation can be depended upon to improve comprehension only when a substantial majority of the members of a jury begin deliberations with a correct understanding of the information at issue."

- Using the deliberating jurors as a basis for comparison, revising the instructions (a single rewrite in this case) was found to increase the performance of deliberating jurors on average from 52% to 67%. Agreeing on an acceptable level of comprehension is a policy issue, not a research question, the authors note, but the results indicate "that a comprehension level of 52% is a cost that neither the legal system as a whole, nor capital defendants in particular, need pay in capital sentencing hearings."

Diamond and Levi reviewed the content of juror discussions during deliberations to determine how the revised instructions "produced greater clarity." They found that "the revised instructions encouraged jurors to consider unenumerated mitigating factors, to determine individually what mitigators are worthy of consideration, and to apply a weighing standard in reaching a decision on the appropriate penalty."

Since the revised instructions gave more attention to mitigation and the weighing standard, it was expected that jurors who received them would be less likely to favor the death penalty than those receiving the pattern instructions, and this was confirmed by the data. However, the authors state, the difference was of only borderline statistical significance. Because the sample was small and the analysis based on one question, the researchers note that further research is needed to determine if this finding holds up. Some additional supporting evidence, however, could be gleaned from this study: Jurors who understood the instructions better were significantly less likely to lean toward a sentence of death.

The research findings support "the District Court's original conclusion that James Free was sentenced to death by a jury that received unnecessarily confusing instructions," the authors argue, "but they came too late for Mr. Free. He was executed on March 22, 1995."

Their experience in this research suggested to Diamond and Levi that the best way to identify and remedy comprehension problems in jury instructions, such as discrepancies between legal terminology and common usage, is through collaborations among attorneys and/or judges, psychologists, and linguists. Further, they say, obtaining input from jurors in posttrial interviews or in simulations can identify "sources of miscomprehension and unintended meanings." Finally, the researchers note, revising instructions is not sufficient. They must be tested to determine when "an acceptable level of performance has been achieved" and to identify areas for further improvement. And the revision and testing process should begin in sentencing hearings, they maintain. "In view of the constitutionally-mandated guidance required in capital cases, improving the clarity of death penalty instructions would appear to be an appropriate and indeed a necessary place to institute reform."

SELECTED BIBLIOGRAPHY

Blanck, What Empirical Research Tells Us: Studying Judges' and Juries' Behavior, 40 American University Law Review 775 (1991).

Blanck, Rosenthal, and Cordell, The Appearance of Justice: Judges' Verbal and Non-verbal Behavior in Criminal Jury Trials, 38 Stanford Law Review 89 (1985).

Conley, O'Barr and Lind, The Power of Language: Presentational Style in the Courtroom, 1978 Duke Law Journal 1375.

Diamond, Instructing on Death, 48 American Psychologist 423 (1993).

Diamond and Levi, Improving Decisions on Death by Revising and Testing Jury Instructions, 79 Judicature 224 (1996).

Ellsworth and Reifman, Juror Comprehension and Public Policy: Perceived Problems and Proposed Solutions, 6 Psychology, Public Policy, and law 788 (2000).

Haney and Lynch, Comprehending Life and Death Matters: A Preliminary Study of California's Capital Penalty Instructions, 18 Law and Human Behavior 411 (1994).

Hannaford, Hans, and Munsterman, Permitting Jury Discussion During Trial: Impact on the Arizona Reform, 24 Law and Human Behavior 359 (2000).

Paglia and Schuller, Jurors' Use of Hearsay Evidence: The Effects of Type and Timing of Instructions, 22 Law and Human Behavior 501 (1998).

Penrod and Heuer, Assessing Aids to Jury Decision Making, 3 Psychology, Public Policy and Law 259 (1997).

Robbennolt, Penrod, and Heuer, Assessing and Aiding Jury Competence. In Handbook of Forensic Psychology (2nd ed.)(I. Weiner and A. Hess eds. 1999).

Rose and Ogloff, Evaluating the Comprehensibility of Jury Instructions: A Method and an Example, 25 Law and Human Behavior 409 (2001).

Saks, Flying Blind In The Courtroom: Trying Cases Without Knowing What Works or Why, 101 Yale Law Journal 1177 (1992).

Stoffelmayr and Diamond, The Conflict Between Precision and Flexibility in Explaining "Beyond a Reasonable Doubt," 6 Psychology, Public Policy, and Law 769 (2000).

Terrance, Matheson, and Spanos, Effects of Judicial Instructions and Case Characteristics in a Mock Jury Trial of Battered Women Who Kill, 24 Law and Human Behavior 207 (2000).

Wissler, Rector and Saks, The Impact of Jury Instructions on the Fusion of Liability and Compensatory Damages, 25 Law and Human Behavior 125 (2001).

Wissler, Kuehn, and Saks, Instructing Jurors on General Damages in Personal Injury Cases: Problems and Possibilities, 6 Psychology, Public Policy, and Law 712 (2000).

DAUBERT v. MERRELL DOW PHARMACEUTICALS

Supreme Court of the United States, 1993.
509 U.S. 579, 113 S.Ct. 2786, 125 L.Ed.2d 469.

■ JUSTICE BLACKMUN delivered the opinion of the Court.

In this case we are called upon to determine the standard for admitting expert scientific testimony in a federal trial.

Petitioners Jason Daubert and Eric Schuller are minor children born with serious birth defects. They and their parents sued respondent [a]lleging that the birth defects had been caused by the mothers' ingestion of Bendectin, a prescription anti-nausea drug marketed by respondent.

[A]fter extensive discovery, respondent moved for summary judgment, contending that Bendectin does not cause birth defects in humans and that petitioners would be unable to come forward with any admissible evidence that it does. In support of its motion, respondent submitted an affidavit of Steven H. Lamm, physician and epidemiologist, who is a well-credentialed expert on the risks from exposure to various chemical substances. Doctor Lamm stated that he had reviewed all the literature on Bendectin and human birth defects—more than 30 published studies involving over 130,000 patients. No study had found Bendectin to be a human teratogen (i.e., a substance capable of causing malformations in fetuses).

[P]etitioners [r]esponded to respondent's motion with the testimony of eight experts of their own, each of whom also possessed impressive credentials. These experts had concluded that Bendectin can cause birth defects. Their conclusions were based upon "in vitro" (test tube) and "in vivo" (live) animal studies that found a link between Bendectin and malformations; pharmacological studies of the chemical structure of Bendectin that purported to show similarities between the structure of the drug and that of other substances known to cause birth defects; and the "reanalysis" of previously published epidemiological (human statistical) studies.

The District Court granted respondent's motion for summary judgment. The court stated that scientific evidence is admissible only if the principle upon which it is based is " 'sufficiently established to have general acceptance in the field to which it belongs.' " 727 F.Supp. 570, 572 (S.D.Cal.1989), quoting United States v. Kilgus, 571 F.2d 508, 510 (C.A.9 1978). The court concluded that petitioners' evidence did not meet this standard. Given the vast body of epidemiological data concerning Bendectin, the court held, expert opinion which is not based on epidemiological evidence is not admissible to establish causation. 727 F.Supp., at 575. Thus, the animal-cell studies, live-animal studies, and chemical-structure analyses on which petitioners had relied could not raise by themselves a reasonably disputable jury issue regarding causation. Ibid. Petitioners' epidemiological analyses, based as they were on recalculations of data in previously published studies that had found no causal link between the drug and birth defects, were ruled to be inadmissible because they had not been published or subjected to peer review. Ibid.

The United States Court of Appeals for the Ninth Circuit affirmed. 951 F.2d 1128 (1991). Citing Frye v. United States, 54 App.D.C. 46, 47, 293 F. 1013, 1014 (1923), the court stated that expert opinion based on a scientific technique is inadmissible unless the technique is "generally accepted" as reliable in the relevant scientific community. 951 F.2d, at 1129–1130.

[I]n the 70 years since its formulation in the *Frye* case, the "general acceptance" test has been the dominant standard for determining the admissibility of novel scientific evidence at trial. Although under increasing attack of late, the rule continues to be followed by a majority of courts.

[T]he *Frye* test has its origin in a short and citation-free 1923 decision concerning the admissibility of evidence derived from a systolic blood pressure deception test, a crude precursor to the polygraph machine. In what has become a famous (perhaps infamous) passage, the then Court of Appeals for the District of Columbia described the device and its operation and declared: "Just when a scientific principle or discovery crosses the line between the experimental and demonstrable stages is difficult to define. Somewhere in this twilight zone the evidential force of the principle must be recognized, and while courts will go a long way in admitting expert testimony deduced from a well-recognized scientific principle or discovery, the thing from which the deduction is made must be sufficiently established to have gained general acceptance in the particular field in which it belongs." 54 App.D.C., at 47, 293 F., at 1014 (emphasis added).

[T]he merits of the *Frye* test have been much debated, and scholarship on its proper scope and application is legion. Petitioners' primary attack, however, is not on the content but on the continuing authority of the rule. They contend that the *Frye* test was superseded by the adoption of the Federal Rules of Evidence. We agree. [R]ule 702, governing expert testimony, provides: "If scientific, technical, or other specialized knowledge will assist the trier of fact to understand the evidence or to determine a fact in issue, a witness qualified as an expert by knowledge, skill, experience, training, or education, may testify thereto in the form of an opinion or otherwise." Nothing in the text of this Rule establishes "general acceptance" as an absolute prerequisite to admissibility. Nor does respondent present any clear indication that Rule 702 or the Rules as a whole were intended to incorporate a "general acceptance" standard. The drafting history makes no mention of *Frye,* and a rigid "general acceptance" requirement would be at odds with the "liberal thrust" of the Federal Rules and their "general approach of relaxing the traditional barriers to 'opinion' testimony." Beech Aircraft Corp. v. Rainey, 488 U.S., at 169 (citing Rules 701 to 705). Given the Rules' permissive backdrop and their inclusion of a specific rule on expert testimony that does not mention "general acceptance," the assertion that the Rules somehow assimilated *Frye* is unconvincing. *Frye* made "general acceptance" the exclusive test for admitting expert scientific testimony. That austere standard, absent from and incompatible with the Federal Rules of Evidence, should not be applied in federal trials.

That the *Frye* test was displaced by the Rules of Evidence does not mean, however, that the Rules themselves place no limits on the admissibility of purportedly scientific evidence. Nor is the trial judge disabled from screening such evidence. To the contrary, under the Rules the trial judge must ensure that any and all scientific testimony or evidence admitted is not only relevant, but reliable.

The primary locus of this obligation is Rule 702, which clearly contemplates some degree of regulation of the subjects and theories about which an expert may testify. [T]he subject of an expert's testimony must be "scientific . . . knowledge." The adjective "scientific" implies a grounding in the methods and procedures of science. Similarly, the word "knowledge" connotes more than subjective belief or unsupported speculation. The term "applies to any body of known facts or to any body of ideas inferred from such facts or accepted as truths on good grounds." Webster's Third New International Dictionary 1252 (1986). Of course, it would be unreasonable to conclude that the subject of scientific testimony must be "known" to a certainty; arguably, there are no certainties in science. But, in order to qualify as "scientific knowledge," an inference or assertion must be derived by the scientific method. Proposed testimony must be supported by appropriate validation—i.e., "good grounds," based on what is known. In short, the requirement that an expert's testimony pertain to "scientific knowledge" establishes a standard of evidentiary reliability.[9]

Rule 702 further requires that the evidence or testimony "assist the trier of fact to understand the evidence or to determine a fact in issue." This condition goes primarily to relevance. "Expert testimony which does not relate to any issue in the case is not relevant and, ergo, non-helpful." 3 Weinstein & Berger P 702[02], p. 702–18. [R]ule 702's "helpfulness" standard requires a valid scientific connection to the pertinent inquiry as a precondition to admissibility.

[F]aced with a proffer of expert scientific testimony, then, the trial judge must determine at the outset, pursuant to Rule 104(a), whether the expert is proposing to testify to (1) scientific knowledge that (2) will assist the trier of fact to understand or determine a fact in issue.[11] This entails a

---

9. We note that scientists typically distinguish between "validity" (does the principle support what it purports to show?) and "reliability" (does application of the principle produce consistent results?). [O]ur reference here is to evidentiary reliability—that is, trustworthiness. [I]n a case involving scientific evidence, evidentiary reliability will be based upon scientific validity.

11. Although the *Frye* decision itself focused exclusively on "novel" scientific techniques, we do not read the requirements of

Rule 702 to apply specially or exclusively to unconventional evidence. Of course, well-established propositions are less likely to be challenged than those that are novel, and they are more handily defended. Indeed, theories that are so firmly established as to have attained the status of scientific law, such as the laws of thermodynamics, properly are subject to judicial notice under Fed. Rule Evid. 201.

preliminary assessment of whether the reasoning or methodology underlying the testimony is scientifically valid and of whether that reasoning or methodology properly can be applied to the facts in issue. We are confident that federal judges possess the capacity to undertake this review. Many factors will bear on the inquiry, and we do not presume to set out a definitive checklist or test. But some general observations are appropriate.

Ordinarily, a key question to be answered in determining whether a theory or technique is scientific knowledge that will assist the trier of fact will be whether it can be (and has been) tested. "Scientific methodology today is based on generating hypotheses and testing them to see if they can be falsified; indeed, this methodology is what distinguishes science from other fields of human inquiry." Green, [Expert Witnesses and Sufficiency of Evidence in Toxic Substances Litigation: The Legacy of Agent Orange and Bendectin Litigation, 86 Nw.U.L.Rev. 643 (1992)] at 645.

Another pertinent consideration is whether the theory or technique has been subjected to peer review and publication. Publication (which is but one element of peer review) is not a sine qua non of admissibility; it does not necessarily correlate with reliability, and in some instances well-grounded but innovative theories will not have been published. Some propositions, moreover, are too particular, too new, or of too limited interest to be published. But submission to the scrutiny of the scientific community is a component of "good science," in part because it increases the likelihood that substantive flaws in methodology will be detected. The fact of publication (or lack thereof) in a peer-reviewed journal thus will be a relevant, though not dispositive, consideration in assessing the scientific validity of a particular technique or methodology on which an opinion is premised.

Additionally, in the case of a particular scientific technique, the court ordinarily should consider the known or potential rate of error, and the existence and maintenance of standards controlling the technique's operation.

Finally, "general acceptance" can yet have a bearing on the inquiry. A "reliability assessment does not require although it does permit, explicit identification of a relevant scientific community and an express determination of a particular degree of acceptance within that community." United States v. Downing, 753 F.2d, at 1238. Widespread acceptance can be an important factor in ruling particular evidence admissible, and "a known technique that has been able to attract only minimal support within the community," Downing, supra, at 1238, may properly be viewed with skepticism.

The inquiry envisioned by Rule 702 is, we emphasize, a flexible one. Its overarching subject is the scientific validity—and thus the evidentiary relevance and reliability—of the principles that underlie a proposed submission. The focus, of course, must be solely on principles and methodology, not on the conclusions that they generate.

[T]o summarize: "general acceptance" is not a necessary precondition to the admissibility of scientific evidence under the Federal Rules of Evidence, but the Rules of Evidence—especially Rule 702—do assign to the trial judge the task of ensuring that an expert's testimony both rests on a reliable foundation and is relevant to the task at hand. Pertinent evidence based on scientifically valid principles will satisfy those demands.

The inquiries of the District Court and the Court of Appeals focused almost exclusively on "general acceptance," as gauged by publication and the decisions of other courts. Accordingly, the judgment of the Court of Appeals is vacated and the case is remanded for further proceedings consistent with this opinion.

■ CHIEF JUSTICE REHNQUIST, with whom JUSTICE STEVENS joins, concurring in part and dissenting in part.

The Court speaks of its confidence that federal judges can make a "preliminary assessment of whether the reasoning or methodology underlying the testimony is scientifically valid and of whether that reasoning or methodology properly can be applied to the facts in issue." The Court then states that a "key question" to be answered in deciding whether something is "scientific knowledge" "will be whether it can be (and has been) tested." Following this sentence are three quotations from treatises, which speak not only of empirical testing, but one of which states that "the criterion of the scientific status of a theory is its falsifiability, or refutability, or testability."

I defer to no one in my confidence in federal judges; but I am at a loss to know what is meant when it is said that the scientific status of a theory depends on its "falsifiability," and I suspect some of them will be, too.

I do not doubt that Rule 702 confides to the judge some gatekeeping responsibility in deciding questions of the admissibility of proffered expert testimony. But I do not think it imposes on them either the obligation or the authority to become amateur scientists in order to perform that role. I think the Court would be far better advised in this case to decide only the questions presented, and to leave the further development of this important area of the law to future cases.

FEDERAL RULES OF EVIDENCE

Rule 104.   Preliminary Questions

(a) Questions of admissibility generally. Preliminary questions concerning the qualification of a person to be a witness, the existence of a privilege, or the admissibility of evidence shall be determined by the court, subject to the provisions of subdivision (b). In making its determination it is not bound by the rules of evidence except those with respect to privileges.

(b) Relevancy conditioned on fact. When the relevancy of evidence depends upon the fulfillment of a condition of fact, the court shall admit it upon, or subject to, the introduction of evidence sufficient to support a finding of the fulfillment of the condition.

(c) Hearing of jury. Hearings on the admissibility of confessions shall in all cases be conducted out of the hearing of the jury. Hearings on other preliminary matters shall be so conducted when the interests of justice require, or when an accused is a witness and so requests.

(d) Testimony by accused. The accused does not, by testifying upon a preliminary matter, become subject to cross-examination as to other issues in the case.

(e) Weight and credibility. This rule does not limit the right of a party to introduce before the jury evidence relevant to weight or credibility.

Rule 201.   Judicial Notice of Adjudicative Facts*

(a) Scope of rule. This rule governs only judicial notice of adjudicative facts.

(b) Kinds of facts. A judicially noticed fact must be one not subject to reasonable dispute in that it is either (1) generally known within the territorial jurisdiction of the trial court or (2) capable of accurate and ready determination by resort to sources whose accuracy cannot reasonably be questioned.

(c) When discretionary. A court may take judicial notice, whether requested or not.

(d) When mandatory. A court shall take judicial notice if requested by a party and supplied with the necessary information.

(e) Opportunity to be heard. A party is entitled upon timely request to an opportunity to be heard as to the propriety of taking judicial notice and the tenor of the matter noticed. In the absence of prior notification, the request may be made after judicial notice has been taken.

(f) Time of taking notice. Judicial notice may be taken at any stage of the proceeding.

(g) Instructing jury. In a civil action or proceeding, the court shall instruct the jury to accept as conclusive any fact judicially noticed. In a

---

* Advisory Committee's Note

56 F.R.D. 183, 201

Subdivision (a). This is the only evidence rule on the subject of judicial notice. It deals only with judicial notice of "adjudicative" facts. No rule deals with judicial notice of "legislative" facts. Judicial notice of matters of foreign law is treated in Rule 44.1 of the Federal Rules of Civil Procedure and Rule 26.1 of the Federal Rules of Criminal Procedure.

The omission of any treatment of legislative facts results from fundamental differ-ences between adjudicative facts and legislative facts. Adjudicative facts are simply the facts of the particular case. Legislative facts, on the other hand, are those which have relevance to legal reasoning and the lawmaking process, whether in the formulation of a legal principle or ruling by a judge or court or in the enactment of a legislative body. The terminology was coined by Professor Kenneth Davis in his article An Approach to Problems of Evidence in the Administrative Process, 55 Harv.L.Rev. 364, 404–407 (1942).

criminal case, the court shall instruct the jury that it may, but is not required to, accept as conclusive any fact judicially noticed.

Rule 401. Definition of "Relevant Evidence"

"Relevant evidence" means evidence having any tendency to make the existence of any fact that is of consequence to the determination of the action more probable or less probable than it would be without the evidence.

Rule 402. Relevant Evidence Generally Admissible; Irrelevant Evidence Inadmissible

All relevant evidence is admissible, except as otherwise provided by the Constitution of the United States, by Act of Congress, by these rules, or by other rules prescribed by the Supreme Court pursuant to statutory authority. Evidence which is not relevant is not admissible.

Rule 403. Exclusion of Relevant Evidence on Grounds of Prejudice, Confusion, or Waste of Time

Although relevant, evidence may be excluded if its probative value is substantially outweighed by the danger of unfair prejudice, confusion of the issues, or misleading the jury, or by considerations of undue delay, waste of time, or needless presentation of cumulative evidence.

Rule 404. Character Evidence Not Admissible to Prove Conduct; Exceptions; Other Crimes

(a) Character evidence generally. Evidence of a person's character or a trait of character is not admissible for the purpose of proving action in conformity therewith on a particular occasion, except:

(1) Character of accused. Evidence of a pertinent trait of character offered by an accused, or by the prosecution to rebut the same, or if evidence of a trait of character of the alleged victim of the crime is offered by an accused and admitted under Rule 404(a)(2), evidence of the same trait of character of the accused offered by the prosecution;

(2) Character of alleged victim. Evidence of a pertinent trait of character of the alleged victim of the crime offered by an accused, or by the prosecution to rebut the same, or evidence of a character trait of peacefulness of the alleged victim offered by the prosecution in a homicide case to rebut evidence that the alleged victim was the first aggressor;

[(b)] Other crimes, wrongs, or acts. Evidence of other crimes, wrongs, or acts is not admissible to prove the character of a person in order to show action in conformity therewith. It may, however, be admissible for other purposes, such as proof of motive, opportunity, intent, preparation, plan, knowledge, identity, or absence of mistake or accident.

Rule 701. Opinion Testimony by Lay Witnesses

If the witness is not testifying as an expert, the witness' testimony in the form of opinions or inferences is limited to those opinions or inferences which are (a) rationally based on the perception of the witness, and (b) helpful to a clear understanding of the witness' testimony or the determination of a fact in issue, and (c) not based on scientific, technical, or other specialized knowledge within the scope of Rule 702.

Rule 702.   Testimony by Experts

If scientific, technical, or other specialized knowledge will assist the trier of fact to understand the evidence or to determine a fact in issue, a witness qualified as an expert by knowledge, skill, experience, training, or education, may testify thereto in the form of an opinion or otherwise, if (1) the testimony is based upon sufficient facts or data, (2) the testimony is the product of reliable principles and methods, and (3) the witness has applied the principles and methods reliably to the facts of the case.

Rule 703.   Bases of Opinion Testimony by Experts

The facts or data in the particular case upon which an expert bases an opinion or inference may be those perceived by or made known to the expert at or before the hearing. If of a type reasonably relied upon by experts in the particular field in forming opinions or inferences upon the subject, the facts or data need not be admissible in evidence in order for the opinion or inference to be admitted. Facts or data that are otherwise inadmissible shall not be disclosed to the jury by the proponent of the opinion or inference unless the court determines that their probative value in assisting the jury to evaluate the expert's opinion substantially outweighs their prejudicial effect.

Rule 704.   Opinion on Ultimate Issue

(a) Except as provided in subdivision (b), testimony in the form of an opinion or inference otherwise admissible is not objectionable because it embraces an ultimate issue to be decided by the trier of fact.

(b) No expert witness testifying with respect to the mental state or condition of a defendant in a criminal case may state an opinion or inference as to whether the defendant did or did not have the mental state or condition constituting an element of the crime charged or of a defense thereto. Such ultimate issues are matters for the trier of fact alone.

Rule 705.   Disclosure of Facts or Data Underlying Expert Opinion

The expert may testify in terms of opinion or inference and give reasons therefor without first testifying to the underlying facts or data, unless the court requires otherwise. The expert may in any event be required to disclose the underlying facts or data on cross-examination.

Rule 706.   Court Appointed Experts

(a) Appointment. The court may on its own motion or on the motion of any party enter an order to show cause why expert witnesses should not be appointed, and may request the parties to submit nominations. The court may appoint any expert witnesses agreed upon by the parties, and may appoint expert witnesses of its own selection. An expert witness shall not be appointed by the court unless the witness consents to act. A witness so appointed shall be informed of the witness' duties by the court in writing, a copy of which shall be filed with the clerk, or at a conference in which the parties shall have opportunity to participate. A witness so appointed shall advise the parties of the witness' findings, if any; the witness' deposition may be taken by any party; and the witness may be called to testify by the court or any party. The witness shall be subject to cross-examination by each party, including a party calling the witness.

(b) Compensation. Expert witnesses so appointed are entitled to reasonable compensation in whatever sum the court may allow. The compensation thus fixed is payable from funds which may be provided by law in criminal cases and civil actions and proceedings involving just compensation under the fifth amendment. In other civil actions and proceedings the compensation shall be paid by the parties in such proportion and at such time as the court directs, and thereafter charged in like manner as other costs.

(c) Disclosure of appointment. In the exercise of its discretion, the court may authorize disclosure to the jury of the fact that the court appointed the expert witness.

(d) Parties' experts of own selection. Nothing in this rule limits the parties in calling expert witnesses of their own selection.

Rule 801.   Definitions

The following definitions apply under this article:

(a) Statement. A "statement" is (1) an oral or written assertion or (2) nonverbal conduct of a person, if it is intended by the person as an assertion.

(b) Declarant. A "declarant" is a person who makes a statement.

(c) Hearsay. "Hearsay" is a statement, other than one made by the declarant while testifying at the trial or hearing, offered in evidence to prove the truth of the matter asserted.

Rule 802.   Hearsay Rule

Hearsay is not admissible except as provided by these rules or by other rules prescribed by the Supreme Court pursuant to statutory authority or by Act of Congress.

Rule 803.   Hearsay Exceptions; Availability of Declarant Immaterial

The following are not excluded by the hearsay rule, even though the declarant is available as a witness:

(1) Present sense impression. A statement describing or explaining an event or condition made while the declarant was perceiving the event or condition, or immediately thereafter.

[18]   Learned treaties. To the extent called to the attention of an expert witness upon cross-examination or relied upon by the expert witness in direct examination, statements contained in published treatises, periodicals, or pamphlets on a subject of history, medicine, or other science or art, established as a reliable authority by the testimony or admission of the witness or by other expert testimony or by judicial notice. If admitted, the statements may be read into evidence but may not be received as exhibits.

INDEX

References are to Pages.

†